London 2015

A SELECTION
OF THE BEST
RESTAURANTS
& HOTELS

Contents

Lists of awards and features 16

In Greater London 320

Index & Maps 494

Dear reader,

We are delighted to present the 2015 edition of the Michelin Guide for London.

All the restaurants within this guide have been chosen first and foremost for the quality of their cooking. You'll find comprehensive information on over 590 dining establishments, ranging from gastropubs and neighbourhood brasseries to internationally renowned restaurants. The diverse and varied selection also bears testament to the rich and buoyant dining scene in London, with the city now enjoying a worldwide reputation for the quality and range of its restaurants.

You'll see that Michelin Stars are not our only awards – look out also for the Bib Gourmands. These are restaurants where the cooking is still carefully prepared but in a simpler style and, priced at under £28 for three courses, they represent excellent value for money.

To complement the selection of restaurants, our team of independent, full-time inspectors have also chosen 50 hotels. These carefully selected hotels represent the best that London has to offer, from the small and intimate to the grand and luxurious. All have been chosen for their individuality and personality.

We are committed to remaining at the forefront of the culinary world and to meeting the demands of our readers. As such, we are always very interested to hear your opinions on the establishments listed in our guide, as well as those you feel could be of interest for future editions. Please don't hesitate to contact us as your contributions are invaluable in directing our work and improving the quality of the information we provide.

Thank you for your support and happy travelling with the 2015 edition of the Michelin Guide for London.

Consult the Michelin Guide at www.viamichelin.com
and write to us at themichelinguide-gbirl@uk.michelin.com

The MICHELIN guide's commitments

Experienced in quality!

Whether they are in Japan, the USA, China or Europe, our inspectors apply the same criteria to judge the quality of each and every hotel and restaurant that they visit. The Michelin guide commands a worldwide reputation thanks to the commitments we make to our readers – and we reiterate these below:

➜ Anonymous inspections

Our inspectors make regular and anonymous visits to hotels and restaurants to gauge the quality of products and services offered to an ordinary customer. They settle their own bill and may then introduce themselves and ask for more information about the establishment. Our readers' comments are also a valuable source of information, which we can follow up with a visit of our own.

➜ Independence

To remain totally objective for our readers, the selection is made with complete independence. Entry into the guide is free. All decisions are discussed with the Editor and our highest awards are considered at a European level.

➜ Selection & choice

The guide offers a selection of the best hotels and restaurants in every category of comfort and price. This is only possible because all the inspectors rigorously apply the same methods.

➜ Annual updates

All the practical information, classifications and awards are revised and updated every year to give the most reliable information possible.

➜ Consistency

The criteria for the classifications are the same in every country covered by the MICHELIN guide. The sole intention of Michelin is to make your travels safe and enjoyable.

How to use this guide...

Restaurants, classified according to comfort (particularly pleasant if in red)

- Quite comfortable
- Comfortable
- Very comfortable
- Top class comfort
- Luxury in the traditional style
- Pubs serving good food

Starred restaurants
Stars for excellent cooking
✿ to ✿✿✿

London area or neighbourhood
Each area is colour coded:
- Central London
- Greater London

Practical information
Name, address and information about the establishment

Prices
Lowest/highest price for a single/double room

Restaurant symbols
- Breakfast
- Small plates
- Vegetarian menu
- Particularly interesting wine list
- Notable cocktail list
- Open late
- Open on Sunday
- Restaurants offering lower priced pre and/or post theatre menus
- Private dining room

Sample menu for starred restaurants

Cuisine type

Birdy Nam-Nam
Fusion
South-West ▸ Plan XVIII
100 Wa…
(020)…
www.r…
Tot…
Closed 2…
Menu

Linda House ✿✿
Seafood
Belgravia • Victoria ▸ Plan IV
▸ Plan XI
Court Road Lancaster St
SW1Y 4AN
(020) 7747 22 00
www.lindahouse.com
Leicester Square
Closed 25-26 December, 1 January, Monday and bank holidays
Menu £14/25 – Carte £20/38

Emile Lepeletier

Linda House is a handsome four storey 18th century building in the heart of Soho. To gain entry, you ring the doorbell and you'll then be ushered into one of the two dining rooms. Regulars may have their favourite but there's little to choose between them – they're both warm and welcoming, although the first floor room is slightly larger than the ground floor.
There is something about being cosseted in a characterful house that makes dining here such a pleasure and it provides the perfect antidote for those feeling bruised and buffeted by the bigger, more boisterous places.
The cooking is modern in its approach and presentation but flavours are far more vigorous and full bodied than one expects and the marriages of various ingredients bear testament to real talent. Evidence of Bob's Welsh roots pops up here and there, from the laver bread to the Welsh cheeses and his homeland provides much of the produce. Tasting and Garden menus are available for those making it an occasion.

First Course	Main Course	Dessert
• Ravioli of shellfish with champagne and chives	• Roast sea bass with black olives, baby squid and creamed fennel	• Lemongrass jelly with pineapple and coconut
• Loin of tuna wrapped in basil with soy, avocado and a salad of radish	• Assiette of lamb with new season garlic, borlotti beans and rosemary	• Vanilla yoghurt parfait with blueberries

194

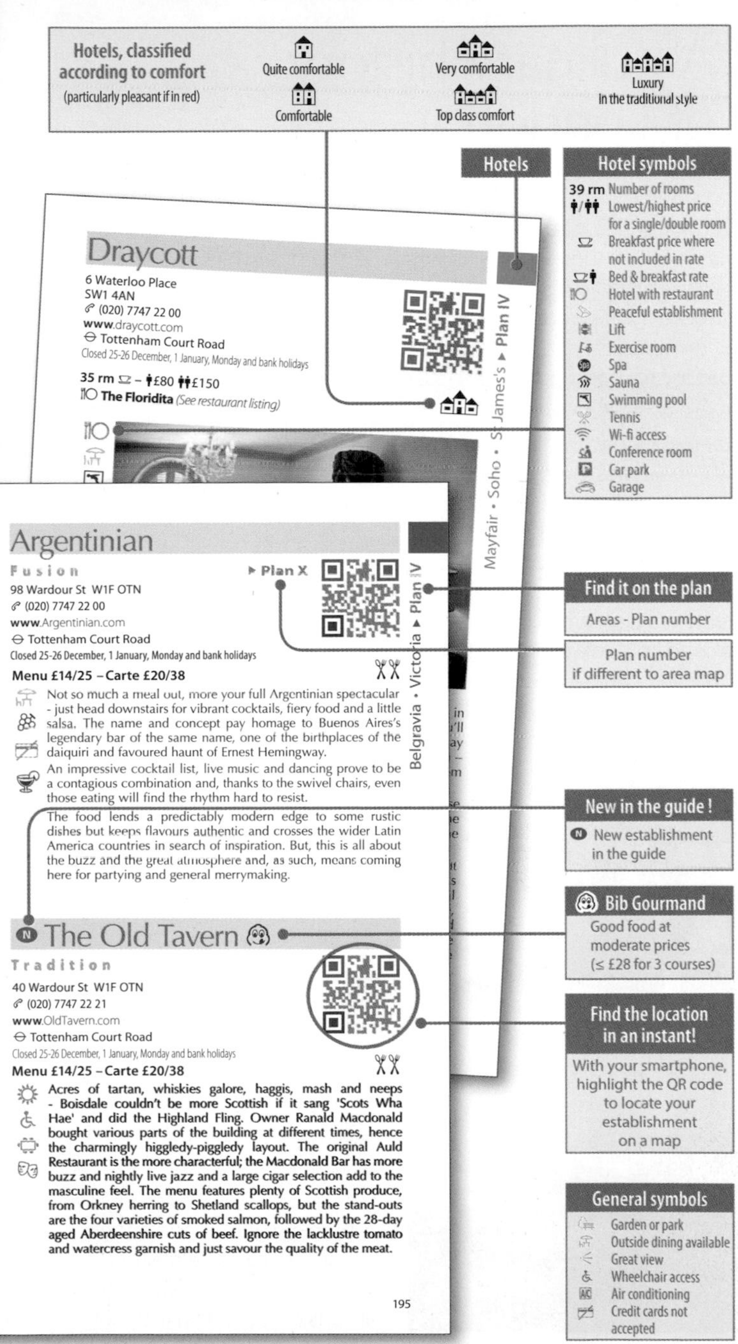

Hotels, classified according to comfort
(particularly pleasant if in red)
Quite comfortable
Comfortable
Very comfortable
Top class comfort
Luxury
In the traditional style
Hotels
Hotel symbols
39 rm Number of rooms
Lowest/highest price for a single/double room
Breakfast price where not included in rate
Bed & breakfast rate
Hotel with restaurant
Peaceful establishment
Lift
Exercise room
Spa
Sauna
Swimming pool
Tennis
Wi-fi access
Conference room
Car park
Garage
Draycott
6 Waterloo Place
SW1 4AN
(020) 7747 22 00
www.draycott.com
Tottenham Court Road
Closed 25-26 December, 1 January, Monday and bank holidays
35 rm – £80 £150
The Floridita (See restaurant listing)
Mayfair • Soho • St James's ▸ Plan IV
Argentinian
Fusion
▸ Plan X
98 Wardour St W1F OTN
(020) 7747 22 00
www.Argentinian.com
Tottenham Court Road
Closed 25-26 December, 1 January, Monday and bank holidays
Menu £14/25 – Carte £20/38
Not so much a meal out, more your full Argentinian spectacular - just head downstairs for vibrant cocktails, fiery food and a little salsa. The name and concept pay homage to Buenos Aires's legendary bar of the same name, one of the birthplaces of the daiquiri and favoured haunt of Ernest Hemingway.
An impressive cocktail list, live music and dancing prove to be a contagious combination and, thanks to the swivel chairs, even those eating will find the rhythm hard to resist.
The food lends a predictably modern edge to some rustic dishes but keeps flavours authentic and crosses the wider Latin America countries in search of inspiration. But, this is all about the buzz and the great atmosphere and, as such, means coming here for partying and general merrymaking.
Belgravia • Victoria ▸ Plan IV
Find it on the plan
Areas - Plan number
Plan number
if different to area map
New in the guide !
New establishment in the guide
The Old Tavern
Tradition
40 Wardour St W1F OTN
(020) 7747 22 21
www.OldTavern.com
Tottenham Court Road
Closed 25-26 December, 1 January, Monday and bank holidays
Menu £14/25 – Carte £20/38
Acres of tartan, whiskies galore, haggis, mash and neeps - Boisdale couldn't be more Scottish if it sang 'Scots Wha Hae' and did the Highland Fling. Owner Ranald Macdonald bought various parts of the building at different times, hence the charmingly higgledy-piggledy layout. The original Auld Restaurant is the more characterful; the Macdonald Bar has more buzz and nightly live jazz and a large cigar selection add to the masculine feel. The menu features plenty of Scottish produce, from Orkney herring to Shetland scallops, but the stand-outs are the four varieties of smoked salmon, followed by the 28-day aged Aberdeenshire cuts of beef. Ignore the lacklustre tomato and watercress garnish and just savour the quality of the meat.
195
Bib Gourmand
Good food at moderate prices
(≤ £28 for 3 courses)
Find the location in an instant!
With your smartphone, highlight the QR code to locate your establishment on a map
General symbols
Garden or park
Outside dining available
Great view
Wheelchair access
Air conditioning
Credit cards not accepted

A culinary history of London

London, influenced by worldwide produce arriving via the Thames, has always enjoyed a close association with its food, though most of the time the vast majority of its people have looked much closer to home for their sustenance.

Even as far back as the 2nd century AD, meat was on the menu: the profusion of wildlife in the woods and forests around London turned it into a carnivore's paradise, thereby setting the tone and the template. Large stoves were employed to cook everything from pork and beef to goose and deer. The Saxons added the likes of garlic, leeks, radishes and turnips to the pot, while eels became a popular staple in later years.

C. Moirenc/hemis.fr

What a lark!

By the 13th century, the taste for fish had evolved to the more exotic porpoise, lamprey and sturgeon, with saffron and spices perking up the common-or-garden meat dish. Not that medieval tastes would have been considered mundane to the average 21st century diner: Londoners of the time would think nothing about devouring roasted thrush or lark from the cook's stalls dotted around the city streets. And you'd have been unlikely to hear the cry "Eat your greens!" In the 15th century, the vegetable diet, such as it was, seemed to run mainly to herbs such as rosemary, fennel, borage and thyme.

As commercial and maritime success burgeoned in the age of the Tudors, so tables began to groan under the weight of London's penchant for feasting. No excess was spared, as oxen, sheep, boars and pigs were put to the griddle; these would have been accompanied by newly arrived yams and sweet potatoes from America and 'washed down' with rhubarb from Asia. People on the streets could 'feast-lite': by the 17th century hawkers were offering all sorts of goodies on the hoof.

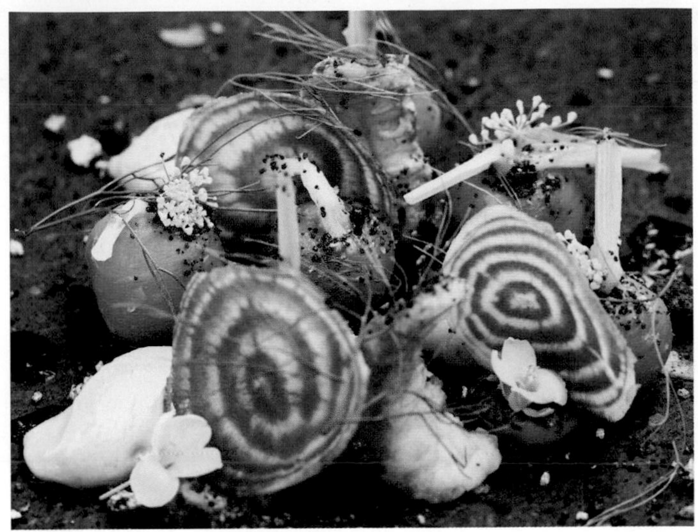

L. Klein/Cultúra Creative/Photononstop

Full of beans

All of this eating was of course accompanied by a lot of drinking. Though much of it took place in the alehouses and taverns - which ran into the thousands - by the 18th century coffee houses had become extraordinarily popular. These were places to do business as well as being convenient 'for passing evenings socially at a very small charge'.

Perhaps the biggest revolution in eating habits came midway through the 19th century when the first cavernous dining halls and restaurants appeared. These 'freed' diners from the communal benches of the cook-house and gave them, for the first time, the chance for a bit of seclusion at separate tables. This private dining experience was an egalitarian movement: plutocrats may have had their posh hotels, but the less well-off were buttering teacakes and scones served by 'nippies' at the local Lyons Corner House.

Influenced by post World War II flavours brought in by immigrants from Asia, the Caribbean and Africa – and, most recently, from Eastern Bloc Countries – Londoners now enjoy an unparalleled cuisine alive with global flavours. Perhaps the Queen's Jubilee and the Olympics have made us more confident about waving the flag for Britain as we are also rediscovering and celebrating our own culinary heritage.

Practical London

Arrival/Departure

If you're coming to London from abroad, it's worth bearing in mind that the capital's airports are (with one exception), a long way from the city itself. The good news is that they're well-served by speedy express train services; the even better news is that if you travel by Eurostar you can go by train direct from the heart of Europe to the heart of London without having to worry about luggage limits, carousels and carbon footprints...

By air

Most people arrive via Heathrow – the UK's busiest airport – or Gatwick. You can catch the Heathrow Express rail service to Paddington every 15 minutes, and that's also about how long the journey takes. Another alternative is to board the Piccadilly line tube train: it's cheaper, but the drawn-out travelling time can make it seem as if you've spent most of your holiday just getting to the centre. Gatwick is further out, south of London's M25 ring road, and the quickest way into the city is via the Gatwick Express rail service, which takes half an hour to reach Victoria station. There are also frequent train services which connect with a host of central London stations, including London Bridge and King's Cross. The capital has three other airports: Stansted, 35 miles northeast of the city; Luton, 30 miles to the north; and London City Airport, which is nine miles to the east and connects to the centre via the Docklands Light Railway.

By train

The days of *having* to fly into London are long gone. Smart travellers from the Continent now jump on the Eurostar from Paris, Brussels or Lille, zip along at 186mph, and step onto the platform at St Pancras International in the time it takes to devour a coffee and a croissant (a big coffee, admittedly). From there, three tube lines from the adjoining King's Cross station whisk you into town. Book Eurostar far enough in advance (which isn't very far, by any means) and you can get tickets for just £69 return.

Getting Around

The pearl that is Oyster

Single, return and day tickets (Travelcards) can be bought from machines and offices at tube, train and bus stations, or from London Travel Information Centres... but your best bet is to buy an Oyster card. This electronic smartcard is the fastest, easiest and cheapest way to pay for journeys around town; just zap it over a yellow reader to let you through the tube gates or onto a bus. Oysters are charged with a pre-paid amount of credit which can cover a week, a month

Superstock/Age fotostock

or be used to 'pay-as-you-go'. The deposit for a card is £5, which will be refunded upon its return, although the pay-as-you-go credit doesn't expire, so you can keep it to use on your next visit.

For details on fares, journey planners, service updates and more:

• visit the Transport for London website www.tfl.gov.uk

• call the 24-hour Travel Information Service on + 44(0) 343 222 1234

• or visit one of the five London Travel Information Centres, which are based at Liverpool Street, Piccadilly Circus, King's Cross, Heathrow Terminals 1, 2 and 3 and Victoria stations.

By Underground and Overground

First, the bad news: the tube can get hot and overcrowded and engineering works can close lines at weekends. But the good news? Generally speaking, the tube is by far the quickest way to get around town. There are 12 lines, plus the automated Docklands Light Railway (DLR); these cover pretty much the whole city and are all clearly shown on the free map you can pick up at any tube station. Trains run from 5am to just past midnight Monday-Saturday, with a reduced timetable on Sundays. There are also four Overground routes which operate across the city, running from Watford and Richmond in the north and south west to Croydon and Barking in the south and east.

By bus

They might move a bit slower than trains but when you ride on the top of a double-decker bus, you get the added bonus of an absorbing, tourist-friendly view. Many bus stops have live arrivals boards and you can pick up a handy central London bus map from a bus station. London buses do not accept cash – you can only pay with a Travelcard, an Oyster card or a UK-issued contactless payment card.

Look out for the updated version of the iconic 'Routemaster' that operates on several routes.

By car

The best advice is not to drive in central London, not if you want your sanity preserved anyway. Roadworks and parking can be the stuff of nightmares, and that's before the Congestion Charge Zone is taken into consideration. This zone covers the central area and is clearly marked by red 'C' signs painted on the road. It's in operation Monday-Friday 7am-6pm (weekends and holidays are free) and you'll need to register the car's number plate on a database at tfl.gov.uk. If it all sounds too much of a headache, you always have the option of hailing a black cab – just stick out your hand when you see one with its 'taxi' light illuminated.

J. Warburton-Lee/Photononstop

By bike

For short journeys, a greener alternative is the humble bike, and those aged 18 and above can hire a so-called 'Boris Bike' from one of the many Barclays Cycle Hire docking points spread across the capital. There's no need to book ahead, they're available 24 hours a day, 7 days a week, and anyone 14 and over can ride. Simply pay the access fee (£2 for 24 hours/£10 for 7 days) at a docking station terminal, using a credit or debit card. You are then charged for your usage but, as the scheme is designed for short journeys, the first 30 minutes are free and it's only £1 for the second 30 minutes. Simply return the bike to any docking station when you're done.

By boat

'Taking to the water' has become increasingly popular over the last few years: the Thames offers some little-seen views of London, and cutting through the open expanse of river can certainly be a most relaxing travel option. Most River Bus services operate every 20-60 minutes and there are piers all over the central area where you can jump on board, from Chelsea Harbour in the west to Woolwich Arsenal in the east. Pay at the pier ticket office and show your Oyster card for a discount; if the office is closed, you can purchase a ticket on-board.

By cable car

Launched in June 2012 for the London Olympics, the Emirates Air Line glides high over the Thames from the Royal Docks (near the Excel Centre) to North Greenwich (by The O2), and offers fantastic views of the Thames Barrier and Canary Wharf. It takes 5-10 minutes to make the crossing and each car can hold around 10 people. You can pay at the ticket office (presenting your Travelcard for a discount), or use your Oyster card at the gates.

Living London Life

It almost goes without saying that visitors to the capital are spoilt for choice when it comes to having a good time. You could visit one of the city's 300 museums or galleries, many of which are free, or you could see for yourself why London's theatre scene is considered the best in the world. Come nightfall, choose from the vast number of globally-influenced restaurants or from one of 5,000 pubs and bars.

At the weekend, an interesting alternative to shopping or sports events is to browse one of the farmers' markets: on a Saturday, the best of the bunch can be found at Ealing, Notting Hill, Pimlico, Wimbledon and Twickenham. On Sundays, two of the favourites are in Marylebone and Blackheath, while, on the same day, the Columbia Road flower market, in the East End, is a wonderful place to while away the hours.

The more mainstream shopper might do well to steer clear of frenetic Oxford Street. Regent Street is a more alluring thoroughfare with its mid-priced fashion stores and hallowed names. If you're after a destination with a real touch of class, then nearby Jermyn Street is the place for bespoke men's clothing, but if your taste is for more outré threads, then Notting Hill or Camden are good bets. Back in the centre of town, Covent Garden is packed with speciality stores, quirky alleyways and – if you choose the wrong time to go – an awful lot of people!

Escape can always be found in the relative quiet of a good bookshop, and London is full of them. Still in Covent Garden, Stanford's is the city's number one travel bookshop, while not far away in Charing Cross Road, the legendary Foyles has thrown over its fusty image with a stylish makeover. But for the marriage of real elegance with a good read, head to Daunt Books in Marylebone High Street, which is set in an Edwardian building with long oak galleries and skylights; the bustle of London's streets will seem a million miles away.

Stéphanie Guillaume/Fotolia.com

Where to **eat**

Lists of awards and features

Starred restaurants

Within the selection, we have highlighted a number of restaurants for their excellent cooking. When awarding one, two or three Michelin Stars there are a number of factors we consider: the quality and compatibility of the ingredients, the technical skill and flair that goes into their preparation, the clarity and combination of flavours, the value for money and, above all, the taste. Equally important is the ability to produce excellent cooking not once but time and time again. Our inspectors make as many visits as necessary, so that you can be sure of the quality and consistency.
A two star restaurant has to offer something very special in its cuisine; a real element of creativity, originality or personality that sets it apart from the rest. Three stars – our highest award – are given to the very best.
Cuisines in any style and of any nationality are eligible for a star; the decoration, service and comfort have no bearing on the award.
For every restaurant awarded a star we include six specialities that are typical of their cooking style.
These specific dishes may not always be available but give an idea as to the type of cuisine you will find.

The awarding of a star is based solely on the quality of the cuisine.

N: highlights those establishments newly promoted to one, two or three stars.

✿✿✿

Exceptional cuisine, worth a special journey.

One always eats extremely well here, sometimes superbly. Distinctive dishes are precisely executed, using superlative ingredients.

Restaurant	Comfort	Page
Alain Ducasse at The Dorchester	XXXXX	41
Gordon Ramsay	XXXX	286

✿✿

Excellent cooking, worth a detour.

Skilfully and carefully crafted dishes of outstanding quality.

Restaurant	Comfort	Page
Dinner by Heston Blumenthal	XX	281
Le Gavroche	XXXX	69
Greenhouse	XXX	72
Hélène Darroze at The Connaught	XXXX	77
Hibiscus	XXX	78
Ledbury	XXX	313
Marcus	XXXX	146
Sketch (The Lecture Room and Library)	XXXX	105
Square	XXXX	109

✿

Very good cooking in its category.

Cuisine prepared to a consistently high standard.

Restaurant	Comfort	Page
Alyn Williams at The Westbury	XXXX	42
Amaya	XXX	140
Ametsa with Arzak Instruction	XXX	141
Angler	XX	223
Arbutus	X	45
L'Atelier de Joël Robuchon	XX	123
L'Autre Pied	XX	161
Barrafina **N**	X	47
Benares	XXX	50
Brasserie Chavot	XX	55
Chez Bruce	XX	433
City Social **N**	XXX	234
Clove Club **N**	X	360
Club Gascon	XX	235
Dabbous	X	191
Fera at Claridge's **N**	XXXX	67
Galvin at Windows	XXX	70
Galvin La Chapelle	XXX	383
The Glasshouse	XX	422
Gymkhana **N**	XX	73
Hakkasan Hanway Place	XX	194
Hakkasan Mayfair	XX	74
Harwood Arms	🍺	413
Hedone	XX	402
HKK	XX	362
Kai	XXX	81
Kitchen Table at Bubbledogs **N**	XX	196
Kitchen W8	XX	311
Launceston Place	XXX	312
Lima	X	169
Locanda Locatelli	XXX	170
Maze	XX	86
Murano	XXX	89
Outlaw's at The Capital	XX	293
Pétrus	XXX	151
Pied à Terre	XXX	199
Pollen Street Social	XX	95
Quilon	XXX	152
Rasoi	XX	297
River Café	XX	421
St John	X	255
Seven Park Place	XXX	103
Social Eating House	X	106
Story	XX	258
Tamarind	XXX	110
Texture	XX	177
Trishna	X	178
La Trompette	XXX	405
Umu	XX	114
Wild Honey	XX	117
Yauatcha	XX	119

Bib Gourmand restaurants

Restaurants offering good quality cooking for £28 or less (price of a 3 course meal, excluding drinks).

Restaurants by cuisine type

Argentinian

Casa Malevo	X	207
Zoilo	X	182

Asian

Bone Daddies	X	53
E and O	XX	308
Eight over Eight	XX	282
Flesh and Buns	X	192
Kopapa	X	195
Singapore Garden	XX	341
Spice Market	XX	107
XO	XX	330

Austrian

Fischer's	XX	166

Basque

Donostia	X	165

British creative

Dairy	X	407
Fera at Claridge's	XXXX ✿	67

British modern

Anchor and Hope	🍺 ☺	222
Berners Tavern	XX	162
Bistro Union	X ☺	406
Bluebird	XX	274
Brown Dog	🍺	394
Chelsea Ram	🍺	279
Chiswell Street Dining Rooms	XX	232
Corrigan's Mayfair	XXX	63
Dean Street Townhouse Restaurant	XX	64
Dinner by Heston Blumenthal	XX ✿✿	281
Drapers Arms	🍺 ☺	355
Fox and Grapes	🍺	434
Great Queen Street	X ☺	193
Hampshire Hog	🍺	418
Harwood Arms	🍺 ✿	413
Hereford Road	X ☺	208
Hoi Polloi	XX	361
Keeper's House	XX	82
Linnea	XX	423
London House	XX	398
Lyle's	X	363
Magdalen	XX	244
Malt House	🍺	414
Market	X ☺	331
The National Dining Rooms	X	90
New Angel	XX	210
1901	XXX	248
Olympic Café + Dining Room	X	395
Pantechnicon	🍺	150
Paradise by way of Kensal Green	🍺	334
Parlour	🍺	335
Peasant	🍺	251
Picture	X ☺	172
Plum + Spilt Milk	XX	338
Prince Arthur	🍺	353
Prince of Wales	🍺	424
Quo Vadis	XXX	98
Restaurant at St Paul's Cathedral	X	254
Rivington Grill (Greenwich)	X	380
Roast	XX	254
Sands End	🍺	415
sixtyone	XX	176
Tate Modern (Restaurant)	X	259
La Trompette	XXX ✿	405
Victoria	🍺	411
Well	🍺	263
Wells	🍺	334

British traditional

Barnyard	X ☺	188
Beagle	X	354
Bedford and Strand	X	125
Bird of Smithfield	X	226
Boisdale of Belgravia	XX	142
Boisdale of Bishopsgate	XX	227
Boisdale of Canary Wharf	XX	375
Builders Arms	🍺	276

Chinese

French

Chez Bruce	XX✿	433
Cigalon	XX	232
Clos Maggiore	XX	125
Club Gascon	XX✿	235
Colbert	XX	280
Le Colombier	XX	280
Comptoir Gascon	X☺	236
Les Deux Salons	XX	127
The Ebury Restaurant and Wine Bar	XX	144
Galvin Bistrot de Luxe	XX	166
Galvin Café a Vin	X☺	382
Galvin La Chapelle	XXX✿	383
Galvin Demoiselle	X	284
Garnier	XX	284
Gauthier - Soho	XXX	68
Le Gavroche	XXXX✿✿	69
Gordon Ramsay	XXXX✿✿✿	286
Green Man and French Horn	X☺	128
Hélène Darroze at The Connaught	XXXX✿✿	77
Henry Root	X	287
High Road Brasserie	X	403
Koffmann's	XXX	145
Little Social	X	83
Lobster Pot	X	381
Luc's Brasserie	XX	243
Marco	XX	290
Marianne	XX	209
Mon Plaisir	XX	197
La Petite Maison	XX	93
Pétrus	XXX✿	151
Le Pont de la Tour	XXX	252
Provender	X☺	366
Racine	XX	296
Rétro Bistrot	XX	429
Roux at the Landau	XXX	175
Sauterelle	XX	256
Sketch (The Lecture Room and Library)	XXXX✿✿	105
Soif	X☺	400
Square	XXXX✿✿	109
10 Cases	X	133
Terroirs	X☺	134
Les Trois Garcons	XX	385
Le Vacherin	XX	392
The Wallace	X	180

Greek

Ergon	X	165
Mazi	X	314
Retsina	X	329

Indian

Amaya	XXX✿	140
Babur	XX	379
Benares	XXX✿	50
Bombay Brasserie	XXXX	275
Cafe Spice Namaste	XX☺	386
Chakra	XX	306
Chutney Mary	XXX	279
The Cinnamon Club	XXX	143
Cinnamon Kitchen	XX	233
Cinnamon Soho	X	62
Dishoom	X	127
Gymkhana	XX✿	73
Hazara	XX	329
Imli Street	X	80
Indian Zilla	XX	394
Indian Zing	XX	419
Kennington Tandoori	XX	381
Malabar	XX	310
Mint Leaf	XX	88
Mint Leaf Lounge	XX	246
Moti Mahal	XX	198
Painted Heron	XX	294
Potli	XX	420
Quilon	XXX✿	152
Rasoi	XX✿	297
Red Fort	XXX	98
Roots at N1	XX☺	348
Roti Chai	X	174
Shayona	X	332
Swagat	X	427
Tamarind	XXX✿	110
Trishna	X✿	178
Veeraswamy	XX	115
Zayna	XX	181
Zumbura	X	408

Italian

A Cena	XX	431
Al Borgo	XX	428
Al Duca	XX	40
Alloro	XX	40
Amaranto	XXX	43
L'Anima	XXX	358
Antico	X	222
Assaggi	X	206
Bibo	X☺	423
Bocca di Lupo	X☺	52

Japanese

Korean

Lebanese

Mediterranean

Light House	X	435
Margaux	X	290
Moro	X	247
Nopi	X	91
Opera Tavern	X ☺	131
The Orange	🍺	149
Ottolenghi	X	356
Palmerston	🍺	378
Pizarro	X	251
Rivea	XX	298
Rosita	X	399
Salt Yard	X ☺	200
Sam's Brasserie	X	404
Winter Garden	XX	180

Mexican

Casa Negra	X	359
Peyote	X	93

North-African

Azou	X ☺	416
Momo	XX	88

North-American

Mishkin's	X	130
One Sixty	X	341
Soho Kitchen and Bar	X	107
Spuntino	X	108

Peruvian

Andina	X	358
Ceviche	X	60
Coya	XX	63
Lima	X ✿	169

Polish

Ognisko	XX	292

Spanish

Barrafina	X ✿	47
Barrica	X ☺	188
Boqueria	X	400
Cambio de Tercio	XX	277
Capote y Toros	X	278
Cigala	X	190
Drakes Tabanco	X	190
El Pirata DeTapas	X	210
Eyre Brothers	XX	361
Fino	XX	192
Iberica Canary Wharf	XX	377
Iberica Marylebone	XX	167
José	X ☺	241
Lola Rojo	X	398
Morito	X ☺	247
Tapas Brindisa (London Bridge)	X	259
Tapas Brindisa (Soho)	X	111
Tendido Cero	X	298
Tendido Cuatro	X	416

Thai

Bangkok	X	273
Blue Elephant	XX	412
Chada	XX	396
Rosa's Carnaby	X	100
Rosa's Soho	X	101
Simply Thai	X	430
Suda	X	133

Vietnamese

Au Lac	X	353
Cây Tre	X	59
Viet Grill	X	365

Fish and chips

Fish and Chip Shop	X	356
Kerbisher and Malt	X	410

Fish and seafood

Angler	XX ✿	223
Bentley's (Grill)	XXX	49
Bentley's (Oyster Bar)	X	51
Bonnie Gull	X	163
Fish Market	X	238
Geales	X	285
J. Sheekey	XX	129
J. Sheekey Oyster Bar	X	130
Olivomare	X	149
One-O-One	XXX	292
Outlaw's at The Capital	XX ✿	293
Poissonnerie	XX	295
Scott's	XXX	102
Wright Brothers	X	264
Wright Brothers Soho	X	118

Innovative

Ametsa with Arzak Instruction	XXX ✿	141
Archipelago	XX	160
Corner Room	X ☺	373
L'Etranger	XX	282

Other world kitchens

Restaurants with outside dining

Restaurants open for breakfast

Restaurant	Category	Page
Al Duca	XX	40
Andina	X	358
Aqua Shard	XX	224
Avenue	XX	44
Balcon	XX	46
Balthazar	XX	124
Berners Tavern	XX	162
Bird of Smithfield	X	226
Bistrot Bruno Loubet	X	226
The Botanist	XX	276
Boulestin	XX	54
Boundary	XXX	359
Brasserie Max	XX	189
Bread Street Kitchen	XX	228
Brumus	XX	56
Caravan (Finsbury)	X	229
Caravan (King's Cross St Pancras)	X	336
Cecconi's	XXX	60
Chapters	XX	374
Chelsea Ram	🍺	279
The Cinnamon Club	XXX	143
Clarke's	XX	307
Clerkenwell Kitchen	X	233
Colbert	XX	280
Dishoom	X	127
Duck and Waffle	XX	237
Electric Diner	X	309
Elliot's	X ☺	237
Fifteen London	X	354
Fischer's	XX	166
Franco's	XX	68
Gail's Kitchen	X ☺	193
Garrison	🍺	239
Granger and Co	X	309
Grazing Goat	🍺	167
Great British	X	71
Hampshire Hog	🍺	418
Ham Yard	XX	75
Harrison's	X	393
Hawksmoor (City of London)	X	240
Hoi Polloi	XX	361
Honey and Co	X ☺	195
Imli Street	X	80
Joe's	XX	288
Jugged Hare	🍺	242
Kopapa	X	195
Lardo	X	352
Manicomio (City of London)	XX	244
The Mercer	XX	245
The Modern Pantry	X	246
Nopi	X	91
Olympic Café + Dining Room	X	395
Only Running Footman	🍺	92
The Orange	🍺	149
Ottolenghi	X	356
Parlour	🍺	335
Pavilion	XX	316
Plum + Spilt Milk	XX	338
Portrait	X	97
Provender	X ☺	366
Quo Vadis	XXX	98
Riding House Café	X	174
Rivea	XX	298
Rivington Grill (Greenwich)	X	380
Rivington Grill (Shoreditch)	X	364
Roast	XX	254
1701	XX	256
Spice Market	XX	107
Toasted	X	379
Tom's Kitchen	X	299
Village East	X	261
The Wolseley	XXX	116

Restaurants open late

Time of last orders in brackets.

Restaurant		Page
Arbutus *(23.30)*	X ✿	45
L'Atelier de Joël Robuchon *(00.00)*	XX ✿	123
Balthazar *(23.30)*	XX	124
Bar Boulud *(23.30)*	XX	273
Bentley's (Oyster Bar) *(23.45)*	X	51
Boisdale of Belgravia *(23.30)*	XX	142
Brasserie Max *(23.30)*	XX	189
Brasserie Zédel *(00.00)*	XX ☺	56
Le Caprice *(23.30)*	XX	59
Cecconi's *(23.15)*	XXX	60
Ceviche *(23.30)*	X	60
Chicken Shop (Kentish Town) *(00.00)*	X	335
China Tang *(23.45)*	XXXX	61
Chutney Mary *(23.30)*	XXX	279
Colbert *(23.30)*	XX	280
Delaunay *(00.00)*	XXX	126
Duck and Waffle *(00.00)*	XX	237
Floridita *(23.30)*	XX	66
Hakkasan Hanway Place *(00.00)*	XX ✿	194
Hakkasan Mayfair *(23.30)*	XX ✿	74
Haozhan *(02.00)*	XX	75
Hoi Polloi *(01.00)*	XX	361
The Ivy *(00.00)*	XXX	129
J. Sheekey *(23.30)*	XX	129
J. Sheekey Oyster Bar *(23.30)*	X	130
Malabar *(23.30)*	XX	310
Momo *(23.15)*	XX	88
Mr Chow *(23.30)*	XX	291
Nobu *(02.15)*	XX	90
Nobu Berkeley St *(00.00)*	XX	91
Palomar *(23.30)*	X ☺	92
Plum Valley *(23.15)*	XX	94
Poissonnerie *(23.30)*	XX	295
Refuel *(00.00)*	XX	99
Roka (Bloomsbury) *(23.30)*	XX	198
Roka (Mayfair) *(23.30)*	XX	100
Shoryu *(23.30)*	X	104
Soho Kitchen and Bar *(01.00)*	X	107
Spuntino *(01.00)*	X	108
Wild Honey *(23.30)*	XX ✿	117
The Wolseley *(00.00)*	XXX	116
Yauatcha *(23.30)*	XX ✿	119

Central London

R. Leaver/Loop Images/Age fotostock

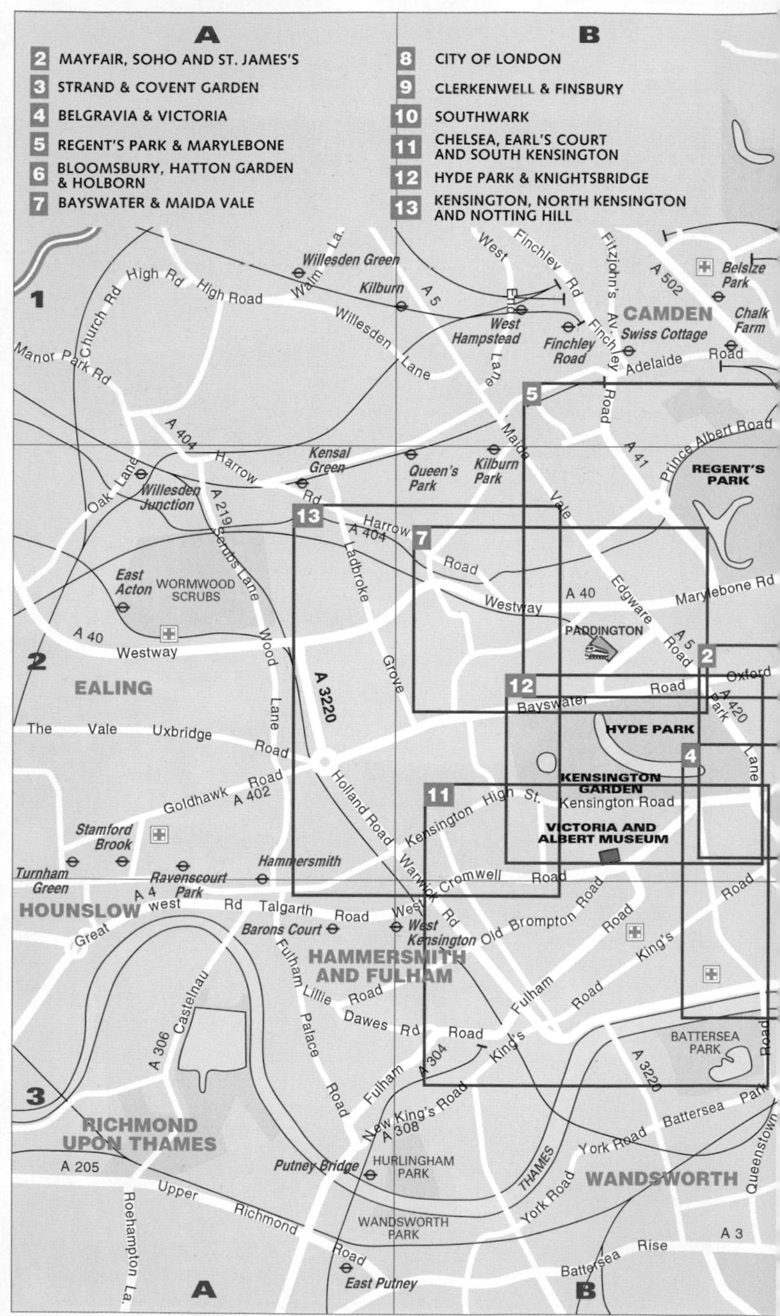
A
B
2 MAYFAIR, SOHO AND ST. JAMES'S
3 STRAND & COVENT GARDEN
4 BELGRAVIA & VICTORIA
5 REGENT'S PARK & MARYLEBONE
6 BLOOMSBURY, HATTON GARDEN & HOLBORN
7 BAYSWATER & MAIDA VALE
8 CITY OF LONDON
9 CLERKENWELL & FINSBURY
10 SOUTHWARK
11 CHELSEA, EARL'S COURT AND SOUTH KENSINGTON
12 HYDE PARK & KNIGHTSBRIDGE
13 KENSINGTON, NORTH KENSINGTON AND NOTTING HILL
1
2
3
Willesden Green
Kilburn
West Hampstead
Finchley Road
Swiss Cottage
Belsize Park
Chalk Farm
CAMDEN
Kensal Green
Queen's Park
Kilburn Park
Willesden Junction
East Acton
WORMWOOD SCRUBS
REGENT'S PARK
PADDINGTON
HYDE PARK
KENSINGTON GARDEN
VICTORIA AND ALBERT MUSEUM
EALING
Stamford Brook
Turnham Green
Ravenscourt Park
Hammersmith
HOUNSLOW
Barons Court
West Kensington
HAMMERSMITH AND FULHAM
BATTERSEA PARK
RICHMOND UPON THAMES
Putney Bridge
HURLINGHAM PARK
WANDSWORTH PARK
East Putney
THAMES
WANDSWORTH
A 404
A 219
A 40
A 3220
A 5
A 41
A 502
A 420
A 402
A 4
A 306
A 304
A 308
A 205
A 3
Westway
The Vale
Uxbridge Road
Goldhawk Road
Holland Road
Kensington High St.
Kensington Road
Cromwell Road
Talgarth Road
Lillie Road
Dawes Rd
Fulham Road
King's Road
New King's Road
York Road
Battersea Park
Battersea Rise
Upper Richmond Road
Roehampton La.
Castelnau
Harrow Road
Ladbroke Grove
Edgware Road
Marylebone Rd
Oxford
Bayswater Road
Maida Vale
Prince Albert Road
Adelaide Road
Fitzjohn's Av.
Finchley Rd
West End Lane
Willesden Lane
High Road
High Rd
Church Rd
Manor Park Rd
Oak Lane
Scrubs Lane
Wood Lane
Warwick Rd
Old Brompton Road
Fulham Palace Road
Great west Rd
Walm La.
Queenstown

Central London Plans
(Plan I)

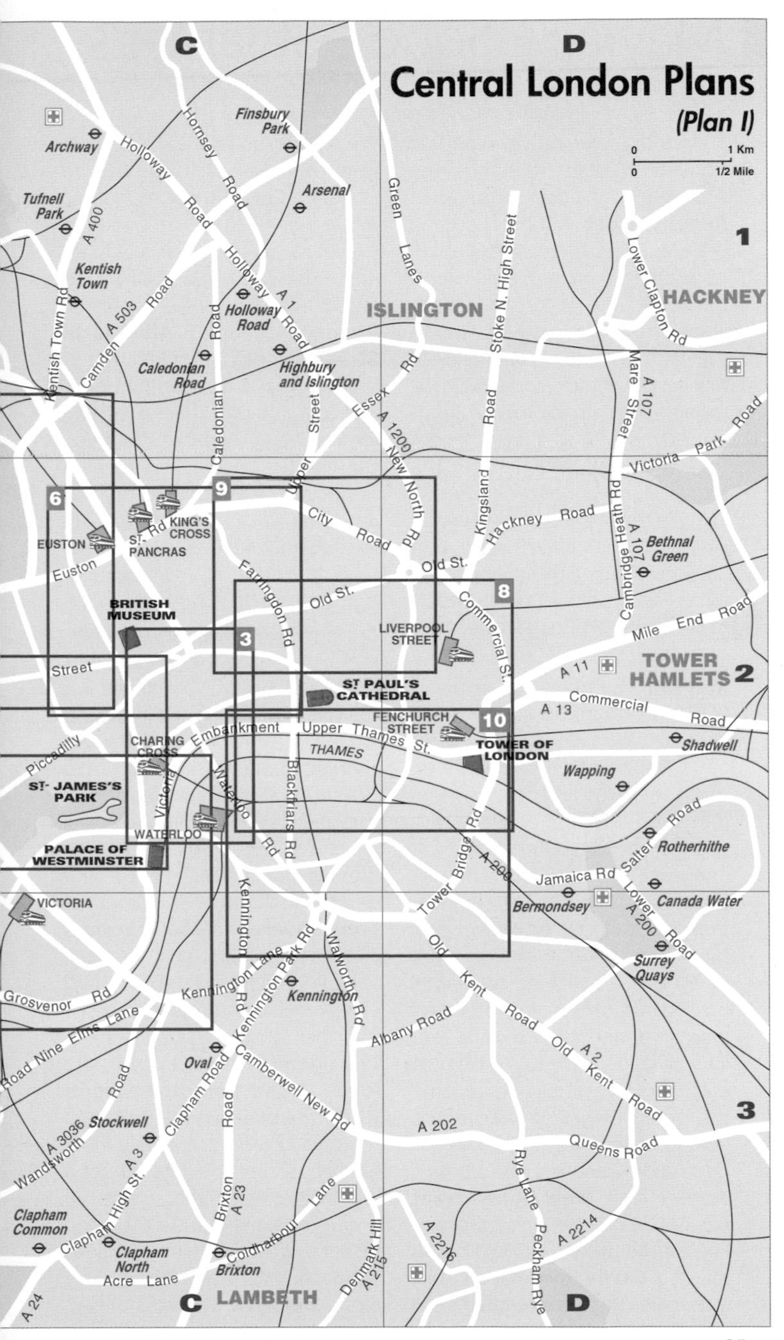

Mayfair · Soho · St James's

There's one elegant dividing line between Mayfair and Soho - the broad and imposing sweep of **Regent Street** - but mindsets and price tags keep them a world apart. It's usual to think of easterly Soho as the wild and sleazy half of these ill-matched twins, with Mayfair to the west the more sedate and sophisticated of the two. Sometimes, though, the natural order of things runs awry: why was rock's legendary wild man Jimi Hendrix, the embodiment of Soho decadence, living in the rarefied air of Mayfair's smart 23 Brook Street? And what induced Vivienne Westwood, punk queen and fashionista to the edgy, to settle her sewing machine in the uber-smart Conduit Street?

Mayfair has been synonymous with elegance for three and a half centuries, ever since the Berkeley and Grosvenor families bought up the local fields and turned them into posh real estate. The area is named after the annual May fair introduced in 1686, but suffice it to say that a raucous street celebration would be frowned upon big time by twenty-first century inhabitants. The grand residential boulevards can seem frosty and imposing, and even induce feelings of inadequacy to the humble passer-by but should he become the proud owner of a glistening gold card, then hey ho, doors will open wide. Claridge's is an art deco wonder, while **New Bond Street** is London's number one thoroughfare for the most chi-chi names in retailing. **Savile Row** may sound a little 'passé' these days, but it's still the place to go for the sharpest cut in town, before sashaying over to compact **Cork Street** to indulge in the purchase of a piece of art at one of its superb galleries. Science and music can also be found here, and at a relatively cheap price: the Faraday Museum in **Albemarle Street** has had a sparkling refurbishment, and the Handel House Museum in Brook Street boasts an impressive two-for-one offer: you can visit the beautifully presented home of the German composer and view his musical scores… before looking at pictures of Hendrix, his 'future' next door neighbour.

Soho challenges the City as London's most famous square mile. It may not have the money of its brash easterly rival, but it sure has the buzz. It's always been fast and loose, since the days when hunters charged through with their cries of 'So-ho!' Its narrow jumbled streets throng with humanity, from the tourist to the tipsy, the libertine to the louche. A lot of the fun is centred round the streets just south of **Soho Square,** where area legends like The Coach & Horses ('Norman's Bar'), Ronnie Scott's and Bar Italia cluster in close proximity. There's 80s favourite, the Groucho Club. The tightest t-shirts in town are found in **Old Compton Street,** where the pink pound jangles the registers in a swathe of gay-friendly bars and restaurants. To get a feel of the 'real' Soho, where old engraved signs enliven the shop fronts and the market stall cries echo back to the 1700s, a jaunt along **Berwick Street** is always

P. Phipp/Travelshots / age fotostock

in vogue, taking in a pint at the eternally popular Blue Posts, an unchanging street corner stalwart that still announces 'Watney's Ales' on its stencilled windows.

Not a lot of Watney's ale was ever drunk in **St James's;** not a lot of ale of any kind for that matter. Champagne and port is more the style here, in the hushed and reverential gentlemen's clubs where discretion is the key, and change is measured in centuries rather than years. The sheer class of the area is typified by **Pall Mall's** Reform Club, where Phileas Fogg wagered that he could zip round the world in eighty days, and the adjacent **St James's Square,** which was the most fashionable address in London in the late seventeenth century, when dukes and earls aplenty got their satin shoes under the silver bedecked tables.

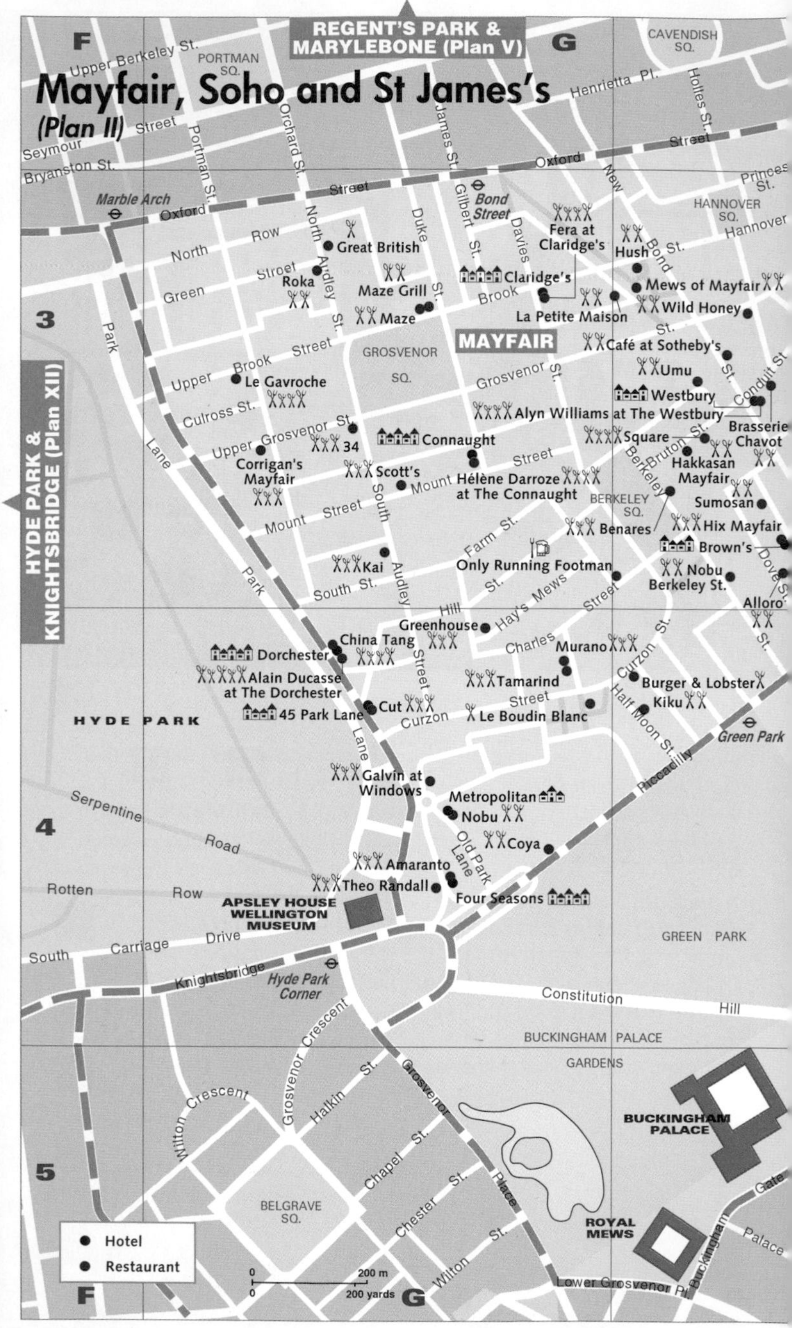
Mayfair, Soho and St James's
(Plan II)
REGENT'S PARK & MARYLEBONE (Plan V)
HYDE PARK & KNIGHTSBRIDGE (Plan XII)
F
G
3
4
5
MAYFAIR
Great British
Roka
Maze Grill
Maze
Claridge's
Fera at Claridge's
Hush
Mews of Mayfair
Wild Honey
La Petite Maison
Café at Sotheby's
Umu
Westbury
Alyn Williams at The Westbury
Brasserie Chavot
Square
Hakkasan Mayfair
Sumosan
Le Gavroche
34
Connaught
Corrigan's Mayfair
Scott's
Hélène Darroze at The Connaught
Benares
Hix Mayfair
Brown's
Kai
Only Running Footman
Nobu Berkeley St.
Alloro
Greenhouse
China Tang
Dorchester
Alain Ducasse at The Dorchester
Murano
Tamarind
Burger & Lobster
Kiku
45 Park Lane
Cut
Le Boudin Blanc
Galvin at Windows
Metropolitan
Nobu
Coya
Amaranto
Theo Randall
Four Seasons
APSLEY HOUSE WELLINGTON MUSEUM
HYDE PARK
GREEN PARK
BUCKINGHAM PALACE GARDENS
BUCKINGHAM PALACE
ROYAL MEWS
BELGRAVE SQ.
GROSVENOR SQ.
BERKELEY SQ.
PORTMAN SQ.
CAVENDISH SQ.
HANNOVER SQ.
Marble Arch
Bond Street
Green Park
Hyde Park Corner
Oxford Street
Piccadilly
Knightsbridge
Constitution Hill
Park Lane
Serpentine Road
Rotten Row
South Carriage Drive
Hotel
Restaurant
0
200 m
200 yards

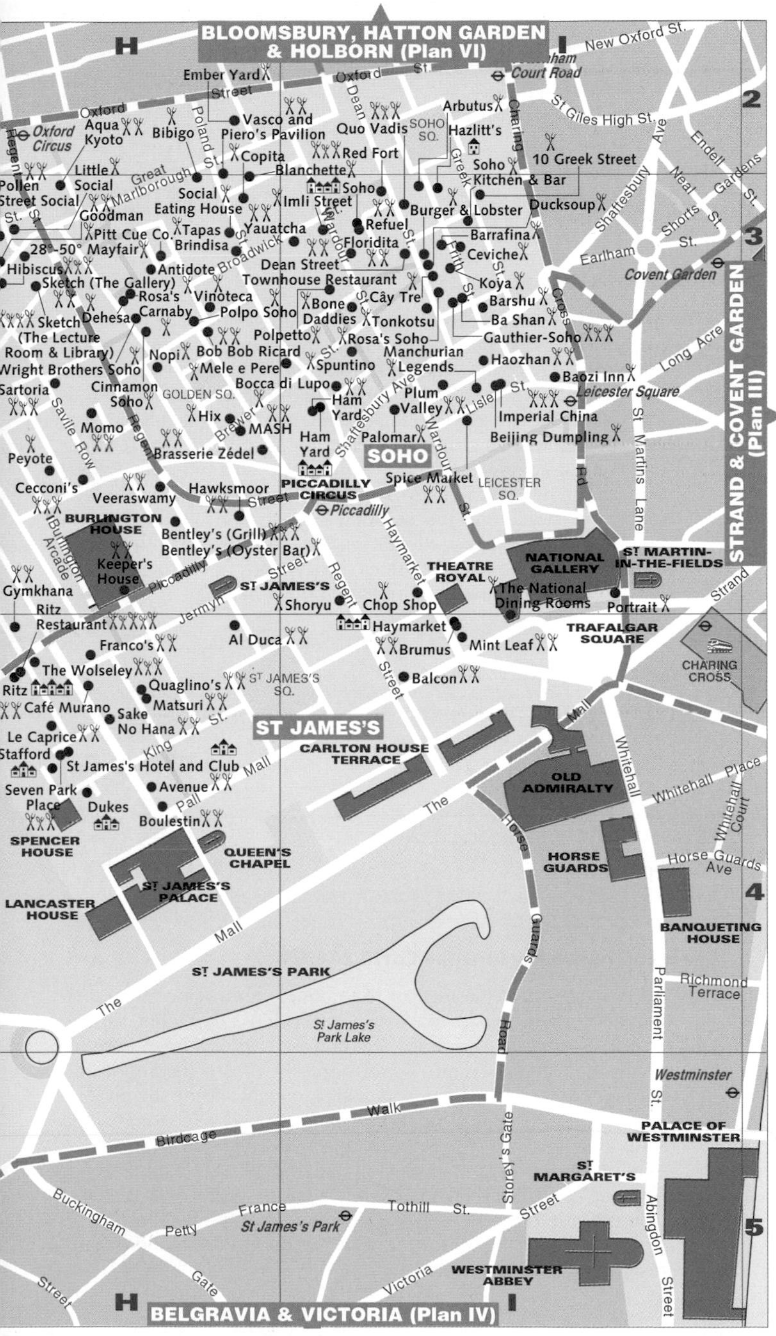
BLOOMSBURY, HATTON GARDEN & HOLBORN (Plan VI)
STRAND & COVENT GARDEN (Plan III)
BELGRAVIA & VICTORIA (Plan IV)
SOHO
ST JAMES'S
PICCADILLY CIRCUS
TRAFALGAR SQUARE
ST JAMES'S PARK
Ember Yard
Vasco and Piero's Pavilion
Quo Vadis
Arbutus
Hazlitt's
Aqua Kyoto
Bibigo
Copita
Red Fort
10 Greek Street
Little Social
Pollen Street Social
Goodman
Social Eating House
Blanchette
Soho Kitchen & Bar
Imli Street
Soho
Burger & Lobster
Ducksoup
Pitt Cue Co.
Tapas Brindisa
Yauatcha
Refuel
Barrafina
28°-50° Mayfair
Floridita
Ceviche
Hibiscus
Antidote
Dean Street Townhouse Restaurant
Koya
Sketch (The Gallery)
Rosa's Carnaby
Vinoteca
Bone Daddies
Cây Tre
Barshu
Sketch (The Lecture Room & Library)
Dehesa
Polpo Soho
Tonkotsu
Ba Shan
Polpetto
Rosa's Soho
Gauthier-Soho
Wright Brothers Soho
Nopi
Bob Bob Ricard
Manchurian Legends
Haozhan
Mele e Pere
Spuntino
Baozi Inn
Sartoria
Cinnamon Soho
Bocca di Lupo
Plum Valley
Imperial China
Hix
Ham Yard
Beijing Dumpling
Momo
MASH
Palomar
Peyote
Brasserie Zédel
Spice Market
Cecconi's
Veeraswamy
Hawksmoor
Bentley's (Grill)
Bentley's (Oyster Bar)
Keeper's House
Gymkhana
Shoryu
Chop Shop
The National Dining Rooms
Portrait
Ritz Restaurant
Al Duca
Haymarket
Brumus
Mint Leaf
Franco's
The Wolseley
Balcon
Quaglino's
Ritz
Matsuri
Café Murano
Sake No Hana
Le Caprice
Stafford
St James's Hotel and Club
Avenue
Seven Park Place
Dukes
Boulestin
BURLINGTON HOUSE
THEATRE ROYAL
NATIONAL GALLERY
ST MARTIN-IN-THE-FIELDS
CHARING CROSS
CARLTON HOUSE TERRACE
OLD ADMIRALTY
HORSE GUARDS
BANQUETING HOUSE
SPENCER HOUSE
QUEEN'S CHAPEL
ST JAMES'S PALACE
LANCASTER HOUSE
PALACE OF WESTMINSTER
ST MARGARET'S
WESTMINSTER ABBEY
Oxford Circus
Tottenham Court Road
Covent Garden
Leicester Square
Piccadilly
Westminster
St James's Park
St James's Park Lake
SOHO SQ.
GOLDEN SQ.
LEICESTER SQ.
ST JAMES'S SQ.
New Oxford St.
Oxford Street
St Giles High St.
Charing Cross Rd
Shaftesbury Ave
Earlham St.
Long Acre
St Martin's Lane
Strand
Whitehall
Whitehall Place
Whitehall Court
Horse Guards Ave
Horse Guards Road
Parliament St.
Richmond Terrace
Birdcage Walk
The Mall
Pall Mall
King St.
Jermyn St.
Piccadilly
Regent Street
Haymarket
Savile Row
Burlington Arcade
Great Marlborough St.
Poland St.
Dean St.
Greek St.
Frith St.
Wardour St.
Lisle St.
Brewer St.
Broadwick St.
Buckingham Gate
Petty France
Tothill St.
Victoria Street
Storey's Gate
Abingdon Street
H
I
2
3
4
5

Al Duca

Italian H4

4-5 Duke of York St ✉ SW1Y 6LA
✆ (020) 7839 3090
www.alduca-restaurant.co.uk
⊖ Piccadilly Circus
Closed Easter, 25 December, Sunday and bank holidays

Menu £20 – Carte approx. £41

A/C

Al Duca has become as much a part of the fabric of St James's as many of the shirt makers who have made neighbouring Jermyn Street home over the years. It is also one of the those restaurants that manage the trick of appearing quiet one minute and full to the rafters the next without anyone noticing and this ensures that the atmosphere is never less than spirited. The serving team are a young, confident bunch and the manager knows who his regulars are. The menu is priced per course; there is plenty of choice and the cooking is crisp and confident, with plenty of well-priced bottles to match. The rib-eye with porcini mushrooms is a highlight. Prices are also pretty keen, especially for a restaurant in this neck of the woods.

Alloro

Italian H3

19-20 Dover St ✉ W1S 4LU
✆ (020) 7495 4768
www.atozrestaurants.com/alloro
⊖ Green Park
Closed 25 December, Saturday lunch and Sunday – booking essential

Menu £36 (weekday lunch) – Carte £44/61

Alloro opened at the turn of the century and this comparative longevity owes much to its sensible prices, confident service and easy-to-eat Italian food. The current chef has been here for nearly half the restaurant's life; he comes from Piedmont and manages to sneak in a few specialties from his home region. The menu offers an appealing and nicely balanced selection, from a crisp chicory salad with bottarga to slow-cooked lamb shoulder, with all breads and pastas being made in-house. It's priced per number of courses taken; having all four represents the best value. Noise drifts in from the adjacent, boisterous baretto and so ensures that the atmosphere in the comfortable and urbane restaurant is always lively.

Alain Ducasse at The Dorchester ✿✿✿

French G4

Dorchester Hotel,
Park Ln ✉ W1K 1QA
✆ (020) 7629 8866 – **www**.alainducasse-dorchester.com
⊖ Hyde Park Corner
Closed 10 August-2 September, 26-30 December, Saturday lunch, Sunday and Monday

Menu £55/90

Alain Ducasse

Alain Ducasse is one of France's greatest post-war chefs and his London team display a confidence in their ability and maturity in their attitude that does justice to his reputation. The service is assured and the meal perfectly paced; the settled, experienced team know when to engage with guests and when to stand back. The room has a serene and luxurious feel and its tables are immaculately set, but try to avoid the raised section by the windows as, although you may have a partial view of the park, you do end up feeling somewhat disengaged from the rest of the room. The kitchen team have steadily lightened the classical French dishes but they remain superbly crafted, with wonderfully complementary flavours and textures. The menu uses the best of British and French produce, from Dorset crab and Scottish lobster to Limousin veal and Anjou pigeon, and some of the dishes will remain long in the memory. The wine list is exemplary, with a particularly impressive selection of Domaine de la Romanée Conti and Château d'Yquem.

First Course

- Sauté of lobster, truffled chicken quenelles and pasta.
- Confit duck foie gras with cherries and fresh almonds.

Main Course

- Fillet of beef Rossini with Périgueux sauce.
- Wild sea bass with courgette flower, basil and olives.

Dessert

- 'Baba like in Monte-Carlo'.
- Summer berry vacherin.

Alyn Williams at The Westbury ✿

modern

H3

Westbury Hotel,
37 Conduit St ✉ W1S 2YF
✆ (020) 7183 6426 – **www**.alynwilliams.com
⊖ Bond Street

Closed first 2 weeks January, last 2 weeks August, Saturday lunch, Sunday and Monday

Menu £28/58

Alyn Williams at The Westbury

Peep inside this restaurant within the Westbury Hotel and the impression you get is one of considerable formality but the good news is that it's a long way from being one of those whispering shrines to gastronomy. Granted, it's a comfortable room, with rosewood panelling and well-spaced, smartly laid tables but the reason the atmosphere never strays into terminal seriousness is largely down to the staff who exude a warmth and sincerity that one all too rarely sees these days. Their willingness to please can also take one by surprise – for instance, they'll gladly let you mix and match the tasting and à la carte menus and if you order a glass of wine they'll happily offer you a taster first. The other reason for its appeal is the relative value for money when one considers the quality of the cooking. Alyn Williams is a man with an innate understanding of flavours; his dishes are colourful and quite elaborate constructions but the combinations of textures and tastes marry happily together. Sourcing of ingredients is key and he displays his foraged herbs in glass pots by the kitchen.

First Course

- Scallops with squid ink, fennel and pumpernickel.
- Wild English rabbit, black radish, celery and truffle.

Main Course

- Wood pigeon, ramsons, morels and honey shallots.
- Veal sirloin with confit garlic, apple and pickled elderflower.

Dessert

- Iced coconut parfait, lime and peanuts.
- Pineapple with Nepali pepper, gingerbread and molasses.

Amaranto

Italian G4

Four Seasons Hotel,
Hamilton Pl, Park Ln ✉ W1J 7DR
✆ (020) 7499 0888
www.fourseasons.com/london/dining
⊖ Hyde Park Corner

Menu £26 (weekday lunch) – Carte £30/72

The Four Seasons hotel emerged from its huge refurbishment programme with a restaurant that's all about flexibility. Amaranto is a bar, a lounge and a dining room, and the idea is that you can have what you want, where you want it, from a largely Italian inspired menu that covers all bases. That means you can enjoy some crab cakes with your drink in the smart bar, share a plate of charcuterie with friends in the comfortable lounge or order a full 3 course meal with business clients in the handsome dining room. No expense was spared on the decoration – the space is full of the colours of the plant after which it is named and there's lots of lacquered wood. Unusually for hotels on Park Lane, there is also a fine terrace attached.

Antidote

modern H3

12A Newburgh St ✉ W1F 7RR
✆ (020) 7287 8488
www.antidotewinebar.com
⊖ Oxford Circus
Closed Sunday – booking advisable

Carte £23/40

Feeling the need to reinvent, the French owners – who ran the place when it was called La Trouvaille – called in Mikael Jonsson from Hedone to consult. Under his guidance, the plan is to offer something a little different in this part of town and to turn the upstairs rooms into a destination restaurant. The cooking is certainly original in style and the dishes are vibrant, fresh and contemporary, if at times a little more elaborate than you expect. The service is keen and charmingly Gallic – the owner likes to see his customers enjoying themselves. Bookings are not taken for the ground floor wine bar, where you can find cheese, charcuterie, 'small plates' and a great selection of organic and biodynamic wines.

Aqua Kyoto

Japanese H3

240 Regent St. (5th floor) (entrance on Argyll St.) ✉ W1F 7EB
✆ (020) 7478 0540
www.aqua-london.com
⊖ Oxford Circus
Closed 25 December and 1 January

Menu £20 (lunch) – Carte £26/88 s

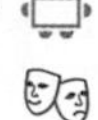

Aqua London occupies all 17,000 square foot of the 5th floor of the former Dickins & Jones department store and boasts, along with a big bar and terrific terraces, two large restaurants. Aqua Kyoto, with its large sushi bar, is the more boisterous of the two, although getting to the table can be a drawn out affair, as you first give your name at the Argyll Street entrance, do so again when you get out of the lift, and only then are you handed over to the restaurant reception. However, it provides a fun night out, more so if you've come in a group – not just so you can compete with the noise, but also because the contemporary Japanese food is designed for sharing. Highlights include the eel teriyaki and the noodle dishes. Service means well but lacks direction.

Avenue

modern H4

7-9 St James's St. ✉ SW1A 1EE
✆ (020) 7321 2111
www.avenue-restaurant.co.uk
⊖ Green Park
Closed Saturday lunch, Sunday dinner and bank holidays

Menu £24 (weekday lunch) – Carte dinner £27/52

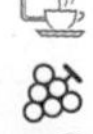

If reinvention is the key to longevity then Avenue should be around for many years to come. In 2014 it went all American, with a new look from Russell Sage and a contemporary menu inspired by what's cooking in Manhattan. So in a street that once epitomised the very essence of Britishness, you can now enjoy a stack of buttermilk pancakes for breakfast, monkfish with Old Bay spice for lunch, and a shared Boston butt for dinner. As the cascading wine 'chandelier' suggests, wine has also been made more of a feature, with US and French wines fighting for supremacy – you can choose the winner by trying some great names by the glass. And as you'd expect from anywhere influenced by NYC, the cocktails at the long, lively bar are great.

Arbutus ✿

modern

I3 

63-64 Frith St. ✉ W1D 3JW
✆ (020) 7734 4545
www.arbutusrestaurant.co.uk
⊖ Tottenham Court Road
Closed 25-26 December and 1 January – booking advisable

Menu £18 (weekday lunch) – Carte £28/40

Arbutus

If you need reminding of what makes a great meal then look no further – Arbutus has it all: a relaxed setting, a terrific wine list that doesn't break the bank, and wonderfully flavoursome cooking. One reason why the food is so satisfying is that the kitchen has an innate understanding of the 'less is more' principle along with an appreciation of what-goes-with-what; and confident, technically assured delivery belies the apparent simplicity on the plate. Rarely seen lesser cuts, such as pig's head or lamb's tripe, vie for your attention next to Dorset crab or wild sea bass; a wonderful egg custard tart needs no adornment. The wine list includes greater numbers of organic wines and most of the wines are available by the carafe which allows for much experimentation and/or indulgence. As it approaches its 10th birthday, the restaurant has been freshened up a little in appearance; the black and white photos of Soho add to the feeling that this is a place at one with its neighbourhood.

First Course

- Squid and mackerel 'burger' with razor clams.
- Heritage tomatoes with goat's curd, watermelon and English peas.

Main Course

- Slow-cooked short rib of Wagyu beef Indonesian style and mango salad.
- Poached sea trout with smoked tomato, mussel broth and chick peas.

Dessert

- Chocolate soup with cardamom ice cream.
- Apricot clafoutis with vanilla ice cream.

Balcon

French

I4

Sofitel London St James Hotel,
8 Pall Mall. ✉ SW1Y 5NG
☏ (020) 7389 7820
www.thebalconlondon.com
⊖ Piccadilly Circus

Menu £21/36 – Carte £33/49

The increasingly ubiquitous Russell Sage was the designer charged with revamping this striking former banking hall and he's wrestled control of the room by installing vast chandeliers, upping the glamour and creating a balcony to house their impressive champagne 'cellar'. The room certainly has a grandeur that raises one's expectations but it needs to be near capacity to create an atmosphere. It's open from breakfast onwards and the classic brasserie menu is designed to appeal at any time of day. Dishes are rooted in French cuisine but most ingredients are British: snails are from Herefordshire, pork for the cassoulet is from Berkshire and their charcuterie, which is a feature, comes from Wales and France. A good value set menu changes weekly.

Baozi Inn

Chinese

I3

25-26 Newport Court ✉ WC2H 7JS
☏ (020) 7287 6877
⊖ Leicester Square
Closed 24-25 December – bookings not accepted

Carte approx. £14

It's camouflaged on the street by the humdrum and the ordinary, so blink and you'll miss this loud, buzzy little place that's great for a quick bite. Granted, the laminated photographs of the dishes in the window don't necessarily inspire confidence but if you like pork buns and big, steaming bowls of noodles along with a hit of Sichuan fire then you won't be disappointed. Only beer, water or tea is on offer but frankly that's all you need; tables are so close together they're almost communal and you can't order too much straight away – not because you won't be able to eat it, but because the dishes simply won't all fit on your table. But who cares? You'll leave feeling energised and rejuvenated without having spent much money.

Barrafina ✿

Spanish

13

54 Frith St. ✉ W1D 3SL
✆ (020) 7813 8016
www.barrafina.co.uk
⊖ Tottenham Court Road
Closed 25 December and 1 January – bookings not accepted

Carte £17/28

Michelin

Great food is all about great sourcing and nowhere is this better demonstrated than at this terrific tapas bar from the Hart brothers. Either join the queue before it opens or chance your luck later for gaps to appear at the counter and you'll find yourself enjoying wonderful, fresh ingredients and expert cooking that allows their natural flavours to shine. Whether it's the bonito and the Dover sole on the special's board or the sardines and octopus on the main menu, you'll soon start wondering why seafood doesn't always taste this good. Meats are pretty damn good too: the hand-carved hams are a must; the chicken thigh is a delight; and the milk-fed lamb is juicy and sweet. Even the pan con tomate will have you looking back with regret at all the inferior versions you've endured over the years. The enthusiasm and pride of the staff behind the counter is palpable and the atmosphere is wonderful. Start and end with a glass of sherry, with a carafe of Albariño in between, and you can't go wrong - or will ever want to leave. A second branch has opened in Adelaide Street.

First Course

- Sardines a la plancha.
- Tortilla.

Main Course

- Pluma Ibérica with confit potatoes.
- Salt cod a la romana.

Dessert

- Crema Catalana.
- Chocolate tart.

Barshu

Chinese

I3

28 Frith St. ✉ W1D 5LF
✆ (020) 7287 8822
www.barshurestaurant.co.uk
⊖ Leicester Square
Closed 24-25 December – booking advisable

Carte £24/56

Those who like their food with a kick won't be disappointed by Barshu as it features the fiery flavours of China's Sichuan province. The menu, which looks more like a brochure, features a photo of each dish along with a chilli rating – a useful aid, as the staff can be a little reluctant to engage with customers. But it's not all mouth-numbingly hot and some of the dishes do display a more subtle balance of flavours. The legendary chillies and peppers are imported directly from China and, with the chef coming from the province too, authenticity is assured, particularly with the 'Five colour appetiser platter', which includes duck tongues and pig intestines. Lots of carved wood and lanterns decorate the place; larger groups should head downstairs.

Ba Shan

Chinese

I3

24 Romilly St. ✉ W1D 5AH
✆ (020) 7287 3266
⊖ Leicester Square
Closed 24-25 December – booking advisable

Carte £15/37

A/C

Whilst there are some Sichuan leanings, this bigger-than-it-looks restaurant excels in specialities from Hunan. What that means is lots of heat and some wonderfully rich colours on the plate. Chillies are used extensively; normally dry roasted and ground so they add flavour as well as spice, but pickling, smoking and curing are also popular techniques. Try pork Chaoshou, dry-wok dishes or specialities like Chairman Mao's red-braised pork – he was born in the area. Staff are sweet and polite if reluctant to make recommendations but there are photos on the menu along with helpful chilli ratings for each dish. Delivery from the kitchen is swift and dishes arrive when ready, making them ideal for sharing.

Beijing Dumpling

Chinese

I3

23 Lisle St. ✉ WC2H 7BA
✆ (0207) 2876 888
⊖ Leicester Square
Closed 24-25 December

Menu £16/20 – Carte £10/40

Flashing neon or hanging roast ducks in the window appear to be the popular Chinatown method of attracting passers-by; this little restaurant catches their attention by showing its chefs hard at work preparing dumplings. It's also a lot less frenzied than many of its more excitable neighbours and a cut above the norm with its food. It serves freshly prepared dumplings of both Beijing and Shanghai styles and, although the range is not quite as comprehensive as the restaurant's name would suggest, they are still the highlight, especially varieties of the famed Siu Lung Bao. The rest of the menu has a wide base but its worth exploring the specials which include the occasional Taiwanese offering like spicy chicken.

Bentley's (Grill)

fish and seafood

H3

11-15 Swallow St. ✉ W1B 4DG
✆ (020) 7734 4756
www.bentleys.org
⊖ Piccadilly Circus
Closed 25 December and 1 January

Menu £29 (dinner) – Carte £34/60

The green neon sign may still be outside but these days the upstairs dining room at Bentley's has a contemporary look, with leather chairs, fabric covered walls and paintings of boats and fish for those who haven't twigged that seafood is the draw here. One thing that will probably never change is the clubby feel and the preponderance of suited male customers, many of whom don't seem to mind paying the anachronistic cover charge. Much of the produce comes from St Ives and Looe in Cornwall and the freshness is palpable. Fish on the bone dissected at the table remains something of a speciality. Dover and Lemon soles feature strongly, as do oysters and soups, whilst the breads and beef remind you that owner Richard Corrigan is Irish.

Benares ✿

Indian

H3

12a Berkeley Square House, Berkeley Sq. ✉ W1J 6BS
✆ (020) 7629 8886
www.benaresrestaurant.com
⊖ Green Park
Closed 24-26 December and 1-2 January

Menu £35/82 – Carte £44/73

Benares

When Benares was re-launched a few years ago after an extended hiatus caused by a kitchen fire, it seemed that not a great deal had changed in its appearance although, apparently, much work did take place behind the scenes. One terrific addition, however, was the 'Chef's Table' with its floor to ceiling windows looking directly into the kitchen; the 'Sommelier's Table' doesn't quite have the same cachet. Another difference came in the subtle evolution of Atul Kochhar's cooking. His dishes appear a little simpler on the plate; the main ingredient takes centre stage, with the Indian spices adding interesting and complementary flavours but without being the dominant force. Those who want to experience as much of the cooking as they can are able to do so thanks to the 'Grazing menu', although those who don't care for too much modernity with their Indian food will find enough recognisable dishes to satisfy them. Much thought has also gone into the wine list and in choosing the right pairings for the food.

First Course

- Chicken tikka pie with wild berry chutney.
- Spiced minced lamb kebab, feta and pomegranate.

Main Course

- Rump of lamb with Calcutta style chickpeas.
- Kashmiri chilli spiced Scottish halibut, white polenta and Alleppey sauce.

Dessert

- Masala chai soufflé, vanilla ice cream.
- Dark chocolate mousse, passion fruit and hot chocolate sauce.

Bentley's (Oyster Bar)

fish and seafood

H3

11-15 Swallow St ✉ W1B 4DG
(020) 7734 4756
www.bentleys.org
Piccadilly Circus
Closed 25 December and 1 December

Menu £29 (early dinner) – Carte £30/59

There's something about Swallow Street that always seems to get the taste buds going. Bentley's small reception area acts for both the upstairs Grill and the ground floor Oyster Bar so be patient; dining on the ground floor means you'll be ushered through the curtain into a dimly lit bar with marbled-topped tables, banquette seating and places laid up at the counter. Oysters are naturally one of the main features, and the fish pie is a popular choice, but there are usually lots of daily specials and these often represent the most appealing option. Bentley's illustrious past is almost tangible and the atmosphere is chummy and clubby, helped along with noise from the bar on the other side and the evening pianist.

Blanchette

French

H3

9 D'Arblay St ✉ W1F 8DR
(020) 7439 8100
www.blanchettesoho.co.uk
Oxford Circus
Closed Sunday dinner – booking essential

Carte £13/20

Opened by three frères – and named after their mother – Blanchette takes classic French bistro food and gives it the 'small plates' treatment. Start with a mini croque monsieur or some bite-sized cheese beignets and then try creamy smoked haddock Arnold Bennett or ox cheek bourguignon which is made to mother Blanche's own recipe – this is the sort of food guaranteed to raise the spirits. The charcuterie is sliced in front of you; the veg section shouldn't be ignored and the wine list offers an interesting variety of styles and a decent selection by the carafe. There are just nine tables, one of which is communal, and the place has an appealing rustic look, with lots of tiles and exposed brick – the counter is a good place to sit.

Bob Bob Ricard

modern H3

1 Upper James St ✉ W1F 9DF
✆ (020) 3145 1000
www.bobbobricard.com
⊖ Oxford Circus
Closed Christmas, Easter and Sunday

Carte £32/80

Everyone needs a little glamour now and again and Bob Bob Ricard is one place that can provide it. This is a restaurant where diners still dress up a little and there's a feeling of exclusivity in the air. Start with a cocktail in their terrific basement bar then snare one of the booths in the restaurant. The room may be quite small but it clearly sees itself as a grand salon and is shiny, plush and elegant – you even get a button to push if you require more champagne. The menu is all encompassing, although the presence of caviar and vodka are clues as to the owner's nationality. For lighter eaters there are oysters, salads and grilled fish; those with heartier appetites can choose beef Wellington, a venison burger or chicken Kiev.

Bocca di Lupo

Italian I3

12 Archer St ✉ WID 7BB
✆ (020) 7734 2223
www.boccadilupo.com
⊖ Piccadilly Circus
Closed 24 December-1 January and 31 August – booking essential

Carte £17/45

Deservedly busy from the day it opened, Bocca di Lupo is one of the best things to have arrived in Soho since the espresso bar. But be sure to sit at the marble counter in front of the chefs rather than at one of the faux-distressed tables at the back – not only is the atmosphere here more fun but the food is often better as it hasn't hung around the waiters' station waiting to be delivered. Each item has its region of origin within Italy noted on the menu and is available in a large or smaller size. The flavours don't hang back and over-ordering in all the excitement is very hard to resist. Highlights include the veal and pork agnolotti, the poussin in bread, and tripe; leave room for dessert or visit their gelato shop opposite.

Bibigo

Korean

H2 

58-59 Great Marlborough St ✉ W1F 7JY
(020) 7042 5225
www.bibigouk.com
⊖ Oxford Circus

Menu £13 (lunch) – Carte £16/30

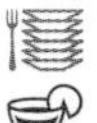

Bibigo represents the first foray into the UK market from Korea's largest food company, 'CJ'. With a little help from Psy, Korea's other famous non-electronic export, their mission is to bring healthy staples such as bibimbap – bowls of rice, vegetables, seeds and nuts finished with a hot pepper paste (gochujang) – to a wider public. Start with a soju-based cocktail then watch the kitchen behind the glass send forth dishes such as kimchi, Bossam (simmered pork belly) and hot stone galbi (chargrilled short ribs). Dishes have been adapted slightly for western tastes and the place may feel a little chainy – you can even buy the sauces at reception on the way out – but it's enthusiastically run and won't break the bank.

Bone Daddies

Asian

I3 

30-31 Peter St ✉ W1F 0AR
(020) 7287 8581
www.bonedaddiesramen.com
⊖ Piccadilly Circus
Closed 25 December – bookings not accepted

Carte £18/29

Maybe ramen is the new rock 'n' roll. Bone Daddies' charismatic young Aussie chef-owner feels that we've only just begun to appreciate the potential of this Japanese speciality; he believes that anything can go into these warming, comforting bowls and that the combinations are endless. Along with the ramen, you'll find other dishes, such as yellowtail sashimi with ponzu and chilli, that owe their influence to the time he spent at Nobu. The staff are a confident, hospitable bunch and the shared tables add to the community spirit. You may have to queue but throughput is apparently quicker than at some of the top floor services offered close by. Those over 30, who probably don't like standing in line, at least get to recognise the music.

Le Boudin Blanc

French

G4

5 Trebeck St ✉ W1J 7LT
✆ (020) 7499 3292
www.boudinblanc.co.uk
⊖ Green Park
Closed Christmas

Menu £15 – Carte £27/53

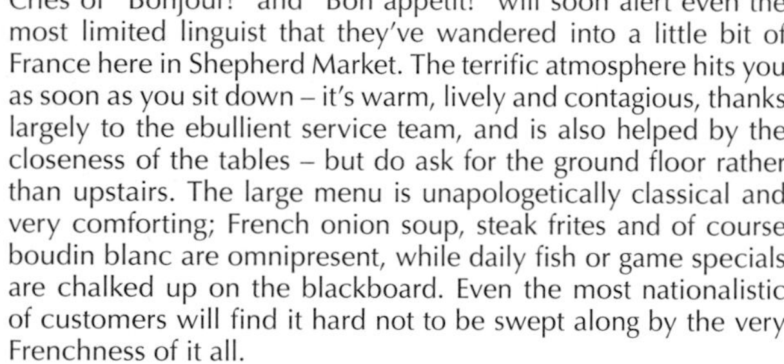

Cries of "Bonjour!" and "Bon appétit!" will soon alert even the most limited linguist that they've wandered into a little bit of France here in Shepherd Market. The terrific atmosphere hits you as soon as you sit down – it's warm, lively and contagious, thanks largely to the ebullient service team, and is also helped by the closeness of the tables – but do ask for the ground floor rather than upstairs. The large menu is unapologetically classical and very comforting; French onion soup, steak frites and of course boudin blanc are omnipresent, while daily fish or game specials are chalked up on the blackboard. Even the most nationalistic of customers will find it hard not to be swept along by the very Frenchness of it all.

Ⓝ Boulestin

French

H4

5 St James's St ✉ SW1A 1EF
✆ (020) 7930 2030
www.boulestin.com
⊖ Green Park
Closed Sunday and bank holidays

Menu £25 (dinner) – Carte £32/61

Nearly a century after Xavier Marcel Boulestin opened his eponymous restaurant showcasing 'Simple French Cooking for English homes', his spirit has been resurrected by another name synonymous with the London dining scene – Joel Kissin. Behind the 17C bay windows, you'll find the cosy bar-cum-simple-bistro Café Marcel with a no-reservations policy and a great value prix fixe; beyond is an elegant brasserie oozing in fin de siècle French charm which opens onto a lovely courtyard terrace. The menu of classic, unfussy and flavoursome dishes is a homage to M. Boulestin's original although some dishes have been lightened a little. Prices can be quite high but this is the sort of restaurant that does make you feel rather special.

Brasserie Chavot ✿

French

H3

41 Conduit St ✉ W1S 2YQ
✆ (020) 7183 6425
www.brasseriechavot.com
⊖ Bond Street

Carte £34/56

The Westbury

The amiable French chef Eric Chavot has found a great spot in which to display his undoubted talents. The brasserie is actually part of the Westbury Hotel, but feels very much like a stand-alone operation and a smart, elegant one at that. A stunning mosaic floor, smoked mirrors, red leather seating and sparkling chandeliers add to the sophisticated look yet the buzz and bonhomie, and the unflustered service, make it all relaxed and easy. Eric's gone back to his roots and the cooking is hearteningly rustic and refreshingly unfussy: daube of beef, filet de canette with orange sauce, rum baba, profiteroles – within minutes you'll find yourself speaking French to the waiters without realising you're doing it. Yet even in relatively simple dishes like grilled poussin or île flottante, you can still see Eric's innate skill; he sees no point in 'reinterpreting' the classics, merely executing them in the best possible way. You'll leave thinking about what dish to order the next time you're here.

First Course

- Deep-fried soft shell crab.
- Waldorf salad with spicy pecan nuts.

Main Course

- Filet de canette à l'orange.
- Roasted cod with peas à la française.

Dessert

- Ile flottante.
- Cheesecake framboise.

Brasserie Zédel

French H3

20 Sherwood St ✉ W1F 7ED
✆ (020) 7734 4888
www.brasseriezedel.com
⊖ Piccadilly Circus
Closed 25 December – booking advisable

Menu £12/20 – Carte £15/26

After bedding in their Delaunay restaurant, Chris Corbin and Jeremy King then opened this grand French brasserie, which is far more about inclusivity and accessibility. Those mourning the old Atlantic Bar and Grill will be pleased to see this big, bustling subterranean space restored to its original art deco glory and this time it also comes with a small café, a bar and a cabaret theatre. The menu is a gloriously unapologetic roll-call of classic French dishes – from escargots to confit de canard – but what is most striking is the exceptionally fair pricing when one considers the location, the glamour, the service and the quality of the cooking. Plenty of tables are kept back for 'walk-ins' so it's always worth trying your luck.

Brumus

modern I4

Haymarket Hotel,
1 Suffolk Pl ✉ SW1Y 4HX
✆ (020) 7470 4000
www.haymarkethotel.com
⊖ Piccadilly Circus

Menu £20 – Carte £22/53

Brumus has always benefitted from its great location – pre-theatre dining is an altogether less frenzied activity when you can actually see the theatre from your table – but it also makes genuine efforts to appeal to wide variety of customer. It's a modern yet elegant space, with switched-on staff adding to the appeal. It's also open from breakfast until late and usually has something to suit the time of day whether that's a shepherd's pie, burger or Dover sole. If you veer away from the set price menus, prices can start to rise quite quickly – although the 'dish of the day' on the à la carte is often the way to go, followed by one of their sundaes. Alternatively, you can share a platter in the busy bar.

Burger & Lobster

meats and grills

I3

36 Dean St ✉ W1D 4PS
✆ (020) 7432 4800
www.burgerandlobster.com
⊖ Leicester Square
Closed bank holidays

Menu £25

Virtually constant queues at the first Burger & Lobster in Mayfair meant that the opening of more branches was pretty inevitable. This one in Soho is a sizeable place, with seating for nearly 140; bookings are only taken for tables of more than six so either come as a group or be prepared to wait – the bar here is as good a place as any, or you can simply leave your phone number and they'll call you when a table becomes available. It's an ingenious concept: you simply decide whether you want a lobster roll in a brioche bun, a 1½lb Maine or Canadian lobster, or a 280g freshly minced burger made from Irish or Nebraskan beef. All are served with salad and fries and, for pudding, there's a choice of a couple of mousses.

Burger & Lobster

meats and grills

H4

29 Clarges St ✉ W1J 7EF
✆ (020) 7409 1699
www.burgerandlobster.com
⊖ Green Park.
Closed Sunday dinner and bank holidays – bookings not accepted

Menu £20

Around the corner from the Curzon cinema, in what was a pub called the Field, is a 'concept' so simple it borders on genius. The choice, if you didn't get the clue in the name, is between a burger, a lobster or a lobster roll, served with chips, salad and sauces, with either chocolate or lime mousse for dessert - that's it. You're given a numbered luggage tag if you want a tab at the bar; there are no menus to read through and no side dishes to choose. There's a small, well-chosen wine and cocktail list under headings B or L (work it out). The lobsters are Canadian; the burgers 10oz and the customers mostly men. Bookings aren't taken so get your name down on the list as soon as you arrive – it may well be a bunfight, but it's a very well organised one.

Café Murano

Italian

H4

33 St. James's St ✉ SW1A 1HD
✆ (0203) 371 5559
www.cafemurano.co.uk
⊖ Green Park
Closed Sunday dinner – booking essential

Menu £22 – Carte £25/53

How satisfying it must have been for Angela Hartnett when she took over this site, considering she worked here over a decade ago when it was Pétrus. True to her roots she has created, along with her chef, a menu of delicious North Italian delicacies with built-in flexibility so you can create your own meal according to the relative sizes of your appetite and wallet; try the truffle arancini with your prosecco while you choose. The lunch and pre/post theatre menu is good value and those who like to eat free from the tyranny of set meal times will appreciate the light selection of antipasti served mid-afternoon. The word 'café' was presumably adopted to imply accessibility but the place has proved so popular that pre-booking is essential.

Cafe at Sotheby's

modern

H3

34-35 New Bond St. ✉ W1A 2AA
✆ (020) 7293 5077
www.sothebys.com/cafe
⊖ Bond Street
Closed 3 weeks August, Christmas and New Year, Saturday, Sunday and bank holidays – booking essential – (lunch only)

Carte £32/42 s

It's usually the seasons that inform the menu of most restaurants but here at Sotheby's they change the style of the dishes according to the art being sold. For instance, experience has shown that modern and Impressionist artists attract a diet-conscious crowd who like their salads, while the Old Masters appeal to those who favour a more substantial, well-lubricated lunch which ends with a proper pudding. The lobster sandwich is a perennial feature and the wine list is brief but appealingly eclectic. Occupying a cosy space just off the lobby of the auction house, this is a little gem of a restaurant which is smarter than the 'café' moniker would suggest. Service is well-judged and the many regulars are discreetly acknowledged.

Le Caprice

modern

H4

Arlington House, Arlington St. ✉ SW1A 1RJ
✆ (020) 7629 2239
www.le-caprice.co.uk
⊖ Green Park
Closed 24-26 December

Menu £25 (dinner) – Carte £32/61

There are two types of customer at Le Caprice: those who are regulars and others who wish they were. This is one of those glamorous restaurants where the atmosphere is effortlessly sophisticated and the clientele confident and urbane; even first-timers feel in safe hands from the moment they enter. The menu offers something for everyone, whether that's a salad or pasta, their famous and very rich salmon fishcake with sorrel sauce, a burger or a more ambitious offering like a well-judged game dish or Asian spiced fish; the kitchen is well-practised and capable. Le Caprice celebrated its 30th anniversary in 2011 by having a little makeover which left it better lit and feeling a little warmer with its different sections more connected.

Cây Tre

Vietnamese

I3

42-43 Dean St ✉ W1D 4PZ
✆ (020) 7317 9118
www.caytresoho.co.uk
⊖ Tottenham Court Road
Booking advisable

Menu £23/29 – Carte £17/28

The West End could do with having plenty more Vietnamese restaurants, so hopefully others will follow the lead of Cây Tre. The bright and sleek surroundings of this Soho branch are smarter than the original in Hoxton and the bustling environment provides plenty of atmosphere. Staff know their menu and go about their business with determined efficiency. Dishes are made for sharing and influences cover all points from north to south. Standouts include Cha La lot (spicy ground pork wrapped in betel leaves) and the fragrant slow-cooked Mekong catfish, with its well-judged sweet and spicy sauce. Pho (noodle soup) is available in six different versions and represents good value; the set menu is a great starting point for neophytes.

Cecconi's

Italian H3

5a Burlington Gdns ✉ W1S 3EP
✆ (020) 7434 1500
www.cecconis.com
⊖ Green Park
Booking essential

Carte £40/49

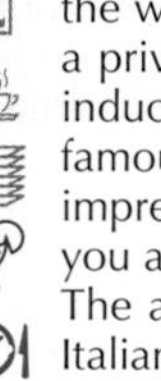

It's obviously a winning formula because Cecconi's are now popping up in various appropriately fashionable cities around the world. One can certainly see the appeal as they do feel like a private members club and even have a roped off VIP area to induce envy amongst those who find themselves insufficiently famous. The bar is the place to sit if you want to give the impression you're a regular who's often in for a quick bite; and if you are one such regular then you'll be assured of good service. The all-day menu offers a good selection of cicchetti, or small Italian tapas; prosciutto is sliced to order; the salads are popular at lunch and the classic, no-nonsense main courses are clearly prepared with care.

Ceviche

Peruvian I3

17 Frith St ✉ W1D 4RG
✆ (020) 7292 2040
www.cevicheuk.com
⊖ Tottenham Court Road

Carte £15/27

Based on a Lima Pisco bar, Ceviche is as loud as it is fun and a great place to pop into for cocktails with a difference and some light dishes to share with friends. The long narrow room has a busy bar specialising in deliriously addictive drinks based on the Peruvian spirit Pisco, a grape brandy, and beyond it you'll find tightly packed tables, posters and photos of 1950s Peru, and waiting staff struggling to keep up. As the name suggests, ceviche, marinated in lime and chilli, is the star of the show, whether that's the sea bass or the Alianza Lima – a mix of prawns, squid and octopus. 3 per person plus perhaps an anticuchos skewer should be enough. Dishes arrive in a random order so ask if you want the ceviche before any hot dish.

China Tang

Chinese

G4

Dorchester Hotel,
Park Ln ✉ W1K 1QA
(020) 7629 9988
www.chinatanglondon.co.uk
Hyde Park Corner
Closed 24-25 December

Menu £28 (lunch) – Carte £28/79

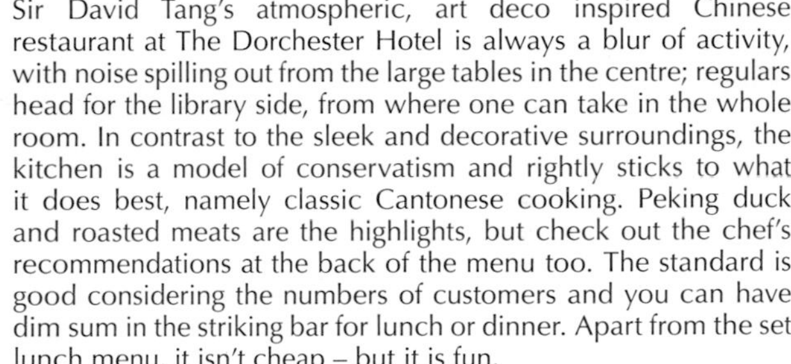

Sir David Tang's atmospheric, art deco inspired Chinese restaurant at The Dorchester Hotel is always a blur of activity, with noise spilling out from the large tables in the centre; regulars head for the library side, from where one can take in the whole room. In contrast to the sleek and decorative surroundings, the kitchen is a model of conservatism and rightly sticks to what it does best, namely classic Cantonese cooking. Peking duck and roasted meats are the highlights, but check out the chef's recommendations at the back of the menu too. The standard is good considering the numbers of customers and you can have dim sum in the striking bar for lunch or dinner. Apart from the set lunch menu, it isn't cheap – but it is fun.

Chop Shop

meats and grills

I3

66 Haymarket ✉ SW1Y 4RF
(020) 7842 8501
www.chopshopuk.com
Piccadilly Circus

Menu £22 (weekday lunch) – Carte £20/48

Things are changing down at Haymarket – a huge redevelopment is planned which will allow new restaurants to give the established chains a run for their money. First off the mark is Chop Shop from New York's Altamarea Group. Spread over two floors and using reclaimed materials for that ersatz industrial look, it would not look out of place in Manhattan's Meatpacking district. The menu too takes its influences from both sides of the Atlantic: start with 'jars' of mousses, 'crocks' of meatballs or 'planks' of cheese; or simply order one of their house cocktails and then head straight for the main event: the steaks and chops. Perfectly matured meats from Cumbria, along with Creekstone USDA steak, are expertly cooked and hit the spot.

Cinnamon Soho

Indian

H3

5 Kingly St ✉ W1B 5PF
✆ (020) 7437 1664
www.cinnamonsoho.com
⊖ Oxford Circus
Closed 1 January – bookings not accepted

Menu £10 (weekday lunch)/35 – Carte £21/33

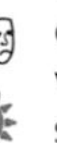

Its catchphrase is 'Joho Soho', Hindi for 'whatever happens' and this Cinnamon outpost is altogether more fun than its two older siblings. Taking our love of Indian food to its logical conclusion, it blends Indian flavours with traditional British dishes, so you can order Rogan Josh shepherd's pie, curried Cullen skink or Cumbrian lamb biryani. It's hard to miss the signature dish as the menu is emblazoned with the word 'Balls': these include crab cakes, potato bondas and even Scotch eggs – and all are served with different pickles. Don't be afraid to ask about relative spiciness, do have one of their fun cocktails and sit on the ground floor rather than in the soulless basement. It's open all day and also has a terrace front and back.

Copita

Mediterranean

H3

27 D'Arblay St ✉ W1F 8EP
✆ (020) 7287 7797
www.copita.co.uk
⊖ Oxford Circus
Closed Sunday and bank holidays – bookings not accepted

Carte £17/29

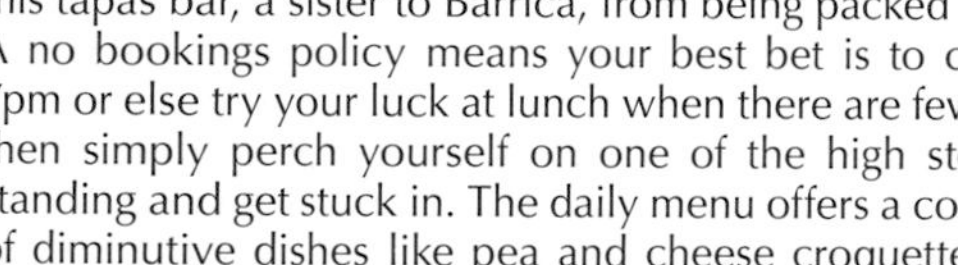

It may not occupy a prime Soho spot but that hasn't stopped this tapas bar, a sister to Barrica, from being packed most nights. A no bookings policy means your best bet is to come before 7pm or else try your luck at lunch when there are fewer drinkers; then simply perch yourself on one of the high stools or stay standing and get stuck in. The daily menu offers a colourful array of diminutive dishes like pea and cheese croquettes, crab and spinach tart, and pumpkin and sage ravioli and you'll find it hard to stop ordering – even the delicate custard tart is delightfully moreish. Staff add to the lively atmosphere and everything on the thoughtfully compiled Spanish wine list is available by the glass or copita.

Corrigan's Mayfair

British modern G3

28 Upper Grosvenor St. ✉ W1K 7EH
✆ (020) 7499 9943
www.corrigansmayfair.com
⊖ Marble Arch
Closed 18-27 August, 25-30 December, Saturday lunch and bank holidays

Menu £29 (lunch and early dinner) – Carte £45/71

Richard Corrigan's flagship restaurant feels as though it has been part of the London scene for years. It's comfortable, clubby yet quite glamorous and Martin Brudnizki's design includes some playful features, such as the feather-covered lamps that give a nod to the restaurant's forte, which is game. The menu is lengthy and the food largely a celebration of British and Irish cooking. It is also fiercely seasonal, which makes having the day's special always a worthwhile choice. This relatively straightforward style of cooking still requires care and precise timing but sometimes the kitchen takes its eye off the ball. Service is smooth and well organised but the anachronistic cover charge is an unwelcome sight.

Coya

Peruvian G4

118 Piccadilly ✉ W1J 7NW
✆ (020) 7042 7118
www.coyarestaurant.com
⊖ Hyde Park Corner
Closed 24-26 December and 1 January – booking advisable

Menu £27 (lunch) – Carte £32/94

It didn't take long for the people behind Roka and Zuma to act upon the realisation that the Next Big Thing on the London restaurant scene was Peruvian food. Their loud and enthusiastically run basement restaurant on Piccadilly provides a lively spot in which to discover this fresh and zesty cuisine. Add in the live music at weekends and it also represents a great night out, especially when fuelled by the deliriously addictive Pisco Sours. Prepared in one of the three kitchens – the main room, the charcoal grill or the ceviche bar – the food is a mix of the authentic, the refined and the more contemporary; ordering a sharp, refreshing ceviche is a must and consider too the huge tiger prawns cooked in the Josper oven.

Cut

meats and grills G4

45 Park Lane Hotel,
45 Park Ln ✉ W1K 1PN
✆ (020) 7493 4545
www.45parklane.com
⊖ Hyde Park Corner
Booking essential

Menu £34 (weekday lunch) – Carte £41/129

Cut is the first European venture from Wolfgang Puck, the US-based Austrian chef whose level of celebrity makes our lot look positively anonymous. Teaming up with the Dorchester's 45 Park Lane hotel, he has created a slick, stylish and sexy room where glamorous people come to eat meat. The steaks – from Kansas, Chile, Australia and Devon— are first presented raw with a few words about their heritage and then cooked over hardwood and charcoal and finished off in a broiler. Sides are as good as the steaks, especially the fries and the macaroni cheese. Artery hardening continues with dessert which eschews the much-needed citrus in favour of lots of cream. You'll leave eminently satisfied, if slightly heavier in weight and lighter in pocket.

Dean Street Townhouse Restaurant

British modern I3

69-71 Dean St. ✉ W1D 3SE
✆ (020) 7434 1775
www.deanstreettownhouse.com
⊖ Tottenham Court Road
Booking essential

Menu £20 – Carte £26/78

A restaurant for every occasion – even shouty ones, as you're hit by a cacophony of sound as soon as you open the heavy door of this attractive Georgian house. It's also a place to be seen, or perhaps not — a ban on flash photography means it's ideal for illicit trysts too. The classic brasserie aesthetic makes it look like it's been here for years and the heartwarming British comfort food fits these surroundings well. Prices for some of the fish and steak dishes can get pretty exclusive but there's plenty more proletariat fare on offer, like faggots with cabbage or mince and potatoes. The salads such as trout with truffled potato or smoked pigeon with Scotch egg are noteworthy and who can resist kipper pâté for afternoon tea?

Dehesa

Mediterranean H3

25 Ganton St ✉ W1F 9BP
✆ (020) 7494 4170
www.dehesa.co.uk
⊖ Oxford Circus
Closed Christmas

Carte £19/29

Dehesa does now take bookings, except for lunch on Saturday, so there's no longer a need to get here quite so early. It's a few streets away from one of its sister restaurants, Salt Yard, and repeats the format of offering delicious Spanish and Italian tapas. The menu is not an exact copy but the bestsellers all feature: the pork belly with cannellini beans; courgette flowers with Monte Enebro and honey; and the soft chocolate cake with Frangelico ice cream. They recommend 2-3 plates per person. Between 3pm and 5pm the kitchen takes a breather so the choice becomes ham on or off the bone, charcuterie and cheese. The drinks list is worthy of a visit in itself. Dehesa is a wooded area of Spain and home to Ibérico pigs who produce such great ham.

Ducksoup

modern I3

41 Dean St ✉ W1D 4PY
✆ (020) 7287 4599
www.ducksoupsoho.co.uk
⊖ Leicester Square
Closed Christmas, Easter, Sunday dinner and bank holidays

Carte £19/35

Bookings are only taken for larger parties so if you're coming to the decoratively unadorned and diminutive Ducksoup then grab a seat at the counter – the basement room does have tables but offers little in the way of atmosphere. The handwritten menu changes every week – with some dishes changing daily – and it's all about simplicity, which is hardly surprising when you know that the owner's family ran the famous Cleveland Tontine near Northallerton for many years. There are just two or three items on each plate, with the kitchen putting its trust in the quality of its ingredients. A concise list of mostly natural and bio-dynamic wines has been thoughtfully compiled, with all choices available by the glass.

Ember Yard

Mediterranean H2

60 Berwick St ✉ W1F 8DX
(020) 7439 8057
www.emberyard.co.uk
⊖ Oxford Circus
Closed 25-26 December and 1 January – booking advisable

Carte approx. £35

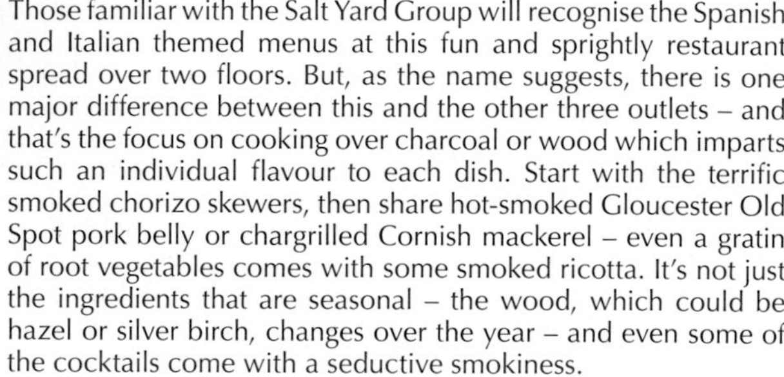

Those familiar with the Salt Yard Group will recognise the Spanish and Italian themed menus at this fun and sprightly restaurant spread over two floors. But, as the name suggests, there is one major difference between this and the other three outlets – and that's the focus on cooking over charcoal or wood which imparts such an individual flavour to each dish. Start with the terrific smoked chorizo skewers, then share hot-smoked Gloucester Old Spot pork belly or chargrilled Cornish mackerel – even a gratin of root vegetables comes with some smoked ricotta. It's not just the ingredients that are seasonal – the wood, which could be hazel or silver birch, changes over the year – and even some of the cocktails come with a seductive smokiness.

Floridita

other world kitchens I3

100 Wardour St ✉ W1F 0TN
(020) 7314 4000
www.floriditalondon.com
⊖ Tottenham Court Road
Closed Sunday, Monday and bank holidays – (dinner only)

Menu £20/38

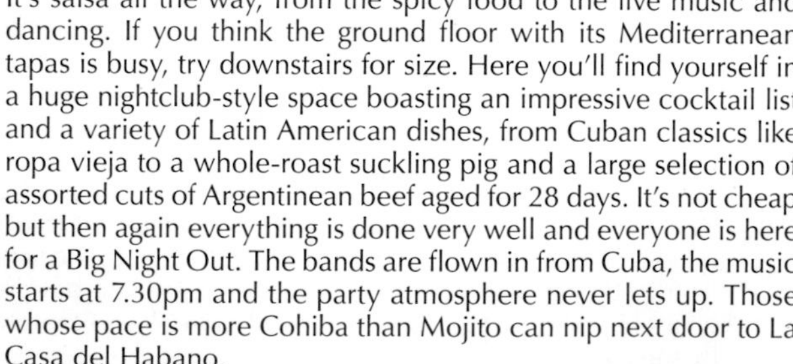

It's salsa all the way, from the spicy food to the live music and dancing. If you think the ground floor with its Mediterranean tapas is busy, try downstairs for size. Here you'll find yourself in a huge nightclub-style space boasting an impressive cocktail list and a variety of Latin American dishes, from Cuban classics like ropa vieja to a whole-roast suckling pig and a large selection of assorted cuts of Argentinean beef aged for 28 days. It's not cheap but then again everything is done very well and everyone is here for a Big Night Out. The bands are flown in from Cuba, the music starts at 7.30pm and the party atmosphere never lets up. Those whose pace is more Cohiba than Mojito can nip next door to La Casa del Habano.

Fera at Claridge's ✿

British creative G3

Claridge's Hotel,
Brook St ✉ W1K 4HR
(020) 7107 8888
www.feraatclaridges.co.uk
Bond Street
Booking advisable

Menu £85/125

Fera at Claridge's

The most eagerly anticipated restaurant opening of 2014 didn't disappoint. Earth-father, forager supreme, farmstead owner and gastronomic alchemist Simon Rogan came down from the boondocks of Cumbria and shook up that bastion of British propriety – Claridge's hotel. The 'wild' of Fera may refer to the influence of nature but this is intricately planned and highly refined cuisine. There's a purity and a natural, unforced style to the cooking that is evident on the plate, yet the wonderfully well-balanced and textured dishes deliver multi-dimensional layers of flavours. The tasting menu is perhaps the best way to go and the wine list offers an intelligent mix of the classic and the more esoteric. For their part, the hotel did a magnificent job in transforming this room into a thing of beauty. The muted tones of green give it an almost herbaceous feel which is juxtaposed by touches of art deco and magnificent detailing, yet the grandeur of the room is tempered by the refreshing lack of pomposity or mannered formality in the service.

First Course

- Prawns from Gairloch, pickled Alexanders, asparagus and shellfish butter.
- Raw beef with smoked broccoli cream and scallop roe.

Main Course

- Goosnargh duck, yellow bean purée, leek and hyssop.
- Brill fillet with razor clams, artichoke, beetroot and nasturtium.

Dessert

- Iced sorrel, nitro sweet cheese and apple.
- Chocolate cream with apple marigold, cultured meringue and rapeseed.

Franco's

Italian H4

61 Jermyn St ✉ SW1Y 6LX
✆ (020) 7499 2211
www.francoslondon.com
⊖ Green Park
Closed Sunday and bank holidays – booking essential

Menu £20/26 – Carte £31/62 XX

There can be few things more English than afternoon tea or the sound of Alan Bennett reading from The Wind in the Willows and, surprisingly enough, both can be enjoyed here at Franco's, one of London's oldest Italian restaurants that was relaunched in the mid-noughties. Open from breakfast onwards, it attracts a largely well-groomed clientele as befits its Jermyn Street address and boasts a clubby feel. Indeed, if you're not a regular visitor, you may find yourself with time to admire the service being enjoyed by other tables. The chef hails from Northern Italy but his menu covers all parts. There is a popular grill section, along with classics like beef Rossini – ideal accompaniment for one of those big Tuscan reds on the wine list.

Gauthier - Soho

French I3

21 Romilly St ✉ W1D 5AF
✆ (020) 7494 3111
www.gauthiersoho.co.uk
⊖ Leicester Square
Closed Monday lunch, Sunday and bank holidays except Good Friday

Menu £18 (lunch) – Carte £45/67

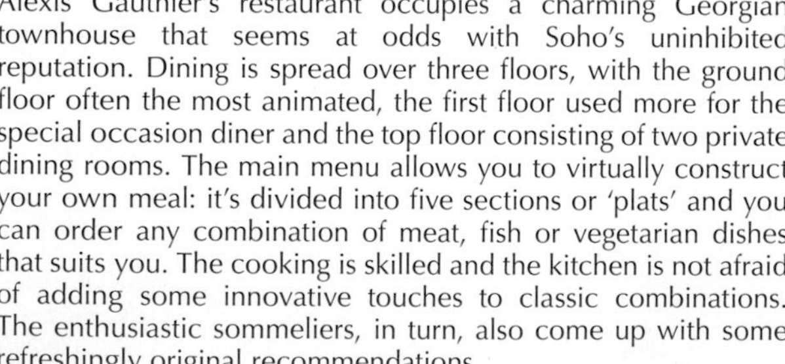

Alexis Gauthier's restaurant occupies a charming Georgian townhouse that seems at odds with Soho's uninhibited reputation. Dining is spread over three floors, with the ground floor often the most animated, the first floor used more for the special occasion diner and the top floor consisting of two private dining rooms. The main menu allows you to virtually construct your own meal: it's divided into five sections or 'plats' and you can order any combination of meat, fish or vegetarian dishes that suits you. The cooking is skilled and the kitchen is not afraid of adding some innovative touches to classic combinations. The enthusiastic sommeliers, in turn, also come up with some refreshingly original recommendations.

Le Gavroche ✿✿

French

G3

43 Upper Brook St ✉ W1K 7QR
(020) 7408 0881
www.le-gavroche.co.uk
⊖ Marble Arch
Closed Christmas-January, Saturday lunch, Sunday and bank holidays – booking essential

Menu £55/124 – Carte £63/156

Le Gavroche

A little indulgence never did anyone any harm and Le Gavroche is all about indulgence. Michel Roux and head chef Rachel Humphrey's unapologetically extravagant French dishes are an exhilarating riposte to all those hectoring health-conscious calorie-counters. The menu is a roll-call of luxury ingredients, the sauces are sublime and the cooking is accompanied by one of London's best wine lists. There are oohs and aahs as trolleys are brought forward and carving knives sharpened; regulars mingle with newcomers and the atmosphere is refreshingly unstuffy, helped along by there being more of a female presence to the service these days. Anyone with an interest in Britain's post-war culinary adventures should be aware of Le Gavroche's significance, not just because of its celebration of, and dedication to, the art of French cuisine but also because of all those chefs who have benefitted from passing through its kitchen. Just avoid sitting too close to the stairs by asking for a table in the main body of this historic restaurant.

First Course

- Mousseline de homard au champagne et caviar.
- Céleri rave rôti et fumé, chou rouge.

Main Course

- Râble de lapin et galette au parmesan.
- Le delice de veau, ravigote aux piments doux et salade aux truffes.

Dessert

- Soufflé aux fruits de la passion et glace Ivoire.
- Truffe chocolat Amedei, cacahuette, caramel et banane.

Galvin at Windows ✿

modern

G4

London Hilton Hotel,
22 Park Ln (28th floor) ✉ W1K 1BE
✆ (020) 7208 4021
www.galvinatwindows.com
⊖ Hyde Park Corner
Closed Saturday lunch and Sunday dinner

Menu £29/68

Galvin at Windows

The lift may take time to drop off its cargo of Hilton Hotel residents as it makes its way up to the 28th floor but the wait will be worth it as the views from up here are spectacular – and it's certainly worth arriving early for a drink in the busy adjacent bar. The restaurant has been cleverly laid out to make the most of the three sides of views and, if you can't secure a window table, the elevated section in the middle of the room is a good compromise. Service is relaxed and friendly which softens some of the formality of the room, although a little more passion would dispel some of the corporate blandness that pervades the atmosphere. It is the food, however, that provides worthy competition to the views. British ingredients like Cornish lamb, Cumbrian beef and Dorset crab proudly feature on the various menus on offer – the Menu du Jour draws in plenty of customers at lunch as it's a steal for this postcode. There's a classical base to the cooking; dishes have bold flavours and come with a pleasing degree of flair and innovation.

First Course

- Scallops with sea vegetables, caviar and lemongrass velouté.
- Ballotine of rabbit with foie gras, ham hock and pistachio.

Main Course

- Rack of lamb with pea purée, spring vegetables, lamb Bolognese and mint jus.
- Roasted monkfish with lemongrass crumbs.

Dessert

- Hot lemon and milk chocolate soufflé with rosemary ice cream.
- Caramelia chocolate crémeux with raspberries and basil sorbet.

Goodman

meats and grills H3

26 Maddox St ✉ W1S 1QH
✆ (020) 7499 3776
www.goodmanrestaurants.com
⊖ Oxford Circus
Closed Sunday and bank holidays – booking essential

Carte £27/73 XX

A/C

Goodman is a Russian-owned New York steakhouse in Mayfair, which sounds like a sketch from the UN's Christmas party. Wood and leather give it an authentic feel and it has captured that macho swagger that often seems to accompany the eating of red meat. Tables are usually full of guffawing men, with their jackets thrown over the back of their chairs and their sleeves rolled up. The American and Irish beef is mostly grain-fed and either dry or wet aged in-house – Australian beef is an option at lunch. It is cooked in a Josper oven using a blend of three types of charcoal and offered with a choice of four sauces. While the steaks, especially the rib-eye, are certainly worth coming for, side dishes tend to be more variable in quality.

Great British

British traditional G3

14 North Audley St ✉ W1K 6WE
✆ (020) 7741 2233
www.eatbrit.com
⊖ Marble Arch
Closed 25 December, 1 January and Sunday dinner

Menu £17 (dinner) – Carte £24/40 X

A/C

There are countless cuisines on offer in Mayfair but, for some reason, this quintessentially British part of London has never exactly been overrun with restaurants serving traditional British food. The Great British seeks to redress this balance by offering the best that Blighty has to offer, from fish pies to sherry trifles. You'll find sausages come with bubble and squeak, fish and chips with curry sauce, and apple crumble with 'proper' custard; and they haven't neglected Britain's greatest gift to the culinary world as breakfast is very popular here too. Perhaps the only gamble they've taken is in making the wine list exclusively English. The three roomed restaurant comes with photos and wood panelling and has a brooding, manly vibe.

Greenhouse ✿✿

innovative

G4

27a Hay's Mews ✉ W1J 5NY
✆ (020) 7499 3331
www.greenhouserestaurant.co.uk
⊖ Hyde Park Corner
Closed Saturday lunch, Sunday and bank holidays

Menu £35/120 – Carte £93/113

The Greenhouse

Chef Arnaud Bignon, who arrived in 2012 from Spondi restaurant in Athens, has taken the cooking at The Greenhouse to new heights. Before choosing your dishes, you have to decide on your menu and there's a plethora of them: a 6 course tasting menu, a set menu, an à la carte and a separate lunch menu, as well as a 6 course vegetable-inspired dinner menu. Whatever you go for, you'll find the food modern, innovative, technically impressive and well-balanced. The chef demonstrates his confidence and understanding of flavour combinations in dishes where coffee, morels and liquorice are matched with a veal chop, and calamansi and citrus powder are coupled with langoustines. His cooking comes with an invigorating freshness and ingredients are sourced from Europe's larder: there's Limousin veal, Dorset lamb, Cornish crab and Challans duck. The breadth of the wine list is astounding and includes vintages of Château Lafite back to 1870, Château Latour to 1900, Château Haut-Brion to 1945 and 14 vintages of La Tâche; the New World is not forgotten – there are 38 vintages of Penfolds Grange.

First Course

- Cornish crab with mint jelly, cauliflower, apple and curry.
- Foie gras with corn, satay and aged balsamic.

Main Course

- Lamb with miso puntarella, mooli and onion.
- Turbot with carrot, coconut, tamarind and ginger.

Dessert

- Orange, saffron, date and filo pastry.
- Manjari chocolate, caramel, vanilla and pear.

Gymkhana ✿

Indian H4

42 Albemarle St ✉ W1S 4JH
✆ (020) 3011 5900
www.gymkhanalondon.com
⊖ Green Park
Closed 22-28 December, 1-4 January and Sunday – booking essential

Menu £25 (lunch and early dinner)/65 – Carte £28/61

Gymkhana

If you enjoyed Trishna then you're really going to love Karam Sethi's Gymkhana – that's if you can get a table. Inspired by Colonial India's gymkhana clubs, the interior is full of wonderful detail and plenty of wry touches, from the hunting trophies and ceiling fans to the glass wall lamps and Grandma Sethi's barometer. If you're on the ground floor ask for one of the booths but it's worth a little persistence to ensure you're downstairs where the beaten brass topped tables, leather banquettes and the dimmest of lighting add to the intimate atmosphere. In such charming surroundings it would be easy for the food to play second fiddle, but far from it. There's an array of dishes inspired by the flavours of North India but don't procrastinate – just go straight for the 6 courser. Included could be wild tiger prawns that show what a charcoal grill can do; kid goat methi keema with its richness and well-judged spicing; the complex flavours of suckling pig vindaloo; and wild muntjac biryani, a triumph of flaky pastry.

First Course

- Lasooni wild tiger prawns with red pepper chutney.
- Aubergine and gourd pakora with coriander and tamarind chutney.

Main Course

- Kid goat methi keema, salli and pao.
- Goan Cafreal bream with tomato kachumber.

Dessert

- Saffron and pistachio kulfi falooda.
- Jaggery and black pepper caramel custard.

Hakkasan Mayfair ✿

Chinese

H3

17 Bruton St ✉ W1J 6QB
✆ (020) 7907 1888
www.hakkasan.com
⊖ Green Park
Closed 25 December – booking essential

Menu £35/130 – Carte £32/72 s

Hakkasan Mayfair

This is less a copy, more a sister to the original Hakkasan; a sister who's just as fun and glamorous but simply lives in a far nicer part of town. As with many of the best addresses, it doesn't draw attention to itself – you could easily walk past the entrance without knowing, and that adds to the appeal. The biggest difference is that this Hakkasan has a funky, more casual ground floor to go with the downstairs dining room; but it's still worth booking for the lower level, as a walk down the stairs will heighten the sense of occasion and add a little mystery. The menu of Cantonese treats is an appealing tome; dim sum must surely be the only way to go at lunch, while the signature dishes, such as silver cod with champagne and honey, and Jasmine tea smoked chicken, can be saved for dinner. Desserts are unashamedly tailored towards European tastes but there's a fine range of speciality teas, as well as an impressive selection of cocktails. The staff, dressed in black – what else? – know their menu backwards, so are more than willing to help those seeking guidance.

First Course

- Crispy duck salad with pomelo, pine nut and shallot.
- Sesame prawn toast with foie gras.

Main Course

- Roasted silver cod with champagne and honey.
- Grilled Wagyu beef with enoki mushrooms.

Dessert

- Tarte Tatin.
- Chocolate marquise, kumquat, macadamia and mandarin.

Ham Yard

modern

Ham Yard Hotel,
1 Ham Yard, ✉ W1D 7DT
✆ (020) 3642 2000
www.firmdalehotels.com
⊖ Piccadilly Circus

I3

Carte £24/35

At Ham Yard's stylish and exuberantly decorated restaurant, you might not even make it past the pewter-topped bar: the bitters, syrups, even the tonic water are homemade using herbs grown in the hotel's rooftop garden and the cocktails are as good as the range of little nibbles they serve. The room comes with bright colours and bold patterns; there are kilim prints from India and silk-lined walls; and the tables are all immaculately laid. The menu moves with the seasons and the kitchen has the confidence to keep the cooking appealingly simple. If it's a nice day the smart money is outside on the courtyard terrace – it may be a thoroughfare but the mature trees and parasols bring a continental air rarely seen in this part of town.

Haozhan

Chinese

8 Gerrard St ✉ W1D 5PJ
✆ (020) 7434 3838
www.haozhan.co.uk
⊖ Leicester Square
Closed 24-25 December

Menu £15/48 – Carte £20/78

A plethora of Chinatown restaurants vie for your attention by offering special deals or just brightening their neon. Haozhan adopts the more worthy policy of serving food that's a cut above the norm. Inside the somewhat garish looking menu is not the usual vast list but rather an interesting collection of dishes that owe more to a fusion style, with mostly Cantonese but other Asian influences too; head straight for the specialities, such as jasmine ribs or wasabi prawns. You'll find there's a freshness to the ingredients that also marks this restaurant out – try the Tom Yum prawns in their pancake cones and leave room for the egg custard buns. Appropriately enough, the name Haozhan translates as "a good place to eat".

Hawksmoor

meats and grills H3

5a Air St ✉ W1B 4EA
✆ (020) 7406 3980
www.thehawksmoor.com
⊖ Piccadilly Circus
Closed 24-26 December – booking advisable

Menu £23 (lunch and early dinner) – Carte £35/74 

For the fourth, and possibly the best Hawksmoor they took over the old L'Odeon restaurant and gave it a great little art deco makeover; there are mirrors down one side and the famous arched windows have been frosted and stained. As with the other branches, the sourcing of British beef is top-notch – the 35-day aged Longhorn beef comes with a charred exterior and a juicy centre – but the difference is that here they also offer great seafood, with charcoal-grilled turbot, Dover sole and monkfish proving popular. The prices are 'Mayfair' but not extreme; there's an excellent Express Menu at lunch and very early evening, and staff are a delightful and well organised lot. Soak up the boisterous atmosphere by first having a cocktail in the bar.

HIX

British traditional H3

66-70 Brewer St. ✉ WIF 9UP
✆ (020) 7292 3518
www.hixsoho.co.uk
⊖ Piccadilly Circus
Closed 25-26 December

Menu £20 (weekday lunch)/28 – Carte £29/59 

Leaded, frosted windows similar to those of The Ivy hint at exclusivity within, as does the huge wooden door and the discreet name plaque. Once entry has been secured, one finds oneself in an enormous space with specially commissioned artwork from Damien Hirst, Sue Webster and Sarah Lucas, reflecting Mark Hix's close relationship with London's artists. Meanwhile, his menu reflects his passion for British recipes and ingredients, which translates as plenty of game in season, unusual cuts of meat, rediscovered classics and proper puddings. Portions aren't over-generous – side dishes are required which makes the bill rise quickly – and sometimes a dish may not quite deliver the promise of the menu, but it's a fun, inclusive place.

Hélène Darroze at The Connaught ✿✿

French G3

Connaught Hotel,
Carlos Pl. ✉ W1K 2AL
✆ (020) 7107 8880
www.the-connaught.co.uk
⊖ Bond Street
Closed 2 weeks August, Sunday and Monday – booking essential

Menu £30/92

Connaught Hotel

Those who prefer to travel in life's leisurely lane will find a meal at Hélène Darroze to be right up their cul-de-sac. For one thing, when you book a table for dinner at this discreet and elegant restaurant it's yours for the evening so no one will be trying to hurry you out of the door after 90 minutes. Moreover, the service team are not only a very professional outfit but also understand the importance of engaging with their customers. In the kitchen there is now even greater emphasis placed on the quality of the ingredients and Hélène Darroze is keen to shine a light on her wonderful French and British suppliers. Her cooking remains largely informed by her homeland, and specifically Landes, but she is not shy of the occasional Asian or North African flavour, in combinations that catch your attention. There's an element of surprise to the dishes although it's worth mentioning that portion sizes will appeal to those who've spent the day reclining in languorous expectation than to anyone who's been labouring in the fields.

First Course

- Oyster 'fine de claire' with oscietra caviar and white beans.
- Foie gras, cherry, pistachio and lemon verbena.

Main Course

- XXL scallop with tandoori spices, citrus and coriander.
- Pigeon with beetroot, strawberry and Mexican mole.

Dessert

- Baba Armagnac, rhubarb and galangal.
- Strawberry, elderflower and bourbon vanilla.

Hibiscus ✿✿

innovative

H3

29 Maddox St ✉ W1S 2PA
✆ (020) 7629 2999
www.hibiscusrestaurant.co.uk
⊖ Oxford Circus
Closed first week January, last week August, Monday except September-December, Sunday and bank holidays

XXX

Menu £35/105

Hibiscus

There's an element of surprise to eating at Claude Bosi's Hibiscus restaurant as only the primary ingredients are listed on the menu. If you plump for more than three courses, the kitchen will decide what dishes you're having. The risk-averse should not worry though – a detailed description of the dishes' make-up is given when they're delivered to the table so you'll know what you're eating. If you really don't like surprises then you can stick to three courses or come for lunch where the good value set menu is accompanied by comprehensive description. Claude spends less time these days travelling to exotic lands, so there's less chance of coming across an unfamiliar ingredient in the course of your meal. However, you'll find his cooking remains innovative in style, with original but well-judged combinations of flavours and textures, supported by some fine produce. The last revamp left the room looking brighter and lighter and whilst the service is smooth and the staff are getting chattier, their patter remains a work in progress.

First Course

- Cardigan Bay prawn, chestnut mushrooms, smoked butter and caviar.
- Pork pie ravioli, broad beans and dried pickled eggs.

Main Course

- Cornish sea bream, morels, coffee, tarragon oil and parmesan.
- Braised pork cheek, girolles, almond and apricot.

Dessert

- Asparagus cream, black olives and lemon.
- Caramelised blond chocolate tart, lentils and bergamot.

Hix Mayfair

British traditional H3

Brown's Hotel,
Albemarle St ✉ W1S 4BP
✆ (020) 7518 4004
www.roccofortecollection.com
⊖ Green Park

Menu £33 – Carte £35/69

Brown's is a thoroughly British hotel with a long history so it makes sense for its restaurant to celebrate Britain's own culinary traditions. Mark Hix – surely one of London's busiest restaurateurs at the moment – was the man entrusted with the task and he has put together an appealing looking menu that's big on seasonality and provenance. Good use is made of ingredients from across the UK, such as Portland crab, Morecambe Bay shrimps and Aberdeenshire beef and there's also a daily roast for lunch, served from the trolley. The traditional feel of the wood-panelled dining room is enlivened by the works from leading contemporary British artists, which ensure that the atmosphere never gets too solemn.

Hush

modern H3

8 Lancashire Ct., Brook St. ✉ W1S 1EY
✆ (020) 7659 1500
www.hush.co.uk
⊖ Bond Street
Closed 25 December and 1 January – booking essential

Carte £21/28

Any time the mercury nudges past 16° Londoners feel the need to eat outside, even if that means battling with passers-by for a few feet of pavement space. There's no such indignity at Hush as you'll find in this courtyard, once used to store materials and cloth for Savile Row, a large and appealing terrace. Its occupants are usually here for the long haul and it's easy to understand why: the menu is a likeable, all-purpose affair which skips merrily around Europe so you might have duck confit, a risotto or a schnitzel; if you want to stay closer to home then order one of their terrific homemade pies. You can also just pop in for cocktails and share some small plates and if you're in no hurry you can simply stay put for afternoon tea.

Imli Street

Indian

I3

167-169 Wardour St ✉ W1F 8WR
✆ (020) 7287 4243
www.imlistreet.com
⊖ Tottenham Court Road
Closed 25-26 December and 1 January – bookings not accepted

Menu £24 – Carte £19/43

No restaurant can afford to stand still these days and Imli has responded to current trends by making a few changes. In terms of looks, the restaurant is now much brighter and that includes the once claustrophobic basement. They've also installed a horse-shoe shaped bar to satisfy the growing demand for cocktails. With the new look comes a new menu; fresh, vibrant sharing plates under the headings 'Railway Cuisine', 'Coastal Shack' and 'Food Cart' are essentially influenced by the south of India; 'Beyond Borders' dishes are more Indo-Chinese in origin. The two things that haven't changed are the service, which remains keen and attentive, and the no booking policy – but with a bar this good, waiting for a table is hardly an ordeal.

Imperial China

Chinese

I3

White Bear Yard, 25a Lisle St ✉ WC2H 7BA
✆ (020) 7734 3388
www.imperialchina-london.com
⊖ Leicester Square
Closed 25 December – booking advisable

Carte £19/51

Heave open the heavy smoked-glass double doors, cross the bamboo bridge and you'll be transported to a calm oasis that seems a world away from the bustle outside. Sharp, well-organised service and comfortable surroundings are not the only things that set this restaurant apart: the Cantonese cooking exudes freshness and vitality, whether that's the steamed dumplings or the XO minced pork with fine beans. Indeed, they pride themselves on seafood and their 'lobster feasts' are very popular - the personable staff are also more than happy to offer recommendations. There are eight private rooms of various sizes available upstairs and these are often in full swing. The owners also run Beijing Dumpling a few doors down.

Kai ✿

Chinese

G3

65 South Audley St ✉ W1K 2QU
✆ (020) 7493 8988
www.kaimayfair.co.uk
⊖ Hyde Park Corner
Closed 25-26 December and 1 January – booking essential

Carte £39/149

Kai

Traditionalists will find a few familiar classics on the menu but Chef Alex Chow's strengths are his modern creations and re-workings of traditional Chinese recipes. There are Cantonese, Shanghainese, Hunanese and Sichuan influences but he also uses the occasional flavour from other Asian countries. The resulting dishes have real depth, use superb ingredients and are wonderfully well balanced. Vegetarians are well catered for and desserts are given a bigger billing than one usually sees. The lunch menu offers further proof that this isn't your typical Chinese restaurant: instead of dim sum, they call their smaller versions of the dinner specialities "little plates of loveliness". The service team in their silk jackets expertly anticipate their customers' needs, whether that's demonstrating how to construct a pork pancake, expertly filleting sea bass or offering jasmine tea to those awaiting a soufflé. The clientele is international and the interior unashamedly glitzy, with the only discordant note being the incongruously clubby music.

First Course

- Sirloin with soy vinaigrette, shallot oil and coriander.
- Wasabi prawns, mild wasabi mayonnaise, mango and basil seeds.

Main Course

- Sea bass with caramelised black vinegar syrup marinade.
- Oriental spiced pork belly with ginger, cinnamon and soy.

Dessert

- Durian soufflé, vanilla and salted caramel.
- Amedei chocolate fondant with pistachio.

Keeper's House

British modern H3

Royal Academy of Arts, Burlington House, Piccadilly
✉ W1J 0BD
✆ (020) 7300 5881
www.keepershouse.org.uk
⊖ Green Park
Closed 25-26 December and Sunday – (dinner only)

Carte £35/53 XX

The Keeper's House, built in the 1860s and fully restored, sits in the corner of the courtyard of Burlington House and acts as a members' club for Royal Academicians and Friends of the RA. In the evenings, though, it's open to all of us – to find it, look for the Tracey Emin neon 'Keep me safe' above the door. The two intimate, interconnecting rooms come with low ceilings and walls lined with green baize and hung with architectural casts; there's also a modern bar which leads out into a hidden garden. The menu is appealingly concise and the emphasis is on seasonality, freshness and contrasts in textures and flavours. The kitchen strives for a certain amount of originality and, when the dishes work, they work very well.

Kiku

Japanese H4

17 Half Moon St. ✉ W1J 7BE
✆ (020) 7499 4208
www.kikurestaurant.co.uk
⊖ Green Park
Closed 25-27 December, 1 January, Sunday and lunch on bank holidays

Menu £22 (weekday lunch) – Carte £23/87 XX

It's not just the fact that it's family owned and has been here for over 35 years that makes Kiku unlike most Mayfair restaurants – this Japanese restaurant is also very sweet. There's an authentic simplicity to its decoration and a pleasing earnestness to the service; most evenings the majority of diners appear to be homesick Japanese. Virtually every style of Japanese cuisine is on offer, from shabu shabu to sukiyaki, yakitori to teriyaki and if you want to try something a little different, like sliced squid and guts or salmon zosui (rice soup), then here's your chance. The extensive à la carte menu is supplemented by a number of set menus and these are worth exploring if you want an all-round experience.

Koya

Japanese I3

49 Frith St ✉ W1D 4SG
✆ (020) 7434 4463
www.koya.co.uk
⊖ Tottenham Court Road
Closed Christmas – bookings not accepted

Carte £10/29

Authenticity is the key to Koya's success: the Japanese wheat is kneaded by foot, while the dashi base stock is freshly made every day. Slurp unselfconsciously to get the full benefit of these delicious noodles with their wonderful chewiness or 'koshi'. They come in three styles: hot in a hot broth, cold with a hot broth or cold with a cold dipping sauce, and arrive on a bamboo mat and with a sprinkling of nori (seaweed). Be sure to order some small plates too, such as the onsen tamago or crisp tempura – and a glass of sake, shochu, beer or wine. The decoration is modest, service is sweet and if you aren't here before the noren curtain is put out then be prepared to queue – or try Koya Bar, their new branch next door, with its similar menu.

Little Social

French H3

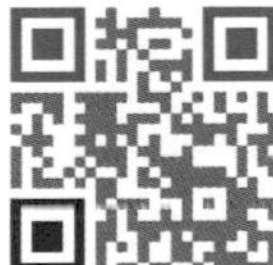

5 Pollen St ✉ W1S 1NE
✆ (020) 7870 3730
www.littlesocial.co.uk
⊖ Oxford Circus
Closed Sunday and bank holidays – booking essential

Menu £21 (lunch) – Carte £29/58

Jason Atherton wisely decided that keeping an eye on your growing restaurant empire is easier when you have two restaurants in the same street. In contrast with the more formal Pollen Street Social, Little Social is a lively French bistro with a clubby, masculine feel and an appealing, deliberately worn look. The best seats are the discreet leather booths at the back; avoid the bar as you can get crowded out by those having a pre-prandial drink. Service is bright, breezy and capable and the French food is fairly classic, with the occasional modern twist. The menu constantly evolves and the choice is enhanced by daily specials; the soups and steaks are winners but, for the more adventurous, there could be pork head terrine or ox cheeks.

Manchurian Legends

Chinese I3

16 Lisle St ✉ WC2H 7BE
✆ (020) 7287 6606
www.manchurianlegends.com
⊖ Leicester Square
Closed Christmas

Menu £16/25 – Carte approx. £46

There's a bewildering choice of Chinese restaurants in these parts so look out for a chef behind the window making the dumplings, which are one of the specialities at this simple yet authentic spot. Also available are specialities from the northeast corner of China – the Dongbei region. They battle the long winters out there with stews and BBQ dishes, along with heartening soups like rib and lotus root. The chillies beside each dish on the menu warn of their relative heat – ignore these at your peril – although the chef cleverly balances the heat with herbs and various other spices. There are ingredients like gizzards, intestines and tripe for the more adventurous eater and it's worth starting with some of the street snacks.

MASH

meats and grills H3

77 Brewer St ✉ W1F 9ZN
✆ (020) 7734 2608
www.mashsteak.co.uk
⊖ Piccadilly Circus
Closed 23-25 December and Sunday lunch

Menu £25 – Carte £48/76

It took a brave team to take on the daunting task of raising the old Titanic restaurant from the depths of Brewer Street but that is what a group of experienced Copenhagen restaurateurs did in 2012. In restoring many of the original art deco features and combining them with contemporary fittings, they have created a striking 350-seater restaurant. Instead of showcasing Danish cuisine, they have gone for a 'Modern American Steak House'. They offer mostly Danish prime and corn-fed Nebraskan and Uruguayan beef and it's clear the kitchen knows what it's doing. Starters are equally robust and include charcuterie and foie gras. Add in a great cocktail bar, slick service and an impressive wine list and you have a seriously grown up restaurant.

Matsuri

Japanese H4

15 Bury St. ✉ SW1Y 6AL
✆ (020) 7839 1101
www.matsuri-restaurant.com
⊖ Green Park
Closed 25 December and 1 January

Menu £40 (lunch) – Carte £32/118

One of the capital's longest running Japanese restaurants remains refreshingly impervious to the contemporary trend towards 'reinterpretation' and instead focuses on traditional dishes and combinations. You're whisked downstairs past the drums, fans and masks by gracious and traditionally costumed ladies to where you can choose between teppan-yaki or a seat at the sushi counter. You'll be assailed by a plethora of menus ranging from a chef's special to a Wagyu beef menu as well as a monthly changing list of seasonal specials such as crab marinated in rice vinegar or pork shabu-shabu. Once decided, you need do nothing except sit and appreciate a bit of knife juggling while enjoying fresh ingredients that taste of what they should.

Maze Grill

meats and grills 

London Marriott Hotel Grosvenor Square,
10-13 Grosvenor Sq ✉ W1K 6JP
✆ (020) 7495 2211
www.gordonramsay.com/mazegrill
⊖ Bond Street

Carte £27/82

Use the Grosvenor Square entrance as it offers a little more charm than if one wanders in from the adjacent Marriott Hotel, for which this restaurant also acts as the breakfast room. But then again, this is less about glamour, more about just enjoying good quality beef. The assorted cuts, from Casterbridge grain-fed and Hereford grass-fed through to Creekstone prime USDA corn-fed and Wagyu, are brought to your table in their raw state for you to hear about their differing personalities. Your preferred steak is then given a blast in the super-hot broiler before being served on a wooden board. The sides and sauces are numerous, varied and individually priced so your wallet can also end up feeling a little tender.

Maze ✿

modern

G3

10-13 Grosvenor Sq ✉ W1K 6JP
☎ (020) 7107 0000
www.gordonramsay.com/maze
⊖ Bond Street

Menu £30 (lunch) – Carte £32/44

Gordon Ramsay Holdings

Standing still should never be an option for any restaurant – however successful – and at Gordon Ramsay's Maze there has been a little tinkering taking place. A cocktail 'mixologist' has arrived to draw in more customers to the bar and there is now a greater element of Asian influence to the cooking. The hallmark precision is evident in all the dishes; combinations are not overworked and flavours and textures have been intelligently thought out. There's a deceptive simplicity here and a playful element too; the Asian tones enhance rather than overpower the ingredients. Four dishes per person should be about right, and the set lunch and early evening menus are bargains. The iPad wine list is more than just a gimmick – it's a great way of running through the list, which may be light on mature vintages but has strength in depth across all regions. The David Rockwell designed room looks as good as ever and the restaurant continues to attract an appealingly mixed crowd, from the romantically inclined to the corporately minded.

First Course

- Beef fillet tataki with wakame seaweed and pickled onion.
- Marinated yellow fin tuna with Iberico ham and avocado purée.

Main Course

- Pigeon breast with consommé, wild garlic and pâté en croûte.
- Salmon Bellevue with watermelon, fennel and citrus salad.

Dessert

- Lemon meringue pie with blackberry sorbet.
- Chocolate and peanut bar with caramelised banana.

Mele e Pere

Italian

I3

46 Brewer St ✉ W1F 9TF
✆ (020) 7096 2096
www.meleepere.co.uk
⊖ Piccadilly Circus
Closed 25-26 December, 1 January and Easter

Menu £16 (dinner) – Carte £26/39

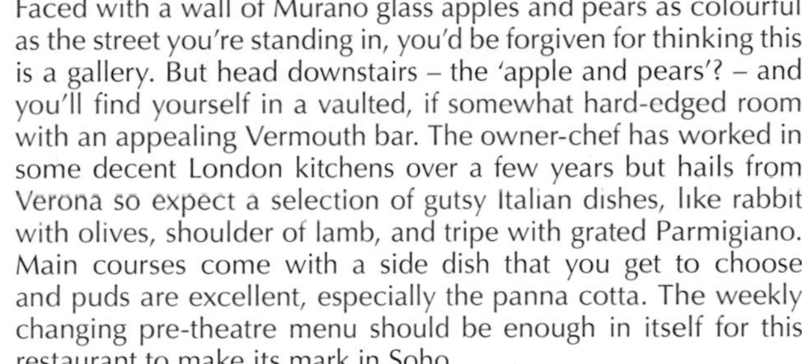

Faced with a wall of Murano glass apples and pears as colourful as the street you're standing in, you'd be forgiven for thinking this is a gallery. But head downstairs – the 'apple and pears'? – and you'll find yourself in a vaulted, if somewhat hard-edged room with an appealing Vermouth bar. The owner-chef has worked in some decent London kitchens over a few years but hails from Verona so expect a selection of gutsy Italian dishes, like rabbit with olives, shoulder of lamb, and tripe with grated Parmigiano. Main courses come with a side dish that you get to choose and puds are excellent, especially the panna cotta. The weekly changing pre-theatre menu should be enough in itself for this restaurant to make its mark in Soho.

Mews of Mayfair

modern

H3

10-11 Lancashire Ct, Brook St (1st floor) ✉ W1S 1EY
✆ (020) 7518 9388
www.mewsofmayfair.com
⊖ Bond Street
Closed 25 December

Carte £21/68

Mews manages that trick of being cool and bright in summer and warm and inviting in winter. The relative serenity of the pretty restaurant is in sharp contrast to the crowds in the narrow lane and busy cocktail bar below, while the private dining room on the next floor up is a very pleasant space. The menu is appealing and sufficiently sensitive to the changing seasons, so expect venison in winter, spring lamb and summer fruit. Simpler dishes are also pepped up, so burgers come with an optional foie gras topping and fish and chips arrive with a wasabi tartare. Flavours are sometimes compromised by an over-eagerness to make dishes look pretty but prices are generally sensible and the atmosphere thoroughly civilised.

Mint Leaf

Indian

I4

Suffolk Pl ✉ SW1Y 4HX
✆ (020) 7930 9020
www.mintleafrestaurant.com
⊖ Piccadilly Circus
Closed 25-26 December, 1 January and lunch Saturday-Sunday

Menu £30/38 – Carte £25/43

Indian restaurants come in a variety of guises these days: Mint Leaf is from the contemporary, slick and designery school. This vast subterranean space with its moody lighting can seat over 250 but it comes divided into seven different areas so you're never rattling around. There is even an enormous bar running the length of the room for those wanting to make a night of it. The menu is also quite a lengthy affair, with many choices available in small or larger sizes. The best bet is to share a few dishes such as the soft shell crab or jumbo prawns, and then have your own curry – the kitchen's strength. The serving team are a mixed bunch: some will explain dishes enthusiastically; others seem keener upselling drinks.

Momo

North-African

H3

25 Heddon St. ✉ W1B 4BH
✆ (020) 7434 4040
www.momoresto.com
⊖ Oxford Circus
Closed 24-25 December and 1 January

Menu £20/52 – Carte £31/48

Lanterns, rugs, trinkets and music all contribute to the authentic Moroccan atmosphere that makes Momo such a fun night out. That being said, it's even more fun if you come with friends as tables of two can get somewhat overawed. The menu is divided into three: a rather expensive set menu, traditional dishes and Momo specialities. The traditional section is the best as here you'll find the classics from pastilla to tagines; the Momo specialities are more contemporary in their make-up. Whatever you order, you'll end up with a pile of couscous and enough good food to last the week. The wine list lacks affordable bottles but there's a great bar downstairs. If it weren't for the absence of cigarette smoke, you could be in Marrakech.

Murano ✿

Italian

G4

20 Queen St ✉ W1J 5PP
✆ (020) 7495 1127
www.muranolondon.com
⊖ Green Park
Closed Christmas and Sunday

Menu £25/95

Murano

Named after the famous glassware from the Venetian island of Murano, Angela Hartnett's restaurant remains as smart and as elegant as ever. It was her Italian grandparents, who came from Bardi in the heart of Emilia-Romagna, who instilled in her a love and appreciation of good food – and her passion shows through in the Italian inspired dishes which are equally appealing to the eye and the palate. There's a choice of 2-5 courses, with four being the best option. Underpinned by a distinctive classical base, the quality of the Italian ingredients really shines through; the dishes are uncluttered and balanced and the flavours clear and defined. Fish dishes are a particular highlight as are the Northern Italian inspired classics like risotto Milanese. Service is structured and comes with a degree of formality but the staff are quite charming and make sure all customers are comfortable and put at ease. It's easy to understand why this restaurant has so many regulars, and Angela is usually on hand to say hello to them.

First Course

- Scallop ceviche with spiced avocado purée, ginger and coriander cress.
- Hand-rolled linguine with clams, artichokes and toasted breadcrumbs.

Main Course

- Cumbrian lamb with pea purée and goat's cheese dauphine.
- Braised turbot with broad beans, tomato and artichoke salad.

Dessert

- Caramelised pear tart, almond crumble and milk ice cream.
- Chocolate ganache, mango cream and passion fruit gel.

The National Dining Rooms

British modern 13/4

Sainsbury Wing, The National Gallery, Trafalgar Sq
✉ WC2N 5DN
✆ (020) 7747 2525
www.peytonandbyrne.co.uk
⊖ Charing Cross
Closed 24-26 December and 1 January – (lunch only and Friday dinner)

Menu £30 – Carte £24/35

There's usually a queue but don't panic – it's either those wanting the bakery section or others realising they should have booked. Oliver Peyton's restaurant on the first floor of the National Gallery's Sainsbury Wing is a bright, open affair, enriched by Paula Rego's complex mural 'Crivelli's Garden'. Ask for a table by the window, not just for the views of Trafalgar Square but also because the other half of the room is darker and under the eaves of the early Renaissance on the floor above. The menu champions British cooking and produce; fish and cheeses are the highlight – pies and puds will write-off the afternoon. The set menu represents decent value and is popular with the customers, who resemble a bridge club up from Winchester for the day.

Nobu

Japanese 

Metropolitan Hotel,
19 Old Park Ln ✉ W1Y 1LB
✆ (020) 7447 4747
www.noburestaurants.com
⊖ Hyde Park Corner
Booking essential

Menu £45 (lunch) – Carte £29/71

These days there are Nobu restaurants stretching from Malibu to Moscow and Beijing to Budapest but back in 1997 when Europe's first branch opened here at the Metropolitan hotel it sent shockwaves through the city. Not only did it add serious sparkle and bags of glamour to the dining out scene but also its innovative cuisine – an intriguing mix of Japanese cuisine and South American ingredients – was unlike anything else at the time. Nobu's heyday may have slipped past but the restaurant remains buzzy and fun, and if you need proof of the influence it has had then simply check out the menus of some of its competitors and imitators and you'll see plenty of evidence of some pretty shameless culinary plagiarism.

Nobu Berkeley St

Japanese H3

15 Berkeley St. ✉ W1J 8DY
✆ (020) 7290 9222
www.noburestaurants.com
⊖ Green Park
Closed 25 December, 1 January and Sunday lunch – booking essential

Menu £35/90 – Carte £28/93

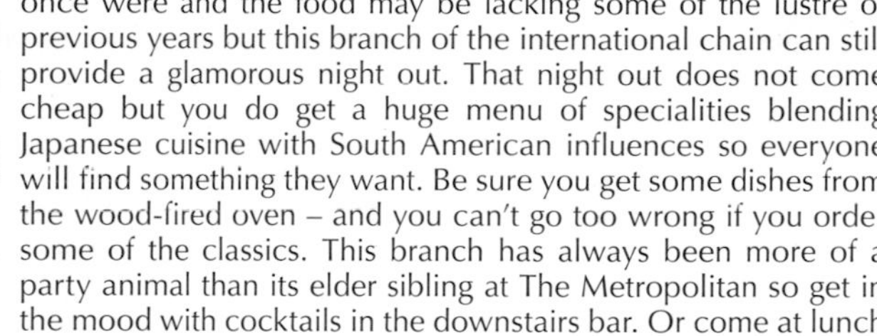

The cries of "irasshaimase" may not be quite as heartfelt as they once were and the food may be lacking some of the lustre of previous years but this branch of the international chain can still provide a glamorous night out. That night out does not come cheap but you do get a huge menu of specialities blending Japanese cuisine with South American influences so everyone will find something they want. Be sure you get some dishes from the wood-fired oven – and you can't go too wrong if you order some of the classics. This branch has always been more of a party animal than its elder sibling at The Metropolitan so get in the mood with cocktails in the downstairs bar. Or come at lunch for a less frenzied experience.

Nopi

Mediterranean H3

21-22 Warwick St. ✉ W1B 5NE
✆ (020) 7494 9584
www.nopi-restaurant.com
⊖ Piccadilly Circus
Closed 25-26 December, 1 January, Sunday and bank holidays

Carte £30/44

There isn't an Aga in the country that doesn't share kitchen space with a few of his cookbooks and his terrific delis are now much copied – so it's no surprise that Yotam Ottolenghi's restaurant is a great success too. It's cleverly designed because you'd think those white walls would make it stark and cold but it actually feels warm and soothing – and the brass lamps and marble add a hint of the exotic. The flavours take in the Med, the Middle East and Asia and whether you share a few smaller dishes or plough your own furrow, you'll find the food refreshing and vibrant and will feel healthy just eating it. This is a relaxed, informal all-day restaurant that is genuinely well run – the staff really make an effort to ensure you enjoy yourself.

Only Running Footman

British traditional G/H3

5 Charles St ✉ W1J 5DF
✆ (020) 7499 2988
www.therunningfootmanmayfair.com
⊖ Green Park.

Menu £35 – Carte £20/49

Apparently the owners added 'only' to the title when they found out that theirs was the only pub in the land called 'The Running Footman'. Spread over several levels, it offers cookery demonstrations and private dinners along with its two floors of dining. Downstairs is where the action usually is, with its menu offering pub classics from steak sandwiches to fishcakes, but you can't book here and it's always packed. Upstairs is where you'll find a surprisingly formal dining room and here they do take reservations. Its menu is far more ambitious and European in its influence but the best dishes are still the simpler ones, with desserts a strength. You can't help feeling that you would be having a lot more fun below stairs, though.

Palomar

other world kitchens I3

34 Rupert St ✉ W1D 6DN
✆ (020) 7439 8777
www.thepalomar.co.uk
⊖ Piccadilly Circus
Closed 25-26 December and Sunday dinner – booking advisable

Carte £19/38

Run by a brother and sister team who used to own a nightclub, Palomar brings a hip slice of modern-day Jerusalem to the heart of theatreland. Inside it's a bit of a squeeze, with a zinc kitchen counter running back to an intimate, wood-panelled dining room, but the limited space, its propensity to get packed and the proximity to the animated chefs make for a high-energy buzz. Like the atmosphere, the food here is fresh and vibrant, with contemporary Middle Eastern cooking taking a tour round Southern Spain and Italy, through North Africa and to the Levant. Starters come from the raw bar, unless you choose the 'Daily 6' assorted mezze, while main dishes come from the stove, the Josper or the plancha and are designed for sharing.

La Petite Maison

French

H3

54 Brooks Mews ✉ W1K 4EG
✆ (020) 7495 4774
www.lpmlondon.co.uk
⊖ Bond Street
Closed Christmas-New Year – booking essential

Carte £31/62 s

A little piece of southern France and Ligurian Italy in Mayfair. The sister operation to the Nice original has a great, buzzy feel which is almost as enticing as the aromas from the kitchen. There's more than a soupçon of glamour and the staff, in their aprons and bow ties, give the impressive that nothing ever fazes them. Simply reading the menus will improve your tan: there are over 20 starters and mains and you can expect lots of healthy olive oil, artichokes, peppers, lemons and tomatoes. There's a fresh pasta of the day, seafood is popular and the whole chicken or gigot of lamb for two are worth ordering. This is a proper neighbourhood restaurant – but as that neighbourhood happens to be Mayfair, don't expect down-to-earth prices.

Peyote

Mexican

H3

13 Cork St ✉ W1S 3NS
✆ (020) 7409 1300
www.peyoterestaurant.com
⊖ Green Park
Closed Saturday lunch and Sunday – booking essential

Carte £26/58

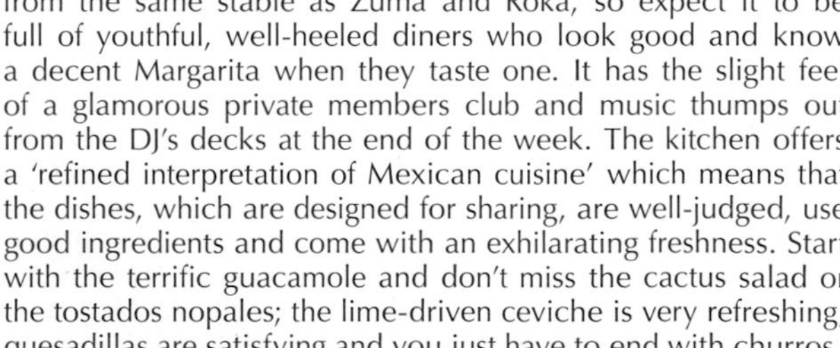

An energetic and moodily lit Mexican restaurant which comes from the same stable as Zuma and Roka, so expect it to be full of youthful, well-heeled diners who look good and know a decent Margarita when they taste one. It has the slight feel of a glamorous private members club and music thumps out from the DJ's decks at the end of the week. The kitchen offers a 'refined interpretation of Mexican cuisine' which means that the dishes, which are designed for sharing, are well-judged, use good ingredients and come with an exhilarating freshness. Start with the terrific guacamole and don't miss the cactus salad or the tostados nopales; the lime-driven ceviche is very refreshing; quesadillas are satisfying and you just have to end with churros.

Pitt Cue Co.

meats and grills H3 

1 Newburgh St ✉ W1F 7RB
✆ (020) 7287 5578
www.pittcue.co.uk
⊖ Oxford Circus
Bookings not accepted

Carte £18/34

When the young owners started selling their version of American barbecue out of a van, word of (electronic) mouth spread so quickly that they soon found this more permanent spot. It's a tiny place, with a bourbon bar on the ground floor – try one of their whiskey sours – and seating for just 18 in the stark basement, so be prepared for some queuing. The menu changes daily but the three constants are house sausage, pulled pork and beef ribs; these are dry-rubbed, smoked in-house for 6 hours and then roasted. All meats come with house pickle and a side dish like bone marrow mash or excellent green chilli slaw and the food's served on enamel tin trays, which adds a little penitentiary chic to proceedings. It's loud, messy, filling and fun.

Plum Valley

Chinese I3

20 Gerrard St. ✉ W1D 6JQ
✆ (020) 7494 4366
⊖ Leicester Square
Closed 23-24 December

Menu £38 – Carte £19/37

Is Chinatown finally casting off its tourist-trap reputation? Plum Valley is the latest venture with genuine aspirations to open in Gerrard Street and its contemporary styling gives the street a much-needed boost. The striking black façade makes it easy to notice, while flattering lighting and layered walls give the interior a dash of sophistication. The chef is from Chiu Chow, a region near Guangdong, and his menu is largely based on Cantonese cooking, with occasional forays into Vietnam and Thailand as well as the odd nod towards contemporary presentation. Dim sum is his kitchen's main strength which fits nicely with the all-day opening of the restaurant. If only those doing the service could muster the same levels of enthusiasm.

Pollen Street Social ✿

innovative

H3

8-10 Pollen St ✉ W1S 1NQ
✆ (020) 7290 7600
www.pollenstreetsocial.com
⊖ Oxford Circus
Closed Sunday and bank holidays – booking essential

Menu £30 (lunch) – Carte £52/69

Pollen Street Social

Jason Atherton may have opened another couple of places in town but there's been no dropping of standards here at his HQ, and Pollen Street Social is now firmly established, with everyone clear about the look and direction of the restaurant. There was a little tinkering done in their second year when Jason stopped with the 'small plates' thing and reverted back to the more traditional starter-main course-dessert format. It's well worth asking for a table in the main room with its 'dessert' bar and glass-fronted kitchen, because this is where the action is. What has never changed is the cooking here, which marries innovation and imagination with sound culinary techniques and an innate understanding of good ingredients. Dishes are elaborately constructed but there are never too many flavours or any discordant notes. Not only has a wine list been created that boasts impressive depth, breadth and variety, but there's also a great cocktail list, which includes their terrific version of a negroni.

First Course	Main Course	Dessert
• Steak tartare, smoked beetroot, wild leaves and berry pearls.	• Pork belly and cheek with black pudding, Jersey Royals and pink apple purée.	• Chocolate marquise, praline, milk mousse and honey ice cream.
• Devon squid cooked in cauliflower, roasted squid juices, ink rice and sea herbs.	• Stuffed loin of young rabbit, cassoulet of white beans and herbs.	• Bergamot and verbena sorbet, frozen citrus and bergamot jam.

(N) Polpetto

Italian I3

11 Berwick St ✉ W1F 0PL
✆ (020) 7439 8627
www.polpetto.co.uk
⊖ Tottenham Court Road
Closed Sunday dinner – (bookings not accepted at dinner)

Carte £12/25

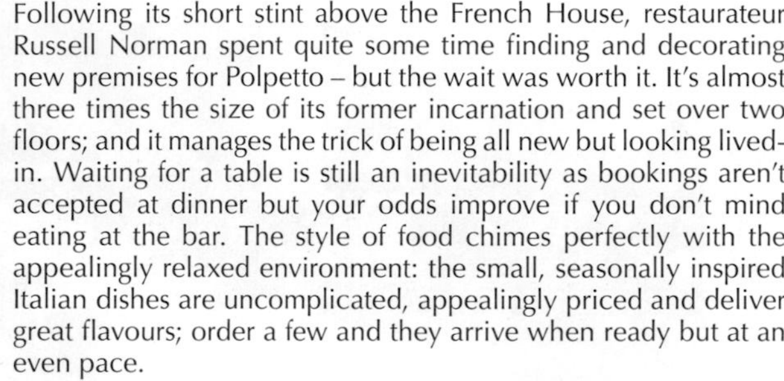

Following its short stint above the French House, restaurateur Russell Norman spent quite some time finding and decorating new premises for Polpetto – but the wait was worth it. It's almost three times the size of its former incarnation and set over two floors; and it manages the trick of being all new but looking lived-in. Waiting for a table is still an inevitability as bookings aren't accepted at dinner but your odds improve if you don't mind eating at the bar. The style of food chimes perfectly with the appealingly relaxed environment: the small, seasonally inspired Italian dishes are uncomplicated, appealingly priced and deliver great flavours; order a few and they arrive when ready but at an even pace.

Polpo Soho

Italian H3

41 Beak St. ✉ W1F 9SB
✆ (020) 7734 4479
www.polpo.co.uk
⊖ Oxford Circus
Closed dinner 24 December, 25-26 and 31 December, 1 January and Sunday dinner – (bookings not accepted at dinner)

Carte £12/24

Opening a Venetian bacaro in an 18C townhouse where Canaletto once lodged does seem providential and Polpo has indeed been packing them in since day one. The stripped-down faux-industrial look is more New York's SoHo than London's Soho, as is the evening no-reservation policy which means you'll probably have to wait. But the fun atmosphere and the appealing prices of the small plates will assuage any impatience you feel in waiting your turn. Order a couple of cicchetti, like arancini or prosciutto; a plate of fritto misto, ham and pea risotto or Cotechino sausage; and a vegetable dish per person and you should leave satisfied - if you do over-order, it's not going to break the bank. Venetian wines, available by the carafe, complete the picture.

Portrait

modern I3

National Portrait Gallery (3rd floor), St Martin's Pl.
✉ WC2H 0HE
✆ (020) 7312 2490 – **www**.searcys.co.uk
⊖ Charing Cross
Closed 24-26 December – booking essential – (lunch only and dinner Thursday-Saturday)

Menu £30 – Carte £32/47

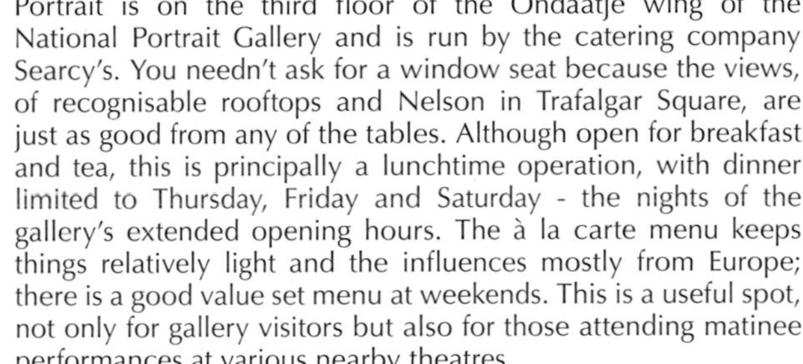

Portrait is on the third floor of the Ondaatje wing of the National Portrait Gallery and is run by the catering company Searcy's. You needn't ask for a window seat because the views, of recognisable rooftops and Nelson in Trafalgar Square, are just as good from any of the tables. Although open for breakfast and tea, this is principally a lunchtime operation, with dinner limited to Thursday, Friday and Saturday - the nights of the gallery's extended opening hours. The à la carte menu keeps things relatively light and the influences mostly from Europe; there is a good value set menu at weekends. This is a useful spot, not only for gallery visitors but also for those attending matinee performances at various nearby theatres.

Quaglino's

modern H4

16 Bury St ✉ SW1Y 6AJ
✆ (020) 7930 6767
www.quaglinos-restaurant.co.uk
⊖ Green Park
Closed Christmas, Easter Monday and Sunday

Menu £20/25 – Carte £34/60

Few London restaurants are as synonymous with the early '90s as Quaglino's when, for a time, securing a table at this vast, glamorous, colourful and glitzy restaurant was the overriding ambition of many. The in-crowd may have since moved on – to other bustling, design-led restaurants which owe a debt to the trail blazed by 'Quag's' – but the old girl can still shake it on a weekend for those wanting a fun night out. The kitchen also feels invigorated and successfully delivers on the promise of the appealing, brasserie-style menu. Classics like pork belly, duck confit and chargrilled steaks are done well, along with shellfish from the 'Crustacea Counter'; look out too for the 'dish of the day'- perhaps a smoked haddock fishcake.

Quo Vadis

British modern I3

26-29 Dean St ✉ W1D 3LL
✆ (020) 7437 9585
www.quovadissoho.co.uk
⊖ Tottenham Court Road
Closed 25-26 December, 1 January and bank holidays

Menu £18 – Carte £26/38 XXX

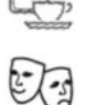

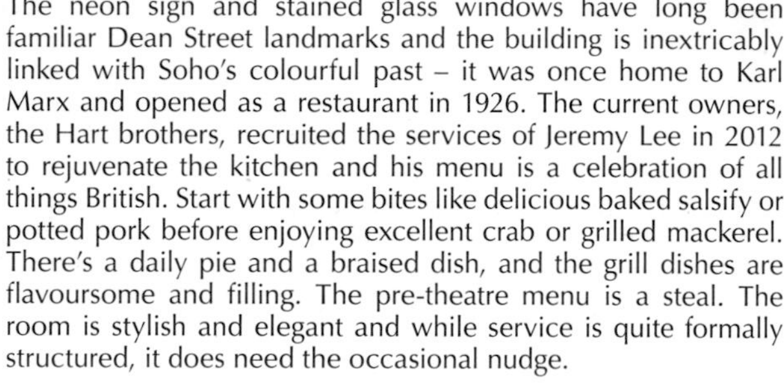

The neon sign and stained glass windows have long been familiar Dean Street landmarks and the building is inextricably linked with Soho's colourful past – it was once home to Karl Marx and opened as a restaurant in 1926. The current owners, the Hart brothers, recruited the services of Jeremy Lee in 2012 to rejuvenate the kitchen and his menu is a celebration of all things British. Start with some bites like delicious baked salsify or potted pork before enjoying excellent crab or grilled mackerel. There's a daily pie and a braised dish, and the grill dishes are flavoursome and filling. The pre-theatre menu is a steal. The room is stylish and elegant and while service is quite formally structured, it does need the occasional nudge.

Red Fort

Indian I3

77 Dean St. ✉ W1D 3SH
✆ (020) 7437 2525
www.redfort.co.uk
⊖ Tottenham Court Road
Closed lunch Saturday-Sunday – bookings advisable at dinner

Menu £15 – Carte £31/59 

Red Fort has been in Soho since 1983, although anyone who hasn't visited for a while will be surprised to see how up-to-date this Indian restaurant now is in the looks department. It's still quite a sizeable place but neatly broken up; the far end even boasts a little waterfall. Service isn't quite so memorable and staff could do with being a little more willing to engage with their customers but the menu does impress. It is not overlong and comes divided between starters, grills and main courses. Much of the produce comes from within the UK, such as Herdwick lamb, and there are also more unusual ingredients like rabbit used. Cooking is nicely balanced but the final bill can be a little high, especially when one has added breads, rice and vegetables.

Refuel

modern

I3

Soho Hotel,
4 Richmond Mews ✉ W1D 3DH
✆ (020) 7559 3007
www.sohohotel.com
⊖ Tottenham Court Road

Menu £21 – Carte £27/57

It comes as no surprise that a hotel as fashionable as The Soho has a restaurant as cool as Refuel. A large part of the room is given over to a slick cocktail bar and the lively atmosphere here tends to seep through into the restaurant through osmosis. Service in the hotel is one of its great strengths and the serving team here are a bright and enthusiastic bunch who are always ready with a smile. The menu is all about ease of eating and includes a popular section of grilled dishes, which could range from Dover sole to a burger, as well as assorted pasta dishes and salads for the image-conscious. Side dishes are needed but can leave you with a sizeable bill so it's worth considering the better value set menu.

Ritz Restaurant

British traditional

H4

Ritz Hotel,
150 Piccadilly ✉ W1J 9BR
✆ (020) 7493 8181
www.theritzlondon.com
⊖ Green Park

Menu £49 (weekday lunch) s – Carte £69/79 s

Dining at The Ritz is not just a mightily grand occasion but also provides a lesson in how things used to be done. The room is certainly unmatched in the sheer lavishness of its Louis XVI decoration; the table settings positively gleam thanks to all that polishing; and there are probably more ranks to the serving team than in a ship's company. Little wonder they insist on jackets and ties. There's a plethora of menus: Ritz Classics could be saddle of Kentish lamb or roast sirloin; Ritz Traditions might include smoked salmon carved at your table or Dover sole filleted in front of you. For the full experience, go at a weekend for a dinner dance, have the six-course Sonata Menu and don't tell your bank manager.

Roka

Japanese G3

30 North Audley St ✉ W1K 6ZF
✆ (020) 7305 5644
www.rokarestaurant.com
⊖ Bond Street

Carte £30/89

Rainer Becker and Arjun Waney's empire now stretches to all parts of the globe but London was where it all began and is where they continue to open new restaurants. For the capital's third Roka they've ventured into the rarefied surroundings of Mayfair and the restaurant's sultry, seductive looks prove a good fit. Tempting aromas fill the air as once again the robata grill takes centre stage – quite literally if you haven't booked and find yourself seated at the Indonesian elm counter that surrounds it. All the favourites from their modern Japanese repertoire are on show here; the tasting menu is often the best way of getting a good all round experience and the dessert platter really is a sight. Even the doggy bags look good.

Rosa's Carnaby

Thai H3

23a Ganton Street ✉ W1F 9BW
✆ (020) 7287 9617
www.rosaslondon.com
⊖ Oxford Circus
Booking essential

Menu £22 (lunch and early dinner) – Carte £17/31

If you have a favourite Thai dish then chances are you'll find it here at this bright and bustling, neat and tidy Thai café spread over two floors. The somewhat alarmingly lengthy menu, which is supplemented by more specialities on the blackboards, celebrates traditional flavours given the occasional modern twist. Go for any dish containing noodles and you won't be disappointed – the pork dishes also stand out. You'll find yourself perching on low red stools at chunky tables so close to your neighbour that you can not only listen to their conversation but feel almost discourteous if you don't join in on it. Staff are unfailingly polite and if any dish really impresses you then grab a recipe card on the way out and try it at home.

Rosa's Soho

Thai

I3

48 Dean St ✉ W1D 5BF
✆ (020) 7494 1638
www.rosaslondon.com
⊖ Leicester Square
Closed Easter and Christmas – booking advisable

Menu £22/32 – Carte £17/31

Those instinctively suspicious of anywhere too shiny and flashy will find Rosa's worn-in appearance suitably reassuring. The simple, pared down look of this authentic Thai café also adds to its intimate feel; the waitresses, in bright red T-shirts to match the colour of the façade, provide cheerful and swift service. The menu is appealing and wide-ranging and the relative heat levels of each dish are indicated. The chef may be from Chiang Mai but his cooking is influenced by all parts of the country. Signature dishes include warm minced chicken salad and a sweet pumpkin red curry; while squid, prawns, mussels and scallops all go into their seafood Pad Cha. The refreshing Tom Yam soup comes with a lovely balance of sweet, sour and spice.

Sake No Hana

Japanese

H4

23 St James's St ✉ SW1A 1HA
✆ (020) 7925 8988
www.sakenohana.com
⊖ Green Park
Closed 25 December and Sunday

Menu £29/65 – Carte £23/62

It's not often one finds good food at the end of an escalator, but then not many restaurants occupy a building like this Grade II listed '60s edifice. What was once the office of The Economist is now home to this modern Japanese restaurant, where an enormous amount of cedar wood and bamboo is used to soften the surroundings. The original tatami seating has been replaced by regular tables and the corner sushi bar adds a little theatre. As with the great cocktails, the menu is best enjoyed when shared with a group; although there is plenty of sushi and sashimi on offer, it's best to stick to the more popular dishes like the snow crab tempura or one of the Iron Pot or Toban dishes like black cod rice or chicken with ginger and garlic.

Sartoria

Italian

H3

20 Savile Row ✉ W1S 3PR
✆ (020) 7534 7000
www.sartoria-restaurant.co.uk
⊖ Green Park
Closed 25 December, Saturday lunch, Sunday and bank holidays

Menu £25 – Carte £33/55

If you're going to have any restaurant occupying a prime site in Savile Row then it might as well be Italian as they know one or two things about tailoring themselves. Sartoria is an elegant, smartly dressed restaurant that always seems to exude a certain poise and self-assurance, along with a little charm. There are subtle allusions to tailoring in the decoration and the sofa-style seating in the middle of the room is very appealing. The à la carte menu is an extensive number and prices can quickly add up, but the cooking, which covers all parts of the country, is undertaken with care and it's apparent that the ingredients are top-notch. Service is also not lacking in confidence and is overseen by assorted suited managers.

Scott's

fish and seafood

G3

20 Mount St ✉ W1K 2HE
✆ (020) 7495 7309
www.scotts-restaurant.com
⊖ Bond Street
Closed 25-26 December

Carte £39/79

Standing in one of Mayfair's smartest streets is one of London's swankiest restaurants. Scott's is both an institution with a long, proud history and also a pretty fashionable hangout – a feat that few restaurants manage to pull off. The room has a wonderful buzz and rhythm to it and the wood panelling juxtaposed with the modern art adds to the clubby, but far from staid, atmosphere. The seafood menu is a comforting thing: there are six types of oyster, super fresh shellfish and fresh fish on the bone; meat eaters aren't forgotten and neither are Veggies. Cooking is unfussy and satisfying, although all this simplicity and freshness doesn't come cheap. The service team are younger, brighter and more enthusiastic than in previous years.

Seven Park Place ✿

modern

St James's Hotel and Club,
7-8 Park Pl ✉ SW1A 1LS
✆ (020) 7316 1615
www.stjameshotelandclub.com
⊖ Green Park
Closed Sunday and Monday – booking essential

H4

Menu £26/72

St James's Hotel and Club

William Drabble describes his food as being "all about the ingredients" and indeed his restaurant at St James's Hotel and Club provides an object lesson in the importance of using the best quality produce available. His dishes may appear relatively simple on the plate but their clarity and precision allow the natural flavours of the ingredients to shine. He forged a close relationship with his butcher in the Lake District when he worked in that part of the world and their loyalty to each other clearly pays off – both know what each animal has eaten and where it is has eaten it. Barbon Fell venison and Lune Valley lamb feature regularly and are a must but you can also expect supremely fresh seafood – his scallops are particularly good. The diminutive, secreted restaurant is in a curious spot as you have to slither past the bar stools in the brasserie to reach it. It's divided into two areas; try to secure one of the three tables in the gilded back room as the outer room lacks the same warmth and you'll find your knees perilously close to those of your neighbour.

First Course

- Lobster tail with cauliflower purée and lobster butter sauce.
- Seared foie gras with roasted peach and hazelnuts.

Main Course

- Assiette of lamb with onions and thyme.
- Sea bass with courgettes and a tomato and basil dressing.

Dessert

- Banana parfait, set chocolate custard and honeycomb.
- Sable of summer fruits with kirsch.

Shoryu

Japanese I3

9 Regent St. ✉ SW1Y 4LR
www.shoryuramen.com
⊖ Piccadilly Circus
Closed 25 December and 1 January – bookings not accepted

Carte £17/35

The restorative powers of ramen are so great it should be prescribed on the NHS. Shoryu is owned by the Japan Centre opposite and specialises in Hakata tonkotsu ramen, which originated in Kyushu in the south and is the most popular style of ramen in Japan. At its base is a milky broth made from pork bones; to this is added springy hosomen noodles made in-house; nitamago (the boiled, marinated egg – an important element); sesame, and extra toppings of your choice; if you want a more robust flavour try a miso-based ramen. The surprisingly large menu includes other items with their roots in Chinese cooking, such as gyoza dumplings. If the queue is too long, try one of the two larger branches in Soho.

Sketch (The Gallery)

modern H3

9 Conduit St ✉ W1S 2XG
(020) 7659 4500
www.sketch.uk.com
⊖ Oxford Circus
Closed 25 December – booking essential – (dinner only)

Carte £34/74

It's been the HQ of RIBA, a safe house for the suffragette movement and an atelier of Christian Dior but it's as a nesting place for London's art, fashion and culinary cognoscenti that this striking Georgian house really shines. Reinvention has always been key here and the Gallery now has a new look from India Mahdavi and artwork from Turner Prize nominated David Shrigley. At dinner the room transmogrifies from art gallery to restaurant when it suddenly reverberates to the rattle of the barman's cocktail shaker and the buzz of contented diners. The menu is a mix of the classic, the modern and the esoteric – beef burger with foie gras, fish and chips with a twist, sweet and sour snails – which suits the surroundings perfectly.

Sketch (The Lecture Room & Library) ✿✿

French H3

9 Conduit St (1st floor) ✉ W1S 2XG
✆ (020) 7659 4500
www.sketch.uk.com
⊖ Oxford Circus
Closed last 2 weeks August, Saturday lunch, Sunday and Monday – booking essential

Menu £35/95 – Carte £97/131

Sketch

We all need a little luxury in our lives from time to time – so praise be for Mourad Mazouz and Pierre Gagnaire's 18C funhouse. As you're whisked past the braided rope and up the stairs to the Lecture Room & Library, you'll feel your expectations rise with every step. The room is lavishly decorated in a kaleidoscope of colours and the impeccably set tables are so far apart they're virtually in different postcodes. The staff are unfailingly polite and professional and it appears that nothing is too much trouble. The French cooking bears all the Pierre Gagnaire hallmarks: the main 'plate' comes surrounded by a number of complementary dishes and at first you don't quite know what to focus on – now is the time to relax into that comfortable armchair and just enjoy the variety of textures and tastes, the complexity and depth of flavours and the quality of the ingredients. The wine list is a tome of epic proportions; take the sommeliers advice, they know what they're talking about. And do make sure you order the array of treats that make up the 'Grand dessert' – pudding it ain't.

First Course

- Langoustine five ways.
- Blue fish and foie gras.

Main Course

- Rack of Querçy lamb, tamarind jus and braised fennel.
- Wild turbot on the bone with baby turnips and chablis sauce.

Dessert

- Pierre Gagnaire's 'Grand Dessert.'
- Chocolate soufflé.

Social Eating House ✿

modern

H3

58 Poland St ✉ W1F 7NR
(020) 7993 3251
www.socialeatinghouse.com
Oxford Circus
Closed Christmas, Sunday and bank holidays

Menu £19 (lunch) – Carte £37/48

Social Eating House

Jason Atherton has created a little bit of Brooklyn in one of Soho's lesser known streets – and by expanding his empire solves the problem of how to hang on to ambitious chefs. It's one of those places where the noise and bustle from the throng of customers hits you as you enter and you instantly feel you've come to the right place. It looks as if it's been around for ages and the bare bricks, raw plastered walls, low ceiling and smoked glass help create what is a very sexy room – one that's bigger than you expect. One of Jason's trusty lieutenants, Paul Hood, runs the kitchen and his style of cooking, with its 'faites simple' approach, would make Escoffier proud. It's pure and nicely balanced, with a touch of originality and refinement but with the emphasis always on flavour, so that you'll find yourself wiping your plate clean. The service is great too – there's a refreshing lack of stuffiness yet the staff are always completely on the ball – and there's a terrific cocktail bar upstairs too.

First Course

- Smoked Shetland salmon, miso crème fraîche, BBQ cucumber and spring truffle.
- Smoked duck ham, Braddock White egg and chips.

Main Course

- Charred côte de porc, heritage carrots, white polenta and spring cabbage.
- Cornish turbot with sweet millet, sour cream and black curry.

Dessert

- Coconut meringue, mango sorbet, calamansi and curry crumble.
- English strawberry bakewell with Amaretto and hibiscus.

Ⓝ Soho Kitchen & Bar

North-American I3

19-21 Old Compton St. ✉ W1D 5JJ
✆ (020) 7734 5656
www.sohodiner.com
⊖ Leicester Square

Carte £17/32

The more we're told to knit our own muesli, sprinkle chia seeds or love quinoa, the more we all just fancy having a burger. Even though there are a few salads on offer at this busy operation with its appealing retro-style diner looks, most of the young punters who pack the place out are here for calorie-clocking classics like mac & cheese, a hot dog or a damn good cheeseburger followed up by a banana split – food that is as comforting as it is familiar. The place has a great vibe and the staff keep things buzzing along. There are also cocktails on tap, so you may find that the surroundings are not alone in being in a mildly distressed state.

Spice Market

Asian I3

W London Hotel,
10 Wardour St ✉ W1D 6QF
✆ (0207) 7581 000
www.wlondon.co.uk
⊖ Leicester Square

Menu £48 – Carte £28/57

Leicester Square might not be as hip as Manhattan's Meatpacking district but this offshoot of Jean-Georges Vongerichten's New York original may just start to change things around here. This London branch certainly learnt about service from its American cousin because staff are all very confident, keen and clued-up. The restaurant is spread over two floors, linked by a spiral staircase, with eye-catching screens of gold mesh, walls of spices and ceilings of upturned woks. The kitchen traverses various Asian countries for influences and dishes are designed for sharing; ingredients are good and curries are a highlight. 'Street food' is how they describe their cooking, although the street in question is clearly a well-to-do one.

Spuntino

North-American I3

61 Rupert St. ✉ W1D 7PW
✆ n/a
www.spuntino.co.uk
⊖ Piccadilly Circus
Closed dinner 24 December, 25-26, 31 December and 1 January – bookings not accepted

Carte £16/23 X

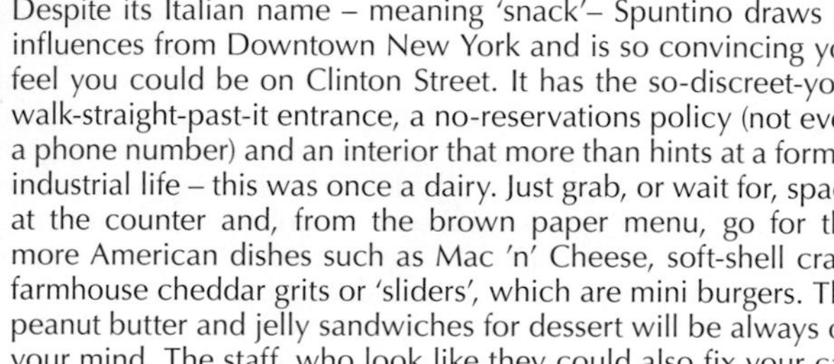

Despite its Italian name – meaning 'snack'– Spuntino draws its influences from Downtown New York and is so convincing you feel you could be on Clinton Street. It has the so-discreet-you-walk-straight-past-it entrance, a no-reservations policy (not even a phone number) and an interior that more than hints at a former industrial life – this was once a dairy. Just grab, or wait for, space at the counter and, from the brown paper menu, go for the more American dishes such as Mac 'n' Cheese, soft-shell crab, farmhouse cheddar grits or 'sliders', which are mini burgers. The peanut butter and jelly sandwiches for dessert will be always on your mind. The staff, who look like they could also fix your car, really add to the fun.

Sumosan

Japanese H3

26 Albemarle St. ✉ W1S 4HY
✆ (020) 7495 5999
www.sumosan.com
⊖ Green Park
Closed lunch Saturday-Sunday and bank holidays

Menu £25 – Carte £19/104 

One minute your restaurant is the hot ticket in town; the next it's celebrating its 10th birthday. In the increasingly ephemeral world of London restaurants, Sumosan's relative longevity is proof that it gets a lot of things right. The large square room in browns and creams provides a stylish backdrop to the Japanese food and the atmosphere is sufficiently strident to drown out the pretty awful muzak. The produce used in the menu is of unimpeachable quality; there's a pleasing balance between the traditional and the more innovative; and the kitchen knows how to make a dish look good. Ignore the fact that the staff lack personality and the bill adds up quicker than a calculator – and just buy yourself a little glamour.

Square ✿✿

French

6-10 Bruton St. ✉ W1J 6PU
✆ (020) 7495 7100
www.squarerestaurant.com
⊖ Green Park
Closed 24-26 December and Sunday lunch

H3

Menu £33/90

The Square

Fame rather than acclaim appears to drive many chefs in this age of celebrity. By contrast, and despite being much in demand and having interests in other restaurants, Philip Howard is a chef who is nearly always to be found in his own kitchen – and this is one of the reasons The Square has been one of London's leading restaurants for two decades. His sophisticated food has its roots in classic French cooking but he isn't put off by new techniques if he thinks they will improve the dish. His menu is one of those that is so appealing it's hard to choose; it changes seasonally but there are some dishes like the crab lasagne that his regulars wouldn't allow him to take off. The dishes are visually appealing and come with a lightness of touch and finesse that few can equal; the tasting menu, with its matching wines, provides a memorable experience. The wine list has an Old World bias and is strong on burgundies. The room is comfortable and understated and the service discreet and detailed.

First Course

- Foie gras with caramelised pineapple, pink grapefruit, honey and mead.
- Tartare of Cornish seabass with Ibizan gazpacho.

Main Course

- Turbot with crushed Jersey Royals, pickled celery, mussels and clams.
- Breast of Dombes duck with black pudding.

Dessert

- Brillat-Savarin cheesecake with rhubarb and cardamom ice cream.
- Blush apricot and green almond soufflé with camomile ice cream.

Tamarind

Indian

G4

20 Queen St. ✉ W1J 5PR
(020) 7629 3561
www.tamarindrestaurant.com
Green Park
Closed 25-26 December, 1 January and Saturday lunch

Menu £21/68 – Carte £35/65

Tamarind

A constant re-laying of tables is required to keep up with the demand for Alfred Prasad's cooking and this, combined with the sometimes slightly hectic service, adds a reassuring buzz to proceedings at Tamarind. It is easy to see the appeal of the cooking: the flavours really shine through and the spicing is so deft that you can taste each component, whether that's the crushed peppercorns on the Jhinga Kalimirch tiger prawns, the green chillies with the Gilafi Reshmi kebab of ground chicken, or the cumin flavouring the side dish of seasonal green vegetables. Tamarind's dishes are mostly influenced by traditional Moghul cuisine so the tandoor oven is used to great effect – the breads and kebabs are terrific and the tandoori pineapple is a refreshing way to end the meal. Those seated closer to the kitchen get to see the chefs at work with the ovens, under Alfred's watchful eye. The basement location adds to the sense of exclusivity and the smoked mirrors and gilded columns lend a dash of Mayfair gloss.

First Course

- Chickpeas, wheat crisps, yoghurt, blueberries and tamarind chutney.
- Steamed shrimps with squid, fennel and ginger dressing.

Main Course

- Chicken tikka, fresh tomato sauce with ginger and fenugreek.
- Fillet of sea bass with fine beans and a tamarind and tomato sauce.

Dessert

- Tandoori grilled pineapple with rose ice cream.
- Nagpuri orange tart served with chocolate sorbet.

Tapas Brindisa

Spanish H3

46 Broadwick St. ✉ W1F 7AF
✆ (020) 7534 1690
www.brindisatapaskitchens.com
⊖ Oxford Circus
Closed dinner 24-27 December – (bookings not accepted at dinner)

Menu £20 (weekday lunch) – Carte £15/25

The owners didn't quite get it right when they first opened this sister to their successful operation in Borough Market, but it didn't take them long before they made the necessary changes – and the place has been packed ever since. In true tapas style, bookings are not taken – they want people to simply stroll in, have a drink and get something to eat and there are now plenty of other places in Soho doing the same thing. Look out for the specialities marked out in bold, such as Basque salt cod with spicy tomato sauce. The owners' expertise in importing Spanish produce is evident; although it's amazing how quickly the bill mounts up. Service is obliging and there's no 'push' to move you off, despite the clamour in the bar.

10 Greek Street

modern I3

10 Greek St ✉ W1D 4DH
✆ (020) 7734 4677
www.10greekstreet.com
⊖ Tottenham Court Road
Closed Christmas, Easter and Sunday

Carte £23/37

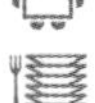

With just 28 seats and a dozen more at the counter, the first challenge is getting a table at this modishly sparse-looking bistro – you can book at lunch but dinner is first-come-first-served. You'll then worry that those at the next table are too close for comfort but soon you'll find yourself caught up with the general bonhomie and start relaxing. The chef-owner's menu is chalked up on a couple of blackboards each day and his cooking comes with Anglo, Med and Middle Eastern elements. Start with some small plates – maybe burrata or sand eels – then try crab rigatoni or Cornish hake with dates; and it's worth choosing a dish for two, like leg of lamb. Wine is the passion of the other owner and the list is constantly evolving.

Theo Randall

Italian G4

Intercontinental Hotel,
1 Hamilton Pl, Park Ln ✉ W1J 7QY
✆ (020) 7318 8747 – **www**.theorandall.com
⊖ Hyde Park Corner
Closed Christmas, Easter, Saturday lunch, Sunday dinner and bank holidays

Menu £27/33 – Carte £46/72

It's no surprise that Theo Randall's menu is so heavily influenced by the River Café, as he spent 17 years there, many of these as Head Chef. It features influences and ingredients from across Italy – including Puglia, his favourite region – as well as produce from the British Isles. The veal chop is a perennial favourite but otherwise it's about what's in season – and when cooking appears this simple there's no room for error. If any dish sums up his philosophy it's his Amalfi lemon tart: he not only uses lemons from Amalfi but eggs too, from chickens fed on corn and carrots, which gives the tart a slight orange tinge. The pleasingly rustic nature of the food is a little at odds with the formal service and the corporate feel of the room.

34

meats and grills G3

34 Grosvenor Sq (entrance on South Audley St) ✉ W1K 2HD
✆ (020) 3350 3434
www.34-restaurant.co.uk
⊖ Marble Arch
Closed 25-26 December, dinner 24 December and lunch 1 January

Menu £28 (weekday dinner) – Carte £32/61

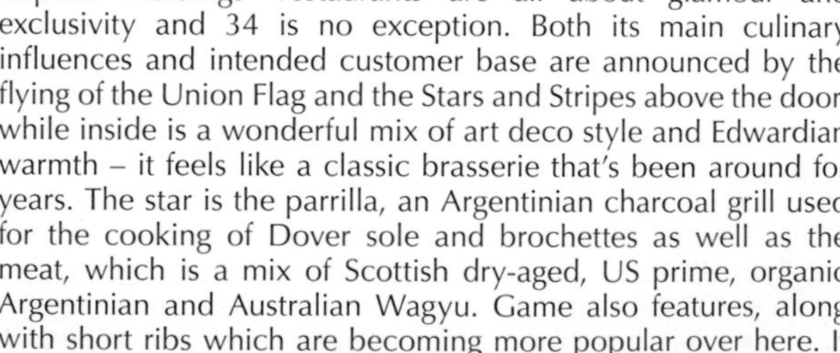

Caprice Holdings' restaurants are all about glamour and exclusivity and 34 is no exception. Both its main culinary influences and intended customer base are announced by the flying of the Union Flag and the Stars and Stripes above the door, while inside is a wonderful mix of art deco style and Edwardian warmth – it feels like a classic brasserie that's been around for years. The star is the parrilla, an Argentinian charcoal grill used for the cooking of Dover sole and brochettes as well as the meat, which is a mix of Scottish dry-aged, US prime, organic Argentinian and Australian Wagyu. Game also features, along with short ribs which are becoming more popular over here. It may not come cheap but then glitz never does.

Tonkotsu

Japanese

I3

63 Dean St ✉ W1D 4QG
✆ (020) 7437 0071
www.tonkotsu.co.uk
⊖ Tottenham Court Road
Bookings not accepted

Carte £19/25

If you want to see why ramen is all the rage in various cities around the world then stand in line and wait for a table at this simple Soho stop. Good ramen is all about the base stock and here 18 hours goes into its preparation to ensure the bowls of soup and homemade wheat-based noodles reach a depth of flavour that seems to nourish one's very soul. Tonkotsu is named after the pork bone broth favoured in southern Japan; you can also try the soy based Tokyo ramen or go for a little northern Japanese influence with the miso base ramen – and when it arrives, with its seasoned egg and assorted toppings like pork belly and bamboo shoots, don't forget to slurp. While you wait for your ramen, share some of the gyoza – handmade Japanese dumplings.

N 28°-50° Mayfair

modern

H3

17-19 Maddox St ✉ W1S 2QH
✆ (020) 7495 1505
www.2850.co.uk
⊖ Oxford Circus
Closed 25 December, 1 January and Sunday

Menu £19 (lunch) – Carte £26/44

The group's third wine-bar-restaurant is possibly their best and, as this is Mayfair, almost certainly their most profitable. The name is not an allusion to some sort of mature, vineous-themed equivalent of an 18-30 holiday but the latitude considered ideal for wine-making grapes. The wines have been cleverly chosen and the Collector's List has an impressive range of Old World classics and a few icons of the New World. The food may be secondary but the modern, unfussy dishes provide great accompaniment, whether that's the crab tortellini with a Grüner Veltliner or the English rib-eye with a Carménère. Sit downstairs for a more intimate experience, although the dim lighting may mean you can't spot that phenolic haze in your red wine.

Umu ✿

Japanese H3

14-16 Bruton Pl. ✉ W1J 6LX
✆ (020) 7499 8881
www.umurestaurant.com
⊖ Bond Street
Closed Christmas, New Year, Saturday lunch, Sunday and bank holidays

Menu £25/115 – Carte £56/124

A/C

Umu

Allowing the natural flavours of the ingredients to shine through is a fundamental element of Japanese cuisine. Accordingly, the search for the best produce is an integral part of any chef's responsibilities. Here at Umu the head chef has been working directly with select Cornish fishermen, training them in the ikejime method of killing fish, to ensure that the fish arrive at the restaurant in as fresh a state as possible - and, as the quality improves, he plans to make his menus a little less westernised and a little more authentic. At the moment the menu choice is extensive, but for the best overall experience choose one of the seasonally changing, multi-course kaiseki menus, where the dishes are both flavoursome and visually appealing. The perfect accompaniment, especially for the sashimi, is sake; not only is the list impressive in its depth and range but the sommelier also offers thoughtful advice. The mostly French wine list is equally extensive in its scope. Warm wood, natural materials and judicious lighting make the restaurant feels as discreet as ever.

First Course

- Sashimi selection.
- Homemade tofu, umadashi, ginger and spring onion.

Main Course

- Wild lobster with shichimi pepper.
- Wagyu beef with miso nut sauce.

Dessert

- Japanese tiramisu with matcha green tea.
- Kinako poached meringue with cream.

Vasco and Piero's Pavilion

Italian **H2/3**

15 Poland St ✉ W1F 8QE
(020) 7437 8774
www.vascosfood.com
Oxford Circus
Closed Saturday lunch, Sunday and bank holidays – booking essential at lunch

Carte £24/44

Not only does Vasco still oversee the kitchen – he keeps a particularly keen eye on the pasta making – but he also likes to help out in the restaurant so he can keep in touch with his regulars, for it is they who have ensured that this institution is still going strong after 40 years. The simply decorated room, closely set tables and matter-of-fact service blend nicely together and there's usually a good mix of customer, including a few tourists, who, by luck or judgement, have stumbled into the right place. The twice daily changing menu is made up of comforting Italian classics but its heart and soul is firmly in Umbria. The presence of Vasco's son will hopefully ensure the future is looking bright for another 40 years.

Veeraswamy

Indian **H3**

Victory House, 99 Regent St (entrance on Swallow St.)
✉ W1B 4RS
(020) 7734 1401
www.realindianfood.com
Piccadilly Circus

Menu £28 (weekday lunch) – Carte £34/64

The manager here knows not to come between a regular and their favourite table: some were first brought here by their grandparents and are now, in turn, introducing their own grandchildren to London's oldest surviving Indian restaurant, which dates from 1926. You'd be excused for thinking it might be a tad old-fashioned but Veeraswamy is anything but: it is awash with vibrant colours and always full of bustle. The Hyderabad lamb biryani may have been on the original menu but there are plenty of other dishes with a more contemporary edge. The meaty Madagascan prawns are a good way of kicking things off; slow-cooked lamb dishes are also done very well. There's a tasting menu available and desserts, prepared with a flourish, shouldn't be ignored.

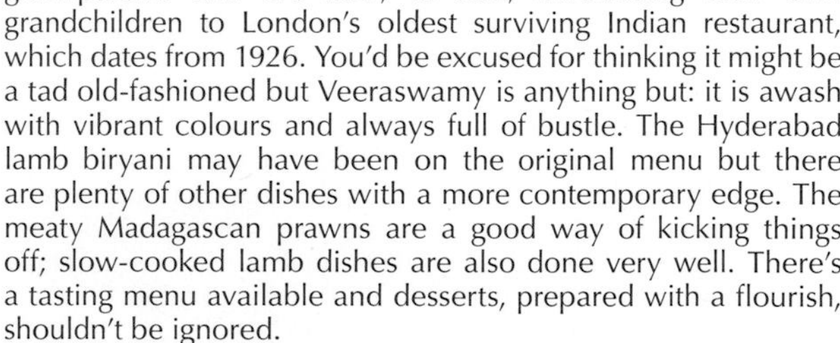

Vinoteca

modern

H3

53-55 Beak St ✉ W1F 9SH
(020) 3544 7411
www.vinoteca.co.uk
Oxford Circus
Closed 24-26 December and 1 January – booking advisable

Carte £18/40

A/C

London is the wine capital of the world – largely because we're not allied to any particular wine producing region – so we should have many more wine bars than we do. This is the third Vinoteca and it's easy to see their appeal. Based on the wine bars and shops of Spain and Italy, the list of wines is terrific and mixes the classic with the esoteric; prices are fair and there's plenty of choice – even under £30. There are biodynamic and organic wines but there's no bandwagon-jumping going on here – emerging markets are also covered and if anything on the shelves catches your eye they're also priced to take away. The food isn't forgotten – cured meats and cheeses are a highlight and European dishes like bavette and risotto also hit the spot.

The Wolseley

modern

H4

160 Piccadilly ✉ W1J 9EB
(020) 7499 6996
www.thewolseley.com
Green Park
Closed dinner 24 December – booking essential

Carte £24/72

The Wolseley didn't take long to earn iconic status, thanks to its stylish décor and celebrity following. Its owners, Chris Corbin and Jeremy King, created a restaurant in the style of a grand European café, all pillars, arches and marble. Open from breakfast until late, the flexible menu offers everything from Austrian and French classics to British staples, so the daily special could be coq au vin or Lancashire hotpot. Pastries come from the Viennoiserie and lunch merges into afternoon tea. So, one table could be tucking into Beluga caviar or a dozen oysters while their neighbours enjoy a salt beef sandwich or eggs Benedict. The large clock and swift service are reminders that there are probably people waiting for your table.

Wild Honey ✿

modern

H3

12 St George St. ✉ W1S 2FB
✆ (020) 7758 9160
www.wildhoneyrestaurant.co.uk
⊖ Oxford Circus
Closed 25-26 December and 1 January

Menu £29/75 (weekdays) – Carte £46/57

XX

Wild Honey

It has proved such a great fit in Mayfair it's hard to believe Wild Honey has only been around since 2007. Once you've done your best Eric Morecambe impression in finding the opening in the velvet curtain, you'll enter into a very elegant restaurant with beautiful oak panelling, modern photographic art and Murano chandeliers. It's very much a room of three parts: in the bright front section you can gaze at the imposing St George's Church opposite; in the middle section you feel part of the general bustle; and at the back you can relax in a more private setting. The menu is a model of understatement and changes with each service; Anthony Demetre and his head chef have also lengthened it a little, in response to the customers' wishes. The cooking continues, without compromise, to use the best quality ingredients and delivers a mix of classically inspired and more modern dishes that are full of flavour but without ostentation. It is this underlying confidence that has contributed to Wild Honey rapidly becoming a much-loved, ageless institution.

First Course

- Scottish crab, guacamole and green mango.
- Summer green vegetable gazpacho with goat's cheese.

Main Course

- Rose veal with root vegetables, gnocchi and black truffles.
- Grilled rib of beef with slow-baked sweet onions.

Dessert

- Wild honey ice cream with honeycomb.
- Cold chocolate fondant with stout ice cream.

Wright Brothers Soho

fish and seafood H3

13 Kingly St. ✉ W1B 5PW
✆ (020) 7434 3611
www.thewrightbrothers.co.uk
⊖ Oxford Circus
Closed 24-28 December, 1-2 January, Easter Sunday and bank holidays

Menu £15 (weekday lunch) – Carte £28/59

It hasn't been around that long but already this casual seafood restaurant has been given a facelift and now comes with a slightly more utilitarian look. The best seats are on the terrace or on one of the high tables; the lower floor is supposed to represent a lobster pot but dining inside a metal cage is surely no one's idea of fun. The menu covers all bases – you can create your own bespoke platter from all the fish and shellfish on offer and there is much that can be shared. Oysters are a speciality and the fish comes mostly from Cornwall and is wonderfully fresh. Lunchtime 'surf boards', such as mackerel with couscous, are ideal for those wanting a quick one course meal – and they even do smaller ones for children.

Bib Gourmand ☺ indicates our inspectors' favourites for good value.

Yauatcha ✿

Chinese

I3

15 Broadwick St ✉ W1F 0DL
✆ (020) 7494 8888
www.yauatcha.com
⊖ Tottenham Court Road
Closed 25 December

Menu £29/55 – Carte £24/57

XX

A/C

Yauatcha

No cuisine or style of eating is immune from revolution, due largely to the changing ways we all live our lives. Go to Hong Kong and you'll see that even dim sum is evolving and has come to mean so much more than merely snacks to accompany the daytime drinking of tea. In London Yauatcha has always been at the heart of this change and its success is not hard to understand. The food is so good and the surroundings so slick and stylish that customers found it hard to be in and out in their allotted time – so now you can keep hold of your table for a couple of hours. They have also put in a bar on the ground floor which means you can wait for your table in a little more comfort. Three dim sum per person followed by some noodles or a stir-fry should be enough. Stand-out dishes are the scallop shui mai, prawn cheung fun, the wonderfully light baked venison puff and the Kung Po chicken. Those who prefer something sweet to accompany their Silver Needle white tea from Fujian can also come for cakes, tarts and pastries during the day.

First Course

- Scallop shui mai.
- Mustard green and edamame dumpling.

Main Course

- Kung Pao chicken.
- Steamed Dover sole with black bean sauce.

Dessert

- Raspberry délice.
- Chocolate and blood orange gateau.

Strand · Covent Garden

It's fitting that Manet's world famous painting 'Bar at the Folies Bergère' should hang in the **Strand** within a champagne cork's throw of theatreland and Covent Garden. This is the area perhaps more than any other which draws in the ticket-buying tourist, eager to grab a good deal on one of the many shows on offer, or eat and drink at fabled shrines like J.Sheekey or Rules. It's here the names already up in lights shine down on their potential usurpers: celeb wannabes heading for The Ivy, West Street's perennially fashionable restaurant. It's here, too, that Nell Gwyn set up home under the patronage of Charles II, while Oscar Wilde revelled in his success by taking rooms at the Savoy.

The hub of the whole area is the piazza at **Covent Garden,** created by Inigo Jones four hundred years ago. It was given a brash new lease of life in the 1980s after its famed fruit and veg market was pulled up by the roots and re-sown in Battersea. Council bigwigs realised then that 'what we have we hold', and any further redevelopment of the area is banned. Where everyone heads is the impressive covered market, within which a colourful jumble of arts and crafts shops gels with al fresco cafés and classical performers proffering Paganini with your cappuccino. Outside, under the portico of St Paul's church, every type of street performer does a turn for the tourist trade. The best shops in Covent Garden, though, are a few streets north of the market melee, emanating out like bicycle spokes from Seven Dials.

For those after a more highbrow experience, one of London's best attractions is a hop, skip and ***grand jeté*** from the market. Around the corner in **Bow Street** is the city's famed home for opera and ballet, where fire – as well as show-stopping performances – has been known to bring the house down. The **Royal Opera House** is now in its third incarnation, and it gets more impressive with each rebuild. The handsome, glass-roofed Floral Hall is a must-see, while an interval drink at the Amphitheatre Café Bar, overlooking the piazza, is de rigeur for show goers. At the other end of the Strand the **London Coliseum** offers more opera, this time all performed in English. Down by Waterloo Bridge, art lovers are strongly advised to stop at **Somerset House** and take in one of London's most sublime collections of art at the Courtauld Gallery. This is where you can get up close and personal to Manet's barmaid, as well as an astonishing array of Impressionist masters and twentieth century greats. The icing on the cake is the compact and accessible eighteenth century building that houses the collection: real icing on a real cake can be found in a super little hidden-away café downstairs.

Of a different order altogether is the huge **National Gallery** at Trafalgar Square which houses more than two thousand Western European pieces (it started off with 38). A visit to the modern Sainsbury Wing is rewarded with some

AGE / PHOTONONSTOP

unmissable works from the Renaissance. It can get just as crowded in the capital's largest Gallery as in the square outside, so a good idea is to wander down **Villiers Street** next to Charing Cross station and breathe the Thames air along the Victoria Embankment. Behind you is the grand Savoy Hotel, which reopened in 2010 after major refurbishment; for a better view of it, you can head even further away from the crowds on a boat trip from the **Embankment,** complete with on-board entertainment. And if the glory of travel in the capital, albeit on the water, has whetted your appetite for more, then pop into the impressively renovated Transport Museum in Covent Garden piazza, where gloriously preserved tubes, buses and trains from the past put you in a positive frame of mind for the real live working version you'll very probably be tackling later in the day.

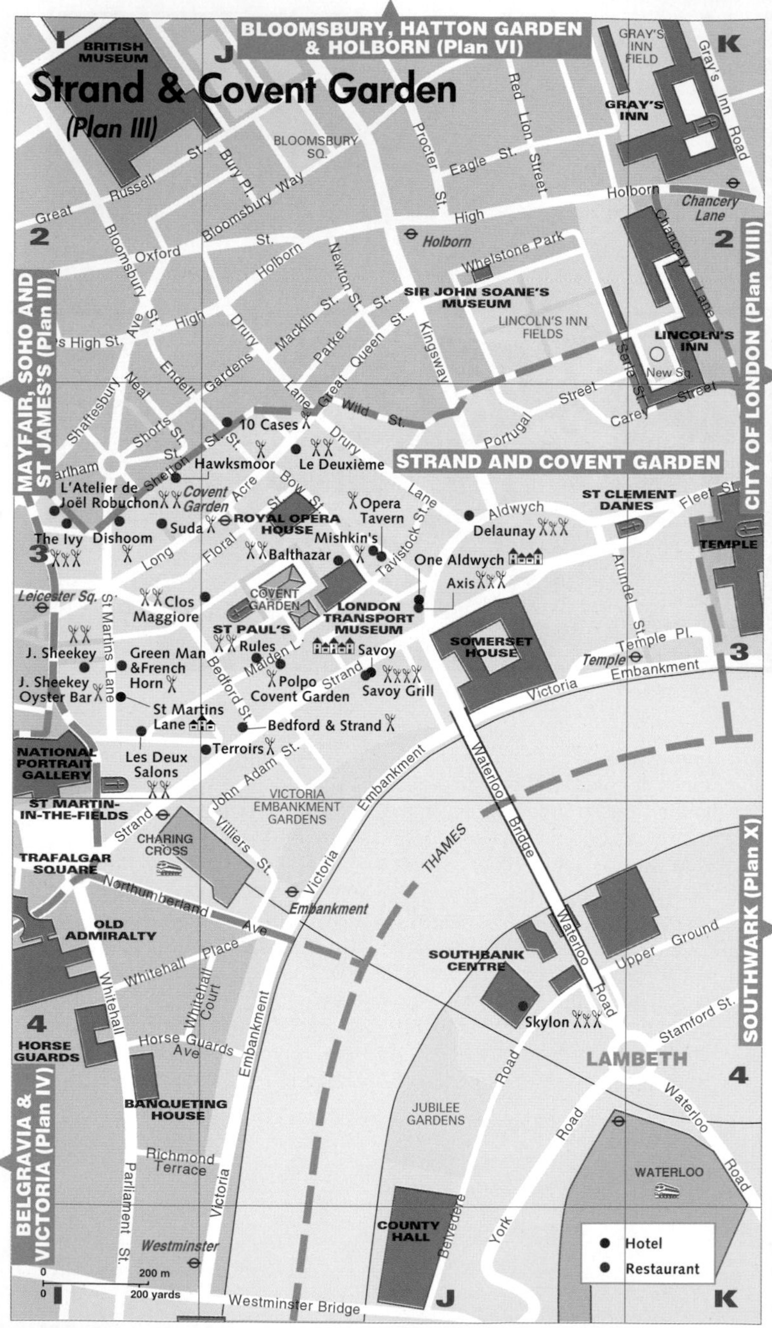

Strand & Covent Garden
(Plan III)
BLOOMSBURY, HATTON GARDEN & HOLBORN (Plan VI)
MAYFAIR, SOHO AND ST JAMES'S (Plan II)
CITY OF LONDON (Plan VIII)
SOUTHWARK (Plan X)
BELGRAVIA & VICTORIA (Plan IV)
STRAND AND COVENT GARDEN
BRITISH MUSEUM
GRAY'S INN FIELD
GRAY'S INN
BLOOMSBURY SQ.
SIR JOHN SOANE'S MUSEUM
LINCOLN'S INN FIELDS
LINCOLN'S INN
Holborn
Chancery Lane
ST CLEMENT DANES
TEMPLE
ROYAL OPERA HOUSE
COVENT GARDEN
LONDON TRANSPORT MUSEUM
ST PAUL'S
SOMERSET HOUSE
Leicester Sq.
Covent Garden
Temple
NATIONAL PORTRAIT GALLERY
ST MARTIN-IN-THE-FIELDS
TRAFALGAR SQUARE
CHARING CROSS
VICTORIA EMBANKMENT GARDENS
Embankment
THAMES
OLD ADMIRALTY
SOUTHBANK CENTRE
HORSE GUARDS
BANQUETING HOUSE
LAMBETH
JUBILEE GARDENS
WATERLOO
COUNTY HALL
Westminster
10 Cases
Hawksmoor
Le Deuxième
L'Atelier de Joël Robuchon
Opera Tavern
Suda
The Ivy
Dishoom
Mishkin's
Balthazar
Delaunay
One Aldwych
Axis
Clos Maggiore
J. Sheekey
Green Man &French Horn
Rules
Savoy
J. Sheekey Oyster Bar
Polpo Covent Garden
Savoy Grill
St Martins Lane
Bedford & Strand
Terroirs
Les Deux Salons
Skylon
Hotel
Restaurant
0 200 m
0 200 yards

L'Atelier de Joël Robuchon ✿

French

13-15 West St. ✉ WC2H 9NE
✆ (020) 7010 8600
www.joelrobuchon.co.uk
⊖ Leicester Square
Closed 25-26 December,1 January, and August bank holiday Monday

I3

Menu £129 – Carte £31/109

L'Atelier de Joel Robuchon

London's L'Atelier de Joël Robuchon differs from his other 'branches' dotted around the world's culinary hotspots by being two restaurants under one roof: on the ground floor is L'Atelier itself, with an open kitchen and large counter; upstairs is the monochrome La Cuisine, a slightly more structured, sleek and more brightly-lit affair with table seating. Apart from a few wood-fired dishes upstairs, the menus are largely similar. The cooking is artistic, creative and occasionally playful; it is technically accomplished and highly labour intensive – there are over thirty chefs in the building – but it is never overworked and each dish is nicely balanced and its flavours true. French is the predominant influence, supported by other Mediterranean flavours, and ordering a number of smaller dishes is the best way to fully appreciate Robuchon's craft and vision, although your final bill can quite quickly get pretty lofty. Service is well timed and confident and sitting at the counter will give you some insight into this polished operation.

First Course

- Scallops with chicory salad and mustard dressing.
- Smoked aubergine caviar with vegetable and spicy tomato sauce.

Main Course

- Quail stuffed with foie gras and mashed potatoes.
- Roasted Scottish lobster, spinach, peppers and pepper sauce.

Dessert

- Orange rum baba, Tahitian vanilla cream.
- Creamy Manjari chocolate mousse, bitter chocolate sorbet and Oreo crumble crumb.

Axis

modern J3

One Aldwych Hotel,
1 Aldwych ✉ WC2B 4RH
✆ (020) 7300 0300
www.onealdwych.com/axis
⊖ Temple
Closed early August-early September, Christmas-New Year and Monday

Menu £25 – Carte £30/41

Expectation is everything and the spiral marble staircase leading down to this restaurant always adds a little excitement. The room, which must have one of the highest ceilings in London, is neatly laid out and service is well-organised, if perhaps a little too formal for its own good. One wise decision was the moving of the bar to downstairs; this means there is always a little noise, even when the restaurant has a lull just after the theatre-goers have left. They have made the menu a little lighter by adding salads and a seafood section. More European influences now also sit alongside the British dishes, so you can have smoked salmon, salt beef and a treacle sponge or scallops with chorizo, beef bourguignon and a crème brûlée.

Balthazar

French J3

4-6 Russell St. ✉ WC2B 5HZ
✆ (020) 3301 1155
www.balthazarlondon.com
⊖ Covent Garden
Closed 25 December – booking essential

Carte £26/62

It's not just musicals and plays that transfer between London and New York – the world's two greatest cities now trade in restaurants as well. Balthazar has long been a landmark in Manhattan's SoHo district but now there's a London version occupying the old Theatre Museum in Covent Garden which, thanks to its red leather seats, mosaic floor, mirrors and flattering lighting, will seem uncannily familiar to anyone who knows the original. This being a London copy of a New York copy of a classic Parisian brasserie means that the Franglais menu plays is safe and focuses on reassuringly familiar dishes like moules frites, coq au vin and duck confit. It's open from breakfast onwards; the cocktails are great; and the atmosphere lively and excitable.

Bedford & Strand

British traditional J3

1a Bedford St ✉ WC2E 9HH
(020) 7836 3033
www.bedford-strand.com
Charing Cross
Closed 24 December-2 January, Sunday and bank holidays – booking essential

Menu £20 – Carte £21/41

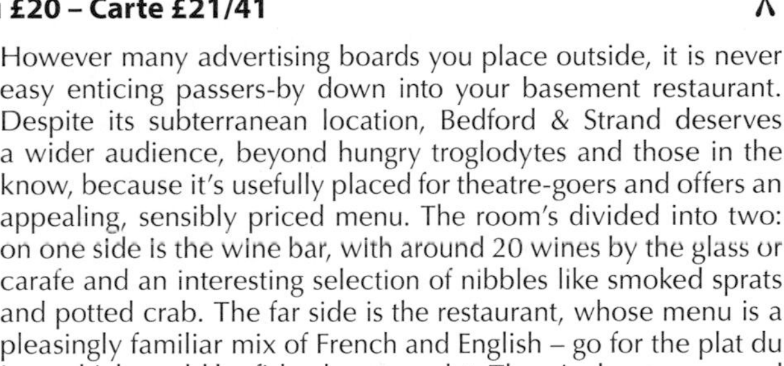

However many advertising boards you place outside, it is never easy enticing passers-by down into your basement restaurant. Despite its subterranean location, Bedford & Strand deserves a wider audience, beyond hungry troglodytes and those in the know, because it's usefully placed for theatre-goers and offers an appealing, sensibly priced menu. The room's divided into two: on one side is the wine bar, with around 20 wines by the glass or carafe and an interesting selection of nibbles like smoked sprats and potted crab. The far side is the restaurant, whose menu is a pleasingly familiar mix of French and English – go for the plat du jour which could be fishcakes or onglet. There's also a very good value lunch and early evening Menu Rapide.

Clos Maggiore

French J3

33 King St ✉ WC2E 8JD
(020) 7379 9696
www.closmaggiore.com
Leicester Square
Closed 24-25 December

Menu £18 (weekdays)/33 – Carte £32/58

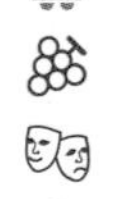

Any West End restaurateurs still half-hearted about pre and post theatre dining should come to Clos Maggiore to see how it can be done: the menu represents excellent value, the kitchen is well organised and the staff get on with the serving, which means the theatregoer doesn't have to keep checking the time. Clos Maggiore is also one of the most romantic restaurants around – just be sure to ask for the table in the enchanting conservatory at the back, with its retractable roof. The chef is from Provence and you can almost smell the lavender when reading his menu. The French dishes are sophisticated in their make-up while the ingredients come mostly from the British Isles. The wine list has great depth and reflects the owner's passion.

Delaunay

modern

J3

55 Aldwych ✉ WC2B 4BB
✆ (020) 7499 8558
www.thedelaunay.com
⊖ Temple
Closed 25 December and dinner 24 December – booking essential

Carte £20/52

Just like The Wolseley, its hugely successful older sibling, The Delaunay was inspired by the grand cafés of Europe and boasts a similar celebrity clientele, yet this is more than a mere replica. It may have opened in 2011, but the 150-seater dining room manages to evoke the 1920s with all its wood panelling, brass and leather. The menu is also more mittel-European, with great schnitzels and wieners featuring prominently. Daily specials could include daube of beef or fish stew, or you could just come for some eggs or a salad – it's that sort of place. There's a nostalgic element too; you'll find Black Forest gateau, banana split, and even a cover charge. The staff are engaging and swift but never make you feel rushed.

Le Deuxième

modern

J3

65a Long Acre ✉ WC2E 9JH
✆ (020) 7379 0033
www.ledeuxieme.com
⊖ Covent Garden
Closed 24-25 December

Menu £15/28 – Carte £27/41

Don't think that because it's busy in the early evening before curtain-up in all the local theatres that's it's going to quieten down when all the early-diners have gone – it seemingly stays busy most of the evening, most nights. This certainly gives the room plenty of energy but it also means that this is the sort of place where, if you get the attention of the waiter or waitress, you'll want to be ready with your order so as not to waste the opportunity. The menu offers an extensive range of dishes, whose influences come largely from within Europe. In amongst the pastas and the salads are some fairly classic French dishes and this is where the kitchen's experience lies. Side dishes, though, can quickly bump up the bill.

Les Deux Salons

French

13

40-42 William IV St ✉ WC2N 4DD
✆ (020) 7420 2050
www.lesdeuxsalons.co.uk
⊖ Charing Cross
Closed 25-26 December and 1 January

Menu £13/23 – Carte £16/48

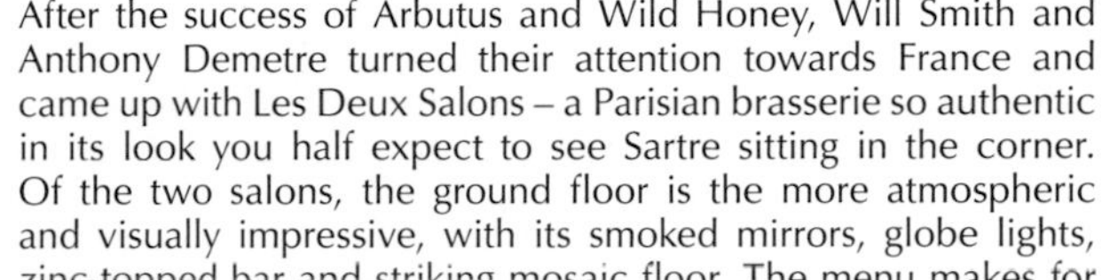

After the success of Arbutus and Wild Honey, Will Smith and Anthony Demetre turned their attention towards France and came up with Les Deux Salons – a Parisian brasserie so authentic in its look you half expect to see Sartre sitting in the corner. Of the two salons, the ground floor is the more atmospheric and visually impressive, with its smoked mirrors, globe lights, zinc-topped bar and striking mosaic floor. The menu makes for an appealing read; you'll find French classics like bouillabaisse, assorted meats grilled on the Josper and even the occasional interloper from this side of The Channel, like cottage pie; desserts are full-on Gallic and all the better for it. It's been busy since opening its doors; service is swift, but not pushy.

Dishoom

Indian

13

12 Upper St Martin's Ln ✉ WC2H 9FB
✆ (020) 7420 9320
www.dishoom.com
⊖ Leicester Square
Closed 24 December dinner, 25-26 December and 1-2 January

Menu £20/35 – Carte £10/26

Dishoom is a facsimile of the sort of café that populated Bombay in the early 20th century. They were opened by Persian immigrants and served snacks and specialities that merged the two countries, along with other dishes displaying some colonial influences; and, because they were classless and casteless, they appealed to everyone. That same inclusiveness is evident here in Covent Garden: the place is usually full of everyone from couples to business-types enjoying a table of shared dishes. It's all about ordering as little or as much as you want, whether that's a full breakfast; some baked roti rolls with chai; vada pav – Bombay's version of the chip butty; a curry; or meats cooked on the grill in the open kitchen.

Green Man & French Horn

French

I3

54 St Martin's Ln ✉ WC2N 4EA
✆ (020) 7836 2645
www.greenmanfrenchhorn.co
⊖ Leicester Square
Closed Christmas and New Year

Carte £23/33

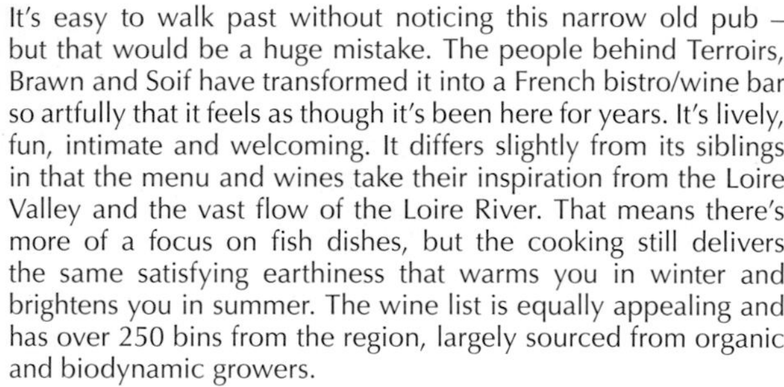

It's easy to walk past without noticing this narrow old pub – but that would be a huge mistake. The people behind Terroirs, Brawn and Soif have transformed it into a French bistro/wine bar so artfully that it feels as though it's been here for years. It's lively, fun, intimate and welcoming. It differs slightly from its siblings in that the menu and wines take their inspiration from the Loire Valley and the vast flow of the Loire River. That means there's more of a focus on fish dishes, but the cooking still delivers the same satisfying earthiness that warms you in winter and brightens you in summer. The wine list is equally appealing and has over 250 bins from the region, largely sourced from organic and biodynamic growers.

Hawksmoor

meats and grills

I3

11 Langley St ✉ WC2H 9JG
✆ (020) 7420 9390
www.thehawksmoor.com
⊖ Covent Garden
Closed 24-26 December

Carte £27/79

Impressive renovation work from those clever Hawksmoor people turned this former brewery cellar into a very atmospheric restaurant whose primary function is the serving and eating of red meat – a suitably apt activity as one 18C owner of the brewery used to host a steak club. You'll get a friendly greeting at the bottom of the stairs and can either eat in the bar or in the large and bustling dining room with its ersatz industrial look. Steaks from Longhorn cattle lovingly reared in North Yorkshire and dry-aged for at least 35 days are the stars of the show. A blackboard shows availability and meat is priced per 100g. But beware as side orders and competitive over-ordering on the size of the cut can push up the final bill.

The Ivy

British traditional

I3

1-5 West St ✉ WC2H 9NQ
✆ (020) 7836 4751
www.the-ivy.co.uk
⊖ Leicester Square
Closed 25 December

Menu £27 – Carte £27/67

The members-only Ivy Club may have siphoned off the top tier of regulars but The Ivy restaurant continues to attract new blood. It's still the sort of place where everyone looks up from their food to see who's just arrived but nowadays that's just as likely to be a reality TV contestant as a theatrical knight. Getting a table is still a challenge; try calling on the day – if they offer the bar, accept, because you may get bumped up into the main room. But the great thing about The Ivy is that it's impossible not to find the menu appealing: perfectly gratinated shepherd's pie, plump fishcakes, eggs Benedict, nursery puddings – they're all here and all done well. Staff earn their crust by frequently but discreetly re-laying the tables.

J. Sheekey

fish and seafood

I3

28-34 St Martin's Ct. ✉ WC2 4AL
✆ (020) 7240 2565
www.j-sheekey.co.uk
⊖ Leicester Square
Closed 25-26 December – booking essential

Carte £32/69

Named after the restaurant's first chef who cooked for its then owner Lord Salisbury, J. Sheekey proves that longevity and tradition need not mean old and crusty. It is as fashionable now as it was in 1896 and remains one of the first choices for the theatrical world and those whose business is show. The wood panelling and silver on the tables add to the timeless British feel and service is as charming and efficient as ever. Fish and seafood are handled deftly: the Arbroath smokie and potted shrimps are permanent fixtures and the fish pie and lemon sole are rightly renowned. Avoiding pre and post-theatre times will shorten the odds of your getting a table; ask for 'dining room 4' which is the largest of the five rooms.

J. Sheekey Oyster Bar

fish and seafood I3

33-34 St Martin's Ct. ✉ WC2 4AL
✆ (020) 7240 2565
www.j-sheekey.co.uk
⊖ Leicester Square
Closed 25-26 December

Carte £22/39

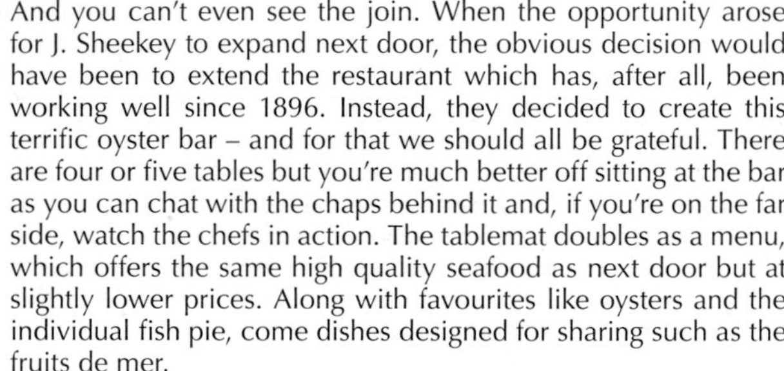

And you can't even see the join. When the opportunity arose for J. Sheekey to expand next door, the obvious decision would have been to extend the restaurant which has, after all, been working well since 1896. Instead, they decided to create this terrific oyster bar – and for that we should all be grateful. There are four or five tables but you're much better off sitting at the bar as you can chat with the chaps behind it and, if you're on the far side, watch the chefs in action. The tablemat doubles as a menu, which offers the same high quality seafood as next door but at slightly lower prices. Along with favourites like oysters and the individual fish pie, come dishes designed for sharing such as the fruits de mer.

Mishkin's

North-American J3

25 Catherine St ✉ WC2B 5JS
✆ (020) 7240 2078
www.mishkins.co.uk
⊖ Covent Garden
Closed 24-26 December and 1-2 January

Carte £14/24

The Jewish-American deli, of the sort found on Manhattan's Lower East Side, was the inspiration behind this fun creation from the Polpo people. The menu is an appealing (non-kosher) blend of classics such as lox beigel, chopped liver and salt beef, along with nibbles like cod cheek popcorn. The Reuben sandwich may not bulge like its transatlantic cousin but it will satisfy most appetites; the crispy lamb belly also hits the spot. Delis aren't often associated with cocktails but it works here and the gin based drinks are great. The place has that ubiquitous distressed urban look; try to book one of the red booths if you're with a group or just grab a seat at the bar. In a further break with tradition, staff are young and accommodating.

Opera Tavern

Mediterranean J3

23 Catherine St. ✉ WC2B 5JS
✆ (020) 7836 3680
www.operatavern.co.uk
⊖ Covent Garden
Closed 25-26 and 31 December, 1 January and Sunday dinner

Carte £12/30

That many of its more touristy areas now boast some decent restaurants is testament to London's maturing dining scene. Opera Tavern shares the same appealing concept of small plates of Spanish and Italian delicacies as its sisters, Salt Yard and Dehesa, and occupies a converted old pub dating from 1879, albeit one that's had a complete makeover. If you haven't booked a table in the upstairs dining room then try your luck on the lively ground floor; order 2 or 3 dishes per person and be prepared to share – stand-outs are the Ibérico ham, chorizo with piquillo pepper and crispy squid. The wine list also swings between Spain and Italy and includes some rare and ancient grape varieties. The staff are all reassuringly confident and clued up.

Polpo Covent Garden

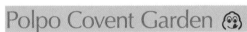

Italian

J3

6 Maiden Ln. ✉ WC2E 7NA
✆ (020) 7836 8448
www.polpo.co.uk
⊖ Leicester Square
Closed 24-26 December – (bookings not accepted at dinner)

Carte £12/26

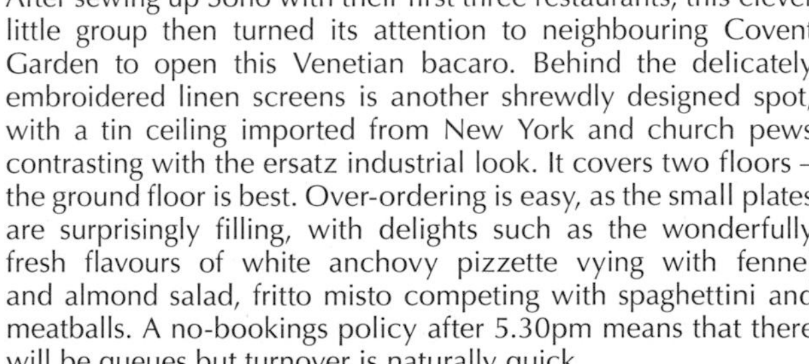

After sewing up Soho with their first three restaurants, this clever little group then turned its attention to neighbouring Covent Garden to open this Venetian bacaro. Behind the delicately embroidered linen screens is another shrewdly designed spot, with a tin ceiling imported from New York and church pews contrasting with the ersatz industrial look. It covers two floors – the ground floor is best. Over-ordering is easy, as the small plates are surprisingly filling, with delights such as the wonderfully fresh flavours of white anchovy pizzette vying with fennel and almond salad, fritto misto competing with spaghettini and meatballs. A no-bookings policy after 5.30pm means that there will be queues but turnover is naturally quick.

Rules

British traditional J3

35 Maiden Ln ✉ WC2E 7LB
✆ (020) 7836 5314
www.rules.co.uk
⊖ Leicester Square
Closed 25-26 December – booking essential

Carte £35/60

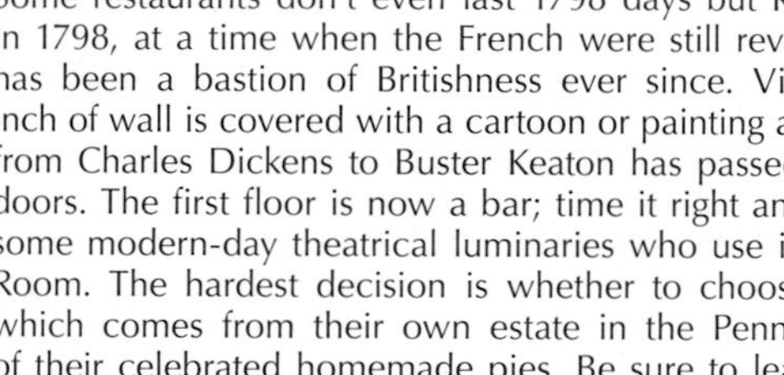

Some restaurants don't even last 1798 days but Rules opened in 1798, at a time when the French were still revolting, and it has been a bastion of Britishness ever since. Virtually every inch of wall is covered with a cartoon or painting and everyone from Charles Dickens to Buster Keaton has passed through its doors. The first floor is now a bar; time it right and you'll spot some modern-day theatrical luminaries who use it as a Green Room. The hardest decision is whether to choose the game, which comes from their own estate in the Pennines, or one of their celebrated homemade pies. Be sure to leave room for their proper puddings, which come with lashings of custard - no wonder John Bull was such a stout fellow. It makes you proud.

Savoy Grill

British traditional 

Savoy Hotel,
Strand ✉ WC2R 0EU
✆ (020) 7592 1600
www.gordonramsay.com/thesavoygrill
⊖ Charing Cross

Menu £30 (lunch) – Carte £34/63

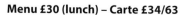

The Savoy Grill prepared for the future by going back to its roots. Archives were explored, designers briefed and much money spent, with the result that it has returned to the traditions that made it famous. As befits the name, it is the charcoal grilling of meats that takes centre stage. Beef from the Lake District and Essex is dry-aged for a minimum of 35 days and offered in an impressive selection of cuts. There's also a daily trolley – it could be beef Wellington one day, leg of lamb the next – and an enticing section entitled 'Roasts, Braises and Pies'. The shiny art deco inspired interior evokes the 1930s, photos of past guests adorn the walls and even the table layout and numbering remains true to the original.

Suda

Thai

I3

23 Slingsby Pl, St Martin's Courtyard ✉ WC2E 9AB
✆ (020) 7240 8010
www.suda-thai.com
⊖ Covent Garden
Closed 25 December and 1 January

Menu £11/26 s – Carte £22/29

This shiny Thai restaurant in the new St Martin's Courtyard development looks remarkably like a branded chain that's about to be rolled out and, as Oscar Wilde said, "It is only shallow people who do not judge by appearances". However, the quality of its food and the care taken in its preparation far exceeds one's expectations. OK, so the 'street' food may have had a wash and brush up and heat warnings on certain dishes are overplayed but the kitchen still delivers enough familiar flavours on a cold January night to transport you back to Sukhumvit Road. Som tam spicy salads are a speciality, as are creamy curries and there's plenty for Veggies. Come in a group, sit upstairs and order cocktails and plenty of dishes to share.

10 Cases

French

J3

16 Endell St ✉ WC2H 9BD
✆ (020) 7836 6801
www.the10cases.co.uk
⊖ Covent Garden
Closed Easter, Christmas-New Year and bank holidays – booking essential

Carte £23/46

It's a simple but effective idea: serve an unpretentious daily changing menu with a choice of 3 starters, 3 main courses and 3 desserts accompanied by a wine list of 10 reds and 10 whites, all available by the glass, carafe or bottle; 10 cases of each wine are bought – hence the name – and when they're finished the wine is changed. The cooking is straightforward and honest and the menu is supplemented by nibbles such as potted crab or roasted garlic. The food suits the cosy bistrot feel of the place and though the portions may be rather small, so too are the prices. The wines are well chosen and the mark-ups limited, so most bottles are priced between £19 and £35; the 50cl carafes are particularly good value.

Terroirs

French J3

5 William IV St ✉ WC2N 4DW
(020) 7036 0660
www.terroirswinebar.com
⊖ Charing Cross
Closed 25-26 December, 1 January, Sunday and bank holidays

Menu £10 (lunch) – Carte £25/34

The ground floor is as busy and as fun as ever but you can also eat 'Downstairs at Terroirs', where the menu is slightly different and there's a greater variety of cooking methods used; there are also dishes for two such as the roast Landaise chicken. Tables down here are a little bigger which makes sharing easier and, despite being two floors down, it is more atmospheric. If you recognise the banquette seating it's because it comes from Mirabelle. Meanwhile, both levels share the same respect for flavoursome and satisfying French cooking, with added Italian and Spanish influences. The wine list is interesting, varied and well-priced. Service remains a mixed bag and can be of the headless chicken variety.

Remember, stars (✿✿✿…✿) are awarded for cuisine only! Elements such as service and décor are not a factor.

K. Garrod/John Warburton-Lee/Photononstop

Belgravia · Victoria

The well-worn cliché 'an area of contrasts' certainly applies to these ill-matched neighbours. To the west, Belgravia equates to fashionable status and elegant, residential calm; to the east, Victoria is a chaotic jumble of backpackers, milling commuters and cheap-and-not-always-so-cheerful hotels. At first sight, you might think there's little to no common ground, but the umbilical cord that unites them is, strange to say, diplomacy and politics. Belgravia's embassies are dotted all around the environs of **Belgrave Square,** while at the furthest end of bustling Victoria Street stands **Parliament Square.**

Belgravia – named after 'beautiful grove' in French - was developed during the nineteenth century by Richard Grosvenor, the second Marquess of Westminster, who employed top architect Thomas Cubitt to come up with something rather fetching for the upper echelons of society. The grandeur of the classical designs has survived for the best part of two centuries, evident in the broad streets and elegant squares, where the rich rub shoulders with the uber-rich beneath the stylish balconies of a consulate or outside a high-end antiques emporium. You can still sample an atmosphere of the village it once was, as long as your idea of a village includes exclusive designer boutiques and even more exclusive mews cottages.

By any stretch of the imagination you'd have trouble thinking of **Victoria** as a village. Its local railway station is one of London's major hubs and its bus station brings in visitors from not only all corners of Britain, but Europe too. Its main 'church', concealed behind office blocks, could hardly be described as humble, either: **Westminster Cathedral** is a grand concoction based on Istanbul's Hagia Sophia, with a view from the top of the bell tower which is breathtaking. From there you can pick out other hidden charms of the area: the dramatic headquarters of Channel 4 TV, the revolving sign famously leading into New Scotland Yard, and the neat little Christchurch Gardens, burial site of Colonel Blood, last man to try and steal the Crown Jewels. Slightly easier for the eye to locate are the grand designs of **Westminster Abbey,** crowning glory and resting place of most of England's kings and queens, and the neo-gothic pile of the **Houses of Parliament.** Victoria may be an eclectic mix of people and architectural styles, but its handy position as a kind of epicentre of the Westminster Village makes it a great place for political chit-chat. And the place to go for that is The Speaker, a pub in Great Peter Street, named after the Commons' centuries-old peacekeeper and 'referee'. It's a backstreet gem, where it's not unknown for a big cheese from the House to be filmed over a pint.

Winston Churchill is someone who would have been quite at home holding forth at The Speaker, and half a mile away in King Charles Street, based within the **Cabinet War Rooms** – the secret underground HQ of the war effort - is

M. Rellini/Sime/Photononstop

the Churchill Museum, stuffed full of all things Churchillian. However, if your passion is more the easel and the brush, then head down to the river where another great institution of the area, **Tate Britain,** gazes out over the Thames. Standing where the grizzly Millbank Penitentiary once festered, it offers, after the National Gallery, the best collection of historical art in London. There's loads of space for the likes of Turner and Constable, while Hogarth, Gainsborough and Blake are well represented, too. Artists from the modern era are also here, with Freud and Hockney on show, and there are regular installations showcasing upwardly mobile British talent. All of which may give you the taste for a trip east along the river to Tate Modern. This can be done every twenty minutes courtesy of the Tate-to-Tate boat service, which handily stops en-route at the London Eye, and, even more handily, sports eye-catching Damien Hirst décor and a cool, shiny bar.

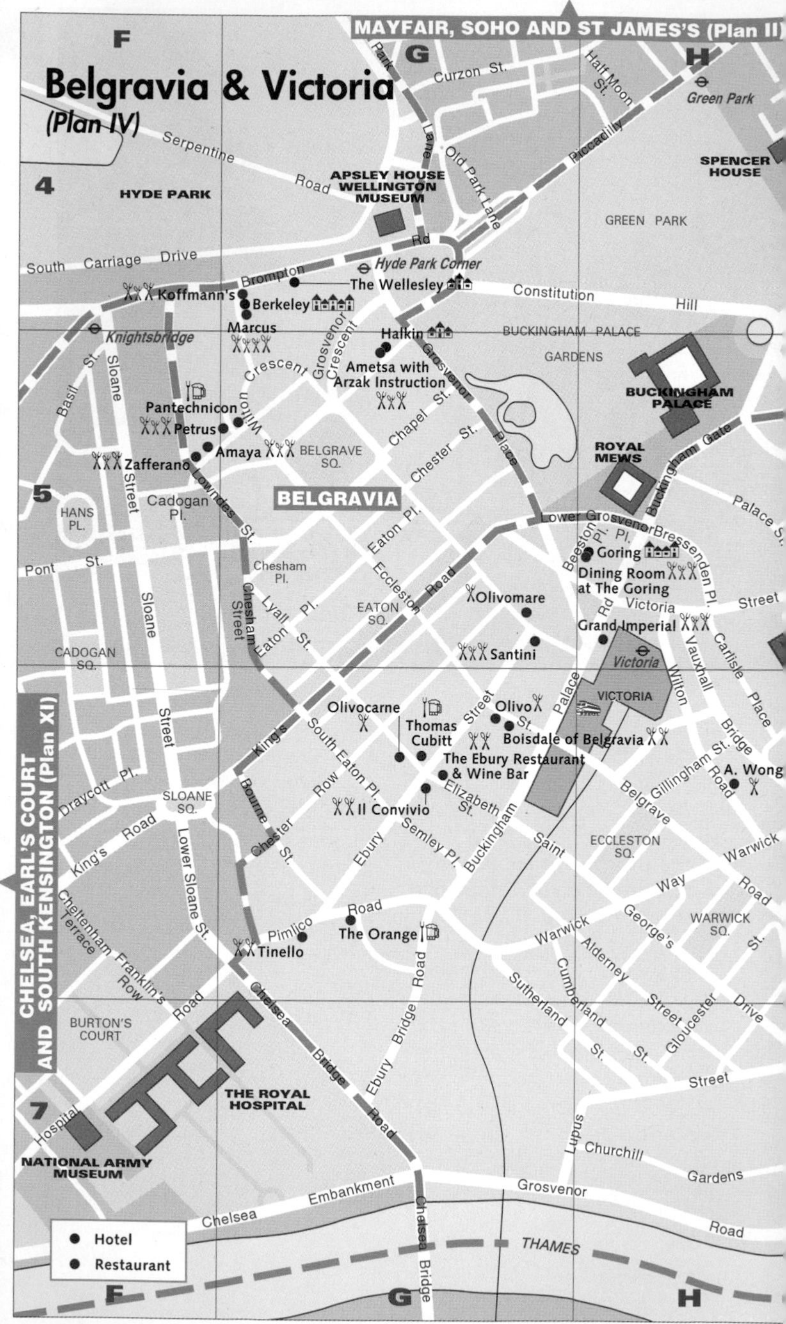

Belgravia & Victoria
(Plan IV)
MAYFAIR, SOHO AND ST JAMES'S (Plan II)
CHELSEA, EARL'S COURT AND SOUTH KENSINGTON (Plan XI)
HYDE PARK
APSLEY HOUSE WELLINGTON MUSEUM
SPENCER HOUSE
GREEN PARK
Green Park
Hyde Park Corner
Knightsbridge
Koffmann's
Berkeley
Marcus
The Wellesley
Halkin
Ametsa with Arzak Instruction
BUCKINGHAM PALACE GARDENS
BUCKINGHAM PALACE
ROYAL MEWS
Pantechnicon
Petrus
Amaya
Zafferano
BELGRAVE SQ.
BELGRAVIA
HANS PL.
Cadogan Pl.
Chesham Pl.
EATON SQ.
CADOGAN SQ.
Goring
Dining Room at The Goring
Olivomare
Grand Imperial
Santini
Victoria
VICTORIA
Olivocarne
Thomas Cubitt
Olivo
Boisdale of Belgravia
The Ebury Restaurant & Wine Bar
A. Wong
Il Convivio
SLOANE SQ.
ECCLESTON SQ.
WARWICK SQ.
Tinello
The Orange
BURTON'S COURT
THE ROYAL HOSPITAL
NATIONAL ARMY MUSEUM
THAMES
Hotel
Restaurant

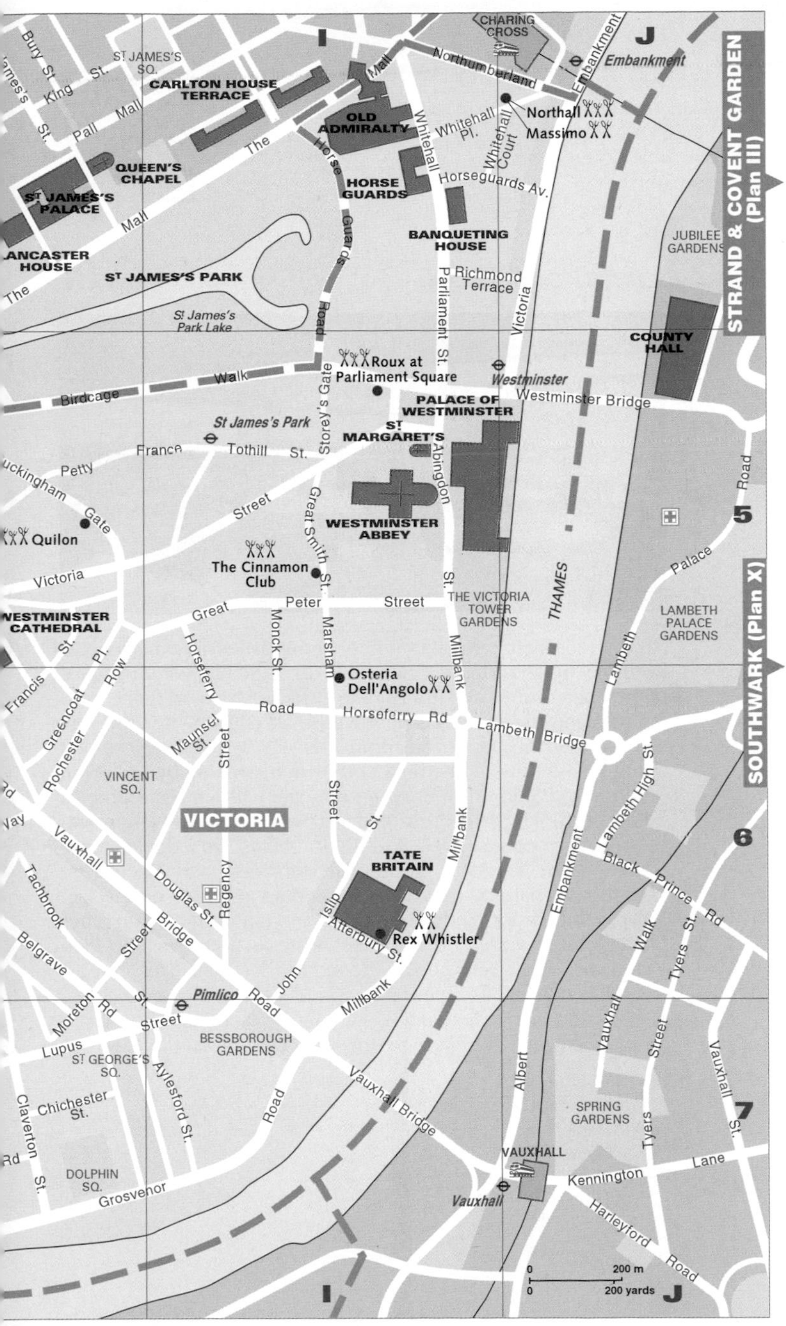
CHARING CROSS
Northumberland
Embankment
J
I
Mall
ST JAMES'S SQ.
CARLTON HOUSE TERRACE
OLD ADMIRALTY
Whitehall
Whitehall Pl.
Whitehall Court
Northall
Massimo
King St.
Bury St.
Pall Mall
The Mall
QUEEN'S CHAPEL
ST JAMES'S PALACE
Horse Guards Road
HORSE GUARDS
Horseguards Av.
BANQUETING HOUSE
LANCASTER HOUSE
ST JAMES'S PARK
St James's Park Lake
Richmond Terrace
Parliament St.
Victoria
JUBILEE GARDENS
STRAND & COVENT GARDEN (Plan III)
COUNTY HALL
Roux at Parliament Square
Birdcage Walk
Westminster
Westminster Bridge
PALACE OF WESTMINSTER
St James's Park
ST MARGARET'S
Storey's Gate
France
Tothill St.
Petty
Buckingham Gate
Abingdon
Street
Great Smith St.
WESTMINSTER ABBEY
Road
5
Quilon
The Cinnamon Club
Victoria
THAMES
Palace
Great Peter Street
THE VICTORIA TOWER GARDENS
LAMBETH PALACE GARDENS
WESTMINSTER CATHEDRAL
SOUTHWARK (Plan X)
Francis St.
Pl.
Row
Horseferry
Monck St.
Marsham
Osteria Dell'Angolo
Millbank
Lambeth
Greencoat
Road
Horseferry Rd
Lambeth Bridge
Rochester
Maunsel St.
Street
Lambeth High St.
VINCENT SQ.
VICTORIA
Street
St.
Vauxhall
Millbank
Embankment
6
TATE BRITAIN
Black Prince Rd
Tachbrook
Douglas St.
Regency
Islip
Rex Whistler
Atterbury St.
Bridge Street
Walk
Tyers St.
Belgrave
Pimlico
John
Road
Millbank
Moreton St
Rd
Street
Vauxhall
Street
BESSBOROUGH GARDENS
Lupus
ST GEORGE'S SQ.
Aylesford St.
Albert
Vauxhall St.
Vauxhall Bridge
SPRING GARDENS
7
Chichester St.
Road
Tyers
Claverton St.
VAUXHALL
Lane
Kennington
DOLPHIN SQ.
Grosvenor
Vauxhall
Harleyford
Road
0 200 m
0 200 yards
I
J

Amaya ✿

Indian

F5

Halkin Arcade, 19 Motcomb St ✉ SW1X 8JT
✆ (020) 7823 1166
www.amaya.biz
⊖ Knightsbridge

Menu £21/55 – Carte £34/64

Amaya

Amaya loosely translates as 'without boundaries' and this reflects both the Indian restaurant's open layout – the kitchen forms part of the main room – and its desire to attract all types of diner, from families and friends to business-types and couples. It is this mix of customer that lends the room its lively atmosphere, helped along by the noise and aroma of the chefs working on the tawa, tandoor and Sigri grills. Bring an appetite with you and order a couple of small plates from the first two sections of the menu then a main course each and some breads; and don't ignore the excellent vegetable dishes like calabrese and sweetcorn. The menu changes regularly but certain popular dishes like grilled lamb chops, griddled scallops and tandoori black pepper chicken rarely come off it. Dishes taste as good as they look – and they look very good indeed. The kitchen takes care to ensure your meal is nicely paced and vegetarians are equally well looked after. The waiting staff are helpful and enthusiastic and if you haven't booked, try the long, communal table.

First Course

- Rock oysters with coconut and ginger moilee sauce.
- Bhojpuri potato.

Main Course

- Slow-roasted leg of baby lamb, cumin and garam masala.
- Chargrilled jumbo Madagascan prawn.

Dessert

- Blood orange brûlée.
- Mango cheesecake.

Ametsa with Arzak Instruction ✿

innovative G5

Halkin Hotel,
5 Halkin St ✉ SW1X 7DJ
☎ (020) 7333 1234
www.comohotels.com/thehalkin
⊖ Hyde Park Corner
Closed 24-26 and 31 December, 1 January and lunch Sunday and Monday

Menu £28/145 – Carte £53/84

A/C

The Halkin

The clever people behind the Halkin hotel always seem to sense when their restaurant has run its course and it's time for a change. The room on the ground floor of the hotel has been an Italian and a Thai, and now it's Spanish – but not just any Spanish restaurant because it's the Arzak father and daughter team who are bringing the Basque country to Belgravia. Despite the rather clumsy name, this isn't a direct copy or a clone of their iconic restaurant in San Sebastián, rather a restaurant specifically for London. The ingredients are largely from the UK yet the flavour combinations are typically Basque, even when dishes are playful or idiosyncratic. The menus are concise and its descriptions fairly economical, so help from the staff will be needed. The dishes are certainly appealing to the eye, without seeming to be overworked, and are often served with a finishing flourish of sauce-pouring at the table. The restaurant is much brighter and the thousands of test tubes filled with spices hanging from the ceiling are its most eye-catching element.

First Course

- Egg with squid noodles.
- Red skin sardines.

Main Course

- Sea bass with leeks.
- Ox cheek with vanilla.

Dessert

- Chocolate wooden board.
- French toast with mango and coconut.

A. Wong

Chinese H6

70 Wilton Rd ✉ SW1V 1DE
(020) 7828 8931
www.awong.co.uk
⊖ Victoria
Closed 23-27 December, 1-2 January, Sunday and Monday lunch – booking essential

Menu £14 – Carte £16/38

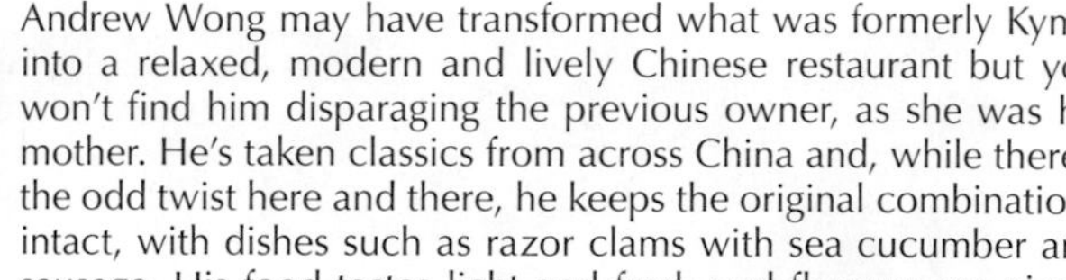

Andrew Wong may have transformed what was formerly Kym's into a relaxed, modern and lively Chinese restaurant but you won't find him disparaging the previous owner, as she was his mother. He's taken classics from across China and, while there's the odd twist here and there, he keeps the original combinations intact, with dishes such as razor clams with sea cucumber and sausage. His food tastes light and fresh and flavours are nicely balanced. Start with snacks like peanuts in vinegar or egg with shredded filo; then, if it's lunch, try their excellent dim sum; otherwise, the 'Taste of China' 8 course menu offers a good summation of his style. Service is keen, as are the prices. Sit at the counter if you want to see the woks in action.

Boisdale of Belgravia

British traditional G6

15 Eccleston St ✉ SW1W 9LX
(020) 7730 6922
www.boisdale.co.uk
⊖ Victoria
Closed 25 December, Saturday lunch, Sunday and bank holidays

Menu £18 – Carte £24/69

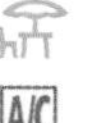

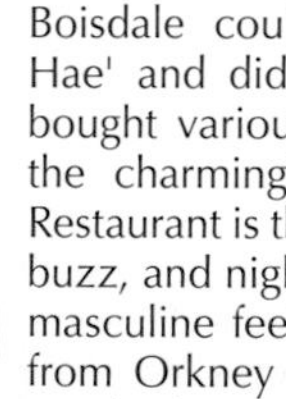

Acres of tartan, whiskies galore, haggis, mash and neeps – Boisdale couldn't be more Scottish if it sang 'Scots Wha Hae' and did the Highland Fling. Owner Ranald Macdonald bought various parts of the building at different times, hence the charmingly higgledy-piggledy layout. The original Auld Restaurant is the more characterful; the Macdonald Bar has more buzz, and nightly live jazz and a large cigar selection add to the masculine feel. The menu features plenty of Scottish produce, from Orkney herring to Shetland scallops, but the stand-outs are the four varieties of smoked salmon, followed by the 28-day aged Aberdeenshire cuts of beef. Ignore the lacklustre tomato and watercress garnish and just savour the quality of the meat.

The Cinnamon Club

Indian

I5

30-32 Great Smith St ✉ SW1P 3BU
✆ (020) 7222 2555
www.cinnamonclub.com
⊖ St James's Park
Closed Sunday and bank holidays

Menu £24 (weekdays) – Carte £31/61

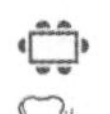

Tourists and locals, politicians and business people – The Cinnamon Club attracts all sorts, which explains why you'll be greeted by that appealing wall of noise enjoyed by all successful restaurants. It certainly makes good use of its surroundings, the listed former Westminster library. You'll be faced with quite a few menus; grab the drinks one first as you'll need time to decide what to eat. Don't come expecting there'll be dishes to share: the style is quite different from most Indian restaurants as the somewhat elaborately constructed dishes arrive fully garnished and spicing is quite subtle – in fact, any watering of eyes is more likely to be caused by some of the prices. Service is supervised by lots of managers in suits.

Il Convivio

Italian

G6

143 Ebury St ✉ SW1W 9QN
✆ (020) 7730 4099
www.ilconvivio.co.uk
⊖ Sloane Square
Closed Christmas-New Year, Easter, Sunday and bank holidays

Menu £18/24 – Carte £29/51

If passing by, you'll find yourself being drawn in by the appealing façade of this handsome Georgian townhouse – and there's usually an eager welcome to boot, whether you're a regular or first-timer. Inside is equally pleasant, with Dante's poetry embossed on the wall to remind you you're in an Italian restaurant and a retractable roof at the back, under which sit the best tables. All pasta is made on the top floor of the house; the squid ink spaghetti with lobster is a menu staple. Dishes are artfully presented but not so showy as to compromise the flavours. Artisanal cheeses are carefully selected and looked after, while service is confident and able. Using the private dining room allows you to imagine being the owner of the house.

Dining Room at The Goring

British traditional **H5**

Goring Hotel,
15 Beeston Pl ✉ SW1W 0JW
✆ (020) 7396 9000
www.thegoring.com
⊖ Victoria
Closed Saturday lunch

Menu £43 (weekday lunch)/53

If you've ever wondered what the difference between a restaurant and a dining room is then book a table here. The Goring hotel is a model of British style and understatement and its ground floor dining room the epitome of grace and decorum. Designed by Viscount Linley, it appeals to those who "like things done properly" and is one of the few spots in London for which everyone appears to dress up. It is supremely well run; even those who decry tradition will be charmed by the well-choreographed service team. The menu respects the hotel's reputation for classic British food while also acknowledging that tastes and techniques move on so you can expect modern, lighter dishes alongside recognisable old favourites.

The Ebury Restaurant & Wine Bar

French **G6**

139 Ebury St. ✉ SW1W 9QU
✆ (020) 7730 5447
www.eburyrestaurant.co.uk
⊖ Victoria
Closed Christmas-New Year

Menu £21/27 – Carte £28/54

There are probably many reasons why The Ebury Wine Bar has been going strong for over 50 years but likeability and adaptability must surely be two. It has an endearing honesty that is largely down to the eagerness of the long-standing staff, and changing habits have meant that the focus is now more on the food than the wine; even the bar offers a decent snack menu. Go through to the dining room, with its trompe l'oeil, and you'll find a kitchen that brings imaginative international influences to some dishes but is equally happy doing the classics such as lamb cutlets or liver and bacon. The set menu includes a glass of champagne; there are separate dairy and gluten free menus; and the wine list is thoughtfully compiled and keenly priced.

Grand Imperial

Chinese H5

Grosvenor Hotel, 101 Buckingham Palace Rd ✉ SW1W 0SJ
✆ (020) 7821 8898
www.grandimperiallondon.com
⊖ Victoria
Closed 25-26 December

Menu £18 (weekday lunch) – Carte £21/110

Grand it most certainly is, as this elegant Chinese restaurant is to be found in the impressive surroundings of The Grosvenor Hotel's former ballroom. In fact, in between the pillars and the ornate ceiling, the only indication that this is a Chinese restaurant is the calligraphy on the walls. The Grand Imperial is a collaboration between the hotel owners and a Malaysian restaurant company and specialises in Cantonese cuisine, particularly the version found in Hong Kong. Techniques of steaming and frying are used to great effect with such signature dishes as diced beef steak with black pepper sauce and steamed lobster with Chinese wine and egg white. There is no fusion food here; just authentic flavours and quality ingredients.

Koffmann's

French G4

Berkeley Hotel,
Wilton Pl ✉ SW1X 7RL
✆ (020) 7235 1010
www.the-berkeley.co.uk
⊖ Knightsbridge

Menu £22/28 (weekdays) – Carte £45/68

There are several talented chefs in the UK who owe much of their success to the time they spent working with Pierre Koffmann. The next generation now have the opportunity to learn from this celebrated chef, here at his eponymous restaurant in The Berkeley hotel where he cooks gutsy, flavoursome dishes close to his heart, from the Gascony region of France. Those with fond memories of his former restaurant, La Tante Claire, will recognise some of his signature dishes – scallops with squid ink, and stuffed pig's trotter – but try too his newer creations such as squid bolognaise. Service is smooth and confident, sommeliers are clued up and the dining room comfortable and discreet. Be sure to ask for a table in the main body of the room.

Marcus ✿✿

modern

G4

Berkeley Hotel,
Wilton Pl ✉ SW1X 7RL
✆ (020) 7235 1200
www.marcus-wareing.com
⊖ Knightsbridge
Closed Sunday

Menu £38 (weekday lunch)/85

Marcus

A shortened moniker wasn't the only change to Marcus Wareing's restaurant in 2014. An announcement was made that it was becoming much more informal to reflect the casual zeitgeist but, in truth, his million pound redecoration has merely made the room lighter and less claustrophobic and it remains as elegant and as comfortable as ever. You'll find the service just as professional and structured as it was but the staff are now just a little more engaging and personable. The most fundamental change, however, has been with the food and the menu. The latter comes with in-built flexibility so that diners can now come along for a couple of courses rather than feel the need to order the tasting menu. The food is also lighter, less elaborate and healthier – Marcus Wareing's style remains classically based but with this simplification come cleaner, more distinct flavours. All restaurants need to reinvent themselves once in a while and the changes undertaken here should ensure its continuing popularity.

First Course

- Foie gras, mango and granola.
- Quail with carrot, corn bread and summer savory.

Main Course

- Beef fillet with potato, cabbage and short rib.
- Turbot with Dorset snails, shallots and gnocchi.

Dessert

- Pineapple pain perdu, coconut and lime.
- Toffee with peanut and milk chocolate nougat.

Massimo

Italian J4

Corinthia Hotel,
10 Northumberland Ave. ✉ WC2N 5AE
✆ (020) 7321 3156
www.corinthia.com/london
⊖ Embankment
Closed Sunday

Menu £30 – Carte £31/76

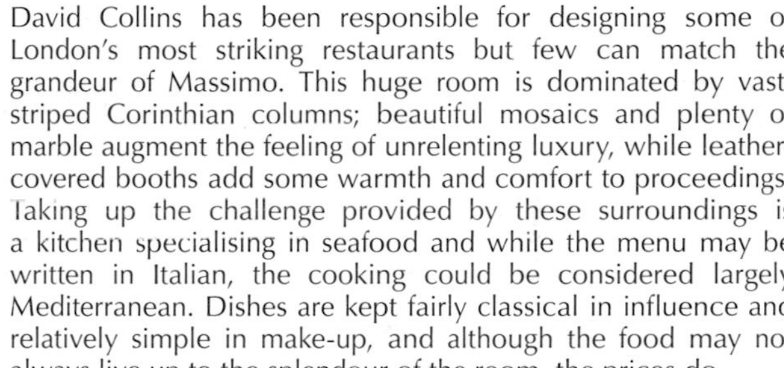

David Collins has been responsible for designing some of London's most striking restaurants but few can match the grandeur of Massimo. This huge room is dominated by vast, striped Corinthian columns; beautiful mosaics and plenty of marble augment the feeling of unrelenting luxury, while leather-covered booths add some warmth and comfort to proceedings. Taking up the challenge provided by these surroundings is a kitchen specialising in seafood and while the menu may be written in Italian, the cooking could be considered largely Mediterranean. Dishes are kept fairly classical in influence and relatively simple in make-up, and although the food may not always live up to the splendour of the room, the prices do.

Northall

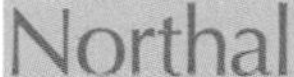

British traditional J4

Corinthia Hotel,
Whitehall Pl. ✉ WC2N 5AE
✆ (020) 7321 3100
www.thenorthall.co.uk
⊖ Embankment

Menu £28/30 – Carte £26/75

The Corinthia Hotel's British restaurant not only celebrates our indigenous food but also champions its producers by acknowledging them all on the menu. It is certainly an appealing document with the likes of potted shrimps, Dover sole meunière and roast venison with swede alongside a grilled section using Cumbrian shorthorn cattle aged for 28 days. The kitchen is also not averse to looking across The Channel for the occasional influence. The restaurant occupies two rooms; the most appealing is the more modern room with its bar counter and booths while the other section is more formally arranged and better suited for a business lunch. An attractive 'market place' set up with cheese and meat displays links the two rooms.

Olivo

Italian G6

21 Eccleston St ✉ SW1W 9LX
✆ (020) 7730 2505
www.olivorestaurants.com
⊖ Victoria
Closed lunch Saturday-Sunday and bank holidays – booking essential

Menu £25 (lunch) – Carte £33/45

A/C

The cooking at Olivo has always been highly capable and reassuringly reliable, which does tend to make up for the service which is never quite as engaging as you hope it will be. Nevertheless this is a popular, pleasant and relaxed little neighbourhood Italian, with vivid blues and yellows, rough wooden floorboards and intimate lighting. The menu showcases the robust flavours of Sardinia and changes fortnightly, although some dishes, such as spaghetti bottarga and linguine with crab, remain permanent features. There are normally a few daily specials – particularly for the regulars – dishes are clearly prepared with care and desserts continue the regional theme; try sebada, a traditional Sardinian cheese fritter.

Olivocarne

Italian G6

61 Elizabeth St ✉ SW1W 9PP
✆ (020) 7730 7997
www.olivorestaurants.com
⊖ Sloane Square

Carte £31/47

Just when you thought Mauro Sanno had this part of town sewn up, he opens another restaurant – this time with the focus on meat dishes. This place is smarter, chicer and larger than his others; head up the steps to the brighter section which has a striking mural themed around Sardinian folklore. Regulars at his other establishments will be familiar with the range of tasty, rustic dishes, but here meat is the principle ingredient, from suckling pig to oxtail as well as a whole section of beef. The dishes are delicious and satisfying; none more so that the roast bone marrow with Mirto salt and crostini. Classic Sardinian pasta dishes like lorighittas with duck sauce are also much in demand. Head upstairs first, for a cocktail in Joe's bar.

Olivomare

fish and seafood G5

10 Lower Belgrave St ✉ SW1W 0LJ
✆ (020) 7730 9022
www.olivorestaurants.com
⊖ Victoria
Closed bank holidays

Carte £35/44

Italian seafood, particularly Sardinian seafood, is celebrated here at Olivomare, a bright and lively restaurant whose design owes as much to Barbarella as it does M.C. Escher. Bottarga naturally features and not just with spaghetti – it also comes with Sardinian artichokes and even burrata. The stews are terrific as are the couscous soups; the octopus, whether in a salad, a stew or just roasted is always worth ordering. For pud the 'gelato allo yoghurt' is good and is just one of the items that can also be bought from their well-stocked deli next door. The wine list is a little limited by the glass but otherwise this is a very warmly run and understandably popular local, where freshness and simplicity combine to great effect.

The Orange

Mediterranean G6

37 Pimlico Rd ✉ SW1W 8NE
✆ (020) 7881 9844
www.theorange.co.uk
⊖ Sloane Square.

Carte £28/42

The former home of the Orange Brewery is a handsome pub that's as charming as its stucco-fronted façade suggests. The locals will no doubt have filled the bar, where the wood-burning oven is quite a feature, but it's still worth trying your luck to get one of the tables here or in the adjacent room; if you book ahead you'll be upstairs which is just as pleasantly decorated but a little more sedate. There's a clear Mediterranean bias to the menu which also includes plenty of salads along with spelt or wheat based pizzas which come with some original toppings; there are also roasts on a Sunday and pies for the traditionalists. Unusually for a London pub, there are bedrooms upstairs: these are stylish and comfortable.

Osteria Dell' Angolo

Italian I6

47 Marsham St ✉ SW1P 3DR
✆ (020) 3268 1077
www.osteriadellangolo.co.uk
⊖ St James's Park
Closed Easter, 17-31 August, 23-27 December, 1-7 January, Saturday lunch, Sunday and bank holidays – booking essential

Menu £18 (lunch) – Carte £30/42

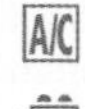

The name may suggest a simple little neighbourhood trattoria but this is, in fact, a rather smart, conscientiously run restaurant offering some authentic, carefully prepared Italian food. As it's opposite the Home Office, lunch is quite a busy time and regulars, who include the odd MP, tend to get the tables on the raised section at the back rather than the less comfortable area by the bar where the Johnny-come-latelys get seated. The kitchen team, visible behind the glass, offer a fairly comprehensive culinary tour of the country's regions and their dishes deliver reassuringly emphatic flavours. There's also a decent selection of wines by the glass for anyone who fears the ignominy of having their expense claims examined.

Pantechnicon

British modern G5

10 Motcomb St ✉ SW1X 8LA
✆ (020) 7730 6074
www.thepantechnicon.com
⊖ Knightsbridge.
Closed 25 December – booking advisable

Carte £29/50

It may be the very antithesis of the spit 'n' sawdust pub, but The Pantechnicon is still a very welcoming and busy local. The brightly run ground floor is crammed with tables and works on a first-come-first-served basis; upstairs you'll find a far more formal, Georgian style dining room and there's even a top floor cocktail bar – this is Belgravia after all. Wisely, the same menu is served throughout – an appealing mix of the refined and the comforting. Castle of Mey 28-day aged steaks and salt and chilli squid are the two most popular choices; home-smoked salmon, burgers and fish pie are also done well. The name comes from the horse-drawn wagons that once transported the belongings of locals to and from a repository on Motcomb Street.

Pétrus ✿

French

G5 

1 Kinnerton St ✉ SW1X 8EA
(020) 7592 1609
www.gordonramsay.com/petrus
⊖ Knightsbridge
Closed 25-26 December, 1 January and Sunday

Menu £35/75

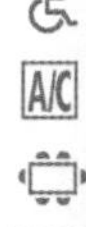

Gordon Ramsay Holdings

Gordon Ramsay's smart Belgravia restaurant is an unapologetically sophisticated and discreet affair, geared to an urbane and international clientele. It is attractively decorated in understated tones of silver, oyster and – to add warmth to the room and as a nod to the name – claret. Tables are immaculately dressed and service is under the watchful eye of an experienced and courteous team who never let proceedings get too reverential. Downstairs is the 'show' kitchen with its horseshoe-shaped chef's table, for those whose enjoyment of a meal is sharpened by watching a large brigade of chefs – in this case around 14 – beavering away in front of them. The uninitiated should initially try lunch, when they'll find a set menu that won't break the bank; there are also vegetarian and chef's menus alongside the appealing à la carte of French-based dishes. The restaurant's name is not just reflected in the décor – the superb wine list includes over 20 vintages of Château Pétrus going back to 1924.

First Course

- Scallops with peas, lettuce, lardo di Colonnata and lemon thyme.
- Rabbit loin wrapped in Bayonne ham, with crayfish and tarragon.

Main Course

- Mutton, smoked aubergine, mint and sheep's yoghurt.
- Cornish monkfish, roast cauliflower, wild garlic and nori.

Dessert

- Coconut soufflé with pineapple sorbet.
- Dark and milk chocolate with Oloroso sherry jelly and prunes.

Quilon ✿

Indian

H5

St James' Court Hotel,
41 Buckingham Gate ✉ SW1E 6AF
☎ (020) 7821 1899
www.quilon.co.uk
⊖ St James's Park
Closed 25 December

Menu £24/53 – Carte £28/55

Quilon

An extensive 2012 makeover left this long-standing Indian restaurant looking slick and contemporary. A stylish bar was added, along with a striking private dining room which comes with its own kitchen. These elegant surroundings provide the ideal backdrop to chef Sriram Aylur's accomplished cooking, which focuses on India's southwest coast. 'Progression' is one of his watchwords and he has overseen a transformation in the food which is now considerably lighter than much Indian cuisine. There's a high degree of originality in some of the dishes, such as his own version of black cod and his imaginative dishes involving game, but traditionalists will still find much to savour, whether that's masala dosa or a fish curry with coconut. The crab cakes are a delight and the colourful and crisp okra is very moreish. The serving team are charming and helpful; the wine list has been thoughtfully compiled to complement the food and there's an interesting selection of beers too. The re-launch of Quilon is something to be celebrated by all lovers of Indian food.

First Course

- Chargrilled scallops.
- Lotus stem and colocasia chop with mango and mint sauce.

Main Course

- Braised lamb shank.
- Herb-crusted tilapia with mustard sauce.

Dessert

- Spiced, cold chocolate fondant.
- Baked yoghurt, confit orange, mango and lychee.

Ⓝ Rex Whistler

British traditional I6

Tate Britain, Millbank ✉ SW1P 4RG
✆ (020) 7887 8825
www.tate.org.uk
⊖ Pimlico
Closed 24-26 December – (lunch only)

Menu £29 XX

When Tate Britain reopened after its £45million renovation, it wasn't just fans of British art who were pleased to see the return of this Victorian landmark. Its restaurant, Rex Whistler, also benefitted from a facelift – but one that remained loyal to its original look. The most striking element remains Whistler's mural, 'The Expedition in Pursuit of Rare Meats', which envelops the room and was painstakingly restored. A 'food historian' works with the chef to produce a monthly menu that is stoutly British and influenced to a degree by the 1920s, the decade in which the restaurant first opened. However, it is the terrific wine list that really leaves an impression: some of the prices are remarkable and the 'half bottle' selection is unrivalled.

Roux at Parliament Square

modern I5

Royal Institution of Chartered Surveyors, Parliament Sq.
✉ SW1P 3AD
✆ (020) 7334 3737 – **www**.rouxatparliamentsquare.co.uk
⊖ Westminster
Closed 22 December-5 January, Saturday, Sunday and bank holidays – bookings advisable at lunch

Menu £35 (lunch) – Carte £38/62

The offices of the Royal Institute of Chartered Surveyors play host to this attractive Westminster restaurant. It's really a Compass-run operation, in conjunction with Michel Roux of Le Gavroche fame. However, instead of the classical French cuisine for which M. Roux is known, here the food is more contemporary in style and adopts some modern techniques. Dishes are still carefully crafted but occasionally you can expect some interesting combinations of flavours. The decoration is cool and comfortable, with plenty of natural light flooding through the Georgian windows. Service, from a well-trained team, comes with personality and there is a particularly attractive private dining room in the library.

Santini

Italian

G5

29 Ebury St ✉ SW1W 0NZ
☎ (020) 7730 4094
www.santinirestaurant.com
⊖ Victoria
Closed 23-26 December, 1 January and Easter

Menu £25 (dinner) – Carte £30/67

Despite the high prices within, and the economic meltdown without, Santini 's loyal and immaculately coiffured customers continue to eschew cheaper alternatives and instead turn up here with impressive regularity. Indeed, it is by looking after its regulars so well for nearly 30 years that the restaurant has managed to remain largely unruffled by the winds of recession. The menu of classic Italian dishes, broadly Venetian in style, is supplemented by daily specials; the cooking is reliable and confident, while pasta dishes and desserts remain the standout courses. If you are one of the regulars, you'll find yourself not only charmed by the flattery you'll receive, but you'll also be offered their excellent Carasau bread.

Thomas Cubitt

modern

G6

44 Elizabeth St ✉ SW1W 9PA
☎ (020) 7730 6060
www.thethomascubitt.co.uk
⊖ Sloane Square.
Booking essential

Carte £28/42

The Thomas Cubitt is a pub of two halves: on the ground floor it's perennially busy and you can't book which means that if you haven't arrived by 7pm then you're too late to get a table. However, you can reserve a table upstairs, in a dining room that's a model of civility and tranquillity. Here, service comes courtesy of a young team where the girls are chatty and the men unafraid of corduroy. Downstairs you get fish and chips; here you get pan-fried fillet of brill with oyster beignet and truffled chips. The cooking is certainly skilled, quite elaborate in its construction and prettily presented. So, take your pick: upstairs can get a little pricey but is ideal for entertaining the in-laws; if out with friends then crowd in downstairs.

Tinello

Italian

G6

87 Pimlico Rd ✉ SW1W 8PH
✆ (020) 7730 3663
www.tinello.co.uk
⊖ Sloane Square
Closed Sunday and bank holidays – booking essential at dinner

Carte £24/52

The brothers Sali have built up a quite a following for their warm and friendly Italian restaurant. These two super Tuscans, who both spent many years working with Giorgio Locatelli, look to their home region for inspiration so you can expect Federico to be busy downstairs preparing dishes like ribollita, liver crostini, pappardelle with wild boar ragout and, to finish, cantucci with vin santo. Meanwhile, Max runs the place with confidence and élan, his team providing earnest, helpful service with plenty of charm and a refreshing absence of upselling. There's a sense of solidity and permanence to the room, where judicious lighting, angled mirrors and exposed brick add an intimate and romantic feel, especially at dinner.

Zafferano

Italian

F5

15 Lowndes St ✉ SW1X 9EY
✆ (020) 7235 5800
www.zafferanorestaurant.co.uk
⊖ Knightsbridge
Booking essential

Menu £23 (weekday lunch) – Carte £35/79

It's hard to believe that Zafferano once felt like an intimate little Italian restaurant – over the years it has steadily been expanded and extended and now it's something of a colossus. Fortunately, it all seems to work, proof being in the high number of impeccably dressed regulars that continue to support it. Large tables are easily absorbed without dominating the space; the atmosphere positively hums along; and an army of staff is on hand to ensure no one has to wait too long for their food. The menu concentrates on recognisable, easy-to-eat classics from all parts of Italy and the portions are quite generous, which is just as well because the prices can be pretty steep – even for Belgravia.

Regent's Park · Marylebone

The neighbourhood north of chaotic Oxford Street is actually a rather refined place where shoppers like to venture for the smart boutiques, and where idlers like to saunter for the graceful parkland acres full of rose gardens and quiet corners. In fact, Marylebone and Regent's Park go rather well together, a moneyed village with a wonderful park for its back garden.

Marylebone may now exude a fashionable status, but its history tells a very different tale. Thousands used to come here to watch executions at Tyburn gallows, a six hundred year spectacle that stopped in the late eighteenth century. Tyburn stream was covered over, and the area's modern name came into being as a contraction of St Mary by the Bourne, the parish church. Nowadays the people who flock here come to gaze at less ghoulish sights, though some of the inhabitants of the eternally popular Madame Tussauds deserved no better fate than the gallows. South across the busy Marylebone Road, the preponderance of swish restaurants and snazzy specialist shops announces your arrival at **Marylebone High Street.** There are patisseries, chocolatiers, cheese shops and butchers at every turn, nestling alongside smart places to eat and drink. At St Marylebone Church, each Saturday heralds a posh market called Cabbages & Frocks, where artisan food meets designer clothing in a charming garden. Further down, the century old Daunt Books has been described as London's most beautiful bookshop: it has long oak galleries beneath graceful conservatory skylights. Close by, the quaintly winding Marylebone Lane boasts some truly unique shops like tiny emporium The Button Queen, which sells original Art Deco, Victorian and Edwardian buttons. In complete contrast, just down the road from here is the mighty **Wigmore Hall,** an art nouveau gem with great acoustics and an unerringly top-notch classical agenda that can be appreciated at rock-bottom prices. Meanwhile, art lovers can indulge an eclectic fix at the **Wallace Collection** in **Manchester Square,** where paintings by the likes of Titian and Velazquez rub shoulders with Sevres porcelain and grand Louis XIV furniture.

Regent's Park – an idyllic Georgian oasis stretching off into London's northern suburbs - celebrated its two hundredth birthday in 2011. Before architect John Nash and his sponsor The Prince Regent gave it its much-loved geometric makeover, it had been farming land, and prior to that, one of Henry VIII's hunting grounds. His spirit lives on, in the sense that various activities are catered for, from tennis courts to a running track. And there are animals too, albeit not roaming free, at **London Zoo,** in the park's northerly section. Most people, though, come here to while away an hour or two around the boating lake or amble the Inner Circle which

C. Eymenier / MICHELIN

contains **Queen Mary's Gardens** and their enchanting bowers of fragrant roses. Others come for a summer sojourn to the Open Air Theatre where taking in a performance of 'A Midsummer Night's Dream' is very much ***de rigueur***. The Regent's Canal provides another fascinating element to the park. You can follow its peaceful waters along a splendid walk from the **Little Venice** houseboats in the west, past the golden dome of the **London Central Mosque,** and on into the north-west confines of Regent's Park as it snakes through London Zoo, before it heads off towards Camden Lock. On the other side of Prince Albert Road, across from the zoo, the scenic glory takes on another dimension with a climb up Primrose Hill. Named after the grassy promontory that sets it apart from its surrounds, to visitors this is a hill with one of the best panoramas in the whole of London; to locals (ie, actors, pop stars, media darlings and the city set) it's an ultra fashionable place to live with pretty Victorian terraces and accordingly sky-high prices. Either way you look at it (or from it), it's a great place to be on a sunny day with the breeze in your hair.

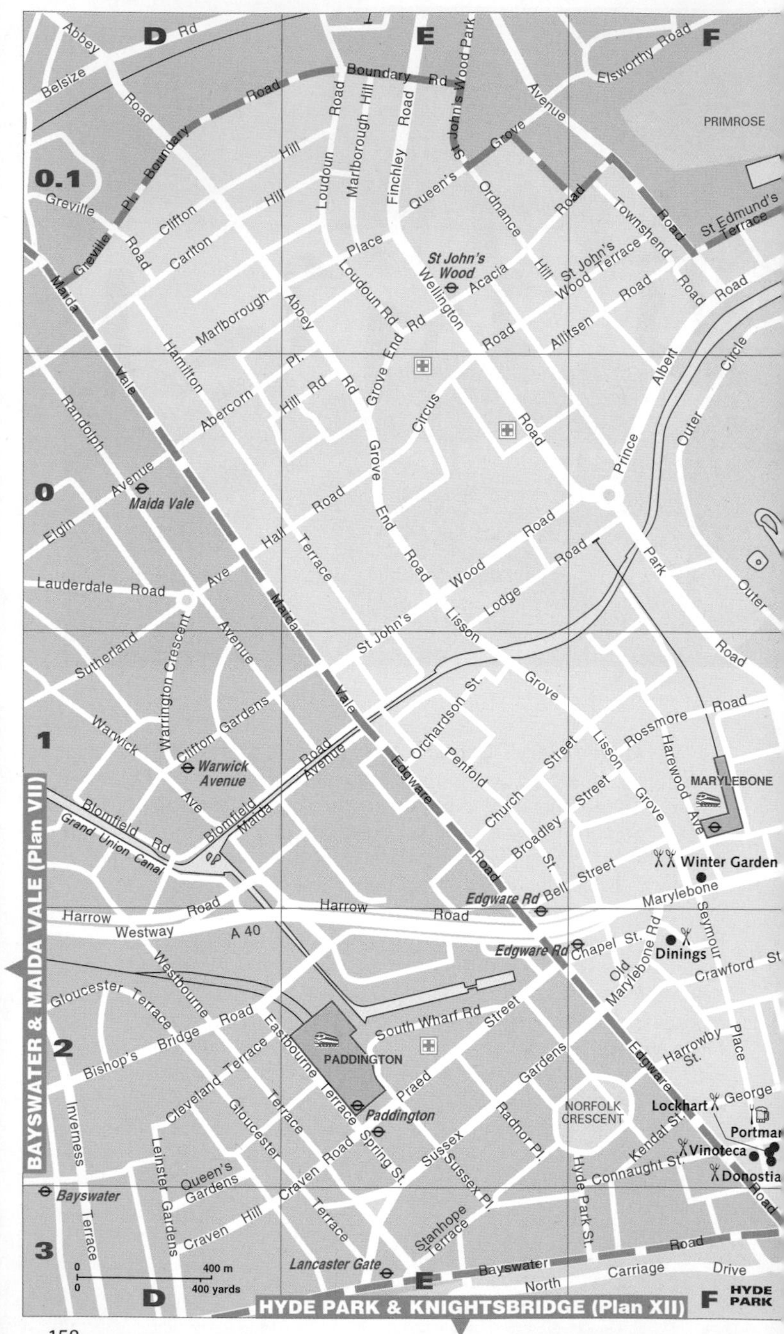

BAYSWATER & MAIDA VALE (Plan VII)
HYDE PARK & KNIGHTSBRIDGE (Plan XII)
PRIMROSE
St John's Wood
Maida Vale
Warwick Avenue
MARYLEBONE
Winter Garden
Edgware Rd
Dinings
PADDINGTON
Paddington
NORFOLK CRESCENT
Lockhart
George
Portman
Vinoteca
Donostia
Bayswater
Lancaster Gate
HYDE PARK
Grand Union Canal
A 40
400 m
400 yards

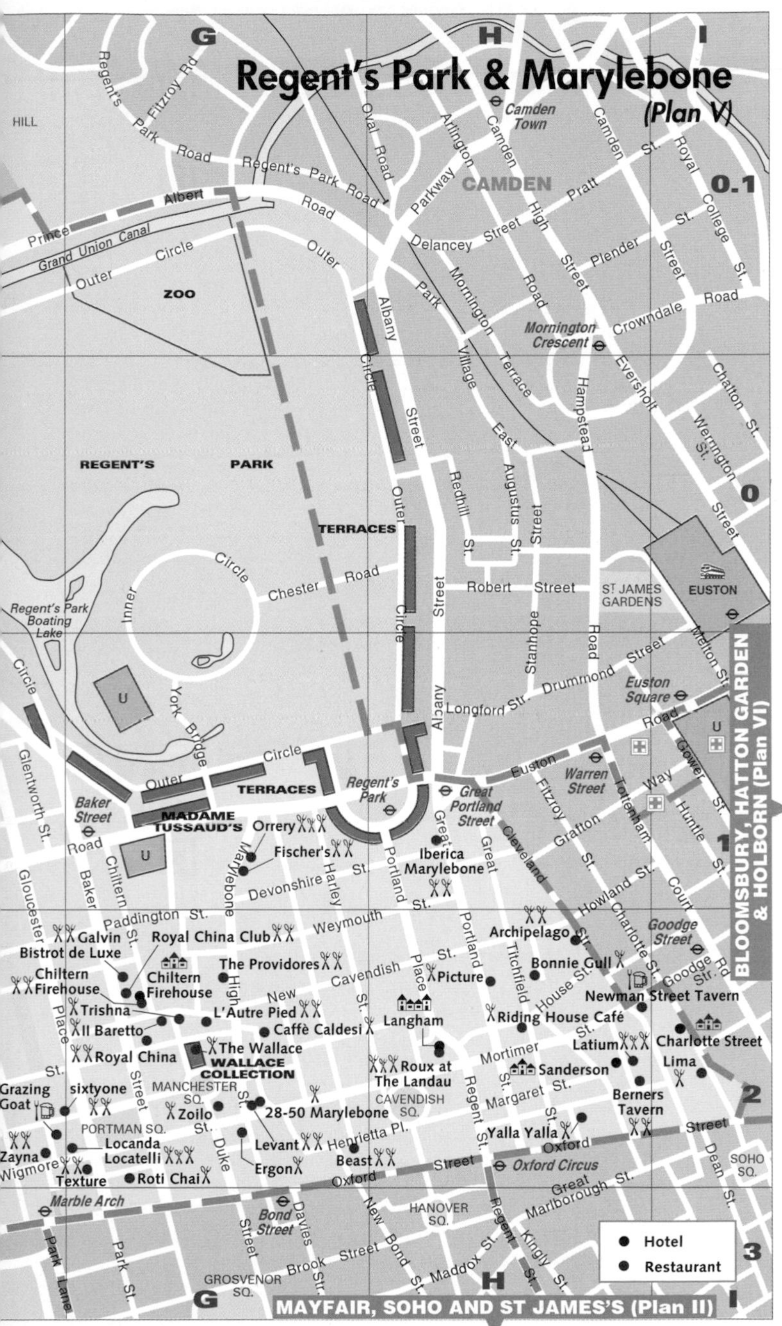
Regent's Park & Marylebone
(Plan V)
Camden Town
CAMDEN
ZOO
REGENT'S
PARK
TERRACES
Regent's Park Boating Lake
Baker Street
MADAME TUSSAUD'S
Regent's Park
Great Portland Street
Warren Street
Euston Square
EUSTON
ST JAMES GARDENS
Mornington Crescent
Goodge Street
Oxford Circus
Bond Street
Marble Arch
Orrery
Fischer's
Iberica Marylebone
Archipelago
Galvin Bistrot de Luxe
Royal China Club
The Providores
Chiltern Firehouse
Trishna
L'Autre Pied
Il Baretto
Caffè Caldesi
Langham
Picture
Bonnie Gull
Newman Street Tavern
Riding House Café
The Wallace
WALLACE COLLECTION
Royal China
Roux at The Landau
Latium
Charlotte Street
Sanderson
Lima
Berners Tavern
Grazing Goat
sixtyone
Zoilo
28-50 Marylebone
Yalla Yalla
Levant
Zayna
Locanda Locatelli
Beast
Ergon
Texture
Roti Chai
MANCHESTER SQ.
PORTMAN SQ.
CAVENDISH SQ.
HANOVER SQ.
GROSVENOR SQ.
SOHO SQ.
Hotel
Restaurant
BLOOMSBURY, HATTON GARDEN & HOLBORN (Plan VI)
MAYFAIR, SOHO AND ST JAMES'S (Plan II)

Archipelago

innovative H2

53 Cleveland St ✉ W1T 4JJ
✆ (020) 7383 3346
www.archipelago-restaurant.co.uk
⊖ Goodge Street
Closed 24-28 December, Saturday lunch, Sunday and bank holidays

Carte £27/43

A/C It may have moved to new premises around the corner but you can expect the same exuberant decoration that makes you feel you're eating in an eccentric Oriental bazaar which is running out of space. The gloriously oddball Archipelago is unlike any other restaurant in London – tales of your meal here can be used to frighten small children. 'Exploring the exotic' is their slogan although 'eating the exotic' would be more exact: the menu reads like an inventory at an omnivore's safari park. Several dishes are given an Asian twist and side dishes include the 'love-bug salad' made with locusts and crickets. Apart from a somewhat laborious reservation system, it's all great fun and the experience will certainly be memorable.

Il Baretto

Italian G2

43 Blandford St. ✉ W1U 7HF
✆ (020) 7486 7340
www.ilbaretto.co.uk
⊖ Baker Street

Menu £26 – Carte £35/83

The discreet entrance and small ground floor bar of this Italian restaurant don't give much away, but downstairs you'll find a large room with a degree of character and quite a lively atmosphere. The menu covers all bases so eating here can be as pricey or an inexpensive as you want: come along for a pizza and a beer and you'll do fine; push the boat out with a three course meal and you could find yourself with a surprisingly large bill. The cooking, though, is reliable and the star of the show is the robata grill – it delivers some very succulent lamb chops; pasta is done well and desserts show some ambition. Service can be a little more hit and miss: some staff members are very confident while others seem a little disinterested.

L'Autre Pied ✿

modern

5-7 Blandford St. ✉ W1U 3DB
✆ (020) 7486 9696
www.lautrepied.co.uk
⊖ Bond Street
Closed 4 days Christmas, 1 January and Sunday dinner

G2

Menu £23/70 – Carte £43/59

XX

A/C

L'Autre Pied

As L'Autre Pied matures so it feels less like a sibling to Pied à Terre and more like a twin. Head Chef Andy McFadden's food is visual and bright and the talent and ability in his kitchen is obvious. Some dishes can appear as quite elaborate constructions but flavour is never sacrificed at the altar of ambition and the modern techniques used are underpinned by a sound understanding of what works best for each ingredient. There is also a slight Scandinavian influence at play here, not least in the kitchen's deft handling of game, which is one of the highlights of the culinary year at L'Autre Pied – if you see roe or sika deer on the menu then you'd be wise to jump at it. Service flows well and the restaurant has that easy, relaxed atmosphere typical of a neighbourhood restaurant, even one where the cooking is seriously good, and there's a nice mix of customer. Some pop in for just a couple of courses, others are here for the full tasting menu; come for lunch or pre-theatre and you'll get a menu that's particularly good value.

First Course

- Ceviche of scallops with crab and horseradish milk.
- Roast quail with black pudding, peas and girolles.

Main Course

- Hogget, red pepper ketchup and violet artichokes.
- Poached cod with brassicas, squid ink and pine nuts.

Dessert

- Valrhona crémeux with pistachio and tonka bean ice cream.
- Apple mousse with fromage frais, olive oil and lime.

Beast

meats and grills G2

3 Chapel Pl ✉ W1G 0BG
(020) 7495 1816
www.beastrestaurant.co.uk
⊖ Bond Street
Closed Sunday-Wednesday, Saturday lunch and bank holidays – booking essential – (set menu only)

Menu £75

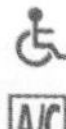

A/C

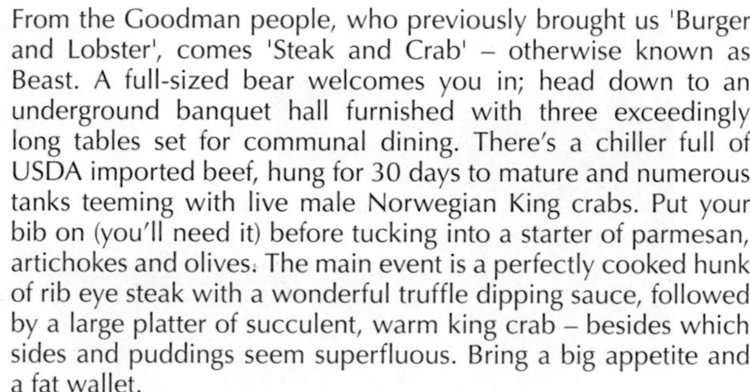

From the Goodman people, who previously brought us 'Burger and Lobster', comes 'Steak and Crab' – otherwise known as Beast. A full-sized bear welcomes you in; head down to an underground banquet hall furnished with three exceedingly long tables set for communal dining. There's a chiller full of USDA imported beef, hung for 30 days to mature and numerous tanks teeming with live male Norwegian King crabs. Put your bib on (you'll need it) before tucking into a starter of parmesan, artichokes and olives. The main event is a perfectly cooked hunk of rib eye steak with a wonderful truffle dipping sauce, followed by a large platter of succulent, warm king crab – besides which sides and puddings seem superfluous. Bring a big appetite and a fat wallet.

Berners Tavern

British modern H2

The London Edition Hotel,
10 Berners St ✉ WIT 3NP
(020) 7908 7979
www.bernerstavern.com
⊖ Tottenham Court Road

Carte £28/61

XX

A/C

There's nothing like a bit of glamour to see off the monochrome days of austerity and Berners Tavern is certainly one of the most beautiful rooms in London – just don't turn up thinking it's a pub. It's like a grand salon and was the original ballroom of the Berners hotel which has been transformed by Ian Shrager in conjunction with Marriott into the London Edition. Every inch of wall is filled with gilt-framed prints, oils and photographs while the vast ceiling, ornate plasterwork and opulent chandeliers keep many pairs of eyes raised towards the heavens. Jason Atherton, whose empire is expanding faster than a trencherman's waistline, has put together an appealing and accessible menu and the cooking is satisfying and assured.

Bonnie Gull

fish and seafood

H2

21a Foley St ✉ W1W 6DS
✆ (020) 7436 0921
www.bonniegull.com
⊖ Goodge Street
Booking essential

Carte £23/56

The very sweet Bonnie Gull calls itself a 'seafood shack' – a reference perhaps to its modest beginnings as a pop-up before it docked permanently here in the West End. It's kitted out in a pretty fishing-village kind of way and the tables are packed into the small room in an appropriately sardine-like manner. There's a decent raw bar to kick things off, offering oysters and cockles, winkles and whelks. The main menu is a mix of traditional favourites and more ambitious dishes, although the kitchen appears to be more adept at the former. Many go for the fish and chips but you can also get a decent Cullen skink and a huge Devon cock crab; it's also worth getting a side order of chunky chips cooked in beef dripping.

Caffé Caldesi

Italian

G2

118 Marylebone Ln. (1st floor) ✉ W1U 2QF
✆ (020) 7487 0754
www.caldesi.com
⊖ Bond Street

Menu £16 (weekday lunch) – Carte £23/54

A/C

This former pub is the hub of the Caldesi family business, which takes in restaurants, cookbooks and cookery schools, and it fits perfectly into the fabric of local Marylebone life. Upstairs is simply but warmly decorated and is enthusiastically run by a young team of Italians – the owners maintain they have staff from all of Italy's 20 regions. The atmosphere is never less than cheery, thanks in no small part to the seasonal menu, which offers up classics from across Italy that have one thing in common – they are generously proportioned and really deliver on flavour; the pasta dishes are particularly satisfying and they do a very good pumpkin soufflé . On the ground floor is a less structured operation with a more accesibly priced menu.

N Chiltern Firehouse

other world kitchens G2

Chiltern Firehouse Hotel,
1 Chiltern St ✉ WIU 7PA
✆ (020) 7073 7676
www.chilternfirehouse.com
⊖ Baker Street

Carte £36/61

What could be more appropriate than the hottest ticket in town being a converted fire station? Everyone from Prime Ministers to pop stars have been papped on their way in to this New York-style brasserie, their smiles revealing the relief they feel in having secured a reservation. A wall of sound hits you as you enter and the room positively bursts with energy, but what makes this celebrity hangout unusual is that the food is good. The kitchen is overseen by Nuno Mendes and he has used all his experience working in North and South America to create a clever menu full of vibrant and flavoursome dishes. If you're more interested in checking out the cooking rather than your fellow diners, ask to sit at the kitchen counter.

Dinings

Japanese F2

22 Harcourt St. ✉ W1H 4HH
✆ (020) 7723 0666
www.dinings.co.uk
⊖ Edgware Road
Closed Christmas and Sunday – booking essential

Carte £16/76

In Tokyo the hanging sign outside would be considered positively flamboyant but in London it's the very definition of discretion, making this sweet little place easy to miss. There are half a dozen seats at the counter on the ground floor and a few tables downstairs in the somewhat claustrophobic basement; but wherever you sit, it's hard not to be charmed by it all. The menu is a very extensive document, supplemented by blackboard specials, and takes many of its influences from the style of Japanese food found at Nobu, the owner's alma mater: accordingly, highlights are the more creative dishes like the 'sashimi four ways'. The temptation is to order plenty to share but beware because the prices can make this an expensive activity.

Donostia

Basque

F2

10 Seymour Pl ✉ W1H 7ND
✆ (020) 3620 1845
www.donostia.co.uk
⊖ Marble Arch
Closed Monday lunch

Menu £36 – Carte £18/40

As London's love affair with tapas continues, many diners are now keen on learning more about Spain's regional specialties. The bright and lively Donostia, which is the Basque name for San Sebastiàn, was opened by two young owners inspired by this coastal municipality. Anyone who has visited the area, known for the quality of its restaurants and its terrific pintxos, will recognise classic Basque dishes like cod with pil-pil sauce, chorizo from the native pig Kintoa and tender, slow-cooked pig's cheeks. Add in a thoughtful wine list along with the traditional drinks of cider and Txakoli and you have a winning recipe. You can book a table but it's worth trying for one of the 10 seats at the marble counter in front of the kitchen.

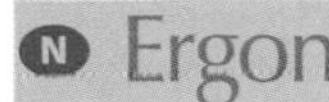

Ergon

Greek

G2

16 Picton Pl ✉ WIU 1BP
✆ (020) 7486 9210
www.ergonproducts.co.uk
⊖ Bond St

Menu £10 (weekday lunch) – Carte £22/37

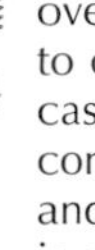

Having opened a number of successful restaurants and delis across Greece, The Ergon group chose London for their first overseas branch, although to get a table Londoners will have to compete with the crowds of homesick émigrés. It's a bright, casual eatery divided into two cosy rooms and offers counter, communal and table dining. The menu is a blend of classic and more modern dishes; sharing is the key and the hard part is deciding what not to order – don't miss the squid, the very moreish 12 hour braised lamb shank or the yoghurt mousse. The wine list is entirely Greek and downstairs is a well-stocked deli of all things Hellenic. Without Zeus they can't change the weather, but Ergon can certainly brighten your day.

Fischer's

Austrian

G1

50 Marylebone High St ✉ W1U 5HN
(020) 7466 5501
www.fischers.co.uk
Baker Street

Carte £19/46

There appears no end to the number of restaurants being opened by Chris Corbin and Jeremy King. Following the success of The Wolseley et al, they took over a site in Marylebone where others have recently struggled and opened a stylish Austrian café and konditorei that summons the spirit of old Vienna. It stays open from 8 until late, with breakfast possibly being the best time to visit – the Viennoiserie are made in-house and are as good as they look. The main menu is a comprehensive document, supplemented by a mittel-European wine list with an impressive choice available by the glass. The schnitzels are first rate – do upgrade to a Holstein – and save room for desserts like the poppy seed parfait.

Galvin Bistrot de Luxe

French

G2

66 Baker St. ✉ W1U 7DJ
(020) 7935 4007
www.galvinrestaurants.com
Baker Street
Closed dinner 24 December, 25-26 December and 1 January

Menu £20/22 – Carte £33/56

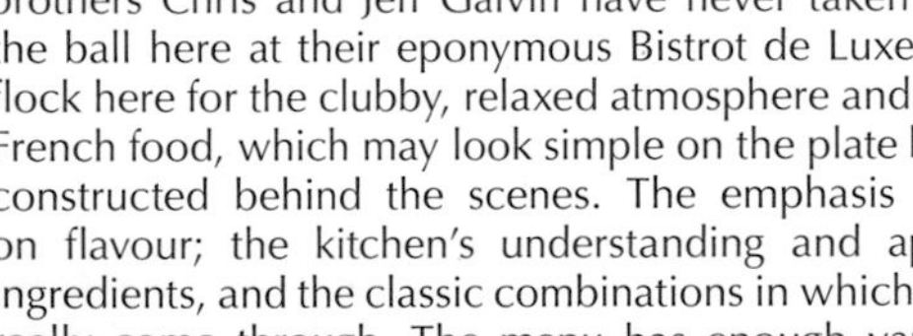

Despite the great success of Galvin La Chapelle in The City, brothers Chris and Jeff Galvin have never taken their eyes off the ball here at their eponymous Bistrot de Luxe. Regulars still flock here for the clubby, relaxed atmosphere and the traditional French food, which may look simple on the plate but is carefully constructed behind the scenes. The emphasis is very much on flavour; the kitchen's understanding and appreciation of ingredients, and the classic combinations in which they are used, really come through. The menu has enough variety to satisfy those happy to indulge but those with one eye on the cost should come for lunch or before 7pm to take advantage of the fixed menu. An elegant basement cocktail bar adds to the comfy feel.

Grazing Goat

British traditional

F2

6 New Quebec St ✉ W1H 7RQ
✆ (020) 7724 7243
www.thegrazinggoat.co.uk
⊖ Marble Arch.
Booking essential at dinner

Carte £31/41

The Portman Estate, owners of some serious real estate in these parts and keen to raise the profile of its investment, encouraged an experienced pub operator more at home in Chelsea and Belgravia to venture a little further north and take over the old Bricklayers Arms. Renamed in homage to a past Lady Portman (who grazed goats in a field where the pub now stands as she was allergic to cows' milk), it is now a smart city facsimile of a country pub. It's first-come-first-served in the bar but you can book in the upstairs dining room. Pub classics are the order of the day, such as pies or Castle of Mey steaks, and Suffolk chicken is cooked on the rotisserie. The eight bedrooms are nicely furnished, with their bathrooms resembling Nordic saunas.

Iberica Marylebone

Spanish

H1

195 Great Portland St ✉ W1W 5PS
✆ (020) 7636 8650
www.ibericalondon.co.uk
⊖ Great Portland Street
Closed 24-26 December, Sunday dinner and bank holidays

Carte £18/46

The original Iberica at the top end of Great Portland Street is a sizeable space spread over two floors and comes divided into assorted areas, so instead of taking the table you're offered, politely ask if you can wander around first – some prefer the intimacy and the sedate pace of upstairs, others the bustle of the ground floor with its bar and deli. Along with an impressive array of Iberico hams, cured meats and cheeses are plenty of tapas style dishes to share. Highlights include the more filling dishes such as glossy black rice with cuttlefish and prawns and a slowly braised beef cheek; if you go for the speciality Spanish omelette, you'll be asked if you'd prefer it medium or well done! Charming young staff are on hand to offer advice.

Latium

Italian H2

21 Berners St. ✉ W1T 3LP
✆ (020) 7323 9123
www.latiumrestaurant.com
⊖ Oxford Circus
Closed 25-26 December, 1 January, lunch Saturday-Sunday and bank holidays

Menu £23 (lunch and early dinner)/36

A/C

The last revamp made it brighter and more contemporary but such is the loyalty of its followers that a simple lick of paint would have been enough. There's now a window into the kitchen for those who like to know where their food comes from, and a chef's table for those who want to watch them at it. Tables by the entrance are given away first but it's worth asking to be seated further in; you'll almost certainly be accommodated as staff are a friendly and considerate bunch. The chef-owner is from Lazio, hence the name, so expect cooking that is free from over-elaboration. Recipes from across Italy also feature; the homemade ravioli is a speciality; and it's always worth ordering the fassone beef. The good value lunch menu changes weekly.

Levant

Lebanese G2

Jason Ct., 76 Wigmore St. ✉ W1U 2SJ
✆ (020) 7224 1111
www.levant.co.uk
⊖ Bond Street
Closed 25-26 December

Menu £10 (lunch)/50 – Carte £23/71

Levant shows how a basement location can be turned into a positive. As you walk down the stairs past the lanterns and the rose petals, with the scent of joss sticks in the air, your expectations start to rise and your pulse begins to quicken – especially if it sounds as though the belly dancing has already started. As with anywhere with a little spice, this is a restaurant best enjoyed in a group: not only because of the principle of safety in numbers but because Lebanese and Middle Eastern food is there to be shared. The best thing to do is order one of the Feast menus as you get a balanced, all-round selection which includes plenty of mezze. And don't bother coming for lunch – it's like arriving at a party the morning after.

Lima ✿

Peruvian

31 Rathbone Pl ✉ W1T 1JH
(020) 3002 2640
www.limalondon.com
Goodge Street
Closed 23 December-3 January and Sunday

I2 

Menu £20 (lunch and early dinner)/48 – Carte £38/52

Lima

Lima is one of those restaurants that just makes you feel good about life – and that's even without the Pisco Sours which, to be honest, will get you in the mood for anything. Peruvian food is the ideal antidote to our recessionary times: it's full of punchy, invigorating flavours and fantastically vivid colours. Virgilio Martinez, who runs the acclaimed 'Central' restaurant in Lima, has created somewhere intimate, informal and fun in which to enjoy his refreshing and exciting cuisine. The menu may be awash with unfamiliar ingredients like tiger's milk and sacha inchi oil but the staff are more than willing to offer help. Most ingredients are from the UK but some are from small suppliers in Peru such as 'huayro potatoes 4000 metres' (a reference to the altitude rather than the depth at which these tubers are grown). Tiradito and its cousin ceviche are popular starters (the former being a slightly punchier version) and there is plenty of originality throughout the menu along with some playfulness, but there's also great skill.

First Course

- Sea bream, tiger's milk, Ají Limo pepper and cancha corn.
- Artichoke Amazonia, radish, red potato and passion fruit.

Main Course

- Beef with wild black quinoa, Cuzco corn and pink molle pepper.
- Hot ceviche of salmon, plantain majado, pepper and ginger.

Dessert

- Dulche de leche ice cream with beetroot emulsion and maca root crust.
- Alfajores with sweet tomato sorbet.

Locanda Locatelli ✿

Italian

G2

8 Seymour St. ✉ W1H 7JZ
✆ (020) 7935 9088
www.locandalocatelli.com
⊖ Marble Arch
Closed 25-26 December and 1 January

Carte £35/63

XXX

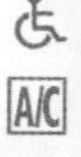

Locanda Locatelli

A few minutes in the company of Giorgio Locatelli, whether face to face or through the medium of television, reveals a man who is passionate about Italian food and it is that very passion that has kept Locanda Locatelli at the top for so long. The restaurant may be into its second decade but it still looks as dapper and as fresh as ever, which is one of the reasons why it has remained in the premier league of London's fashionable addresses since the day it opened. The layout and style of the room were clearly designed with conviviality in mind and this is further helped along by service that is smooth but never intrusive. The other reason for its enduring popularity is the great food and the consistency that the kitchen maintains. The hugely appealing menu covers many of the regions of Italy and provides plenty of choice for everyone including coeliacs, as the terrific pasta dishes available include gluten-free options. Unfussy presentation and superlative ingredients allow natural flavours to shine through.

First Course

- Ox tongue with green sauce.
- Braised cuttlefish with black ink and white polenta.

Main Course

- Sea bass with artichoke purée, tomato crust and vernaccia wine sauce.
- Spring lamb, stewed peppers and aubergine caviar.

Dessert

- Chocolate and Gianduiotto liqueur fondant with milk ice cream.
- Amalfi lemon 'Eton mess'.

Lockhart

other world kitchens F2

22-24 Seymor Pl ✉ W1H 7NL
✆ (020) 3011 5400
www.lockhartlondon.com
⊖ Marble Arch
Closed Sunday dinner and Monday

Carte £22/47

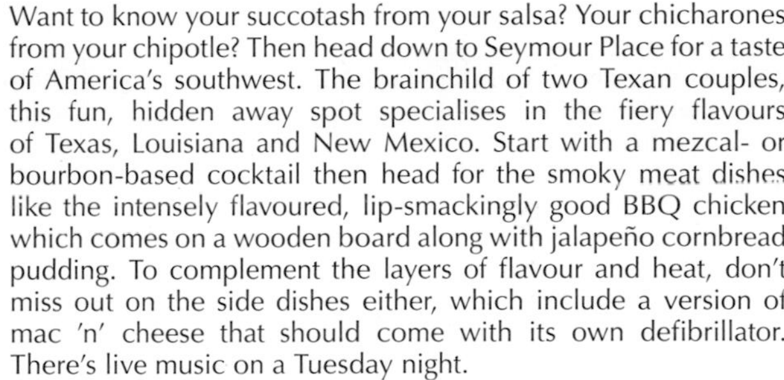

Want to know your succotash from your salsa? Your chicharones from your chipotle? Then head down to Seymour Place for a taste of America's southwest. The brainchild of two Texan couples, this fun, hidden away spot specialises in the fiery flavours of Texas, Louisiana and New Mexico. Start with a mezcal- or bourbon-based cocktail then head for the smoky meat dishes like the intensely flavoured, lip-smackingly good BBQ chicken which comes on a wooden board along with jalapeño cornbread pudding. To complement the layers of flavour and heat, don't miss out on the side dishes either, which include a version of mac 'n' cheese that should come with its own defibrillator. There's live music on a Tuesday night.

Newman Street Tavern

British traditional H2

48 Newman St ✉ W1T 1QQ
✆ (020) 3667 1445
www.newmanstreettavern.co.uk
⊖ Goodge Street.
Closed 24 December, 1 January, Sunday dinner and bank holidays

Menu £20 – Carte £24/42

Provided it isn't preceded by "ye" and "olde", there's something very comforting about the word "tavern". The experienced foursome behind Newman Street Tavern chose the word deliberately as they wanted to create a genuinely warm and welcoming place for customers to come and celebrate British food – and they got it spot on. The menu has been thoughtfully compiled and, with its soused Cornish anchovies, Blackface lamb, game tea, and Banbury cakes, is instantly appealing. There are no shortcuts in the kitchen: they do their own butchery, smoke their own fish, work closely with their suppliers and take issues of sustainability seriously. You can eat in the bustle of the bar or the charming and more sedate first floor dining room.

Orrery

modern

G1

55 Marylebone High St ✉ W1U 5RB
✆ (020) 7616 8000
www.orrery-restaurant.co.uk
⊖ Regent's Park
Booking essential

Menu £25 (weekday lunch)/65

Enthusiastic post-prandial shopping can be a perilously expensive pastime – the danger is doubled here as Orrery is perched temptingly above a Conran shop. These are actually converted stables from the 19C but, such is the elegance and style of the building, you'd never know. What is sure is the long, narrow restaurant looks its best when the daylight floods in; on warm days make time to have a drink on the terrific rooftop terrace. To complement these charming surroundings you'll be offered a bewildering array of menus, all of which feature quite elaborate, modern European cooking. Dishes are strong on presentation and there is the occasional twist but it's usually done with some meaning rather than merely straining for effect.

Picture

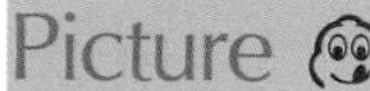

British modern

H2

110 Great Portland St. ✉ W1W 6PQ
✆ (020) 7637 7892
www.picturerestaurant.co.uk
⊖ Oxford Circus
Closed Sunday and bank holidays

Carte £24/28

Two chefs and a manager, who all made their reputations at Arbutus and Wild Honey, set out on their own in 2013 and opened this terrific place in an underdeveloped part of Central London. The look may be a little stark – there's a large counter at the front fashioned out of recycled flooring and tables at the back beneath a skylight – but the service team add enormous warmth to the place and their enthusiasm is palpable. What was saved on the decoration was clearly spent on the shiny new kitchen downstairs, and it's paying dividends for these very skilful chefs. The small plates are vibrant, fresh and colourful; the flavours are assured and the contrasting textures a delight. And at these prices, Picture deserves success.

Portman

modern

F2

51 Upper Berkeley St ✉ W1H 7QW
✆ (020) 7723 8996
www.theportmanmarylebone.com
⊖ Marble Arch.

Menu £32/38 – Carte £20/48

When it went by the name of The Masons Arms this pub was widely known for its gruesome history. It was here that the condemned, on their way to Tyburn Tree gallows, would take their last drink, which purportedly led to the phrase "one for the road". Reincarnated as The Portman, the pub these days boasts a less disreputable clientele who are more attracted by the quality of the cooking. Food is served all day and you can choose to eat in the busy ground floor bar or in the unexpectedly formal upstairs dining room, all thick-pile carpet and starched tablecloths. Fortunately, the style of food remains thoroughly down-to-earth and satisfying and is accompanied by a well-organised wine list and an interesting selection of cocktails.

The Providores

innovative

G2

109 Marylebone High St. ✉ W1U 4RX
✆ (020) 7935 6175
www.theprovidores.co.uk
⊖ Bond Street
Closed 25-26 December

Carte £38/51

'Marylebone Village' offers so many restaurants and cafés that it's becoming a destination in itself. Included in the roll call is this fusion restaurant within a former Edwardian pub. The warmth of the staff and the general buzz hit you immediately in the ground floor Tapa Room, where tables and tapas are shared. Upstairs is a slightly more sedate room but the staff are equally charming. Here all dishes come in starter size to "minimise food envy" and allow for sharing; three courses plus a dessert should suffice. There is no doubting the originality or the quality of the ingredients, but sometimes there's a flavour or two too many on the plate. The wine list champions New Zealand. Bookings are needed upstairs; downstairs, it's first-come-first-served.

Riding House Café

modern

H2

43-51 Great Titchfield St ✉ W1W 7PQ
✆ (020) 7927 0840
www.ridinghousecafe.co.uk
⊖ Oxford Circus
Closed 25-26 December

Menu £11/18 – Carte £17/40

For their third project, the owners of The Garrison and Village East ventured uptown, albeit to an area hitherto untroubled by the presence of decent restaurants. It's less a café, more an all-day Manhattan-style brasserie and cocktail bar, with some charming touches of quirky design. You turn left for the restaurant but it's more fun in the main section where you can't book – either at a counter facing the kitchen or on a large refectory table where you rub shoulders with strangers. It's the same menu throughout, starting with breakfast and followed by a choice of 'small plates' along with more straightforward main courses like steak or burgers. It's easy to over-order so stick with the small plates which have a bit more zing to them.

Roti Chai

Indian

G2

3 Portman Mews South ✉ W1H 6HS
✆ (020) 7408 0101
www.rotichai.com
⊖ Marble Arch
Closed 25 December

Carte £15/31

Making great use of a big concrete shell is this modern Indian restaurant which is split in two: you can book downstairs in the smarter and more formally run dining room, with its own kitchen and menu of updated regional classics, but you're far better off, quite literally, if you get a table on the ground floor. It looks not unlike a school canteen, is buzzy and fun and has a menu modelled on street food and roadside 'dhaba' cafés. It's worth coming just for the 'Railway' lamb curry but also try the gloriously moreish chilli chicken bun with a tamarind glaze. Finish with great kulfi which arrives as a lollipop, and a masala chai packed-full-of spices. Come with a group and order to your heart's content – you can even buy the T-shirt.

Roux at The Landau

French

H2 

Langham Hotel,
1c Portland Pl., Regent St. ✉ W1B 1JA
✆ (020) 7636 1000
www.langhamhotels.com
⊖ Oxford Circus
Closed Saturday lunch and Sunday

Menu £35 – Carte £43/95

It does have its own street entrance but it's best to enter this grand, oval-shaped restaurant from the hotel, as you don't often get the chance to walk through a 'wine corridor'. The hotel brought in the considerable experience of the Roux organisation – which means Albert and Michel Jr – to add vigour and ambition to the operation. Classical, French-influenced cooking is the order of the day but one can detect the emergence of a lighter style of cuisine with the odd twist. The restaurant is also sensible enough to keep its more traditionally minded regulars happy by ensuring that their favourites, like grilled Dover Sole, remain constants. The daily special from the trolley goes down well with the busy lunchtime corporates.

Royal China

Chinese

G2 

24-26 Baker St ✉ W1U 7AB
✆ (020) 7487 4688
www.royalchinagroup.co.uk
⊖ Baker Street

Menu £30/38 – Carte £18/74

It could be just as at home in Hong Kong's Wanchai or Central districts but, as it is, Royal China sits very comfortably in Baker Street. The large kitchen is staffed exclusively by Chinese chefs, including the early rising dim sum chef, who is responsible for the specialities served between midday and 5pm each day. The Cantonese dishes are strong on aroma and colour and, while the restaurant does not sell a great deal of seafood due to a lack of tank space, the lobster dishes remain one of the more popular choices. However, it is the barbecued meats, assorted soups, stir-fries and the choice of over 40 different types of dim sum that draw the large groups and ensure that this branch of the Royal China group remains as bustling as ever.

Royal China Club

Chinese

G2

40-42 Baker St ✉ W1U 7AJ
✆ (020) 7486 3898
www.royalchinagroup.co.uk
⊖ Baker Street
Closed 25-27 December

Carte £23/71

'The Club' is the glittering bauble in the Royal China chain but along with the luxurious feel of the room comes an appealing sense of intimacy and calm. The service helps in this regard, as the staff are personable, offer sound advice and seem able to anticipate their customers' needs. At first glance the menu appears similar to the other branches but it soon becomes apparent that the ingredients here are from the luxurious end of the spectrum, especially when it comes to seafood and shellfish – just check out the large tanks, holding everything from eels and lobsters to sea bass and crabs. The best time to come is for lunch and their very good dim sum. At dinner, look out for the Cantonese dishes and the Chef's seasonal specials.

sixtyone

British modern

G2

61 Upper Berkeley St ✉ W1H 7PP
✆ (020) 7958 3222
www.sixtyonerestaurant.co.uk
⊖ Marble Arch
Closed Sunday dinner

Menu £15 (weekday lunch) – Carte £26/42

A joint venture between chef Arnaud Stevens and Searcy's and occupying space leased from the Montcalm hotel, sixtyone is a modern, smoothly run operation in a useful central location. The crisply furnished room, with its mirrored columns and eye-catching ceiling display of hanging copper tubes, comes with a certain style and a degree of elegance. The modern menu is largely European and clearly much thought went into its construction; it also gives the impression it was designed to allow the kitchen to show off its full repertoire of techniques and its lightness of touch. This is elaborate and at times quite playful cooking, although the best dishes often turn out to be the simplest ones, like the rabbit bolognaise.

Texture ✿

innovative G2

34 Portman St ✉ W1H 7BY
✆ (020) 7224 0028
www.texture-restaurant.co.uk
⊖ Marble Arch
Closed 5-18 August, 1 week Easter, Christmas, New Year, Sunday and Monday

Menu £25/107 – Carte £53/79

Texture

Chef-owner Agnar Sverrisson and his business partner Xavier Rousset, who trained as a sommelier, have steadily gone about creating an exceedingly good restaurant. The Champagne Bar at the front has become a destination in itself and is separated from the restaurant by a large cabinet so you never feel too detached from it. The high ceilings add a little grandeur and the service is very pleasant, with staff all ready with a smile. Agnar's cooking is a little less showy than when Texture opened in 2007 and is all the better for that; you feel he's now cooking the food he wants to cook rather than the food he thought he should be cooking. Iceland is his country of birth so it is no surprise to find lamb, cod (whose crisp skin is served with drinks), langoustine and skyr, the dairy product that nourished the Vikings. There's considerable technical skill and depth to the cooking but dishes still appear light and refreshing and, since the use of cream and butter is largely restricted to the desserts, you even feel they're doing you good.

First Course

- Chargrilled pigeon, sweetcorn, bacon popcorn and red wine essence.
- Norwegian king crab, new season garlic and Jersey Royals.

Main Course

- Salted cod, smoked quinoa, sorrel and cauliflower.
- Pyrénées lamb, best end and shoulder with lamb broth.

Dessert

- Skyr with Gariguette strawberries and ice cream.
- Valrhona chocolate, muscatel grapes and anise ice cream.

Trishna ✿

Indian

G2

15-17 Blandford St. ✉ W1U 3DG
(020) 7935 5624
www.trishnalondon.com
⊖ Baker Street
Closed 24-28 December and 1-4 January

Menu £19 (lunch)/60 – Carte £22/49

Trishna

They may have opened Gymkhana but they haven't forgotten about Trishna: its recent makeover resulting in an elegant, understated style. The coast of southwest India provides many of the influences and the menu is full of appealing dishes, ranging from the playful – try their own mini version of 'fish and chips' as a starter – to the original; the succulent guinea fowl comes with lentils, fennel seed and star anise. However, the undoubted star of the show is a version of the dish made famous by the original Trishna in Mumbai: brown crab, in this case from Dorset, comes with lots of butter and a little kick of wild garlic; it is so wondrously rich no man alone can finish a bowl, and you'll be licking your lips for days afterwards. All the dishes are as fresh tasting as they are colourful, and wine is taken seriously too, with a list impressive in its breadth, well-thought out recommendations next to each dish, and even monthly wine nights. Doing things a little differently also extends to the cocktail list, although the mango chutney martini is perhaps one brave step too far.

First Course

- Baby squid with turmeric, samphire, mango and ginger.
- Yellow lentil and rice dumplings with yoghurt, papad and pickle.

Main Course

- Bream with green chilli and tandoor-smoked tomato kachumber.
- Guinea fowl tikka with masoor lentils, star anise and fennel.

Dessert

- Warm heritage carrot pudding, samosa and masala chai ice cream.
- Alphonso mango cream with raw mango chutney.

28°-50° Marylebone

modern G2

15-17 Marylebone Ln. ✉ W1U 2NE
✆ (020) 7486 7922
www.2850.co.uk
⊖ Bond Street
Closed 25-26 and 31 December, 1 January and Sunday

Menu £16 (weekday lunch) – Carte £22/53

If only wine bars had looked like this in the '80s. The second 28°-50° from the people behind Texture restaurant follows the successful formula adopted in their first branch in The City. That means a well-priced wine list where everything is offered in sizes ranging from a mouthful or a glass to a carafe or a bottle, and a supplementary "Collectors' List" with an impressive roll-call of largely Old World classics. On the food-front, grilled meats from their coal burning oven are the highlight of the menu, while salads, soups and starters all come in a choice of size. You can also simply pop in for a plate of charcuterie, salmon or cheese to share with your wine. Service is as bright as the room which is dominated by the central bar counter.

Vinoteca

modern F2

15 Seymour Pl. ✉ W1H 5BD
✆ (020) 7724 7288
www.vinoteca.co.uk
⊖ Marble Arch
Closed Christmas, bank holidays and Sunday dinner – booking advisable

Carte £25/40

They've transferred the winning formula from their Clerkenwell original, so expect a great selection of wines, gutsy and wholesome cooking, young and enthusiastic staff and almost certainly a wait for a table. One side of the room is given over to shelves of wine; not only is the selection immeasurably appealing but the staff display both a knowledge and, more importantly, enormous enthusiasm when giving advice. The daily changing menu takes its cue from the sunnier parts of Europe and includes thoughtfully compiled salads and good charcuterie. There are also some firmly British dishes too, like mutton and oyster pie, and each one comes with its own wine pairing recommendation. It's great fun, basic in comfort and always very busy.

The Wallace

French G2

Hertford House, Manchester Sq ✉ W1U 3BN
(020) 7563 9505
www.peytonandbyrne.co.uk/the-wallace-restaurant/index.html
⊖ Bond Street
Closed 24-26 December – (lunch only and dinner Friday-Saturday)

Menu £23/26 – Carte £31/44

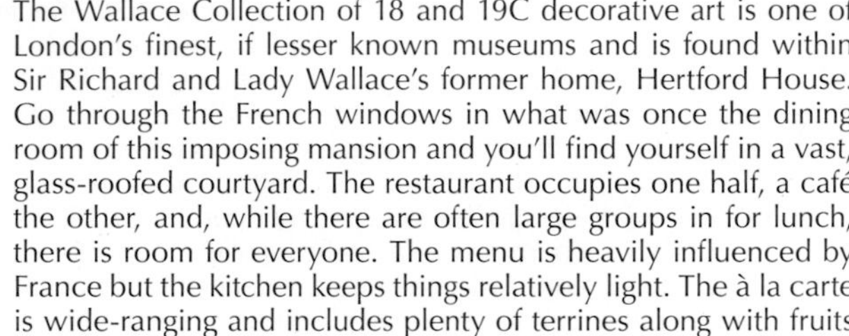

The Wallace Collection of 18 and 19C decorative art is one of London's finest, if lesser known museums and is found within Sir Richard and Lady Wallace's former home, Hertford House. Go through the French windows in what was once the dining room of this imposing mansion and you'll find yourself in a vast, glass-roofed courtyard. The restaurant occupies one half, a café the other, and, while there are often large groups in for lunch, there is room for everyone. The menu is heavily influenced by France but the kitchen keeps things relatively light. The à la carte is wide-ranging and includes plenty of terrines along with fruits de mer, but the menu du jour represents much better value and usually offers a nicely balanced selection of dishes.

Winter Garden

Mediterranean F1

The Landmark London Hotel,
222 Marylebone Rd ✉ NW1 6JQ
(020) 7631 8000
www.landmarklondon.co.uk
⊖ Edgware Road

Menu £30/40 – Carte £36/50

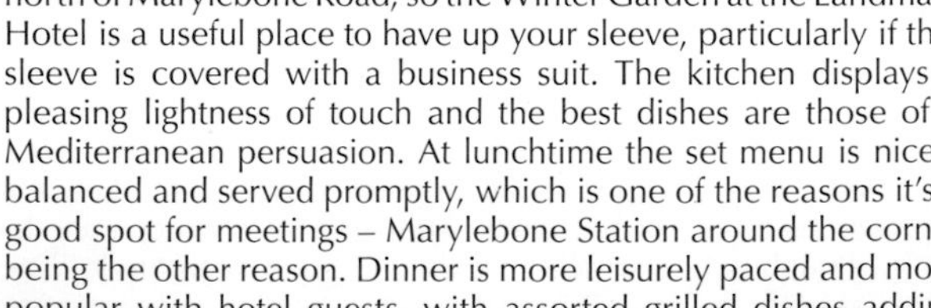

Dining options tend to get more limited once you find yourself north of Marylebone Road, so the Winter Garden at the Landmark Hotel is a useful place to have up your sleeve, particularly if that sleeve is covered with a business suit. The kitchen displays a pleasing lightness of touch and the best dishes are those of a Mediterranean persuasion. At lunchtime the set menu is nicely balanced and served promptly, which is one of the reasons it's a good spot for meetings – Marylebone Station around the corner being the other reason. Dinner is more leisurely paced and more popular with hotel guests, with assorted grilled dishes adding to the choice. A pianist gallantly tries to help fill the enormous atrium in which the restaurant sits.

Yalla Yalla

Lebanese H2

12 Winsley St. ✉ W1W 8HQ
✆ (020) 7637 4748
www.yalla-yalla.co.uk
⊖ Oxford Circus
Closed 25-26 December, 1 January and Sunday

Carte £19/29

If you get here to find there's a queue (they don't take bookings), just remember that the name means "Hurry up!" so you shouldn't have to wait for long. And come with a few friends because Beirut street food is designed for sharing and you'll want to try as much as you can. The place is loud, the tables are packed in and the lighting a little dull so just ask for recommendations rather than spending time staring at the menu – that's if you can hear what they're saying above the noise. Start with a rich hommos or baba ghannouj then order homemade soujoc (spicy sausages) or sawda djej (chicken livers) and you can't go wrong with any of the succulent lamb dishes. There are cocktails, juices, and wines from the Bekaa valley.

Zayna

Indian 

25 New Quebec St. ✉ W1H 7SF
✆ (020) 7723 2229
www.zaynarestaurant.co.uk
⊖ Marble Arch

Carte £20/37 

Generic menus no longer cut the mustard – these days we all want more regional specialities and greater authenticity. The owner of this sweet and enthusiastically run little restaurant spent his formative years in Kashmir and Punjab and so his kitchen's focus is on the cuisine of Pakistan and northerly parts of India. Start with creamy Papdi Chanaa Chaat and then choose your preferred cooking method: from the pan comes Ishtu, a succulent lamb dish; from the tawa you can choose Murgh Chatkhara, slices of chicken with ginger and chilli; and from the grill try Lahori Pusli, marinated lamb chops. Only halal meat and free-range chicken are used but vegetarians will also find much to savour. End with tooth-achingly sweet Gulab Jamun.

Zoilo

Argentinian

G2 

9 Duke St. ✉ W1U 3EG
✆ (020) 7486 9699
www.zoilo.co.uk
⊖ Bond Street

Menu £10 (weekdays) – Carte £14/46

London's current crush on all things South American shows no sign of waning. Zoilo comes from the same people behind Casa Malevo but whereas that restaurant focuses on meat and Malbec this venture introduces us to Argentina's regional specialities. It's also all about sharing so plonk yourself down at the counter and order away. Highlights include a wonderfully chewy melted provoleta cheese, a great beetroot salad with goat's curd and garrapiñada (candied nuts with a soft centre: a Buenos Aires street snack) and an expert mackerel escabeche. The beef is naturally good but why not try grilled sweetbreads with lemon instead? The ground floor is livelier but if you want to know how it's all done then sit downstairs in front of the kitchen.

The sun is out – let's eat alfresco! Look for 🍽.

SuperStock/Age Fotostock

Bloomsbury · Hatton Garden · Holborn

A real sense of history pervades this central chunk of London. From the great collection of antiquities in the British Museum to the barristers who swarm around the Royal Courts of Justice and Lincoln's Inn; from the haunts of Charles Dickens to the oldest Catholic church in Britain, the streets here are dotted with rich reminders of the past. Hatton Garden's fame as the city's diamond and jewellery centre goes back to Elizabethan times while, of a more recent vintage, Bloomsbury was home to the notorious Group (or Set) who, championed by Virginia Woolf, took on the world of art and literature in the 1920s.

A full-on encounter with **Holborn** is, initially, a shock to the system. Coming up from the tube, you'll find this is where main traffic arteries collide and a rugby scrum regularly ensues. Fear not, though; the relative calm of London's largest square, part-flanked by two quirky and intriguing museums, is just round the corner. The square is **Lincoln's Inn Fields,** which boasts a canopy of characterful oak trees and a set of tennis courts. On its north side is **Sir John Soane's Museum,** a gloriously eccentric place with twenty thousand exhibits where the walls open out like cabinets to reveal paintings by Turner and Canaletto. On its south side, the Hunterian Museum, refitted a few years ago, is a fascinating repository of medical bits and pieces. Visitors with a Damien Hirst take on life will revel in the likes of animal digestive systems in formaldehyde, or perhaps the sight of half of mathematician Charles Babbage's brain. Others not so fascinated by the gory might flee to the haunting silence of **St Etheldreda's church** in Ely Place, the only surviving example of thirteenth-century Gothic architecture in London. It survived the Great Fire of 1666, and Latin is still the language of choice.

Contemplation of a different kind takes centre stage in the adjacent **Hatton Garden.** This involves eager-eyed couples gazing at the glittering displays of rings and jewellery that have been lighting up the shop fronts here for many generations, ever since the leafy lane and its smart garden environs took the fancy of Sir Christopher Hatton, a favourite of Elizabeth I. After gawping at the baubles, there's liquid refreshment on hand at one of London's most atmospheric old pubs, the tiny Ye Old Mitre hidden down a narrow passageway. The preserved trunk of a cherry tree stands in the front bar, and, by all accounts, Elizabeth I danced the maypole round it (a legend that always seems more believable after the second pint).

Bloomsbury has intellectual connotations, and not just because of the writers and artists who frequented its townhouses in the twenties. This is where the University of London has its headquarters, and it's also home to the **British Museum,** the vast treasure

C. Eymenier / MICHELIN

trove of international artefacts that attracts visitors in even vaster numbers. As if the exhibits themselves weren't lure enough, there's also the fantastic glass-roofed Great Court, opened to much fanfare at the start of the Millennium, which lays claim to being the largest covered public square in Europe. To the north of here by the Euston Road is the **British Library,** a rather stark red brick building that holds over 150 million items and is one of the greatest centres of knowledge in the world. Meanwhile, Dickens fans should make for the north east corner of Bloomsbury for the great man's museum in **Doughty Street:** this is one of many London houses in which he lived, but it's the only one still standing. He lived here for three years, and it proved a fruitful base, resulting in Nicholas Nickleby and Oliver Twist. The museum holds manuscripts, letters and Dickens' writing desk. If your appetite for the written word has been truly whetted, then a good tip is to head back west half a mile to immerse yourself in the bookshops of Great Russell Street.

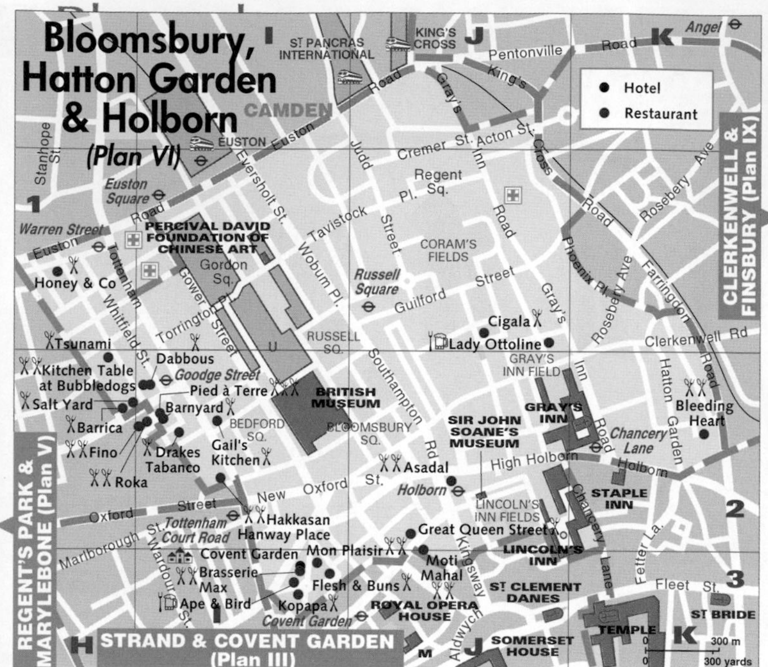
Bloomsbury, Hatton Garden & Holborn (Plan VI)
Hotel
Restaurant
ST PANCRAS INTERNATIONAL
KING'S CROSS
CAMDEN
EUSTON
Euston Square
Warren Street
PERCIVAL DAVID FOUNDATION OF CHINESE ART
Honey & Co
Tsunami
Kitchen Table at Bubbledogs
Salt Yard
Barrica
Fino
Roka
Drakes Tabanco
Dabbous
Goodge Street
Pied à Terre
Barnyard
Gail's Kitchen
BRITISH MUSEUM
RUSSELL SQ.
Russell Square
CORAM'S FIELDS
Cigala
Lady Ottoline
GRAY'S INN FIELD
GRAY'S INN
SIR JOHN SOANE'S MUSEUM
Asadal
Holborn
Chancery Lane
Bleeding Heart
STAPLE INN
LINCOLN'S INN FIELDS
Great Queen Street
LINCOLN'S INN
Tottenham Court Road
Hakkasan
Hanway Place
Covent Garden
Mon Plaisir
Brasserie Max
Ape & Bird
Flesh & Buns
Moti Mahal
Kopapa
ROYAL OPERA HOUSE
ST CLEMENT DANES
SOMERSET HOUSE
TEMPLE
ST BRIDE
CLERKENWELL & FINSBURY (Plan IX)
REGENT'S PARK & MARYLEBONE (Plan V)
STRAND & COVENT GARDEN (Plan III)
300 m
300 yards

Ape & Bird

modern

I3

142 Shaftesbury Ave ✉ WC2H 8HJ
✆ (020) 7836 3119
www.apeandbird.com
⊖ Leicester Square
Closed 25 December and 1 January

Carte £24/34

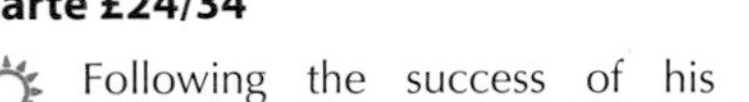

Following the success of his ever-expanding empire of restaurants, Ape & Bird is Russell Norman's first venture into pubs. The style is stripped back and simple, but look closer and you notice the attention to detail: tin tiles shipped from the USA; chandeliers inspired by Balham tube station and a mural featuring famous Soho residents. It's a big place which at first can be a bit bewildering; go into the basement for cocktails, stay in the busy bar for snacks like sausage rolls or Welsh rarebit, or head up to the airy dining room with views over Cambridge Circus. Dishes are British, but their construction owes more to Italian principles: a few, top quality ingredients cooked with care to create plates full of flavour, aroma and appeal.

Asadal

Korean

J2

227 High Holborn ✉ WC1V 7DA
✆ (020) 7430 9006
www.asadal.co.uk
⊖ Holborn
Closed 25-26 December, 1 January and Sunday lunch

Carte £20/30

If it was any nearer Holborn Tube station you'd need an Oyster card to get in. But head down the stairs and you'll soon be oblivious to what's going on at street level, thanks to a comfortable room which is divided up and kitted out with lots of wood. Those unfamiliar with Korean food will find that, by and large, the menu explains itself, since many of the dishes have had their photo taken. One thing to note is that the more there are in your party the better, as sharing is the key. Kimchi provides the perfect starter; there's plenty of seafood but the stars of the show are the hotpots, the delicate dumplings and the barbecues where meats are cooked on the hot-plate on the table. The young staff cope well with the early evening rush.

Barnyard

British traditional I2

18 Charlotte St ✉ W1T 2LZ
✆ (020) 7580 3842
www.barnyard-london.com
⊖ Goodge Street
Closed Sunday dinner – bookings not accepted

Carte £20/25

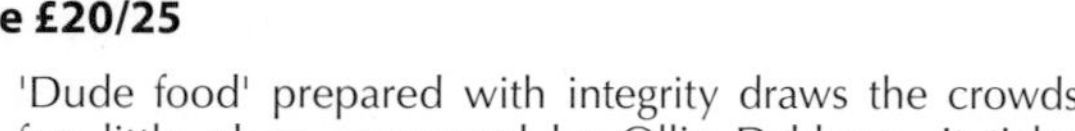

'Dude food' prepared with integrity draws the crowds to this fun little place co-owned by Ollie Dabbous. It ticks all the boxes demanded by your average hipster, from its look which mixes ersatz industrial distress with picket-fence Americana to its appealing menu of dishes divided up by animal. The food arrives all at once on enamel plates, and dishes are full of rustic goodness, whether that's a sausage roll, crispy chicken or simply lard on toast – they may seem simple but there's a care and precision to them one rarely sees in similarly styled restaurants. You won't exactly lose weight eating here but you will certainly leave feeling better about life. Just be prepared to queue, as it seats fewer than 50.

Barrica

Spanish H2

62 Goodge St ✉ W1T 4NE
✆ (020) 7436 9448
www.barrica.co.uk
⊖ Goodge Street
Closed 25-26 December, 1 January, Sunday and bank holidays – booking essential

Menu £12/26

Staff at this lively little tapas bar all appear to be Spanish so perhaps it's national pride that makes them run it with a passion lacking in many of their competitors. They make a concerted effort to look after their diners, of whom there are always many, so it's worth booking ahead unless you're okay squeezing onto a seat at the counter. When it comes to the food, authenticity is high on the agenda and it's hard to avoid temptation. Lamb chop with romesco sauce, and smoked duck breast with cherry butter, are a couple of standouts and it's worth ordering another savoury dish or one of their Spanish cheeses in place of dessert. They also offer an interesting selection of around 20 sherries and assorted Spanish wines – try one from the blackboard.

Bleeding Heart

French K2

Bleeding Heart Yard (off Greville St.) ✉ EC1N 8SJ
✆ (020) 7242 2056
www.bleedingheart.co.uk
⊖ Farringdon
Closed 24 December-1 January, Saturday, Sunday and bank holidays – booking essential

Menu £25 (lunch and early dinner) s – Carte £27/56 s

Dickensian tales of murder and intrigue still haunt the wonderfully evocative Bleeding Heart Yard, while contented bankers and modern day industrialists sit in its candlelit and atmospheric restaurant, feasting on classic French cuisine. Weekly changing set menus sit alongside the fairly pricey à la carte, which comes written in French and English, and well-drilled French staff exhibit a fair degree of personality. The kitchen can sometimes overcomplicate dishes so you're better off going for the more traditional choices with their relative simplicity. The wine list is a splendid affair and the owners have their own estate in New Zealand. If you want something altogether less formal then cross the yard for the bistro.

Brasserie Max

meats and grills I3

Covent Garden Hotel,
10 Monmouth St ✉ WC2H 9HB
✆ (020) 7806 1007
www.firmdalehotels.com
⊖ Covent Garden
Booking essential

Menu £24 (lunch and early dinner) – Carte £34/65

It may do a brisk trade in afternoon tea but this is much more than your usual hotel restaurant. For a start, the room is refreshingly free from chintz and has its own identity. The menu is appealingly accessible and will always have something on it that fits the bill, whether you're grabbing a bite before the theatre or making an evening of it. There's also an interesting cocktail list, as one end of the room is dominated by a large zinc-topped bar. Expect Asian and Mediterranean influences, carefully compiled salads and plenty of grilled meats; they also do a 'dish of the day' which could be fish pie or surf 'n' turf, but be aware of getting too enthusiastic about side dishes otherwise your final bill will be bigger than expected.

Cigala

Spanish J1

54 Lamb's Conduit St. ✉ WC1N 3LW
(020) 7405 1717
www.cigala.co.uk
⊖ Russell Square
Closed 25-26 December, 1 January, Easter Sunday and Easter Monday – booking essential

Menu £18 (weekday lunch) – Carte £23/51

Cigala may be more restaurant than bar but it was serving authentic Spanish food when all those fashionable little tapas bars were still in short pantelones. The reason for its longevity is that it gives the punters exactly what they want: an extensive menu that regularly changes but also recognises that some dishes must remain perennials, and a lively and convivial atmosphere. The owner personally seeks out producers in Spain and this care is particularly evident in the dried hams, which are a must. Chicken livers in sherry and salt cod fritters are always winners and it's well worth waiting the 30 minutes for a paella. Staff are approachable and it's wise to heed their counsel on what and how much to order.

Ⓝ Drakes Tabanco

Spanish I2

3 Windmill St ✉ W1T 2HY
(020) 7637 9388
www.drakestabanco.com
⊖ Goodge Street
Closed Sunday and bank holidays

Carte £20/34

Taking advantage of London's newfound fondness for fino is this simple tabanco, courtesy of the people behind nearby Barrica and Copita and named after Sir Francis in honour of the booty of butts he returned home with. Typical of Jerez, these taverns' unique feature is that they serve sherry straight from the barrel using a venencia; order a glass of Rare Old India or Oloroso and you'll wonder why you haven't been drinking sherry for years. The small, Andalusian-inspired tapas menu uses imported produce from Spain alongside British ingredients. Truffled goat's cheese and the pork and oxtail meatballs are musts, as is the board of charcuterie. They even do a tasting menu with a different sherry matched to each course.

Dabbous ✿

modern

I2

39 Whitfield St ✉ W1T 2SF
(020) 7323 1544
www.dabbous.co.uk
⊖ Goodge Street
Closed 3 weeks Christmas-New Year, 2 weeks August, 1 week Easter, Sunday and Monday – booking essential

Menu £28/59

Dabbous

The look is stark, dark and ersatz-industrial and, as owner chef Ollie Dabbous admits, "the only luxurious thing in this place is the food". So once you've managed to get a table, simply follow the majority of customers by going for the Tasting menu and you'll be rewarded with seven courses of thrilling culinary magic. Visually stunning, the dishes deliver clean, fresh and distinctive flavours; some creations come with clever modern twists; others owe more to classical combinations. However, this is not a kitchen that relies on trickery or technique to create an effect – there is a sublime purity to the cooking here, along with a certain restraint too – and that's what makes the food so easy to eat. There may be a hard edge to the room but it is not without some charm. The staff help enormously in this regard, providing service that is evenly paced, very knowledgeable and refreshingly devoid of arrogance or conceit. Dabbous remains one of the hottest tickets in town – and it's very easy to see why.

First Course

- Speckled endive with gingerbread, mint and bergamot.
- Avocado, basil and almonds in a chilled osmanthus broth.

Main Course

- Cod wrapped in wood shavings, honey and turnip dressing.
- Chicken with fenugreek, lettuce and clove.

Dessert

- Ripe peach in its own juice.
- Burrata with wild strawberries and fennel pollen.

Fino

Spanish I2

33 Charlotte St (entrance on Rathbone St.) ✉ W1T 1RR
✆ (020) 7813 8010
www.finorestaurant.com
⊖ Goodge Street
Closed Saturday lunch, Sunday and bank holidays

Menu £18 (weekday lunch) – Carte £15/29

Fino's basement location and discreet entrance engender in its clientele that warm, satisfyingly smug feeling of being 'in the know'. While it is more formally structured than most restaurants that serve tapas, the atmosphere is always lively and the crowd, particularly at night, is pleasingly mixed. Start with a sherry and some croquetas while you scour the sensibly laid out menu. The young staff all know what's on offer and the more effort you put in with them the more they'll be inclined to offer guidance. Then order a bottle of Albariño and dig in; seafood is a delight, especially the squid from the plancha. Dishes are easy to share and, as in life, the more people in your party, the greater will be your enjoyment.

Ⓝ Flesh & Buns

Asian I3

41 Earlham St ✉ WC2H 9LX
✆ (020) 7632 9500
www.fleshandbuns.com
⊖ Leicester Square
Closed 24-25 December and 1 January – booking advisable

Menu £20 (lunch and early dinner) – Carte £21/42

Hot on the heels of the successful ramen shop Bone Daddies comes another hip joint where Japanese and Asian influences are refracted through the prism of New York. This time it's a loud, fun, subterranean spot next to the Donmar, occupying what was previously a micro-brewery. You can expect sashimi, rolls, teriyaki and tempura but star billing, as the slightly unappetising name of the place suggests, quite rightly goes to the hirata bun – the soft little Taiwanese-style steamed pillows of delight that sandwich your choice of meat or fish filling and come with a dipping sauce. Add to the equation communal tables, cocktails, beers and an easy to navigate wine and sake list and you have all the makings of a fun night out with friends.

Gail's Kitchen

Mediterranean

I2 

11-13 Bayley St ✉ WC1B 3HD
✆ (020) 7323 9694
www.gailskitchen.co.uk
⊖ Goodge Street
Closed 25 December

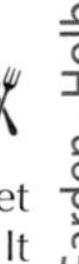

Carte £14/21

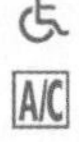

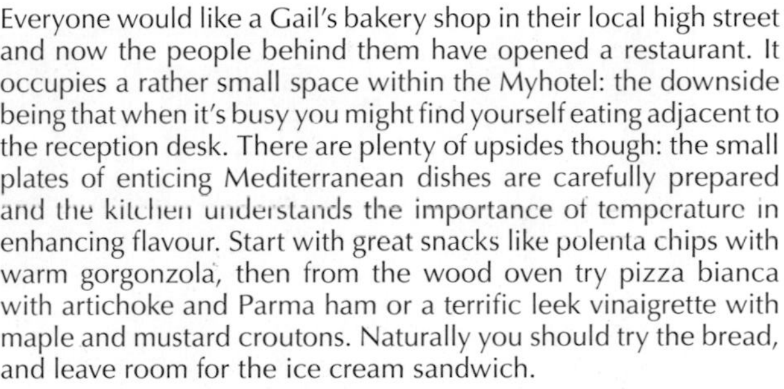

Everyone would like a Gail's bakery shop in their local high street and now the people behind them have opened a restaurant. It occupies a rather small space within the Myhotel: the downside being that when it's busy you might find yourself eating adjacent to the reception desk. There are plenty of upsides though: the small plates of enticing Mediterranean dishes are carefully prepared and the kitchen understands the importance of temperature in enhancing flavour. Start with great snacks like polenta chips with warm gorgonzola, then from the wood oven try pizza bianca with artichoke and Parma ham or a terrific leek vinaigrette with maple and mustard croutons. Naturally you should try the bread, and leave room for the ice cream sandwich.

Great Queen Street 

British modern

J2

32 Great Queen St ✉ WC2B 5AA
✆ (020) 7242 0622
www.greatqueenstreetrestaurant.co.uk
⊖ Holborn
Closed Christmas-New Year, Sunday dinner and bank holidays – booking essential

Menu £15 (weekday lunch) – Carte £19/37

This is one of those restaurants that feels the perfect choice on a cold winter's night, thanks to its bustling atmosphere and its heartwarming food. Its popularity does mean that service can sometimes need a prompt but there is no doubting the staff's enthusiasm for the food they serve. The menu descriptions are unapologetically concise but then dishes come equally unembellished. There's little difference between what constitutes a starter or main course and there's always a daily special or two. Highlights are the shared dishes such as the roast chicken crown or the shoulder of lamb, but offal is also done very well. Wine is served in tumblers and the list is thoughtfully put together.

Hakkasan Hanway Place ✿

Chinese

I2

8 Hanway Pl. ✉ W1T 1HD
(020) 7927 7000
www.hakkasan.com
⊖ Tottenham Court Road
Closed 24-25 December

Menu £35/118 – Carte £34/91

Hakkasan

Over recent years Hakkasans have opened in many cities around the world but it all started here in 2001 in this unexceptional alleyway just off Tottenham Court Road. Thanks to its sensual looks, air of exclusivity and glamorous atmosphere – characteristics now synonymous with the brand – the original Hakkasan wowed London back then and, judging by the crowds, continues to do so today. The restaurant has always managed the art of coping equally well with all types of customers, from large parties out to celebrate to couples on a date and the well-organised and helpful staff are a fundamental part of that success. Lunchtime dim sum here is a memorable and more relaxed experience; at dinner try the Signature menus which represent better value than the à la carte. Thanks to the brigade of about twenty chefs in the kitchen, the Cantonese specialities are prepared with care and consistency; dishes are exquisitely presented and while there are moments of inventiveness they never come at the expense of flavour.

First Course

- Dim sum platter.
- Turbot soup with wild fungus and goji berry.

Main Course

- Roasted silver cod with champagne and honey.
- Sweet and sour Duke of Berkshire pork.

Dessert

- Jivara bomb.
- Tarte Tatin, blackberries, almond and vanilla.

Honey & Co

other world kitchens H1

25a Warren St ✉ W1T 5LZ
✆ (020) 7388 6175
www.honeyandco.co.uk
⊖ Warren Street
Closed last week August, 25-26 December and Sunday – booking essential

Menu £16/30 – Carte £22/29

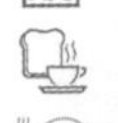

When Itamar and Sarit decided to open their own place they did so knowing that they didn't have to worry too much about the kitchen – they'd both been head chefs at Ottolenghi restaurants. The philosophy at their sweet little café is to offer the same sort of food and hospitality you'd get if you were guests in their home. The friendly girls certainly provide charming, chatty and tactile service and the cooking is full of freshness and colour. The influences stretch beyond Israel to the wider Middle East; start by sharing some mezze, follow with roasted baby chicken or delicious lamb shawarma. Breads are great, cakes are hard to resist and the prices are commendable – which is another reason why the place is packed most evenings.

Kopapa

Asian I3

32-34 Monmouth St ✉ WC2H 9HA
✆ (020) 7240 6076
www.kopapa.co.uk
⊖ Covent Garden
Closed 25-26 December – booking advisable

Menu £22 (dinner) – Carte £30/42

Stroll past in the early evening and it looks like another tourist trap but Peter Gordon's cleverly disguised restaurant is a more than useful spot for those in search of some West End refuelling. There are broadly two parts to the menu: the left side offers fairly predictable fare like Caesar salad, burgers and charcuterie boards; but head to the right and you'll find small or large plates of Peter Gordon's signature style of cooking: dishes that use plenty of ingredients and fuse all sorts of influences from around the world. These could be Asian, Mediterranean or Middle Eastern and, while the combinations may appear ambitious, they're well-judged and so stimulating so that you almost forget about the disorganised service.

Kitchen Table at Bubbledogs ✿

modern **H2**

70 Charlotte St ✉ W1T 4QG
✆ (020) 7637 7770
www.kitchentablelondon.co.uk
⊖ Goodge Street
Closed 1-14 January, 18-25 April, 19 August-2 September, 23-27 December, Sunday and Monday – booking essential – (dinner only) – (set menu only)

Menu £78

Michelin

Fight your way past the throngs enjoying the curious combination of hot dogs with champagne and head for the curtain – for behind it is where you'll find a horseshoe counter and a look of expectation on the faces of your fellow diners. This is Kitchen Table where chef-owner James Knappett and his small team prepare a no-choice menu of around 12 dishes. Each one is described on the blackboard in a single noun so you have to put your trust in the kitchen. The produce is some of the best you can find and while the cooking has a classical base, the small dishes come with a clever creative edge; they aren't made up of lots of ingredients – instead it is the combinations of flavours and textures that give them depth. With seating for just 19, the atmosphere is very convivial, especially if you're a fully paid up member of the foodie community. The chefs interact with their customers over the counter and offer more comprehensive explanations of each dish; they are helped out by James' wife Sandia who is charm personified.

First Course

- Scallop with ginger mayonnaise and dried coral.
- Crispy chicken skin with chive mascarpone and bacon jam.

Main Course

- Lamb sweetbreads, peas and girolles.
- Onglet with wild garlic cream and Ticklemore cheese.

Dessert

- Strawberry salad, coconut jelly and tips of the Christmas tree.
- Ricotta with black cherries and pepper.

Lady Ottoline

British traditional J1

11a Northington St ✉ WC1N 2JF
✆ (020) 7831 0008
www.theladyottoline.com
⊖ Chancery Lane.
Closed 24 December-2 January and bank holidays

Menu £28 (lunch and early dinner) – Carte £24/35 

Apart from some repair work on the cornicing and the tiled floor, this substantial red-brick Victorian pub is largely unchanged from when it was called The Kings Arms. The menus in the packed and slightly chaotic ground floor bar and the Queen Anne style upstairs dining room are not hugely different: cold winter nights see dishes like braised pig cheeks with lentils or venison haunch with squash purée. The kitchen takes more care with its cooking than one expects and dishes deliver on flavour. There's also a large selection of wine by the glass. This is the second pub for this husband and wife team and a sister to the Princess of Shoreditch. It is named after the society hostess who was a friend to the Bloomsbury set.

Mon Plaisir

French I3

19-21 Monmouth St. ✉ WC2H 9DD
✆ (020) 7836 7243
www.monplaisir.co.uk
⊖ Covent Garden
Closed Christmas-New Year, Sunday and bank holidays

Menu £13/25 – Carte £28/42 

Mon Plaisir couldn't be more French if it wore a beret and whistled La Marseillaise; but because this institution has been around since the 1940s, and under the current ownership since the '70s, it can also give one an unexpected but palpable sense of old London. It's divided into four rooms, all of which have slightly different personalities but share the Gallic theme; even the bar was reportedly salvaged from a Lyonnais brothel. Service may lack some of the exuberance of the past but the serving team do get the job done. All the classics are on offer, from snails to terrines, duck to coq; the set menu represents good value while the à la carte can be a little pricey.

Moti Mahal

Indian

J2

45 Great Queen St. ✉ WC2B 5AA
✆ (020) 7240 9329
www.motimahal-uk.com
⊖ Holborn
Closed 25-28 December, Saturday lunch, Sunday and bank holidays

Menu £16/23 – Carte £27/43

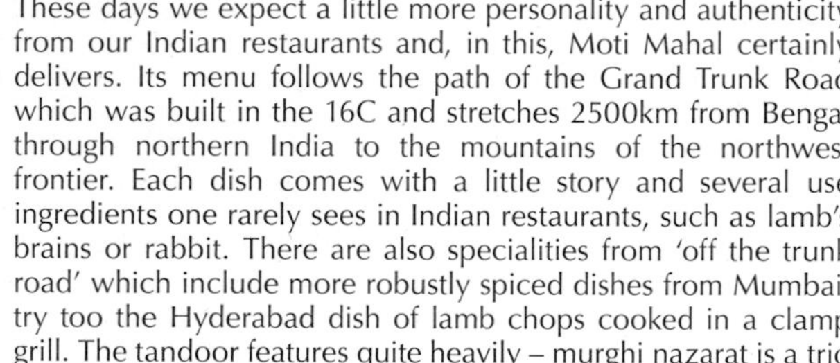

These days we expect a little more personality and authenticity from our Indian restaurants and, in this, Moti Mahal certainly delivers. Its menu follows the path of the Grand Trunk Road which was built in the 16C and stretches 2500km from Bengal through northern India to the mountains of the northwest frontier. Each dish comes with a little story and several use ingredients one rarely sees in Indian restaurants, such as lamb's brains or rabbit. There are also specialities from 'off the trunk road' which include more robustly spiced dishes from Mumbai; try too the Hyderabad dish of lamb chops cooked in a clamp grill. The tandoor features quite heavily – murghi nazarat is a trio of chicken tikka dishes served in copper pots.

Roka

Japanese

I2

37 Charlotte St ✉ W1T 1RR
✆ (020) 7580 6464
www.rokarestaurant.com
⊖ Goodge Street
Closed 25 December

Carte £18/89

Roka has one of those appealingly perceptible pulses that only really busy, well-run restaurants enjoy. It attracts a handsome crowd although they don't just come to glory in their mutual attractiveness but to share food that's original, easy to eat and just as pretty as they are. The kitchen takes the flavours, delicacy and strong presentation standards of Japanese food and adds its own contemporary touches. The menu can appear bewildering but just skip the set menus and order an assortment from the various headings; ensure you have one of the specialities from the on-view Robata grill. Sometimes too many dishes can arrive at once but the serving team are a friendly and capable bunch and they'll ease up on the delivery if you ask.

Pied à Terre ✿

innovative

I2 

34 Charlotte St ✉ W1T 2NH
✆ (020) 7636 1178
www.pied-a-terre.co.uk
⊖ Goodge Street
Closed last week December-5 January, Saturday lunch, Sunday and bank holidays – booking essential

Menu £28/65

A/C

Pied a Terre

Hard to believe that when David Moore opened Pied à Terre back in 1991 some questioned whether a quality restaurant could ever survive on Charlotte Street – these days this busy street is one of the most sought-after spots in town, with restaurateurs virtually queuing up to get their hands on a lease. Marcus Eaves is the fourth chef to have led the kitchen since the restaurant's inception and his cooking is confident and bold, both in flavour and presentation. His menus are a good read – nicely balanced and with plenty of choice on offer – and while his dishes are quite elaborate in their make-up, they never feel overcrowded and the contrasts in textures make them very easy to eat. Wine remains a very strong element here: the two weighty tomes list over 700 bins, with considerable depth and quality across all major regions. Each year a different artist is commissioned to decorate the room which, despite its relatively small size, is cleverly designed so that no single table can dominate proceedings.

First Course

- Roast breast, crispy leg and Kiev of quail, Douglas Fir purée and hazelnut vinaigrette.
- Salad of spring vegetables with smoked duck breast.

Main Course

- Monkfish with blackened spices, onion squash and mussels.
- Slow-cooked daube of beef with asparagus and pain d'épices crumb.

Dessert

- Rhubarb and cardamom millefeuille, rhubarb sorbet.
- Valrhona chocolate mousse with honeycomb.

Salt Yard

Mediterranean H2

54 Goodge St. ✉ W1T 4NA
(020) 7637 0657
www.saltyard.co.uk
Goodge Street
Closed 25-26 and dinner 24 and 31 December, 1 January and Sunday

Carte £13/32

The ground floor is the more boisterous and you'll feel like you're in the middle of a fun party; downstairs is better if you don't know your dining companion that well, although it too is full of life. This is all about tapas, although not just about Spanish tapas. One side of the menu has bar snacks, charcuterie and cheese but after ordering some olives or boquerones, turn over and you'll find three headings: Fish, Meat and Vegetable – one plate of each per person should do it. Unusual dishes, like braised gurnard with smoked Jersey Royals, sit alongside more traditional pairings like duck breast with parsnip purée. Prices are excellent; sharing is encouraged and service, young and sincere. Spain and Italy dominate the wine list.

Tsunami

Japanese H2

93 Charlotte St. ✉ W1T 4PY
(020) 7637 0050
www.tsunamirestaurant.co.uk
Goodge Street
Closed Christmas-New Year, Saturday lunch and Sunday

Carte £18/46 s

You'll find that this Japanese restaurant, at the less excitable end of Charlotte Street, is smaller and less likely to be dominated by large groups than the original branch in Clapham. It's prettily decorated with lacquered walls and a delicate pink floral motif and comes with colour changing lights and lounge music. Despite their reticence in making recommendations, staff do an efficient job and the food arrives quickly from the kitchen. The menu covers all points and is a mix of the familiar and the more original. Seafood, whether grilled, as tempura or as sashimi salad, is often a highlight and much can be shared without breaking the bank – which is not something you can say about many places in this neighbourhood.

Bayswater · Maida Vale

There may not appear to be an obvious link between Maida Vale and Italy, but the name of this smart area to the west of central London is derived from a battle fought over two hundred years ago in Southern Italy, and the most appealing visitor attraction in the neighbourhood is the charming canalside **Little Venice.** To stroll around here on a summer's day brings to mind promenading in a more distant European clime; it's hard to believe that the ear-shattering roar of the Westway is just a short walk away. South of this iconic elevated roadway – a snaking route out from Marylebone to the western suburbs – is Bayswater, a busy area of imposing nineteenth century buildings that's the epicentre of London's Middle Eastern community.

During its Victorian heyday, **Bayswater** was a grand and glamorous address for affluent and elegant types who wanted a giant green space (Hyde Park) on their doorstep. The whole area had been laid out in the mid 1800s, when grand squares and cream stuccoed terraces started to fill the acres between Brunel's curvy Paddington station and the park. But during the twentieth century Bayswater's cachet nose-dived, stigmatised as 'the wrong side of the park' by the arrivistes of Knightsbridge and Kensington. Today it's still a backpacker's paradise: home to a bewildering number of shabby tourist hotels, bedsits and B&Bs, converted from the grand houses. But this tells only a fraction of the modern story, because the area is undergoing a massive facelift that will transform it forever. The hub of this makeover is the **Paddington Basin,** a gigantic reclamation of the old Grand Union Canal basin in the shadow of the rail terminus. From a ramshackle wasteground, it's now a shimmering zone of metal, steel and glass, a phantasmagoria of blue chip HQs, homes, shops and leisure facilities. Even the barges have been turned into permanently moored 'retail opportunities'. Tree-lined towpaths along the perimeter complete the picture of a totally modern waterscape.

Lovers of the old Bayswater can still relish what made it famous in the first place: radiating out from **Lancaster Gate,** away from Hyde Park, is a web of streets with handsome squares and tucked-away mews, and it still retains pockets of close-knit communities, such as Porchester Square, west of Paddington station. Meanwhile, the 'cathedral' of the area, Whiteleys shopping centre in **Queensway**, remains a pivotal landmark, as it has been for more than a century. Just beyond Whiteleys heading away from central London, **Westbourne Grove** is still reassuringly expensive, or at least the bit that heads determinedly towards Notting Hill. But the wind of change has rustled other parts of the neighbourhood: Connaught

R. Leaver/Loop Images/Photononstop

Street has evolved into a villagey quarter of boutiques, galleries and restaurants, while, further west, Craven Hill Gardens is the height of chic.

Little Venice pretty much acts as a dividing line between Bayswater and Maida Vale. Technically, it's the point where the Paddington arm of the Grand Union Canal meets the **Regent's Canal,** but the name, coined by poet Robert Browning who lived close by, has come to encompass the whole area just to the north of the soaring Westway. Narrow boat moorings vie for attention alongside the cafés and pubs that mercifully lack the frantic high street buzz so typical of their kind away from the water's edge. The permanently moored boats were here a long time before those upstarts at Paddington Basin. This is where you can find old-time favourites including a floating art gallery and a puppet theatre barge, and all overseen by the Warwick Castle pub, a stalwart of the area that's a minute's walk from the canal. Suitably refreshed, a wander round the residential streets of Maida Vale is very pleasant, dominated by the impressive Edwardian blocks of flats that conjure up a distinctive well-to-do scene.

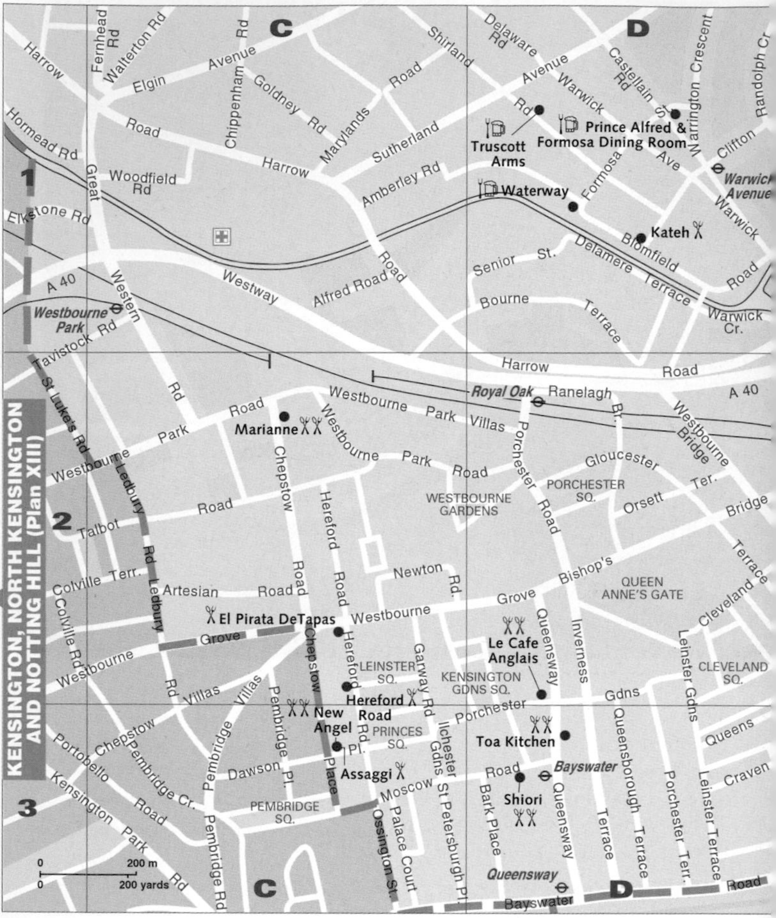

KENSINGTON, NORTH KENSINGTON AND NOTTING HILL (Plan XIII)

C
D
1
2
3

Truscott Arms
Prince Alfred & Formosa Dining Room
Waterway
Kateh
Marianne
El Pirata DeTapas
Le Cafe Anglais
Hereford Road
New Angel
Toa Kitchen
Assaggi
Shiori

Westbourne Park
Royal Oak
Bayswater
Queensway
Warwick Avenue

Harrow Road
Westway
A 40
Fernhead Rd
Walterton Rd
Elgin Avenue
Chippenham Rd
Goldney Rd
Marylands Road
Shirland Road
Delaware Rd
Castellain Rd
Warrington Crescent
Randolph Cr.
Hormead Rd
Woodfield Rd
Great Western Rd
Elkstone Rd
Sutherland Ave
Amberley Rd
Alfred Road
Formosa St.
Clifton Gdns
Warwick Ave
Blomfield Road
Delamere Terrace
Senior St.
Bourne Terrace
Warwick Cr.
Tavistock Rd
St Luke's Rd
Westbourne Park Road
Westbourne Park Villas
Ranelagh Br.
Westbourne Bridge
Porchester Road
Gloucester Ter.
Orsett Ter.
Bishop's Bridge Road
Talbot Road
Ledbury Rd
Chepstow Road
Hereford Road
Westbourne Park Road
WESTBOURNE GARDENS
PORCHESTER SQ.
Newton Rd.
Westbourne Grove
QUEEN ANNE'S GATE
Cleveland Terrace
Colville Terr.
Colville Rd
Artesian Road
Queensway
Inverness Terrace
Leinster Gdns
CLEVELAND SQ.
LEINSTER SQ.
KENSINGTON GDNS SQ.
Garway Rd
Porchester Gdns
Westbourne Villas
Chepstow Villas
Pembridge Villas
Pembridge Pl.
Chepstow Place
Hereford Rd
PRINCES SQ.
Ilchester Gdns
Queensborough Terrace
Queens Gdns
Portobello Road
Pembridge Cr.
Pembridge Rd
Dawson Pl.
PEMBRIDGE SQ.
Moscow Road
Ossington St.
Palace Court
St Petersburgh Pl.
Bark Place
Porchester Terr.
Leinster Terrace
Craven
Kensington Park Rd
Bayswater Road

0 200 m
0 200 yards

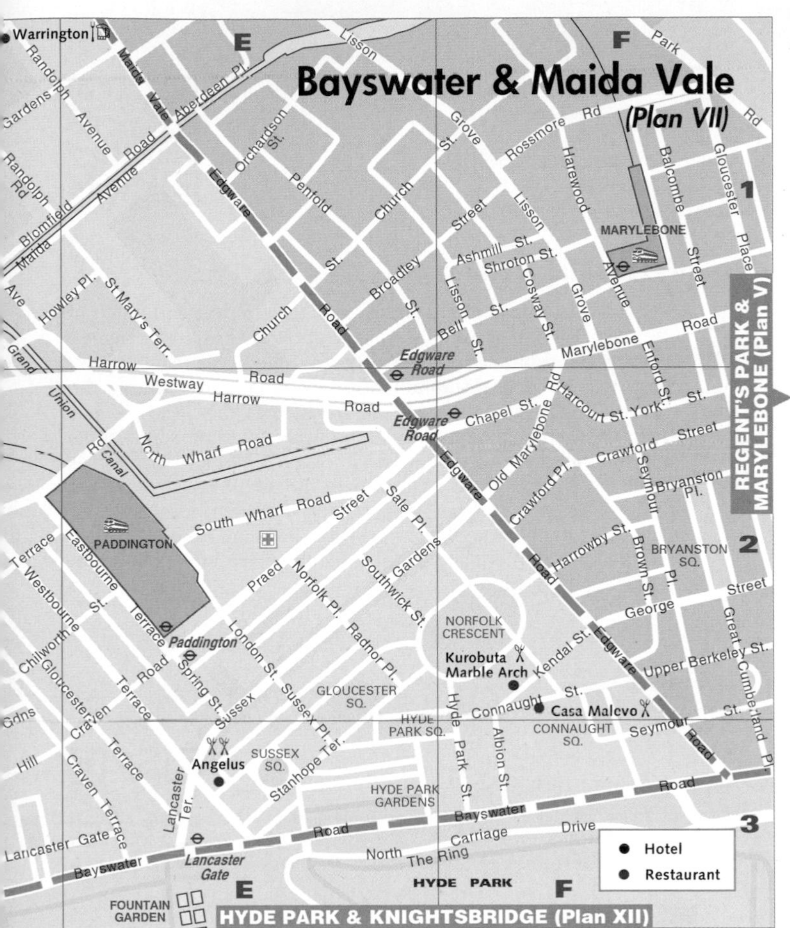
Bayswater & Maida Vale
(Plan VII)
E
F
1
2
3
Warrington
Randolph Gardens
Randolph Avenue
Randolph Rd
Maida Vale
Aberdeen Pl.
Blomfield Road
Maida Avenue
Maida Ave
Howley Pl.
St Mary's Terr.
Grand Union Canal
Lisson Grove
Park Rd
Rossmore Rd
Harewood Avenue
Balcombe Street
Gloucester Place
MARYLEBONE
Orchardson St.
Penfold St.
Church St.
Broadley St.
Bell St.
Ashmill St.
Shroton St.
Lisson St.
Cosway St.
Edgware Road
Marylebone Road
Harrow Road
Westway
Chapel St.
Old Marylebone Rd
Harcourt St.
York St.
Enford St.
Crawford Street
Crawford Pl.
Seymour Pl.
Bryanston Pl.
Bryanston St.
BRYANSTON SQ.
Harrowby St.
Brown St.
George Street
Great Cumberland Pl.
Upper Berkeley St.
North Wharf Road
South Wharf Road
Praed Street
Sale Pl.
Norfolk Pl.
Southwick Gardens
Southwick St.
Radnor Pl.
London St.
Sussex Gardens
Sussex Pl.
NORFOLK CRESCENT
Kurobuta Marble Arch
Kendal St.
Connaught St.
Casa Malevo
CONNAUGHT SQ.
Seymour St.
HYDE PARK SQ.
Hyde Park St.
Albion St.
GLOUCESTER SQ.
PADDINGTON
Paddington
Eastbourne Terrace
Westbourne Terrace
Chilworth St.
Gloucester Terrace
Craven Road
Craven Hill Gdns
Craven Terrace
Spring St.
Angelus
SUSSEX SQ.
Stanhope Ter.
Lancaster Ter.
HYDE PARK GARDENS
Bayswater Road
Lancaster Gate
North Carriage Drive
The Ring
HYDE PARK
FOUNTAIN GARDEN
REGENT'S PARK & MARYLEBONE (Plan V)
HYDE PARK & KNIGHTSBRIDGE (Plan XII)
Hotel
Restaurant

Angelus

French

E3

4 Bathurst St ✉ W2 2SD
(020) 7402 0083
www.angelusrestaurant.co.uk
⊖ Lancaster Gate
Closed 24 December-2 January

Menu £22 (lunch) – Carte £38/64

Angelus has a delightfully warm and inclusive feel and much of the credit for that goes to its amiable and truly hospitable owner, Thierry Tomasin – if you're not already one of his regulars, you soon will be. The restaurant occupies what was formerly the Archer Tavern and the building dates from the 1850s. It has been charmingly decorated with art nouveau mirrors and prints and the bell that his mother would ring to call him in for meals when he was a boy growing up in the south of France takes pride of place in the bar. The cooking is French in its base but English in its ingredients; game will always be a highlight here but the kitchen is equally adept at lightly grilling some halibut or whipping up a soufflé.

Assaggi

Italian

C3

39 Chepstow Pl, (1st Floor) ✉ W2 4TS
(020) 7792 5501
⊖ Bayswater
Closed 2 weeks Christmas, Sunday and bank holidays – booking essential

Carte £42/56

A/C

There's nothing like getting off to a good start, whether that's a book, a film or a meal out. Here at Assaggi you're pretty much guaranteed a warm welcome, whether it's your first visit or you're one of its many regulars. As well as wonderful hospitality, the other reason for eating in this simply decorated room above a former pub is the Italian food. It doesn't come cheap but the prices are driven by the quality of the ingredients, and the menu of classics – which is written in Italian as the owner enjoys the process of translating it verbally and being able to gauge his diners' feelings – is very appealing. Preparations are straightforward and, with only two or three ingredients on the plate, natural flavours are allowed to shine through.

Le Café Anglais

Mediterranean

D2

8 Porchester Gdns ✉ W2 4BD
✆ (020) 7221 1415
www.lecafeanglais.co.uk
⊖ Bayswater
Closed 25-26 December, 1 January and 31 August

Menu £30 (weekday lunch) – Carte £25/54

To get the full effect of this handsome brasserie with its art deco looks, take the lift up from the dedicated entrance on Porchester Gardens instead of walking through Whiteley's. At the 'pass' you're more likely than not to catch sight of Rowley Leigh, a chef who knows all about simplicity, seasonality and delivering good flavours. The menu is very appealing and dishes usually comprise three or four complementary ingredients. Influences are surprisingly global, with the Med leading the way. The place tends not to fill up until mid-evening which causes a dilemma: come early and you may be rushed through; arrive at the height of the rush and service slows up. If you haven't booked, try your luck at the oyster bar.

Casa Malevo

Argentinian

F2

23 Connaught St ✉ W2 2AY
✆ (020) 7402 1988
www.casamalevo.com
⊖ Marble Arch
Closed 21-26 December – (dinner only)

Carte £21/45

Accordion music playing in the background and photos of gauchos on the wall are the two most obvious clues as to the nationality of this warm, country style restaurant – welcome to the 'Cocina Argentina'. This is all about robust flavours and tasty combinations. Kick things off with empanadas or homemade chorizo then head for the mainstay of the menu – premium cuts of Argentinian beef, with the rib-eye and the skirt being the popular choices. Side dishes are not quite premier league, but sauces like Malbec and bone marrow really hit the spot. Non-carnivores are not wholly ignored and there is usually a fish dish on the daily specials board. Larger groups should consider booking the lovely little basement room which resembles a kitchen.

Hereford Road

British modern C2

3 Hereford Rd ✉ W2 4AB
✆ (020) 7727 1144
www.herefordroad.org
⊖ Bayswater
Closed 24 December-3 January and 27-29 August – booking essential

Menu £14 (weekday lunch) – Carte £23/32

Hereford Road is, first and foremost, a local restaurant. Lunch is usually a relaxed affair, with the room brightened by the large domed skylight, while dinner is the livelier feast, where everyone gives the impression that they live near enough to have walked here. The delightful owner-chef Tom Pemberton is often the first person you see, as the open kitchen is by the entrance – this was once a butcher's shop. He is an acolyte of St John and his cooking shares the same principles but not the same prices. So expect seasonal, British ingredients in very tasty dishes devoid of frippery. Offal is handled with aplomb and dishes designed for two, such as the shoulder of lamb or the whole oxtail, are so good you won't actually want to share them.

Kateh

Mediterranean D1

5 Warwick Pl ✉ W9 2PX
✆ (020) 7289 3393
www.kateh.net
⊖ Warwick Avenue
Closed 25-26 December – booking essential – (dinner only and lunch Friday-Sunday)

Carte £21/36

Booking is imperative if you want to join those locals who have already discovered what a little jewel they have here in the form of this buzzy, busy Persian restaurant. Kateh is a type of rice from the Gilan Province in Iran; the fishermen there cook it to a sticky consistency and mix it with their daily catch. It features as a traditional accompaniment here, along with herbs and fruits. The baby calamari is delicious, the stews are very satisfying and the grilling is expertly done over charcoal. Warm sesame-coated flatbreads are moreish and be sure to finish with an authentic dessert like 'kolouche' (date and walnut pastries) along with tea made with cardamom. There's a delightful decked terrace at the back.

Kurobuta Marble Arch

Japanese F2

17-20 Kendal St ✉ W2 2AW
(020) 3475 4158
www.kurobuta-london.com
⊖ Marble Arch
Closed 25 December

Carte £40/60

Having practiced with a pop-up in Chelsea, the Australian chef-owner hit the ground running when he opened his flagship Japanese restaurant – which was just as well because the crowds soon piled in. It's modelled somewhat on a Japanese izakaya, although it's bigger than anything usually seen in Tokyo. The bar is the best place to sit – start with a cocktail or a beer with a frozen head and then get ordering. The robata grill provides the stickiest BBQ pork belly, which is served in steamed buns; the lamb chops are lip-tinglingly good; the black pepper soft shell crabs fly out of the kitchen; and the yuzu tart is the star of the desserts. The place is a lot of fun and the staff are knowledgeable and helpful.

Marianne

French C2

104a Chepstow Rd ✉ W2 5QS
(020) 3675 7750
www.mariannerestaurant.com
⊖ Westbourne Park
Closed 22-24 August and Monday – booking essential – (dinner only and lunch Friday-Sunday)

Menu £55

Marianne Lumb spent several years travelling the world as a private chef to a host of names from the sunny side of Celebrity Street. She then entered BBC's 'MasterChef: The Professionals' and reached the final. Now she has her own restaurant and it's a delightful little place, with just six tables in a pleasant, panelled corner room. As she has the minimum amount of assistance, the daily menu is kept quite concise, but it still allows for her own style of cooking to come through – you can just about see her in action behind the fearsome line of kitchen knives. In essence, the cooking is quite classically based using sound French principles and while flavours are pronounced, it also comes with a pleasing lightness of touch.

New Angel

British modern C3

39 Chepstow Pl ✉ W2 4TS
(020) 7221 7620
www.thenewangel-nh.co.uk
Bayswater
Closed 25 December, Sunday dinner, Monday and bank holidays

Menu £32/54

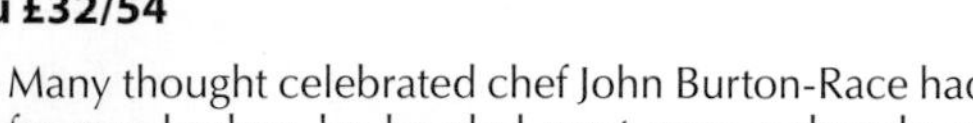

Many thought celebrated chef John Burton-Race had left London for good when he headed west over a decade ago. But now he's back and this time he's in a converted Victorian pub on the fringes of Notting Hill. The place has been prudently revamped and now has the feel of a bistrot-deluxe – sit in the lighter front section if you want to see the comings-and-goings or at the back if you want more privacy. Despite the classical French nature to the cooking there's a hint of modernity to the presentation and a refinement to the flavours – one can sense there's an experienced hand here in the kitchen. There are plenty of luxurious ingredients from France and the UK and the evening tasting Menu shows the kitchen's talents to the full.

El Pirata DeTapas

Spanish C2

115 Westbourne Grove ✉ W2 4UP
(020) 7727 5000
www.elpiratadetapas.co.uk
Bayswater
Closed 24-26 December, 24-25 August and 1 January

Menu £10/25 – Carte £19/29

Spanish restaurants and tapas-style eating satisfy our appetite for a shared, less structured dining experience and El Pirata is no exception. It's spread over two floors, although you wouldn't want to be the first table downstairs, and is decorated in a contemporary yet warm style. The staff give helpful advice on a menu that is quite lengthy but helpfully divided up into sections, from charcuterie to fish, croquettes to vegetarian, meat to paellas; there are also a couple of appealing and balanced set menus and the pricing structure is far from piratical. The kitchen shows respect for traditional flavours but is not afraid of trying new things or adding a note of playfulness to some dishes. A good place to come with friends.

Prince Alfred & Formosa Dining Room

modern D1

5A Formosa St ✉ W9 1EE
✆ (020) 7286 3287
www.theprincealfred.com
⊖ Warwick Avenue.

Carte £24/41

The Prince Alfred is a wonderful example of a classic Victorian pub and its period features include ornate tiles, plate glass, panels and snugs. Unfortunately, the eating is done in the Formosa Dining Room extension on the side but at least it's a lively room and the open kitchen adds to the general bonhomie. There's more than a rustic edge to the appealing menu which will please all traditionalists; the mature steaks, pork belly and sticky toffee pudding are perennials but there are also dishes geared to those whose tastes are a tad more continental, such as sea bream with couscous and peppers. The service team could perhaps try revealing a little more personality but prices are kept realistic and the place still feels like a local.

Ⓝ Shiori

Japanese D3

45 Moscow Rd ✉ W2 4AH
✆ (020) 7221 9790
www.theshiori.com
⊖ Bayswater
Closed Sunday and Monday – booking essential

Menu £70/95

Moscow Road is no match for the beauty of Kyoto but Takashi and Hitomi Takagi's restaurant brings a little of Japan's former Imperial capital to west London. Kaiseki – the very traditional multi-course Japanese equivalent of haute cuisine – follows a formal structure in both the order in which specific dishes are served and the ceremony with which they are presented. Two monthly-changing menus are served here; the 8 course Hana and 10 course Kokoro. The finest ingredients from Britain are supplemented by vegetables imported directly from Japan and the resulting dishes are beautifully presented, delicate and balanced but also show plenty of original touches. With seating for just 16 it's a small but immaculately dressed room.

Toa Kitchen

Chinese

D3

100 Queensway ✉ W2 3RR
(020) 7792 9767
www.toakitchen.com
Bayswater
Closed 25 December

Carte £14/54

Take a pre-prandial stroll along Queensway and you'll be faced with an overwhelming choice of Chinese restaurants, so keep an eye out for Toa Kitchen. At first glance the menu may seem dispiritingly long but search out the "Chef's Specials" and you won't go wrong. These carefully prepared Cantonese specialities, together with the hotpot dishes, are the ones to go for: portions are generous, ingredients good and the flavours authentic. Service is also a cut above average and you'll be well looked after by owner Mr Fung and his team of very capable and friendly ladies. For a more comfortable table, head to the back of the restaurant where the blossom the restaurant gets its name from is attractively displayed.

Truscott Arms

modern

D1

55 Shirland Rd ✉ W9 2JD
(020) 7266 9198
www.thetruscottarms.com
Warwick Avenue

Menu £32 (dinner) – Carte £24/43

A Victorian pub not so much revamped but resuscitated and restored. There's nothing quite like private ownership for putting the love back into a pub and the husband and wife team who took over this big old place invested considerable sums and are now deservedly reaping the benefits. There's a lovely pewter-topped bar where the locals gather and the pub is getting known too for the regularly changing local artwork it displays, particularly in the upstairs dining room which comes with a beautifully intricate corniced ceiling. The kitchen shows obvious ambition and uses fairly modern techniques to produce dishes featuring quite a number of ingredients and some interesting flavour combinations.

Waterway

modern

D1

54 Formosa St ✉ W9 2JU
✆ (020) 7266 3557
www.thewaterway.co.uk
⊖ Warwick Avenue.

Carte £23/39

It sits by the canal offering refreshment to passing narrowboaters, its large terrace gets besieged by drinkers and there's live music on a Thursday night – it sounds like a pub, it has the warmth and bustle of a pub, but it's all surprisingly smart. A bar occupies one side of the room and a restaurant the other – and there's no evidence anywhere of any spit or sawdust. The menu and cooking also sit somewhere between a restaurant and an urban gastropub, with dishes like rump of lamb with couscous sitting alongside more delicate offerings, such as scallops with pea purée, which reveal the kitchen's lighter touch. Desserts keep up the standard and prices are kept sensible. Service is youthful, bubbly and capable.

City of London · Clerkenwell Finsbury · Southwark

Say what you like about London, **The City** is the place where it all started. The Romans developed this small area – this square mile – nearly two thousand years ago, and today it stands as the economic heartbeat of not only the capital, but the country as a whole. Each morning it's besieged with an army of bankers, lawyers and traders, and each evening it's abandoned to an eerie ghost-like fate. Of course, this mass exodus is offset by the two perennial crowd-pullers, **St Paul's** and the **Tower of London**, but these are both on the periphery of the area, away from the frenetic commercial zone within. The casual visitor tends to steer clear of the City, but for those willing to mix it with the daytime swarm of office workers, there are many historical nuggets hidden away, waiting to be mined. You can find here, amongst the skyscrapers, a tempting array of Roman ruins, medieval landmarks and brooding churches designed by Wren and Hawksmoor. One of the best ways of encapsulating everything that's happened here down the centuries is to visit the Museum of London, on London Wall, which tells the story of the city from the very start, and the very start means 300,000 BC.

For those seeking the hip corners of this part of London, the best advice is to head slightly north-west, using the brutalist space of the **Barbican Arts Centre** as your marker. You're now entering **Clerkenwell**. Sliding north/south through here is the bustling and buzzy **St John Street,** home to some of the funkiest eating establishments in London, their proximity to **Smithfield** meat market giving a clue as to much of their menus' provenance. Clerkenwell's revivalist vibe has seen the steady reclamation of old factory space: during the Industrial Revolution, the area boomed with the introduction of breweries, print works and the manufacture of clocks and watches. After World War II, decline set in, but these days city professionals and loft-dwellers are drawn to the area's zeitgeist-leading galleries and clubs, not to mention the wonderful floor-to-ceiling delicatessens. Clerkenwell is home to The Eagle, one of the city's pioneering gastropubs and still a local favourite, which even has its own art gallery upstairs. Meanwhile, the nearby **Exmouth Market** teems with trendy bars and restaurants, popular with those on their way to the perennially excellent dance concerts at Sadler's Wells Theatre.

The area was once a religious centre, frequented by monks and nuns; its name derives from the parish clerks who performed Biblical mystery plays around the Clerk's Well set in a nunnery wall. This can be found in **Farringdon Lane** complete with an exhibition explaining all. Close by in St John's Lane is the 16C gatehouse which is home to the Museum of the Order of St John (famous today for its

C. Eymenier / MICHELIN

ambulance services), and chock full of fascinating objects related to the Order's medieval history.

Not too long ago, a trip over London Bridge to **Southwark** was for locals only, its trademark grimness ensuring it was well off the tourist map. These days, visitors treat it as a place of pilgrimage as three of London's modern success stories reside here in the shadow of The Shard. **Tate Modern** has become the city's most visited attraction, a huge former power station that generates a blistering show of modern art from 1900 to the present day, its massive turbine hall a must-see feature in itself. Practically next door but a million miles away architecturally is Shakespeare's **Globe,** a wonderful evocation of medieval showtime. Half a mile east is the best food market in London: **Borough Market.** Foodies can't resist the organic, feel-good nature of the place, with, its mind-boggling number of stalls selling produce ranging from every kind of fruit and veg to rare-breed meats, oils, preserves, chocolates and breads. And that's just for hors-d'œuvres…

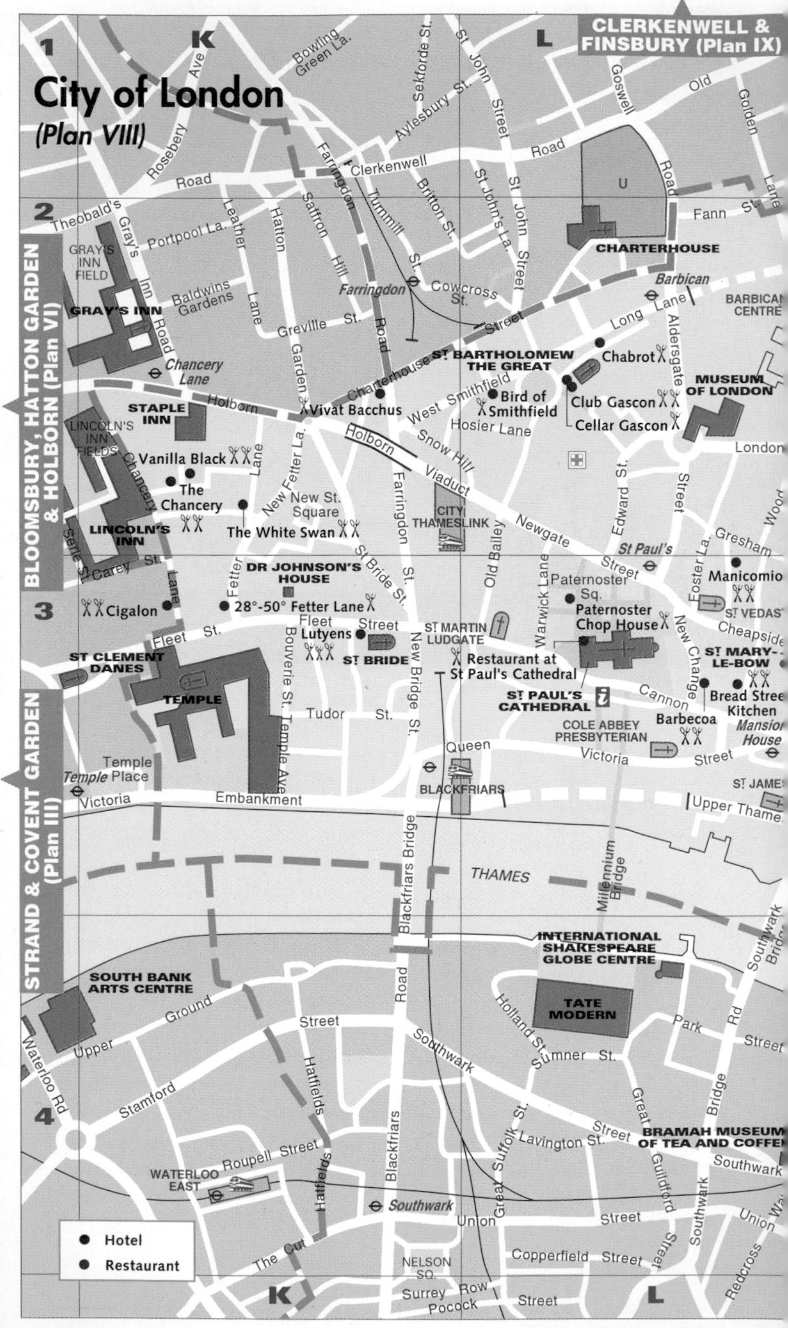
City of London
(Plan VIII)
CLERKENWELL & FINSBURY (Plan IX)
BLOOMSBURY, HATTON GARDEN & HOLBORN (Plan VI)
STRAND & COVENT GARDEN (Plan III)
CHARTERHOUSE
BARBICAN CENTRE
GRAY'S INN
STAPLE INN
LINCOLN'S INN
ST BARTHOLOMEW THE GREAT
MUSEUM OF LONDON
DR JOHNSON'S HOUSE
ST MARTIN LUDGATE
ST BRIDE
ST CLEMENT DANES
TEMPLE
ST PAUL'S CATHEDRAL
COLE ABBEY PRESBYTERIAN
ST MARY-LE-BOW
BLACKFRIARS
CITY THAMESLINK
INTERNATIONAL SHAKESPEARE GLOBE CENTRE
TATE MODERN
SOUTH BANK ARTS CENTRE
BRAMAH MUSEUM OF TEA AND COFFEE
WATERLOO EAST
Chabrot
Club Gascon
Cellar Gascon
Bird of Smithfield
Vivat Bacchus
Vanilla Black
The Chancery
The White Swan
Cigalon
28°-50° Fetter Lane
Lutyens
Restaurant at St Paul's Cathedral
Paternoster Chop House
Manicomio
Bread Street Kitchen
Barbecoa
THAMES
Hotel
Restaurant

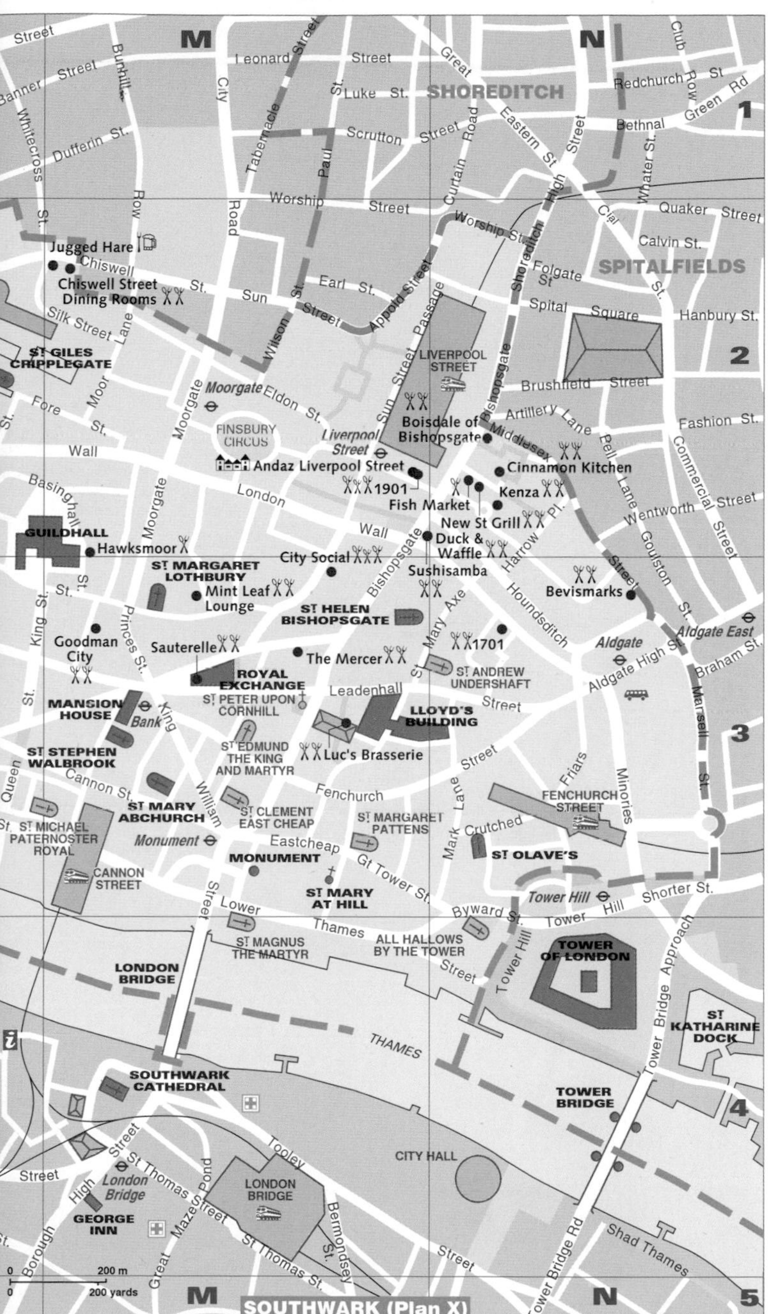
M
N
SHOREDITCH
SPITALFIELDS
Jugged Hare
Chiswell Street Dining Rooms
ST GILES CRIPPLEGATE
Moorgate
FINSBURY CIRCUS
Liverpool Street
LIVERPOOL STREET
Boisdale of Bishopsgate
Andaz Liverpool Street
1901
Fish Market
Cinnamon Kitchen
Kenza
New St Grill
Duck & Waffle
Sushisamba
GUILDHALL
Hawksmoor
City Social
ST MARGARET LOTHBURY
Mint Leaf Lounge
Bevismarks
ST HELEN BISHOPSGATE
Goodman City
Sauterelle
The Mercer
1701
Aldgate
Aldgate East
ROYAL EXCHANGE
ST ANDREW UNDERSHAFT
MANSION HOUSE
Bank
ST PETER UPON CORNHILL
LLOYD'S BUILDING
ST STEPHEN WALBROOK
ST EDMUND THE KING AND MARTYR
Luc's Brasserie
ST MARY ABCHURCH
ST CLEMENT EAST CHEAP
ST MARGARET PATTENS
FENCHURCH STREET
ST MICHAEL PATERNOSTER ROYAL
Monument
MONUMENT
ST OLAVE'S
CANNON STREET
ST MARY AT HILL
Tower Hill
ST MAGNUS THE MARTYR
ALL HALLOWS BY THE TOWER
TOWER OF LONDON
LONDON BRIDGE
THAMES
ST KATHARINE DOCK
SOUTHWARK CATHEDRAL
TOWER BRIDGE
CITY HALL
London Bridge
LONDON BRIDGE
GEORGE INN
0 200 m
0 200 yards
SOUTHWARK (Plan X)
1
2
3
4
5

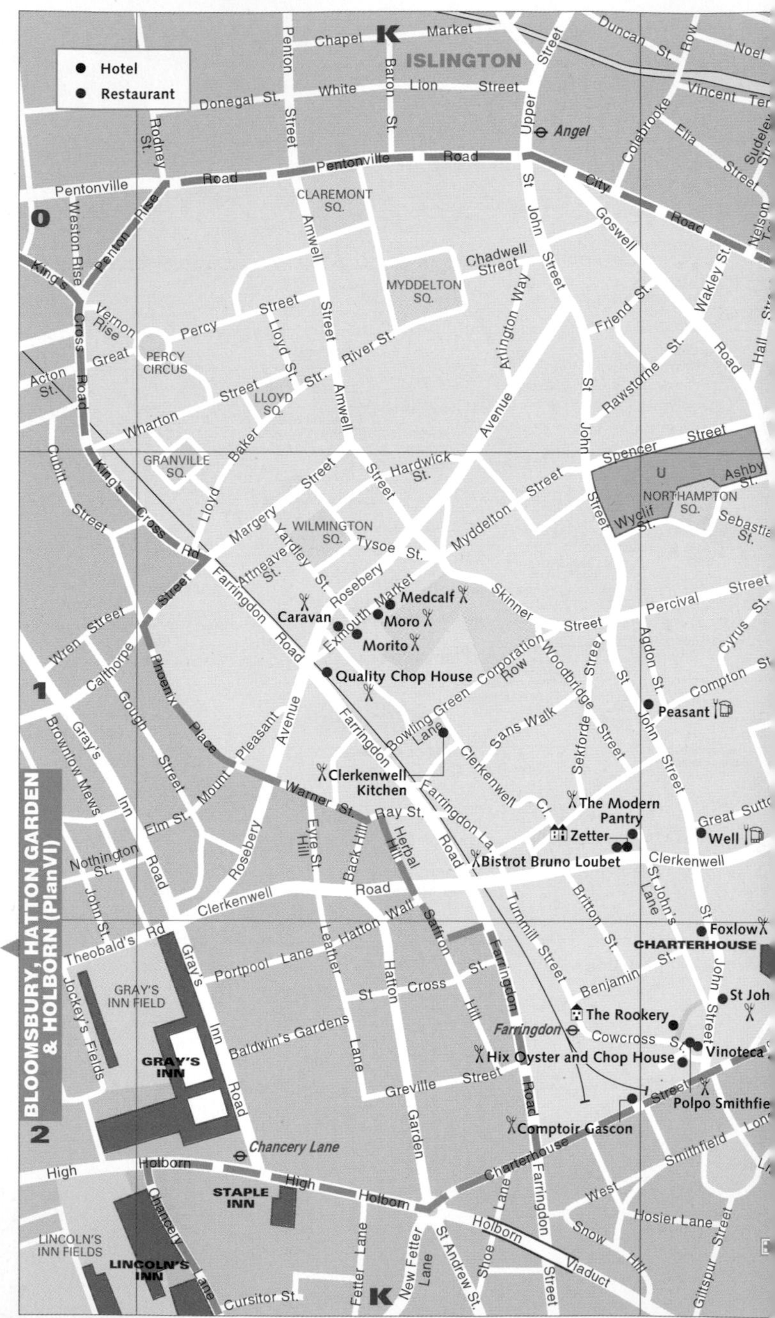

Hotel
Restaurant
ISLINGTON
K
Chapel Market
White Lion Street
Donegal St.
Penton Street
Baron St.
Rodney St.
Pentonville Road
Upper Street
Angel
Duncan St.
Noel
Vincent Ter.
Colebrooke Row
Elia Street
City Road
Goswell Road
St John Street
Pentonville
Penton Rise
Weston Rise
King's Cross Road
CLAREMONT SQ.
Amwell Street
MYDDELTON SQ.
Chadwell Street
Arlington Way
Friend St.
Wakley St.
Vernon Rise
Great Percy Street
PERCY CIRCUS
Lloyd St.
River St.
Acton St.
Wharton Street
LLOYD SQ.
Lloyd Baker Street
Avenue
Rawstorne St.
GRANVILLE SQ.
Cubitt Street
Hardwick St.
Spencer Street
Ashby St.
NORTHAMPTON SQ.
Wyclif St.
Sebastian St.
Margery Street
WILMINGTON SQ.
Yardley St.
Tysoe St.
Myddelton Street
Attneave St.
Rosebery Avenue
Farringdon Road
Exmouth Market
Medcalf
Moro
Morito
Caravan
Skinner Street
Percival Street
Cyrus St.
Quality Chop House
Corporation Row
Woodbridge Street
Agdon St.
Compton St.
Peasant
Wren Street
Calthorpe Street
Phoenix Place
Gough Street
Gray's Inn Road
Brownlow Mews
Mount Pleasant
Bowling Green Lane
Sans Walk
Sekforde Street
Clerkenwell Kitchen
Clerkenwell Cl.
The Modern Pantry
Zetter
Great Sutton St.
Well
Warner St.
Ray St.
Farringdon La.
Elm St.
Eyre St. Hill
Back Hill
Herbal Hill
Bistrot Bruno Loubet
Clerkenwell Road
Nothington St.
John St.
Theobald's Rd
Hatton Wall
Saffron Hill
Turnmill Street
Britton St.
St John's Lane
Foxlow
CHARTERHOUSE
Portpool Lane
Leather Lane
Hatton Garden
Cross St.
St.
Farringdon Road
Benjamin St.
St John
GRAY'S INN FIELD
Jockey's Fields
The Rookery
Farringdon
Cowcross St.
Vinoteca
Baldwin's Gardens
Hix Oyster and Chop House
Greville Street
Polpo Smithfield
GRAY'S INN
Comptoir Gascon
Chancery Lane
Charterhouse Street
Smithfield
High Holborn
STAPLE INN
West
Hosier Lane
Chancery Lane
Holborn Viaduct
Snow Hill
LINCOLN'S INN FIELDS
LINCOLN'S INN
Fetter Lane
New Fetter Lane
St Andrew St.
Shoe Lane
Farringdon Street
Giltspur Street
Cursitor St.
0
1
2
U
BLOOMSBURY, HATTON GARDEN & HOLBORN (Plan VI)

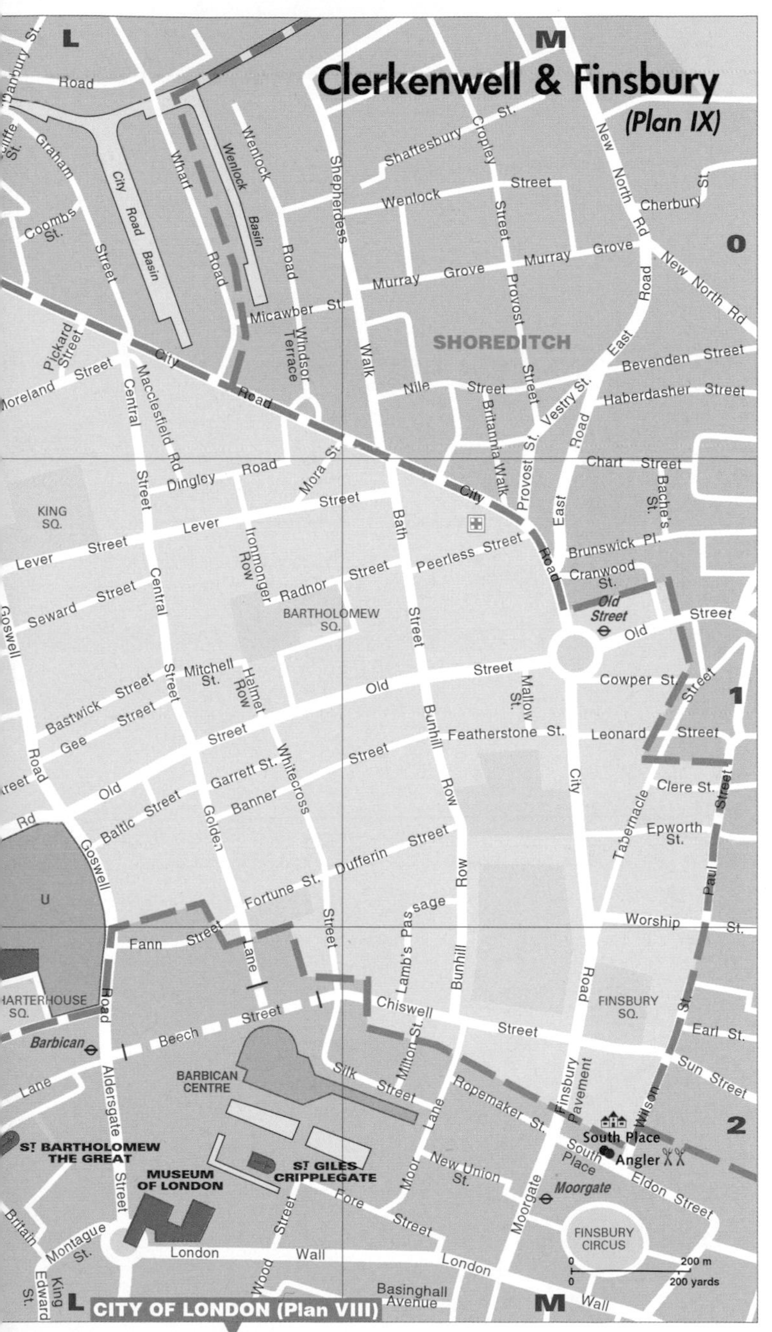

Clerkenwell & Finsbury
(Plan IX)
SHOREDITCH
BARTHOLOMEW SQ.
KING SQ.
FINSBURY SQ.
FINSBURY CIRCUS
BARBICAN CENTRE
ST BARTHOLOMEW THE GREAT
MUSEUM OF LONDON
ST GILES CRIPPLEGATE
CHARTERHOUSE SQ.
South Place
Angler
Barbican
Old Street
Moorgate
CITY OF LONDON (Plan VIII)
200 m
200 yards

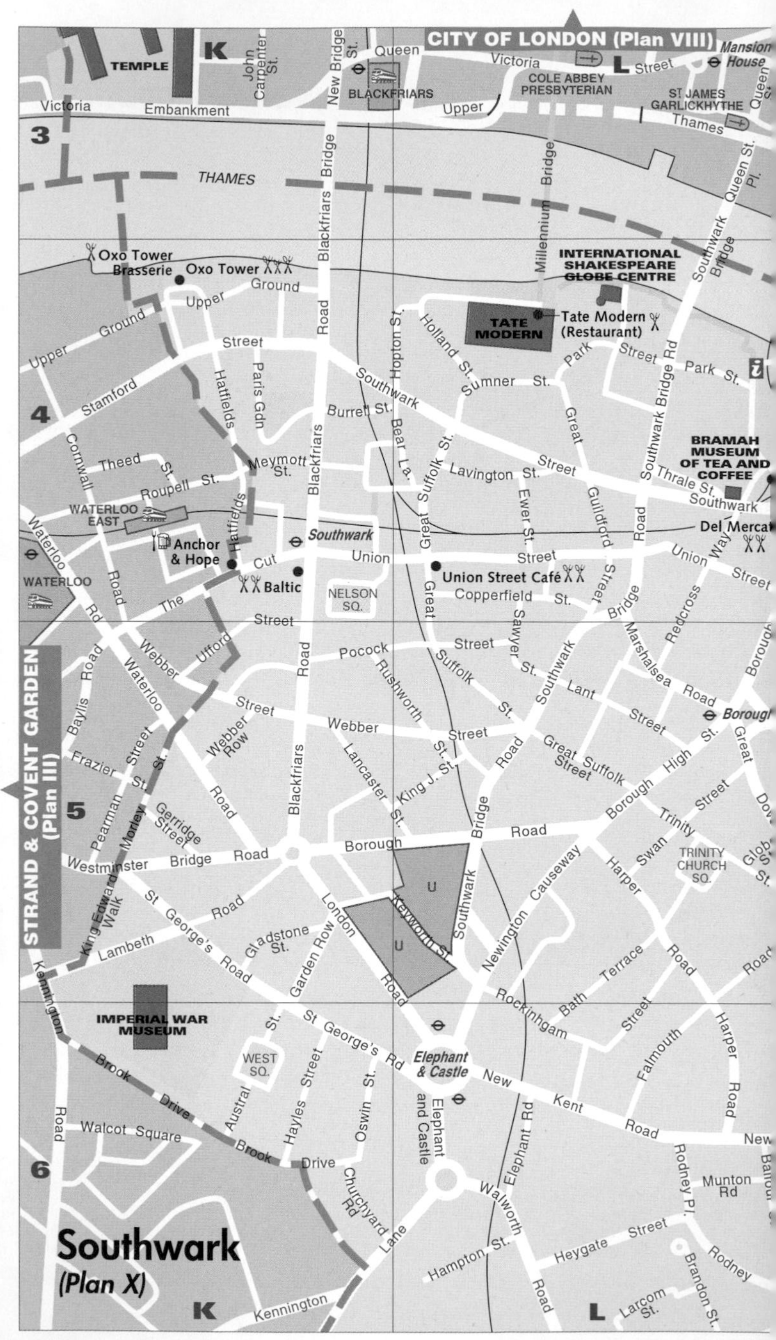
CITY OF LONDON (Plan VIII)
Mansion House
TEMPLE
K
L
John Carpenter St.
New Bridge St.
Queen
Victoria Street
BLACKFRIARS
COLE ABBEY PRESBYTERIAN
ST JAMES GARLICKHYTHE
Queen St.
Victoria Embankment
Upper Thames Street
3
4
5
6
THAMES
Blackfriars Bridge
Millennium Bridge
Southwark Bridge
Queen St. Pl.
Oxo Tower Brasserie
Oxo Tower
INTERNATIONAL SHAKESPEARE GLOBE CENTRE
Upper Ground
TATE MODERN
Tate Modern (Restaurant)
Hopton St.
Holland St.
Park Street
Sumner St.
Stamford Street
Hatfields
Paris Gdn
Southwark Street
Burrell St.
Bear La.
Great Suffolk St.
Lavington St.
Great Guildford Street
Southwark Bridge Rd
BRAMAH MUSEUM OF TEA AND COFFEE
Thrale St.
Cornwall
Theed St.
Meymott St.
Roupell St.
WATERLOO EAST
Ewer St.
Del Mercato
Anchor & Hope
Southwark
Waterloo Rd
WATERLOO
The Cut
Union Street
Union Street Café
Baltic
NELSON SQ.
Copperfield St.
Redcross Way
Southwark Bridge Road
Sawyer St.
Marshalsea Road
Pocock Street
Rushworth St.
Suffolk St.
Lant Street
Borough
Webber Street
Ufford
Baylis Road
Webber Row
Great Suffolk Street
Borough High St.
Great Dover
Frazier St.
Lancaster St.
King J. St.
Trinity Street
Pearman St.
Morley St.
Gerridge Street
Swan
TRINITY CHURCH SQ.
Globe St.
STRAND & COVENT GARDEN (Plan III)
Westminster Bridge Road
Borough Road
Harper
U
Keyworth St.
Newington Causeway
St George's Road
London Road
Gladstone St.
Garden Row
King Edward Walk
Lambeth Road
Bath Terrace
Rockingham
Kennington Road
IMPERIAL WAR MUSEUM
St George's Rd
Elephant & Castle
New Kent Road
Harper Road
Falmouth
WEST SQ.
Austral St.
Hayles Street
Oswin St.
Elephant and Castle
Elephant Rd
Brook Drive
Walcot Square
Churchyard Rd
Walworth Road
Rodney Pl.
Munton Rd
Heygate Street
Hampton St.
Rodney
Southwark (Plan X)
Kennington Lane
Larcom St.
Brandon St.

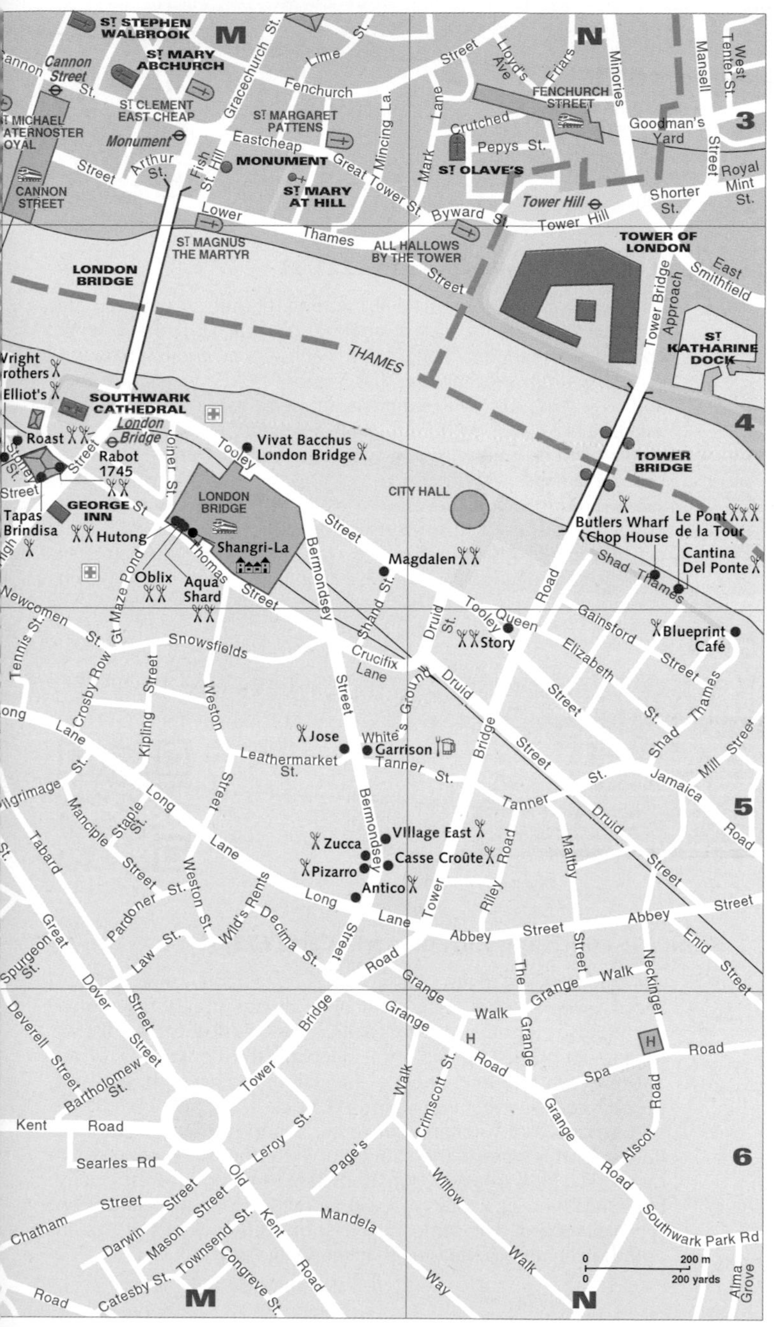

ST STEPHEN WALBROOK
ST MARY ABCHURCH
ST CLEMENT EAST CHEAP
ST MICHAEL PATERNOSTER ROYAL
CANNON STREET
Cannon Street
Monument
MONUMENT
ST MARGARET PATTENS
ST MARY AT HILL
ST MAGNUS THE MARTYR
ALL HALLOWS BY THE TOWER
ST OLAVE'S
FENCHURCH STREET
Tower Hill
TOWER OF LONDON
ST KATHARINE DOCK
LONDON BRIDGE
THAMES
TOWER BRIDGE
SOUTHWARK CATHEDRAL
London Bridge
CITY HALL
GEORGE INN
LONDON BRIDGE
Shangri-La
Wright Brothers
Elliot's
Roast
Rabot 1745
Tapas Brindisa
Hutong
Oblix
Aqua Shard
Vivat Bacchus London Bridge
Magdalen
Story
Butlers Wharf Chop House
Le Pont de la Tour
Cantina Del Ponte
Blueprint Café
Jose
White Garrison
Village East
Zucca
Casse Croûte
Pizarro
Antico
M
N
3
4
5
6
0 200 m
0 200 yards

Anchor & Hope

British modern **Plan X K4**

36 The Cut ✉ SE1 8LP
(020) 7928 9898
www.anchorandhopepub.co.uk
⊖ Southwark.
Closed Christmas-New Year, Sunday dinner, Monday lunch and bank holidays – bookings not accepted

Menu £15 (weekday lunch) – Carte £21/33

The Anchor & Hope is still running at full steam and its popularity shows no sign of abating. It's not hard to see why: combine a menu that changes with each service and is a paragon of seasonality, with cooking that is gutsy, bold and wholesome, and you end up with immeasurably rewarding dishes like suckling kid chops with wild garlic, succulent roast pigeon with lentils or buttermilk pudding with poached rhubarb. The place has a contagiously congenial feel and the staff all pull in the same direction; you may spot a waiter trimming veg or a chef delivering dishes. The no-reservation policy remains, so either get here early or be prepared to wait – although you can now book for Sunday lunch, when everyone sits down at 2pm for a veritable feast.

Antico

Italian **Plan X M5**

214 Bermondsey St ✉ SE1 3TQ
(020) 7407 4682
www.antico-london.co.uk
⊖ London Bridge
Closed 25 December, 1 January and Monday

Menu £15 (lunch and early dinner) – Carte £23/34

Art galleries, markets, pubs, bars, restaurants, independent shops, even a local festival...if only all our streets resembled Bermondsey Street. In 2012 Antico was added to the list of dining options along the strip following the conversion of an antiques warehouse – hence the name. This is a bright and breezy corner spot, with exposed brick walls acknowledging its past and a downstairs lounge bar a nod to the present. The Italian food is honest and straightforward; the homemade pasta dishes like slow-roasted pork shoulder tortelloni are especially tasty and there is always a seasonal ragu, risotto and sorbet on the blackboard. The atmosphere is fun, the cocktails are good and the clientele is pleasingly mixed in age and affluence.

Angler ✿

fish and seafood **Plan IX M2**

South Place Hotel,
3 South Pl ✉ EC2M 2AF
✆ (020) 3215 1260
www.anglerrestaurant.com
⊖ Moorgate

Closed 26 December-1 January (except dinner 31 December), Saturday lunch and Sunday – booking advisable

Menu £25/65 – Carte £36/67

Angler

The rooftop restaurant of D&D's South Place hotel is a bright, light and supremely comfortable space; its adjoining bar and terrace the perfect place for a pre-prandial cocktail. Sloping floor to ceiling windows allow the light to flood in and the contemporary styling represents something of an antidote to all those clubby, masculine rooms that have recently opened. Service is smooth and detailed and gets the balance between formality and friendliness just right. The menu champions the best of British seafood: there are oysters from Mersea, langoustines from Orkney and crab and cod from Cornwall. The cooking is confidently executed and the freshness of the ingredients really shines through; cheeses are British and puddings hit the spot.

The glass-fronted wine cabinets are more than just a feature at one end of the restaurant – they have also been thoughtfully stocked. The ever-changing selection by the glass is first-rate and the Enomatic machine keeps the wines fresh and at the perfect temperature.

First Course

- Yellow fin tuna tartare, lime and chilli.
- Chilled tomato and basil minestrone with borlotti beans.

Main Course

- Angler and lobster pie, button mushrooms and mashed potato.
- Roast Anjou pigeon with peas and smoked bacon.

Dessert

- Chocolate fondant, pistachio ice cream.
- Flourless orange cake with Grand Marnier and roasted almond ice cream.

Aqua Shard

modern **Plan X M4**

Level 31, The Shard, 31 St Thomas St ✉ SE1 9RY
(020) 3011 1256
www.aquashard.co.uk
⊖ London Bridge
Closed 25 December and 1 January

Menu £26 (weekday lunch) – Carte £33/68

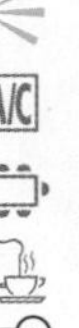

The Shard's most accessible restaurant covers all bases by serving breakfast, brunch, lunch, afternoon tea and dinner. You can even come here just for a drink and a gander which is surely preferable to paying for the viewing platform, but be warned – at weekends the queue is at street level and can be dispiritingly long. If you have booked to eat then the express lift will whisk you straight up here to the 31st floor where you should ask to sit on the west side for the better views. The contemporary cooking makes good use of British ingredients and comes with a degree of finesse in both flavour and presentation. The à la carte prices can be a little steep though, so your best bet is to come for lunch and go for the Market Menu.

Baltic

other world kitchens **Plan X K4**

74 Blackfriars Rd ✉ SE1 8HA
(020) 7928 1111
www.balticrestaurant.co.uk
⊖ Southwark
Closed 24-26 December and Monday lunch – bookings advisable at dinner

Menu £20/23 – Carte £25/36

There's nothing like a nondescript façade to lower expectations and Baltic's dull exterior goes even further by giving few clues as to what lies within: a large, bright restaurant housed in what was once an 18C coach builder's works. The menu is an appealing read and specialises in dishes from various countries out east – Poland, Russia, Bulgaria, even Siberia. Expect two types of beetroot soup, Barszcz and Chlodnik; assorted dumplings including pierogi and spaetzle, which are done well; lots of meat dishes such as pork schnitzel and lamb shashlik – and great vodkas. The cooking is executed with more subtlety that you expect and the largely Polish staff are clearly proud and pleased to be serving food with which they are familiar.

Barbecoa

meats and grills Plan VIII L3

20 New Change Passage ✉ EC4M 9AG
✆ (020) 3005 8555
www.barbecoa.com
⊖ St Paul's
Closed 24-26 December and 1 January – booking essential

Carte £30/58 XX

Good barbecue is about using prime ingredients and choosing the appropriate cooking method. At Jamie Oliver's Barbecoa the kitchen uses fire pits, smokers, tandoors, grills and ovens to ensure maximum flavour on your plate, whether you've chosen prawns, ribs, pulled pork shoulder or dry-aged British steak. Another thing BBQ needs is a good appetite: ideally you'd have spent the morning chopping down trees although, judging by the clientele and the suit jackets hanging off the backs of the chairs, it seems that working in finance does just as well. Don't ignore the starters, like pig's cheek or beetroot salad, as they're more than a run-up to the main course – and if you manage dessert too then you won't need to eat again for days.

Ⓝ Bevismarks

other world kitchens Plan VIII N3

3 Middlesex St ✉ E1 7AA
✆ (020) 7247 5474
www.bevismarkstherestaurant.com
⊖ Aldgate
Closed Saturday and Sunday

Menu £19 (lunch) – Carte £31/47

Before establishing itself in its current site, this kosher restaurant, which is licensed by the Sephardi Kashrut Authority & Beth Din (Glatt), was based at the nearby Bevis Marks Synagogue for 10 years – hence the name. While the room and service could both do with a little more personality, the menu offers enough choice to keep both traditionalists and progressives happy. Influences are Ashkenazi as well as Sephardi but there are also Asian touches and some dishes that can only be described as 'modern British'. So, you can come here to order holishkes or to test the lightness of the matzo ball in the chicken soup; you can try shredded salt beef in a Thai noodle salad; or you can simply plump for a beef and ale pie.

Bird of Smithfield

British traditional **Plan VIII L2**

26 Smithfield St ✉ EC1A 9LB
✆ (020) 7559 5100
www.birdofsmithfield.com
⊖ Farringdon
Closed Christmas, New Year, Sunday and bank holidays – booking essential

Carte £28/61

No, it's not a reference to any fowl or feathered variety – Alan Bird is the owner-chef of his appealing townhouse. The place has the relaxed look and atmosphere of a private members' club but without the smugness, and the five floors of fun include a cocktail bar, small but friendly restaurant, a lounge with its own menu, a rooftop terrace with views over Smithfield Market and a private dining room. There's a worthy British stoutness to the menu, which makes good use of the country's larder. Dishes are inherently satisfying, unadorned and full of flavour with the emphasis lying firmly on the main ingredient, whether that's Dorset crab, Suffolk pork or Devon slip soles and beef.

Bistrot Bruno Loubet

French **Plan IX K1**

Zetter Hotel,
St John's Sq, 86-88 Clerkenwell Rd. ✉ EC1M 5RJ
✆ (020) 7324 4444
www.bistrotbrunoloubet.com
⊖ Farringdon
Closed 24-26 December – booking advisable

Menu £20 (weekday lunch) – Carte £27/43

Bruno Loubet may have surprised a few people by pitching up in Clerkenwell after his sojourn in Australia, but the trendy Zetter hotel is actually a very good fit for his satisfying and rustic cooking. The restaurant has been busy from day one, and it is clear that he's attracting plenty of new followers because not everyone here is old enough to remember 1994 when he made his name in Soho. The menu is largely influenced by bistro classics but the dishes here come with a greater degree of depth and sophistication than one expects; and neither are they exclusively French, as the occasional touch of Asian spicing finds its way in. The closely set tables ensure the room has plenty of buzz and staff provide informed, unhurried service.

Blueprint Café

modern **Plan X N5**

Design Museum, Shad Thames, Butlers Wharf ✉ SE1 2YD
✆ (020) 7378 7031
www.blueprintcafe.co.uk
⊖ London Bridge
Closed 26-27 December, 1-4 January and Sunday dinner

Menu £15/20 – Carte £28/39

It may have been open for over twenty years but it is still very much business as usual at this bright white restaurant above the Design Museum. The cooking remains light, uncomplicated and easy to eat as they make the most of seasonal ingredients and use them in complementary ways. The set menus come with very appealing price tags and this is a great choice of restaurant on a sunny day thanks to the retractable windows and views of the river and Tower Bridge. The local area has far more bustle to it than when the restaurant opened at the end of the '80s and the opera glasses allow those with window tables to zoom in on the passers-by below, with the knowledge that, as you're one floor up, they won't notice you doing so.

Boisdale of Bishopsgate

British traditional **Plan VIII N2**

Swedeland Crt, 202 Bishopsgate ✉ EC2M 4NR
✆ (020) 7283 1763
www.boisdale.co.uk
⊖ Liverpool Street
Closed Saturday lunch, Sunday and bank holidays

Carte £29/59

In this age of austerity and healthy living, spare a thought for the old school bon viveur. Fortunately for him – and it's almost always a him – there are still places like Boisdale around: clubby, traditional, unapologetically masculine and reassuringly clandestine. Cigars, champagne and oysters – surely three of the Almighty's most pleasurable creations – are on offer on the ground floor. The serious action, though, takes place downstairs where you'll find old fashioned Scottish hospitality and live jazz. There are comforting classics like Scottish salmon, scallops, haggis and game in season but most customers are here for the dry-aged, grass-fed Aberdeenshire beef. The wine list has an Old World bias, with plenty of choice at the top end.

Bread Street Kitchen

modern **Plan VIII L3**

10 Bread St ✉ EC4M 9AJ
✆ (020) 3030 4050
www.breadstreetkitchen.com
⊖ St Paul's
Closed 25-26 December – booking advisable

Carte £37/59

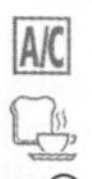

Influenced perhaps by the time he has spent in the US in recent years, Bread Street Kitchen is Gordon Ramsay's take on New York loft-style dining. With floor-to-ceiling windows, a large bar, thumping music, an open kitchen running down one side and enough zinc ducting on the ceiling to kit out a small industrial estate, the space is big, butch and full of buzz. In a further departure from his usual style of operation, the food is quite simple and rustic – think modern bistro dishes with the odd touch of refinement – and there is enough choice to provide something for everyone. The short rib burger is a best seller; the wood oven is used to good effect with dishes like braised pork collar; and the desserts are particularly well done.

Butlers Wharf Chop House

British traditional **Plan X N4**

36e Shad Thames, Butlers Wharf ✉ SE1 2YE
✆ (020) 7403 3403
www.chophouse-restaurant.co.uk
⊖ London Bridge

Carte £29/64

A chophouse means meat and, where there is meat, there are usually men. You'll see plenty of them here, their suit jackets slung over their seats as they get stuck into a charcoal-grilled rib-eye or prepare to wrestle with a game bird. The menu is a paean to all things British so other choices such as steak and kidney pudding or lamb with haggis are equally sturdy; finish off with a sticky toffee pudding and you'll wonder if you'll ever be hungry again. The large room comes with light wood panelling that'll prompt cricketers to think of linseed oil, and the bar at the entrance offers a simpler and cheaper menu. Come in the summer for a table on the fantastic terrace – few restaurants can match the stunning views.

Cantina Del Ponte

Italian **Plan X N4**

36c Shad Thames, Butlers Wharf ✉ SE1 2YE
✆ (020) 7403 5403
www.cantina.co.uk
⊖ London Bridge
Closed 24-26 December

Menu £13/23 – Carte £18/50

A refurbishment a few years back revitalised this Italian stalwart. They kept the large mural on one wall and created a pleasantly relaxing, faux-rustic environment. The menu was also tweaked: it was out with the pizzas and in with a greater degree of authenticity. The focus is on appealing and flavoursome dishes and the set menu represents decent value. There's a good selection on offer, with the focus very much on recognisable standards and old favourites; flavours are well-defined and portions are bigger than expected. The wine list covers all of Italy and there's ample choice by the glass. The first tables to go on a summer's day are naturally those on the riverside terrace under the awning.

Caravan

other world kitchens **Plan IX K1**

11-13 Exmouth Market ✉ EC1R 4QD
✆ (020) 7833 8115
www.caravanonexmouth.co.uk
⊖ Farringdon
Closed Sunday – booking advisable

Carte £19/45

A discernible Antipodean vibe pervades this casual eatery, from the laid-back, easy-going charm of the serving team to the kitchen's confident combining of unusual flavours; even in the excellent flat-whites served by the barista. There's an ersatz industrial feel to the room and a randomness to the decorative touches that belies the seriousness of the ambition. The 100% Arabica beans are roasted daily in the basement, the wine list features an unusual selection of producers and plenty of organic wines, and the owners' travels (hence the name) inform the innovative and inventive cooking. There's something for everyone, from breakfast to small plates to share, or even main courses for two – this really is a caravan of love.

Ⓝ Casse Croûte

French **Plan X M5**

109 Bermondsey St ✉ SE1 3XB
✆ (020) 7407 2140
www.cassecroute.co.uk
⊖ London Bridge
Closed Sunday dinner – booking essential

Carte £25/32

The joys of Bermondsey Street are legion and the variety of restaurants on offer is considerable but if you'd still prefer to feel you're somewhere else then squeeze into this tiny bistro and you'll be instantly transported to rural France. From the fleur de lys decoration and the tiled flooring to the red leather seating and the gingham table cloths, this place is so French that if a film studio had created it they would be accused of perpetuating cultural clichés. The blackboard menu offers just three choices for each course but does evolve during the day, with new dishes added as others run out. The cooking is rustic and authentic and the flavours heartening and wholesome; go the whole way and have the cheese course too.

Cellar Gascon

French **Plan VIII L2**

59 West Smithfield ✉ EC1A 9DS
✆ (020) 7600 7561
www.cellargascon.com
⊖ Barbican
Closed Christmas-New Year, Saturday, Sunday and bank holidays – booking essential at lunch

Menu £9 (lunch) – Carte £15/24

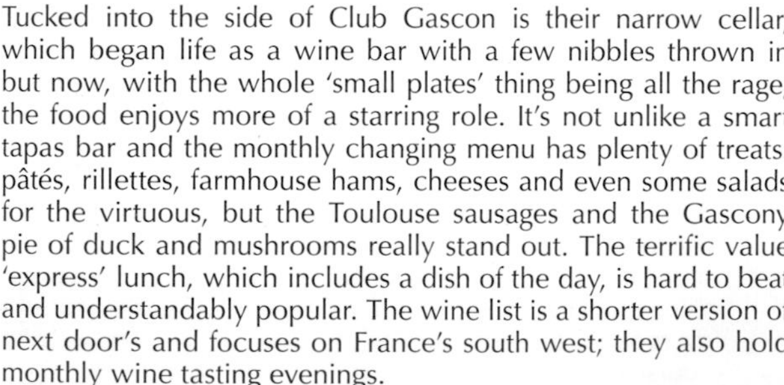

Tucked into the side of Club Gascon is their narrow cellar, which began life as a wine bar with a few nibbles thrown in but now, with the whole 'small plates' thing being all the rage, the food enjoys more of a starring role. It's not unlike a smart tapas bar and the monthly changing menu has plenty of treats: pâtés, rillettes, farmhouse hams, cheeses and even some salads for the virtuous, but the Toulouse sausages and the Gascony pie of duck and mushrooms really stand out. The terrific value 'express' lunch, which includes a dish of the day, is hard to beat and understandably popular. The wine list is a shorter version of next door's and focuses on France's south west; they also hold monthly wine tasting evenings.

Chabrot

French — **Plan IX L2**

62-63 Long Ln ✉ EC1A 9EJ
✆ (020) 7796 4550
www.chabrot.com
⊖ Barbican
Closed August, Christmas, Saturday and Sunday

Menu £15 (lunch and early dinner) – Carte £25/42

If you're yearning to relive that romantic weekend in Paris then a meal at this classic French bistrot could help, although its location opposite Smithfield meat market may reduce some of your ardour. This is the second Chabrot, following the success of the original branch in Knightsbridge, and it shares the same reassuringly familiar Gallic look and lively, inclusive atmosphere. If you're looking for value head for the keenly priced set menu, otherwise enjoy the rustic delights of the main menu, where gutsy classics like tête de veau, confit de canard and boudin noir are there in all their glory. If you're still not sated after that, then finish with some French farmhouse cheeses or a classic crème brûlée.

The Chancery

modern — **Plan VIII K2**

9 Cursitor St ✉ EC4A 1LL
✆ (020) 7831 4000
www.thechancery.co.uk
⊖ Chancery Lane
Closed 23-30 December, 1 January, Saturday lunch, Sunday and bank holidays

Menu £29/35

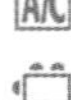

The Chancery is an elegant, discreet restaurant that's so close to the law courts you'll assume your fellow diners are all barristers, jurors or the recently acquitted. The ground floor, with its contemporary artwork and smartly laid tables, is slightly more comfortable than the basement. The menu is appealingly concise and understated and most of the dishes have a reassuringly classical backbone, whether that's the mackerel escabeche or the saddle of rabbit. The kitchen clearly knows what it is doing – flavours are bold and sauces are a particular highlight. The service team can seem a little withdrawn at first – maybe it's dealing with all those formal legal types – but they do get the job done.

Chiswell Street Dining Rooms

British modern **Plan VIII M2**

Montcalm London City at The Brewery Hotel,
56 Chiswell St ✉ EC1Y 4SA
✆ (020) 7614 0177
www.chiswellstreetdining.com
⊖ Barbican
Closed 25-26 December, 1 January, Saturday and Sunday

Carte £29/55

The Martin brothers used their successful Botanist restaurant as the model for their corner spot at the former Whitbread brewery. It may double as a dining room for the Montcalm Hotel, but the place really comes alive in the evening, thanks in no small part to its lively cocktail bar. There's a pleasing Britishness to the menu and the kitchen makes good use of nearby Billingsgate, with classics like whole Cornish lemon sole, and poached langoustines. Those who prefer more muscular cooking can head for the Hereford snail and smoked bacon pie or Aberdeen Angus rib-eye; and who cannot fail to smile when they see 'Knickerbocker Glory' on a menu? The smartly kitted-out staff cope well and help with the buzzy atmosphere.

Cigalon

French **Plan VIII K3**

115 Chancery Ln ✉ WC2A 1PP
✆ (020) 7242 8373
www.cigalon.co.uk
⊖ Chancery Lane
Closed Christmas and New Year, Saturday, Sunday and bank holidays

Menu £15/27 – Carte £22/40

A huge skylight bathes the room in light while the kitchen pays homage to the food of Provence – this is a restaurant that really comes into its own in the summer. A former auction house for law books, the space is stylishly laid out, with the booths in the centre being the prized seats – ask for No.9 if you want to watch the chefs in action. Along with the traditional dishes such as soupe au pistou, bouillabaisse, salade niçoise and pieds et paquets are popular grilled dishes such as venison, and there's even the occasional detour to Corsica. Equal thought went into the name: it refers to both a 1935 Marcel Pagnol film about a haughty chef and the local name for the summer cicada. There's also a busy bar downstairs in the cellar.

Cinnamon Kitchen

Indian **Plan VIII N2**

9 Devonshire Sq ✉ EC2M 4YL
(020) 7626 5000
www.cinnamon-kitchen.com
⊖ Liverpool Street
Closed Saturday lunch, Sunday and bank holidays

Menu £21 (lunch and early dinner) – Carte £24/52

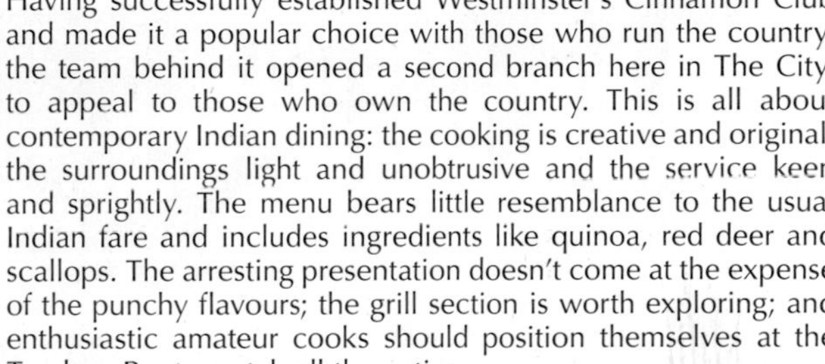

Having successfully established Westminster's Cinnamon Club and made it a popular choice with those who run the country, the team behind it opened a second branch here in The City, to appeal to those who own the country. This is all about contemporary Indian dining: the cooking is creative and original, the surroundings light and unobtrusive and the service keen and sprightly. The menu bears little resemblance to the usual Indian fare and includes ingredients like quinoa, red deer and scallops. The arresting presentation doesn't come at the expense of the punchy flavours; the grill section is worth exploring; and enthusiastic amateur cooks should position themselves at the Tandoor Bar to watch all the action.

Clerkenwell Kitchen

modern **Plan IX K1**

27-31 Clerkenwell Cl ✉ EC1R 0AT
(020) 7101 9959
www.theclerkenwellkitchen.co.uk
⊖ Farringdon
Closed Christmas-New Year, Saturday, Sunday and bank holidays – booking advisable – (lunch only)

Carte £17/23

Time spent working in Dorset with Hugh Fearnley-Whittingstall has clearly influenced Emma, the owner of this busy, tucked away eatery: she sources her ingredients from small producers who use traditional methods and is committed to sustainability, recycling and the reduction of food miles. But this is more than just a worthy enterprise – the food is rather good too. Local office workers flock in for breakfast and takeaway sandwiches but it is well worth booking for the appealing daily changing lunch menu. Two of the six main courses will be vegetarian and offer, along with dishes like venison and pancetta pie, plenty of freshness and flavour. Even the juices are seasonal and the tarts, pies and cakes are all made daily.

City Social

modern Plan VIII M3

Tower 42 (24th floor), 25 Old Broad St ✉ EC2N 1HQ
☎ (020) 7877 7703
www.citysociallondon.com
⊖ Liverpool Street
Closed Sunday

Carte £34/55

City Social

One of the first things Jason Atherton insisted on when he took over the space in Tower 42 – previously occupied by Gary Rhodes – was having a separate lift for the restaurant; getting up to the 24th floor is now a far less tortuous experience. The other major change is that the place is far bigger as further office space was commandeered to create a large bar. The handsome restaurant has a darker, moodier look with a subtle art deco twist – larger parties should ask for one of the comfortable circular booths – while the views of the City's ever-changing skyline are as impressive as ever, especially if you ask for tables 10 or 15. The menu is the same lunch and dinner, but has some flexibility built in, and the influences are largely European. The kitchen has a deft touch but also wisely acknowledges its customer base by making dishes quite robust in flavour and generous in size – this is elegant, refined but satisfying cooking, without the frills and fripperies. The wine list is also noteworthy, with a good mix of styles and prices.

First Course

- Pig's trotter and ham hock with black pudding, apple and Madeira.
- Yellow fin tuna tataki, cucumber salad, radish, avocado and ponzu dressing.

Main Course

- Braised Isle of Gigha halibut with chorizo & red pepper stew, crispy squid and fennel.
- Rack of Romney Marsh lamb, shepherd's pie.

Dessert

- White chocolate mousse, caramel hazelnuts and salted caramel ice cream.
- Rum baba, English summer berries and strawberry sorbet.

Club Gascon ✿

French **Plan VIII L2**

57 West Smithfield ✉ EC1A 9DS
✆ (020) 7600 6144
www.clubgascon.com
⊖ Barbican
Closed Christmas-New Year, Saturday lunch, Sunday and bank holidays – booking essential

Menu £25/60 – Carte £39/55

A/C

Club Gascon

Those living in Gascony enjoy a diet with the highest fat content in France yet they tend to live longer than their compatriots. Leaving aside the magical powers of Armagnac, this 'Gascony paradox' is surely reason enough to explore further this most indulgent of cuisines. Chef-owner Pascal Aussignac is passionate about all things south-western: get him started on the quality of the produce and he'll talk the hind legs off an âne. Whilst familiar ingredients appear on the menu, the cooking is surprisingly contemporary and often quite original; the ambition may not always be matched by the execution but the dishes will certainly grab your attention. Lunch is a slightly pared down version of the evening menu but the tasting menu remains the benchmark and comes with some intelligent and well-considered wine matches. Service is appropriately and unapologetically Gallic, while marble pillars, panelling and huge floral displays add grandeur to the high-ceilinged room, which was once a Lyons Corner House.

First Course

- Razor clams with hay-infused emulsion and truffle vinaigrette.
- Gillardeau oysters, seaweed crush, cured foie gras and lime.

Main Course

- Cappuccino of black pudding, lobster and asparagus.
- French rabbit, octopus and chorizo chutney, ink sauce.

Dessert

- Black olive 'millionaire'.
- Cherries, smoked berries, elderflower and black tea tuile.

Comptoir Gascon

French **Plan IX K2**

61-63 Charterhouse St. ✉ EC1M 6HJ
✆ (020) 7608 0851
www.comptoirgascon.com
⊖ Farringdon
Closed Christmas-New Year, Sunday, Monday and bank holidays – booking essential

Menu £15 (weekday lunch) – Carte £17/45 

A/C This buzzy restaurant should be subsidised by the French Tourist Board as it does more to illustrate one component of Gascony's famed 'douceur de vivre' – sweetness of life – than any glossy brochure. The wines, breads, foie gras, duck and cheeses all celebrate SW France's reputation for earthy, proper man-food. The menu is divided into 'mer', 'vegetal' and 'terre'; be sure to order duck, whether as rillettes, confit or in a salade Landaise. After these big flavours, it'll come as a relief to see that the desserts, displayed in a cabinet, are delicate little things. The prices are also commendable; even the region's wine comes direct from the producers to avoid the extra mark-up. There's further booty on the surrounding shelves.

Del Mercato

Italian **Plan X L4**

Park St ✉ SE1 9AD
✆ (020) 7407 3651
www.delmercato.co.uk
⊖ London Bridge
Closed 25-26 December, 1-2 January, Saturday lunch and Sunday

Menu £18/30 – Carte £27/38 

 Just when you thought every wharf and warehouse in this part of town had been converted into something shiny and new, along came Del Mercato, from the Vinopolis people. It occupies 3,000 sq ft of space under railway arches and is divided up into a bakery, a little espresso bar that's open for breakfast, a trattoria that does a brisk trade in pizzas and homemade pastas, and upstairs, a more formal restaurant. This room is bright and contemporary yet still manages to evoke something of its past. The on-view kitchen is an accomplished one: the à la carte is extensive and traverses Italy, offering everything from Sicilian caponata to Caprese cake to Venetian mackerel 'in saor'; there is also a competitively priced set menu run alongside.

Duck & Waffle

modern — **Plan VIII N2**

Heron Tower (40th floor), 110 Bishopsgate ✉ EC2N 4AY
✆ (020) 3640 7310
www.duckandwaffle.com
⊖ Liverpool Street
Booking essential

Carte £27/64

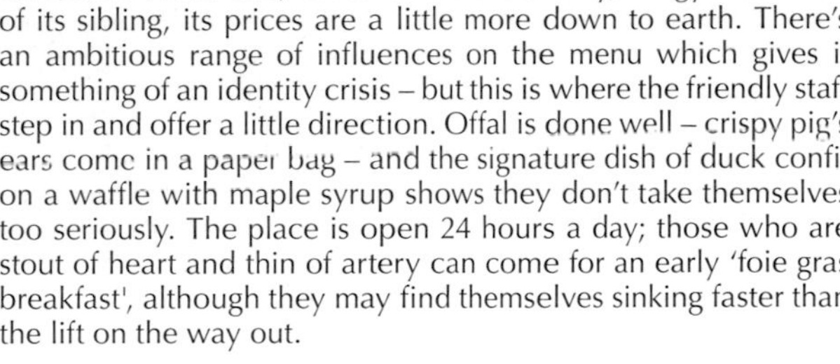

The UK's highest restaurant sits one floor up from Sushisamba in the Heron Tower and, while it lacks the shouty, blingy showiness of its sibling, its prices are a little more down to earth. There's an ambitious range of influences on the menu which gives it something of an identity crisis – but this is where the friendly staff step in and offer a little direction. Offal is done well – crispy pig's ears come in a paper bag – and the signature dish of duck confit on a waffle with maple syrup shows they don't take themselves too seriously. The place is open 24 hours a day; those who are stout of heart and thin of artery can come for an early 'foie gras breakfast', although they may find themselves sinking faster than the lift on the way out.

Elliot's

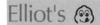

modern — **Plan X M4**

12 Stoney St., Borough Market ✉ SE1 9AD
✆ (020) 7403 7436
www.elliotscafe.com
⊖ London Bridge
Closed Sunday and bank holidays – booking advisable

Carte £17/35

If you want to satisfy the powerful Pavlovian pangs induced by the bounty on display in Borough Market then head for Elliot's. This unpretentious spot sources its ingredients directly from the market and has a kitchen that's wise enough not to muck about with them too much. It's open from breakfast-time onwards and the menu is concise, regularly changing and instantly appealing. Earthy and uncomplicated dishes like squid with aioli and dukkah, and beef cheek with market-fresh winter vegetables, will leave anyone feeling sated and satisfied; many just pop in for their burger which has quickly established its own fan-base. The appeal of Elliot's lies in the fact that it does the simple things well.

Fish Market

fish and seafood **Plan VIII N2**

16b New St ✉ EC2M 4TR
✆ (020) 3503 0790
www.fishmarket-restaurant.co.uk
⊖ Liverpool Street
Closed 25-26 December,1 January, Sunday and bank holidays – booking advisable

Menu £17/25 – Carte £24/52

An antidote to the plethora of steakhouses comes in the form of this traditional seafood restaurant, courtesy of the D&D group. Housed within a former warehouse of the East India Company, it has an appealing ersatz industrial look, with cast-iron pillars, rough-hewn walls and limed oak; the chef shucking oysters behind the full-length marble-topped bar adds to the feeling that you've stepped from Liverpool Street straight into St Ives. From its lengthy menu of classics, the kitchen concentrates on delivering familiar flavours – and by using Cornish crab, oysters from Colchester and West Mersea, day-boat plaice, line-caught cod and farmed bass from Greece – demonstrates it has the appropriate sustainability credentials.

Ⓝ Foxlow

meats and grills **Plan IX L2**

69-73 St John St ✉ EC1M 4AN
✆ (020) 7014 8070
www.foxlow.co.uk
⊖ Farringdon
Closed 24-31 December and Sunday dinner

Carte £20/37

When those clever people behind the Hawksmoor chain took over the site of the former North Road restaurant, they decided it would make the ideal spot in which to serve something a little different to the usual offerings found in their various steakhouses. Granted, there are steaks on offer but there are plenty of other choices whose influences come from Italy, Asia and the Middle East – highlights include the 8-hour bacon rib which is smoked overnight, assorted fresh salads and ice cream sundaes in a myriad of flavours. The vibe is fun and lively, especially on the ground floor and the place has a funky look too, with a reclaimed oak floor, glazed bricks from the tube and chemistry lab tops from a Yorkshire school.

Garrison

Mediterranean **Plan X M5**

99-101 Bermondsey St ✉ SE1 3XB
(020) 7089 9355
www.thegarrison.co.uk
⊖ London Bridge.
Closed 25-26 December – booking essential at dinner

Menu £12/16 – Carte £21/35

You'd be hard pressed to find a more charming pub than The Garrison. With its appealing vintage look, warm atmosphere and delightful staff, it's the perfect antidote to those hard-edged boozers that we've all accidentally found ourselves in at some point. Open from 8am for smoothies and breakfast, it gets busier as the day goes on – and don't bother coming for dinner if you haven't booked. Booth numbers 4 and 5, opposite the open kitchen, are the most popular while number 2 at the back is the cosiest. Daily specials on the blackboard supplement the nicely balanced menu and the cooking is perky and bright, with a subtle Mediterranean slant. Salads are done well and there's a daily steak, while puds are of a more traditional bent.

Goodman City

meats and grills **Plan VIII M3**

11 Old Jewry ✉ EC2R 8DU
(020) 7600 8220
www.goodmanrestaurants.com
⊖ Bank
Closed Saturday, Sunday and bank holidays

Menu £19 (lunch) – Carte £43/66

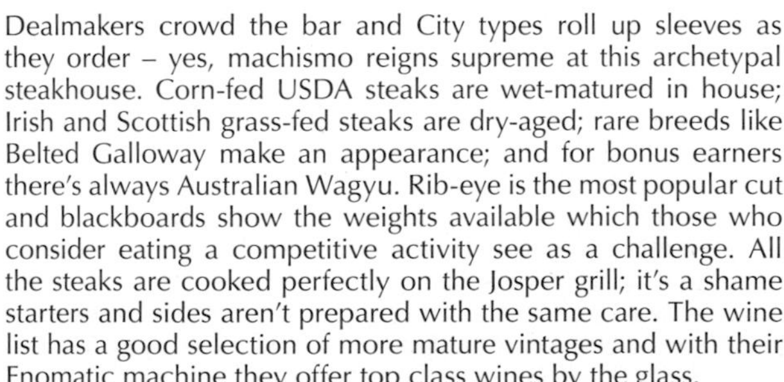

Dealmakers crowd the bar and City types roll up sleeves as they order – yes, machismo reigns supreme at this archetypal steakhouse. Corn-fed USDA steaks are wet-matured in house; Irish and Scottish grass-fed steaks are dry-aged; rare breeds like Belted Galloway make an appearance; and for bonus earners there's always Australian Wagyu. Rib-eye is the most popular cut and blackboards show the weights available which those who consider eating a competitive activity see as a challenge. All the steaks are cooked perfectly on the Josper grill; it's a shame starters and sides aren't prepared with the same care. The wine list has a good selection of more mature vintages and with their Enomatic machine they offer top class wines by the glass.

Hawksmoor

meats and grills **Plan VIII M2**

10-12 Basinghall St ✉ EC2V 5BQ
✆ (020) 7397 8120
www.thehawksmoor.com
⊖ Bank

Closed 24 December-2 January, Saturday, Sunday and bank holidays – booking essential

Carte £34/79

Fast and furious, busy and boisterous, Hawksmoor provides another testosterone filled celebration of the serious business of beef eating – this is about red meat, red wine and red-faced City types in duels to see who can order the biggest steak. It's a handsome room, with its low ceiling, leather seating and wood panelling which was once used in specimen cupboards at the Natural History Museum. The place comes with a great cocktail list and an impressive wine list offering plenty of Mouton Rothschild for the big earners. The Longhorn steaks are nicely aged, particularly the D-Rump, and well-rested before coming to the table. With notice you can order 'meat feasts' which take you on a 7-course 'tour of a cow'.

Hix Oyster and Chop House

British traditional **Plan IX L2**

36-37 Greenhill Rents ✉ EC1M 6BN
✆ (020) 7017 1930
www.hixoysterandchophouse.co.uk
⊖ Farringdon

Closed 25-29 December, Saturday lunch, Sunday dinner and bank holidays

Menu £20 (lunch and early dinner) – Carte £27/54

Utilitarian surroundings, seasonal British ingredients, plenty of offal and prissy-free cooking: this may sound like a description of St John but was in fact Mark Hix's first solo venture and the start of his rapidly expanding restaurant empire. Smithfield Market seems an appropriate location for a restaurant that not only celebrates Britain's culinary heritage with old classics like rabbit brawn, nettle soup and beef and oyster pie but also reminds us of our own natural bounty, from sand eels to asparagus, whiting to laver bread. It's also called an Oyster and Chop House for a reason, with four types of oyster on offer as well as plenty of meat, including Aberdeen beef aged for 28 days and served on the bone.

Hutong

Chinese **Plan X M4**

Level 33, The Shard, 31 St Thomas St ✉ SE1 9RY
✆ (020) 3011 1257
www.hutong.co.uk
⊖ London Bridge
Closed 25-26 December and 1 January – booking essential

Carte £23/50 XX

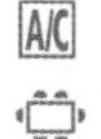

The views may not quite match those of Victoria Harbour enjoyed by Hutong in Tsim Sha Tsui but at least you no longer have to fly out to Hong Kong to get a good vista with your Peking duck. London's branch is on the 33rd floor of The Shard and comes divided into two – if you're looking east you're in the room called Shanghai; if the outlook is westward you're sitting in Beijing which is more atmospheric. The menu focuses on the northern Chinese regions – the specialities include crispy deboned lamb ribs, soft shell crab with chilli and, of course, roast duck served in two parts. Prices are unapologetically vertiginous and service can get a little overwhelmed but so far there's no let-up in its popularity.

José

Spanish **Plan X M5**

104 Bermondsey St ✉ SE1 3UB
✆ (020) 7403 4902
www.josepizarro.com
⊖ London Bridge
Closed 24-26 December and Sunday dinner

Carte approx. £25 X

Included on any list of 'things to be enjoyed while standing up' must surely be the eating of tapas. Here at this snug Bermondsey tapas bar they don't take bookings, but fear not – just turn up and you'll get in because they pack 'em in like boquerones and that adds to the charm. The eponymous José was formerly with Brindisa in Borough Market, so he knows what he's doing and is usually found at the counter carving the wonderful acorn-fed Iberico ham. Five plates per person should be more than enough but it's hard to stop ordering when you see what the person next to you has got. The food is dictated by the markets; you'll find the daily fishy dishes on the blackboard. There's a great list of sherries and all wines are available by the glass.

Jugged Hare

British traditional **Plan VIII M3**

42 Chiswell St ✉ EC1Y 4SA
(020) 7614 0134
www.thejuggedhare.com
⊖ Barbican.
Closed 25-26 December – booking advisable

Menu £38 (dinner) – Carte £29/59

The famous 18C recipe created by Hannah Glasse, the UK's first domestic goddess, provided the inspiration for the renaming of this Grade II listed pub, previously known as The King's Head. It's an apt name because committed vegetarians may feel ill at ease – and not just because of the collection of glass cabinets in the bar which showcase the art of taxidermy. The atmospheric and appealingly noisy dining room, which has a large open kitchen running down one side, specialises in stout British dishes, with Denham Estate venison, Yorkshire guinea fowl and Cumbrian Longhorn steaks from the rotisserie and the grill being the highlights. If the main course doesn't fill you, puddings like treacle tart or bread and butter pudding will.

Kenza

Lebanese **Plan VIII N2**

10 Devonshire Sq. ✉ EC2M 4YP
(020) 7929 5533
www.kenza-restaurant.com
⊖ Liverpool Street
Closed 24-25 December, Saturday lunch and bank holidays

Menu £15/30 – Carte £29/69

Proving that a party atmosphere and good food are not mutually exclusive, Kenza's Middle Eastern exotica instantly transports you away from the city institutions above. It's not easy to find which adds a frisson of expectation, as does descending the staircase into a room full of Moroccan tiles, beaded lamps, lanterns, silk cushions, mosharabi screens and thumping lounge music. Most of the menu is Lebanese but with Moroccan influences; meze is varied and satisfying and the best main courses are slow-cooked lamb shoulder, chargrilled chicken and marinated swordfish; all meat is Halal. Larger parties need not waste time choosing and can order the 'feasting' menus thus allowing more time to appreciate the skills of the belly dancers.

Luc's Brasserie

French **Plan VIII M3**

17-22 Leadenhall Mkt ✉ EC3V 1LR
✆ (020) 7621 0666
www.lucsbrasserie.com
⊖ Bank
Closed Christmas, New Year, Saturday, Sunday and bank holidays – booking essential – (lunch only and dinner Tuesday-Thursday)

Menu £20 – Carte £25/65

An object lesson in understanding your market: Luc's Brasserie regularly serves around 120 people for lunch, many of whom have not just come for the food but because they know they can be in and out within the magical 45 minutes. It's in a great spot looking down over the Victorian splendour of Leadenhall Market and its staff go about their business with impressive efficiency yet still manage to smile and engage with their customers. The menu has all the French favourites you'll ever need, from onion soup to duck rillettes, but many go for the grill section which includes steaks in all sizes and chops aplenty. Needless to say, descending the narrow staircase at the end of the meal requires considerably less resolve than climbing up it.

Lutyens

modern **Plan VIII K3**

85 Fleet St. ✉ EC4Y 1AE
✆ (020) 7583 8385
www.lutyens-restaurant.com
⊖ Blackfriars
Closed 1 week Christmas-New Year, Saturday, Sunday and bank holidays

Menu £22 (lunch and early dinner) – Carte £33/58

This impressive building, designed by Sir Edwin Lutyens and previously Reuters' HQ, is now the ideal backdrop to Sir Terence Conran's elegant and understated restaurant. It's a smoothly run operation, with staff dealing promptly and efficiently with the lunchtime full house; dinner is a far more languid affair. The menu closely follows the seasons and is an appealing blend of the classic, like Dover sole, and the more contemporary, such as squid with ink sauce or smoked venison carpaccio. The cooking is crisp and confident, game is handled well and the kitchen avoids any lily-gilding. Over 30 wines are offered by the glass; from the young and exciting to the fine and rare, and in a super range of measures.

Magdalen

British modern **Plan X M4**

152 Tooley St. ✉ SE1 2TU
✆ (020) 7403 1342
www.magdalenrestaurant.co.uk
⊖ London Bridge
Closed Sunday, Saturday lunch and bank holidays

Menu £16 (lunch) – Carte £28/41

A/C

The Magdalen's kitchen is a clever one: super sourcing and direct contact with farmers take care of the ingredients; the cooking demonstrates a solid, unshowy technique and the influences are kept largely from within the British Isles. Shoulder of Middle White pork with fennel and lemon is a highlight and the rabbit leg with broad beans leaves you wondering why this meat isn't sold in every supermarket. French toast with apricots and vanilla ice cream provides a suitably comforting finale. The lunch menu is a steal, the wine list has been thoughtfully put together by someone who knows the menu well and staff are an eager, genial bunch. The restaurant is divided between two floors; it's more fun on the ground floor.

Manicomio

Italian **Plan VIII L3**

6 Gutter Ln ✉ EC2V 8AS
✆ (020) 7726 5010
www.manicomio.co.uk
⊖ St Paul's
Closed 1 week Christmas, Saturday, Sunday and bank holidays

Menu £23 (dinner) – Carte £28/51

A/C

They've got most of the angles covered here at this City branch of Manicomio: they serve breakfast, cater for private parties, operate a café, provide takeaway, serve drinks and run a restaurant – all within this Norman Foster designed building. The restaurant has a bright, modern feel and the Italian food comes with an unexpected degree of sophistication, although portions are big enough to satisfy anyone who does more than sit at a desk. The homemade breads are good, as are the pasta dishes such as pappardelle which may come with ox cheek or rabbit. Desserts, if you make it that far, continue the theme of adding a modern edge to traditional dishes. Wine, cheese, even the furniture, is all imported from Italy.

Medcalf

British traditional **Plan IX K1**

40 Exmouth Mkt. ✉ EC1R 4QE
✆ (020) 7833 3533
www.medcalfbar.co.uk
⊖ Farringdon
Closed 25 December-1 January, Sunday dinner and bank holidays – booking essential

Menu £15 (weekday dinner) – Carte £23/32

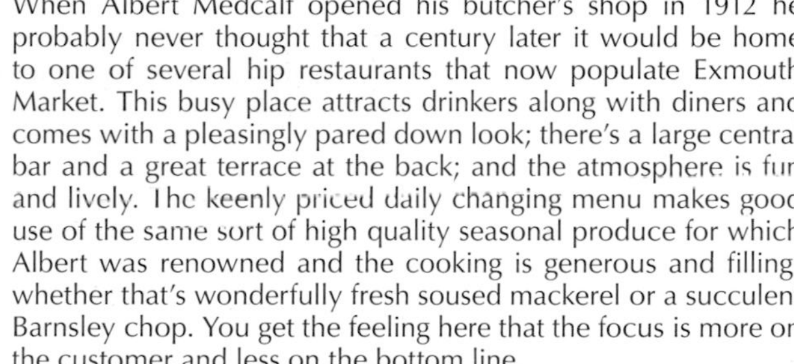

When Albert Medcalf opened his butcher's shop in 1912 he probably never thought that a century later it would be home to one of several hip restaurants that now populate Exmouth Market. This busy place attracts drinkers along with diners and comes with a pleasingly pared down look; there's a large central bar and a great terrace at the back; and the atmosphere is fun and lively. The keenly priced daily changing menu makes good use of the same sort of high quality seasonal produce for which Albert was renowned and the cooking is generous and filling, whether that's wonderfully fresh soused mackerel or a succulent Barnsley chop. You get the feeling here that the focus is more on the customer and less on the bottom line.

The Mercer

British traditional **Plan VIII M3**

34 Threadneedle St ✉ EC2R 8AY
✆ (020) 7628 0001

www.themercer.co.uk

⊖ Bank
Closed 25-26 December, Saturday, Sunday and bank holidays

Carte £27/53

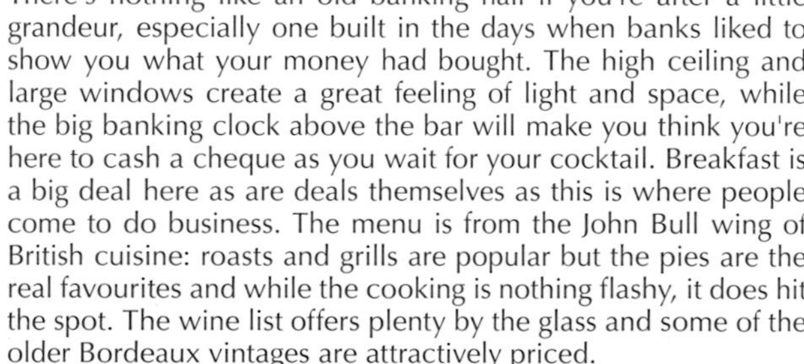

There's nothing like an old banking hall if you're after a little grandeur, especially one built in the days when banks liked to show you what your money had bought. The high ceiling and large windows create a great feeling of light and space, while the big banking clock above the bar will make you think you're here to cash a cheque as you wait for your cocktail. Breakfast is a big deal here as are deals themselves as this is where people come to do business. The menu is from the John Bull wing of British cuisine: roasts and grills are popular but the pies are the real favourites and while the cooking is nothing flashy, it does hit the spot. The wine list offers plenty by the glass and some of the older Bordeaux vintages are attractively priced.

Mint Leaf Lounge

Indian **Plan VIII M3**

12 Angel Ct, Lothbury ✉ EC2R 7HB
✆ (020) 7600 0992
www.mintleaflounge.com
⊖ Bank
Closed 25-26 December, 1 January, Saturday, Sunday and bank holidays

Menu £30 (lunch and early dinner) – Carte £27/43

The 'lounge' in the name is a bit of a clue because the first thing you see when you walk into this impressively proportioned building is a bright and shiny bar. This area is quite a lot larger than the dining room opposite and is a place where many no doubt sought sanctuary during the banking crisis – an added irony being that this was once NatWest's HQ. There's an array of menus on offer, including a number of sharing menus. The à la carte comes with a slight slant towards southern India; the cooking has a contemporary edge and the tandoor oven, chargrill and tawa plate are all used extensively. Staff are irreproachably attentive and, in a sign of improving fortunes, there's a busy champagne bar on the mezzanine floor.

The Modern Pantry

other world kitchens **Plan IX K1**

47-48 St John's Sq. ✉ EC1V 4JJ
✆ (020) 7553 9210
www.themodernpantry.co.uk
⊖ Farringdon
Closed 25-26 December – booking advisable

Menu £22 (weekday lunch)/45 – Carte £26/39

This Georgian building has been everything from a foundry to a carpentry workshop but these days plays host to New Zealander Anna Hansen's fusion restaurant. The smart glass doors lead into a simple, crisp space; there's an upstairs too, split between two rooms, which offers a little more intimacy but lacks the buzz of downstairs. The kitchen's travels are reflected in a menu that has few boundaries. You'll probably need to ask for an explanation of at least one ingredient but the staff are clued up, which is no mean feat since menus change daily as ingredients come in. Despite all that's happening on the plate, flavours are well-judged and complementary. Most dishes also come with thoughtfully suggested wine matches.

Morito

Spanish **Plan IX K1**

32 Exmouth Mkt ✉ EC1R 4QE
✆ (020) 7278 7007
www.morito.co.uk
⊖ Farringdon
Closed 24 December-2 January, Sunday dinner and bank holidays – (bookings not accepted at dinner)

Carte £16/23

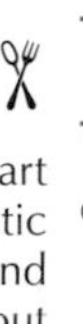

Morito may not seduce you with its looks but once you start eating you'll find it hard to tear yourself away. This authentic tapas bar comes courtesy of the owners of next door Moro and shares their passion for Moorish cuisine. It's modestly kitted out but endearingly so, with a two-tone formica counter and half a dozen small tables; just turn up and if they haven't got space they'll take your number and you can have a drink in Exmouth Market while you wait. Seven or eight dishes between two should be enough but at these prices you can never overspend. Highlights of the immensely appealing menu include jamon and chicken croquetas and succulent lamb chops with cumin and paprika, all served in authentic earthenware dishes.

Moro

Mediterranean **Plan IX K1**

34-36 Exmouth Mkt ✉ EC1R 4QE
✆ (020) 7833 8336
www.moro.co.uk
⊖ Farringdon
Closed dinner 24 December-2 January, Sunday dinner and bank holidays – booking essential

Carte £30/40

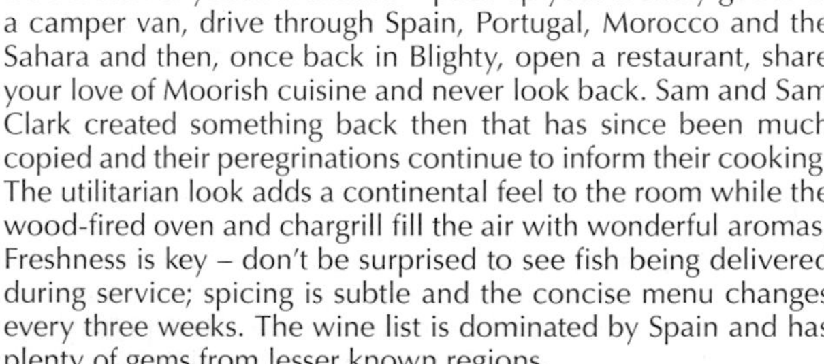

It's the stuff of youthful dreams – pack up your worldly goods in a camper van, drive through Spain, Portugal, Morocco and the Sahara and then, once back in Blighty, open a restaurant, share your love of Moorish cuisine and never look back. Sam and Sam Clark created something back then that has since been much copied and their peregrinations continue to inform their cooking. The utilitarian look adds a continental feel to the room while the wood-fired oven and chargrill fill the air with wonderful aromas. Freshness is key – don't be surprised to see fish being delivered during service; spicing is subtle and the concise menu changes every three weeks. The wine list is dominated by Spain and has plenty of gems from lesser known regions.

New St Grill

meats and grills **Plan VIII N2**

16a New St ✉ EC2M 4TR
✆ (020) 3503 0785
www.newstreetgrill.com
⊖ Liverpool Street
Closed 23 December-7 January except dinner 31 December, Saturday lunch and Sunday dinner

Menu £22 (lunch and early dinner) – Carte £28/58

The people at D&D, who recognise a trend when they see one, converted this 18th century warehouse to satisfy London's ever increasing appetite for red meat. Out of a building that was once used by the East India Company to store spices, they have created an intimate and atmospheric space, with a chic bar attached. The kitchen has a sure hand when it comes to classics like lobster cocktail, Cornish dressed crab and rack of lamb, but beef is the main event here, with steaks cooked on a Josper grill. They use Black Angus and the choice is between grass-fed British beef, aged for 28 days, or corn-fed American beef, aged for 40 days. The wine list is strong on older red Bordeaux and mixes the classic with the more esoteric.

1901

British modern **Plan VIII M2**

Andaz Liverpool Street Hotel,
Liverpool St. ✉ EC2M 7QN
✆ (020) 7618 7000
www.andaz.com
⊖ Liverpool Street
Closed Christmas, Saturday lunch, Sunday and bank holidays

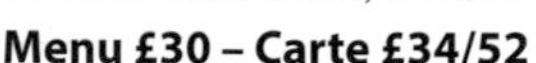

Menu £30 – Carte £34/52

The flagship restaurant in the Andaz hotel occupies what was the ballroom of the original railway hotel – and it's a mightily impressive space. The crisp white decoration and judicious lighting highlight the immense Doric columns, the cornicing and the beautiful cupola above. The 'floating' cocktail bar in the centre of the room takes a little getting used to: the dining tables are fanned out around it so you may find yourself in close proximity to a group of bankers who've just popped in for a bottle or two of Pomerol after work. The menu champions British produce and the cooking is modern and quite ambitious in its reach. A battalion of staff are on hand to provide eager and helpful service and afternoon tea is also served.

Oblix

meats and grills **Plan X M4**

Level 32, The Shard, St Thomas St. ✉ SE1 9RY
✆ (020) 7268 6700
www.oblixrestaurant.com
⊖ London Bridge

Carte £42/124

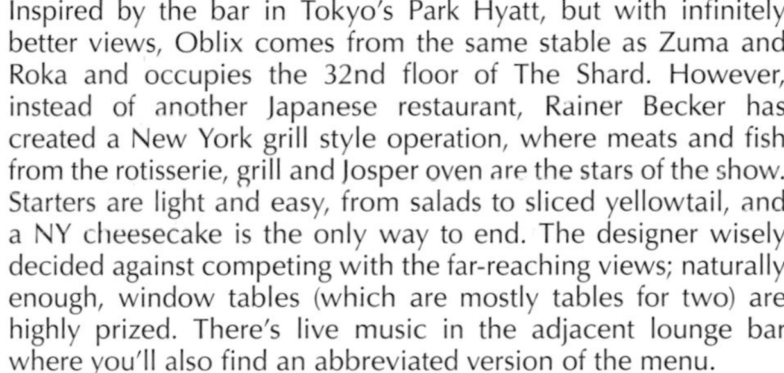

Inspired by the bar in Tokyo's Park Hyatt, but with infinitely better views, Oblix comes from the same stable as Zuma and Roka and occupies the 32nd floor of The Shard. However, instead of another Japanese restaurant, Rainer Becker has created a New York grill style operation, where meats and fish from the rotisserie, grill and Josper oven are the stars of the show. Starters are light and easy, from salads to sliced yellowtail, and a NY cheesecake is the only way to end. The designer wisely decided against competing with the far-reaching views; naturally enough, window tables (which are mostly tables for two) are highly prized. There's live music in the adjacent lounge bar where you'll also find an abbreviated version of the menu.

Oxo Tower

modern **Plan X K4**

Oxo Tower Wharf (8th floor), Barge House St ✉ SE1 9PH
✆ (020) 7803 3888
www.harveynichols.com
⊖ Southwark
Closed 25 December and dinner 24 December

Menu £35 (early dinner) – Carte £42/75

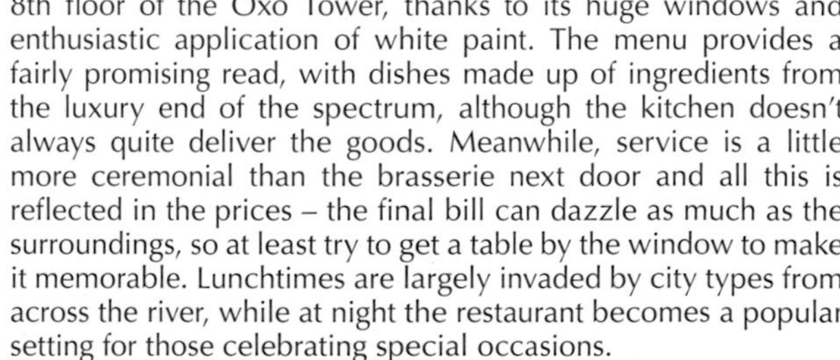

There can be few brighter restaurants than this one on the 8th floor of the Oxo Tower, thanks to its huge windows and enthusiastic application of white paint. The menu provides a fairly promising read, with dishes made up of ingredients from the luxury end of the spectrum, although the kitchen doesn't always quite deliver the goods. Meanwhile, service is a little more ceremonial than the brasserie next door and all this is reflected in the prices – the final bill can dazzle as much as the surroundings, so at least try to get a table by the window to make it memorable. Lunchtimes are largely invaded by city types from across the river, while at night the restaurant becomes a popular setting for those celebrating special occasions.

Oxo Tower Brasserie

modern **Plan X K4**

Oxo Tower Wharf (8th floor), Barge House St ✉ SE1 9PH
✆ (020) 7803 3888
www.harveynichols.com
⊖ Southwark
Closed 25 December and dinner 24 December

Menu £30 (lunch and early dinner) – Carte £35/59

The light-filled, glass-encased brasserie on the eighth floor of the iconic Oxo Tower makes much of its riverside location but that's not to say that this is just a spot for a summer's day as the bold, zingy Mediterranean flavours ensure that the cooking is bright and sunny even when it's dull outside. They've moved the bar to the front so that everyone gets a better view these days. Even so, if you've never asked for a window table before, then now is the time to start. Better still, ask for the terrace and face east towards St Paul's for the best views. Staff do their bit by being a responsive bunch and the place really rocks in the evenings. It's much more fun than their restaurant and the prices are friendlier too.

Paternoster Chop House

British traditional **Plan VIII L3**

Warwick Ct., Paternoster Sq. ✉ EC4M 7DX
✆ (020) 7029 9400
www.paternosterchophouse.co.uk
⊖ St Paul's
Closed Christmas, Saturday and dinner Sunday

Menu £23 – Carte £26/46

If you could make just one restaurant legally obliged to serve British food then it would probably be the one that lies in the shadow of St Paul's Cathedral, one of Britain's most symbolic landmarks. Fortunately, Paternoster Chop House negates the need for a bye-law by offering classics from all parts of these isles. The first thing you see on the neatly laid-out menu is the comfortingly patriotic sight of a 'Beer of the Day'. Their livestock comes from small farms, their fish from day boats in the southwest and all the old favourites are present and correct: native oysters, cottage pie, potted hough, liver and bacon, and apple crumble. The dining room is large and open; you might have to fight your way through the busy bar.

Peasant

British modern — **Plan IX L1**

240 St John St ✉ EC1V 4PH
✆ (020) 7336 7726
www.thepeasant.co.uk
⊖ Farringdon.
Closed 25 December-1 January and bank holidays except Good Friday – booking essential

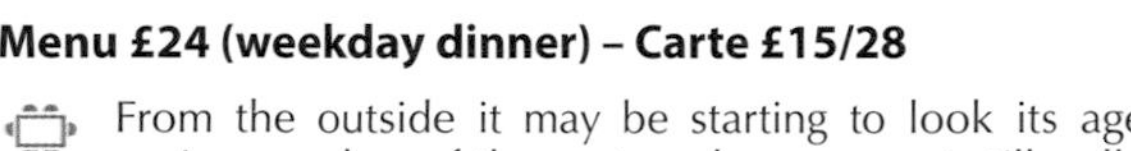

Menu £24 (weekday dinner) – Carte £15/28

From the outside it may be starting to look its age, but this senior member of the gastropub movement still pulls in plenty of punters. Come evening, you have two choices: stay in the bar and compete for a spare table with the City boys having a post-work pint, or book a table in the sanctuary of the sedate upstairs dining room with its circus-themed prints and posters. Downstairs comes with an easy, eat-on-the-hoof type of menu: squid tempura and sharing boards such a cheese or meze stand out and are ideal accompaniments to a pint. In the restaurant dishes such as sea bream with capers and brown shrimps, and honey-roast duck with celeriac purée, come with a greater degree of sophistication but still deliver on flavour.

Pizarro

Mediterranean — **Plan X M5**

171-173 Bermondsey St ✉ SE1 3UW
✆ (020) 7378 9455
www.josepizarro.com
⊖ Borough
Closed 24-28 December

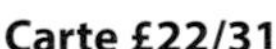

Carte £22/31

José Pizarro has a refreshingly simple way of naming his establishments: first came José, a bustling little tapas bar, and then Pizarro, a larger, more structured restaurant a few doors down. The good news is that Pizarro now takes bookings so you no longer need to hang around waiting for a window seat or a place at the large communal table; in fact, when you do book it's worth asking for one of the prized semi-circular booths. The atmosphere in the restaurant is great and the food equally enjoyable. The menu offers a selection of small and large plates; dishes such as prawns with piquillo peppers and jamón are as tasty as they are easy on the eye. Larger plates could include hake with artichoke, and pork fillet with almonds.

Polpo Smithfield

Italian **Plan IX L2**

3 Cowcross St ✉ EC1M 6DR
✆ (020) 7250 0034
www.polpo.co.uk
⊖ Farringdon.
Closed Christmas, New Year and Sunday dinner

Carte £12/24

If you've been to a Polpo, or even if you've just bought the cookbook, then you'll know what to expect here – refreshingly uncomplicated and inherently satisfying dishes designed for sharing. For his third Venetian-style bacaro, Russell Norman converted a former meat market storage facility and the place has a charming, elegantly battered feel. Head first to the Negroni bar downstairs, with its appealingly wicked atmosphere, and order the eponymous cocktail. Afterwards, you'll find yourself eagerly over-ordering such delights as crisp pizzette or hearty meatballs. The Venetian and North Italian wines come by the glass, carafe and bottle; staff are cool and calm and the atmosphere terrific. Bookings are only taken up to 5.30pm.

Le Pont de la Tour

French **Plan X N4**

36d Shad Thames, Butlers Wharf ✉ SE1 2YE
✆ (020) 7403 8403
www.lepontdelatour.co.uk
⊖ London Bridge
Closed 26 December and 1 January

Menu £15/25 – Carte £36/68

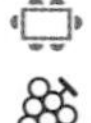

For over 20 years, Le Pont de la Tour has been the flagship restaurant of the Butlers Wharf development. Decoratively, it may not look quite as striking as it did in 1991 but there is no doubting the glory of its location, especially in summer when you can sit on the terrace and look out over the river and Tower Bridge. During the week the place is largely populated by noisier corporate types but at weekends the room takes on a more romantic air. The set price menu, which includes a few dishes which carry supplements, is not dissimilar to that found in a bistro moderne, but if you want even more rustic choices such as pork rillettes or coq au vin then sit in the livelier cocktail bar and grill, with its evening pianist.

Quality Chop House

British traditional **Plan IX K1**

92-94 Farringdon Rd ✉ EC1R 3EA
✆ (020) 7278 1452
www.thequalitychophouse.com
⊖ Farringdon
Closed Sunday dinner and bank holidays – booking advisable

Menu £10 (weekdays)/35 – Carte £22/44

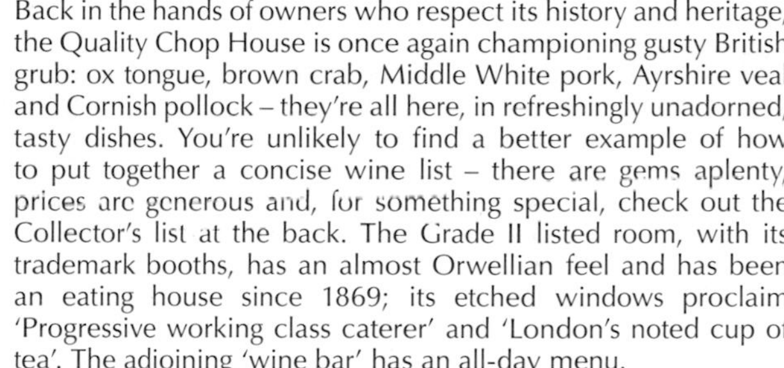

Back in the hands of owners who respect its history and heritage, the Quality Chop House is once again championing gusty British grub: ox tongue, brown crab, Middle White pork, Ayrshire veal and Cornish pollock – they're all here, in refreshingly unadorned, tasty dishes. You're unlikely to find a better example of how to put together a concise wine list – there are gems aplenty, prices are generous and, for something special, check out the Collector's list at the back. The Grade II listed room, with its trademark booths, has an almost Orwellian feel and has been an eating house since 1869; its etched windows proclaim 'Progressive working class caterer' and 'London's noted cup of tea'. The adjoining 'wine bar' has an all-day menu.

Rabot 1745

modern **Plan X M4**

2-4 Bedal St, Borough Mkt ✉ SE1 9AL
✆ (020) 7378 8226
www.rabot1745.com
⊖ London Bridge
Closed 25-26 December, Sunday dinner and Monday

Menu £18 (weekday lunch) – Carte £29/49

Bored by the ordinary? Looking for something different? Then try Rabot 1745, from the owners of Hotel Chocolat, which celebrates the cocoa bean in all its infinite majesty. Named after their estate in St Lucia and its founding year, the restaurant uses wood from the island to add to the plantation feel of the upstairs room. A light-hearted yet knowledgeable introduction is given at the start of the meal explaining how, in its natural state, the flavour of the bean is bitter with a little spice. These flavours are then used in the classically based cooking, with crushed nibs playing a key role, and the resulting dishes have genuine substance. Naturally enough, the desserts are a highlight – don't miss the trio of chocolate mousses.

Restaurant at St Paul's Cathedral

British modern **Plan VIII L3**

St Paul's Churchyard ✉ EC4M 8AD
(020) 7248 1574
www.restaurantatstpauls.co.uk
St Paul's
Closed 25-26 December, 1 January and Good Friday – booking advisable – (lunch only)

Menu £22/26

Tired tourists and weary worshippers in search of sustenance are ably served by this earnest little restaurant, which is tucked away in a corner of the crypt of Sir Christopher Wren's 17C masterpiece. The kitchen prepares everything from scratch and, appropriately enough, promotes and celebrates all things British, and that includes the drinks menu – refresh yourself by ordering 'Britain in a glass'. The monthly changing menu is reassuringly concise and follows the seasons; try soused mackerel, Scottish pollock or free range chicken with black pudding, followed by some cheeses from Neal's Yard or a rice pudding with Bramley apple compote. Service is well meaning and if you linger long enough, they'll start serving afternoon tea.

Roast

British modern **Plan X M4**

The Floral Hall, Borough Mkt ✉ SE1 1TL
(0845) 0347 300
www.roast-restaurant.com
London Bridge
Closed 25 December and 1 January – booking essential

Menu £30 (weekdays)/35 – Carte £30/60

These days every restaurant seemingly name-checks its suppliers – but Roast was one of the first and has always been known for promoting British producers, whether they rear pigs or make cider. Mind you, could they do anything else considering their location – bang in the heart of Borough Market? There's a new energy to the kitchen these days and greater care shown in the preparation of the dishes. The highlight is often the 'dish of the day' which could be rare breed suckling pig with apple sauce; prices can be a little high though, as most main courses need side dishes. Service is also more personable and the bar, which hosts live music at night, is becoming a destination in its own right. Ask for a window table on the market side.

St John ✿

British traditional Plan IX L2

26 St John St ✉ EC1M 4AY
✆ (020) 7251 0848
www.stjohnrestaurant.com
⊖ Farringdon
Closed Christmas-New Year, Saturday lunch, Sunday dinner and bank holidays – booking essential

Carte £25/59

St John

There's no standing on ceremony here at St John; indeed, very little ceremony at all, and that makes eating here such a joyful experience as one's focus is directed entirely at the food. There's little distraction from the surroundings either, which come in a shade of detention centre white. You can play it safe and go for some crab and then roast beef but this is the place to try new flavours, whether that's cuttlefish or ox tongue. Game is a real favourite and the only gravy will be the blood of the bird – this is natural, 'proper' food. Seasonality is at its core – the menu is rewritten for each service – and nothing sums up the philosophy more than the potatoes and greens: they are always on the menu but the varieties and types change regularly. The waiters wear chef's jackets and spend time in the kitchen so they know what they're talking about and are worth listening to. There are dishes for two as well as magnums of wine for real trenchermen – and be sure to order a dozen warm madeleines to take home.

First Course

- Roast bone marrow with parsley salad.
- Smoked sprats with horseradish.

Main Course

- Roast Tamworth loin, turnips and trotter.
- Smoked haddock, saffron and courgettes.

Dessert

- Pear and sherry trifle.
- Eccles cakes with Lancashire cheese.

Sauterelle

French **Plan VIII M3**

The Royal Exchange ✉ EC3V 3LR
✆ (020) 7618 2483
www.royalexchange-grandcafe.co.uk
⊖ Bank
Closed Easter, Saturday, Sunday and bank holidays

Menu £20 – Carte £34/59 

It can't be easy for this D&D restaurant as it's in the somewhat unenviable position of having to compete with the grandeur of its own setting. It occupies the mezzanine floor of the Royal Exchange overlooking what was once the trading floor and is now the Grand Café. This City landmark was twice destroyed by fire and was rebuilt in 1844, but its layout remains largely true to Sir Thomas Gresham's 1566 original. In this most British of scenes one finds a menu of a largely European persuasion, with a particular fondness for all things French, although the ingredients are largely from within the UK. It's easy to find something appealing and, whilst prices are quite high, the kitchen doesn't skimp on luxury ingredients.

1701

innovative **Plan VIII N3**

Bevis Marks Synagogue, Bevis Marks ✉ EC3A 5DQ
✆ (020) 7621 1701
www.restaurant1701.co.uk
⊖ Aldgate

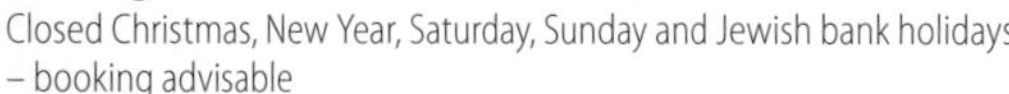

Closed Christmas, New Year, Saturday, Sunday and Jewish bank holidays – booking advisable

Menu £25 (lunch) – Carte £35/51 

This kosher restaurant is housed in a modern extension to Bevis Marks Synagogue – 1701 was the year the synagogue was built, making it the oldest in Britain and one of the oldest in Europe. The dining room is bright and light, thanks to a large glass roof, and service is attentive and helpful. The menu is an extensive document that explains the origins of the dishes but also gives some clues as to how the kitchen will reinterpret them – this is all about fusing different elements of Jewish cuisine in a modern style. The chef's ambition is palpable and, whilst there is the occasional overreliance on presentation, there is no doubting the skill of his kitchen and its mastery of a range of cooking techniques.

Skylon

modern **Plan III J4**

1 Southbank Centre, Belvedere Rd ✉ SE1 8XX
✆ (020) 7654 7800
www.skylon-restaurant.co.uk
⊖ Waterloo
Closed 25 December and Sunday dinner

Menu £29/48

The original Skylon was a steel structure built for the Festival of Britain in 1951 to promote better quality design. Its name now lives on as the restaurant within the Royal Festival Hall, which was built just yards from where this 'vertical feature' once stood. The South Bank is now a much appreciated area of London and the restaurant offers wonderful river views. It's a large space, with a busy central cocktail bar, a formally laid out restaurant on one side and a simpler grill-style operation on the other. The latter serves fishcakes, burgers, steaks and the like; the restaurant uses more expensive ingredients and puts a modern spin on classic combinations. Be sure to ask for a window table.

Sushisamba

Japanese **Plan VIII N2**

Heron Tower (38th and 39th Floor), 110 Bishopsgate
✉ EC2N 4AY
✆ (020) 3640 7330
www.sushisamba.com
⊖ Liverpool Street
Booking essential

Carte £33/73

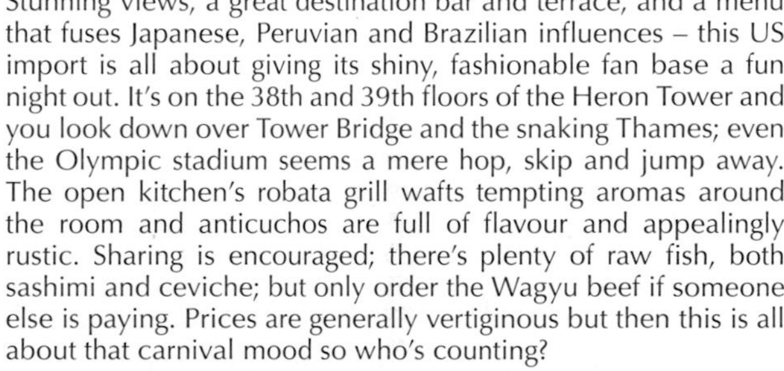

Stunning views, a great destination bar and terrace, and a menu that fuses Japanese, Peruvian and Brazilian influences – this US import is all about giving its shiny, fashionable fan base a fun night out. It's on the 38th and 39th floors of the Heron Tower and you look down over Tower Bridge and the snaking Thames; even the Olympic stadium seems a mere hop, skip and jump away. The open kitchen's robata grill wafts tempting aromas around the room and anticuchos are full of flavour and appealingly rustic. Sharing is encouraged; there's plenty of raw fish, both sashimi and ceviche; but only order the Wagyu beef if someone else is paying. Prices are generally vertiginous but then this is all about that carnival mood so who's counting?

Story ✿

modern **Plan X N5**

201 Tooley St. ✉ SE1 2UE
✆ (020) 7183 2117
www.restaurantstory.co.uk
⊖ London Bridge
Closed 2 weeks Christmas-New Year, 2 weeks August-September, Sunday and Monday – booking essential

Menu £35 (weekday lunch)/80

Story

It's amazing what you can create out of an old public toilet on a traffic island in Bermondsey. Tom Sellers is the young chef who's not only making waves with his cooking but also helped design this purpose-built restaurant. From a distance the wooden structure resembles some sort of Nordic eco-lodge; from the inside, the huge picture window allows the light to flood in, and at night the wood burning stove adds warmth to the room. But the real story is the food – and the food is very good. There are two set menus (presented in old Charles Dickens books – he lived on Tooley Street) of 6 or 10 courses; go for the 10, as 6 is too few. Whilst one can see the obvious influences of Tom's alma maters such as Noma in the food and in the style of service (the chefs occasionally bring the dishes to the table), there is also much originality, not least in the candle made from beef dripping that melts when lit. The food is governed by the seasons; it's earthy yet always delicate, playful but also easy to eat. With just 13 tables, getting in is another story.

First Course

- Onion, apple and gin.
- Scallops, cucumber and dill ash.

Main Course

- Lamb, grilled salad and sheep's yogurt.
- Wild stems, langoustine and clam broth.

Dessert

- Almond and dill.
- Hay, prune and cereal.

Tapas Brindisa

Spanish **Plan X M4**

18-20 Southwark St, Borough Market ✉ SE1 1TJ
✆ (020) 7357 8880
www.tapasbrindisa.com
⊖ London Bridge
Bookings not accepted

Carte £20/32

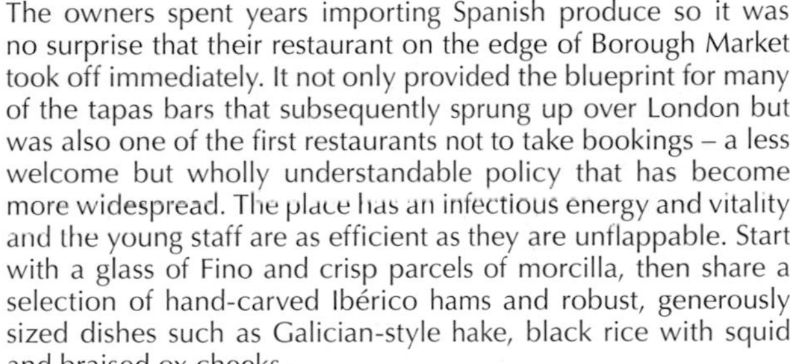

The owners spent years importing Spanish produce so it was no surprise that their restaurant on the edge of Borough Market took off immediately. It not only provided the blueprint for many of the tapas bars that subsequently sprung up over London but was also one of the first restaurants not to take bookings – a less welcome but wholly understandable policy that has become more widespread. The place has an infectious energy and vitality and the young staff are as efficient as they are unflappable. Start with a glass of Fino and crisp parcels of morcilla, then share a selection of hand-carved Ibérico hams and robust, generously sized dishes such as Galician-style hake, black rice with squid and braised ox cheeks.

Tate Modern (Restaurant)

British modern **Plan X L4**

Tate Modern (6th floor), Bankside ✉ SE1 9TG
✆ (020) 7887 8888
www.tate.org.uk
⊖ Southwark
Closed 24-26 December – (lunch only and dinner Friday-Saturday)

Menu £24 – Carte £29/43

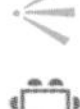

The first thing you'll notice when you get up to Tate Modern's restaurant on Level 6 is the view of St Paul's – and that's about the time you wish you'd asked for a window table. The huge, bright restaurant can seat nearly 150 people so getting a table should never be a problem and there's usually no shortage of atmosphere; black and white is the chosen canvas and tables are surprisingly well spaced. The menu is very seasonal and dishes are largely British; the kitchen keeps things relatively light, even with wintry dishes like venison with red cabbage – so lunch need never impinge on plans for post-prandial art appreciation. Each dish comes with a suggested wine pairing and plenty of thought has gone into creating the drinks selection.

28°-50° Fetter Lane

modern **Plan VIII K3**

140 Fetter Ln ✉ EC4A 1BT
✆ (020) 7242 8877
www.2850.co.uk
⊖ Temple
Closed Saturday, Sunday and bank holidays

Carte £27/40

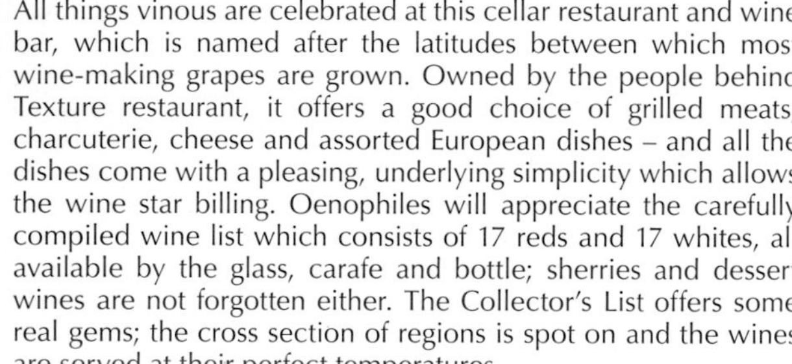

All things vinous are celebrated at this cellar restaurant and wine bar, which is named after the latitudes between which most wine-making grapes are grown. Owned by the people behind Texture restaurant, it offers a good choice of grilled meats, charcuterie, cheese and assorted European dishes – and all the dishes come with a pleasing, underlying simplicity which allows the wine star billing. Oenophiles will appreciate the carefully compiled wine list which consists of 17 reds and 17 whites, all available by the glass, carafe and bottle; sherries and dessert wines are not forgotten either. The Collector's List offers some real gems; the cross section of regions is spot on and the wines are served at their perfect temperatures.

Ⓝ Union Street Café

Italian **Plan X L4**

47 - 51 Great Suffolk Street ✉ SE1 0BS
✆ (020) 7592 7977
www.gordonramsay.com
⊖ London Bridge
Closed 25-26 December and 1 January

Menu £25 (lunch and early dinner) – Carte £29/48

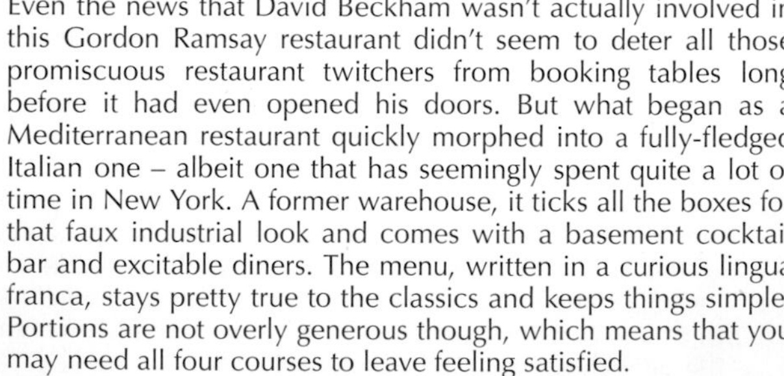

Even the news that David Beckham wasn't actually involved in this Gordon Ramsay restaurant didn't seem to deter all those promiscuous restaurant twitchers from booking tables long before it had even opened his doors. But what began as a Mediterranean restaurant quickly morphed into a fully-fledged Italian one – albeit one that has seemingly spent quite a lot of time in New York. A former warehouse, it ticks all the boxes for that faux industrial look and comes with a basement cocktail bar and excitable diners. The menu, written in a curious lingua franca, stays pretty true to the classics and keeps things simple. Portions are not overly generous though, which means that you may need all four courses to leave feeling satisfied.

Vanilla Black

innovative — Plan VIII K2

17-18 Tooks Ct. ✉ EC4A 1LB
✆ (020) 7242 2622
www.vanillablack.co.uk
⊖ Chancery Lane
Closed 2 weeks Christmas and bank holidays

Menu £20/40

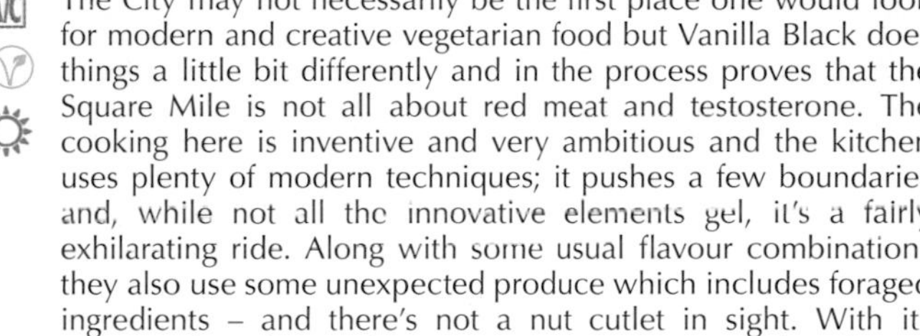

The City may not necessarily be the first place one would look for modern and creative vegetarian food but Vanilla Black does things a little bit differently and in the process proves that the Square Mile is not all about red meat and testosterone. The cooking here is inventive and very ambitious and the kitchen uses plenty of modern techniques; it pushes a few boundaries and, while not all the innovative elements gel, it's a fairly exhilarating ride. Along with some usual flavour combinations they also use some unexpected produce which includes foraged ingredients – and there's not a nut cutlet in sight. With its polite and professional service, smart racing green façade and understated interior, it dispels a few other clichés too.

Village East

modern — Plan X M5

171-173 Bermondsey St ✉ SE1 3UW
✆ (0207) 3576 082
www.villageeast.co.uk
⊖ London Bridge
Closed 24-26 December

Menu £14/24 – Carte £19/45

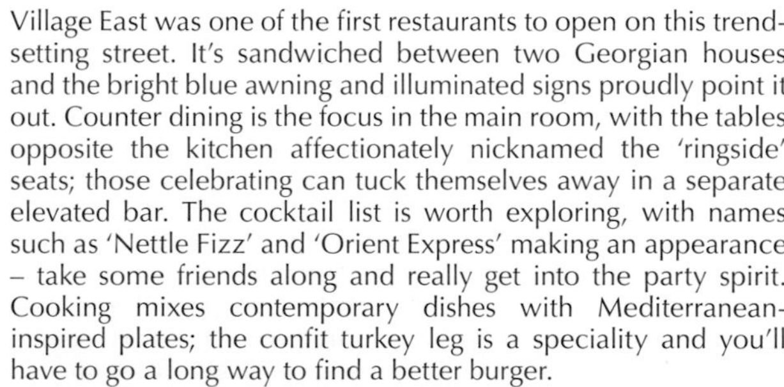

Village East was one of the first restaurants to open on this trend-setting street. It's sandwiched between two Georgian houses and the bright blue awning and illuminated signs proudly point it out. Counter dining is the focus in the main room, with the tables opposite the kitchen affectionately nicknamed the 'ringside' seats; those celebrating can tuck themselves away in a separate elevated bar. The cocktail list is worth exploring, with names such as 'Nettle Fizz' and 'Orient Express' making an appearance – take some friends along and really get into the party spirit. Cooking mixes contemporary dishes with Mediterranean-inspired plates; the confit turkey leg is a speciality and you'll have to go a long way to find a better burger.

Vinoteca

modern **Plan IX L2**

7 St John St. ✉ EC1M 4AA
✆ (020) 7253 8786
www.vinoteca.co.uk
⊖ Farringdon
Closed 25-26 December, 1 January, Sunday and bank holidays

Carte £24/32

Vinoteca, a self-styled 'bar and wine shop', comes divided into two tiny rooms and is always so busy that you'll almost certainly have to wait for a table. But what makes this frenetic place so special is the young and very passionate team who run it so well. The wine list is thrilling: it is constantly evolving and covers all regions, including less familiar territories along with the organic and the biodynamic. In circumstances such as these, the food can often be an afterthought but here it isn't. Alongside the cheeses and the cured meats that are available all day are classic dishes like pear, chicory and Roquefort salad; potted shrimps; bavette steak; and panna cotta – all fresh tasting, well-timed and enjoyable.

Vivat Bacchus

meats and grills **Plan VIII K2**

47 Farringdon St ✉ EC4A 4LL
✆ (020) 7353 2648
www.vivatbacchus.co.uk
⊖ Farringdon
Closed Christmas and New Year, Saturday, Sunday and bank holidays

Carte £22/47

Both the name and the Paul Cluver barriques outside offer clues about the make-up of this bustling City spot: it revolves around wine and the owner is South African. From four cellars come a hugely impressive 500 labels and 15,000 bottles, not only paying homage to major players like Château Latour, d'Yquem, Lafite and Romanée Conti, but also featuring South African jewels like Meerlust Rubicon – if you can button-hole owner Gerrie, he'll give you a tour. The restaurant attracts an ebullient City crowd and the menu complements the wine: steaks and charcuterie dominate and the sharing platters are perfect with a glass or three. Ostrich and kangaroo also feature and you can choose your perfectly ripened cheese from the cheese room.

Vivat Bacchus London Bridge

meats and grills **Plan X M4**

4 Hays Ln ✉ SE1 2HB
✆ (020) 7234 0891
www.vivatbacchus.co.uk
⊖ London Bridge
Closed Christmas-New Year, Saturday lunch, Sunday and bank holidays

Carte £24/47

Here at Vivat Bacchus, wine is regarded as the starting point rather than a supplement. Friends sharing a bottle or two after work make up a healthy part of the business and the menu looks as though it was devised to complement the wine rather than vice versa. As the owners are South African, wines from that country feature heavily, many of which have the necessary muscle for the meat-based menu which includes everything from kangaroo steaks to biltong. Avoid the more ambitious dishes and choose one of the many sharing boards which are largely themed around different countries, perhaps a platter of Italian hams or South African BBQ. It's also worth visiting their cheese room to make your own selection.

Well

British modern **Plan IX L1**

180 St John St ✉ EC1V 4JY
✆ (020) 7251 9363
www.downthewell.com
⊖ Farringdon.
Closed 25-26 December

Carte £23/41

One of the smallest pubs in the Martin Brothers' portfolio is also one of the easiest to find, thanks to its wide expanse of blue canopy. This well-supported neighbourhood pub comes with the sort of food that is reassuringly familiar yet still done well, and service that instills confidence in the customer – just be sure to eat on the ground floor, rather than in the basement. Whether it's asparagus soup or veal Holstein, dishes are cooked with care and deliver on flavour. A side dish between two is needed – the macaroni cheese is worth ordering even if it doesn't necessarily match up to what you're eating – and who isn't reassured by the presence of a crumble on a menu? The only let-down is a lack of draught beers.

The White Swan

modern **Plan VIII K2**

108 Fetter Ln (1st floor) ✉ EC4A 1ES
✆ (020) 7242 9696
www.thewhiteswanlondon.com
⊖ Chancery Lane
Closed 25-26 December, Saturday, Sunday and bank holidays

Menu £29 (lunch) – Carte £26/42

A/C A brunoise here, a glossy sauce there – the evidence of a classical culinary education is insurmountable. There's obvious care and refinement to the cooking as well as an innate understanding of exactly what goes with what. The British provenance of the ingredients is unimpeachable but if the kitchen thinks some Mediterranean flavours will suit a dish better then that is exactly what it gets. The wine list is unapologetically Old World and even comes in a heavy leather binder and the clubby surroundings also fit the bill: the walls are half-panelled and the copper-topped bar has been enthusiastically polished. To reach this haven of serenity and propriety one first has to fight through the hordes of drinkers in the ground floor bar.

Wright Brothers

fish and seafood **Plan X M4**

11 Stoney St., Borough Market ✉ SE1 9AD
✆ (020) 7403 9554
www.thewrightbrothers.co.uk
⊖ London Bridge
Closed dinner 24 December-dinner 28 December, 1-2 January, Easter Sunday and bank holidays – booking advisable

Carte £28/53

If you want to take a breather from the crowds at Borough Market then nip into Wright Brothers, but do it early as it quickly fills. Their motto is 'not just oysters' but then they do excel in them – hardly surprising when you consider that this small place started as an oyster wholesaler. Grab a table and enjoy them raw or cooked, by candlelight, along with the perfect accompaniment – a glass of porter – or else share a bench or the counter and opt for a platter of fruits de mer and a bottle of chilled Muscadet. If the bivalve is not your thing, then there are daily specials such as skate knobs, as well as pies and, for dessert, either chocolate truffles or crème brûlée. An air of contentment reigns.

Zucca

Italian **Plan X M5**

184 Bermondsey St ✉ SE1 3TQ
✆ (020) 7378 6809
www.zuccalondon.com
⊖ Borough

Closed 24 December-7 January, Sunday dinner and Monday – booking essential at dinner

Carte £23/39

The suitably fresh faced young chef-owner seems to have got it all pretty spot-on: the simple but informed Italian cooking is driven by the ingredients, the prices are more than generous, the room is bright and crisp and the service, sweet and responsive. The antipasti forms the largest part of the weekly changing menu and the hard part – especially if you're sharing – is knowing when to stop ordering; but do always include the zucca fritti – the pumpkin speciality. The kitchen team are an unflustered group, largely because they don't fiddle with the food and know that less equals more. The freshly baked breads come with Planeta olive oil; there are usually two pasta dishes and the aromas that fill the room make it hard to leave.

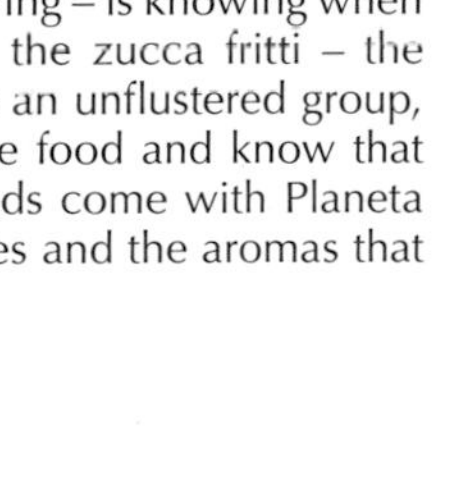

Do not confuse ✗ with ✿ ! ✗ defines comfort, while ✿ are awarded for the best cuisine. Stars are awarded across all categories of comfort.

Chelsea · Earl's Court · Hyde Park · Knightsbridge · South Kensington

Though its days of unbridled hedonism are long gone - and its 'alternative' tag is more closely aligned to property prices than counter-culture - there's still a hip feel to **Chelsea.** The place that put the Swinging into London has grown grey, distinguished and rather placid over the years, but tourists still throng to the **King's Road,** albeit to shop at the chain stores which have steadily muscled out SW3's chi-chi boutiques. It's not so easy now to imagine the heady mix of clans that used to sashay along here, from Sixties mods and models to Seventies punks, but for practically a quarter of a century, from the moment in 1955 when Mary Quant opened her trend-setting Bazaar, this was the pavement to parade down.

Chelsea's most cutting-edge destination these days is probably the gallery of modern art that bears the name of Margaret Thatcher's former favourite, Charles Saatchi. Which isn't the only irony, as Saatchi's outlandishly modish exhibits are housed in a one-time military barracks, the Duke of York's headquarters. Nearby, the traffic careers round **Sloane Square,** but it's almost possible to distance yourself from the fumes by sitting amongst the shady bowers in the centre of the square, or watching the world go by from a prime position in one of many cafés. Having said that, *the* place to get away from it all, and yet still be within striking distance of the King's Road, is the delightful **Physic Garden,** down by the river. Famous for its healing herbs for over 300 years, it's England's second oldest botanic garden.

Mind you, if the size of a green space is more important to you than its medicinal qualities, then you need to head up to **Hyde Park,** the city's biggest. Expansive enough to accommodate trotting horses on Rotten Row, swimmers and rowers in the Serpentine, up-to-the-minute art exhibitions at the Serpentine Gallery, and ranting individualists at Speakers' Corner, the park has also held within its borders thousands of rock fans for concerts by the likes of the Rolling Stones, Simon and Garfunkel and Pink Floyd.

Just across from its southern border stands one of London's most imperious sights, The **Royal Albert Hall,** gateway to the cultural hotspot that is South Kensington. Given its wings after the 1851 Great Exhibition, the area round **Cromwell Road** invested heavily in culture and learning, in the shape of three world famous museums and three heavyweight colleges. But one of its most intriguing museums is little known to visitors, even though it's only a few metres east of the Albert Hall: the Sikorski is, by turns, a moving

C. Eymenier/MICHELIN

and spectacular showpiece for all things Polish.

No one would claim to be moved by the exhibits on show in nearby **Knightsbridge,** but there are certainly spectacular credit card transactions made here. The twin retail shrines of Harvey Nichols and Harrods are the proverbial honey-pots to the tourist bee, where a 'credit crunch' means you've accidentally trodden on your visa. Between them, in **Sloane Street,** the world's most famous retail names line up like an A-lister's who's who. At the western end of Knightsbridge is the rich person's Catholic church of choice, the Brompton Oratory, an unerringly lavish concoction in a baroque Italianate style. Behind it is the enchanting Ennismore Gardens Mews, a lovely thoroughfare that dovetails rather well with the Oratory.

Further west along Old Brompton Road is **Earl's Court,** an area of grand old houses turned into bedsits and spartan hotels. An oddly bewitching contrast sits side by side here, the old resting alongside the new. The old in this case is Brompton Cemetery, an enchanting wilderness of monuments wherein lie the likes of Samuel Cunard and Emmeline Pankhurst. At its southwest corner, incongruously, sits the new, insomuch as it's the home of a regular influx of newcomers from abroad, who are young, gifted and possessed of vast incomes: the players of Chelsea FC.

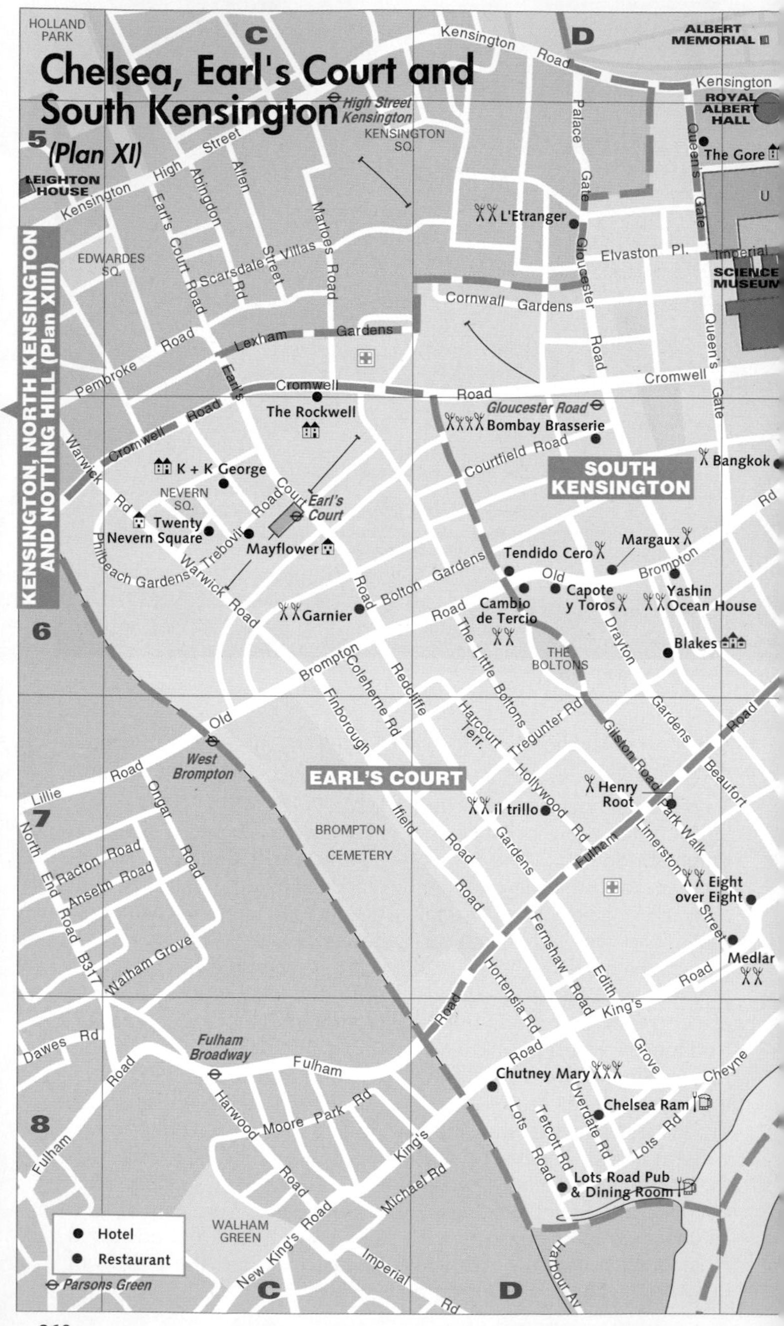

Chelsea, Earl's Court and South Kensington
(Plan XI)
HOLLAND PARK
C
D
5
6
7
8
ALBERT MEMORIAL
ROYAL ALBERT HALL
The Gore
L'Etranger
LEIGHTON HOUSE
EDWARDES SQ.
KENSINGTON SQ.
High Street Kensington
KENSINGTON, NORTH KENSINGTON AND NOTTING HILL (Plan XIII)
SCIENCE MUSEUM
The Rockwell
Gloucester Road
Bombay Brasserie
K + K George
NEVERN SQ.
Twenty Nevern Square
Mayflower
Earl's Court
SOUTH KENSINGTON
Bangkok
Tendido Cero
Margaux
Capote y Toros
Yashin Ocean House
Cambio de Tercio
Garnier
Blakes
THE BOLTONS
West Brompton
EARL'S COURT
BROMPTON CEMETERY
Henry Root
il trillo
Eight over Eight
Medlar
Fulham Broadway
Chutney Mary
Chelsea Ram
Lots Road Pub & Dining Room
WALHAM GREEN
Hotel
Restaurant
Parsons Green
Kensington Road
Kensington High Street
Palace Gate
Queen's Gate
Elvaston Pl.
Cornwall Gardens
Gloucester Road
Cromwell Road
Earl's Court Road
Abingdon Rd
Allen Street
Scarsdale Villas
Marloes Road
Lexham Gardens
Pembroke Road
Warwick Rd
Courtfield Road
Trebovir Road
Philbeach Gardens
Warwick Road
Bolton Gardens
Old Brompton Road
Drayton Gardens
The Little Boltons
Coleherne Rd
Redcliffe
Finborough
Harcourt Terr.
Tregunter Rd
Gilston Road
Beaufort
Hollywood Rd
Park Walk
Limerston Street
Fulham Road
Lillie Road
Ongar Road
North End Road B317
Racton Road
Anselm Road
Walham Grove
Ifield Road
Gardens
Fernshaw Road
Hortensia Rd
Edith Grove
King's Road
Cheyne
Dawes Rd
Fulham Road
Harwood Road
Moore Park Rd
King's Road
Michael Rd
Lots Road
Tetcott Rd
Uverdale Rd
Lots Rd
New King's Road
Imperial Rd
Harbour Av

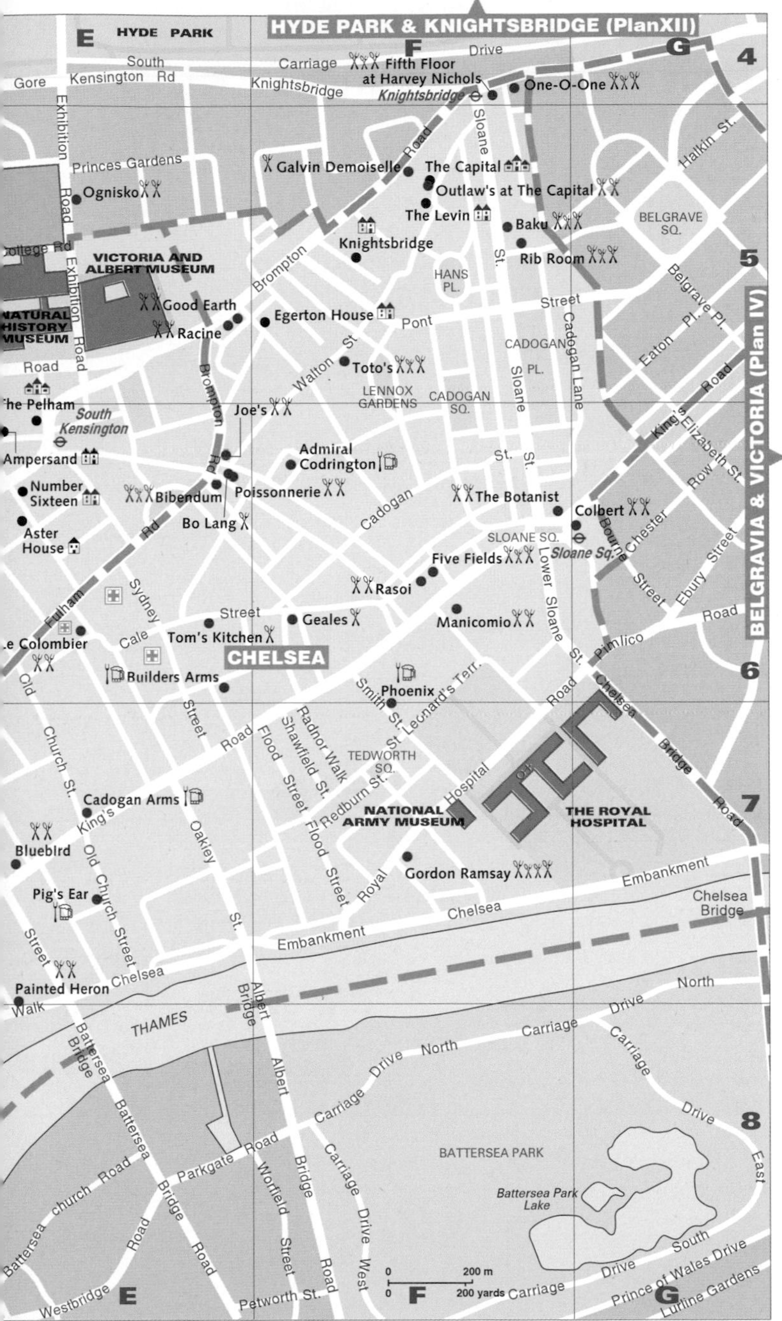
HYDE PARK & KNIGHTSBRIDGE (PlanXII)
BELGRAVIA & VICTORIA (Plan IV)
HYDE PARK
Fifth Floor at Harvey Nichols
One-O-One
Knightsbridge
Galvin Demoiselle
The Capital
Outlaw's at The Capital
The Levin
Baku
Knightsbridge
Rib Room
Ognisko
VICTORIA AND ALBERT MUSEUM
NATURAL HISTORY MUSEUM
Good Earth
Racine
Egerton House
Toto's
The Pelham
South Kensington
Joe's
Ampersand
Admiral Codrington
Number Sixteen
Bibendum
Poissonnerie
Bo Lang
Aster House
The Botanist
Colbert
Sloane Sq.
Five Fields
Rasoi
Geales
Manicomio
Tom's Kitchen
CHELSEA
Le Colombier
Builders Arms
Phoenix
Cadogan Arms
NATIONAL ARMY MUSEUM
THE ROYAL HOSPITAL
Bluebird
Gordon Ramsay
Pig's Ear
Painted Heron
THAMES
BATTERSEA PARK
Battersea Park Lake
200 m
200 yards

Hyde Park & Knightsbridge
(Plan XII)

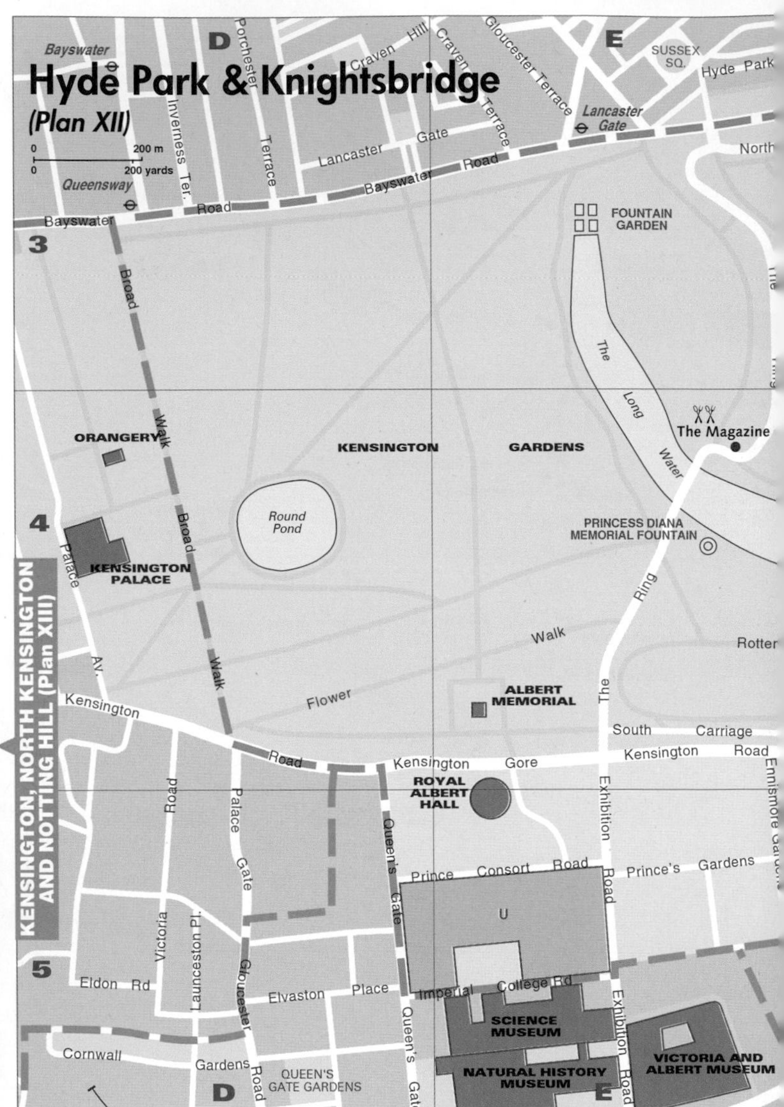

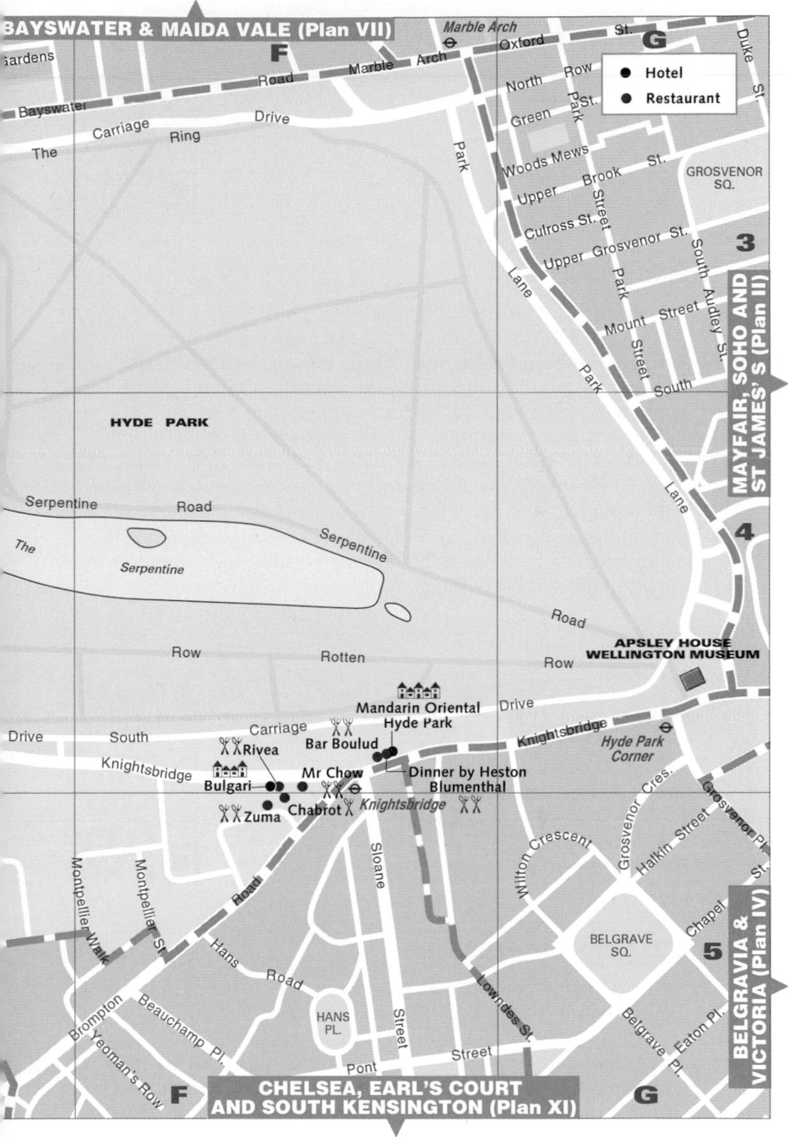
BAYSWATER & MAIDA VALE (Plan VII)
Hotel
Restaurant
HYDE PARK
The Serpentine
Serpentine Road
Rotten Row
South Carriage Drive
Knightsbridge
Mandarin Oriental Hyde Park
Bar Boulud
Rivea
Bulgari
Mr Chow
Dinner by Heston Blumenthal
Zuma
Chabrot
Knightsbridge
Hyde Park Corner
APSLEY HOUSE WELLINGTON MUSEUM
Park Lane
GROSVENOR SQ.
BELGRAVE SQ.
HANS PL.
MAYFAIR, SOHO AND ST JAMES'S (Plan II)
BELGRAVIA & VICTORIA (Plan IV)
CHELSEA, EARL'S COURT AND SOUTH KENSINGTON (Plan XI)
Marble Arch
Oxford St.
Bayswater Road
North Row
Green St.
Woods Mews
Upper Brook St.
Culross St.
Upper Grosvenor St.
Mount Street
South Audley St.
Duke St.
Park Street
Wilton Crescent
Grosvenor Cres.
Halkin Street
Sloane Street
Lowndes St.
Hans Road
Brompton Road
Beauchamp Pl.
Yeoman's Row
Montpellier Walk
Montpellier St.
Pont Street
Chapel St.
Eaton Pl.
Belgrave Pl.
F
G
3
4
5

Admiral Codrington

modern **Plan XI F6**

17 Mossop St ✉ SW3 2LY
✆ (020) 7581 0005
www.theadmiralcodrington.com
⊖ South Kensington.
Closed 24-26 December

Carte £25/45

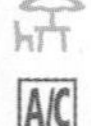

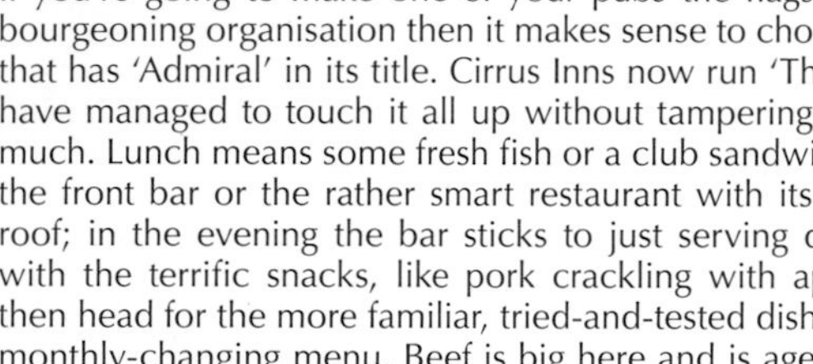

If you're going to make one of your pubs the flagship of your bourgeoning organisation then it makes sense to choose the one that has 'Admiral' in its title. Cirrus Inns now run 'The Cod' and have managed to touch it all up without tampering with it too much. Lunch means some fresh fish or a club sandwich in either the front bar or the rather smart restaurant with its retractable roof; in the evening the bar sticks to just serving drinks. Start with the terrific snacks, like pork crackling with apple sauce, then head for the more familiar, tried-and-tested dishes from the monthly-changing menu. Beef is big here and is aged in-house; the burgers have become popular, with new combinations communicated by Twitter.

Baku

other world kitchens **Plan XI F5**

164 Sloane St (1st Floor) ✉ SW1X 9QB
✆ (020) 7235 5399
www.bakulondon.com
⊖ Knightsbridge

Menu £17/27 – Carte £28/63

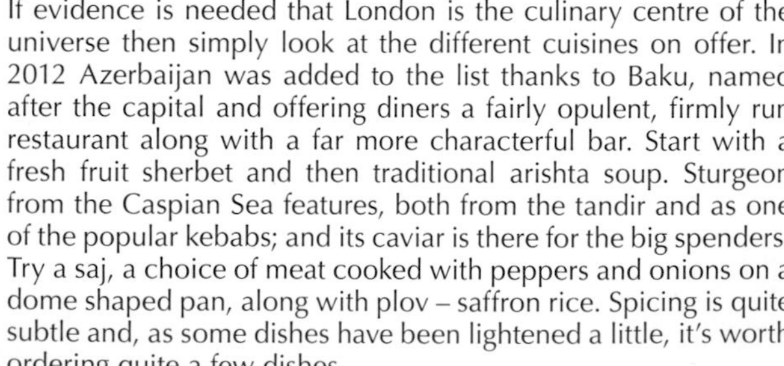

If evidence is needed that London is the culinary centre of the universe then simply look at the different cuisines on offer. In 2012 Azerbaijan was added to the list thanks to Baku, named after the capital and offering diners a fairly opulent, firmly run restaurant along with a far more characterful bar. Start with a fresh fruit sherbet and then traditional arishta soup. Sturgeon from the Caspian Sea features, both from the tandir and as one of the popular kebabs; and its caviar is there for the big spenders. Try a saj, a choice of meat cooked with peppers and onions on a dome shaped pan, along with plov – saffron rice. Spicing is quite subtle and, as some dishes have been lightened a little, it's worth ordering quite a few dishes.

Bangkok

Thai

Plan XI E6

9 Bute St ✉ SW7 3EY
✆ (020) 7584 8529
www.bangkokrestaurant.co.uk
⊖ South Kensington
Closed 24 December-2 January and Sunday

Carte £24/40

A/C You don't survive for over 40 years in London's capricious restaurant scene without doing something right. Bangkok opened at a time when few knew what a wok was and it was the first restaurant to introduce us to fresh and zesty soups, delicate fishcakes, rich curries and moreish noodles. Over the years, Thai restaurants have sprung up throughout the UK, many of them smart and sophisticated, but Bangkok remains resolutely traditional in both its cooking and its uncomplicated surroundings and for that we should be grateful. The laminated menu lists about 20 dishes and the cooking is so fresh and satisfying that, such down-to-earth prices, you feel the restaurant should be sponsored by Thailand's Tourist Board.

Bar Boulud

French

Plan XII F4

Mandarin Oriental Hyde Park Hotel,
66 Knightsbridge ✉ SW1X 7LA
✆ (020) 7201 3899
www.barboulud.com
⊖ Knightsbridge

Menu £19 (lunch and early dinner) – Carte £23/53

A/C    

Lyon-born Daniel Boulud built his considerable reputation in New York and these two cities now inform the menu here at his London outpost. Order a plate of excellent charcuterie while you look at the menu; sausages are a highlight and there are plenty of classic French dishes, from fruits de mer to coq au vin, but it's the burgers that steal the show. Designed by Adam Tihany, the restaurant makes the best of its basement location which was previously used by the Mandarin Oriental Hotel as a storeroom. Don't think you'll be in exile if they lead you to a table around the corner: it's a good spot and you'll be facing the open kitchen. Service is fast and furious; prices are sensible and the place is noisy, fashionable and fun.

Bibendum

French **Plan XI E6**

Michelin House, 81 Fulham Rd. ✉ SW3 6RD
✆ (020) 7581 5817
www.bibendum.co.uk
⊖ South Kensington
Closed dinner 24 December, 25-26 December and 1 January

Menu £28 (weekdays)/36 – Carte £37/72

Bibendum is now well into its twenties but very little has changed over those years, which is why it remains a favourite restaurant for so many. Matthew Harris' cooking continues to produce the sort of food that Elizabeth David would adore – it's French with a British point of view. The set lunch menu is joined by a small à la carte selection; evening menus are handwritten and the roast chicken with tarragon for two remains a perennial presence. Side dishes can bump the final bill up but the food is easy to eat and satisfying; and you've always got the oyster bar downstairs. The striking character of Michelin's former HQ, dating from 1911, is perhaps best appreciated at lunch when the sun lights up the glass Bibendum – the Michelin Man.

Bluebird

British modern **Plan XI E7**

350 King's Rd. ✉ SW3 5UU
✆ (020) 7559 1000
www.bluebird-restaurant.co.uk
⊖ South Kensington

Menu £20 – Carte £21/62

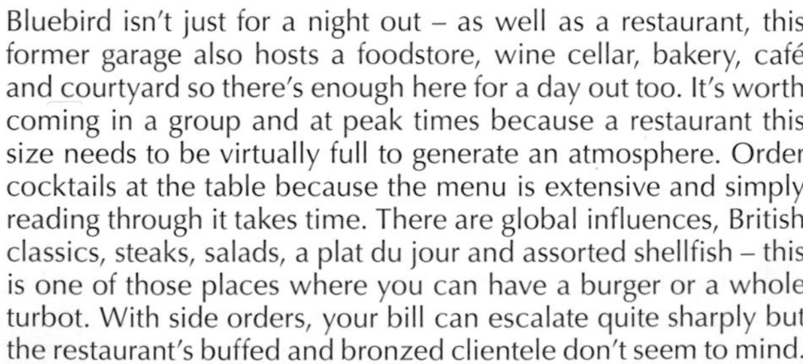

Bluebird isn't just for a night out – as well as a restaurant, this former garage also hosts a foodstore, wine cellar, bakery, café and courtyard so there's enough here for a day out too. It's worth coming in a group and at peak times because a restaurant this size needs to be virtually full to generate an atmosphere. Order cocktails at the table because the menu is extensive and simply reading through it takes time. There are global influences, British classics, steaks, salads, a plat du jour and assorted shellfish – this is one of those places where you can have a burger or a whole turbot. With side orders, your bill can escalate quite sharply but the restaurant's buffed and bronzed clientele don't seem to mind.

Ⓝ Bo Lang

Chinese **Plan XI E6**

100 Draycott Ave ✉ SW3 3AD
✆ (020) 7823 7887
www.bolangrestaurant.com
⊖ South Kensington

Menu £22 (weekday lunch) – Carte £25/48

It's all about dim sum at this diminutive Hakkasan wannabe and they get a lot of things right: the kitchen has a deft touch; the cocktails are very good; the service is polite; the look is cool and the lighting moody. While there are more substantially sized 'main courses' on the menu you're better off sticking with the dim sum, particularly the traditional steamed items, and sharing with friends to mitigate the effects of some fairly ambitious pricing. What doesn't quite work are those dishes made up of more unusual flavour combinations, the small tables, which are not particularly conducive to this style of eating, and the intrusively loud music which, in such a small space, hints at a lack of nerve on someone's part.

Bombay Brasserie

Indian **Plan XI D6**

Courtfield Rd. ✉ SW7 4QH
✆ (020) 7370 4040
www.bombaybrasserielondon.com
⊖ Gloucester Road
Closed 25 December – bookings advisable at dinner

Menu £24 (lunch and early dinner) – Carte £29/52

Going strong since 1982, The Bombay Brasserie has always been one of the smartest Indian restaurants around, but a few years ago it emerged with a brand new look which revitalised the whole place. Plushness abounds, from the deep carpet and huge chandeliers of the large main room to the show kitchen of the conservatory and the very smart bar. The staff also got a new look with their burgundy waistcoats, but they continue to offer charming and professional service. The menu wasn't forgotten either and was overhauled by Hemant Oberoi. They replaced the predictable with the more creative, while at the same time respecting traditional philosophies; influences are a combination of Bori, Parsi, Maharashtrian and Goan cuisine.

The Botanist

modern **Plan XI F6**

7 Sloane Sq ✉ SW1W 8EE
✆ (020) 7730 0077
www.thebotanistonsloanesquare.com
⊖ Sloane Square
Closed 25-26 December

Menu £21 (dinner) – Carte £29/54

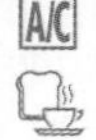

The jury may be out on whether this is a restaurant with a bar attached, or a bar with a restaurant attached but what is certain is that you can get a decent cocktail before ordering dinner. The restaurant is open from breakfast onwards and the menu covers all bases, although its prices can vary quite considerably. The best dishes are usually the simplest ones, which are also usually the most fairly priced – this is the sort of place to have fishcakes, pasta or a big salad; many come here early evening to grab a quick bite before curtain-up at the Royal Court or Cadogan Hall. The waiting staff are a confident lot, perpetually in motion, but for some reason always seem to be on the other side of the room when you need them.

Builders Arms

British traditional **Plan XI E6**

13 Britten St ✉ SW3 3TY
✆ (020) 7349 9040
www.geronimo-inns.co.uk
⊖ South Kensington.
Bookings not accepted

Carte £26/40

The Builders Arms is very much like a packed village local – the only difference being that, in this instance, the village is Chelsea and the villagers are all young and prosperous. The inside delivers on the promise of the smart exterior but don't expect it to be quiet as drinkers are welcomed just as much as diners. In fact, bookings are only taken for larger parties but just tell the staff that you're here to eat and they'll sort you out. The cooking reveals the effort that has gone into the sourcing of some decent ingredients; the rib of beef for two is a perennial favourite. Dishes are robust and satisfying and are not without some flair in presentation. Wine is also taken seriously and their list has been thoughtfully put together.

Cadogan Arms

British traditional **Plan XI E7**

298 King's Rd ✉ SW3 5UG
✆ (020) 7352 6500
www.thecadoganarmschelsea.com
⊖ South Kensington.
Closed 25-26 December – bookings advisable at dinner

Carte £23/42

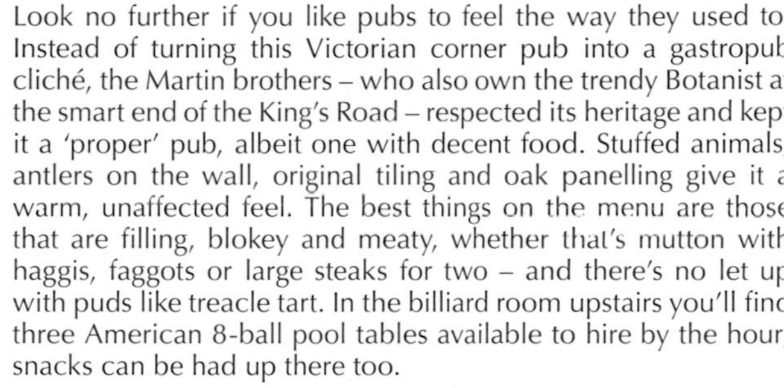

Look no further if you like pubs to feel the way they used to. Instead of turning this Victorian corner pub into a gastropub cliché, the Martin brothers – who also own the trendy Botanist at the smart end of the King's Road – respected its heritage and kept it a 'proper' pub, albeit one with decent food. Stuffed animals, antlers on the wall, original tiling and oak panelling give it a warm, unaffected feel. The best things on the menu are those that are filling, blokey and meaty, whether that's mutton with haggis, faggots or large steaks for two – and there's no let up with puds like treacle tart. In the billiard room upstairs you'll find three American 8-ball pool tables available to hire by the hour; snacks can be had up there too.

Cambio de Tercio

Spanish **Plan XI D6**

163 Old Brompton Rd. ✉ SW5 0LJ
✆ (020) 7244 8970
www.cambiodetercio.co.uk
⊖ Gloucester Road
Closed 2 weeks December and 2 weeks August

Carte £30/60 s

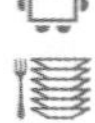

There has been no laurel resting from the owners of this longstanding Spanish restaurant as they are seemingly snapping up every available property in SW5. In 2012 they bought next door but instead of creating another tapas bar they extended this, their flagship restaurant. Nothing changed with the waiters though, who still run around like hormigas looking after all their regulars, many of whom are homesick nationals. The single page menu is divided into Traditional Tapas, their own Signature Tapas – some of which are inspired by El Bulli, such as the excellent omelette – and main courses like the popular Pluma Iberica pork. They also offer a superb selection of sherries and a wine list that proves there is life beyond Rioja.

Capote y Toros

Spanish **Plan XI D6**

157 Old Brompton Road ✉ SW5 0LJ
✆ (020) 7373 0567
www.cambiodetercio.co.uk
⊖ Gloucester Road
Closed 2 weeks Christmas, Sunday and Monday – (dinner only)

Carte £15/39

From the owners of not-quite-next-door Cambio de Tercio comes the compact and vividly coloured Capote y Toros which celebrates sherry, tapas and ham. Named after the matador's cape and his foe, there are enough bullfighting references to satisfy enthusiasts of Hemingway proportions, including a large wall of photos. However, it is sherry that takes centre stage and there's a huge variety and choice on offer. Those as yet unmoved by this most underappreciated of wines should start by trying 5 varieties in a 'flight'. Meanwhile, the menu revolves around about 25 dishes; try 3 per person. The Iberico ham is excellent and the octopus will make the queuing worthwhile – bookings aren't taken. A guitarist plays in the evenings.

Chabrot

French **Plan XII F5**

9 Knightsbridge Grn ✉ SW1X 7QL
✆ (020) 7225 2238
www.chabrot.co.uk
⊖ Knightsbridge
Closed 25 December and 1 January

Carte £23/46

To be honest, you wouldn't give this a place a second glance if you were just strolling down the alley – but all perceptions change when you step inside. Chabrot is a true French bistrot that's warm, cosy and well run. All the classic decorative touches are here and that includes some fearsome Opinel knives to help you get stuck in. The menu is not overlong but what it lacks in length it more than makes up in authenticity. The kitchen looks to the SW of France and Pays Basque for inspiration, so along with snails in parsley butter, cassoulet and coq au vin you'll find Basque charcuterie, sea bream with piperade, and gâteau Amatxi. Dishes are hearty and tasty and many of the regulars plan their visit according to the plat du jour.

Chelsea Ram

British modern **Plan XI D8**

32 Burnaby St ✉ SW10 0PL
✆ (020) 7351 4008
www.geronimo-inns.co.uk/thechelsearam
⊖ Fulham Broadway.

Carte £22/29

The Chelsea Ram stands out from the crowd because it's got heart and soul – this is a pub that just feels right as soon as you walk in. It has always been a proper local and comes with a palpable sense of community, but not to the extent that interlopers are given the evil eye by the regulars at the bar. Thursday is steak night and Friday, fish night; you can come for brunch at weekends and can even join the Geronimo Club for regular cheese and wine tastings. Dining tables wind themselves around the bar, with quieter ones nestling at the back under a glass roof. Blackboard specials supplement the menu of sturdy pub classics and seasonal dishes. Alternatively, you can stand at the bar for a pint and a pork pie.

Chutney Mary

Indian **Plan XI D8**

535 King's Rd. ✉ SW10 0SZ
✆ (020) 7351 3113
www.realindianfood.com
⊖ Fulham Broadway
(dinner only and lunch Saturday-Sunday)

Menu £26 – Carte £34/58

When Chutney Mary opened in 1990 it signalled the arrival of a new-wave of cosmopolitan Indian restaurants. Instead of the basic beer and curry house aesthetic we got smart surroundings, regional specialities, cocktails and even suggested wine pairings for the meal – and it's a combination that is still working successfully today. The place is deceptively large and comes with framed silks, mirrors, candles and prints; if you're a couple then ask for a table in the slightly less hectic conservatory. Dishes come from all across India and range in style from redefined street food to luxurious fish dishes from the south. The kitchen uses plenty of British produce and employs chefs from the different Indian regions to ensure authenticity.

Colbert

French G6

50-52 Sloane Sq ✉ SW1W 8AX
✆ (020) 7730 2804
www.colbertchelsea.com
⊖ Sloane Square
Closed 25 December and dinner 24 December – booking advisable

Carte £18/55 XX

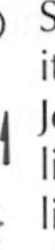

With its posters, chessboard tiles and red leather seats, Colbert bears more than a passing resemblance to a Parisian pavement café and there can't be a better spot for one than here on Sloane Square, next to the Royal Court. This is the old Oriel café and it was transformed by seasoned restaurateurs Chris Corbin and Jeremy King. It's an all-day, every day operation and the menu lists all the French classics; you can pop in for a croque monsieur, linger over a steak Diane or come for breakfast at any time of day. The best dishes are the simpler ones and if you haven't booked, try the bar. Despite the somewhat dispiriting sight of an anachronistic cover charge, this place feels set to become part of the local fabric for some time.

Le Colombier

French Plan XI E6

145 Dovehouse St. ✉ SW3 6LB
✆ (020) 7351 1155
www.le-colombier-restaurant.co.uk
⊖ South Kensington

Menu £20 (weekday lunch) – Carte £34/57

Le Colombier is as warm and welcoming as it is honest and reliable and thereby offers proof that being a good neighbourhood restaurant takes more than just being in a good neighbourhood. French influences abound, from the accents of the staff and the menu content to the inordinate amount of double cheek kissing that occurs – most of the customers appear to know one another or feel they should like to know one another. In summer, when the full-length windows fold back, the terrace is the place to sit although the underfloor heating ensures the place is equally welcoming in winter. Oysters, game in season, veal in various forms and regional cheeses are the highlights, as are the classic desserts from crêpe Suzette to crème brûlée.

Dinner by Heston Blumenthal ✿✿

British modern Plan XII F4

Mandarin Oriental Hyde Park Hotel,
66 Knightsbridge ✉ SW1X 7LA
✆ (020) 7201 3833
www.dinnerbyheston.com
⊖ Knightsbridge
Closed 2 days Christmas

Menu £38 (weekday lunch) – Carte £63/75

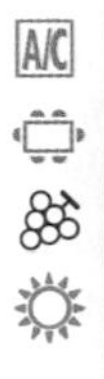

Mandarin Oriental Hyde Park

For a country with a less than stellar reputation for the quality of its food, we need reminding sometimes about the glories of our own culinary heritage. So hats off then to Heston Blumenthal because his mischievously named restaurant at the Mandarin Oriental Hyde Park should stir feelings of pride in all of us regarding our native cuisine. Don't come expecting 'molecular' alchemy; the menu reads like a record of historic kitchen triumphs, with the date of origin attached to each dish and a fashionably terse list of its parts; on the reverse you can read more. A kitchen brigade of 45 works with calm efficiency, meticulous attention to detail and intelligence to produce food that looks deceptively 'simple' but tastes sublime. The large, light room has quirky touches, like wall sconces shaped as jelly moulds, but the main focus is on the open kitchen, with its oversized watch mechanics powering the spit to roast the pineapple that goes with the Tipsy Cake (c.1810).

First Course

- Scallops with cucumber ketchup, roasted cucumber and borage.
- Mandarin, chicken liver and foie gras parfait with grilled bread.

Main Course

- Spiced pigeon, onion, ale and artichokes.
- Roast turbot with mussel and seaweed ketchup, salmon roe and sea rosemary.

Dessert

- Tipsy cake with spit-roast pineapple.
- Chocolate bar with passion fruit jam and ginger ice cream.

Eight over Eight

Asian **Plan XI E7**

392 King's Rd ✉ SW3 5UZ
✆ (020) 7349 9934
www.rickerrestaurants.com
⊖ South Kensington
Closed 25 December and 1 January

Menu £35/50 – Carte £15/45 

A/C 

A major fire a few years ago meant that Eight over Eight stayed shut for quite a few months, but anyone who missed it too much during this period needed only to nip up to Notting Hill to find another one of Will Ricker's trendy Asian restaurants. From the day it reopened it has been full, so maybe its customers are more loyal than anyone thought; they are certainly a handsome bunch and many of them seem to know one another. The restaurant was largely unchanged in its look; it just feels a little plusher and is better lit. Wisely, they didn't change the menu either; its influences stretch across a number of countries in South East Asia and dishes are designed for sharing. Highlights are the creamy curries and anything that's crispy.

L'Etranger

innovative **Plan XI D5**

36 Gloucester Rd. ✉ SW7 4QT
✆ (020) 7584 1118
www.etranger.co.uk
⊖ Gloucester Road
Booking essential

Menu £18/26 – Carte £35/61 

A/C   

Messing around with classic French cooking is considered sacrilegious in certain parts of France but L'Etranger has escaped the tyranny of tradition by locating itself in South Kensington, London's own little Gallic ward. It offers an eclectic mix off French dishes that are heavily influenced by Japan, so a veal chop will come with wasabi sauce and salmon is poached in sake. Not every dish has a Nipponese constituent but it certainly makes for an original experience. The room is dark and moody and better suited to evenings, while service is a little more formal than it need be. The clientele is a mix of well-heeled locals and homesick French and Japanese émigrés, who also appreciate the depth and breadth of the impressive wine list.

Fifth Floor at Harvey Nichols

modern **Plan XI F4**

109-125 Knightsbridge ✉ SW1X 7RJ
✆ (020) 7235 5250
www.harveynichols.com
⊖ Knightsbridge
Closed Christmas, Easter and Sunday dinner

Menu £22/32 – Carte £45/52

Competition for customers in this part of town gets stiffer by the day so it's all change once again on the Fifth Floor of Harvey Nicks. The biggest difference is in the style of the food. A new kitchen team has been assembled and charged with improving the quality of the cooking. Whilst it remains largely European in its influences and classically French in its techniques, the menu now boasts quite a degree of sophistication and the elaborately constructed dishes clearly demonstrate talent and ambition. The room itself is as handsome as ever, even though it has had more new looks than many of its glamorous customers – the challenge is giving it its own sense of identity among all the other delights on offer on this floor.

Five Fields

modern **Plan XI F6**

8-9 Blacklands Terr ✉ SW3 2SP
✆ (020) 7838 1082
www.fivefieldsrestaurant.com
⊖ Sloane Square
Closed first 2 weeks January, first 2 weeks August, Sunday and Monday – (dinner only)

Menu £50

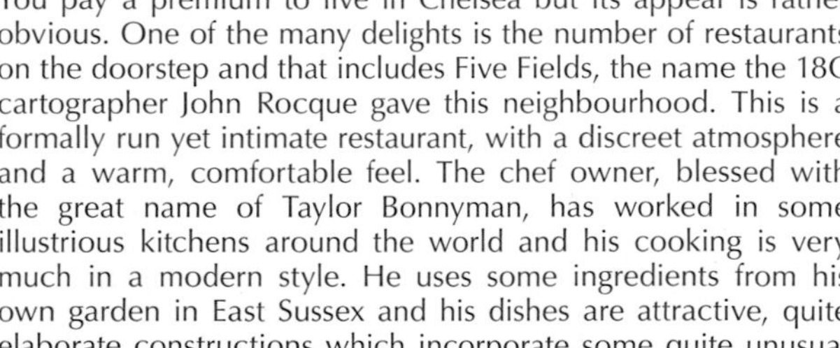

You pay a premium to live in Chelsea but its appeal is rather obvious. One of the many delights is the number of restaurants on the doorstep and that includes Five Fields, the name the 18C cartographer John Rocque gave this neighbourhood. This is a formally run yet intimate restaurant, with a discreet atmosphere and a warm, comfortable feel. The chef owner, blessed with the great name of Taylor Bonnyman, has worked in some illustrious kitchens around the world and his cooking is very much in a modern style. He uses some ingredients from his own garden in East Sussex and his dishes are attractive, quite elaborate constructions which incorporate some quite unusual combinations of flavours, particularly in the desserts.

Galvin Demoiselle

French — **Plan XI F5**

Ground Floor Food Hall, Harrods, 87-135 Brompton Rd
✉ SW1X 7XL
✆ (020) 7893 8590
www.galvinrestaurants.com
⊖ Knightsbridge
Closed 25 December and Sunday dinner – bookings not accepted

Carte £34/46

A/C The Galvin brothers' bourgeoning company now includes this smart and distinctively dressed café, which you'll find on the mezzanine floor of Harrods' food hall. Their French-accented menu sensibly acknowledges the unavoidable truth that most people are in the building primarily to shop and so you won't find anything too heavy, elaborate or time consuming. A different soup is served each day, along with a choice of five salads; there's assorted charcuterie and carefully prepared, easy-to-eat dishes like cocottes or their popular baked lobster fishcake. You can also pop in for morning coffee and a pastry or afternoon tea and a French Fancy and, although it's not inexpensive, they have got the tone and style of the service just right.

Garnier

French — **Plan XI C6**

314 Earl's Court Rd ✉ SW5 9QB
✆ (020) 7370 4536
www.garnier-restaurant-london.co.uk
⊖ Earl's Court

Menu £18 (lunch) – Carte £35/61

A/C

Earl's Court has never been overburdened by decent restaurants so local residents must have considered getting out the bunting when the experienced Garnier brothers decided to open a brasserie on their doorstep. Sandwiched by nondescript shops, it has an authentic traditional Gallic feel, thanks to a wall of mirrors and rows of simply dressed tables. But the decoration is not the point – it's all about the comforting food here. London was once full of French restaurants but these days finding escargots, pigeon rôti and crêpes Suzette all on the same menu is not so easy, and the extensive menu of reassuring classics is such a good read, you'll find it hard to choose. The wine list has good representation from Burgundy and Bordeaux.

Geales

fish and seafood **Plan XI F6**

1 Cale St ✉ SW3 3QT
✆ (020) 7965 0555
www.geales.com
⊖ South Kensington
Closed 22 December-3 January and Monday

Menu £13 (weekday lunch) – Carte £23/39

Good fish and chips shouldn't just be the preserve of tourists hoping to catch up on new episodes of the Benny Hill Show while they're here – we all need reminding of their appeal sometimes and, for this, there is Geales. Don't be fooled by the "Established 1939" sign outside, as this branch opened in 2010. It occupies the site of Tom Aikens' short-lived chippy but the extraction system has clearly improved as there has been no uprising by locals worried about frying fumes permeating their Colefax and Fowler. The place is charmingly decorated, cosy and warmly run and the menu successfully mixes the classics with the more modern, so there's fried haddock along with soft shell crab tempura. Puds are wholesome and homemade.

Good Earth

Chinese **Plan XI E5**

233 Brompton Rd. ✉ SW3 2EP
✆ (020) 7584 3658
www.goodearthgroup.co.uk
⊖ Knightsbridge
Closed 23-31 December

Carte £23/46

The menu might seem a little predictable but this long-standing Chelsea Chinese has always proved a reliable choice in an area where tourist-traps are not entirely unknown. Although there is no particular geographical bias, the cooking is fresh and carefully executed and dishes neatly presented and authentic. Shanghai chilli chicken and the clay pots are the popular choices; there's a decent selection of vegetarian dishes; and the kitchen uses some pretty high-end ingredients without charging the earth. The restaurant has a smart, slighter lighter look these days; choose between the larger, more comfortable basement and the ground floor room with its smart horseshoe bar for those who like counter dining.

Gordon Ramsay ✿✿✿

French **Plan XI F7**

68-69 Royal Hospital Rd. ✉ SW3 4HP
✆ (020) 7352 4441
www.gordonramsay.com
⊖ Sloane Square
Closed 23-27 December, Saturday and Sunday – booking essential

Menu £55/185

Gordon Ramsay

It's not just the kitchen at Gordon Ramsay's flagship restaurant that has evolved – the room itself has also had a makeover to keep it fresh and it is now a lot brighter, with light wood panels all fashioned from the same tree. Reassuringly, the ever-reliable Jean-Claude is ever-present, as he has been since the day the restaurant opened. He has instilled in his team the same care and passion for the art of service as he has demonstrated over the years; they are not only effortlessly composed but also undertake their work without the slightest arrogance or aloofness. The result is that an air of calm pervades the room. In the kitchen, head chef Clare Smyth continues to reveal more of her own personality through her cooking, with the menu being a little more daring and the combinations more original. The Menu Prestige offers the complete experience, with G. Ramsay classics alongside Clare's newer creations, but her passion is most evident in the exquisite dishes from the Seasonal Inspiration dinner menu.

First Course

- Cheltenham beetroot with clementine and smoked goat's curd.
- Butter baked young cauliflower, Iberico ham and Lincolnshire Poacher.

Main Course

- Turbot, seaweed, palourde clams, fennel and romanesco.
- Lamb, spring vegetable 'Navarin', best end and braised shank.

Dessert

- Smoked chocolate cigar with blood orange and cardamom ice cream.
- Lemonade parfait with honey and yogurt sorbet.

Henry Root

French Plan XI D7

9 Park Walk ✉ SW10 0AJ
✆ (020) 7352 7040
www.thehenryroot.com
⊖ South Kensington
Closed 25-27 December – booking advisable

Carte £20/37 X

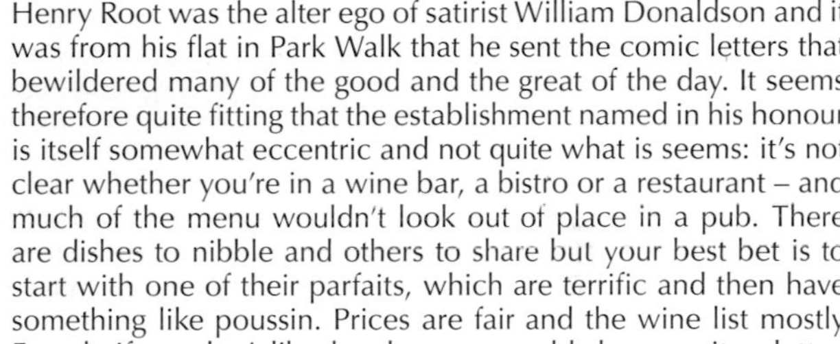

Henry Root was the alter ego of satirist William Donaldson and it was from his flat in Park Walk that he sent the comic letters that bewildered many of the good and the great of the day. It seems therefore quite fitting that the establishment named in his honour is itself somewhat eccentric and not quite what is seems: it's not clear whether you're in a wine bar, a bistro or a restaurant – and much of the menu wouldn't look out of place in a pub. There are dishes to nibble and others to share but your best bet is to start with one of their parfaits, which are terrific and then have something like poussin. Prices are fair and the wine list mostly French. If you don't like the place you could always write a letter.

il trillo

Italian Plan XI D7

4 Hollywood Rd ✉ SW10 9HY
✆ (020) 3602 1759
www.iltrillo.net
⊖ Earl's Court
Closed 25-26 December – (dinner only and lunch Saturday-Sunday)

Menu £28 – Carte £25/54

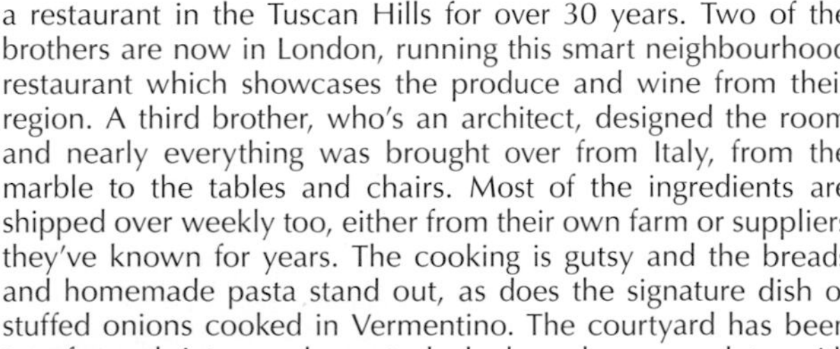

The Bertuccelli family have been making wine and running a restaurant in the Tuscan Hills for over 30 years. Two of the brothers are now in London, running this smart neighbourhood restaurant which showcases the produce and wine from their region. A third brother, who's an architect, designed the room and nearly everything was brought over from Italy, from the marble to the tables and chairs. Most of the ingredients are shipped over weekly too, either from their own farm or suppliers they've known for years. The cooking is gutsy and the breads and homemade pasta stand out, as does the signature dish of stuffed onions cooked in Vermentino. The courtyard has been transformed into a pleasant decked garden, complete with lemon trees.

Joe's

modern **Plan XI E6**

126 Draycott Ave ✉ SW3 3AH
✆ (020) 7225 2217
www.joseph.co.uk
⊖ South Kensington
Closed 25 December and dinner Sunday-Monday

Carte £24/46

A/C

Most restaurants rely on a certain amount of passing business to keep the credit side of their ledgers looking positive. Joe's faces a challenge here because its narrow entrance makes it resemble a bar more than a restaurant and this is a shame because this is a place that deserves to do well. For one thing, it understands the importance of giving its glamorous customers what they want, which means an appealing mix of Mediterranean influenced favourites and various light, healthy choices. Dishes may be quite simple but the kitchen does things with care and flavours are clearly defined. The attractive room is framed by bookcases full of wine and magazines. Service hits the spot too, as the good-looking staff really do seem to care.

Lots Road Pub & Dining Room

British traditional **Plan XI D8**

114 Lots Rd ✉ SW10 0RJ
✆ (020) 7352 6645
www.lotsroadpub.com
⊖ Fulham Broadway.
Closed 25 December

Carte £22/35

A/C

At lunch expect to be joined by those from the nearby Design Centre; at dinner the place is colonised by good-looking locals; and at weekends it's full of folk who've been busy buying antiques. The pub may be looking a little worn around the edges but when a kitchen occupies half the bar you just know they take their food seriously. The menu may be short and at first glance rather safe but they use good produce and cook it with care and respect. Blackboards offer "season's eatings" and there's a daily recipe too. Look out too for the weekly 'wicked wines' selection where you can pick up a bargain. Steak is still a speciality and it's worth coming on Sunday for a roast and a Bloody Mary. They also have a great customer loyalty scheme.

The Magazine

modern — **Plan XII E4**

Serpentine Sackler Gallery, West Carriage Dr,
Kensington Gardens ✉ W2 2AR
✆ (020) 7298 7552
www.magazine-restaurant.co.uk
⊖ Lancaster Gate
Closed Sunday dinner, Tuesday dinner and Monday

Carte £27/51

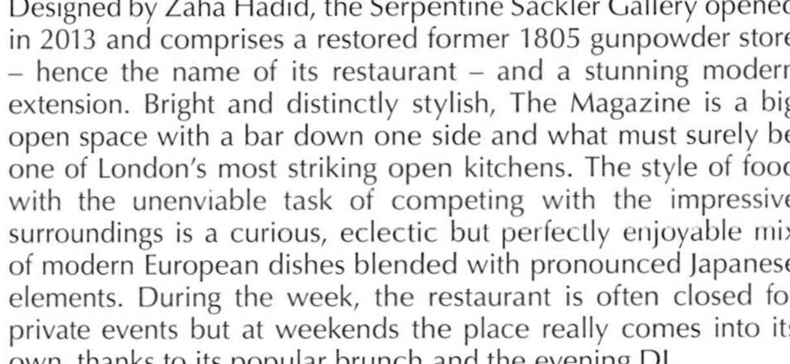

Designed by Zaha Hadid, the Serpentine Sackler Gallery opened in 2013 and comprises a restored former 1805 gunpowder store – hence the name of its restaurant – and a stunning modern extension. Bright and distinctly stylish, The Magazine is a big open space with a bar down one side and what must surely be one of London's most striking open kitchens. The style of food with the unenviable task of competing with the impressive surroundings is a curious, eclectic but perfectly enjoyable mix of modern European dishes blended with pronounced Japanese elements. During the week, the restaurant is often closed for private events but at weekends the place really comes into its own, thanks to its popular brunch and the evening DJ.

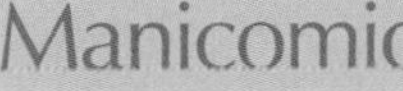

Manicomio

Italian — **Plan XI F6**

85 Duke of York Sq, King's Rd ✉ SW3 4LY
✆ (020) 7730 3366
www.manicomio.co.uk
⊖ Sloane Square
Closed 25 December-1 January

Menu £23 (lunch and early dinner) – Carte £29/49

If anywhere encapsulates King's Road's journey from counterculture hub to retail playground it is Duke of York Square and its outlets. Among these is Manicomio, a glossy Italian restaurant which doesn't need to rely solely on weary shoppers as it also draws visitors from the Saatchi Gallery next door, a fact that shows just what an inspired location this was. Its success is also helped by an accessible menu, offering a greatest hits of easy-to-eat Italian food. Cooking is undertaken with care and the simplest dishes are the best ones, although prices do reflect the Chelsea postcode. Service remains sufficiently perky for one to forgive occasional moments of forgetfulness. The terrific front terrace fills quickly in nearly all seasons.

Marco

French **Plan XVIII T2**

Stamford Bridge, Fulham Rd. ✉ SW6 1HS
✆ (020) 7915 2929
www.marcorestaurant.org
⊖ Fulham Broadway
Closed Sunday-Monday – booking advisable – (dinner only)

Carte £24/44

A/C

A section of Manchester United fans was once derided as being prawn sandwich eaters; London expectations being what they are, at Chelsea's ground you get a brasserie from Marco Pierre White. Some will inevitably cry foul and shed a tear for football's working class roots; others will cheer for this evidence of our growing culinary maturity. Both sides, though, should applaud the menu, which offers classics galore such as grilled Dover sole, assorted roasts and Scottish steaks. This being a polyglot club means other nationalities are also represented, in this case a bit of Italy and France, and more sophisticated fare such as foie gras terrine or duck confit is available. Puddings are a particular highlight.

Margaux

Mediterranean **Plan XI D6**

152 Old Brompton Rd ✉ SW5 0BE
✆ (020) 7373 5753
www.barmargaux.co.uk
⊖ Gloucester Road
Closed 1 week Christmas

Menu £15 (weekday lunch) – Carte £30/56

A/C

Spain and Italy are the primary culinary influences at this appealing modern bistro and a glance at the menu would suggest there's nothing here to scare les chevaux. You can expect classics aplenty made using good quality, Mediterranean ingredients like porcini risotto or veal chop but, on closer inspection, there is also clear evidence of some boundary-pushing with dishes such as duck leg confit with cocoa and blackberry, and Iberico pork with fennel and pineapple. The wine list by the glass and carafe provides a good choice of varietals from quality producers along with plenty of gems from top growers. While the kitchen's influences are largely European, the ersatz industrial look of the place is far more Downtown Manhattan.

Medlar

modern **Plan XI E7**

438 King's Rd ✉ SW10 0LJ
✆ (020) 7349 1900
www.medlarrestaurant.co.uk
⊖ South Kensington
Closed 24-26 December and 1 January

Menu £27 (weekday lunch)/45

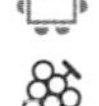
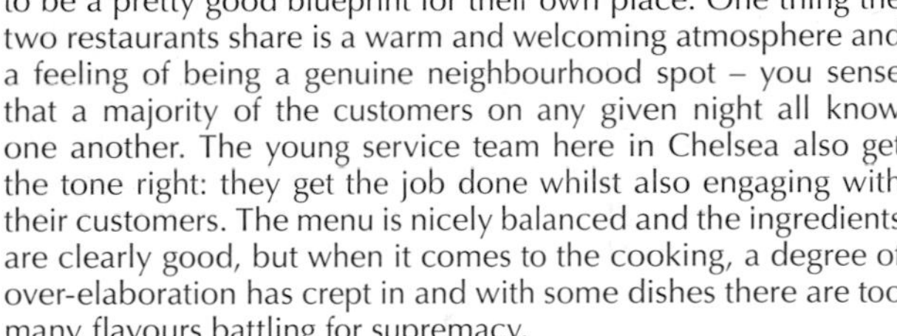

The two young owners are alumni of Chez Bruce which proved to be a pretty good blueprint for their own place. One thing the two restaurants share is a warm and welcoming atmosphere and a feeling of being a genuine neighbourhood spot – you sense that a majority of the customers on any given night all know one another. The young service team here in Chelsea also get the tone right: they get the job done whilst also engaging with their customers. The menu is nicely balanced and the ingredients are clearly good, but when it comes to the cooking, a degree of over-elaboration has crept in and with some dishes there are too many flavours battling for supremacy.

Mr Chow

Chinese **Plan XII F4**

151 Knightsbridge ✉ SW1X 7PA
✆ (020) 7589 7347
www.mrchow.com
⊖ Knightsbridge
Closed 24-26 December, 1 January, Easter Monday dinner and Monday lunch

Menu £26/50 – Carte £39/63

Chinese food, Italian waiters, swish surroundings, steep prices and immaculately coiffured regulars: it's an unusual mix that clearly works because Mr Chow has already celebrated its fortieth birthday. Even if you're not recognisable, you'll get a friendly welcome and the champagne chariot will be wheeled towards you. The laminated menu is long but clearly divided between sections entitled 'from the sea', 'from the land' and 'from the sky'; chickens will be pleased to find themselves in this last category. The cooking is far better than you expect, with genuine care shown. The desserts are thoroughly European and come on a trolley, with tarts the speciality. Your final bill won't be clearly itemised but this doesn't seem to bother anyone.

Ognisko

Polish — **Plan XI E5**

55 Prince's Gate, Exhibition Rd ✉ SW7 2PN
✆ (020) 7589 0101
www.ogniskorestaurant.co.uk
⊖ South Kensington
Closed 24-26 December and 1 January

Menu £17 (lunch and early dinner) – Carte £24/36

Ognisko Polskie Club was founded in 1940 and became an important cultural centre for the Polish community in exile after the war. It is housed in the magnificent surroundings of an impressive 1870s townhouse and now, thanks to experienced restaurateur Jan Woroniecki, its restaurant is open to the public. Head first to the bar for a quick sharpener provided by home-flavoured vodka, then plunge straight into the unapologetically traditional menu that celebrates cooking that is without pretence and truly from the heart. The dumplings are good and available as starters or mains; the roast duck is popular and the Krupnik or Bigos just perfect for a winter's day. On a summer's day ask for a table on the terrace overlooking Prince's Gardens.

One-O-One

fish and seafood — **Plan XI F4**

Park Tower Knightsbridge Hotel,
101 Knightsbridge ✉ SW1X 7RN
✆ (020) 7290 7101
www.oneoonerestaurant.com
⊖ Knightsbridge

Menu £21 (lunch) – Carte £55/98

Walking past the Sheraton Park Tower hotel, one of London's less majestic buildings, you'd never know there was a restaurant behind those heavy net curtains, and a rather good one to boot. Granted, the room size and shape can mean an animated atmosphere remains elusive – but the food is good and that food is mostly fish. There are tasting menus along the appealing à la carte so there is something for everyone and all occasions, whether that means sharing a whole turbot or just enjoying a bowl of bouillabaisse. Much of the produce comes from Brittany and Norway; the latter gives us the King crab legs which are the stars of the show. The kitchen is also unafraid of adding a little playfulness to its classical base.

Outlaw's at The Capital ✿

fish and seafood **Plan XI F5**

The Capital Hotel,
22-24 Basil St. ✉ SW3 1AT
✆ (020) 7591 1202
www.capitalhotel.co.uk
⊖ Knightsbridge
Closed Sunday – booking essential

Menu £27 (lunch) – Carte £47/65

The Capital

In an effort to reinvent this cosy dining room at The Capital hotel, Nathan Outlaw was persuaded to bring his award-winning formula from Cornwall to Chelsea. Nathan not only has the greatest name in Chefland but probably knows more about cooking fish than anyone else in the country. He's installed one of his trusted lieutenants in the kitchen and dishes very much reflect his distinct style. Essentially, it's all about the quality of the fish, which comes up daily from Cornwall and includes wreckfish, found in deep waters around shipwrecks. The cooking may appear effortless but the combination of flavours on the plate harmonises perfectly and any elements of originality are there to enhance rather than hoodwink. The room has also been given a new look, the main feature being views into the kitchen through the large picture window. Service is a little less starchy and stiff than in the restaurant's previous incarnations and is all the better for it. The well-structured wine list features the ever popular Levin Sauvignon Blanc from the owner's estate in the Loire.

First Course

- Lobster risotto, orange, basil and lobster dressing.
- Barbecued wood pigeon, chicory tart, pistachio and pink grapefruit.

Main Course

- Turbot with crispy oysters, cabbage, bacon and oyster sauce.
- Lamb saddle and belly, aubergine, anchovy and tarragon.

Dessert

- Quince and ginger cheesecake, quince and cider sorbet.
- Gooseberry crumble tart with elderflower ice cream.

Painted Heron

Indian **Plan XI E7**

112 Cheyne Walk ✉ SW10 0DJ
✆ (020) 7351 5232
www.thepaintedheron.com
⊖ Fulham Broadway
Closed Monday

Menu £20/65 – Carte £26/37

Ever fancied a Cohiba after your curry? Proof that The Painted Heron is not your typical Indian restaurant – this is Cheyne Walk after all – comes in the form of a smart, heated cigar terrace with a retractable roof for those who like a post-prandial puff. The restaurant itself is consciously run, stylishly kitted out and cleverly designed so that it always feels more intimate than it size would suggest. But what really sets it apart is the food: the influences come from across all parts of India but instead of the ubiquitous classics, the kitchen concentrates on seasonality. Dishes are quite elaborate in their construction and game is a speciality. The tasting menu offers the best overview of the kitchen's ability.

Phoenix

modern **Plan XI F6**

23 Smith St ✉ SW3 4EE
✆ (020) 7730 9182
www.geronimo-inns.co.uk/thepheonix
⊖ Sloane Square.
Closed dinner 25 December

Carte £15/42

The same menu is served throughout and, while the bar has plenty of seating and a civilised feel, head to the warm and comfortable dining room at the back if you want a more structured meal or you're impressing a date. Blackboard specials supplement the menu which keeps things traditional: fish on a Friday, a pasta of the day and the likes of fishcakes or sausage and mash with red onion jam. For lunch, you'll find some favourites for late-risers, like eggs Benedict and, in winter, expect the heartening sight of crumbles or plum pudding. Wines are organised by their character, with nearly 30 varieties offered by the glass. The side dishes can bump up the final bill but The Phoenix remains a friendly and conscientiously run Chelsea local.

Pig's Ear

British traditional Plan XI E7

35 Old Church St ✉ SW3 5BS
✆ (020) 7352 2908
www.thepigsear.info
⊖ South Kensington.

Carte £14/38

This Chelsea pub may not look much like a foodie spot from the outside, or indeed from the inside, but it does have a refreshing honesty to it. Lunch is in the rough-and-ready ground floor bar, decorated with everything from 'Tintin' pictures to covers of 'Sounds' newspaper. There's a decent choice of 5-6 main courses and a wine list on a blackboard. With its wood panelling and dressed tables, the upstairs dining room provides quite a contrast, but the atmosphere is still far from starchy. Here the menu displays a little more ambition but cooking remains similarly earthy and the wine list has plenty of bottles under £30. The kitchen knows its way around an animal: slow-cooked dishes such as pork cheeks are done particularly well.

Poissonnerie

fish and seafood Plan XI E6

82 Sloane Ave. ✉ SW3 3DZ
✆ (020) 7589 2457
www.poissonnerie-chelsea.co.uk
⊖ South Kensington
Closed Easter and 25-26 December

Menu £28/35 – Carte £41/54

Old-school is a term often used pejoratively but, in the stampede for all things new, deference should always be paid to the pioneers. Poissonerie has been a feature in Sloane Avenue for over 50 years and remains stoically and unapologetically traditional; this is a restaurant where things are done 'properly'. The owner, now aged over fourscore years, greets his immaculately groomed customers like old friends, which indeed is what many of them have become. The menu is full of classic seafood dishes and the freshness of the fish remains a given; oysters are of unimpeachable quality and all the shellfish is particularly good. The panelled room, hung with nautical-themed oil paintings, gives the impression you're dining on an old liner.

Racine

French

Plan XI E5

239 Brompton Rd ✉ SW3 2EP
✆ (020) 7584 4477
www.racine-restaurant.com
⊖ South Kensington
Closed 25 December

Menu £18/20 – Carte £30/53

Racine is as authentic a French brasserie as you can get at this end of the tunnel. The accents are thick; the baguettes are fresh; and the room's wood and leather have that reassuring lived-in look. Some of the clientele, who are a mature and confident bunch, give the impression that they come here on a weekly basis and it's easy to understand why: along with the authentically prepared classics, such as steak tartare, tête de veau or fruits de mer, are plenty of other dishes that hit the spot, along with well priced lunch and early evening menus. Try to avoid the tables in the middle of the room because, on windier days, you'll find yourself assailed by the gusts of wind whenever somebody opens the front door.

Rib Room

meats and grills

Plan XI F5

Jumeirah Carlton Tower Hotel,
Cadogan Pl ✉ SW1X 9PY
✆ (020) 7858 7250
www.theribroom.co.uk
⊖ Knightsbridge

Menu £28/58 – Carte £50/116

The Rib Room is something of a London institution and a restaurant designed for those who didn't get where they are today by wasting time looking at prices. The menu would delight the most traditional of British trenchermen: one can start with smoked salmon or half a dozen Angel oysters then move on to Dover sole, a steak or, more appropriately, rib of Aberdeen Angus. The kitchen does things properly and wisely avoids trying to be too clever. The last designer successfully managed to add a little elegance to the room while also maintaining the overriding sense of masculinity that's often associated with this style of dining. The bar is an integral part of the set up and lends the place a pleasant buzz.

Rasoi ✿

Indian Plan XI F6

10 Lincoln St ✉ SW3 2TS
✆ (020) 7225 1881
www.rasoirestaurant.co.uk
⊖ Sloane Square
Closed 25-26 December, 1-2 January and Saturday lunch

Menu £23/89 – Carte £65/86

Rasoi

With his outposts in Geneva, Mauritius and Dubai, Vineet Bhatia proves that Indian food is as open to innovation and interpretation as any other cuisine. Fortunately for fans of his original branch here in Chelsea, he has a team of loyal lieutenants who are more than capable of ensuring that things remain consistently good. What really comes across in his modern Indian food is the delicate balance of flavours and the superb quality of the ingredients. For a rounded experience of his unique style, go for the 7-course 'Prestige' menu. On the à la carte, the 'street food' chaats are almost a meal in themselves; the vegetarian dishes are as colourful as they are delicious; and the desserts, such as 'Chocolate Cravings' come with more of a Western personality. Be sure to ask for a table in the larger room at the back of the house which has more personality than the one at the front, especially when filled with the sweet aroma of the smoke rising from the racks of lamb. Alternatively, come with friends and book one of the richly decorated private rooms on the first floor.

First Course

- Smoked tandoori salmon, herb mash, cucumber and dill raita.
- Banana wrapped mustard tilapia with asparagus couscous.

Main Course

- Grilled duck, peppercorn jus and sesame duck confit tikki.
- Lamb fillet, cinnamon lamb jus and sundried tomato upma.

Dessert

- Chocolate cravings.
- Orange gulab jamun cheese cake and cocoa tuile.

Ⓝ Rivea

Mediterranean **Plan XII F4**

Bulgari Hotel,
171 Knightsbridge ✉ SW7 1DW
✆ (020) 7151 1025
www.rivealondon.com
⊖ Knightsbridge

Menu £35 (lunch) – Carte £22/42

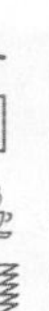
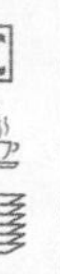
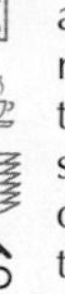

In the basement, beneath the Bulgari Hotel's sleek bar, is the not-quite-so-sunny sister to the 'Rivea' restaurant in St Tropez; an elegantly appointed room where blues and whites make reference to warmer climes. Unfussy cooking also focuses on the French – and Italian – Riviera, offering an interesting range of small plates which are vibrant in both colour and flavour. Four or five dishes per person should suffice and sharing is the way to go for those who just can't quite decide. Alongside the must-try pasta dishes you'll find the likes of roasted duck with tender turnips and beetroots, and sea bass with violin courgettes and flowers. These are accompanied by an eclectic wine list which showcases varietals purely from the Med.

Tendido Cero

Spanish **Plan XI D6**

174 Old Brompton Rd. ✉ SW5 0LJ
✆ (020) 7370 3685
www.cambiodetercio.co.uk
⊖ Gloucester Road
Closed 2 weeks Christmas-New Year

Menu £23.15 – Carte £17/51

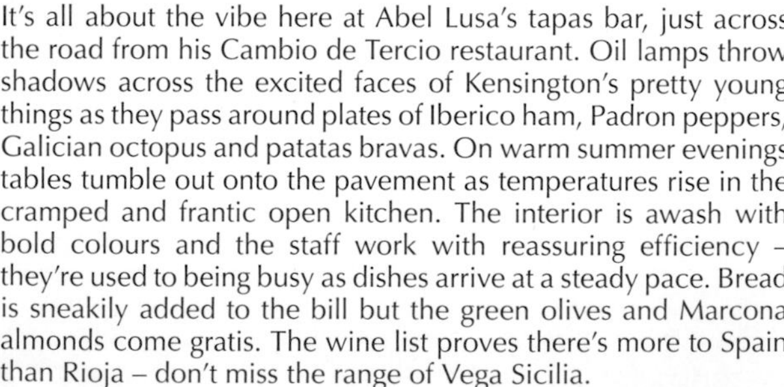

It's all about the vibe here at Abel Lusa's tapas bar, just across the road from his Cambio de Tercio restaurant. Oil lamps throw shadows across the excited faces of Kensington's pretty young things as they pass around plates of Iberico ham, Padron peppers, Galician octopus and patatas bravas. On warm summer evenings tables tumble out onto the pavement as temperatures rise in the cramped and frantic open kitchen. The interior is awash with bold colours and the staff work with reassuring efficiency – they're used to being busy as dishes arrive at a steady pace. Bread is sneakily added to the bill but the green olives and Marcona almonds come gratis. The wine list proves there's more to Spain than Rioja – don't miss the range of Vega Sicilia.

Tom's Kitchen

modern **Plan XI E6**

27 Cale St. ✉ SW3 3QP
✆ (020) 7349 0202
www.tomskitchen.co.uk
⊖ South Kensington
Closed 25-26 December

Carte £29/55

The locals may not have taken to his fish and chip shop but they do seem to like his kitchen. This is a restaurant with a thoroughly sound plan: it's open from early in the morning until late at night and offers satisfying comfort food in relaxed surroundings. The tiled walls and open kitchen work well and there's an upstairs room for the overspill. With its shepherd's pie, sausage and mash, and belly of pork, the menu wouldn't look out of place in a pub; although, as the eponymous Tom is Tom Aikens, a few luxury ingredients like foie gras do sneak in. Bread, olives and side dishes can push up the final bill but it's a friendly place with a stress-free atmosphere. There's a less convincing second branch in Somerset House.

N Toto's

Italian **Plan XI F5**

Walton House, Lennox Garden Mews (off Walton St)
✉ SW3 2JH
✆ (020) 7589 2062
www.totosrestaurant.com
⊖ South Kensington
Booking essential at dinner

Menu £25 – Carte £39/54

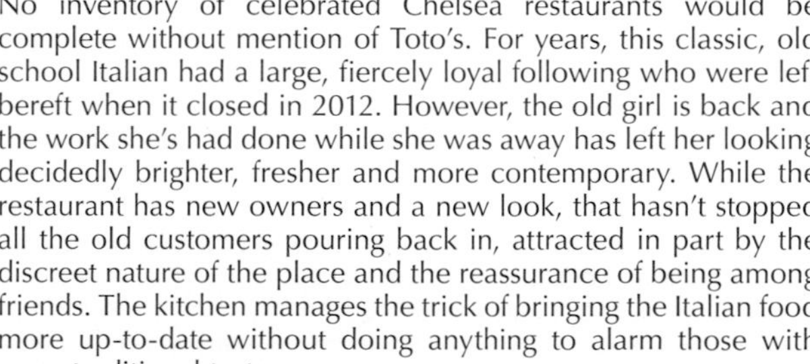

No inventory of celebrated Chelsea restaurants would be complete without mention of Toto's. For years, this classic, old school Italian had a large, fiercely loyal following who were left bereft when it closed in 2012. However, the old girl is back and the work she's had done while she was away has left her looking decidedly brighter, fresher and more contemporary. While the restaurant has new owners and a new look, that hasn't stopped all the old customers pouring back in, attracted in part by the discreet nature of the place and the reassurance of being among friends. The kitchen manages the trick of bringing the Italian food more up-to-date without doing anything to alarm those with more traditional tastes.

Ⓝ Yashin Ocean House

Japanese **Plan XI D6**

117-119 Old Brompton Rd ✉ SW7 3RN
✆ (020) 7373 3990
www.yashinocean.com
⊖ Gloucester Road
Closed 24-26 December, dinner 31 December and 1 January

Menu £20 (lunch) – Carte £25/58

It seems you can't open a restaurant these days without it having a 'concept'. The USP of this modern Japanese restaurant – sister to Yashin in Kensington – is 'head to tail' eating although, as there's nothing here for carnivores, perhaps 'fin to scale' would be more accurate. The stylish interior includes large cabinets of dry-aged fish to get you in the mood for this style of eating which is actually pretty commonplace in Japan. Take a seat at the counter or grab a table opposite the curiously incongruous full-sized horse lampstand and get cracking with a few small dishes like mackerel bone and fish skin for a joyous umami hit. Some dishes work better than others so stick with the specialities, like the whole dry-aged sea bream.

Zuma

Japanese **Plan XII F5**

5 Raphael St ✉ SW7 1DL
✆ (020) 7584 1010
www.zumarestaurant.com
⊖ Knightsbridge
Closed 25 December

Carte £26/70

Zuma may have become a global brand, with branches stretching from Istanbul to Hong Kong, but this is the original and it's still giving its fashionable band of fans – which includes a high quotient of celebrities and enough footballers to make up a whole team – exactly what they want. Glamorous surroundings with an open kitchen, a great cocktail bar, intelligent service and easy-to-share modern Japanese food mean that the large, stylish space is rarely less than bursting, especially at night. The menu covers all bases but instead of sushi, sashimi or tempura your best bet is to head straight for the delicately presented, modern constructions as well as those dishes cooked on the robata grill, which range from beef to sea bass.

D. Pearson/agency Jon Arnold Images/Age fotostock

Kensington · North Kensington · Notting Hill

It was the choking air of 17C London that helped put **Kensington** on the map: the little village lying to the west of the city became the favoured retreat of the asthmatic King William III who had Sir Christopher Wren build **Kensington Palace** for him. Where the king leads, the titled follow, and the area soon became a fashionable location for the rich. For over 300 years, it's had no problem holding onto its cachet, though a stroll down Kensington High Street is these days a more egalitarian odyssey than some more upmarket residents might approve of.

The shops here mix the everyday with the flamboyant, but for a real taste of the exotic you have to take the lift to the top of the Art Deco Barkers building and arrive at the Kensington Roof Gardens, which are open to all as long as they're not in use for a corporate bash. The gardens are now over seventy years old, yet still remain a 'charming secret'. Those who do make it up to the sixth floor discover a delightful woodland garden and gurgling stream, complete with pools, bridges and trees. There are flamingos, too, adding a dash of vibrant colour.

Back down on earth, Kensington boasts another hidden attraction in **Leighton House** on its western boundaries. The Victorian redbrick façade looks a bit forbidding as you make your approach, but step inside and things take a dramatic turn, courtesy of the extraordinary Arab Hall, with its oriental mosaics and tinkling fountain creating a scene like something from ***The Arabian Knights.*** Elsewhere in the building, the Pre-Raphaelite paintings of Lord Leighton, Burne-Jones and Alma-Tadema are much to the fore. Mind you, famous names have always had a hankering for W8, with a particular preponderance to dally in enchanting **Kensington Square,** where there are almost as many blue plaques as buildings upon which to secure them. William Thackeray, John Stuart Mill and Edward Burne-Jones were all residents.

One of the London's most enjoyable green retreats is **Holland Park,** just north of the High Street. It boasts the 400 year-old Holland House, which is a fashionable focal point for summer-time al fresco theatre and opera. Holland Walk runs along the eastern fringe of the park, and provides a lovely sojourn down to the shops; at the Kyoto Garden, koi carp reach hungrily for the surface of their pool, while elsewhere peacocks strut around as if they own the place.

Another world beckons just north of here – the seedy-cum-glitzy environs of **Notting Hill.** The main drag itself, Notting Hill Gate, is little more than a one-dimensional thoroughfare only enlivened by second hand record shops, but to its south are charming cottages with pastel shades in leafy streets,

B. Gardel/hemis.fr

while to the north the appealing **Pembridge Road** evolves into the boutiques of Westbourne Grove. Most people heading in this direction are making for the legendary Portobello Road market – particularly on Saturdays, which are manic. The market stretches on for more than a mile, with a chameleon-like ability to change colour and character on the way: there are antiques at the Notting Hill end, followed further up by food stalls, and then designer and vintage clothes as you reach the Westway. Those who don't fancy the madding crowds of the market can nip into the Electric Cinema and watch a movie in supreme comfort: it boasts two-seater sofas and leather armchairs. Nearby there are another two film-houses putting the hip into the Hill – the Gate, and the Coronet, widely recognised as one of London's most charming 'locals'.

Hidden in a mews just north of **Westbourne Grove** is a fascinating destination: the Museum of Brands, Packaging and Advertising, which does pretty much what it says on the label. It's both nostalgic and evocative, featuring thousands of items like childhood toys, teenage magazines…and HP sauce bottles.

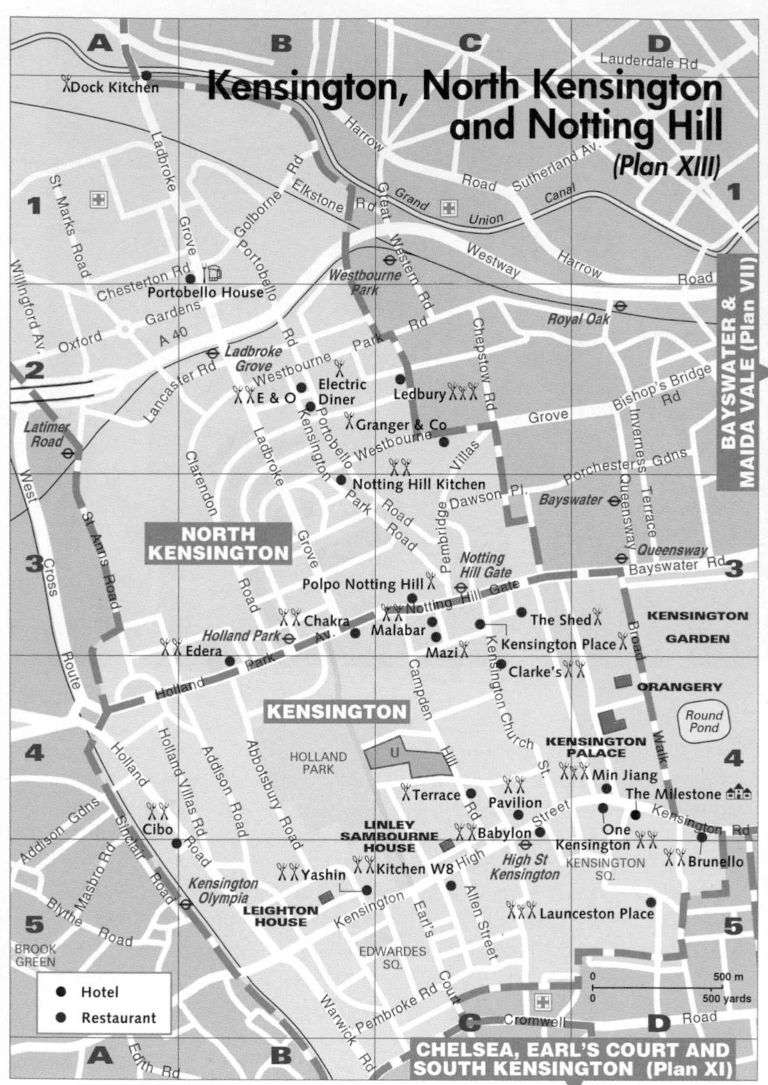
Kensington, North Kensington and Notting Hill
(Plan XIII)
A
B
C
D
1
2
3
4
5
Dock Kitchen
Portobello House
Electric Diner
E & O
Ledbury
Granger & Co
Notting Hill Kitchen
Polpo Notting Hill
Chakra
Malabar
Mazi
The Shed
Kensington Place
Clarke's
Edera
Min Jiang
The Milestone
Terrace
Pavilion
Babylon
One Kensington
Brunello
Cibo
Yashin
Kitchen W8
Launceston Place
NORTH KENSINGTON
KENSINGTON
HOLLAND PARK
KENSINGTON GARDEN
ORANGERY
Round Pond
KENSINGTON PALACE
LINLEY SAMBOURNE HOUSE
LEIGHTON HOUSE
KENSINGTON SQ.
EDWARDES SQ.
BROOK GREEN
Westbourne Park
Ladbroke Grove
Latimer Road
Royal Oak
Bayswater
Queensway
Notting Hill Gate
Holland Park
High St Kensington
Kensington Olympia
Lauderdale Rd
Harrow Road
Sutherland Av.
Grand Union Canal
Westway
Elkstone Rd
Great Western Rd
Golborne Rd
Portobello Rd
Ladbroke Grove
St Marks Road
Chesterton Rd
Oxford Gardens
Willingford Av.
A 40
Lancaster Rd
Westbourne Park Rd
Westbourne Grove
Bishop's Bridge Rd
Chepstow Rd
Inverness Terrace
Porchester Gdns
Queensway
Dawson Pl.
Pembridge Villas
Kensington Park Road
Clarendon Road
Ladbroke Grove
Ledbury Road
Bayswater Rd
Notting Hill Gate
Holland Park Av.
Holland Park
West Cross Route
St Anns Road
Campden Hill
Kensington Church St.
Broad Walk
Kensington Rd
Holland Road
Holland Villas Rd
Addison Road
Abbotsbury Road
Addison Gdns
Sinclair Road
Masbro Rd
Blythe Road
Terrace Rd
Kensington High Street
Allen Street
Earl's Court Rd
Pembroke Rd
Warwick Rd
Cromwell Road
Edith Rd
0 500 m
0 500 yards
Hotel
Restaurant
BAYSWATER & MAIDA VALE (Plan VIII)
CHELSEA, EARL'S COURT AND SOUTH KENSINGTON (Plan XI)

Babylon

modern C4

The Roof Gardens, 99 Kensington High St (entrance on Derry St) ✉ W8 5SA
✆ (020) 7368 3993
www.roofgardens.virgin.com
⊖ High Street Kensington
Closed 24-30 December, 1-2 January and Sunday dinner

Menu £23/48 – Carte £29/73

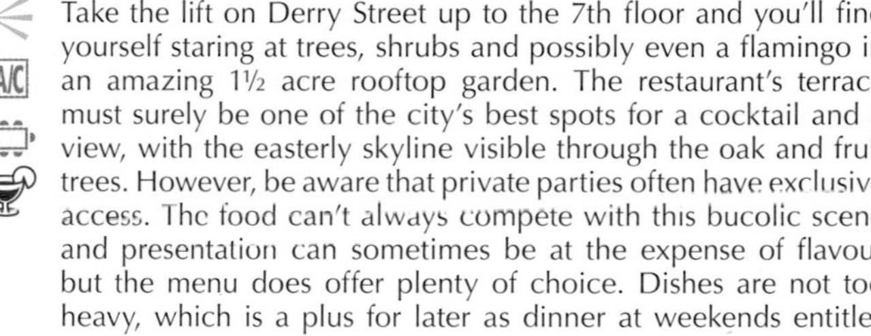

Take the lift on Derry Street up to the 7th floor and you'll find yourself staring at trees, shrubs and possibly even a flamingo in an amazing 1½ acre rooftop garden. The restaurant's terrace must surely be one of the city's best spots for a cocktail and a view, with the easterly skyline visible through the oak and fruit trees. However, be aware that private parties often have exclusive access. The food can't always compete with this bucolic scene and presentation can sometimes be at the expense of flavour but the menu does offer plenty of choice. Dishes are not too heavy, which is a plus for later as dinner at weekends entitles you to access to The Club. You could also consider coming on a Tuesday as that's jazz night.

Brunello

Italian D4

Baglioni Hotel,
60 Hyde Park Gate ✉ SW7 5BB
✆ (020) 7368 5900
www.baglionihotels.com
⊖ High Street Kensington

Menu £23 (lunch) – Carte £39/64

It takes time for some restaurants to find the chef that suits them best. Brunello, the Italian restaurant on the ground floor of the Baglioni hotel, has tried a couple in the last few years but now seems to have sensibly settled on a brigade that is less about showiness and more about delivering recognisable Italian classics. This works because there's frankly more than enough drama in the exuberant decoration – with all that velvet, glass, black and gold, you need something reassuringly familiar to stop you thinking you've wandered onto the stage in the middle of a performance of Turandot. Many ingredients come from Italy and there are dishes from all regions. Service is friendly and endearingly proud.

Chakra

Indian B3

157-159 Notting Hill Gate ✉ W11 3LF
✆ (020) 7229 2115
www.chakralondon.com
⊖ Notting Hill Gate
Closed 25-26 December and 1 January – booking advisable

Menu £10/20 – Carte £21/41 

Indian 'street food' may be all the rage these days but here at Chakra – which is named after the body's energy points – the influences come from the Royal kitchens of the Maharajahs, particularly those from the North Western province of Lucknow. A different chef is credited with running each section on the menu, whether that's the charcoal grill, griddle, clay oven or veg pan, and dishes are designed for sharing, although some of the prices tend to discourage too much ordering. The spicing is more subtle than usual, the aroma fresher and the presentation more striking, with the best dishes being the more traditional ones. Divided into two smart rooms, one white and one brown, the place is run by charming and elegant young ladies.

Cibo

Italian A4/5

3 Russell Gdns ✉ W14 8EZ
✆ (020) 7371 6271
www.ciborestaurant.net
⊖ Kensington Olympia
Closed 1 week Christmas, Easter and bank holidays

Menu £20 (weekday lunch) – Carte £27/40 

Some of the sparkle may have dimmed since Cibo opened in 1989 but its band of local followers remain committed in their enthusiasm for this friendly Italian restaurant. The interior looks a tad weary these days but the quirky pictures celebrating the naked female form are still there and the imported hand-painted crockery is a nice touch. The ever-popular platter of grilled seafood dictates that the menu pretty much changes on a daily basis, although certain dishes can never be altered too much; some regulars can even guess who's in the kitchen that day by the degree of spicing. Service is friendly if a touch chaotic at times and while the opening front façade is a boon in summer, it can be draughty in winter, so ask for a table at the back.

Clarke's

modern C4

124 Kensington Church St ✉ W8 4BH
✆ (020) 7221 9225
www.sallyclarke.com
⊖ Notting Hill Gate
Closed Christmas-New Year, Sunday and bank holidays – booking advisable

Menu £35 (dinner) – Carte £35/50

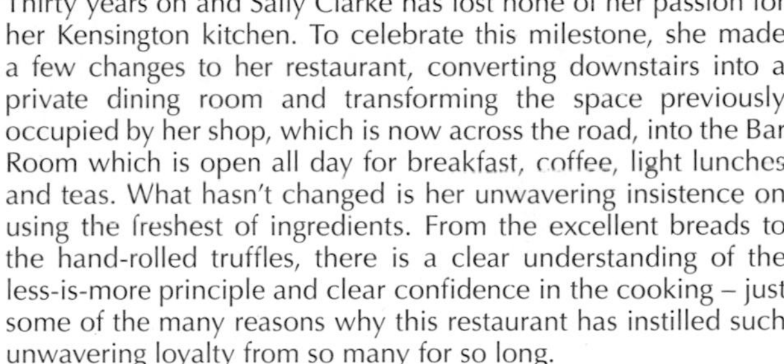

Thirty years on and Sally Clarke has lost none of her passion for her Kensington kitchen. To celebrate this milestone, she made a few changes to her restaurant, converting downstairs into a private dining room and transforming the space previously occupied by her shop, which is now across the road, into the Bar Room which is open all day for breakfast, coffee, light lunches and teas. What hasn't changed is her unwavering insistence on using the freshest of ingredients. From the excellent breads to the hand-rolled truffles, there is a clear understanding of the less-is-more principle and clear confidence in the cooking – just some of the many reasons why this restaurant has instilled such unwavering loyalty from so many for so long.

Dock Kitchen

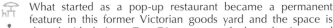

Mediterranean A0/1

Portobello Dock, 342-344 Ladbroke Grove ✉ W10 5BU
✆ (020) 8962 1610
www.dockkitchen.co.uk
⊖ Ladbroke Grove
Closed Christmas, Sunday dinner and bank holidays

Menu £18/45 – Carte £30/44

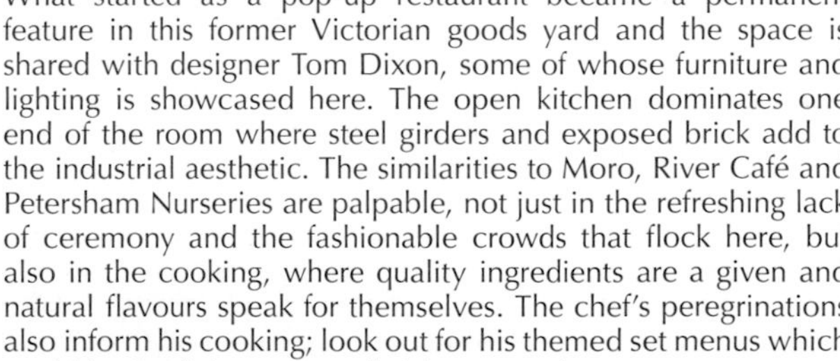

What started as a pop-up restaurant became a permanent feature in this former Victorian goods yard and the space is shared with designer Tom Dixon, some of whose furniture and lighting is showcased here. The open kitchen dominates one end of the room where steel girders and exposed brick add to the industrial aesthetic. The similarities to Moro, River Café and Petersham Nurseries are palpable, not just in the refreshing lack of ceremony and the fashionable crowds that flock here, but also in the cooking, where quality ingredients are a given and natural flavours speak for themselves. The chef's peregrinations also inform his cooking; look out for his themed set menus which could be Sardinian one week, Moroccan the next.

E&O

Asian

B2

14 Blenheim Cres. ✉ W11 1NN
✆ (020) 7229 5454
www.rickerrestaurants.com
⊖ Ladbroke Grove
Closed 25 December

Menu £20/59 – Carte £22/55

Once you've sidestepped the full-on bar of this Notting Hill favourite, a step from Portobello Road, you'll find yourself in a moodily sophisticated restaurant packed with the beautiful and the hopeful. The room is understatedly urbane, with slatted walls, large circular lamps and leather banquettes, while noise levels are at the party end of the auditory index. Waiting staff are obliging, pleasant and often among the prettiest people in the room. E&O stands for Eastern and Oriental and the menu journeys across numerous Asian countries, dividing itself into assorted headings which include dim sum, salads, tempura, curries and roasts. Individual dishes vary in size and price so sharing, as in life, is often the best option.

Edera

Italian

B4

148 Holland Park Ave. ✉ W11 4UE
✆ (020) 7221 6090
www.edera.co.uk
⊖ Holland Park

Carte £26/52

The last makeover made Edera warmer and more comfortable and, while it actually holds up to 75 people, it still manages to feel quite intimate. On a typical night it seems as though the vast majority of customers have been before, that they know one another and probably walked here. In comparison, the staff are a youthful bunch, but they are well-marshalled and quietly efficient. The menu is quite broad and portions are on the generous side so if you're having a pasta dish you may struggle with a fourth course. The list of daily specials is wisely printed so you don't have to try to memorise the waiter's recital; there is a Sardinian element to the cooking, with bottarga omnipresent, and the ingredients are first-rate.

Electric Diner

meats and grills B2

191 Portobello Rd ✉ W11 2ED
✆ (0207) 8908 9696
www.electricdiner.com
⊖ Ladbroke Grove
Closed 24-25 August and 25 December – bookings not accepted

Carte £15/36

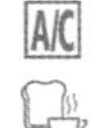

Any cinema that's over 100 years old deserves to be shown respect, so treat your visit to the Electric Cinema as a special occasion and start, or finish, with a meal next door at the Electric Diner. It's a loud, fun and brash all-day operation with a simple but all-encompassing menu that changes daily. The long counter, red leather booths and low ceiling certainly create the mood and look of the classic American diner – even the music comes from a reel-to-reel. Au Cheval diner in Chicago has supplied most of the influences so be prepared for big portions that are heavy on flavour. The room fills with smoke from the grill; the steak and pork chops could easily feed two and the lemon meringue pie is of Desperate Dan dimensions.

Granger & Co

modern C2

175 Westbourne Grove ✉ W11 2SB
✆ (020) 7229 9111
www.grangerandco.com
⊖ Bayswater
Closed August bank holiday weekend and 25-26 December – bookings not accepted

Carte £19/44

Having relocated from the sun of Sydney to the cool of Notting Hill, Bill Granger decided to open a local restaurant. He's brought with him that disarmingly charming 'matey' service that only Australians can do, his breakfast sweetcorn fritters and ricotta hotcakes and a zesty menu that features everything from pasta to pork chops. At dinner a BBQ section is added along with a daily fish dish, while various puds replace the cakes offered during the day. The room is bright and open, prices are reasonable and the Asian accents lend many of the dishes an easy-to-eat quality which makes you feel healthier than when you arrived and allows you to forget that you probably had to queue for a table.

Kensington Place

modern

C3

201-209 Kensington Church St. ✉ W8 7LX
✆ (020) 7727 3184
www.kensingtonplace-restaurant.co.uk
⊖ Notting Hill Gate
Closed Sunday dinner, Monday lunch and bank holidays

Menu £25 (lunch) – Carte £24/39

It must have been quite difficult for the D&D group to re-establish Kensington Place, especially as Rowley Leigh, its well-known former chef, now operates in nearby Bayswater. But one thing about all iconic restaurants is that many out there never forget the soft spot they once had for the old place and will often return. The food is reassuringly familiar and offers a host of brasserie favourites, with the emphasis very much on fresh fish. The cooking is modern and quite dainty at times and desserts are done well. Service is swift and copes easily with the numbers when it needs to. The addition of cushions has succeeded in softening the acoustics so it's also easier to have a conversation these days.

Malabar

Indian

C3

27 Uxbridge St. ✉ W8 7TQ
✆ (020) 7727 8800
www.malabar-restaurant.co.uk
⊖ Notting Hill Gate
Closed 1 week Christmas – (buffet lunch Sunday)

Menu £18 (lunch and early dinner) s – Carte £16/31 s

One of the reasons why Malabar has been going strong since 1983 is that it keeps on top of its appearance, as, it seems, do most of its Notting Hill customers. These days the front has a sleek, understated look; the interior is a fashionable grey and the staff do their bit by dressing in black. What doesn't change is the quality of the food, from the breads to the piping hot thalis. The favourites remain but the seafood section has been beefed up with the addition of a monkfish curry and a whole gilt-head bream; and just because the tandoori dishes sit beside the starters on the menu, don't assume they come in starter sizes. The excellent value Sunday buffet lunch, when children under 12 eat for free, still packs them in.

Kitchen W8 ✿

modern

C5

11-13 Abingdon Rd ✉ W8 6AH
☏ (020) 7937 0120
www.kitchenw8.com
⊖ High Street Kensington
Closed 25-26 December and bank holidays

Menu £25 (lunch and early dinner)/60 – Carte £35/54

Kitchen W8

Kitchen W8 is the sort of restaurant every neighbourhood should have because it succeeds on so many levels. Whether you're here for a special occasion on a Saturday night or a quick bite for lunch during the week, the staff will get the tone of the service just right and the food will be meticulously prepared yet very easy to eat. The restaurant is a joint venture between experienced restaurateur Rebecca Mascarenhas and Philip Howard of The Square. Head Chef Mark Kempson, a Square alumni himself but very much his own man, puts as much care into the great value lunch and early evening menu as he does the main à la carte; all are produce driven and his cooking delivers great flavours and subtle degrees of originality so that the dishes have both personality and depth. The restaurant may not be quite as informal as the name suggests but it is certainly free of pomp or pomposity. On Sunday the restaurant entices even more locals in by making it a corkage free night which encourages them to open up their own cellars.

First Course

- Smoked eel with Cornish mackerel, leek hearts and sweet mustard.
- Gazpacho jelly with focaccia, red onions, smoked anchovies and goat's milk.

Main Course

- Bresse pigeon with heritage beetroots, bulgur wheat, hazelnuts and bacon.
- Slow-poached Cornish cod with violet artichoke, aioli and sardine.

Dessert

- Chocolate pavé with thyme salted caramel, banana and popcorn.
- Macerated English strawberries with watermelon, vanilla and lime.

Launceston Place ✿

modern D5

1a Launceston Pl ✉ W8 5RL
✆ (020) 7937 6912
www.launcestonplace-restaurant.co.uk
⊖ Gloucester Road
Closed 22-30 December, 1 January, Tuesday lunch and Monday – bookings advisable at dinner

Menu £30 (weekday lunch)/70

Launceston Place

Under the watchful eye of head chef Tim Allen, this longstanding Kensington restaurant continues to deliver food that is original and highly polished – as you could expect from a man who has worked with Martin Burge and John Burton-Race. But, unsurprisingly for a Yorkshireman, his cooking also comes with guts and substance so you're unlikely to leave without feeling satisfied. The engaging service team are personable and confident and you'll find they'll eagerly elaborate on the make-up of any of the dishes, be they from the great value lunch menu, the Market menu or, for those pushing the boat out, the tasting menu - the only option on Friday and Saturday nights. Such passion is also evident in the impressive wine list – a selection that not only contains all the finest labels but also champions lesser known regions and a number of family-made wines. Elegant, discreet and cosy, the restaurant has a discernible local atmosphere and you get the impression that many of the diners feel a genuine sense of proprietorial pride in the place.

First Course

- Pigeon, hazelnut, crumbled frozen foie gras, chicory and pear.
- Scallops with truffle cassonade, confit chicken wings and sorrel.

Main Course

- Suckling pig, loin and belly with black pudding and Braeburn apple.
- Turbot with crab mousse and Jersey Royals.

Dessert

- Yorkshire rhubarb, candied ginger tapioca and iced apple.
- Raspberry delice with white chocolate Aero.

Ledbury ✿✿

modern C2

127 Ledbury Rd. ✉ W11 2AQ
✆ (020) 7792 9090
www.theledbury.com
⊖ Notting Hill Gate
Closed 25-26 December, August bank holiday and lunch Monday-Tuesday

Menu £45/110

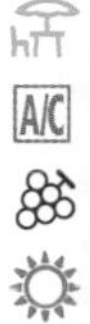

Ledbury

Brett Graham is a chef who understands his ingredients. His deep-rooted knowledge of husbandry and his close working relationship with his suppliers are revealed through his menus and reflected on the plate. The quality of the produce really shines through and the kitchen's ability and deft touch means that the strikingly original flavour combinations will linger long in the memory. Lovers of game have much to savour in the season and it is not unknown for Brett to head off up to Norfolk after service to shoot some venison. The wine list offers good value at all levels, is strong across the regions and includes a great selection by the glass. The Ledbury has always had to work hard to attract lunchtime business so the fixed price lunch menu represents excellent value and often includes some unexpectedly luxurious ingredients, like Red Ruby beef or hand-dived scallops. At weekends, only a tasting menu is offered for dinner. Whenever you come, you'll find this a smart yet unshowy restaurant with a satisfying hum and smooth yet engaging service.

First Course

- Flame-grilled fillet of mackerel, pickled cucumber, Celtic mustard and shiso.
- Almonds, green beans and white peach.

Main Course

- Roast breast and confit leg of pigeon with quince.
- Fillet of turbot with brassicas, chopped oysters and sake.

Dessert

- Brown sugar tart with stem ginger ice cream.
- Tartlet of English strawberries with honey cream.

Mazi

Greek

C2

12-14 Hillgate St ✉ W8 7SR
✆ (020) 7229 3794
www.mazi.co.uk
⊖ Notting Hill Gate
Closed 24-26 December and 1-2 January

Menu £13 (weekday lunch) – Carte £23/52

Apart from one or possibly two exceptions, Greek restaurants in the capital have been less than inspiring over the years – but that may start to change thanks to Mazi, which means 'together'. The kitchen seeks inspiration from traditional recipes then adds contemporary twists to create vibrant, colourful and fresh tasting dishes. It's all about sharing here, with cold dishes such as tarama with lemon confit served in glass jars; bigger, more robust dishes include braised saddle of lamb with its shoulder, and rabbit ragout with pasta. The wine list is exclusively Greek and much of the imported produce is available to buy. The simple room is bright and fresh and there are few more charming spots than the garden terrace at the back.

Min Jiang

Chinese

Royal Garden Hotel,
2-24 Kensington High St (10th Floor) ✉ W8 4PT
✆ (020) 7361 1988
www.minjiang.co.uk
⊖ High Street Kensington

Menu £40/80 – Carte £25/92

It's got great views of Kensington Palace and Gardens below (ask for tables 11 or 16) but because of its own good looks and its collection of vases influenced by the Ming Dynasty, this stylish Chinese restaurant on the 10th floor of the Royal Garden hotel can more than hold its own. The speciality is wood-fired Beijing duck in two servings - order it in advance; its glistening meat is carved at the table and one then has the difficult task of choosing one of the four options offered for the second serving. The cuisine covers all provinces, although Cantonese and Sichuanese are the most dominant. Signature dishes include sea bass with shredded chicken, sautéed Gong Bao chicken and spicy pork belly with leeks.

Notting Hill Kitchen

modern B3

92 Kensington Park Rd ✉ W11 2PN
✆ (020) 7313 9526
www.nottinghillkitchen.co.uk
⊖ Notting Hill Gate
Closed 25-26 December, 1 January and Sunday dinner-Wednesday lunch

Menu £32 (weekday lunch) – Carte £36/56

A/C The discreet terracotta tiles outside are the only clue that it's Iberian cooking happening inside these converted Edwardian townhouses. The three roomed restaurant has an understated, pared down look and the wine racks hint at the fact that wine is an important part of the experience here – indeed, you'll find some good vintages from serious producers that are very generously priced. The menu is appealingly concise and it's apparent that much work has gone into finding quality ingredients, especially the Pata Negra and the seafood from the Atlantic like the red mullet. Go for the simpler dishes as some of the combinations of the more creative dishes don't always quite sing as well – or stay in the bar for the tapas.

One Kensington

other world kitchens D4

1 Kensington High St ✉ W8 5NP
✆ (020) 7795 6533
www.one-kensington.com
⊖ High Street Kensington
Closed Monday lunch

Menu £25/29 – Carte £34/51

Just when restaurant menus have become less generic and more focused on specific regions of their chef's homeland, along comes a restaurant that's positively global in its reach. This striking Grade II listed Victorian Gothic building and former bank is now home to a partnership between Massimiliano Blasone, formerly of Apsleys, and the people behind Tamarind – and the kitchen does a bit of everything. There's homemade tagliolini, beef pie, veal schnitzel, salads and Sunday roasts; Friday's daily dish could be fritto misto; Saturday's, sausage and mash. The cooking is perfectly competent but this lack of identity, coupled with the awkwardness of the room's layout, makes you think they've got their work cut out making it a success.

Ⓝ Pavilion

modern

C4

96 Kensington High St ✉ W8 4SG
✆ (020) 7221 2000
www.kensingtonpavilion.com
⊖ High Street Kensington
Closed Christmas-New Year and Sunday dinner

Carte £27/59

Kensington High Street has always been more about shopping rather than eating, so it's quite a surprise when you first walk past this smart and stylish restaurant. A central bar dominates the room, with a few tables dotted around it; there are also seats on a separate marble-topped counter for those who like the watch chefs prepare their food. The appealing contemporary menu comes with a fair amount of originality and the produce is exemplary – especially the steaks. The kitchen makes its own bread, as well as the croissants and jams for breakfast. This is one of those places where you can quite happily pop in for one quick course or really push the boat out. Sadly the terrace at the back is exclusively for members of the club upstairs.

Ⓝ Polpo Notting Hill

Italian

C3

126-128 Notting Hill Gate ✉ W11 3QG
✆ (020) 7229 3283
www.polpo.co.uk
⊖ Notting Hill Gate
Closed 25-26 December and 1 January

Carte £22/40

The fourth Polpo is perhaps the most commercially minded one in Russell Norman's growing group – it's certainly unusual to find one of his Venetian-style bacaros in the middle of a high street, albeit a high street in Notting Hill. However, judging by the crowds, the 'small plates' formula is as popular in W11 as it is elsewhere in the city. It's all about the whole package here – come with a group of friends, get in the aperitifs along with some cicheti, then order a selection of in-house baked breads, hearty meatballs and assorted fish and meat dishes to share. The buzz is great and the lack of pretence is very appealing. Bookings are not taken after 3pm, although the bar is a good place is to wait.

Portobello House

modern

B1

225 Ladbroke Grove ✉ W10 6HQ
✆ (020) 3181 0920
www.portobellohouse.com
⊖ Ladbroke Grove.
Closed 25 December

Carte £18/31

A/C

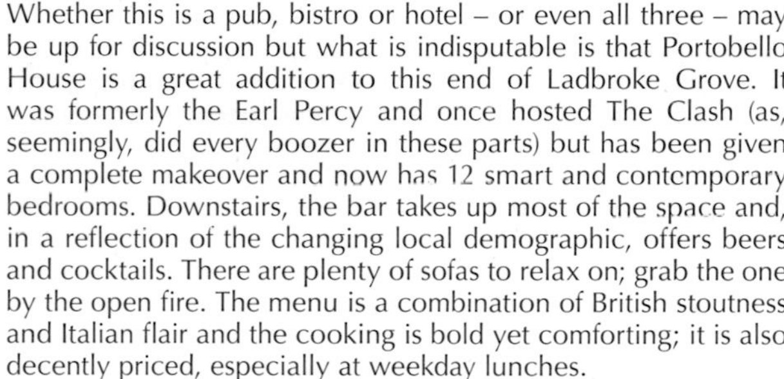

Whether this is a pub, bistro or hotel – or even all three – may be up for discussion but what is indisputable is that Portobello House is a great addition to this end of Ladbroke Grove. It was formerly the Earl Percy and once hosted The Clash (as, seemingly, did every boozer in these parts) but has been given a complete makeover and now has 12 smart and contemporary bedrooms. Downstairs, the bar takes up most of the space and, in a reflection of the changing local demographic, offers beers and cocktails. There are plenty of sofas to relax on; grab the one by the open fire. The menu is a combination of British stoutness and Italian flair and the cooking is bold yet comforting; it is also decently priced, especially at weekday lunches.

The Shed

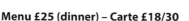

British traditional

C3

122 Palace Gardens Terr. ✉ W8 4RT
✆ (020) 7229 4024
www.theshed-restaurant.com
⊖ Notting Hill Gate
Closed Monday lunch and Sunday

Menu £25 (dinner) – Carte £18/30

Names add to expectations, so if you call your place the Grand Palace it really doesn't give you anywhere to hide. The Gladwin brothers behind The Shed instead opted for understatement and it works a treat. This is the old Ark restaurant and is obviously more than just a shed, even though it comes with a healthy dose of the outdoors. There are farming tools around, upturned barrels for tables and even an old tractor engine, all adding to its higgledy-piggledy charm. One brother cooks, one manages and the third runs the farm in West Sussex from where much of the produce comes. The cooking is appropriately British, earthy and satisfying, with the small plates divided into 'slow' or 'fast': a reference to the cooking process.

Ⓝ Terrace

modern

C4

33c Holland St ✉ W8 4LX
✆ (020) 7937 9252
www.theterraceonhollandstreet.co.uk
⊖ High Street Kensington

Menu £18 (weekday lunch) – Carte £25/45

Terrace is a sweet little neighbourhood restaurant, tucked away in a corner spot on a quiet residential street, close to – but light years away from – the hustle and bustle of High Street Ken. With space for less than twenty diners, it's cosy rather than cavernous – although capacity does double in fine weather when the eponymous outside space comes into use. Muted hues and serene staff help create a relaxed but professional feel here; it has fast become a favourite of the locals, so be sure to book ahead. The short menu changes daily and concentrates on seasonal, British-inspired dishes with classic combinations and bold flavours; from crisp, feather-light crab croquettes to succulent venison or an indulgent apple tart.

Yashin

Japanese

B5

1A Argyll Rd. ✉ W8 7DB
✆ (020) 7938 1536
www.yashinsushi.com
⊖ High Street Kensington
Closed 24-25 and 31 December,1 January – booking essential

Carte £24/95

Two experienced sushi chefs joined forces to create this contemporary restaurant with its crisp, appealing black and white theme. Their worthy ambition to wean diners off fermented soya bean is reflected in their grammatically challenging but charmingly equitable slogan: "without soy sauce...but if you want to". There are three omakase choices offering 8, 11 or 15 pieces of sushi selected by the chefs and served together. The quality of the fish is clear and originality comes in the form of minuscule garnishes adorning each piece and the odd bit of searing. Service is knowledgeable and endearing but be sure to ask for a counter seat as one of the joys of sushi comes from watching the dextrous knife skills and the deft handling of the fish.

Greater London

M. Jones/Age fotostock

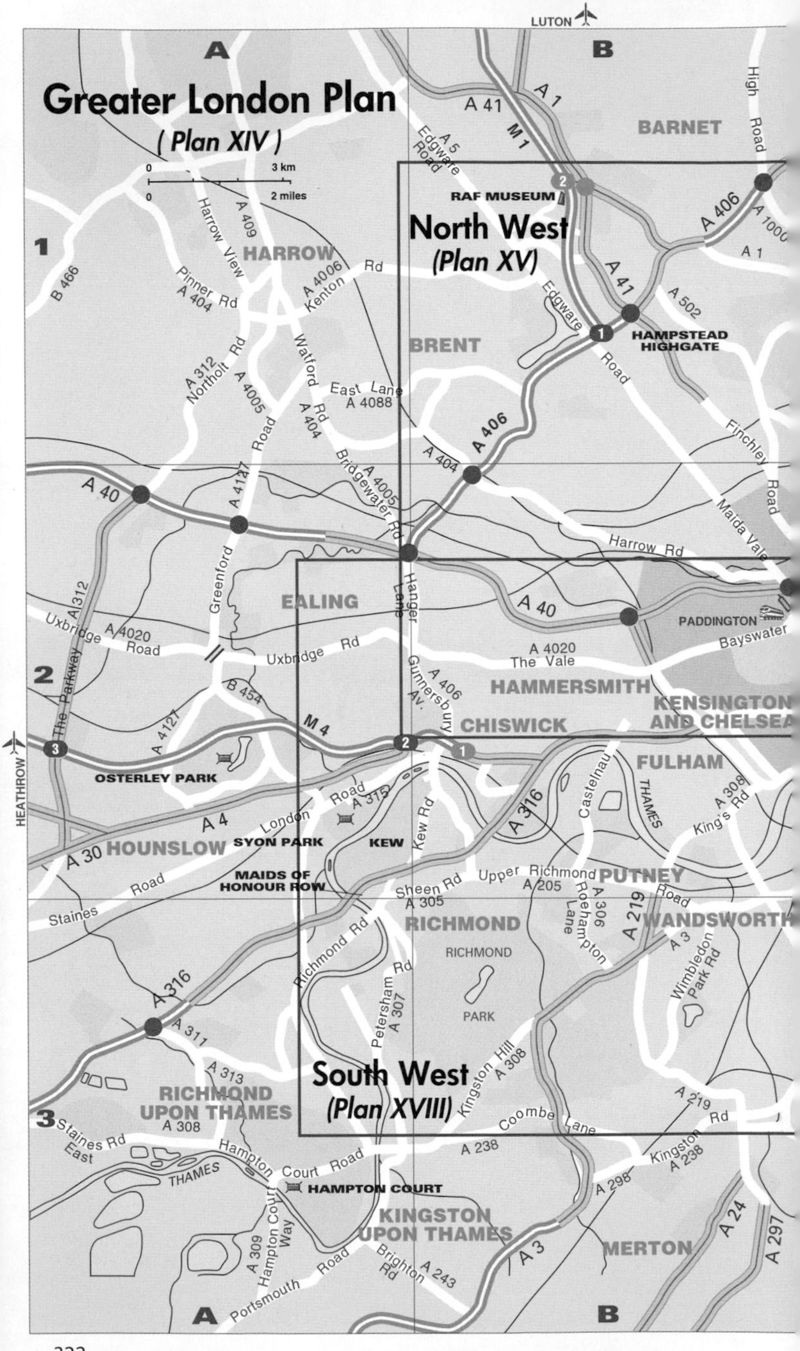
Greater London Plan
(Plan XIV)
0 3 km
0 2 miles
LUTON
A
B
1
2
3
HEATHROW
North West
(Plan XV)
South West
(Plan XVIII)
BARNET
HARROW
BRENT
HAMPSTEAD
HIGHGATE
RAF MUSEUM
EALING
PADDINGTON
HAMMERSMITH
KENSINGTON
AND CHELSEA
CHISWICK
FULHAM
OSTERLEY PARK
HOUNSLOW
SYON PARK
KEW
MAIDS OF
HONOUR ROW
PUTNEY
WANDSWORTH
RICHMOND
RICHMOND
PARK
RICHMOND
UPON THAMES
HAMPTON COURT
KINGSTON
UPON THAMES
MERTON
THAMES
M 1
M 4
A 1
A 41
A 5 Edgware Road
A 406
A 1000
A 502
High Road
Edgware Road
Finchley Road
Maida Vale
Harrow Rd
Harrow View
A 409
Pinner Rd A 404
A 4006 Kenton Rd
B 466
A 312 Northolt Rd
A 4005 Road
Watford Rd A 404
East Lane A 4088
A 404
A 4005 Bridgewater Rd
A 40
A 4127
Greenford
Hanger Lane
A 312 The Parkway
Uxbridge Road A 4020
Uxbridge Rd
A 4020 The Vale
Bayswater
B 454
A 406 Gunnersbury Av.
A 4127
A 4
A 30
London Road A 315
Kew Rd
A 316
Castelnau
A 308 King's Rd
Staines Road
Upper Richmond Road A 205
Sheen Rd A 305
A 306 Roehampton Lane
A 219
A 3
Wimbledon Park Rd
Richmond Rd
Petersham Rd A 307
Kingston Hill A 308
A 316
A 311
A 313
A 308
Staines Rd East
Hampton Court Road
Coombe Lane
A 238
A 219
Kingston Rd A 238
A 298
A 309 Hampton Court Way
Portsmouth Road
Brighton Rd
A 243
A 3
A 24
A 297

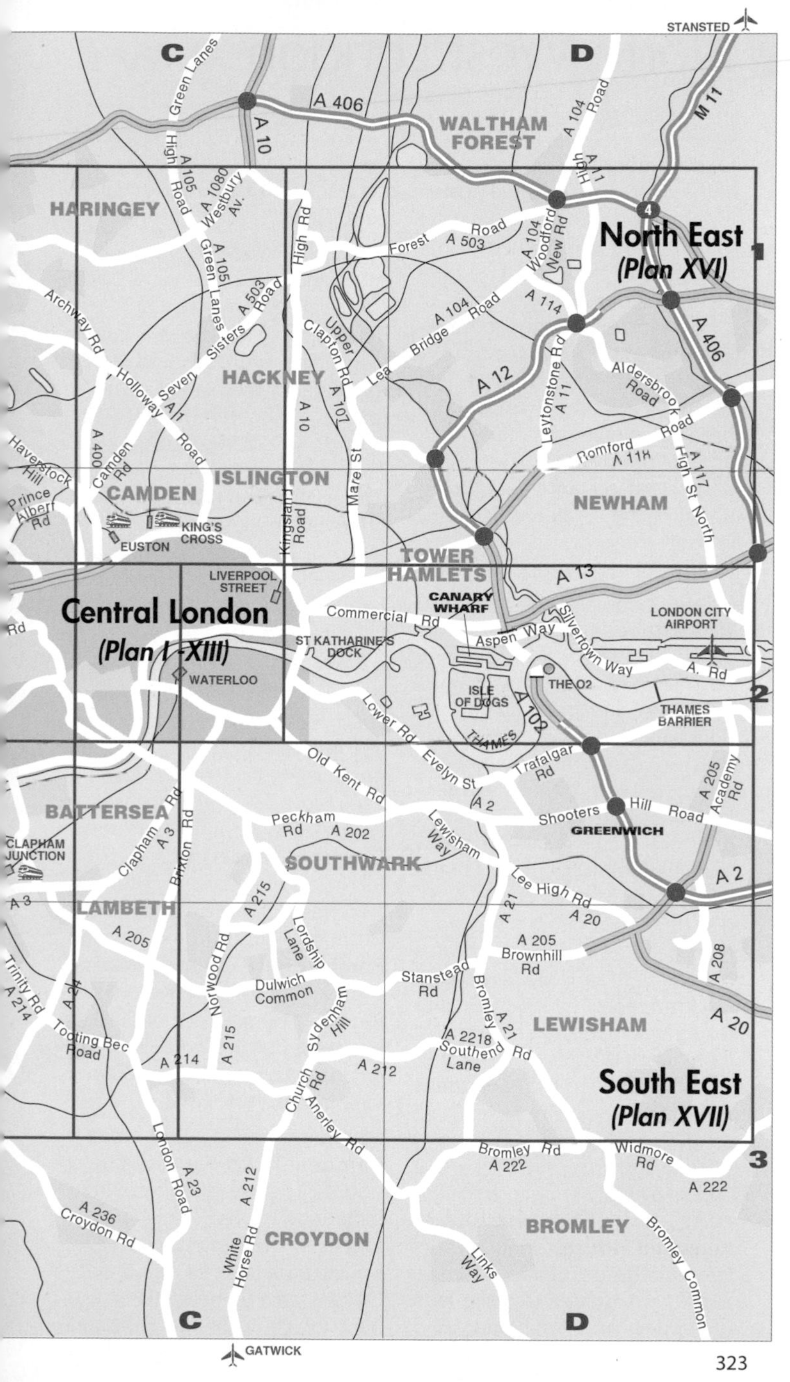

STANSTED
C
D
North East
(Plan XVI)
Central London
(Plan I -XIII)
South East
(Plan XVII)
HARINGEY
WALTHAM FOREST
HACKNEY
ISLINGTON
CAMDEN
TOWER HAMLETS
NEWHAM
BATTERSEA
SOUTHWARK
LAMBETH
LEWISHAM
CROYDON
BROMLEY
GREENWICH
EUSTON
KING'S CROSS
LIVERPOOL STREET
WATERLOO
CANARY WHARF
ST KATHARINE'S DOCK
ISLE OF DOGS
THE O2
LONDON CITY AIRPORT
THAMES BARRIER
CLAPHAM JUNCTION
THAMES
1
2
3
GATWICK

North-West London

Heading north from London Zoo and Regent's Park, the green baton is passed to two of the city's most popular and well-known locations: Hampstead Heath and Highgate Wood. In close proximity, they offer a favoured pair of lungs to travellers emerging from the murky depths of the Northern Line. Two centuries ago, they would have been just another part of the area's undeveloped high ground and pastureland, but since the building boom of the nineteenth century, both have become prized assets in this part of the metropolis.

People came to seek shelter in **Hampstead** in times of plague, and it's retained its bucolic air to this day. Famous names have always enjoyed its charms: Constable and Keats rested their brush and pen here, while the sculptors Henry Moore and Barbara Hepworth were residents in more recent times. Many are drawn to such delightful places as Church Row, which boasts a lovely Georgian Terrace. You know you're up high because the thoroughfares bear names like Holly Mount and Mount Vernon. The Heath is full of rolling woodlands and meadows; it's a great place for rambling, particularly to the crest of **Parliament Hill** and its superb city views. There are three bathing ponds here, one mixed, and one each for male and female swimmers, while up on the Heath's northern fringes, **Kenwood House,** along with its famous al fresco summer concerts, also boasts great art by the likes of Vermeer and Rembrandt. And besides all that, there's an ivy tunnel leading to a terrace with idyllic pond views.

Highgate Wood is an ancient woodland and conservation area, containing a leafy walk that meanders enchantingly along a former railway line to **Crouch End,** home to a band of thespians. Down the road at Highgate Cemetery, the likes of Karl Marx, George Eliot, Christina Rossetti and Michael Faraday rest in a great entanglement of breathtaking Victorian over-decoration. The cemetery is still in use – most recent notable to be buried here is Alexander Litvinenko, the Russian dissident.

Next door you'll find **Waterlow Park,** another fine green space, which, apart from its super views, also includes decorative ponds on three levels. Lauderdale House is here, too, a 16C pile which is now an arts centre; more famously, Charles II handed over its keys to Nell Gwynn for her to use as her North London residence. Head back south from here, and **Primrose Hill** continues the theme of glorious green space: its surrounding terraces are populated by media darlings, while its vertiginous mass is another to boast a famously enviable vista.

Of a different hue altogether is **Camden Town** with its buzzy edge, courtesy of a renowned indie music scene, goths, punks, and six earthy markets selling everything from tat to exotica. Charles Dickens grew up here, and he was none too complimentary; the area

S. Vidler/age fotostock

still relishes its seamy underside. A scenic route out is the **Regent's Canal,** which cuts its way through the market and ambles to the east and west of the city. Up the road, the legendary Roundhouse re-opened its arty front doors in 2006, expanding further the wide range of Camden's alt scene.

One of the music world's most legendary destinations, the **Abbey Road** studios, is also in this area and, yes, it's possible to join other tourists making their way over that zebra crossing. Not far away, in Maresfield Gardens, stands a very different kind of attraction. The Freud Museum is one of the very few buildings in London to have two blue plaques. It was home to Sigmund during the last year of his life and it's where he lived with his daughter Anna (her plaque commemorates her work in child psychiatry). Inside, there's a fabulous library and his working desk. But the pivotal part of the whole house is in another corner of the study – the psychiatrist's couch!

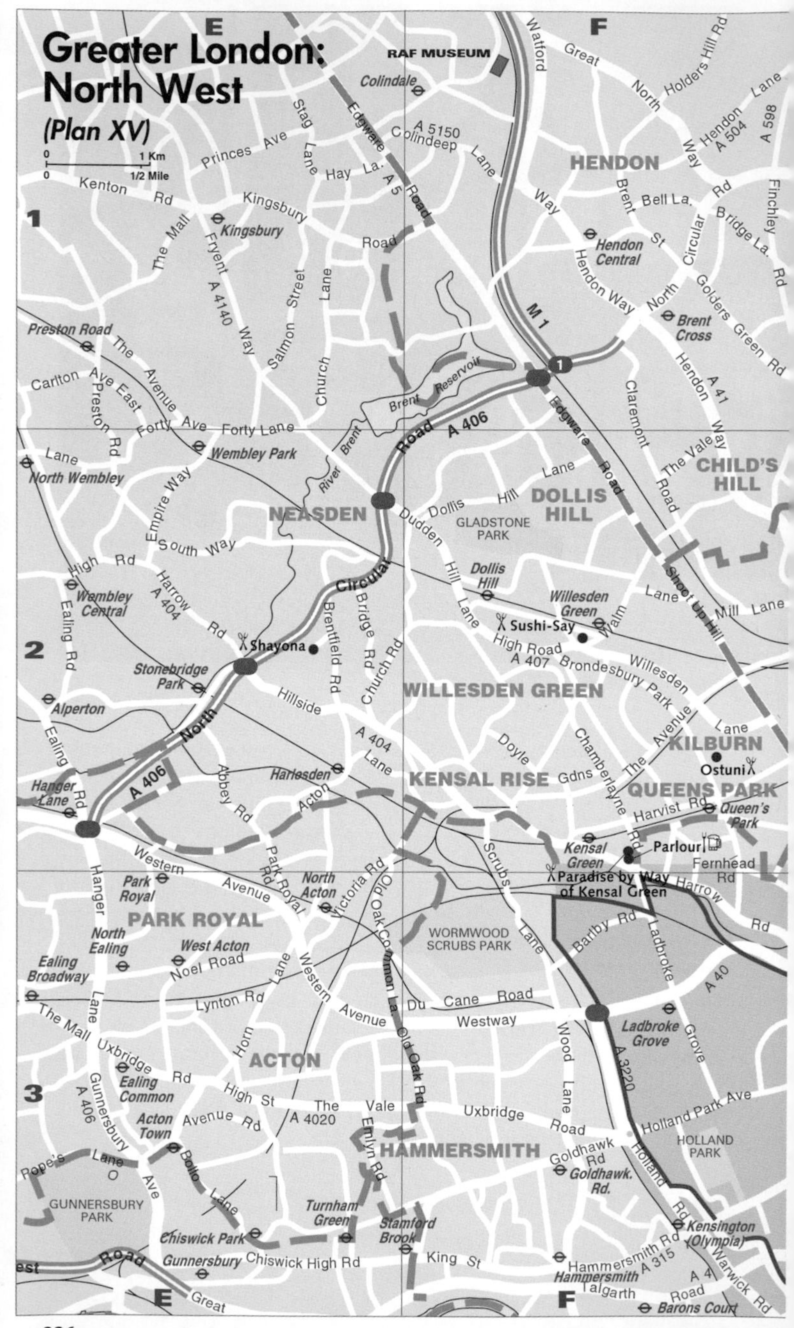

Greater London: North West
(Plan XV)
0 1 Km
0 1/2 Mile
E
F
1
2
3
RAF MUSEUM
Colindale
A 5150
Colindeep Lane
Edgware Road
A 5
Watford Way
Great North Way
Holders Hill Rd
Hendon Lane
A 504
A 598
HENDON
Brent St
Bell La.
Circular Rd
Bridge La.
Finchley Rd
Hendon Central
Hendon Way
North Circular
Brent Cross
Golders Green Rd
Princes Ave
Stag Lane
Hay La.
Kenton Rd
Kingsbury Road
Kingsbury
The Mall
Fryent Way
A 4140
Salmon Street
Church Lane
M 1
1
Preston Road
The Avenue
Carlton Ave East
Preston Rd
Forty Ave
Forty Lane
Brent Reservoir
River Brent
Road A 406
Edgware Road
Claremont Road
Hendon Way
A 41
The Vale
CHILD'S HILL
Lane
North Wembley
Wembley Park
Empire Way
NEASDEN
Dudden Hill Lane
Dollis Hill Lane
GLADSTONE PARK
DOLLIS HILL
Shoot Up Hill
South Way
High Rd
Wembley Central
Ealing Rd
Harrow Rd
A 404
Circular
Brentfield Rd
Bridge Rd
Church Rd
Dollis Hill
Willesden Green
Walm Lane
Mill Lane
Sushi-Say
High Road
A 407
Brondesbury Park
Willesden Lane
Shayona
Stonebridge Park
Alperton
Hillside
WILLESDEN GREEN
North
A 406
The Avenue
KILBURN
Ostuni
Ealing Rd
Hanger Lane
Abbey Rd
Acton Lane
Harlesden
A 404
Doyle Gdns
Chamberlayne Rd
KENSAL RISE
QUEENS PARK
Harvist Rd
Queen's Park
Kensal Green
Parlour
Paradise by Way of Kensal Green
Fernhead Rd
Harrow Rd
Western Avenue
Park Royal
Park Royal Rd
North Acton
Victoria Rd
Old Oak Common La.
Scrubs Lane
Hanger Lane
PARK ROYAL
North Ealing
West Acton
Noel Road
WORMWOOD SCRUBS PARK
Barlby Rd
Ladbroke Grove
Rd
A 40
Ealing Broadway
Lynton Rd
Horn Lane
Western Avenue
Du Cane Road
Westway
The Mall
Uxbridge Rd
Ealing Common
ACTON
Wood Lane
Ladbroke Grove
A 3220
High St
The Vale
A 4020
Old Oak Rd
Uxbridge Road
Holland Park Ave
HOLLAND PARK
Gunnersbury Ave
A 406
Acton Town
Avenue Rd
Emlyn Rd
HAMMERSMITH
Goldhawk Rd
Goldhawk Rd.
Holland Rd
Pope's Lane
Bollo Lane
GUNNERSBURY PARK
Turnham Green
Stamford Brook
Chiswick Park
Gunnersbury
Chiswick High Rd
King St
Hammersmith Rd
A 315
Kensington (Olympia)
Hammersmith
Talgarth Road
A 4
Warwick Rd
Barons Court
Great West Road

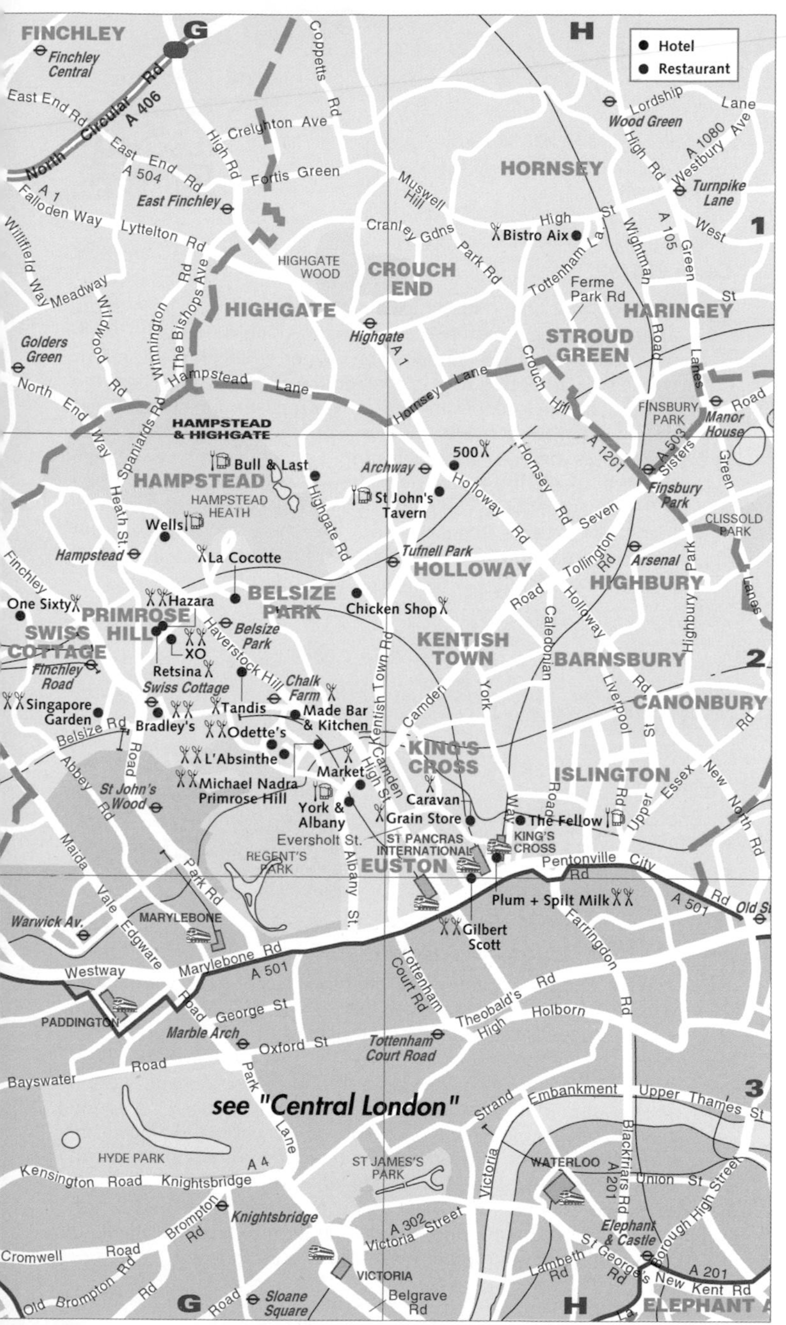
Hotel
Restaurant
FINCHLEY
G
H
Finchley Central
HORNSEY
Wood Green
Turnpike Lane
CROUCH END
HIGHGATE
HIGHGATE WOOD
Highgate
Golders Green
HARINGEY
STROUD GREEN
HAMPSTEAD & HIGHGATE
HAMPSTEAD
HAMPSTEAD HEATH
FINSBURY PARK
Manor House
Finsbury Park
Archway
Bull & Last
St John's Tavern
500
Wells
La Cocotte
Hampstead
Tufnell Park
HOLLOWAY
HIGHBURY
Arsenal
CLISSOLD PARK
BELSIZE PARK
One Sixty
Hazara
Chicken Shop
PRIMROSE HILL
SWISS COTTAGE
XO
Retsina
Belsize Park
KENTISH TOWN
BARNSBURY
Finchley Road
Swiss Cottage
Chalk Farm
CANONBURY
Singapore Garden
Tandis
Made Bar & Kitchen
Bradley's
Odette's
KING'S CROSS
L'Absinthe
Market
ISLINGTON
Michael Nadra Primrose Hill
St John's Wood
York & Albany
Caravan
Grain Store
The Fellow
ST PANCRAS INTERNATIONAL
KING'S CROSS
REGENT'S PARK
EUSTON
Plum + Spilt Milk
Gilbert Scott
Warwick Av.
MARYLEBONE
PADDINGTON
Marble Arch
Tottenham Court Road
see "Central London"
HYDE PARK
ST JAMES'S PARK
WATERLOO
Knightsbridge
Elephant & Castle
VICTORIA
Sloane Square
ELEPHANT
1
2
3
North Circular Rd
A 406
East End Rd
A 504
A 1
Falloden Way
Lyttelton Rd
Creighton Ave
Fortis Green
High Rd
Coppetts Rd
Muswell Hill
Cranley Gdns
Park Rd
Tottenham La.
Ferme Park Rd
Lordship Lane
A 1080
Westbury Ave
Wightman Road
A 105
Green Lanes
Hampstead Lane
Hornsey Lane
Crouch Hill
Seven Sisters
A 503
A 1201
Holloway Rd
Hornsey Rd
Highgate Rd
Spaniards Rd
Heath St.
North End Way
Wildwood Rd
Winnington Rd
The Bishops Ave
Meadway
Willifield Way
Finchley Rd
Haverstock Hill
Kentish Town Rd
Camden Rd
Camden High St
York Way
Caledonian Road
Liverpool Rd
Upper St
Essex Rd
New North Rd
Tollington Rd
Highbury Park
Belsize Rd
Abbey Rd
Maida Vale
Edgware Road
Park Rd
Albany St.
Eversholt St.
Pentonville Rd
City Rd
Old St
A 501
Farringdon Rd
Marylebone Rd
Westway
Tottenham Court Rd
Theobald's Rd
High Holborn
George St
Oxford St
Bayswater Road
Park Lane
Strand
Embankment
Upper Thames St
Blackfriars Rd
A 201
Union St
Borough High Street
Victoria
A 4
Kensington Road
Knightsbridge
Brompton Rd
A 302
Victoria Street
Cromwell Road
Old Brompton Rd
Belgrave Rd
Lambeth Rd
St George's Rd
New Kent Rd

500

Italian

Archway

782 Holloway Rd ✉ N19 3JH
(020) 7272 3406 – **www**.500restaurant.co.uk
⊖ Archway
Closed 2 weeks summer and 2 weeks Christmas-New Year – booking essential – (dinner only and lunch Friday-Sunday)

H2

Carte £24/32

Named after the cute little Fiat and that couldn't be more appropriate because here is a restaurant which is small, fun, well-priced and ideal for London. The owner is an ebullient fellow who takes an active role in the service, as does the chef who likes to see the look of satisfaction on his customers' faces. Their shared passion is evident in the cooking: homemade breads and pastas are very good; the fluffy gnocchi with sausage ragu delivers a kick; the tender veal chop is a winner and the rabbit is the house special. The menu, which has occasional Sardinian leanings, changes regularly and the sheet of daily specials includes great little snacks to have with a drink. Black and white photos of old Holloway are the only incongruity.

St John's Tavern

modern

Archway

91 Junction Rd ✉ N19 5QU
(020) 7272 1587 – **www**.stjohnstavern.com
⊖ Archway.
Closed 25-26 December and 1 January – booking advisable – (dinner only and lunch Friday-Sunday)

H2

Carte £25/35

Having undergone an English Heritage restoration a few years ago, St John's Tavern stands as something of a beacon of hope on the sluggishly smartening thoroughfare that is Junction Road. It doesn't disappoint inside either: the laid-back front bar does an appealing line in snacks like salt cod croquettes and mutton pasties, and there are few more warming spots in North London on a cold night than the large, boldly decorated rear dining room. The chefs list the provenance of their ingredients on a board next to the open kitchen, with Devon and Dorset seemingly the favoured counties. The daily menu is largely hardy and British but with nods to the Med; heartening terrines are a highlight, as is the delicious sourdough which is baked in-house.

Hazara

Indian

G2

Belsize Park

44 Belsize Ln ✉ NW3 5AR

✆ (020) 7423 1147 – **www**.hazararestaurant.com

⊖ Belsize Park

Closed 25-26 December and 1 January – (dinner only and lunch Saturday-Sunday)

Carte £25/50

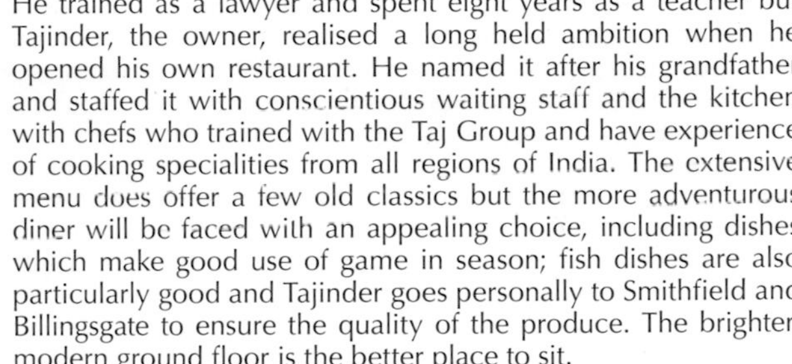

A/C

He trained as a lawyer and spent eight years as a teacher but Tajinder, the owner, realised a long held ambition when he opened his own restaurant. He named it after his grandfather and staffed it with conscientious waiting staff and the kitchen with chefs who trained with the Taj Group and have experience of cooking specialities from all regions of India. The extensive menu does offer a few old classics but the more adventurous diner will be faced with an appealing choice, including dishes which make good use of game in season; fish dishes are also particularly good and Tajinder goes personally to Smithfield and Billingsgate to ensure the quality of the produce. The brighter, modern ground floor is the better place to sit.

Retsina

Greek

G2

Belsize Park

48-50 Belsize Ln ✉ NW3 5AR

✆ (020) 7431 5855

www.retsina-london.com

⊖ Belsize Park

Closed 25-26 December, 1 January, Monday lunch and bank holidays

Menu £19 (lunch) – Carte £22/36

As private equity companies and international conglomerates continue on the path to world domination, there's something very reassuring about finding a restaurant that's still family-owned and part of the neighbourhood. It's quite a simple-looking place – bright, airy and enlivened with some modern artwork. Regulars across all age groups are literally welcomed with open arms and, with a little wishful thinking and a touch of imagination, one could almost be eating with the locals on a Greek island. The menu has all the Greek classics, from dolmathes to spanagopita, kleftico to moussaka but, bearing in mind they have a proper charcoal grill in the kitchen, the kebabs, cutlets and souvla are worthy choices.

Tandis

other world kitchens **G2**

Belsize Park

73 Haverstock Hill ✉ NW3 4SL

✆ (020) 7586 8079

www.tandisrestaurant.com

⊖ Chalk Farm

Closed 25 December

Carte £18/28

Haverstock Hill's maturing restaurant scene has now acquired a little exoticism thanks to Tandis and its enticing Iranian cooking. The appeal of this contemporary looking restaurant stretches way beyond the Iranian diaspora – plenty of locals also appear to have been seduced as soon as they tasted the traditional flat bread baked in a clay oven. A varied selection of invigorating 'koresht' stews and succulent 'kababs' form the mainstay of the menu but other specialities such as 'sabzi polo' and the rich and complex flavours of 'kashke bademjaan' are well worth exploring. Finish with some of their fine teas and a 'faloodeh', where rose water sorbet is matched with a sour cherry syrup. The best seats are to be found at the back.

XO

Asian **G2**

Belsize Park

29 Belsize Ln ✉ NW3 5AS

✆ (020) 7433 0888

www.rickerrestaurants.com/xo

⊖ Belsize Park

Closed 25-26 December, 1 January and bank holidays

Menu £18 (lunch) – Carte £20/52

Who knew Belsize Park was so trendy? Apart from estate agents, obviously. This branch of Will Ricker's small chain of glossy pan-Asian restaurants may not be quite as frenetic as the others but it still attracts plenty of shiny happy people, many of whom are holding hands. It follows the same theme as the others: a busy front bar that serves decent cocktails, behind which is the slick, uncluttered restaurant in shades of lime. The menu trawls through most of Asia; start with some warm edamame while reading through it. Highlights include the ever-popular crispy squid and the tender and tasty Indonesian lamb rendang curry. Sharing is the key, especially as those who come in large parties get the booths.

Made Bar & Kitchen

other world kitchens G2

Camden Town

Roundhouse, Chalk Farm Rd ✉ NW1 8EH

✆ (020) 7424 8495

www.roundhouse.org.uk/made

⊖ Chalk Farm

Closed 25 December, 1-2 January, Sunday dinner and Monday

Carte £21/33

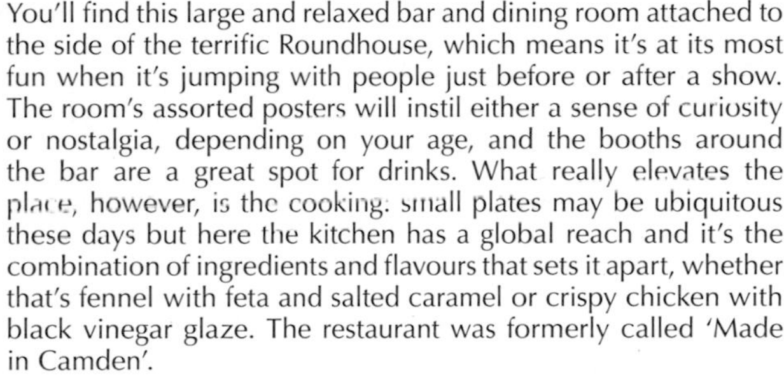

You'll find this large and relaxed bar and dining room attached to the side of the terrific Roundhouse, which means it's at its most fun when it's jumping with people just before or after a show. The room's assorted posters will instil either a sense of curiosity or nostalgia, depending on your age, and the booths around the bar are a great spot for drinks. What really elevates the place, however, is the cooking: small plates may be ubiquitous these days but here the kitchen has a global reach and it's the combination of ingredients and flavours that sets it apart, whether that's fennel with feta and salted caramel or crispy chicken with black vinegar glaze. The restaurant was formerly called 'Made in Camden'.

Market

British modern G2

Camden Town

43 Parkway ✉ NW1 7PN

✆ (020) 7267 9700 – **www**.marketrestaurant.co.uk

⊖ Camden Town

Closed 25 December-3 January, Sunday dinner and bank holidays – booking essential

Menu £10 (weekday lunch) – Carte £27/38

The name is spot on because this is all about market fresh produce, seasonality and cooking that is refreshingly matter of fact, with big, bold flavour and John Bull Britishness. Dishes come as advertised, with no pointless ornamentation, and you can expect to find the likes of brawn, ox tongue fritters and devilled kidneys alongside stews and shepherd's pie in winter, followed by proper puddings, not desserts. But be sure to have lamb or beef dripping on toast as a pre-starter – it'll leave you licking your lips for the next few hours. The exposed brick walls, zinc-topped tables and old school chairs work very well and the atmosphere is fun without ever becoming too excitable. The terrific prices entice in plenty of passers-by.

York & Albany

modern G2

Camden Town

127-129 Parkway ✉ NW1 7PS

(020) 7388 3344

www.gordonramsay.com/yorkandalbany

Camden Town.

Booking essential

Menu £24 (weekday lunch) – Carte £31/41

These days things are more egalitarian down at the York & Albany, a handsome 1820s John Nash coaching inn rescued by Gordon Ramsay after lying virtually derelict for years. Gone is the separation of bar and restaurant dining – you are now offered the same menu wherever you want to sit, whether that's in the bar, the back restaurant or downstairs next to the open kitchen. The menu has also been made a little more inclusive and includes wood-fired pizzas and pasta dishes alongside more adventurous choices like lamb shoulder with braised celery and duck with hispi cabbage. It works well because the kitchen treats a burger with the same respect as they do a rib-eye steak, although service can still wobble at times. The bedrooms have character.

Shayona

Indian E2

Church End

54-62 Meadow Garth ✉ NW10 8HD

(020) 8965 3365

www.shayonarestaurants.com

Stonebridge Park

Closed 23-24 October, 11-12 November and 25 December

Menu £8 (weekday lunch) – Carte £14/20

Shayona sits in the shadow of Neasden's remarkable Shri Swaminarayan Mandir and is actually owned by the temple. In contrast to the splendour of this Hindu gem, the restaurant is housed within a building that looks, from the outside, a little like a supermarket and indeed somewhat resembles one on the inside too — but head past the sweet counter and you'll find yourself in a comfortable and vibrantly decorated room. The fresh, balanced cooking here is sattvic which means it is vegetarian and 'pure' and so avoids certain foods like onion or garlic. The large and varied menu covers all parts of India and includes curries from the north, dosas from the south and street snacks from Mumbai. There is no alcohol available so choose a refreshing lassi instead.

Bistro Aix

French

Crouch End

H1

54 Topsfield Par, Tottenham Ln ✉ N8 8PT
✆ (020) 8340 6346 – **www**.bistroaix.co.uk
⊖ Crouch Hill
Closed 26 December and 1 January – (dinner only and lunch Friday-Sunday)

Menu £18 – Carte £26/50

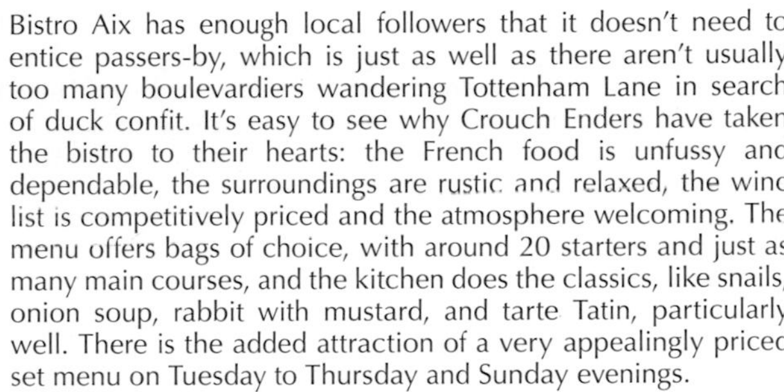

Bistro Aix has enough local followers that it doesn't need to entice passers-by, which is just as well as there aren't usually too many boulevardiers wandering Tottenham Lane in search of duck confit. It's easy to see why Crouch Enders have taken the bistro to their hearts: the French food is unfussy and dependable, the surroundings are rustic and relaxed, the wine list is competitively priced and the atmosphere welcoming. The menu offers bags of choice, with around 20 starters and just as many main courses, and the kitchen does the classics, like snails, onion soup, rabbit with mustard, and tarte Tatin, particularly well. There is the added attraction of a very appealingly priced set menu on Tuesday to Thursday and Sunday evenings.

Bull & Last

British traditional

Dartmouth Park

G2

168 Highgate Rd ✉ NW5 1QS
✆ (020) 7267 3641
www.thebullandlast.co.uk
⊖ Tufnell Park.
Closed 24-25 December – booking essential

Carte £23/42

Dartmouth Park locals know a good thing when they see it and The Bull and Last, always full of character and life, is most certainly a good thing. If you haven't booked, it's still worth trying your luck as they keep the odd table back – mind you, with enticing bar snacks like pig's trotter wontons and soft shell crab tempura, you may simply find happiness at the bar ordering some of these to go with your pint. The cooking is gloriously robust and generous and the menu mainly British with some pasta dishes thrown in. The kitchen knows its way around an animal too – the charcuterie boards are very popular. Puds are traditional; cheese is in good order and the homemade ice creams are a hit. And where else can you get marrowbone for your dog?

Wells

British modern

G2

Hampstead

30 Well Walk ✉ NW3 1BX

✆ (020) 7794 3785

www.thewellshampstead.co.uk

⊖ Hampstead.

Carte £25/35

The Wells is named after Chalybeate Well which, in 1698, was given to the poor of Hampstead – it's about 30 yards away, next to that BMW. Equidistant between Heath and High Street, this handsome pub is split in two: downstairs is the busier, more relaxed part of the operation, while upstairs you'll find a formally dressed dining room. Apart from a couple of extra grilled dishes downstairs, the two areas share a menu, which is cleverly balanced to satisfy all appetites from spirited dog walker to leisurely shopper. Salads or seared scallops can be followed by sea bass, assorted pasta or duck confit; puds are good and they do a decent crumble. Add a commendable range of ales and wines and you have a pub for all seasons.

Paradise by way of Kensal Green

British modern

F2

Kensal Green

19 Kilburn Ln ✉ W10 4AE

✆ (020) 8969 0098

www.theparadise.co.uk

⊖ Kensal Green.

(dinner only and lunch Saturday and Sunday)

Menu £30 – Carte £24/41

Calling 'Paradise' a pub hardly does it justice – this is a veritable fun palace. Named after a line from a GK Chesterton poem, this gloriously bohemian place is spread over three floors and means different things to different people: some come along for comedy nights and cocktails or party nights and DJs; others pop in for drinks in the Reading room or snacks in the bar; many come to eat in the restaurant; and you can even get married here. The food is a reassuring mix of British favourites and European themed dishes, all made using good ingredients from trusted suppliers and prepared with obvious care. The surroundings are wonderfully quirky and idiosyncratic, the staff are contagiously enthusiastic and the vibe effortlessly cool.

Ⓝ Parlour

British modern F2

Kensal Green

5 Regent St ✉ NW10 5LG
(020) 8969 2184
www.parlourkensal.com
⊖ Kensal Green
Closed 24 December-1 January

Menu £10 (weekday lunch) – Carte £25/36

It may not quite be a pub but nor is it a restaurant so let's focus more on what Parlour actually is – a fun, warmly run and slightly quirky neighbourhood hangout. Open from breakfast until late, it has one room dominated by a large bar and the other set up for eating with an appealingly higgledy-piggledy look. They do a decent cocktail and a great range of beers and the menu is a wonderfully unabashed mix of tradition, originality and reinvention. Approaching legendary status is their cow pie which even Dan, however Desperate, would struggle to finish. The vegetable 'ravioli' is a cleverly thought-out construction and the marshmallow Wagon Wheel something for the children. On warm nights ask for one of the cabanas in the garden.

Chicken Shop

meats and grills G2

Kentish Town

79 Highgate Rd ✉ NW5 1TL
(020) 3310 2020
www.chickenshop.com
⊖ Kentish Town
Bookings not accepted – (dinner only and lunch Saturday-Sunday)

Carte £16/21

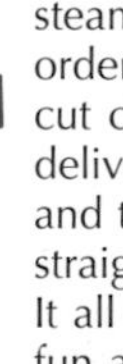
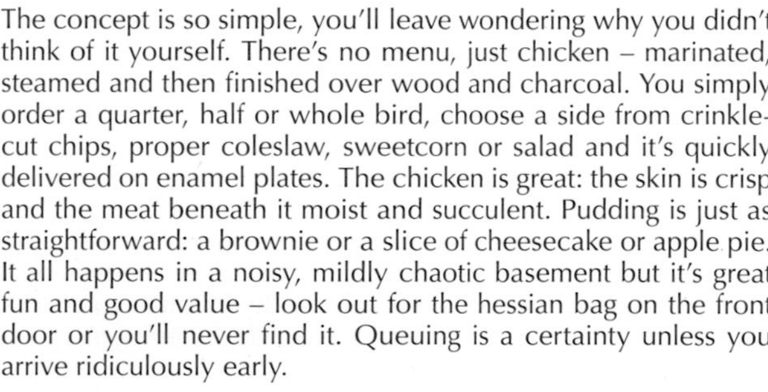

The concept is so simple, you'll leave wondering why you didn't think of it yourself. There's no menu, just chicken – marinated, steamed and then finished over wood and charcoal. You simply order a quarter, half or whole bird, choose a side from crinkle-cut chips, proper coleslaw, sweetcorn or salad and it's quickly delivered on enamel plates. The chicken is great: the skin is crisp and the meat beneath it moist and succulent. Pudding is just as straightforward: a brownie or a slice of cheesecake or apple pie. It all happens in a noisy, mildly chaotic basement but it's great fun and good value – look out for the hessian bag on the front door or you'll never find it. Queuing is a certainty unless you arrive ridiculously early.

Caravan

other world kitchens **H2**

King's Cross St Pancras

The Granary Building, 1 Granary Sq. ✉ N1C 4AA

✆ (020) 7101 7661

www.caravankingscross.co.uk

⊖ King's Cross St Pancras

Closed Sunday dinner – booking essential

Carte £19/45

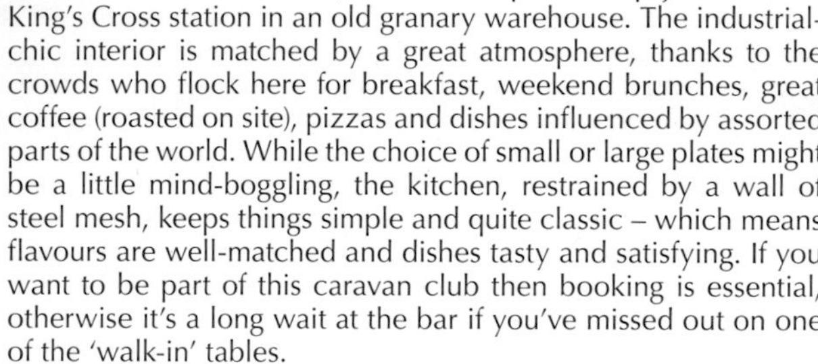

For their second Caravan, the owners pitched up just north of King's Cross station in an old granary warehouse. The industrial-chic interior is matched by a great atmosphere, thanks to the crowds who flock here for breakfast, weekend brunches, great coffee (roasted on site), pizzas and dishes influenced by assorted parts of the world. While the choice of small or large plates might be a little mind-boggling, the kitchen, restrained by a wall of steel mesh, keeps things simple and quite classic – which means flavours are well-matched and dishes tasty and satisfying. If you want to be part of this caravan club then booking is essential, otherwise it's a long wait at the bar if you've missed out on one of the 'walk-in' tables.

Fellow

modern **H2**

King's Cross St Pancras

24 York Way ✉ N1 9AA

✆ (020) 7833 4395

www.thefellow.co.uk

⊖ King's Cross St Pancras.

Closed 25-27 December

Carte £25/37

This clever Fellow established itself well before the regeneration of King's Cross finished so was all ready for the influx of new customers. Don't be fooled by its rather anonymous façade – this is a pub de nos jours, complete with a slick cocktail bar and a kitchen with worthy ingredient-sourcing credentials. Most of the action takes place on the ground floor which looks a little dark and moody but the atmosphere is brightened considerably by the staff who make a genuine effort to look after their customers. A relatively small kitchen means they keep the menu lean and clean and influences remain largely within Europe. Fish from Cornish day boats is often a highlight; cheeses are British and puds are well worth a flutter.

Gilbert Scott

British traditional **H2/3**

King's Cross St Pancras

St Pancras Renaissance Hotel,
Euston Rd ✉ NW1 2AR
✆ (020) 7278 3888
www.thegilbertscott.co.uk
⊖ King's Cross St Pancras

Menu £21 (lunch and early dinner) – Carte £28/61

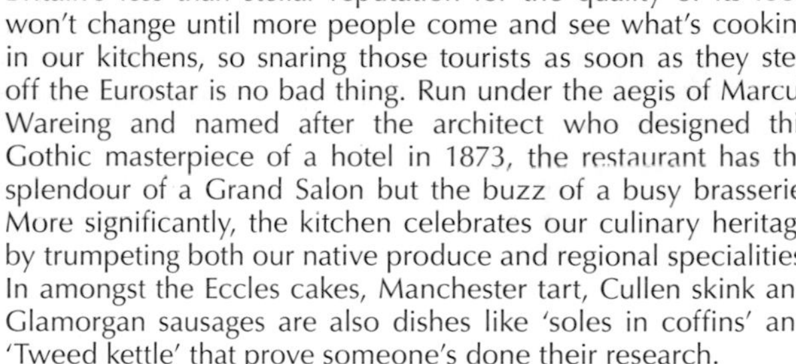

Britain's less than stellar reputation for the quality of its food won't change until more people come and see what's cooking in our kitchens, so snaring those tourists as soon as they step off the Eurostar is no bad thing. Run under the aegis of Marcus Wareing and named after the architect who designed this Gothic masterpiece of a hotel in 1873, the restaurant has the splendour of a Grand Salon but the buzz of a busy brasserie. More significantly, the kitchen celebrates our culinary heritage by trumpeting both our native produce and regional specialities. In amongst the Eccles cakes, Manchester tart, Cullen skink and Glamorgan sausages are also dishes like 'soles in coffins' and 'Tweed kettle' that prove someone's done their research.

Grain Store

modern **H2**

King's Cross St Pancras

Granary Sq, 1-3 Stable St ✉ N1C 4AB
✆ (020) 7324 4466
www.grainstore.com
⊖ King's Cross St Pancras
Closed 24-25 December, 1 January and Sunday dinner

Carte £22/32

The redevelopment of King's Cross may be far from finished, yet already train travellers and locals have a wealth of eating places close by. Grain Store is a big, buzzing 'canteen' from Bruno Loubet and the people behind the Zetter hotel, so you know it's going to be run properly. However, don't come expecting the same style of cooking – here it's about bringing together Bruno's experiences from around the world. On offer is an exciting array of eclectic, well-priced dishes that show thought, imagination and intelligence; they're packed with interesting tastes and textures, and vegetables often take the principle role. Sustainability and seasonality are more than mere buzz words here and the large kitchen rightly takes centre stage.

Plum + Spilt Milk

British modern

H2

King's Cross St Pancras

Great Northern Hotel London,
Pancras Rd ✉ N1C 4TB
✆ (020) 3388 0818
www.plumandspiltmilk.com
⊖ Kings Cross St Pancras

Menu £21 (lunch) – Carte £32/53

Whether you've just arrived or are preparing to depart, King's Cross St Pancras offers a number of dining options these days and these include this smart brasserie on the first floor of the Grade II listed Great Northern hotel. It's quite a small room but with windows on three sides; it's a bright and very pleasant spot. The menu is sensibly accessible and should appeal to all tastes with its classic British dishes that include potted shrimps, a 'pie of the day' and meats from the grill; follow that with bread and butter pudding and you'll feel full and also grateful that there's no weight restriction on trains. The restaurant's unusual moniker refers to the name given to the livery of the first dining cars on the Flying Scotsman.

L'Absinthe

French

G2

Primrose Hill

40 Chalcot Rd ✉ NW1 8LS
✆ (020) 7483 4848
www.labsinthe.co.uk
⊖ Chalk Farm
Closed August and Christmas

Menu £10 (weekday lunch) – Carte £21/40

In thoroughly English-sounding Primrose Hill is a bistro so Gallic you'll find yourself unwittingly summoning the spirit of Serge Gainsbourg or at least contemplating an affair. The menu has all the great classics, from cassoulet to onion soup, steak frites to duck confit. Okay, so the execution doesn't always quite live up to the promise of the menu but no one seems to mind because the wine list is terrific — the owner just charges corkage on the retail price – and the atmosphere's great, although do try to get a table on the ground floor as it's more appealing than downstairs. Next door you'll find their traiteur, an ideal spot for morning coffee or a lunchtime plat du jour – or for a bottle of wine at any time.

Michael Nadra Primrose Hill

modern

G2

Primrose Hill

42 Gloucester Ave ✉ NW1 8JD

✆ (020) 7722 2800

www.restaurant-michaelnadra.co.uk/primrose

⊖ Camden Town

Closed 24-28 December and 1 January

Menu £20/55

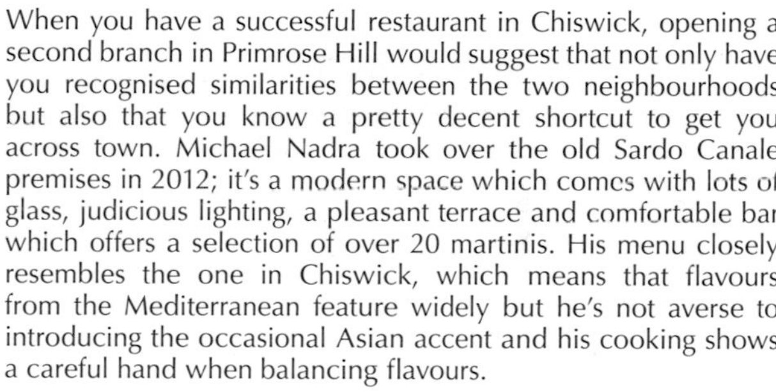

When you have a successful restaurant in Chiswick, opening a second branch in Primrose Hill would suggest that not only have you recognised similarities between the two neighbourhoods but also that you know a pretty decent shortcut to get you across town. Michael Nadra took over the old Sardo Canale premises in 2012; it's a modern space which comes with lots of glass, judicious lighting, a pleasant terrace and comfortable bar which offers a selection of over 20 martinis. His menu closely resembles the one in Chiswick, which means that flavours from the Mediterranean feature widely but he's not averse to introducing the occasional Asian accent and his cooking shows a careful hand when balancing flavours.

Odette's

modern

G2

Primrose Hill

130 Regent's Park Rd. ✉ NW1 8XL

✆ (020) 7586 8569

www.odettesprimrosehill.com

⊖ Chalk Farm

Closed 25-26 December and 1 January

Menu £15 (weekday lunch) – Carte £30/40

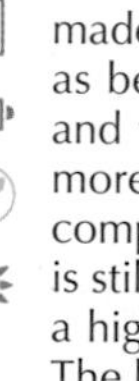
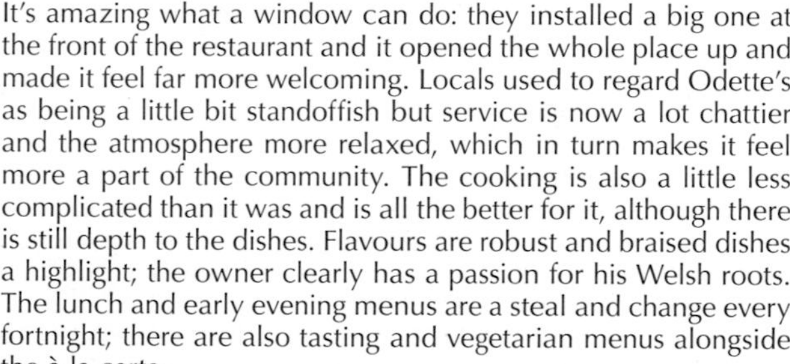

It's amazing what a window can do: they installed a big one at the front of the restaurant and it opened the whole place up and made it feel far more welcoming. Locals used to regard Odette's as being a little bit standoffish but service is now a lot chattier and the atmosphere more relaxed, which in turn makes it feel more a part of the community. The cooking is also a little less complicated than it was and is all the better for it, although there is still depth to the dishes. Flavours are robust and braised dishes a highlight; the owner clearly has a passion for his Welsh roots. The lunch and early evening menus are a steal and change every fortnight; there are also tasting and vegetarian menus alongside the à la carte.

Ostuni

Italian

Queens Park

F2

43-45 Lonsdale Rd ✉ NW6 6RA

✆ (020) 7624 8035

www.ostuniristorante.co.uk

⊖ Queen's Park

Menu £20/40 – Carte £15/37

A/C

The cuisine of Puglia, the red hot heel in Italy's boot, is celebrated at Ostuni. Start with some great olives or taralli, then order the creamy burrata or mackerel before heading to the orecchiette – the region's ear-shaped pasta made from durum wheat. For the main course, carnivores should look no further than the sausages or bombette (cheese encased in pork) from the charcoal oven, or the ox cheek which comes with another speciality – fava bean purée. Even dessert celebrates all things Pugliese: the panna cotta is topped with a sweet reduction of Primitivo. The room has an appealing, rustic look and a large terrace; seats at the bar and at the counter of the open kitchen are kept for locals who haven't booked.

Bradley's

modern

Swiss Cottage

G2

25 Winchester Rd. ✉ NW3 3NR

✆ (020) 7722 3457

www.bradleysnw3.co.uk

⊖ Swiss Cottage

Closed Sunday dinner

Menu £16/28 – Carte £33/43

A/C

Simon Bradley has been steadily going about his business for nigh on 20 years and has engendered such loyalty in his regulars that many of them wouldn't countenance a visit to a competitor until it had been going for at least a couple of years. Whilst there is an appealing and nicely balanced à la carte, the real draw here are the very well priced set menus. This affordability is achieved by proper 'cheffing' such as braising beef and buying less fashionable and underused fish like ling to create dishes with clear, complementary flavours. Simon is also a proper neighbourhood restaurateur: he can often be found at the local farmers' market. This is the ideal choice for those going to the splendid Hampstead Theatre around the corner.

Singapore Garden

Asian

G2

Swiss Cottage

83 Fairfax Rd. ✉ NW6 4DY

✆ (020) 7328 5314

www.singaporegarden.co.uk

⊖ Swiss Cottage

Closed 24-28 December

Menu £20 (lunch) – Carte £23/49

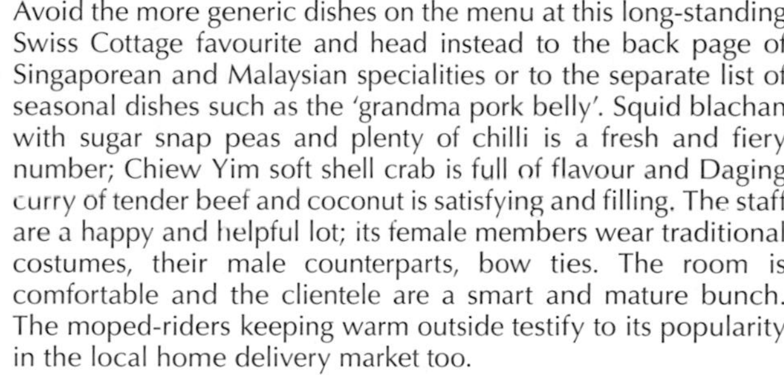

Avoid the more generic dishes on the menu at this long-standing Swiss Cottage favourite and head instead to the back page of Singaporean and Malaysian specialities or to the separate list of seasonal dishes such as the 'grandma pork belly'. Squid blachan with sugar snap peas and plenty of chilli is a fresh and fiery number; Chiew Yim soft shell crab is full of flavour and Daging curry of tender beef and coconut is satisfying and filling. The staff are a happy and helpful lot; its female members wear traditional costumes, their male counterparts, bow ties. The room is comfortable and the clientele are a smart and mature bunch. The moped-riders keeping warm outside testify to its popularity in the local home delivery market too.

N One Sixty

North-American

G2

West Hampstead

291 West End Ln. ✉ NW6 1RD

✆ (020) 77949 786 – **www**.one-sixty.co.uk

⊖ West Hampstead

Closed 24 December-2 January – (dinner only and lunch Saturday-Sunday)

Carte £19/33

The battle for supremacy between independents and chains in West Hampstead has intensified in recent years. In 2014, reinforcements for those fighting high street homogenisation arrived in the form of One Sixty, a lively local bar and restaurant based on an American smokehouse. It's a loud, buzzy, stripped back sort of place, with the kind of food you eat with your fingers. The pork ribs, ox cheek and lamb are smoked in-house for 8 hours to a temperature of 160°f – hence the name – and food comes in enamel bowls; the dry-aged burger is also proving very popular. Extras like mac & cheese and corn on the cob can be ordered on the side and there's an impressive choice of over 50 craft beers from around the world – the ideal accompaniment.

Sushi-Say 

Japanese F2

Willesden Green

33B Walm Ln. ✉ NW2 5SH

✆ (020) 8459 2971

⊖ Willesden Green

Closed 2 weeks August, 25 December-2 January, Wednesday after bank holidays, Monday and Tuesday – (dinner only and lunch Saturday-Sunday)

Carte £18/38

One of the delights of Willesden Green must surely be this long-standing Japanese restaurant which has never looked back since its last revamp and which is nearly always full. As the name suggests, sushi is the reason why many come and a seat at the counter, watching owner Mr Shimizu's expertise with his knife, is the place to be; if you're tempted to supplement your selection with some creamy uni or rich, warmed unagi then just ask him and he'll oblige. If you prefer other styles of Japanese cookery then you'll find plenty of choice; it's often worth considering the monthly specials menu; the yakitori is particularly good and there's a well-priced selection of sake and shochu. Mrs Shimizu leads her team with alacrity and efficiency.

Look out for **red** symbols, indicating a particularly pleasant ambiance.

SuperStock/Age fotostock

North-East London

If northwest London is renowned for its leafy acres, then the area to its immediate east has a more urban, brick-built appeal. Which has meant, over the last decade or so, a wholesale rebranding exercise for some of its traditionally shady localities. A generation ago it would have been beyond the remit of even the most inventive estate agent to sell the charms of Islington, Hackney or Bethnal Green. But then along came Damien Hirst, Tracey Emin et al, and before you could say 'cow in formaldehyde' the area's cachet had rocketed.

Shoreditch and **Hoxton** are the pivotal points of the region's hip makeover. Their cobbled brick streets and shabby industrial remnants were like heavenly manna to the artists and designers who started to colonise the old warehouses twenty years ago. A fashionable crowd soon followed in their footsteps, and nowadays the area around **Hoxton Square** positively teems with clubs, bars and galleries. Latest must-see space is Rivington Place, a terrific gallery that highlights visual arts from around the world. Nearby are Deluxe (digital installations), and Hales (galleries).

Before the area was ever trendy, there was the Geffrye Museum. A short stroll up Hoxton's **Kingsland Road,** it's a jewel of a place, set in elegant 18C almshouses, and depicting English middle-class interiors from 1600 to the present day. Right behind it is St. Mary's Secret Garden, a little oasis that manages to include much diversity including a separate woodland and herb area, all in less than an acre. At the southern end of the area, in Folgate Street, Dennis Severs' House is an original Huguenot home that recreates 18 and 19C life in an original way – cooking smells linger, hearth and candles burn, giving you the impression the owners have only just left the place. Upstairs the beds remain unmade: did a certain local artist pick up any ideas here?

When the Regent's Canal was built in the early 19C, **Islington's** fortunes nose-dived, for it was accompanied by the arrival of slums and over-crowding. But the once-idyllic village managed to hold onto its Georgian squares and handsome Victorian terraces through the rough times, and when these were gentrified a few years ago, the area ushered in a revival. **Camden Passage** has long been famed for its quirky antique emporiums, while the slinky Business Design Centre is a flagship of the modern Islington. Cultural icons established themselves around the Upper Street area and these have gone from strength to strength. The **Almeida** Theatre has a habit of hitting the production jackpot with its history of world premieres, while the King's Head has earned itself a reputation for raucous scene-stealing; set up in the seventies, it's also London's very first theatre-pub. Nearby, the Screen on the Green boasts a wonderful old-fashioned neon billboard.

C. Eymenier / MICHELIN

Even in the 'bad old days', Islington drew in famous names, and at Regency smart **Canonbury Square** are the one-time homes of Evelyn Waugh (no.17A) and George Orwell (no.27). These days it houses the Estorick Collection of Modern Italian Art; come here to see fine futuristic paintings in a Georgian villa. To put the history of the area in a proper context, head to St. John Street, south of the City Road, where the Islington Museum's shiny new headquarters tells the story of a colourful and multi-layered past.

Further up the A10, you come to **Dalston,** a bit like the Islington of old but with the buzzy Ridley Road market and a vibrant all-night scene including the blistering Vortex Jazz Club just off Kingsland Road. A little further north is **Stoke Newington,** referred to, a bit unkindly, as the poor man's Islington. Its pride and joy is Church Street, which not only features some characterful bookshops and eye-catching boutiques, but also lays claim to Abney Park Cemetery, an enchanting old place with a wildlife-rich nature reserve.

Greater London: North East
(Plan XVI)
HORNSEY
CROUCH END
HARINGEY
STROUD GREEN
TOTTENHAM HALE
STOKE NEWINGTON
HOLLOWAY
HIGHBURY
SHACKLEWELL
KENTISH TOWN
BARNSBURY
CANONBURY
KING'S CROSS
ISLINGTON
HACKNEY
HOXTON
EUSTON
SHOREDITCH
SPITALFIELDS
WHITECHAPEL
WAPPING
ELEPHANT AND CASTLE
Au Lac
Primeur
White Rabbit
Trullo
Prince Arthur
Lardo
Canonbury Kitchen
Roots at N1
Rotorino
Empress
Market Café
Beagle
Viet Grill
Clove Club
Tramshed
Fifteen London
Rivington Grill
Hoi Polloi
Casa Negra
Merchants Tavern
Boundary
Andina
Princess of Shoreditch
Lyle's
HKK
Eyre Brothers
L'Anima
see "Central London"

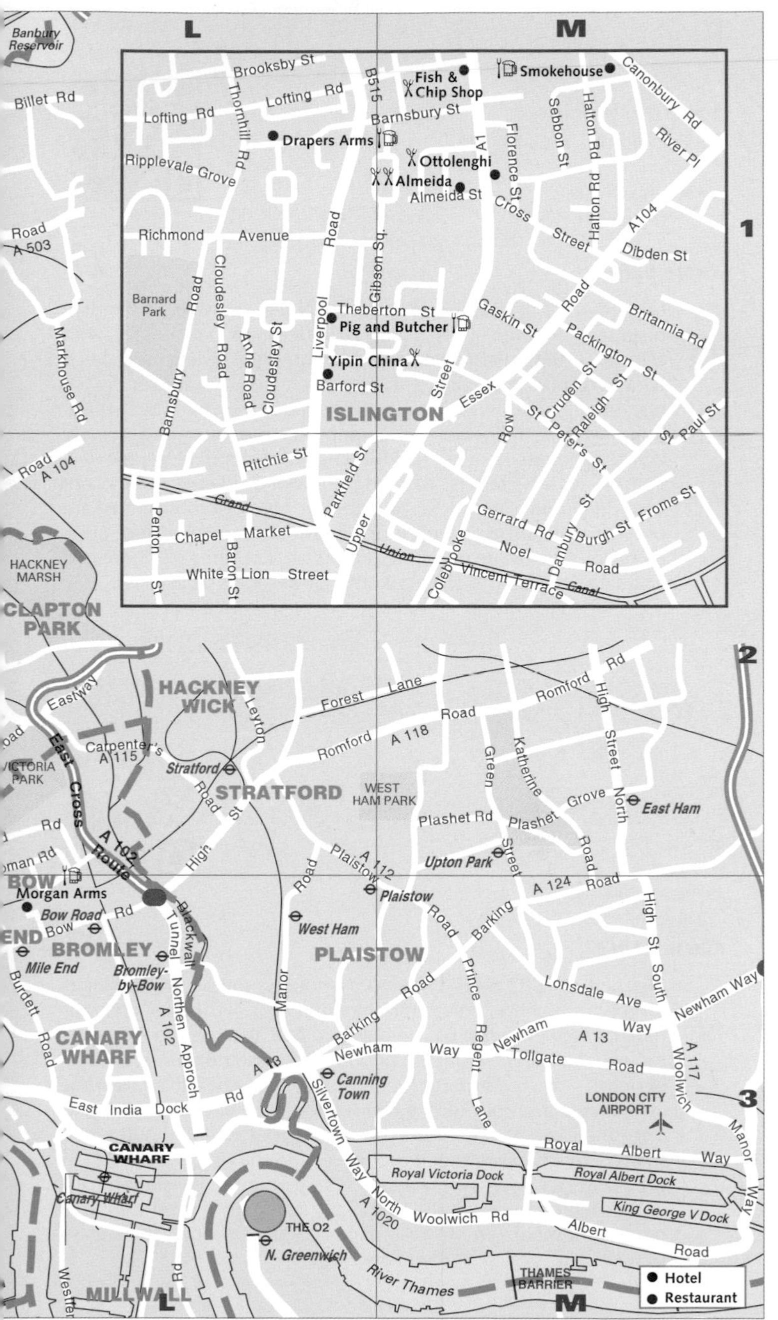

L
M
Smokehouse
Fish & Chip Shop
Drapers Arms
Ottolenghi
Almeida
Pig and Butcher
Yipin China
ISLINGTON
Brooksby St
Lofting Rd
Barnsbury St
Canonbury Rd
River Pl
Ripplevale Grove
Richmond Avenue
Almeida St
Cross Street
Dibden St
Theberton St
Gaskin St
Britannia Rd
Packington St
Barford St
Essex Road
Ritchie St
Chapel Market
White Lion Street
Gerrard Rd
Noel Road
Vincent Terrace
Frome St
Burgh St
Grand Union Canal
Barnard Park
1
2
3
Banbury Reservoir
Billet Rd
Markhouse Rd
HACKNEY MARSH
CLAPTON PARK
HACKNEY WICK
Forest Lane
Romford Road
A 118
Stratford
STRATFORD
WEST HAM PARK
Plashet Rd
Plashet Grove
East Ham
Upton Park
Plaistow
West Ham
PLAISTOW
BOW
Morgan Arms
Bow Road
BROMLEY
Mile End
Bromley-by-Bow
CANARY WHARF
Barking Road
Newham Way
A 13
Tollgate Road
Lonsdale Ave
Newham Way
Canning Town
LONDON CITY AIRPORT
East India Dock Rd
Royal Albert Way
Royal Victoria Dock
Royal Albert Dock
King George V Dock
Woolwich Rd
Albert Road
THE O2
N. Greenwich
River Thames
THAMES BARRIER
MILLWALL
Hotel
Restaurant

Roots at N1

Indian

J2

Barnsbury

115 Hemingford Rd ✉ N1 1BZ

✆ (020) 7697 4488

www.rootsatn1.com

⊖ Caledonian Road

Closed 25-26 December and Monday – booking essential – (dinner only)

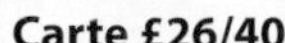

Carte £26/40

Citizens of N1 must surely be delighted to have this Indian restaurant in their midst. This old Victorian pub comes with a touch of colonial splendour, and the high ceilings and large windows lend it an airy feel. The three friends who set up the restaurant, after working together at Benares for three years, run it with a palpable sense of pride and offer a genuinely warm welcome to their customers. The menu is appealingly concise with 8 starters, 8 main courses – and side dishes kept to a minimum: freshness is the key here. Combinations are original and spicing is well-judged; tandoor-cooked dishes are a highlight, breads are plump and moreish, and the kulfi is creamy and satisfying. This is a restaurant that deserves its success.

Morgan Arms

British traditional

L3

Bow

43 Morgan St ✉ E3 5AA

✆ (020) 8980 6389

www.morganarmsbow.com

⊖ Bow Road.

Closed 25 December

Carte £18/37

Opened in 1892 and encircled by houses, the Morgan Arms is a proper neighbourhood pub. In summer it gets bedecked with hanging flowers while quiz nights and real ales keep spirits up on long winter nights. Drinkers huddle on sofas and friends occupy benches scattered around the impressive structure that is the bar and there's a proper dining room filled with books at the back. The cooking certainly offers more than your standard pub fare – the weekly changing menu provides everything from the Morgan burger to sea bass with polenta. It's tasty, fresh, sensibly priced and delivered by a friendly team who are clearly keen to see you enjoy your meal. On Monday nights come for 'onglet and a glass of Cab Sauv' which is a veritable steal.

Canonbury Kitchen

Italian

J2

Canonbury

19 Canonbury Ln ✉ N1 2AS
✆ (020) 7226 9791
www.canonburykitchen.com
⊖ Highbury & Islington

Closed Sunday dinner – (dinner only and lunch Saturday-Sunday)

Carte £23/36

Inserting the word 'kitchen' into the name of one's restaurant is becoming more and more common as it instantly evokes images of simple food and unpretentious dining. That certainly applies to Canonbury Kitchen, which comes with an appropriately light, fresh look, thanks to its exposed brick walls, high ceiling and painted floorboards. With seating for just forty it also feels like the very epitome of a neighbourhood restaurant. Owner Max and his team provide gently reassuring service and the kitchen – on-view at the far end – sensibly keeps things simple. That includes an ever-popular fritto misto made with cuttlefish and octopus, pan-fried hake with herbs, and a lemon tiramisu with limoncello replacing the marsala.

Ⓝ Primeur

modern

K2

Canonbury

116 Petherton Rd ✉ N5 2RT
www.primeurn5.co.uk
⊖ Canonbury

Closed Christmas, Monday, dinner Sunday and lunch Tuesday-Thursday

Carte £20/31

Housed in a former garage, with the huge concertina doors still in place and the sign 'Barnes Motors' above them, Primeur is the realisation of a dream for a group of friends who've spent years gaining experience in many of London's top restaurants. This time they're doing things their way, meaning tap water on the tables, communal and counter seating and no phone reservations; the feel here is laid-back and a little bit quirky and the place is run with passion, confidence and a refreshing humility. The menu offers a mix of Mediterranean and classic British dishes, of which sharing is encouraged and the seasonal ingredients are brought together with the minimum of fuss, a clear understanding of technique and plenty of vibrancy and flavour.

Smokehouse

modern

M1

Canonbury

63-69 Canonbury Rd ✉ N1 2DG

✆ (020) 7354 1144 – **www**.smokehouseislington.co.uk

⊖ Highbury & Islington.

Closed 24-26 December – booking advisable –
(dinner only and lunch Saturday-Sunday)

Carte £26/37

If barbecuing to you means a burnt chicken leg, warm wine and a wet garden then a visit to Smokehouse will set you straight. You can smell the oak chips in the smoker as you approach this warm, modern pub, which was previously called The House. Meat is the mainstay of the very appealing menu – the peppered ox cheeks have understandably become a firm favourite – but whilst the flavours are undeniably gutsy, the smoking and barbecuing manages to add a little something to the ingredients without ever overpowering them. With portion sizes to appease Desperate Dan, only the committed may make it to dessert but chocolate lovers should try the Friday pie. The pub is enthusiastically run and staff are eager to recommend dishes.

Trullo

Italian

J2

Canonbury

300-302 St Paul's Rd ✉ N1 2LH

✆ (020) 7226 2733

www.trullorestaurant.com

⊖ Highbury & Islington

Closed Christmas-New Year and Sunday dinner – booking essential

Menu £15 (lunch) – Carte £24/37

It's named after the conical-shaped buildings of southern Italy used primarily by farm workers for meeting and eating: a most appropriate moniker for a restaurant always full of noisily contented diners. While the ground floor has kept its well-worn, homely feel, the basement has a new, all-American look, with exposed brick, industrial ducting and red banquettes – the three booths being the most sought-after seats in the house. Its style may be reminiscent of a U.S. diner, but the food stays resolutely Italian: expect rustic, well-priced dishes bursting with flavour, including meats and fish cooked on the charcoal grill and great pasta, hand-rolled fresh before each service. Young, enthusiastic and cheery staff deliver dishes with aplomb.

Rotorino

Italian

K2

Dalston

434 Kingsland Rd ✉ E8 4AA
✆ (020) 7249 9081 – **www**.rotorino.com
⊖ Dalston Junction

Closed 23 December-2 January – (dinner only and lunch Saturday-Sunday)

Carte £15/35

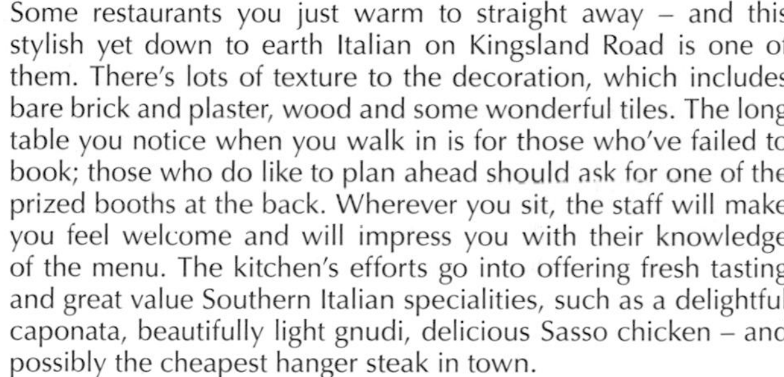

Some restaurants you just warm to straight away – and this stylish yet down to earth Italian on Kingsland Road is one of them. There's lots of texture to the decoration, which includes bare brick and plaster, wood and some wonderful tiles. The long table you notice when you walk in is for those who've failed to book; those who do like to plan ahead should ask for one of the prized booths at the back. Wherever you sit, the staff will make you feel welcome and will impress you with their knowledge of the menu. The kitchen's efforts go into offering fresh tasting and great value Southern Italian specialities, such as a delightful caponata, beautifully light gnudi, delicious Sasso chicken – and possibly the cheapest hanger steak in town.

White Rabbit

modern

K2

Dalston

15-16 Bradbury St ✉ N16 8JN
✆ (020) 7682 0163
www.whiterabbitdalston.com
⊖ Dalston Kingsland

(dinner only and lunch Saturday-Sunday)

Menu £18 (early dinner) – Carte £23/35

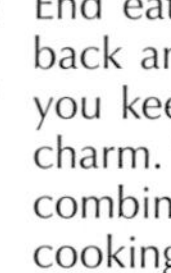

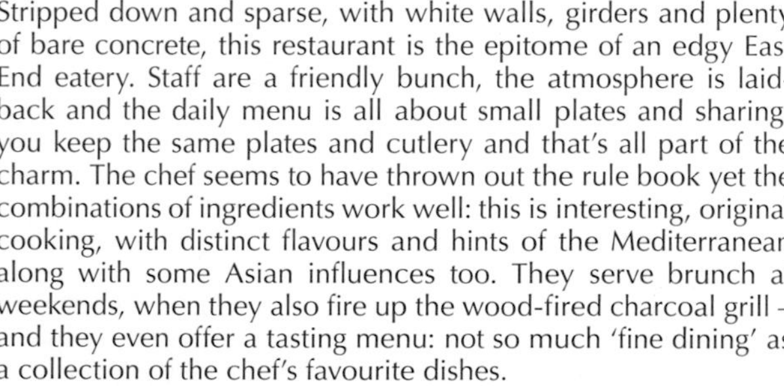

Stripped down and sparse, with white walls, girders and plenty of bare concrete, this restaurant is the epitome of an edgy East End eatery. Staff are a friendly bunch, the atmosphere is laid-back and the daily menu is all about small plates and sharing; you keep the same plates and cutlery and that's all part of the charm. The chef seems to have thrown out the rule book yet the combinations of ingredients work well: this is interesting, original cooking, with distinct flavours and hints of the Mediterranean along with some Asian influences too. They serve brunch at weekends, when they also fire up the wood-fired charcoal grill – and they even offer a tasting menu: not so much 'fine dining' as a collection of the chef's favourite dishes.

Lardo

Italian

Hackney

K2

197-205 Richmond Rd ✉ E8 3NJ
✆ (020) 8985 2683
www.lardo.co.uk
⊖ Dalston Junction

Carte £17/30

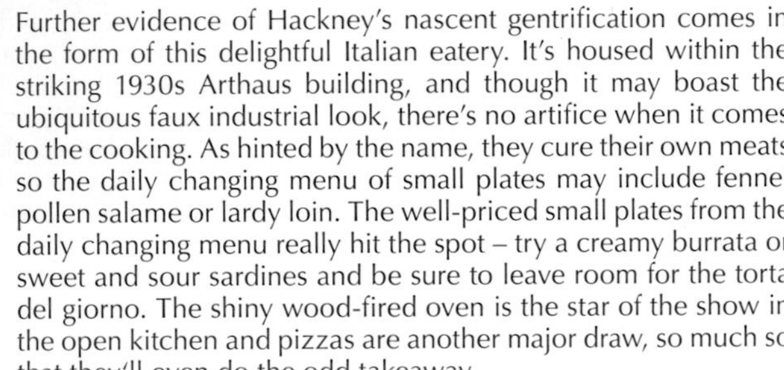

Further evidence of Hackney's nascent gentrification comes in the form of this delightful Italian eatery. It's housed within the striking 1930s Arthaus building, and though it may boast the ubiquitous faux industrial look, there's no artifice when it comes to the cooking. As hinted by the name, they cure their own meats so the daily changing menu of small plates may include fennel pollen salame or lardy loin. The well-priced small plates from the daily changing menu really hit the spot – try a creamy burrata or sweet and sour sardines and be sure to leave room for the torta del giorno. The shiny wood-fired oven is the star of the show in the open kitchen and pizzas are another major draw, so much so that they'll even do the odd takeaway.

Market Cafe

modern

Hackney

K2

2 Broadway Mkt ✉ E8 4QG
✆ (020) 7249 9070
www.market-cafe.co.uk
⊖ Bethnal Green
Closed 25-26 December

Menu £20 (dinner) – Carte £21/32

Forget data studies and economic analysis – an area's gentrification can be largely gauged by the arrival of two things: delis and restaurants. Broadway Market's steady advance towards middle class hipdom was given a nudge by the opening of Market Cafe, a former pub beside the canal. Research was clearly done because it ticks all the zeitgeist boxes, from the Formica table tops to the salvaged chairs, the pierced-and-inked young staff to the terse menu descriptions. There's a distinct Italian accent to many of the dishes, with homemade pastas a feature. The kitchen uses the local market for its meat, bread and coffee, the cooking is fresh and generous and the prices fair – especially the 'workers lunch'. Weekend brunches are very popular.

Prince Arthur

British modern K2

Hackney

95 Forest Rd ✉ E8 3BH

✆ (020) 7249 9996

www.theprincearthurlondonfields.com

⊖ Dalston Junction.

Closed 25 December – (dinner only and lunch Saturday-Sunday)

Menu £10 (weekdays) – Carte £25/41

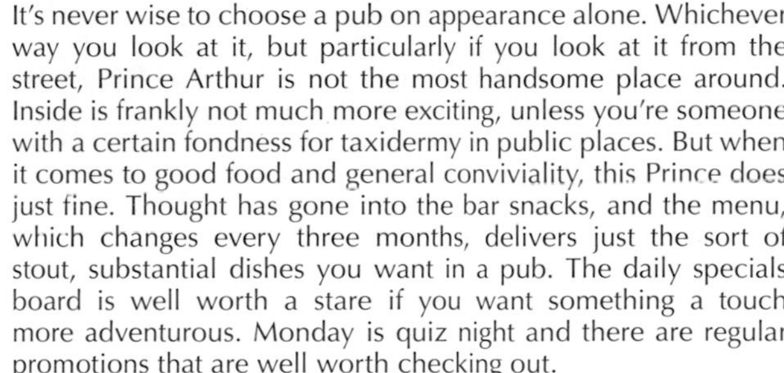

It's never wise to choose a pub on appearance alone. Whichever way you look at it, but particularly if you look at it from the street, Prince Arthur is not the most handsome place around. Inside is frankly not much more exciting, unless you're someone with a certain fondness for taxidermy in public places. But when it comes to good food and general conviviality, this Prince does just fine. Thought has gone into the bar snacks, and the menu, which changes every three months, delivers just the sort of stout, substantial dishes you want in a pub. The daily specials board is well worth a stare if you want something a touch more adventurous. Monday is quiz night and there are regular promotions that are well worth checking out.

Au Lac

Vietnamese J2

Highbury

82 Highbury Park ✉ N5 2XE

✆ (020) 7704 9187 – **www**.aulac.co.uk

⊖ Arsenal

Closed 24-26 December, 1-2 January and 1 week early August – (dinner only and lunch Thursday-Friday)

Menu £14/18 – Carte £12/24

It's unlikely to ever attract passers-by on its looks alone but fortunately enough people know about this longstanding Vietnamese restaurant, run by two brothers, to ensure that its phone rings red hot most nights. The comforts inside may also be fairly unremarkable but that just allows everyone to focus their attention on the lengthy menu, to which new dishes are added regularly. The pho noodle soup is a favourite but along with the traditional dishes there are plenty of more contemporary creations, all exhibiting the same freshness and lively flavours. The prices are kept honest, especially as the generous portion sizes mean that you don't have to order too many dishes to feel satisfied. They also do a roaring trade in takeaways.

Beagle

British traditional K2

Hoxton

397-400 Geffrye St ✉ E2 8HZ

✆ (020) 7613 2967

www.beaglelondon.co.uk

⊖ Hoxton

Closed lunch Monday-Tuesday – booking essential

Menu £15 (lunch and early dinner) – Carte £21/36

Occupying three converted railway arches, and named after the steam train that ran on the line above, Beagle is a big, bustling operation. One arch is used as a bar; one as the dining room; and the third is a kitchen and private dining room. Lots of brick, reclaimed materials and clever lighting add to the atmosphere and the terrace, overlooking The Geffrye, is a good spot to enjoy one of their cocktails. The British menu changes twice a day and its contents are largely determined by whatever seasonal produce arrives at the kitchen door – the descriptions are derivatively terse. There are occasional Italian touches, like a braised beef shin pappardelle, and blackboards announce the dishes for two, such as whole steamed sea bass.

Fifteen London

modern K3

Hoxton

15 Westland Pl ✉ N1 7LP

✆ (020) 3375 1515

www.fifteen.net

⊖ Old Street

Closed 25-26 December and 1 January – booking essential

Menu £19 (lunch) – Carte £27/41

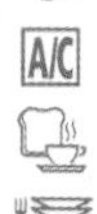

When it reached its 10th anniversary in 2012, Jamie Oliver's Fifteen got itself a new look and a new style of food – but what didn't change were the principles behind its creation, namely the training and development of youngsters who've faced difficulties in their lives. The focus is now on seasonal British food rather than Italian and the menu is mostly made up of small tasting plates. The cooking certainly has personality and the wood-fired oven is used to good effect, delivering some great flavours. Service is keen and eager; the same menu is offered in both the ground floor restaurant and the livelier, noisier cellar below; and the bar is a great place to come for a cocktail. Fifteen may not come cheap but it's a very worthy cause.

Almeida

French M1

Islington

30 Almeida St. ✉ N1 1AD

✆ (020) 7354 4777

www.almeida-restaurant.com

⊖ Angel

Closed 26 December, 1 January, Sunday dinner and Monday lunch

Menu £17 (lunch and early dinner) – Carte £24/47

To keen historians, Almeida is the Portuguese town known for two key sieges of the Peninsular War; to the rest of us, the name conjures up images of theatre and food. The Almeida Theatre is a 325-seater studio, built in 1980 and rejuvenated in 2003, which is unquestionably one of the jewels of Islington; opposite is this propitiously placed restaurant from the D&D people which wisely shares the name and is thus virtually assured of being busy at certain times of the evening. It's a smoothly run operation, where the well-spaced tables add to the comfortable feel. There's a classical edge to the cooking, which is reliably consistent, and a definite Mediterranean bias; in contrast to the à la carte, the theatre menus are a bargain.

Drapers Arms

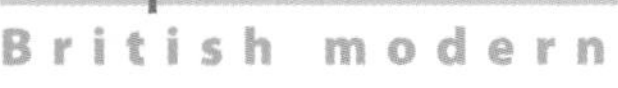

British modern L1

Islington

44 Barnsbury St ✉ N1 1ER

✆ (020) 7619 0348

www.thedrapersarms.com

⊖ Highbury & Islington.

Closed 25-26 December – bookings advisable at dinner

Carte £22/33

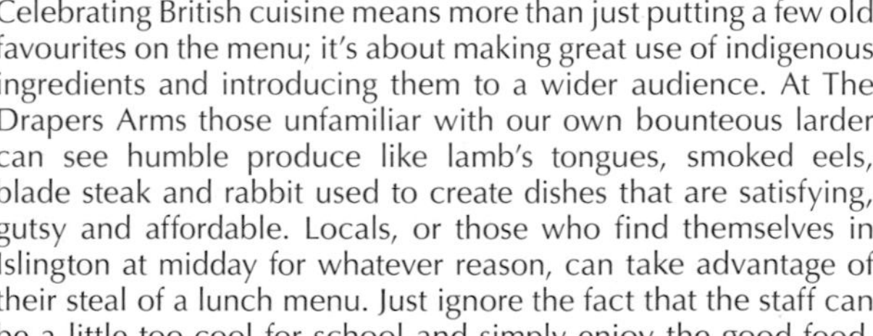

Celebrating British cuisine means more than just putting a few old favourites on the menu; it's about making great use of indigenous ingredients and introducing them to a wider audience. At The Drapers Arms those unfamiliar with our own bounteous larder can see humble produce like lamb's tongues, smoked eels, blade steak and rabbit used to create dishes that are satisfying, gutsy and affordable. Locals, or those who find themselves in Islington at midday for whatever reason, can take advantage of their steal of a lunch menu. Just ignore the fact that the staff can be a little too cool for school and simply enjoy the good food, unpretentious atmosphere and shabby chic interior of this busy Georgian pub, with its handsome façade.

Ⓝ Fish & Chip Shop

fish and chips M1

Islington

189 Upper St ✉ N1 1RQ
✆ (020) 3227 0979
www.thefishandchipshop.uk.com
⊖ Highbury and Islington
Closed Sunday – booking essential at dinner

Carte £18/39

Having worked for Caprice Holdings, the owner knows a thing or two about successful restaurants. For his first solo project, he unexpectedly opened this fish and chip shop, although the fact that you can order cocktails and have brunch at weekends tells you this is not your run-of-the-mill chippy. It comes with an appealing post-war feel with booths and counters. The menu, on brown paper, is also different. Starters are hearty affairs – the Isle of Man crab on toast is almost a main course in itself. Butties are fun for a quick snack and puds are the real deal, with Knickerbocker Glory in summer and fruit cobbler in winter – but most punters are here simply for the Camden Hells battered fish. They do takeaway and more shops are planned.

Ottolenghi

Mediterranean  M1

Islington

287 Upper St. ✉ N1 2TZ
✆ (020) 7288 1454 – **www**.ottolenghi.co.uk
⊖ Highbury & Islington
Closed 25-26 December, Sunday dinner and bank holidays – booking essential

Menu £17 (lunch) – Carte dinner approx. £27

A/C

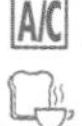

The few people in the country yet to buy one of Yotam Ottolenghi's cookbooks will find that a single visit to his crisp and coolly decorated spot on Upper Street will send them scurrying off to the nearest bookshop. If you haven't booked one of the tables for two, just sit at one of the two large communal tables and check out what everyone else is ordering. Whether you choose a dish from the kitchen or the counter, the freshness and vitality of the food is palpable and you'll never think of salad again in the same way; vegetarians will sob with gratitude. There are vibrant flavours from the Med, North Africa, the Middle East, and even the occasional Asian note. Service is well-paced and the delightful staff all know their stuff.

Pig and Butcher

British traditional

L1

Islington

80 Liverpool Rd ✉ N1 0QD

✆ (020) 7226 8304 – **www**.thepigandbutcher.co.uk

⊖ Angel.

Closed 25-27 December – booking advisable – (dinner only and lunch Friday-Sunday)

Carte £26/46

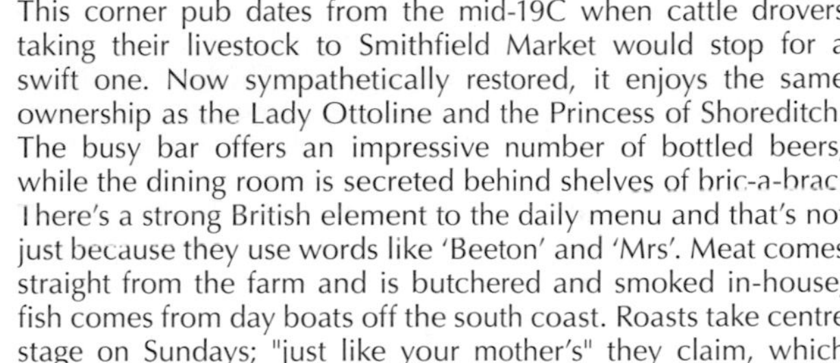

This corner pub dates from the mid-19C when cattle drovers taking their livestock to Smithfield Market would stop for a swift one. Now sympathetically restored, it enjoys the same ownership as the Lady Ottoline and the Princess of Shoreditch. The busy bar offers an impressive number of bottled beers, while the dining room is secreted behind shelves of bric-a-brac. There's a strong British element to the daily menu and that's not just because they use words like 'Beeton' and 'Mrs'. Meat comes straight from the farm and is butchered and smoked in-house; fish comes from day boats off the south coast. Roasts take centre stage on Sundays; "just like your mother's" they claim, which presumably means something different to us all.

Yipin China

Chinese

L1

Islington

70-72 Liverpool Rd ✉ N1 0QD

✆ (020) 7354 3388

www.yipinchina.co.uk

⊖ Angel

Closed 25 December

Carte £19/42

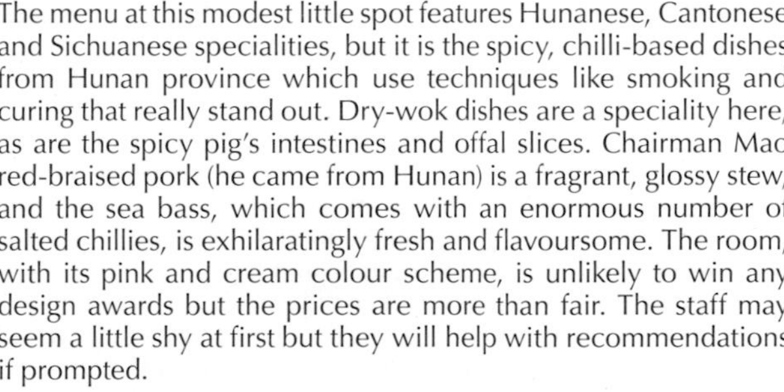

The menu at this modest little spot features Hunanese, Cantonese and Sichuanese specialities, but it is the spicy, chilli-based dishes from Hunan province which use techniques like smoking and curing that really stand out. Dry-wok dishes are a speciality here, as are the spicy pig's intestines and offal slices. Chairman Mao red-braised pork (he came from Hunan) is a fragrant, glossy stew, and the sea bass, which comes with an enormous number of salted chillies, is exhilaratingly fresh and flavoursome. The room, with its pink and cream colour scheme, is unlikely to win any design awards but the prices are more than fair. The staff may seem a little shy at first but they will help with recommendations if prompted.

Ⓝ Andina

Peruvian K3

Shoreditch

1 Redchurch St ✉ E2 7DJ

✆ (020) 7920 6499

www.andinalondon.com

⊖ Shoreditch High Street

Booking essential

Menu £9 (weekday lunch) – Carte £11/30

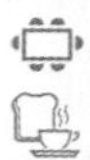

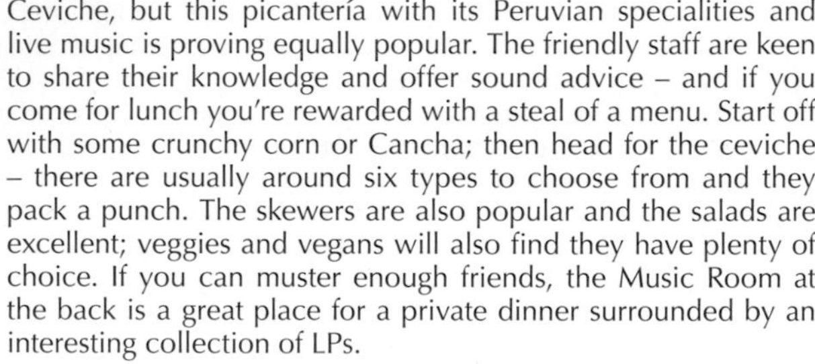

Andina may be smaller and slightly more chaotic that its sister Ceviche, but this picantería with its Peruvian specialities and live music is proving equally popular. The friendly staff are keen to share their knowledge and offer sound advice – and if you come for lunch you're rewarded with a steal of a menu. Start off with some crunchy corn or Cancha; then head for the ceviche – there are usually around six types to choose from and they pack a punch. The skewers are also popular and the salads are excellent; veggies and vegans will also find they have plenty of choice. If you can muster enough friends, the Music Room at the back is a great place for a private dinner surrounded by an interesting collection of LPs.

L'Anima

Italian K3

Shoreditch

1 Snowden St. ✉ EC2A 2DQ

✆ (020) 7422 7000 – **www**.lanima.co.uk

⊖ Liverpool Street

Closed 25-26 December, Saturday lunch, Sunday and bank holidays – booking essential

Carte £35/70

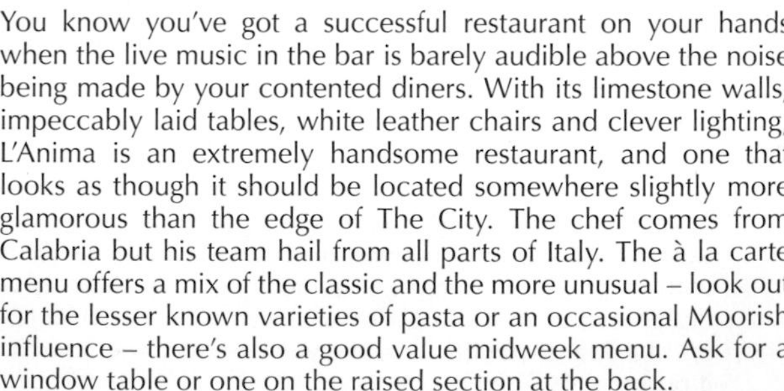

You know you've got a successful restaurant on your hands when the live music in the bar is barely audible above the noise being made by your contented diners. With its limestone walls, impeccably laid tables, white leather chairs and clever lighting, L'Anima is an extremely handsome restaurant, and one that looks as though it should be located somewhere slightly more glamorous than the edge of The City. The chef comes from Calabria but his team hail from all parts of Italy. The à la carte menu offers a mix of the classic and the more unusual – look out for the lesser known varieties of pasta or an occasional Moorish influence – there's also a good value midweek menu. Ask for a window table or one on the raised section at the back.

Boundary

French

Shoreditch

2-4 Boundary St ✉ E2 7DD

✆ (020) 7729 1051

www.theboundary.co.uk

⊖ Shoreditch High Street

Closed Sunday dinner – (dinner only and Sunday lunch)

Menu £22 – Carte £34/58

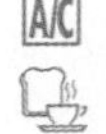

When the management team took over his restaurant group, many thought Sir Terence Conran's days of opening restaurants were over. Not a bit of it, because he was soon back with a bang with Boundary. As is his way, he has taken an interesting building, in this case a large warehouse and former printworks, and turned it into a veritable house of fun. From the top, you have a roof terrace with an open fire; Albion is a ground floor 'caff' alongside a shop and bakery, and Boundary is the French-inspired 'main' restaurant below. The room is stylish, good-looking and works well, while the kitchen serves up reassuringly familiar cross-Channel treats, including fruits de mer. The fourth part of the equation are the comfy, individually designed bedrooms.

N Casa Negra

Mexican

Shoreditch

54-56 Great Eastern St ✉ EC2A 3QR

✆ (020) 7033 7360

www.casanegra.co.uk

⊖ Old Street

Closed Saturday lunch, Sunday and Monday – booking essential at dinner

Carte £24/54

You don't become a successful restaurateur without recognising a trend or two. With South America all the rage, Will Ricker turned his former Great Eastern Dining Room into this lively Mexican bar and restaurant and, judging by the crowds and the wall of sound that slaps you as you enter, has another hit to go with his La Bodega Negra in Soho. The food is largely traditional and dishes deliver all the spice and heat you'd expect. The braised beef rib and the fried poblano chilli are the two standout dishes; instead of dessert just order an extra taco. As the music pumps, the bar becomes the place to be, especially as the cocktails are good too. If you haven't booked then try sharing at the huge 'kitchen table'.

Clove Club ✿

modern K3

Shoreditch

380 Old St ✉ EC1V 9LT

✆ (020) 7729 6496 – **www**.thecloveclub.com

⊖ Old Street

Closed 2 weeks Christmas-New Year, August bank holiday, Monday lunch and Sunday – bookings advisable at dinner – (set menu only)

Menu £35/55

Michelin

Nowhere captures the zeitgeist of London's restaurant scene quite like The Clove Club. For a start, it was set up by three 'young Turks' who made their names in pop-ups. For their first permanent site they chose the Grade II listed Shoreditch Town Hall, whose ornate façade contrasts with the unrelentingly sparse nature of the room – it is clear that their money was spent on the smart kitchen which stands centre stage and is an integral part of the room. The cooking is certainly bang on-trend, with only a set menu of 5 or 6 courses offered – very Scandinavian – although you can also pre-order the longer Tasting menu. What becomes immediately apparent is that this is a kitchen obsessed with sourcing great produce, including some interesting and underused ingredients. The meal starts with a few bite-sized canapés which set the tone: there is originality, verve and flair but flavours are always expertly judged and complementary. There's also an adjacent bar, packed out with local hipsters, where a simpler menu is served.

First Course

- Smoked wild pollan with caviar and crème fraîche.
- Buttermilk fried chicken with pine salt.

Main Course

- Salt-baked duck, gingerbread and turnip.
- Hebridean lamb, January King cabbage and seaweed sauce.

Dessert

- Amalfi lemonade and Sarawak black pepper ice cream.
- Clove Club chocolate bar.

Eyre Brothers

Spanish

K3

Shoreditch

70 Leonard St ✉ EC2A 4QX
✆ (020) 7613 5346 – **www.**eyrebrothers.co.uk
⊖ Shoreditch High Street

Closed 24 December-4 January, Saturday lunch, Sunday and bank holidays

Menu £12 (lunch and early dinner) – Carte £25/51

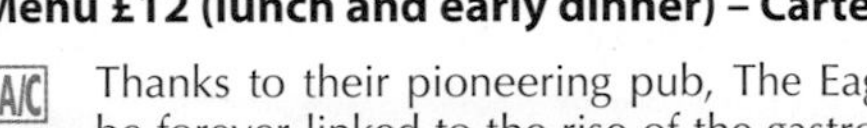

Thanks to their pioneering pub, The Eagle, the Eyre name will be forever linked to the rise of the gastropub, but this sleek and confidently run 100-seater shows that they know how to do restaurants as well. Drawing on memories of their upbringing in Mozambique, the menu celebrates all things Iberian. Tiger prawns piri-piri has been on since day 1; the 'Cinco Jotas' ham is deliciously sweet and the meats are all cooked over lumpwood charcoal which adds a wonderful aroma to proceedings. If you're coming in a larger party, then pre-order paella or the whole suckling pig. The wine list is equally Iberian, with Riojas for every pocket as well as a great selection of Madeira and Jerez. Everyone leaves feeling full and eminently satisfied.

N Hoi Polloi

British modern

K3

Shoreditch

Ace Hotel,
100 Shoreditch High St ✉ E1 6JQ
✆ (020) 8880 6100
www.hoi-polloi.co.uk
⊖ Shoreditch High Street

Carte £22/48

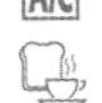

The boys from Bistrotheque and Shrimpy's are the brains behind this modern brasserie. It's open from early morning to the wee small hours so whenever you drop in they'll have something on the menu that just seems right, whether that's a banana and soy shake first thing, mackerel with sea vegetables for lunch, an evening featherblade with marrow or a midnight burger. The largely British ingredients are good and the cooking is undertaken with more care than one expects from somewhere so damn hip. There are a couple of irritations, apart from the name: the entrance, for some reason, is via a florist and the menu resembles a student newspaper and takes an age to read, but overall this is a good fit for the neighbourhood.

HKK ✿

Chinese

North-East ▸ Plan XVI

Shoreditch

K3

Broadgate West, 88 Worship St ✉ EC2A 2BE
✆ (020) 3535 1888
www.hkklondon.com
⊖ Liverpool Street
Closed 25 December and Sunday

Menu £29/98 – Carte lunch £26/62

HKK

From the people behind Hakkasan comes this most sophisticated of Cantonese restaurants. The room is understated, elegant and graceful; the service smooth, assured and unobtrusive. As time is money in this part of town, the lunch menu has been designed with consideration towards those who have to return to work – to really experience what HKK is all about, come for dinner when you'll be presented with their expertly paced 16 course menu, which evolves on a monthly basis. Cantonese has always been considered the finest of the Chinese cuisines and here at HKK it is given an extra degree of refinement. One can still expect the classic combinations of flavours but just delivered in a more modern way, whether that's abalone in truffle rice wine sauce or osmanthus flower with crispy taro milk cake. One highlight is the duck: roasted to order in a cherry wood fired oven, it is expertly carved and served in three different ways. The presentation of all of the dishes is sublime and they come with well-considered wine pairings.

First Course

- Cherry wood roasted Peking duck.
- Alaskan King crab salad with Tobiko.

Main Course

- Jasmine tea smoked Wagyu beef.
- Cantonese-style steamed halibut.

Dessert

- Almond brûlée tart with wine-poached plum.
- Salted cashew nut and milk chocolate parfait.

Lyle's

British modern K3

Shoreditch

Tea Building, 56 Shoreditch High St ✉ E1 6JJ
✆ (020) 3011 5911
www.lyleslondon.com
⊖ Shoreditch High Street
Closed Saturday lunch, Sunday and bank holidays

Menu £39 (dinner) – Carte lunch £18/29

A/C

One glance at the menu tells immediately of the influence of Fergus Henderson – and sure enough, the young chef-owner ran the kitchen at St John Bread and Wine before opening his own place. Where his operation differs is that only a set menu is offered at dinner – although for lunch you can choose an array of dishes in smaller sizes – and in the occasional use of modern cooking techniques. Where they converge is in the use of superb seasonal British ingredients which result in flavours that are clean, natural, unadulterated and a joy to eat. This pared-down approach extends to the decoration: the open kitchen and bar are really the only notable features of the semi-industrial room which is high on functionality, low on warmth.

Merchants Tavern

British traditional K3

Shoreditch

36 Charlotte Rd ✉ EC2A 3PG
✆ (020) 7060 5335
www.merchantstavern.co.uk
⊖ Old Street
Closed 25-26 December and Monday

Menu £18 (weekday lunch) – Carte £32/49

It sounds like a pub, looks like one and even feels like one, but once you're settled in you'll soon realise there's more to this place than you initially thought. The 'pub' part – a Victorian warehouse –morphs into a big restaurant with an open kitchen and some very appealing booths beneath the skylight – the prized seats. Neil Borthwick and his partner Angela Hartnett are part-owners, along with the founders of Canteen, and the cooking is founded on the simple yet sublime pleasures of seasonal British cooking. The kitchen has the confidence to stick to recognisable combinations in order to deliver flavours that are reassuringly familiar and satisfying: the quail with hazelnut pesto, remoulade and foie gras is already a huge favourite.

Princess of Shoreditch

British traditional K3

Shoreditch

76-78 Paul St ✉ EC2A 4NE

✆ (020) 7729 9270

www.theprincessofshoreditch.com

⊖ Old Street

Closed 24-26 December – booking essential

Menu £28 (lunch and early dinner) – Carte £24/34

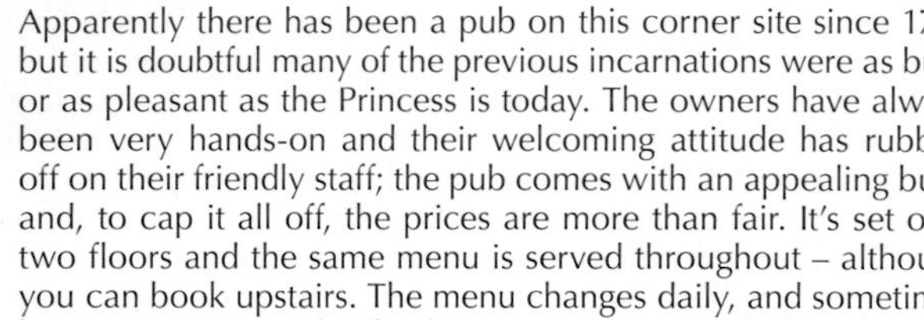

Apparently there has been a pub on this corner site since 1742 but it is doubtful many of the previous incarnations were as busy or as pleasant as the Princess is today. The owners have always been very hands-on and their welcoming attitude has rubbed off on their friendly staff; the pub comes with an appealing buzz and, to cap it all off, the prices are more than fair. It's set over two floors and the same menu is served throughout – although you can book upstairs. The menu changes daily, and sometimes between services; the food appears quite simple but the best dishes are those that come with a satisfying rustic edge, whether that's the buttery goose rillettes, the chicken pie with terrific mash or the tender pulled pork.

Rivington Grill

British traditional K3

Shoreditch

28-30 Rivington St ✉ EC2A 3DZ

✆ (020) 7729 7053

www.rivingtonshoreditch.co.uk

⊖ Old Street

Closed 25-26 December

Carte £22/42

A converted warehouse surrounded by design studios, galleries and printing premises means not only that this place is popular with the artistically inclined but that it also shows artwork itself, including a Tracey Emin neon "Life without you, never". However, it is also close to The City so head left when you enter as larger groups tend to occupy the tables on the right. The British menu will fill you with patriotic fervour – if this was what John Major had meant when he referred to 'back-to-basics' there wouldn't have been such derision. There's a section 'on toast' and oysters are a speciality; there are pies, chops and faggots, even fish fingers and bubble and squeak. There are also plenty of bottles under £30 and weekend lunches.

Tramshed

meats and grills

K3

Shoreditch

32 Rivington St ✉ EC2A 3LX
(020) 7749 0478
www.chickenandsteak.co.uk
⊖ Old Street
Closed 25-26 December

Menu £10 (weekday lunch) – Carte £19/64

Mark Hix's impressive brasserie is housed within a Grade II listed warehouse that was built in 1905 to house the generators for the trams and is best enjoyed, like most things in life, in the company of friends. The striking piece of work by Damien Hirst of a tank containing a Hereford cow and a cockerel in formaldehyde is not just an impressive feature in the cavernous room, but also a clue as to what's on the menu. The Swainson House Farm chickens and the various cuts of Glenarm beef are accurately cooked and delicious; sides are good too and there are regularly changing starters and puds. The best seats are the booths around the wall. Service is alert and capable – when the staff aren't busy trying to arrest former Prime Ministers.

Viet Grill

Vietnamese

K2

Shoreditch

58 Kingsland Rd ✉ E2 8DP
(020) 7739 6686
www.vietgrill.co.uk
⊖ Hoxton

Menu £10/23 – Carte £17/30

Vietnamese restaurants are proving very popular in this part of town, so perhaps it's about time that Hackney was twinned with Hanoi. The reason Viet Grill attracts so many customers is not down to its bright neon lighting, but because it is owned by the same team behind Cây Tre, which means that the service is charming and helpful and the food is fresh and authentic. From the slurpable pho noodle soups to Devon crab (most ingredients are sourced within the UK) and La Vong monkfish for two, you'll find dishes packed with flavour and vibrancy; meats grilled on the robata also stand out. Those who don't plan ahead can take advantage of their takeaway menu; those who do can order one of their 'feast' menus, which require 48 hours' notice.

Empress

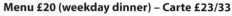

Mediterranean K2

South Hackney

130 Lauriston Rd, Victoria Park ✉ E9 7LH
(020) 8533 5123
www.empresse9.co.uk
⊖ Homerton.

Closed 25 December and Monday lunch except bank holidays

Menu £20 (weekday dinner) – Carte £23/33

The name of this 1850s pub was changed from the Empress of India as some customers arrived expecting chicken tikka – information which will dishearten history teachers everywhere. Queen Victoria has been demoted to the Empress of E9 but then everything is about being 'local' these days and that includes this re-launched pub. Sourdough comes from the baker down the road and their butcher and fishmonger are within walking distance; the menu is pleasingly seasonal and the cooking is several notches above usual pub fare. Dishes like risotto made with pearl barley and feta, or lamb's liver with lentils demonstrate that this is a kitchen with confidence and ability. Prices are kept in check and Sunday lunch is a very languid affair.

Provender

French

Wanstead

17 High St ✉ E11 2AA
(020) 8530 3050
www.provenderlondon.co.uk
⊖ Snaresbrook

Menu £16 (weekdays) – Carte £20/41

Wanstead High Street may not necessarily be the first place one would expect to find great French bourgeois cooking but the locals must be mightily glad that Max Renzland decided to pitch up in their arrondissement. Max's reputation for creating terrific French restaurants was forged in the suburbs, albeit at the opposite end of town, and Provender has his stamp all over it. That means you can expect authentic and satisfying food; plenty of choice; and prices, for the menus and the exclusively French wine list, that are very competitive. The fish is good here, as are the charcuterie boards, and there are dishes to share and even a separate menu for 'les enfants'. It's no wonder the split-level room hums with the sound of contentment.

R. Herrett /Loop Images/Age fotostock

South-East London

Once considered not only the wrong side of the tracks, but also most definitely the wrong side of the river, London's southeastern chunk has thrived in recent times courtesy of the Docklands Effect. As the gleaming glass peninsula of **Canary Wharf** (ironically, just north of the Thames) sprouted a personality of its own – with bars, restaurants, slinky bridges and an enviable view, not to mention moneyed residents actually putting down roots – the city's bottom right hand zone began to achieve destination status on a par with other parts of London. You only have to stroll around the glossy and quite vast **Limehouse Basin** – a slick marina that was once a hard-grafting East End dock – to really see what's happened here.

Not that the area hasn't always boasted some true gems in the capital's treasure chest. **Greenwich,** with fabulous views across the water to the docklands from its delightfully sloping park, has long been a favourite of kings and queens: Henry VIII and Elizabeth I resided here. The village itself bustles along with its market and plush picturehouse, but most visitors make their way to the stand-out attractions, of which there are many. The **Royal Observatory** and the Meridian Line draw star-gazers and hemisphere striders in equal number, while the palatial Old Royal Naval College is a star turn for lovers of Wren, who designed it as London's answer to Versailles. On the northern edge of Greenwich Park, the **National Maritime Museum** has three floors of sea-faring wonders; down by the pier, the real thing exists in the shape of the **Cutty Sark**. Up on the peninsula, the O2 Arena's distinctive shape has become an unmistakable landmark, but if you fancy a contrast to all things watery, the Fan Museum on Crooms Hill has more hand-held fans (over 3,000 of them) than anywhere else on earth. Strolling south from Greenwich park you reach **Blackheath,** an alluring suburban village, whose most striking feature is the towering All Saints' Church, standing proud away from the chic shops and restaurants.

Of slightly less spectacular charms, but a real crowd-pleaser nevertheless, is **Dulwich Village,** hidden deeper in the southeastern enclaves. It's a leafy oasis in this part of the world, with a delightful park that boasts at its western end, next to the original buildings of the old public school, the Dulwich Picture Gallery. This was designed in 1811, and its pedigree is evident in works by the likes of Rembrandt, Rubens, Van Dyck and Canaletto. Half an hour's walk away across the park is the brilliant Horniman Museum, full of natural history and world culture delights – as well as a massive aquarium that seems to take up much of southeast London.

C. Eymenier / MICHELIN

A bit further east along the South Circular, there's the unexpected gem of Eltham Palace, originally the childhood home of Henry VIII with a magnificent (and still visible) Great Hall. What makes it unique is the adjacent Art Deco mansion built for millionaires in the 1930s in Ocean Liner style. It's the closest you'll ever get to a setting fit for hog roast and champagne. Heading back towards London, a lifestyle of bubbly and banquets has never really been **Peckham**'s thing, but it boasts a couple of corkers in the shape of the South London Gallery with its zeitgeist-setting art shows, and the Peckham Library, a giant inverted 'L' that after a decade still looks like a lot of fun to go into.

Back in the luxury flat-lands of the **Docklands, Wapping** has become an interesting port of call, its new-build architecture mixing in with a still Dickensian feel, in the shape of glowering Victorian warehouses and Wapping New Stairs, where the bodies of pirates were hanged from a gibbet until seven tides had showered their limp bodies. You can catch a fascinating history of the whole area in the nearby Museum in Docklands.

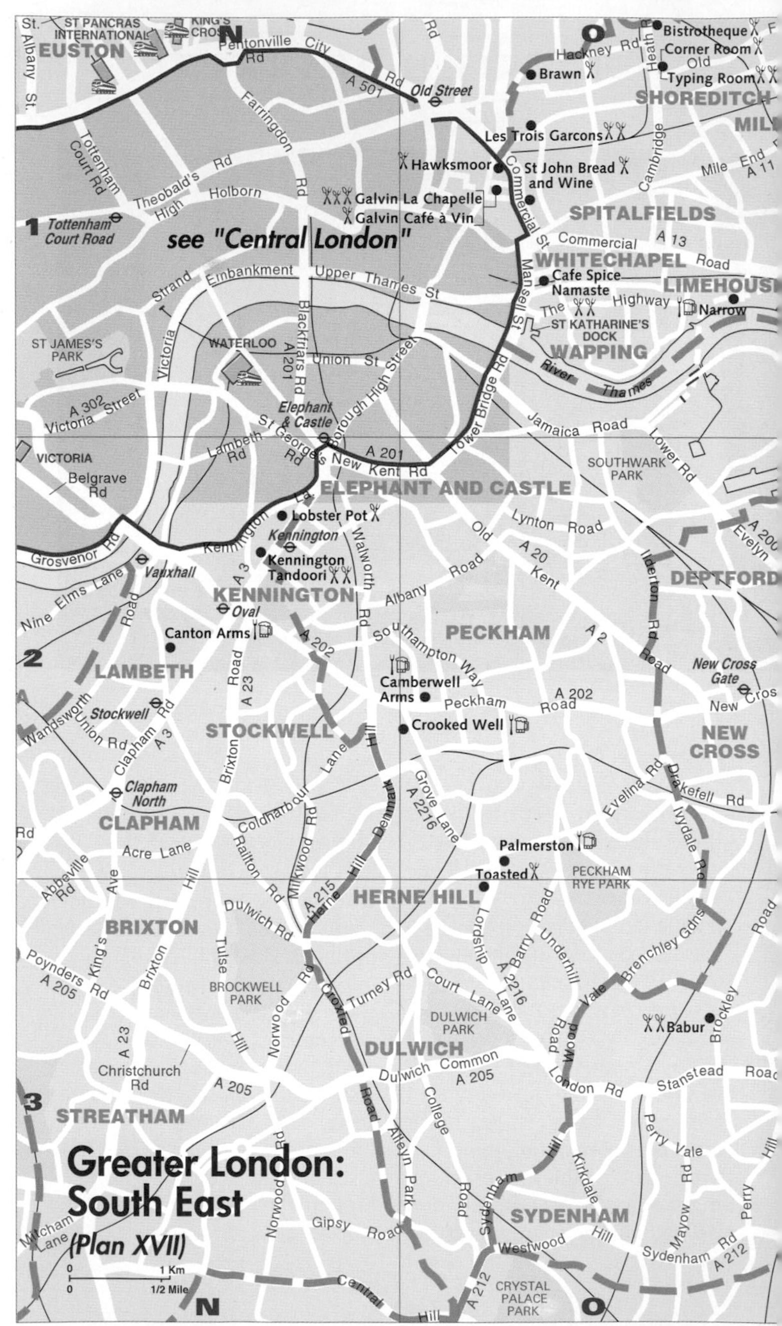
Greater London:
South East
(Plan XVII)
0 1 Km
0 1/2 Mile
N
O
1
2
3
see "Central London"
ST PANCRAS INTERNATIONAL
KING'S CROSS
EUSTON
Pentonville Rd
City Rd
A 501
Old Street
Albany St.
Farringdon Rd
Tottenham Court Rd
Theobald's Rd
High Holborn
Tottenham Court Road
Hawksmoor
Galvin La Chapelle
Galvin Café à Vin
St John Bread and Wine
Les Trois Garcons
Brawn
Bistrotheque
Corner Room
Typing Room
Hackney Rd
Old
Heath Rd
Cambridge
SHOREDITCH
Mile End
A 11
SPITALFIELDS
Commercial St
Commercial Road
A 13
WHITECHAPEL
Cafe Spice Namaste
Mansell St
The Highway
Narrow
LIMEHOUSE
ST KATHARINE'S DOCK
WAPPING
River Thames
Strand
Embankment
Upper Thames St
ST JAMES'S PARK
Victoria
WATERLOO
Union St
Blackfriars Rd
A 201
Borough High Street
Tower Bridge Rd
A 302
Victoria Street
Elephant & Castle
Lambeth Rd
St George's Rd
New Kent Rd
A 201
Jamaica Road
SOUTHWARK PARK
Lower Rd
VICTORIA
Belgrave Rd
ELEPHANT AND CASTLE
Lobster Pot
Kennington
Kennington La.
Kennington Tandoori
Lynton Road
Old Kent
A 20
A 2
Evelyn
DEPTFORD
Grosvenor Rd
Vauxhall
Nine Elms Lane
Road
A 3
KENNINGTON
Oval
Walworth Rd
Albany Road
Ilderton Rd
Road
Canton Arms
Southampton Way
PECKHAM
A 202
LAMBETH
Road
A 23
Camberwell Arms
Peckham Road
A 202
New Cross Gate
New Cross
NEW CROSS
Wandsworth
Stockwell
Union Rd
Clapham Rd
A 3
STOCKWELL
Crooked Well
Lane
Hill
Denmark
Grove Lane
A 2216
Evelina Rd
Drakefell Rd
Brixton
Clapham North
CLAPHAM
Coldharbour
Milkwood Rd
Railton Rd
Acre Lane
Palmerston
Toasted
PECKHAM RYE PARK
Ivydale Rd
Abbeville Rd
Ave
Hill
A 215
Herne Hill
HERNE HILL
Dulwich Rd
Lordship Lane
A 2216
Barry Road
Underhill
Brenchley Gdns
Road
BRIXTON
Poynders Rd
A 205
King's
Brixton
Tulse Hill
BROCKWELL PARK
Norwood Rd
Croxted Road
Turney Rd
Court Lane
DULWICH PARK
Vale
Wood Road
Babur
Brockley
A 23
Christchurch Rd
A 205
DULWICH
Dulwich Common
A 205
College
London Rd
Stanstead Road
STREATHAM
Perry Vale
Rd
Mayow
Perry
Hill
Norwood Rd
Alleyn Park
Road
Sydenham Hill
Kirkdale
SYDENHAM
Mitcham Lane
Gipsy Road
Westwood Hill
Sydenham Rd
A 212
Central Hill
A 212
CRYSTAL PALACE PARK

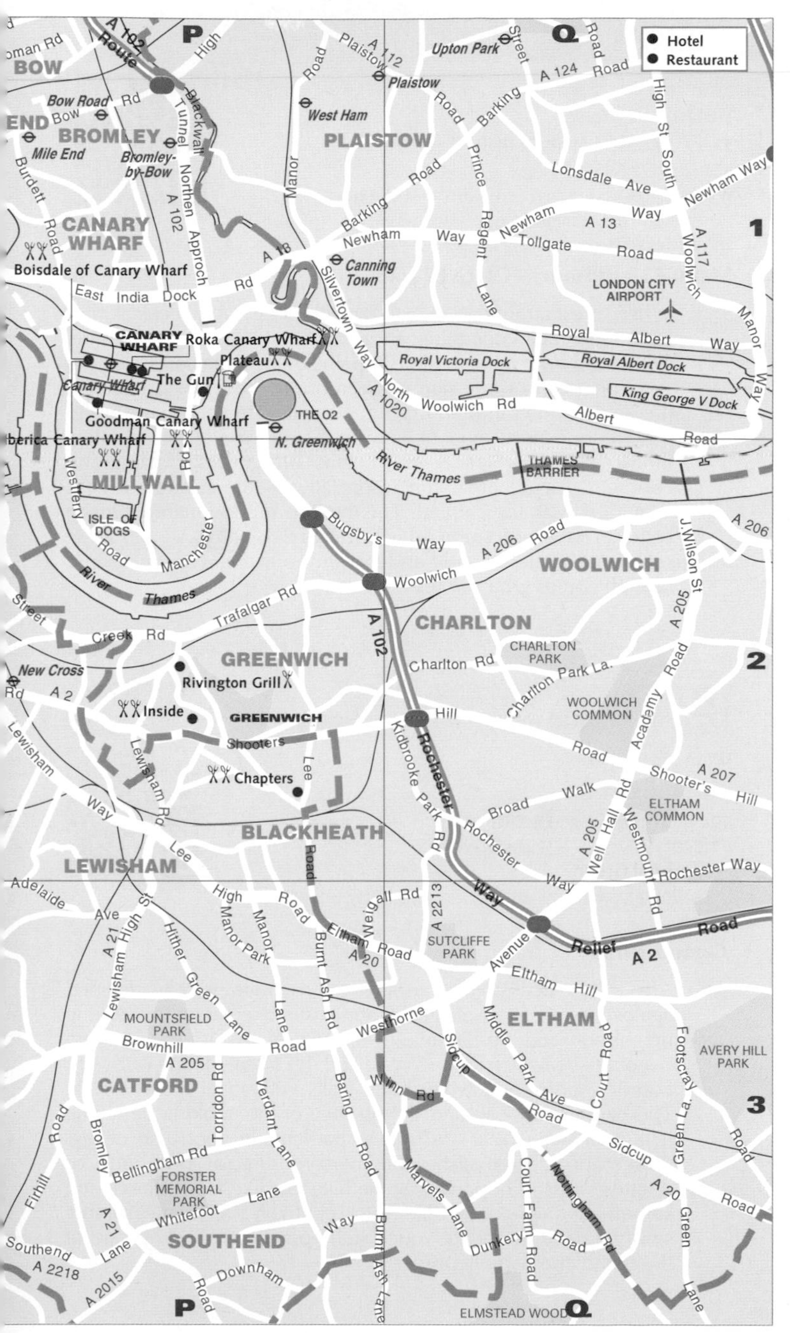

Hotel
Restaurant
P
Q
1
2
3
BOW
BROMLEY
Mile End
Bromley-by-Bow
CANARY WHARF
Boisdale of Canary Wharf
PLAISTOW
Upton Park
Plaistow
West Ham
Canning Town
LONDON CITY AIRPORT
Royal Victoria Dock
Royal Albert Dock
King George V Dock
CANARY WHARF
Roka Canary Wharf
Plateau
The Gun
Goodman Canary Wharf
Iberica Canary Wharf
THE O2
N. Greenwich
River Thames
THAMES BARRIER
MILLWALL
ISLE OF DOGS
WOOLWICH
CHARLTON
CHARLTON PARK
GREENWICH
Rivington Grill
Inside
GREENWICH
WOOLWICH COMMON
Chapters
ELTHAM COMMON
BLACKHEATH
LEWISHAM
New Cross
SUTCLIFFE PARK
ELTHAM
MOUNTSFIELD PARK
AVERY HILL PARK
CATFORD
FORSTER MEMORIAL PARK
SOUTHEND
ELMSTEAD WOOD

Bistrotheque

modern

Bethnal Green

23-27 Wadeson St ✉ E2 9DR
✆ (020) 8983 7900
www.bistrotheque.com – ⊖ Bethnal Green

Closed 24 and 26 December – booking advisable – (dinner only and lunch Saturday-Sunday)

01

Menu £18 (dinner) – Carte £21/48

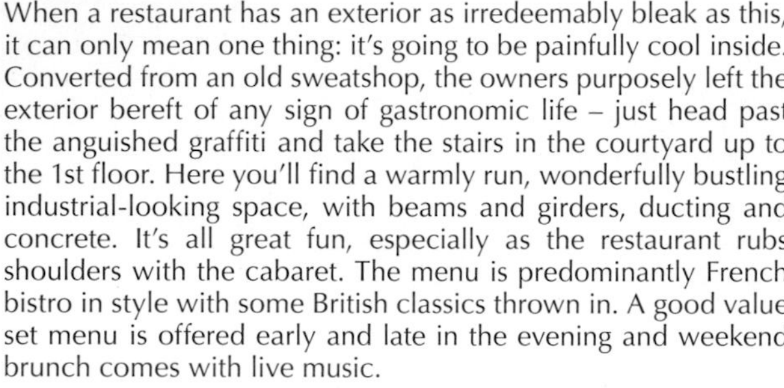

When a restaurant has an exterior as irredeemably bleak as this, it can only mean one thing: it's going to be painfully cool inside. Converted from an old sweatshop, the owners purposely left the exterior bereft of any sign of gastronomic life – just head past the anguished graffiti and take the stairs in the courtyard up to the 1st floor. Here you'll find a warmly run, wonderfully bustling industrial-looking space, with beams and girders, ducting and concrete. It's all great fun, especially as the restaurant rubs shoulders with the cabaret. The menu is predominantly French bistro in style with some British classics thrown in. A good value set menu is offered early and late in the evening and weekend brunch comes with live music.

Brawn

modern

Bethnal Green

01

49 Columbia Rd. ✉ E2 7RG
✆ (020) 7729 5692 – **www**.brawn.co
⊖ Bethnal Green

Closed Christmas-New Year, Sunday dinner, Monday lunch and bank holidays

Carte £19/33

After the success of Terroirs, the owners wisely decided against trying to duplicate it and instead created this terrific neighbourhood restaurant in a Victorian former furniture warehouse, away from the West End. It's simply kitted out, with Formica tables and white brick walls with local artists' work. The name really captures the essence of the cooking perfectly: it is rustic, muscular and makes particularly good use of pig. Order about three dishes per person, such as prosciutto or rillettes; mussels or prawns; something raw like Tuscan beef; and something slow-cooked like duck confit. It's all immeasurably satisfying and the polite young staff appear genuinely proud of the menu and happily proffer advice.

Corner Room

innovative

01

Bethnal Green

Town Hall Hotel,
Patriot Sq ✉ E2 9NF
(020) 7871 0461
www.cornerroom.co.uk
⊖ Bethnal Green

Menu £19 (lunch) – Carte £21/43

Hidden upstairs above the Typing Room in the old town hall is a warm and intimate space called Corner Room. It comes with wood panelling juxtaposed with bright white tiles and a backdrop of ornate and antique hanging light fittings for a little bit of whimsy. It's worth getting here a touch early to have a drink beforehand in the delightful little bar next door. The core ingredient of each dish is British, be it Longhorn beef or Tamworth pork, and the cooking is assured and very effective – there is no needless elaboration and you feel you're getting a real taste of nature. They say the dishes are for sharing but you don't have to – you certainly won't want to give up your braised short rib or sweetbreads to anyone.

Typing Room

modern

01

Bethnal Green

Town Hall Hotel, Patriot Sq ✉ E2 9NF
(020) 7871 0461
www.typingroom.com
⊖ Bethnal Green

Closed Sunday dinner, Monday and Tuesday

Menu £27 (lunch) – Carte £38/51

When Nuno Mendes left and took the name 'Viajante' with him, there was no real surprise when it was chef du jour Jason Atherton who took over the premises. The kitchen is headed by one of his protégés and the restaurant seems ready for its second act. The open kitchen, packed with chefs, remains the dominant feature of the room and there is a splash more colour to the place than before or indeed when this really was home to the town hall's typing pool. It's worth ordering a few of the 'snacks' straight off; the breads are also very good. The dishes are attractive and feature lots of textures without falling into the trap of becoming overwrought – this is clever cooking where flavours are distinct and complementary.

Chapters

modern

P2

Blackheath

43-45 Montpelier Vale ✉ SE3 0TJ

✆ (020) 8333 2666

www.chaptersrestaurants.com

Closed 2-3 January

Menu £15/18 – Carte £21/34

Flexibility has been the key to Chapters' success. This classic brasserie seems to know just what the locals want and they reward it by coming in their droves. It's open for breakfast and brunch at weekends; it has a great value menu Monday to Thursday and their à la carte has something for everyone. Specialities from the Josper grill are a highlight, especially the double Barnsley chop, though there's also steak from Cumbria, Omaha and Limousin for meat-eating enthusiasts. Add in main courses with a Mediterranean slant; blackboard specials; a kids' menu; and a good size wine list with plenty by the glass or pichet, and you can see why it seems as though all of Blackheath is in the room. Ask for the ground floor, rather than the basement.

N Camberwell Arms

British traditional

O2

Camberwell

65 Camberwell Church St ✉ SE5 8TR

✆ (020) 7358 4364 – **www**.thecamberwellarms.co.uk

⊖ Denmark Hill

Closed 27 December-2 January, Sunday dinner, Monday lunch, Tuesday lunch after bank holidays and bank holiday Mondays – bookings not accepted

Carte £24/34

The people behind the Anchor & Hope and Canton Arms not only know how to open great pubs but also seem to have a knack for identifying areas that are 'up and coming', although it could be said that their pubs very presence is often a contributory factor in this process. The open plan kitchen and much-coveted adjoining counter separates the front bar from the rear dining room and as the pub doesn't take bookings you may find yourself sharing your table with others. The daily menu is refreshingly short, simple and supplemented by blackboard specials in the evening – and the serving team know it inside out. Starters are quite light to prepare you for the punchy, earthy flavours of the main course, many of which come courtesy of the BBQ grill.

Crooked Well

modern

O2

Camberwell

16 Grove Ln ✉ SE5 8SY

✆ (020) 7252 7798

www.thecrookedwell.com

⊖ Denmark Hill (Rail).

Closed Monday lunch

Menu £10 (weekday lunch) – Carte £21/39

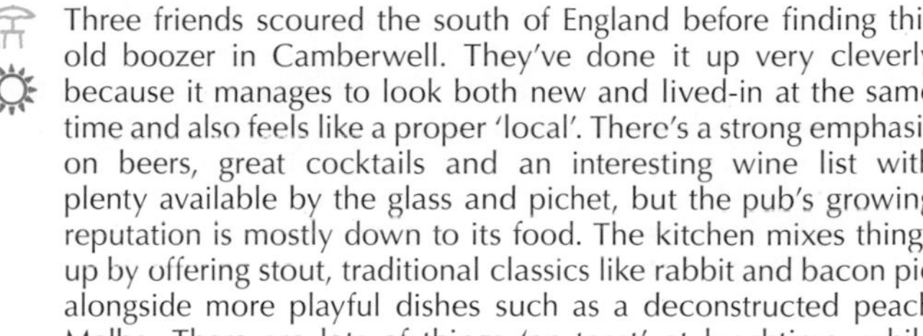

Three friends scoured the south of England before finding this old boozer in Camberwell. They've done it up very cleverly because it manages to look both new and lived-in at the same time and also feels like a proper 'local'. There's a strong emphasis on beers, great cocktails and an interesting wine list with plenty available by the glass and pichet, but the pub's growing reputation is mostly down to its food. The kitchen mixes things up by offering stout, traditional classics like rabbit and bacon pie alongside more playful dishes such as a deconstructed peach Melba. There are lots of things 'on toast' at lunchtime, while dishes like Scotch egg with Heinz tomato soup are designed to evoke memories of childhood.

Boisdale of Canary Wharf

British traditional

P1

Canary Wharf

Cabot Pl ✉ E14 4QT

✆ (020) 7715 5818

www.boisdale.co.uk

⊖ Canary Wharf

Closed bank holidays – booking advisable

Menu £18 – Carte £26/64

This is two operations under one roof: get out of the lift on the 1st floor for the art deco inspired Oyster Bar: a richly decorated, tartan room centred around a marble topped bar. Here it's about relaxed dining, with an impressive selection of crustacea along with burgers and steaks. It has a lovely terrace overlooking Cabot Square and a walk-in humidor with an impressive selection of Cuban cigars. Climb out on the 2nd floor and three things hit you: the fabulous bay window, a stage and a remarkable wall of whiskies. Things here are grander and more comfortable and there's live jazz for which a charge is made. In amongst the caviar, steaks and assorted dishes of Scottish persuasion is the more moderately priced Great British Menu.

Goodman Canary Wharf

meats and grills P1

Canary Wharf

Discovery Dock East, 3 South Quay ✉ E14 9RU

✆ (020) 7531 0300 – **www**.goodmanrestaurants.com

⊖ South Quay (DLR)

Closed 25-26 December, 1 January, Saturday lunch, Sunday and bank holidays – booking advisable

Carte £25/67

No one likes their meat more than those whose business is business, so Canary Wharf was a logical location for this growing group. Whether you're thinking corn or grass fed Scottish fillet, rib on the bone or US strip loin, the delightful staff will show you what's on offer and explain the maturation process. It can be wet and vac-packed from the US or dry hung from Scotland and Ireland; even the Aussies get in on the act with their Wagyu. You then decide on the cut and the weight, which depends on the relative sizes of your appetite and wallet. The quality of the beef is excellent, as are the side dishes like truffle chips. The lively brasserie-style room, with semi-private booths, offers great waterfront views.

The Gun

British traditional P1

Canary Wharf

27 Coldharbour ✉ E14 9NS

✆ (020) 7515 5222

www.thegundocklands.com

⊖ Blackwall (DLR).

Closed 25-26 December – booking essential

Carte £28/54

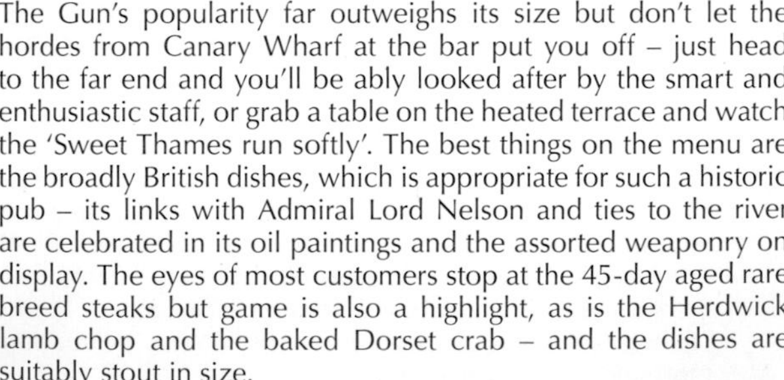

The Gun's popularity far outweighs its size but don't let the hordes from Canary Wharf at the bar put you off – just head to the far end and you'll be ably looked after by the smart and enthusiastic staff, or grab a table on the heated terrace and watch the 'Sweet Thames run softly'. The best things on the menu are the broadly British dishes, which is appropriate for such a historic pub – its links with Admiral Lord Nelson and ties to the river are celebrated in its oil paintings and the assorted weaponry on display. The eyes of most customers stop at the 45-day aged rare breed steaks but game is also a highlight, as is the Herdwick lamb chop and the baked Dorset crab – and the dishes are suitably stout in size.

Iberica Canary Wharf

Spanish

P1

Canary Wharf

Cabot Sq ✉ E14 4QQ
✆ (020) 7636 8650 – **www**.ibericalondon.co.uk
⊖ Canary Wharf
Closed 24-25 December, 1 January and dinner on Sunday and bank holidays

Carte £18/46

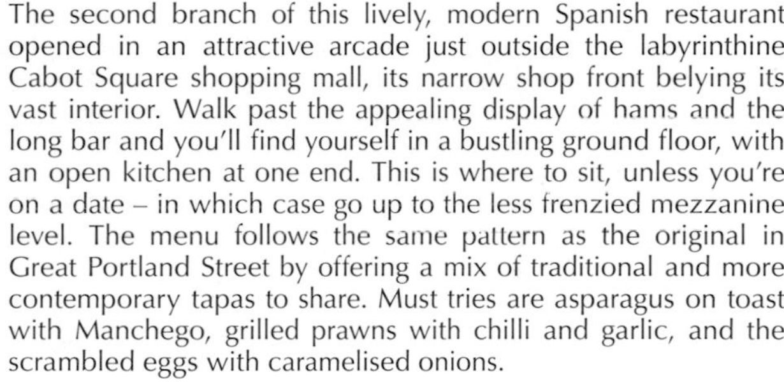

The second branch of this lively, modern Spanish restaurant opened in an attractive arcade just outside the labyrinthine Cabot Square shopping mall, its narrow shop front belying its vast interior. Walk past the appealing display of hams and the long bar and you'll find yourself in a bustling ground floor, with an open kitchen at one end. This is where to sit, unless you're on a date – in which case go up to the less frenzied mezzanine level. The menu follows the same pattern as the original in Great Portland Street by offering a mix of traditional and more contemporary tapas to share. Must tries are asparagus on toast with Manchego, grilled prawns with chilli and garlic, and the scrambled eggs with caramelised onions.

Plateau

modern

P1

Canary Wharf

Canada Place (4th floor), Canada Square ✉ E14 5ER
✆ (020) 7715 7100
www.plateaurestaurant.co.uk
⊖ Canary Wharf
Closed 25 December, 1 January and Sunday

Menu £15/25 – Carte £29/60

In a building that wouldn't look out of place in Manhattan is a restaurant that harks back to a time when bankers ruled the world. This striking room, with its subtle 1950s design influences, is an impressive open-plan space and its dramatic glass walls and ceilings make the surrounding monolithic office blocks seem strangely appealing, for some reason. There are two choices: the Grill where, as the name suggests, the choice is from rotisserie meats and classic grilled dishes, or the formal restaurant beyond it, which comes with more comfortable surroundings. Here, the range is more eclectic and dishes are constructed with more global influences. They also come in ample sizes, though, so ignore the enthusiastic selling of the side dishes.

Roka Canary Wharf

Japanese

Canary Wharf

P1

4 Park Pavilion (1st Floor) ✉ E14 5FW
✆ (020) 7636 5228
www.rokarestaurant.com
⊖ Canary Wharf
Closed 25 December – booking essential

Carte £20/89

London's second Roka restaurant sits in the shadow of Canary Wharf Tower, now the UK's second tallest building, and the first thing to hit you, once you've actually found the entrance, is a wall of sound. This is a big, open and perennially busy affair, with tightly packed tables which are usually occupied by large groups of City folk – and is not somewhere for a quiet dinner à deux. The menu follows the format of the Charlotte Street branch by offering a wide selection of mostly contemporary Japanese dishes. The easiest option is to head straight for one of the tasting menus which offer a balanced picture of what the food is all about. The robata grill is the centrepiece of the kitchen's operation – the lamb chops are particularly good.

Palmerston

Mediterranean

East Dulwich

O2

91 Lordship Ln ✉ SE22 8EP
✆ (020) 8693 1629
www.thepalmerston.co.uk
⊖ East Dulwich (Rail).
Closed 25-26 December and 1 January

Menu £14 (weekday lunch) – Carte £28/64

The Palmerston has long realised that success for any pub lies in being at the heart of the local community. Since its last makeover, this Victorian pub has been popular with families – just look at all those highchairs – and local artists' work decorates the walls. It has a comfortable, lived-in feel, along with a snug, wood-panelled rear dining room with an original and quite beautiful mosaic floor. The menu is as reassuring as the service and the cooking has a satisfying, gutsy edge. There's plenty of choice, from chowders and soups to well-judged fish but it's the meat dishes that stand out, like the mature steaks or lamb chops – and if they have grouse on the menu, then forsake all others and get in quick.

Toasted

modern

East Dulwich

38 Lordship Ln ✉ SE22 8HJ
✆ (020) 8693 9250
www.toasteddulwich.co.uk
Closed Sunday dinner

03

Carte £18/42

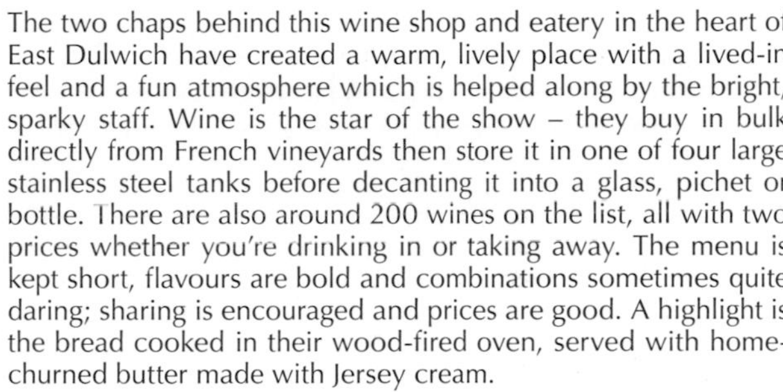

The two chaps behind this wine shop and eatery in the heart of East Dulwich have created a warm, lively place with a lived-in feel and a fun atmosphere which is helped along by the bright, sparky staff. Wine is the star of the show – they buy in bulk directly from French vineyards then store it in one of four large stainless steel tanks before decanting it into a glass, pichet or bottle. There are also around 200 wines on the list, all with two prices whether you're drinking in or taking away. The menu is kept short, flavours are bold and combinations sometimes quite daring; sharing is encouraged and prices are good. A highlight is the bread cooked in their wood-fired oven, served with home-churned butter made with Jersey cream.

Babur

Indian

Forest Hill

119 Brockley Rise ✉ SE23 1JP
✆ (020) 8291 2400
www.babur.info
⊖ Honor Oak Park
Closed dinner 25 December-lunch 27 December

Carte £25/32

It's not just its good looks and innovative cooking that set Babur apart – this long-standing Indian restaurant is also run with great passion and enthusiasm. Regular customers are invited to tastings and can even have an input on the quarterly changing menus – and the makeup of each dish is fully explained when dishes are presented at the table. The south and north-west of India feature most predominantly on the menu but there are also Western-influenced dishes available, like crab claws with asparagus and saffron. Seafood is certainly a highlight, so look out for the periods of the year when the separate 'Treasures of the Sea' menu appears. You'll find suggested wine pairings for each dish, along with some inventive cocktails.

Inside

modern

Greenwich

P2

19 Greenwich South St ✉ SE10 8NW
✆ (020) 8265 5060
www.insiderestaurant.co.uk
⊖ Greenwich
Closed 25-26 December, Sunday dinner and Monday

Menu £18/25 – Carte £26/39

A/C

The advantage of having an unremarkable façade is that it dampens unrealistic expectations. Indeed, 'Inside' was so named because the chef and his fellow owners had very little money when they opened, so wisely concentrated on the interior. With seating for just under forty, the room is tidy, comfortable and uncluttered, although it does take a few diners to generate an atmosphere. On offer is an appealingly priced set menu, elements of which change every fortnight. Dishes are attractively presented, relatively elaborate in their make-up and clearly prepared with care; most of the influences come from within Europe but staples do include the chicken and coriander spring rolls. There's also a decent choice of wine for under £25.

Rivington Grill

British modern

Greenwich

P2

178 Greenwich High Rd ✉ SE10 8NN
✆ (020) 8293 9270
www.rivingtongreenwich.co.uk
⊖ Greenwich (DLR)
Closed 25-26 December

Carte £20/40

A/C

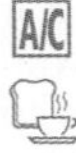

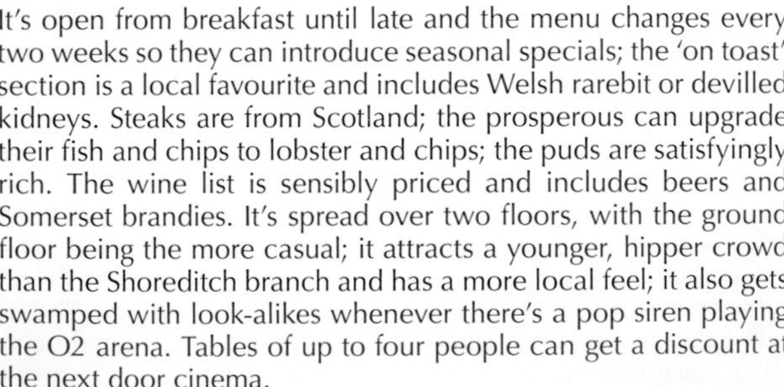

It's open from breakfast until late and the menu changes every two weeks so they can introduce seasonal specials; the 'on toast' section is a local favourite and includes Welsh rarebit or devilled kidneys. Steaks are from Scotland; the prosperous can upgrade their fish and chips to lobster and chips; the puds are satisfyingly rich. The wine list is sensibly priced and includes beers and Somerset brandies. It's spread over two floors, with the ground floor being the more casual; it attracts a younger, hipper crowd than the Shoreditch branch and has a more local feel; it also gets swamped with look-alikes whenever there's a pop siren playing the O2 arena. Tables of up to four people can get a discount at the next door cinema.

Kennington Tandoori

Indian

Kennington

N2

313 Kennington Rd ✉ SE11 4QE
✆ (020) 7735 9247
www.kenningtontandoori.com
⊖ Kennington

Closed 25 December – booking advisable

Menu £20 (lunch) – Carte £20/33

A/C

Known affectionately as KT, the Hoque family's long-standing Indian restaurant was reinvigorated a couple of years ago when their son Kowsar took over. He brought the look up-to-date and then set about raising the standards all round. The result is that he now has a very pleasant neighbourhood restaurant that is clearly a cut above the norm. The menu is made up of recognisable classics and old favourites but the kitchen's skill is evident in the execution. Vegetarian dishes stand out and everything is made from scratch, from the chutneys to the kulfi. Mind you, many of the regulars, who make up the vast majority of customers – and include plenty of cricket fans and politicians – don't even bother with the menu and just ask for their 'usual'.

Lobster Pot

French

Kennington

N2

3 Kennington Ln. ✉ SE11 4RG
✆ (020) 7582 5556
www.lobsterpotrestaurant.co.uk
⊖ Kennington

Closed 25 December-2 January, Sunday and Monday

Carte £28/65

A/C

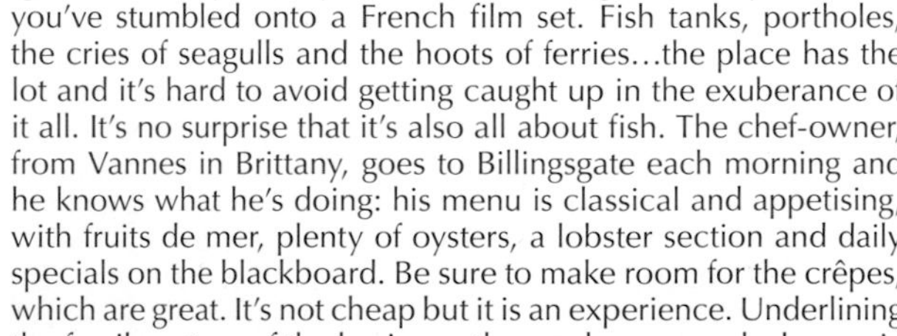

Ignore the fairly shabby exterior, dive straight in and you'll think you've stumbled onto a French film set. Fish tanks, portholes, the cries of seagulls and the hoots of ferries...the place has the lot and it's hard to avoid getting caught up in the exuberance of it all. It's no surprise that it's also all about fish. The chef-owner, from Vannes in Brittany, goes to Billingsgate each morning and he knows what he's doing: his menu is classical and appetising, with fruits de mer, plenty of oysters, a lobster section and daily specials on the blackboard. Be sure to make room for the crêpes, which are great. It's not cheap but it is an experience. Underlining the family nature of the business, the son has opened a brasserie next door.

Narrow

British traditional 01

Limehouse

44 Narrow St ✉ E14 8DP

✆ (020) 7592 7950

www.gordonramsay.com

⊖ Limehouse (DLR).

Booking essential

Carte £31/42

There can't be many London pubs with better views than The Narrow and Gordon Ramsay's group has certainly made the most of the Thames-side location by wrapping a conservatory around this Grade II listed former dockmaster's house. The place has a real buzz, thanks largely to the many regulars drinking at the bar, the weekly quiz nights and the occasional live music, and the large number of diners which includes plenty of tourists who have made a special trek down here. The menu gives them an opportunity to discover Blighty's more traditional culinary offerings such as Scotch egg, cottage pie, toad in the hole and the ubiquitous fish and chips. Dishes on the whole hit the mark, although the kitchen can be a little heavy-handed at times.

Galvin Café a Vin

French 01

Spitalfields

35 Spital Sq (entrance on Bishops Sq) ✉ E1 6DY

✆ (020) 7299 0404

www.galvinrestaurants.com

⊖ Liverpool Street

Closed 24-26 December and 1 January

Menu £17 (lunch and early dinner) – Carte £26/36

In the same building as La Chapelle, but with a separate entrance around the corner, is this simpler but no less professionally run operation from the Galvin brothers. The room may not have the grandeur of next door but what it does offer is classic French bistro food at very appealing prices. Snails, confit of duck and rum baba are all here – tasty and satisfying dishes to evoke memories of French holidays and have you reaching for the Gauloises. So, if you want the fillet or the loin, go next door; if you're happy with the leg or bavette then come here. The place is loud, fun and friendly, and the atmosphere is helped along by a cheerful team and a thoughtfully compiled wine list which is also well-priced.

Galvin La Chapelle ✿

French

01

Spitalfields

35 Spital Sq ✉ E1 6DY

(020) 7299 0400 – **www**.galvinrestaurants.com

Liverpool Street

Closed dinner 24-26 December and 1 January

Menu £24 (lunch and early dinner)/29 – Carte £37/62

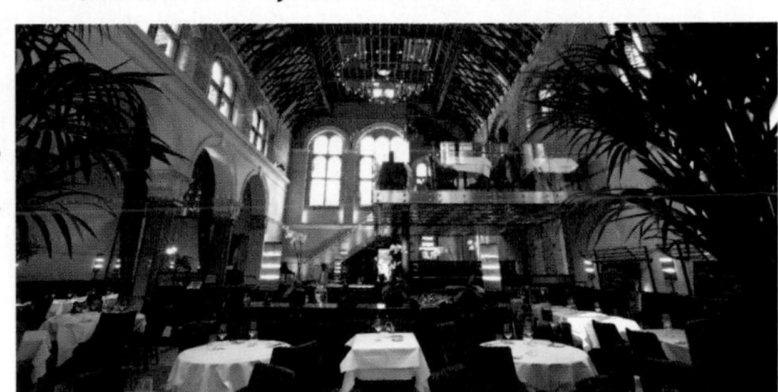

Galvin La Chapelle

These days, it is rare to walk into a restaurant in London and be taken back with the grandeur and sheer scale of a room. However, this venture from the Galvin Brothers, who have already proved themselves expert restaurateurs, is one that will dazzle the most jaded of diner. The Victorian splendour of St Botolph's Hall, with its vaulted ceiling, arched windows and marble pillars, lends itself effortlessly to its role as a glamorous restaurant. There are tables in booths, in the wings or in the middle of the action and those who like some comfort with their food will not be disappointed. It is also a fitting backdrop to the cooking, which is, in essence, bourgeois French but with a sophisticated edge, which means it is immensely satisfying. There are no unnecessary fripperies, just three courses of reassuringly familiar combinations with the emphasis on bold, clear flavours. Add in a service team who are a well-drilled, well-versed outfit and you have somewhere that will be part of the restaurant landscape for years to come.

First Course

- Smoked eel, caramelised pineapple, Alsace bacon, parsley and horseradish.
- Cured organic salmon with fennel, avocado and Ruby Red grapefruit.

Main Course

- Tagine of pigeon, couscous, confit lemon and harissa sauce.
- Roast John Dory, cauliflower purée and pine nut dressing.

Dessert

- Chilled Valrhona chocolate, banana and yoghurt ice cream.
- Tarte Tatin with Normandy crème fraîche.

Hawksmoor

meats and grills 01

Spitalfields

157a Commercial St ✉ E1 6BJ

✆ (020) 7426 4850

www.thehawksmoor.com

⊖ Shoreditch High Street

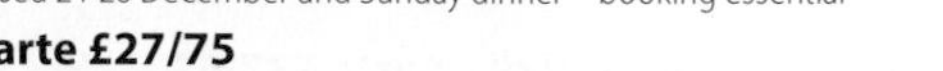

Closed 24-26 December and Sunday dinner – booking essential

Carte £27/75

Hawksmoor was a 17C architect and a student of Sir Christopher Wren so you could expect this steakhouse to be found in a building of note rather than in this modern edifice of little aesthetic value. Inside is equally unremarkable but no matter because this place is all about beef and, more specifically, British beef which has been hung for 35 days. It comes from Longhorn cattle raised by the Ginger Pig Co in the heart of the North Yorkshire Moors and the quality and depth of flavour is exceptional. Just choose your preferred weight – go for 400g if you're hungry. Starters and puds don't come close in quality but again, no matter, because when you've got some fantastic red meat in front of you, all you need is a mate and a bottle of red wine.

St John Bread and Wine

British traditional 01

Spitalfields

94-96 Commercial St ✉ E1 6LZ

✆ (020) 7251 0848

www.stjohnbreadandwine.com

⊖ Shoreditch

Closed 25-26 December and 1 January

Carte £19/30

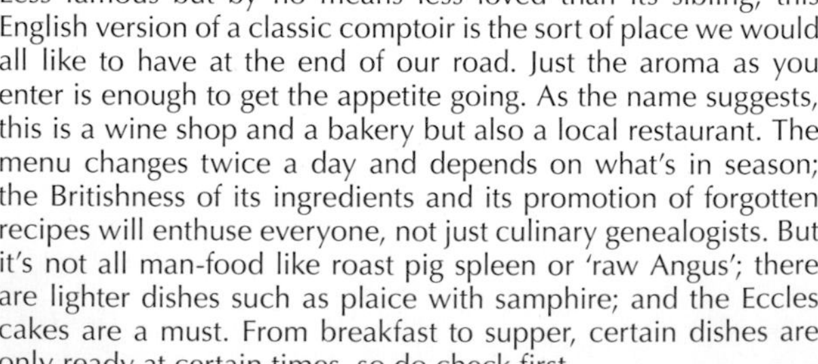

Less famous but by no means less loved than its sibling, this English version of a classic comptoir is the sort of place we would all like to have at the end of our road. Just the aroma as you enter is enough to get the appetite going. As the name suggests, this is a wine shop and a bakery but also a local restaurant. The menu changes twice a day and depends on what's in season; the Britishness of its ingredients and its promotion of forgotten recipes will enthuse everyone, not just culinary genealogists. But it's not all man-food like roast pig spleen or 'raw Angus'; there are lighter dishes such as plaice with samphire; and the Eccles cakes are a must. From breakfast to supper, certain dishes are only ready at certain times, so do check first.

Les Trois Garcons

French

Spitalfields

O1

1 Club Row ✉ E1 6JX

✆ (020) 7613 1924 – **www**.lestroisgarcons.com

⊖ Shoreditch High Street

Closed 23 December-3 January and Sunday – (dinner only and lunch Wednesday-Friday)

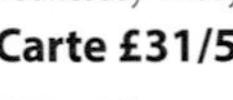

Carte £31/56

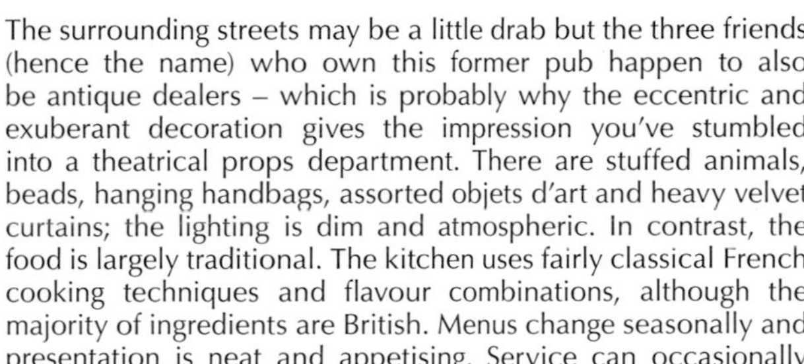

The surrounding streets may be a little drab but the three friends (hence the name) who own this former pub happen to also be antique dealers – which is probably why the eccentric and exuberant decoration gives the impression you've stumbled into a theatrical props department. There are stuffed animals, beads, hanging handbags, assorted objets d'art and heavy velvet curtains; the lighting is dim and atmospheric. In contrast, the food is largely traditional. The kitchen uses fairly classical French cooking techniques and flavour combinations, although the majority of ingredients are British. Menus change seasonally and presentation is neat and appetising. Service can occasionally veer from the efficient to the over-confident.

Canton Arms

British traditional

Stockwell

N2

177 South Lambeth Rd ✉ SW8 1XP

✆ (020) 7582 8710 – **www**.cantonarms.com

⊖ Stockwell.

Closed Christmas-New Year, Monday lunch, Sunday dinner and bank holidays – bookings not accepted

Carte £19/31

Its appreciative audience prove that the demand for fresh, honest, seasonal food is not just limited to smart squares in Chelsea or Islington. The oval-shaped bar dominates the room; the front half busy with drinkers and the back laid up for diners, although it's all very relaxed and you can eat where you want. The kitchen's experience in places like the Anchor & Hope and Great Queen Street is obvious on their menu which features rustic, earthy British food, of the sort that suits this environment so well. Lunch could be a kipper or tripe and chips; even a reinvented toasted sandwich. Dinner sees a short, no-nonsense menu offering perhaps braised venison or grilled haddock, with daily specials like steak and kidney pie for two.

Cafe Spice Namaste 

Indian

O1

Whitechapel

16 Prescot St. ✉ E1 8AZ

✆ (020) 7488 9242

www.cafespice.co.uk

⊖ Tower Hill

Closed Saturday lunch, Sunday and bank holidays

Menu £35 – Carte £22/33

Cyrus Todiwala has built up quite a following since opening in this former Victorian magistrate's court back in 1995. In that time he's also cooked for the Queen, grown a little empire and collected an OBE – not bad for someone who only planned on staying for 5 years. The menu here is extensive and appealing and makes good use of seasonal British ingredients. The Parsee and tandoor dishes are specialities; there are dishes to share; and vegetables get their own special menu. There may be no artificial colouring in the food but they certainly went to town on the room which is awash with bright yellows and blues – even the jaunty waistcoats of the staff catch your eye. Cyrus' wife Pervin oversees the service and she rarely misses a thing.

Good food without spending a fortune? Look for the Bib Gourmand.

R. Leaver/Loop Images/Photononstop

South-West London

Meandering like a silver snake, **The Thames** coils serenely through south-west London, adding definition to the area's much-heralded middle-class enclaves and leafy suburbs. It's the focal point to the annual **university boat race** from **Putney** to **Mortlake,** and it serves as the giant glass pond attractively backing countless bank-side pubs. This area has long been regarded as the cosy bourgeois side of town, though within its postcode prowls the lively and eclectic **Brixton,** whose buzzing street markets and lauded music venues add an urban lustre and vibrant edge.

In most people's minds, though, south-west London finds its true colours in the beautiful terrace view from the top of **Richmond Hill,** as the river bends majestically through the meadows below. Or in the smart **Wimbledon Village,** its independent boutiques ranged prettily along its own hill, with the open spaces of the Common for a back garden. Or, again, in the Italianate architecture that makes **Chiswick House** and grounds a little corner of the Mediterranean close to the Great West Road.

Green space is almost as prolific in this zone as the streets of Victorian and Edwardian villas. **Richmond Park** is the largest royal park in the whole of London and teems with kite flyers, cyclists and deer – though not necessarily in that order. From here, round a southerly bend in the river, delightful grounds surround **Ham House,** which celebrated its 400th birthday in 2010, although not so excessively as during the seventeenth century when it was home to Restoration court life. Head slightly north to **Kew Gardens** and its world famous 300 acres can now be viewed from above – the treetop walkway, takes you 60 feet up to offer some breath-taking views. Just across the river from here is another from the historical hit-list: **Syon Park,** which boasts water meadows still grazed by cattle, giving it a distinctly rural aspect. Syon House is considered one of architect Robert Adam's finest works; it certainly appealed to Queen Victoria, who spent much of her young life here. Up the road in bourgeoning Brentford, two unique museums bring in hordes of the curious: the Musical Museum includes a huge Wurlitzer theatre organ (get lucky and watch it being played), while almost next door, the Kew Bridge Steam Museum shows off all things steamy on a grand scale, including massive beam engines which pumped London's water for over a century.

Hammersmith may be known for its bustling Broadway and flyover, but five minutes' walk from here is the Upper Mall, which has iconic riverside pubs and Kelmscott House, the last home of artistic visionary William Morris: down in the basement and coach house are impressive memorabilia related to his life plus changing exhibitions of designs and drawings. From here, it's just a quick jaunt across **Hammersmith Bridge** and down the arrow-straight Castelnau to the

D. Chapuis / MICHELIN

Wetland Centre in Barnes, which for ten years has lured wildlife to within screeching distance of the West End. **Barnes** has always revelled in its village-like identity – it juts up like an isolated peninsula into the Thames and boasts yummy boutiques and well-known restaurants. The Bulls Head pub in Lonsdale Road has featured some of the best jazz in London for half a century.

In a more easterly direction, the urbanised areas of **Clapham** and **Battersea** have re-established themselves as desirable places to live over the last decade. **Clapham Common** is considered prime southwest London turf, to the extent that its summer music festivals are highly prized. It's ringed by good pubs and restaurants, too. Battersea used to be famous for its funfair, but now the peace pagoda in the park lends it a more serene light. And if you're after serenity on a hot day, then a cool dip in the wondrous **Tooting** Lido is just the thing.

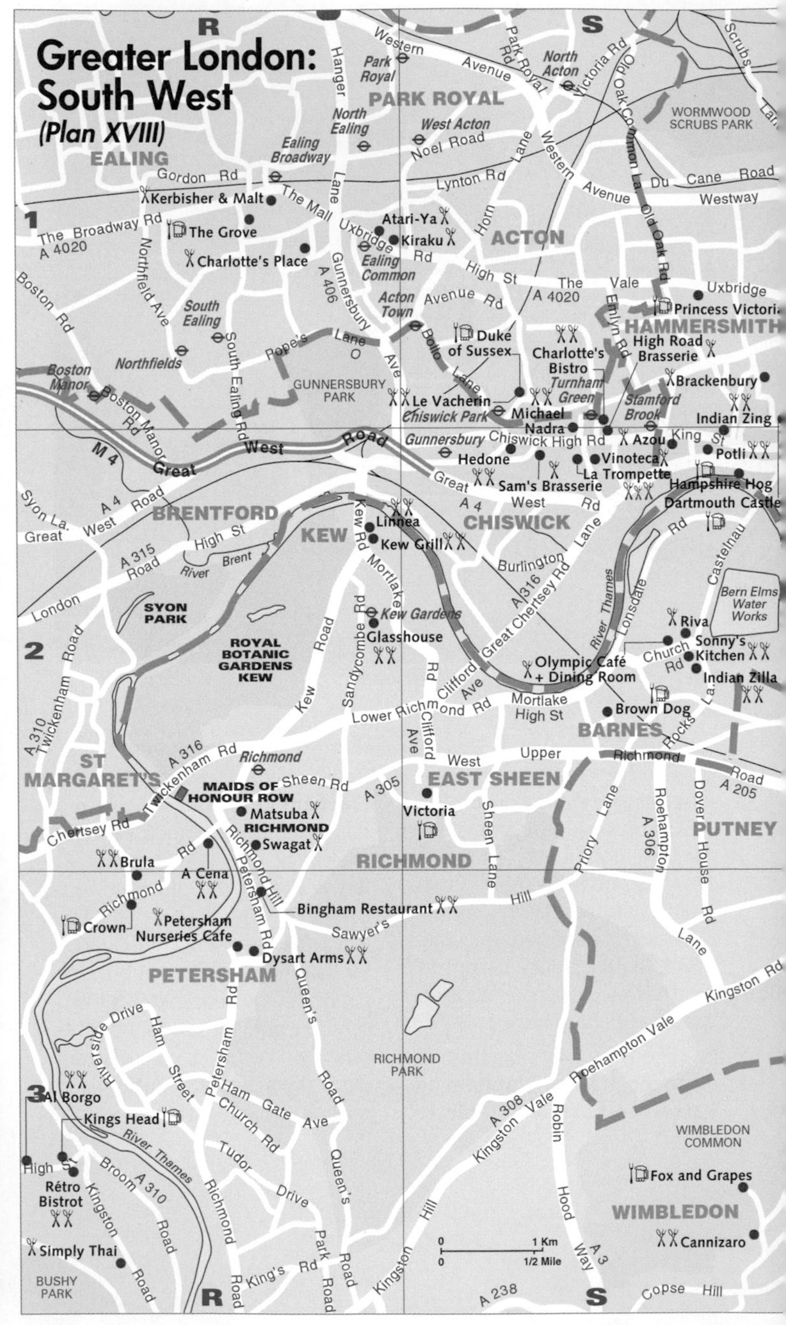
Greater London: South West
(Plan XVIII)
EALING
PARK ROYAL
ACTON
HAMMERSMITH
BRENTFORD
KEW
CHISWICK
ROYAL BOTANIC GARDENS KEW
SYON PARK
ST MARGARET'S
MAIDS OF HONOUR ROW
RICHMOND
EAST SHEEN
BARNES
PUTNEY
PETERSHAM
RICHMOND PARK
WIMBLEDON COMMON
WIMBLEDON
BUSHY PARK
WORMWOOD SCRUBS PARK
GUNNERSBURY PARK
Bern Elms Water Works
Kerbisher & Malt
The Grove
Charlotte's Place
Atari-Ya
Kiraku
Princess Victoria
Duke of Sussex
Charlotte's Bistro
High Road Brasserie
Brackenbury
Le Vacherin
Michael Nadra
Indian Zing
Hedone
Azou
Potli
Vinoteca
La Trompette
Sam's Brasserie
Hampshire Hog
Dartmouth Castle
Linnea
Kew Grill
Glasshouse
Riva
Sonny's Kitchen
Olympic Café + Dining Room
Indian Zilla
Brown Dog
Victoria
Matsuba
Swagat
Brula
A Cena
Bingham Restaurant
Crown
Petersham Nurseries Cafe
Dysart Arms
Al Borgo
Kings Head
Rétro Bistrot
Simply Thai
Fox and Grapes
Cannizaro
1 Km
1/2 Mile

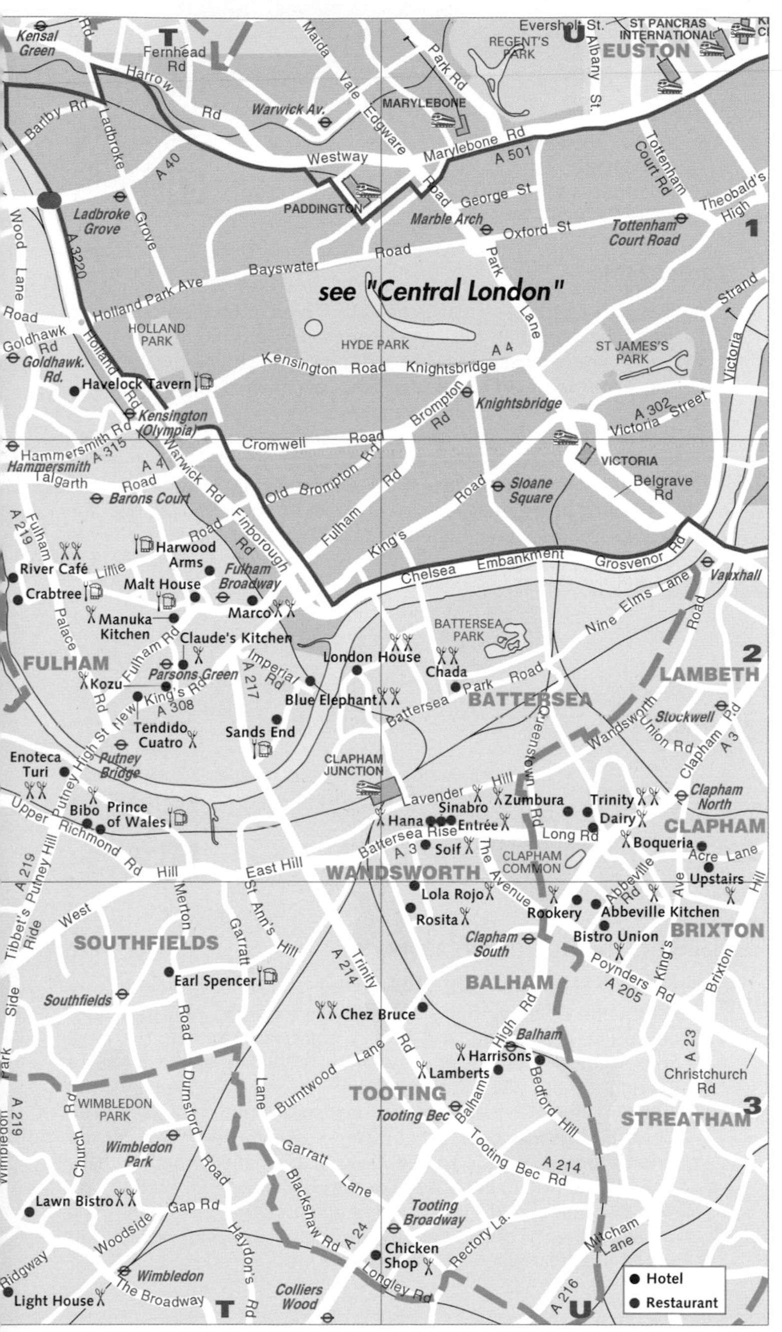
see "Central London"
Kensal Green
Fernhead Rd
Harrow Rd
Warwick Av.
Maida Vale
Edgware Road
Park Rd
REGENT'S PARK
Eversholt St.
Albany St.
ST PANCRAS INTERNATIONAL
EUSTON
MARYLEBONE
Marylebone Rd
A 501
Westway
A 40
Barlby Rd
Ladbroke Grove
Ladbroke Grove
PADDINGTON
George St
Marble Arch
Oxford St
Tottenham Court Rd
Tottenham Court Road
Theobald's
High
1
Wood Lane
A 3220
Bayswater Road
Park Lane
Holland Park Ave
HOLLAND PARK
HYDE PARK
Strand
Goldhawk Rd
Goldhawk Rd.
Holland Rd
Kensington Road
Knightsbridge
A 4
ST JAMES'S PARK
Victoria
Havelock Tavern
Kensington (Olympia)
Brompton Rd
Knightsbridge
A 302
Victoria Street
Hammersmith Rd
A 315
Hammersmith
Cromwell Road
VICTORIA
Talgarth Road
A 4
Warwick Rd
Old Brompton Rd
Fulham Rd
King's Road
Sloane Square
Belgrave Rd
Barons Court
A 219
Fulham Palace Rd
Lillie Road
Finborough Rd
Harwood Arms
River Café
Crabtree
Malt House
Fulham Broadway
Marco
Chelsea Embankment
Grosvenor Rd
Vauxhall
Nine Elms Lane
Manuka Kitchen
Claude's Kitchen
Fulham Rd
BATTERSEA PARK
London House
Chada
2
FULHAM
Imperial Rd
A 217
LAMBETH
Kozu
Parsons Green
New King's Rd
A 308
Blue Elephant
Battersea Park Road
BATTERSEA
Queenstown Rd
Wandsworth Rd
Stockwell
Union Rd
Clapham Rd
A 3
Tendido Cuatro
Putney Bridge
Sands End
CLAPHAM JUNCTION
Enoteca Turi
Putney High St
Lavender Hill
Sinabro
Zumbura
Trinity
Dairy
Clapham North
Upper Richmond Rd
Bibo
Prince of Wales
Hana
Entrée
Long Rd
CLAPHAM
Battersea Rise
A 3
Soif
The Avenue
Boqueria
Acre Lane
Hill
East Hill
CLAPHAM COMMON
A 219
WANDSWORTH
Upstairs
Putney Hill
Merton
Garratt
St Ann's Hill
Lola Rojo
Abbeville Rd
Ave
West
Rookery
Abbeville Kitchen
Tibbet's Ride
SOUTHFIELDS
Rosita
Clapham South
Bistro Union
BRIXTON
A 214
Trinity
King's
Brixton
Earl Spencer
BALHAM
Poynders Rd
A 205
Side
Southfields
Road
Chez Bruce
High Rd
Balham
Harrisons
A 23
Park
Lane
Rd
Burntwood Lane
Lamberts
Christchurch Rd
Church Rd
WIMBLEDON PARK
Durnsford Road
TOOTING
Balham
Bedford Hill
3
A 219
Tooting Bec
STREATHAM
Wimbledon Park
Garratt Lane
Blackshaw Rd
Tooting Bec Rd
A 214
Lawn Bistro
Gap Rd
Tooting Broadway
Woodside
Haydon's Rd
A 24
Chicken Shop
Rectory La.
Mitcham Lane
Ridgway
Wimbledon
The Broadway
Longley Rd
Colliers Wood
A 216
Light House
Hotel
Restaurant

Duke of Sussex

Mediterranean S1

Acton Green

75 South Par ✉ W4 5LF

(020) 8742 8801

www.realpubs.co.uk

⊖ Chiswick Park.

Carte £23/36

The Duke of Sussex may seem like a typical London pub, even from the front bar, but step through into the dining room and you'll find yourself in what was once a variety theatre from the time when this was a classic gin palace, complete with proscenium arch, glass ceiling and chandeliers. If that wasn't unusual enough, you could then find yourself eating cured meats or fabada, as the menu has a strong Spanish influence. Traditionalists can still get their steak pies and treacle tart but it's worth being more adventurous and trying the sardines, the paella and the crema Catalana. This is a fun, enthusiastically run and bustling pub and the kitchen's enthusiasm is palpable. On Mondays it's BYO; Sunday is quiz night.

Le Vacherin

French S1

Acton Green

76-77 South Par ✉ W4 5LF

(020) 8742 2121

www.levacherin.com

⊖ Chiswick Park

Closed Monday lunch

Menu £19 (lunch) – Carte £28/48

Le Vacherin calls itself a bistro but, with its brown leather banquette seating, mirrors and belle époque prints, it feels more like a brasserie, and quite a smart one at that. The most important element of the operation is the appealing menu of French classics which rarely changes, largely because they don't need to but also because the regulars wouldn't allow it. The checklist includes oeufs en cocotte, escargots, confit of duck and crème brûlée. Beef is something of a speciality, whether that's the côte de boeuf, the rib-eye or the chateaubriand. Portions are sensible, flavours distinct and ingredients good. The only thing missing in terms of authenticity are some insouciant French staff and a little Piaf playing in the background.

Harrison's

modern

U3

Balham

15-19 Bedford Hill ✉ SW12 9EX
✆ (020) 8675 6900
www.harrisonsbalham.co.uk
⊖ Balham
Closed 24-28 December

Menu £17 (weekdays) – Carte £27/39

Sam Harrison's Balham brasserie may not occupy quite as impressive a building as his place in Chiswick but it does emit a welcoming glow to passers-by and is just as popular with the locals. It's cleverly laid out, with drinkers and diners gathered around the central bar and kitchen which results in a lively buzz. Cooking is fresh, simple and unfussy and dishes arrive with a polite smile and in good time; 'Harrison's burgers' are top sellers, as are the fish and chips. The midweek set menus are very good value, BYO Mondays work well and weekend brunches are particularly popular with local families. Those who prefer a room free of children, however, can take advantage of the smart cocktail bar in the basement.

Lamberts

British traditional

U3

Balham

2 Station Par, Balham High Rd. ✉ SW12 9AZ
✆ (020) 8675 2233
www.lambertsrestaurant.com
⊖ Balham
Closed 25-26 December, 1 January, Sunday dinner and Monday

Menu £15 (weekday lunch) – Carte £27/42

Mr Lambert and his eponymous restaurant have succeeded by offering the locals exactly what they want: relaxed surroundings, hospitable service and tasty, seasonal food. The menu is updated each month and small suppliers have been sought out. The cooking is quite British in style and has a satisfying wholesomeness to it; Sunday's ribs of Galloway beef or legs of Salt Marsh lamb are hugely popular. Equal thought and passion have gone into the commendably priced wine list, which includes some favourites offered in 300ml decanters. Other nice touches include filtered water delivered gratis and velvety truffles brought with the coffee. The owner's enthusiasm has rubbed off on his team, for whom nothing is too much trouble.

Brown Dog

British modern

Barnes

S2

28 Cross St ✉ SW13 0AP
(020) 8392 2200
www.thebrowndog.co.uk
⊖ Barnes Bridge (Rail).
Closed 25 December

Carte £20/37

Thankfully, changes of ownership don't appear to mean much here – perhaps you really can't teach an old dog new tricks – because The Brown Dog remains a terrific neighbourhood pub and the locals clearly love it just the way it is. Mind you, this pretty Victorian pub is so well hidden in the maze of residential streets that it's a wonder any new customers ever find it anyway. The look fuses the traditional with the modern and service is bubbly and enthusiastic. Jugs of iced water arrive without prompting and the cleverly concise menu changes regularly. A lightly spiced crab salad or pint of prawns could be followed by a succulent rump of lamb, while puddings like sticky toffee date pudding or gooseberry cheesecake are also commendably priced.

Indian Zilla

Indian

Barnes

S2

2-3 Rocks Ln. ✉ SW13 0DB
(020) 8878 3989
www.indianzilla.co.uk
Closed 25 December – (dinner only and lunch Saturday-Sunday)

Carte £20/38

Judging by the crowds, Barnes' locals are clearly delighted that their district was chosen as the third location for this bourgeoning little group, following on from the success of Indian Zing and Indian Zest. The bright restaurant has a lovely buzz to it and the young, eager-to-please service team are very attentive. The new-wave Indian cooking is surprisingly light yet full of flavour, with many of the dishes using organic ingredients. Whilst a few old favourites are offered, it is the more delicate options that really stand out, such as lobster Balchao and specialities from the owner's home province of Maharashtra, like vegetable Bhanavla. The breads are super as is the lemon and ginger rice, and be sure to end with the Tandoori figs.

Olympic Café + Dining Room

British modern S2

Barnes

117-123 Church Rd ✉ SW13 9HL

✆ (020) 8912 5161

www.olympiccinema.co.uk

Bookings advisable at dinner

Carte £16/41

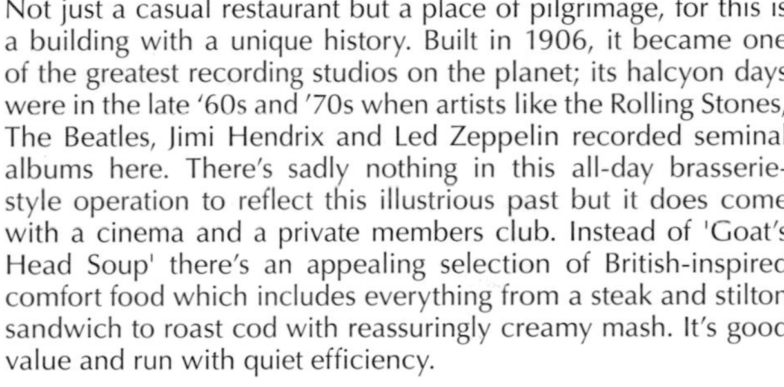

Not just a casual restaurant but a place of pilgrimage, for this is a building with a unique history. Built in 1906, it became one of the greatest recording studios on the planet; its halcyon days were in the late ‘60s and ’70s when artists like the Rolling Stones, The Beatles, Jimi Hendrix and Led Zeppelin recorded seminal albums here. There’s sadly nothing in this all-day brasserie-style operation to reflect this illustrious past but it does come with a cinema and a private members club. Instead of 'Goat’s Head Soup' there’s an appealing selection of British-inspired comfort food which includes everything from a steak and stilton sandwich to roast cod with reassuringly creamy mash. It’s good value and run with quiet efficiency.

Riva

Italian S2

Barnes

169 Church Rd. ✉ SW13 9HR

✆ (020) 8748 0434

Closed 2 weeks August, Christmas-New Year, Saturday lunch and bank holidays

Carte £29/52

Customer loyalty is the sine qua non of any successful restaurant; those seeking guidance on how to build it should get down to Barnes and learn from Andrea Riva. His secret is to shower so much attention on his regulars that all other diners sit imagining the day when they will be treated in the same way – when he will tell them what he’s going to cook especially for them. That could be some milk-fed lamb, game, suckling pig or risotto; all expertly rendered using tip-top, seasonal ingredients. While you wait for graduation, you’ll be served by a friendly young female team and still get to enjoy some gutsy, flavoursome food. Andrea is also a keen wine collector so if you can talk oenology it could improve your chances of joining the club.

Sonny's Kitchen

modern

S2

Barnes

94 Church Rd ✉ SW13 0DQ

(020) 8748 0393

www.sonnyskitchen.co.uk

Closed 25 December, 1 January and bank holiday Mondays

Menu £18/25 – Carte £26/44

Long-time owner Rebecca Mascarenhas has been joined by Philip Howard, celebrated chef of The Square and local Barnes resident, but instead of creating a brand new restaurant as they did at Kitchen W8, here they've been busy rejuvenating this much-loved neighbourhood favourite. The menu is appealingly all-encompassing and the kitchen takes good ingredients, treats them with respect and keeps dishes simple and easy to eat. The room has a bright, somewhat Scandinavian feel and weekends here are especially popular, due to the brunches, roasts and Sunday night BYO, for which no corkage is charged. What hasn't changed is the very pleasant atmosphere and the interesting artwork from Rebecca's private collection.

Chada

Thai

U2

Battersea

208-210 Battersea Park Rd. ✉ SW11 4ND

(020) 7622 2209

www.chadathai.com

⊖ Clapham Junction

Closed Sunday and bank holidays – (dinner only)

Carte £17/34

Chada, whose positively resplendent façade marks it out on Battersea Park Road, is still going strong after 20 years, although it doesn't face huge competition. A striking carved Buddha dominates the simply dressed room but check out the owner's gilded headdress, displayed in a cabinet, which she uses for festivals. This may never be the busiest restaurant around but the welcome is always warm, the service polite and endearing and the Thai cooking satisfying and keenly priced. The menu is still a very long affair but it's easy to navigate through and the seafood selection is an undoubted highlight. Several dishes can be made with a choice of chicken, duck, prawn or vegetables; portions are generous and presentation is appealing.

Entrée

modern

U2

Battersea

2 Battersea Rise ✉ SW11 1ED
✆ (020) 7223 5147 – **www**.entreebattersea.co.uk
⊖ Clapham Junction
Closed 24-28 December, Sunday dinner and Monday – (dinner only and lunch Saturday-Sunday)

Carte £27/45

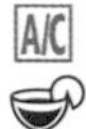

The name doesn't quite fit as it implies a devotion to all things French and a degree of pretentiousness that is thankfully absent. In reality they have gone more for a casual bistro look which, along with an intimate basement bar and weekend pianist, appears to have hit the right note with the locals. The style of food is a little harder to categorise: the attractively priced menu offers a selection of French classics together with dishes of a more modern European persuasion, as well as other choices that could be considered as being more from the '80s. It is this third section which actually provides some of the highlights, such as the scallop and crab lasagne. Haunch of venison and the ubiquitous pork belly are also popular choices.

Hana

Korean

U2

Battersea

60 Battersea Rise ✉ SW11 1EG
✆ (020) 7228 2496
www.hanakorean.co.uk
⊖ Clapham Junction
Closed 24-26 December

Carte £16/26

Most of the decent local restaurants are up at the Common end, so it's nice to see a few places opening further down the hill. The young owners of this sweet, warmly run little Korean restaurant are also benefitting from the growing popularity of Korean food in the capital. The cooking style may have been slightly westernised but the dishes still have plenty of vibrancy and freshness, and the aromas fill the air. Yang Yeum chicken and the Pa Jeon seafood pancake are popular starters; the bibimbap mixed rice dishes burst with flavour; they have their own take on the classic Bossam dish; and seafood cooked on the barbeque is particularly good. You can also try Korean teas, beers, wine and soju.

Lola Rojo

Spanish

Battersea

U3

78 Northcote Rd ✉ SW11 6QL

✆ (020) 7350 2262

www.lolarojo.net

⊖ Clapham Junction

Closed 25-26 December and lunch 1 January – booking essential

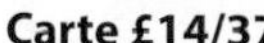

Carte £14/37

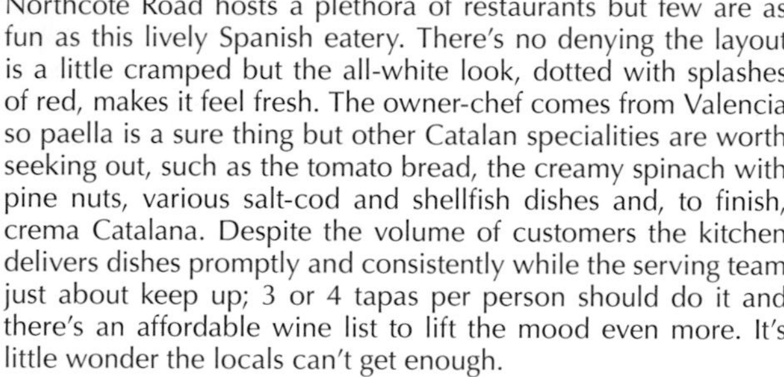

Northcote Road hosts a plethora of restaurants but few are as fun as this lively Spanish eatery. There's no denying the layout is a little cramped but the all-white look, dotted with splashes of red, makes it feel fresh. The owner-chef comes from Valencia so paella is a sure thing but other Catalan specialities are worth seeking out, such as the tomato bread, the creamy spinach with pine nuts, various salt-cod and shellfish dishes and, to finish, crema Catalana. Despite the volume of customers the kitchen delivers dishes promptly and consistently while the serving team just about keep up; 3 or 4 tapas per person should do it and there's an affordable wine list to lift the mood even more. It's little wonder the locals can't get enough.

London House

British modern

Battersea

T2

7-9 Battersea Sq, Battersea Village ✉ SW11 3RA

✆ (020) 7592 8545 – www.gordonramsay.com/londonhouse

⊖ Clapham Junction

Closed Monday except bank holidays – (dinner only and lunch Friday-Sunday)

Menu £28/35

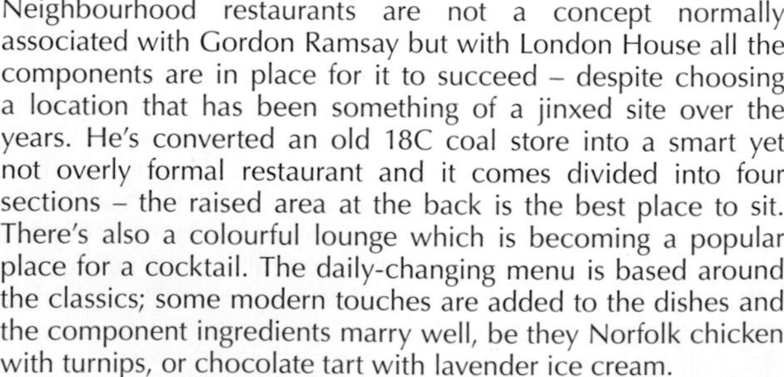

Neighbourhood restaurants are not a concept normally associated with Gordon Ramsay but with London House all the components are in place for it to succeed – despite choosing a location that has been something of a jinxed site over the years. He's converted an old 18C coal store into a smart yet not overly formal restaurant and it comes divided into four sections – the raised area at the back is the best place to sit. There's also a colourful lounge which is becoming a popular place for a cocktail. The daily-changing menu is based around the classics; some modern touches are added to the dishes and the component ingredients marry well, be they Norfolk chicken with turnips, or chocolate tart with lavender ice cream.

Rosita

Mediterranean

Battersea

U3

124 Northcote Rd ✉ SW11 6QU
✆ (020) 7998 9093 – **www**.rositasherry.net
⊖ Clapham Junction
Closed 25-26 December, 1 January and Monday – (dinner only and lunch Friday-Sunday)

Carte £15/26

From the same team as Lola Roja down the road comes this fun sherry and tapas bar, which is named after the owner's aunt. Brightly painted ceramic tiles and brass lanterns lend a subtle Moorish look to the room and cheery service adds to the buzzy atmosphere. Plate sizes vary from the diminutive to the generous – the latter being the more flavoursome and expensive dishes involving meats and seafood cooked by the Josper grill. The best action is to ask for advice as the staff are great at guiding you through ordering – and they are also keen to know you're enjoying yourself. The other aim of the place is to showcase the versatility of sherry: there's plenty of choice by the glass as well as suggested pairings with certain dishes.

N Sinabro

modern

Battersea

U2

28 Battersea Rd ✉ SW11 1EE
✆ (0203) 302 3120
www.sinabro.co.uk
⊖ Clapham Junction
Closed 1 week August, 25 December, 1 January and Monday

Menu £29

'Sinabro' is Korean for 'slowly but surely without noticing', and is a fitting name for Yoann Chevet's restaurant, which is gradually establishing itself as part of the local dining scene. The main room feels almost kitchen-like, courtesy of a wall of stainless steel; sit at the wooden counter – made by Yoann's father – and sit back and watch the show. Menus evolve constantly and give just a hint at what is to come, with descriptions such as 'salmon, pomegranate, spinach' or 'duck, polenta, peach'. Confidently prepared dishes allow quality ingredients to speak for themselves; they rely largely on classic French flavours but are modern in style. Brunch is served at weekends and the Tuesday-Friday lunch 'plat du jour' is particularly good value.

Soif

French

U2

Battersea

27 Battersea Rise ✉ SW11 1HG
✆ (020) 7233 1112 – **www**.soif.co
⊖ Clapham Junction
Closed Christmas and New Year, Sunday dinner, Monday lunch and bank holidays – booking essential at dinner

Carte £22/32

Eminently satisfying food, an appealingly louche look and a thoughtfully compiled wine list – yes, it's another terrific eaterie from the team behind the hugely successful Terroirs and Brawn. This busy bistro-cum-wine bar has a predominantly French list which includes plenty of 'natural' wines. The food menu is compiled daily and the cooking is gloriously no-nonsense and comes with bags of flavour. All things piggy are done particularly well – the charcuterie is well worth ordering; there's Lardo di Colonnata to spread on the great sourdough and the Montbéliard sausage will satisfy most hungers. Add in fair prices, a great atmosphere and delightfully natural service and it's no surprise they have another hit on their hands.

Boqueria

Spanish

U2

Brixton

192 Acre Ln. ✉ SW2 5UL
✆ (020) 7733 4408
www.boqueriatapas.com
⊖ Clapham North
(dinner only and lunch Saturday-Sunday)

Carte £10/17

Named after – and inspired by – Barcelona's famous food market, this contemporary tapas bar is a welcome addition to the neighbourhood and has quickly established a local fan-base. The menu doubles as a place mat and is a mix of recognisable classics and more adventurous offerings; it is also supplemented by specials on the blackboard. As everyone involved appears to hail from Andalucía, it makes sense to kick off with a glass of sherry. The Ibérico hams are in excellent order, the lamb medallions are full of flavour and be sure to save room for a particularly good crema Catalana. It's worth sitting at the counter as the main dining area at the back lacks a little personality. Their café next door serves coffee and churros.

Upstairs

modern

U2

Brixton

89b Acre Ln. ✉ SW2 5TN

✆ (020) 7733 8855 – **www**.upstairslondon.com

⊖ Clapham North

Closed 24 December-7 January, 5-14 April, 16 August-1 September, Sunday and Monday – (dinner only)

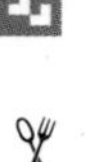

Menu £29

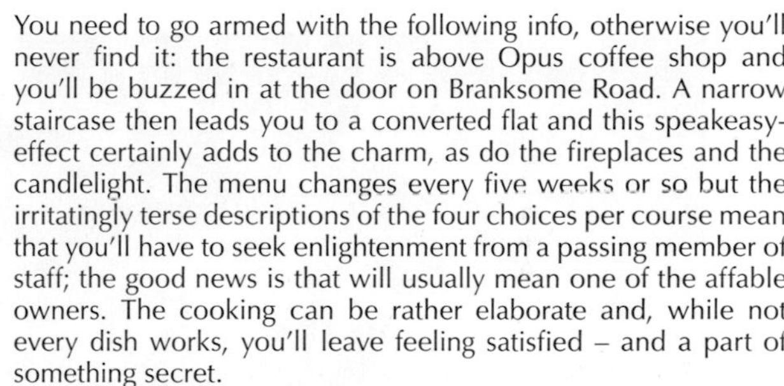

You need to go armed with the following info, otherwise you'll never find it: the restaurant is above Opus coffee shop and you'll be buzzed in at the door on Branksome Road. A narrow staircase then leads you to a converted flat and this speakeasy-effect certainly adds to the charm, as do the fireplaces and the candlelight. The menu changes every five weeks or so but the irritatingly terse descriptions of the four choices per course mean that you'll have to seek enlightenment from a passing member of staff; the good news is that will usually mean one of the affable owners. The cooking can be rather elaborate and, while not every dish works, you'll leave feeling satisfied – and a part of something secret.

Charlotte's Bistro

modern

S1

Chiswick

6 Turnham Green Terr ✉ W4 1QP

✆ (020) 8742 3590

www.charlottes.co.uk

⊖ Turnham Green

Booking advisable

Menu £16/27 – Carte £25/33

Unlike some desirable London neighbourhoods, Chiswick has always had plenty of restaurants, so locals never feel the need to venture too far from home for dinner. This little sister to nearby Ealing's Charlotte's Place provides them with another pleasantly unpretentious option. A large bar takes up most of the front section and then it's a few steps up to the bright dining room with a glass roof. The menu changes regularly and has a European accent, with such dishes as crab and celeriac tian, cod brandade, pan-fried halloumi, rolled leg of lamb and fishcakes. There's also a nice little cheese menu. Wines are listed by character and include bottles from some small producers. Service and prices are equally friendly.

Hedone ✿

modern S2

Chiswick

301-303 Chiswick High Rd ✉ W4 4HH

✆ (020) 8747 0377 – **www**.hedonerestaurant.com

⊖ Chiswick Park

Closed two weeks in summer, two weeks Christmas-New Year, Sunday and Monday – (dinner only and lunch Thursday-Saturday)

Menu £45/95

Hedone

Mikael Jonsson's restaurant continues to flourish but this former lawyer and food blogger turned chef is not one for complacency so it also continues to evolve. Out has gone the à la carte and in have come set menus, including for lunch. At dinner the choice is between the tasting menu, which does include some choice, and the Carte Blanche menu where you place your faith entirely in the hands of the kitchen; even the wine selection is made easy with a choice of Classic or Prestige pairings. The content of all menus is governed entirely by what ingredients are in their prime and it is this passion for seeking out the best seasonal produce, be it suckling pig or salt marsh lamb, which underpins the superlative cooking. Just a glance at the open kitchen also reveals the attention to detail and respect which the ingredients are shown. This results in refined, immeasurably satisfying dishes where the combinations of flavours ooze personality. All this and his basement bakery delivers some of the finest sourdough you'll find in the city.

First Course

- Luberon asparagus, avocado, pistachio and wild primrose.
- Dorset wild turbot, bok choi, shrimp mayonnaise and Asian flavours.

Main Course

- Rack of salt marsh lamb with fresh peas, carrots and spinach.
- Suckling pig 'Noir de Bigorre', green peas, morels and vin jaune.

Dessert

- Warm chocolate, passion fruit jelly, Madagascan vanilla ice cream.
- Gariguette strawberries, hibiscus and biscuit.

High Road Brasserie

French

Chiswick

S2

High Road House Hotel, 162 Chiswick High Rd. ✉ W4 1PR
✆ (020) 8742 7474
www.highroadhouse.co.uk
⊖ Turnham Green
Booking essential

Carte £20/36

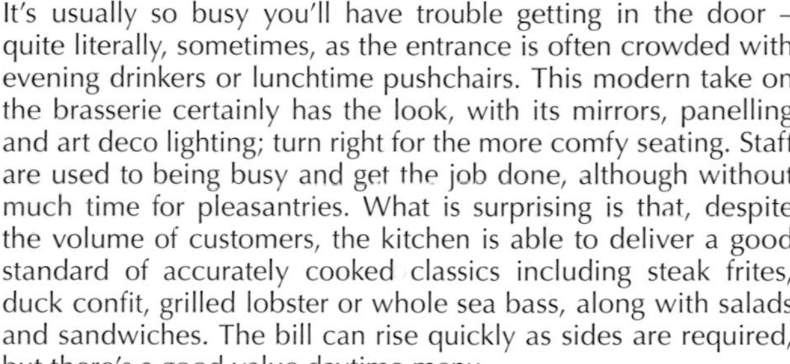

It's usually so busy you'll have trouble getting in the door – quite literally, sometimes, as the entrance is often crowded with evening drinkers or lunchtime pushchairs. This modern take on the brasserie certainly has the look, with its mirrors, panelling and art deco lighting; turn right for the more comfy seating. Staff are used to being busy and get the job done, although without much time for pleasantries. What is surprising is that, despite the volume of customers, the kitchen is able to deliver a good standard of accurately cooked classics including steak frites, duck confit, grilled lobster or whole sea bass, along with salads and sandwiches. The bill can rise quickly as sides are required, but there's a good value daytime menu.

Michael Nadra

modern

Chiswick

S1/2

6-8 Elliott Rd ✉ W4 1PE
✆ (020) 8742 0766
www.restaurant-michaelnadra.co.uk
⊖ Turnham Green
Closed 24-26 December, 1 January and Sunday dinner

Menu £20/55

Michael Nadra may have another restaurant in Primrose Hill but the regulars here in Chiswick give the impression they wouldn't be backward in coming forward in letting him know if standards slip back in W4. Hidden down a side street, this is a small, intimate place where the closely set tables add to the general bonhomie. The cooking is influenced by the Mediterranean and it is the fish dishes that particularly stand out. The kitchen does have a slight tendency towards over-elaboration but the ingredients are good and the prices are set at sensible levels – and that includes the six course tasting menu which appeals to many of those regulars. The two window tables are the prized seats and service is warm and responsive.

Sam's Brasserie

Mediterranean

S2

Chiswick

11 Barley Mow Passage ✉ W4 4PH
✆ (020) 8987 0555
www.samsbrasserie.co.uk
⊖ Turnham Green
Closed 24-26 December

Menu £14 (lunch and early dinner) – Carte £25/41

The building was once a Sanderson wallpaper mill and the industrial feel works well in this bustling brasserie environment. An added helping of hipness comes courtesy of the artwork from local resident, and occasional diner here, Sir Peter Blake. Look out too for the regular Soul and Jazz evenings. Dining is on two levels; the mezzanine is the quieter one, while the larger room looks into the kitchen and has plenty of bustle. The modern brasserie food is prepared with more care and expertise than one expects when one considers the size of the operation and, with a wine list offering over half its bottles for under £30, it's no surprise that the place gets busy. Service is efficient but could be a little more communicative.

Vinoteca

modern

S2

Chiswick

18 Devonshire Rd ✉ W4 2HD
✆ (020) 3701 8822
www.vinoteca.co.uk
⊖ Turnham Green
Closed 25 December

Carte £25/42

It was a brave move opening opposite La Trompette but this 4th outpost of the group has established itself in double quick time. Booking is a must at dinner, although the bar area is first come, first wined and dined. The short menu has strong Italian roots and the dishes rely on quality ingredients for the fresh flavours – it's not unusual to see fish being delivered mid-service. Sunday sees a more traditional roast which goes down a storm with the locals, as do Monday nights when all wine sales are at shop prices; at lunch the plat du jour and glass of wine deal is hard to beat. Wine certainly plays a large part here and the keenly priced wine flights provide an opportunity to try something a little different.

La Trompette ✿

British modern

Chiswick

5-7 Devonshire Rd ✉ W4 2EU
✆ (020) 8747 1836
www.latrompette.co.uk
⊖ Turnham Green

Closed 24-26 December and 1 January – booking essential

S2

Menu £28 (lunch and early dinner)/45

La Trompette

One of the reasons for the success of La Trompette is that it has always looked after its customers – when the shop next door was bought and the restaurant expanded, the owners didn't add more tables, they merely used the extra room to add more space between the existing ones. The very pleasant service team also ensure that customers keep returning – they manage the feat of making service seem effortless and the diners do their bit by creating a warm, congenial atmosphere. These days there is a greater distinction between the lunch and dinner menus. Lunch is all about great value; dishes are quite simple but just as skilfully prepared and the kitchen uses lesser known cuts and fewer luxury ingredients. At dinner the mackerel is replaced by turbot and the cooking is a tad more ambitious, but it's never over-elaborate. Another reason for La Trompette's continued success is that, despite the very accomplished cooking, it never gives the impression that it would rather be in Mayfair – it suits Chiswick and the locals clearly like having it.

First Course

- Scallops with raisin, pomegranate, pine nut and coriander dressing.
- Tomato and smoked aubergine with bocconcini and savoury granola.

Main Course

- Suckling pig with creamed potato, kale and carrot.
- Breast and croustillant of guinea fowl with mousserons and peas.

Dessert

- Rhubarb crumble soufflé with rhubarb ripple ice cream.
- Buttermilk panna cotta with English strawberries and peach.

Abbeville Kitchen

Mediterranean U3

Clapham Common

47 Abbeville Rd ✉ SW4 9JX

✆ (020) 8772 1110 – **www**.abbevillekitchen.com

⊖ Clapham Common

Closed 25-26 December – bookings advisable at dinner – (dinner only and lunch Friday-Sunday)

Carte £20/31

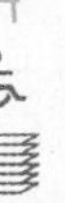

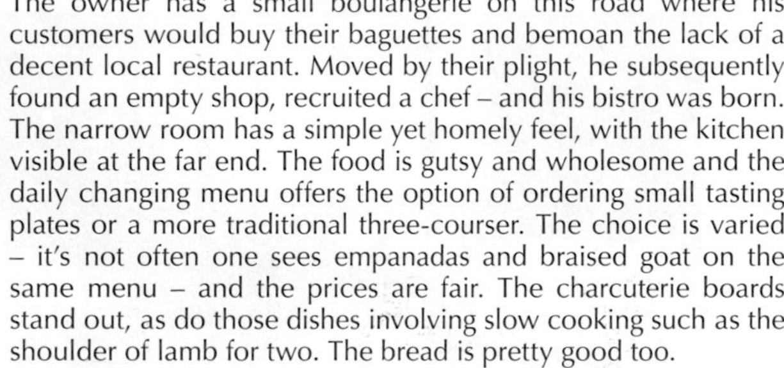

The owner has a small boulangerie on this road where his customers would buy their baguettes and bemoan the lack of a decent local restaurant. Moved by their plight, he subsequently found an empty shop, recruited a chef – and his bistro was born. The narrow room has a simple yet homely feel, with the kitchen visible at the far end. The food is gutsy and wholesome and the daily changing menu offers the option of ordering small tasting plates or a more traditional three-courser. The choice is varied – it's not often one sees empanadas and braised goat on the same menu – and the prices are fair. The charcuterie boards stand out, as do those dishes involving slow cooking such as the shoulder of lamb for two. The bread is pretty good too.

Bistro Union

British modern U3

Clapham Common

40 Abbeville Rd ✉ SW4 9NG

✆ (020) 7042 6400

www.bistrounion.co.uk

⊖ Clapham Common

Closed 24-28 December and Sunday dinner – booking advisable

Carte £18/37

'Comforting' is the word that comes to mind at Bistro Union, chef Adam Byatt's affordable and bustling offspring of his Trinity restaurant. Whether it's the menus written in old school exercise books or the rolled sheet of brown paper listing the day's snacks, there is something reassuring and familiar about everything at this fun neighbourhood spot. The food is hearteningly British and manages to evoke feelings of nostalgia while simultaneously being bang on-trend. Start with some snacks like the fish finger sarnie, beef with dripping toast or pickled quail eggs. Then share a spit-roast chicken, or try the Toad in the Hole or the cottage pie along with one of their great ales – and finish off with their homemade Eccles cake ice cream.

Dairy

British creative U2

Clapham Common

15 The Pavement ✉ SW4 0HY

✆ (020) 7622 4165 – **www**.the-dairy.co.uk

⊖ Clapham Common

Closed Christmas, Sunday dinner, Monday and Tuesday lunch – booking essential at dinner

Carte £20/25

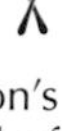

Much of the furniture and crockery has come from London's markets and the higgledy-piggledy look and homemade feel of this fun, lively restaurant add to its charm. What one doesn't expect to find in this environment is food that is so innovative and unusual. The chef-owner's cooking is informed by his extensive travels and from experience gleaned in some famous kitchens. The menu is driven by the available ingredients – they grow their own herbs and some fruit and veg on the rooftop, and have three beehives – and all the modern techniques such as pickling and fermenting are there. The food is earthy, original, very labour intensive but also easy to eat – the set menu, with some unusual drink pairings, is the best option.

Rookery

British traditional U3

Clapham Common

69 Clapham Common South Side ✉ SW4 9DA

✆ (020) 8673 9162

www.therookeryclapham.co.uk

⊖ Clapham Common

Closed 25-26 December – (dinner only and lunch Saturday-Sunday)

Carte £20/34

The on-trend Rookery shows that Soho doesn't have a monopoly on ersatz Brooklyn speakeasies. It was set up by a former Guardian journalist who regularly lunched at The Eagle, and he has stayed true to his principles by naming it after the colloquial term for a city slum. Downstairs is dominated by the bar, which comes with an impressive selection of artisan beers, but if you don't want to jostle for space with the drinkers then try the upstairs – and in summer head for the large outdoor terrace. Food is an important part of the operation; the menu may be short but usually includes a soup, a salad, a pasta dish, some charcuterie or offal, and a daily pie for sharing. The kitchen doesn't muck around and delivers some punchy flavours.

Trinity

innovative

Clapham Common

U2

4 The Polygon ✉ SW4 0JG
✆ (020) 7622 1199
www.trinityrestaurant.co.uk
⊖ Clapham Common
Closed 23-29 December, Monday lunch and Sunday dinner

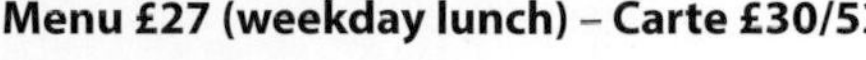

Menu £27 (weekday lunch) – Carte £30/53

A/C

Trinity is smarter and a little more formal than your average neighbourhood restaurant and residents of Clapham Old Town have clearly taken to it, especially as it means they don't have to schlep up to the West End for a 'proper' night out. The cooking is suitably sophisticated, with the kitchen adding some innovative combinations to what is a fairly classical base. Offal dishes are often the highlight and the pig's trotter on toasted sourdough has become a signature dish. The lunch menu is simpler in style and content but is priced very appealingly. To underline its neighbourhood credentials, the restaurant also offers cookery classes. In summer, ask for a table by the windows, which open up to add a little continental colour.

Ⓝ Zumbura

Indian

Clapham Common

U2

36a Old Town ✉ SW4 0LB
✆ (020) 7720 7902
www.zumbura.com
⊖ Clapham Common
Closed 1 January – (dinner only)

Carte £13/28

A/C

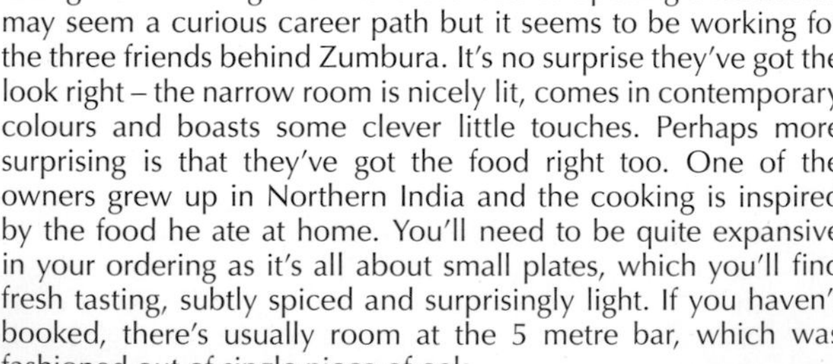

Going from running a furniture business to opening a restaurant may seem a curious career path but it seems to be working for the three friends behind Zumbura. It's no surprise they've got the look right – the narrow room is nicely lit, comes in contemporary colours and boasts some clever little touches. Perhaps more surprising is that they've got the food right too. One of the owners grew up in Northern India and the cooking is inspired by the food he ate at home. You'll need to be quite expansive in your ordering as it's all about small plates, which you'll find fresh tasting, subtly spiced and surprisingly light. If you haven't booked, there's usually room at the 5 metre bar, which was fashioned out of single piece of oak.

Atari-ya

Japanese

R1 

Ealing

1 Station Par, Uxbridge Rd ✉ W5 3LD

✆ (020) 8202 2789

www.atariya.co.uk

⊖ Ealing Common

Closed bank holiday Mondays

Carte £12/26 

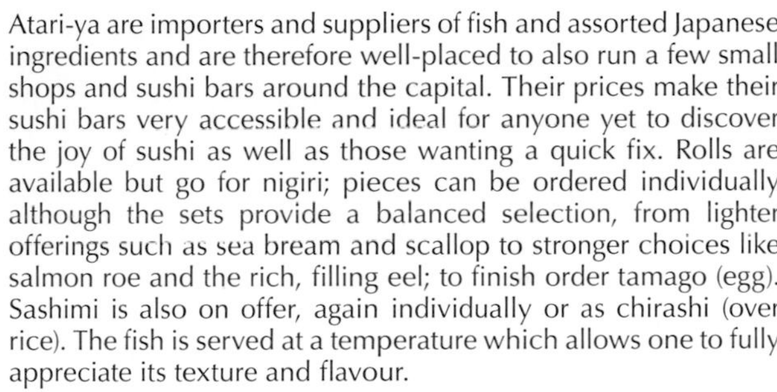

Atari-ya are importers and suppliers of fish and assorted Japanese ingredients and are therefore well-placed to also run a few small shops and sushi bars around the capital. Their prices make their sushi bars very accessible and ideal for anyone yet to discover the joy of sushi as well as those wanting a quick fix. Rolls are available but go for nigiri; pieces can be ordered individually although the sets provide a balanced selection, from lighter offerings such as sea bream and scallop to stronger choices like salmon roe and the rich, filling eel; to finish order tamago (egg). Sashimi is also on offer, again individually or as chirashi (over rice). The fish is served at a temperature which allows one to fully appreciate its texture and flavour.

Charlotte's Place

modern

R1 

Ealing

16 St Matthew's Rd ✉ W5 3JT

✆ (020) 8567 7541

www.charlottes.co.uk

⊖ Ealing Common

Closed 26 December and 1 January

Menu £18/33

It's been a sweet shop, a transport café and a private club but really found its niche as an honest and warmly run local restaurant. The ground floor offers views over the Common so is more popular at lunch; downstairs is ideal for couples who only have eyes for each other. The à la carte offers ample choice and the cooking is largely British, with smoked fish, traditional Sunday lunches and homely puddings done well; there are also one or two Mediterranean influences and the beef onglet enjoys a constant presence. There is a small cover charge but it does pays for bread and unlimited amounts of filtered water, rather than being an accountant's wheeze for squeezing more money out of the customers.

The Grove

modern

Ealing

R1 

The Green ✉ W5 5QX
✆ (020) 8567 2439
www.thegrovew5.co.uk
⊖ Ealing Broadway.

Menu £13 (weekday lunch) – Carte £22/36 

It's hard to avoid this beast of a place in central Ealing but then, why would you? It may be brewery owned and have undergone a typical London gastropub makeover, but it'll hit the spot – whether you're out with friends or after a candle-lit dinner. There's a huge front terrace dominated by drinkers but inside it's spilt into half-bar, half-restaurant; you can eat anywhere but the restaurant at the back is the quieter choice. The menus change monthly – lunch is pretty standard issue, but at dinner the skilful kitchen celebrates its classical roots. The easy-to-eat dishes add a distinctive French accent to the largely British ingredients; desserts are mostly crowd-pleasing classics and are equally satisfying.

Kerbisher & Malt

fish and chips

Ealing

R1 

53 New Broadway ✉ W5 5AH
✆ (020) 8840 4418
www.kerbisher.co.uk
⊖ Ealing Broadway

Carte £12/20 

There may have been a revolution in British cooking over the last two decades, but for many people, especially tourists, fish and chips will always be our national dish. Restaurants have been doing decent versions for years but Kerbisher & Malt represents a new wave of ethical fish and chip shops that are raising this classic dish to new heights. The fish here is fresh, sustainably sourced and cooked to order in rapeseed oil (which is then turned into biofuel); chips are made from British spuds and are fried separately; and all packaging is biodegradable. Choose your fish and a side order of thick 'Yorkshire caviar' or pickled onion rings, along with a pot of great tartare sauce. There's another branch in Hammersmith.

Kiraku

Japanese R1

Ealing

8 Station Par, Uxbridge Rd. ✉ W5 3LD
✆ (020) 8992 2848 – **www**.kiraku.co.uk
⊖ Ealing Common
Closed Christmas-New Year, Tuesday following bank holidays and Monday

Carte £15/37

Ayumi and Erica became so frustrated with the lack of a decent local Japanese restaurant that they decided to open one themselves; and now it is not just the bourgeoning Japanese community who flock to this cute little place. It's modestly styled and brightly lit, but service is very charming. Look out for the daily changing dishes on the blackboard. Zensai, or starters, include the popular Agedashi dofu; these can then be followed by assorted skewers, noodles and rice dishes. Fish is purchased daily and their sushi now displays a more modern touch; Bara Chirashi is the house speciality. Be sure to end with matcha ice cream or green tea sponge cake. The restaurant's name means 'relax and enjoy' and it's hard not to.

Victoria

British modern S2

East Sheen

10 West Temple Sheen ✉ SW14 7RT
✆ (020) 8876 4238
www.thevictoria.net
⊖ Mortlake (Rail).

Menu £15 (lunch and early dinner) – Carte £23/44

Many pubs claim to be genuine locals – The Victoria is the real deal: it sponsors local clubs and the chef is patron of the local food festival; he also holds cookery workshops at the school next door. This is a beautifully decorated pub, with a restored bar, a wood burning stove and plenty of nooks and crannies; a few steps down and you're in the more formal conservatory overlooking the terrace. The cooking is modern British with the odd international note. Warm homemade bread could be followed by Scotch egg with roast beetroot, cod with a white bean stew and, to finish, blood oranges with rhubarb sorbet. Produce is local where possible: veg is from Surrey and honey from Richmond. Service is engaging and there are bedrooms available.

Blue Elephant

Thai

Fulham

The Boulevard, Imperial Wharf ✉ SW6 2UB
✆ (020) 7751 3111 – **www**.blueelephant.com
⊖ Imperial Wharf

T2

Closed 25-26 December, 1 January and Monday lunch – booking advisable

Menu £38 (lunch and early dinner) – Carte £27/54

The Blue Elephant was a Fulham Road landmark for so long that everyone was taken by surprise when it packed its trunk and relocated. Fortunately for its followers, it didn't wander too far and these swankier premises within the large development that is Imperial Wharf have given it a new lease of life. Spread over two floors, the decoration is as exotic as one would expect – except that instead of the koi ponds you have the Thames outside, along with two terrific terraces; even the golden dragon made the journey from the old address but can now be found in a different guise at the bar. The appealing menu traverses Thailand and in amongst the classic dishes are a few more contemporary offerings; the curries here are always worth ordering.

Claude's Kitchen

modern

Fulham

51 Parsons Green Ln ✉ SW6 4JA
✆ (020) 7371 8517 – **www**.amusebouchelondon.com
⊖ Parsons Green.

T2

Closed Sunday dinner – booking essential – (dinner only and lunch Saturday-Sunday)

Carte £23/33

The eponymous Claude has created two little operations within one converted Victorian pub. On the ground floor is 'Amuse Bouche', a champagne bar where the bubbles are sold at competitive prices, along with assorted boards of cheese or cured meats. Upstairs is a small and intimate dining room where you'll find a concise but nicely balanced à la carte menu which changes every Tuesday. Indeed, if you actually come on a Tuesday (or 'guinea pig night' as it is known), you get to enjoy three courses at a considerably reduced price. Everything is homemade here, including the terrific bread, and the food is colourful and fresh, although Claude does have the occasional urge to drop in one or two challenging flavour combinations.

Harwood Arms ✿

British modern T2

Fulham

Walham Grove ✉ SW6 1QP
✆ (020) 7386 1847
www.harwoodarms.com
⊖ Fulham Broadway.
Closed 24-27 December, 1 January and Monday lunch – booking essential

Menu £25 (weekday lunch) – Carte £38/46

Harwood Arms

It may be a very handsome pub in a smart postcode and with all its tables laid up for dining but there's nothing stuck-up or snooty about this place – in fact, the only thing that's superior is the cooking. It's British to its core, with its reassuringly concise, daily changing menu resolutely governed by our country's own seasonal produce. Cornish fish, Herdwick lamb, Cumbrian chicken and Wiltshire pork can all feature and game is a real strength of the kitchen whether it's the rabbit, grouse, or Hampshire Muntjac. Dishes have real depth and flavours are bold and satisfying. Service is smooth and assured and comes courtesy of a young yet experienced team and the well-chosen wine list offers a particularly good choice of mature claret. If you're sitting beneath the skylight then look up and you'll spot the roof-top vegetable and herb 'garden'. As this is still a pub, you can just pop in for a drink at the bar but if you do then be sure to order some of the great bar snacks like game rissoles or venison Scotch egg.

First Course

- Berkshire game faggots with celeriac and pickled walnuts.
- Hereford snails with oxtail, stout and smoked bone marrow.

Main Course

- Cod with Jersey Royals, purple sprouting broccoli and laverbread.
- Shoulder of Tamworth pork with pickled hops and pear.

Dessert

- Buttermilk pudding with English strawberries and toasted almonds.
- Warm semolina cake with rapeseed oil and chamomile ice cream.

Kozu

Japanese

Fulham

T2

58 New King's Rd ✉ SW6 4LS
✆ (020) 7731 2520
www.kozu.co.uk
⊖ Parsons Green
Closed 24-26 December and Monday

Carte £31/54

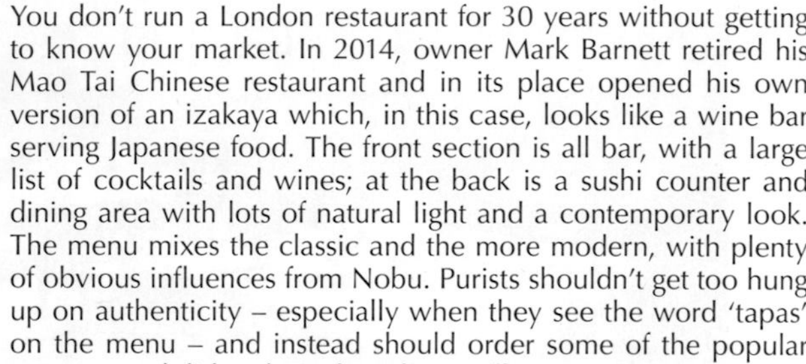

You don't run a London restaurant for 30 years without getting to know your market. In 2014, owner Mark Barnett retired his Mao Tai Chinese restaurant and in its place opened his own version of an izakaya which, in this case, looks like a wine bar serving Japanese food. The front section is all bar, with a large list of cocktails and wines; at the back is a sushi counter and dining area with lots of natural light and a contemporary look. The menu mixes the classic and the more modern, with plenty of obvious influences from Nobu. Purists shouldn't get too hung up on authenticity – especially when they see the word 'tapas' on the menu – and instead should order some of the popular tempura and dishes from the robata grill.

Malt House

British modern

Fulham

T2

17 Vanston Pl ✉ SW6 1AY
✆ (020) 7084 6888
www.malthousefulham.co.uk
⊖ Fulham Broadway.
Closed 25 December

Carte £23/42

Inside is so pristine and well-ordered, you begin to wonder if the bottles of sauce on the tables are there primarily to remind everyone that this really is still a pub. There are plenty of tables laid up for dining but there are also some sofas to add a more leisurely note and the general atmosphere is welcoming and friendly – the keen young staff help enormously in this regard. The appealing menu is all-encompassing enough to attract both the traditionalist and the more adventurous eater. Dishes are appealingly presented; meats grilled on the barbecue are something of a speciality and on Sundays three different roasts are offered. To further prove this is not your typical London boozer, there are six elegant bedrooms upstairs.

Manuka Kitchen

modern

Fulham

510 Fulham Rd ✉ SW6 5NJ
✆ (020) 7736 7588
www.manukakitchen.com
⊖ Fulham Broadway

Closed 16-30 August, 25-26 December, Sunday dinner and Monday

Menu £12 (weekday lunch) – Carte £22/29

A chef and an ex hotel manager chanced upon this former Italian restaurant and thought it the perfect spot for a venture of their own. Using only their own funds, they subsequently created this simply furnished little place, which they run with great enthusiasm. Their aim is to provide wholesome food at keen prices without compromising on the quality of the ingredients. Tyler, the chef, is from New Zealand, as is Manuka honey which is purported to have magical powers. His menu is appealing in its variety and dishes come with plenty of punch; the crispy squid is proving a very popular choice, as is the bolognese which uses Wagyu beef. Honey does also make occasional appearances – perhaps with the cheese or in a crème brûlée.

Sands End

British modern

Fulham

135-137 Stephendale Rd ✉ SW6 2PR
✆ (020) 7731 7823
www.thesandsend.co.uk
⊖ Fulham Broadway.

Closed 25 December – booking advisable

Menu £11 (weekday lunch) – Carte £28/39

Sands End is probably not the best known part of London, or indeed Fulham, but no doubt its residents prefer it that way so they can keep their eponymous pub to themselves. It's a cosy, warm and welcoming one, with a central bar offering some nifty homemade snacks, but try resisting because the main menu – which changes every few days – is pretty appealing itself. There's a distinct British bias which amounts to more than merely name-checking the birthplace of the ingredients. Winter dishes like braised lamb neck or roast partridge with Savoy cabbage are particularly pleasing and West Mersea oysters a good way of starting things off. There's a well-chosen and equally equitably priced wine list that sticks mostly to the Old World.

Tendido Cuatro

Spanish T2

Fulham

108-110 New Kings Rd ✉ SW6 4LY

✆ (020) 7371 5147

www.cambiodetercio.co.uk

⊖ Parsons Green

Closed 2 weeks Christmas

Menu £30 (lunch and early dinner) – Carte £24/46 

Any resemblance to their other restaurant in Old Brompton Road is entirely intentional: here too the front panels burst open in summer to reveal a warm interior where vivid colours are used with wild abandon. The main difference is that, along with tapas, the speciality is the Valencian classic, paella. Using bomba rice, the choice varies from seafood to quail and chorizo; vegetarian to cuttlefish ink. They are designed for two but that assumes a more than eager appetite, especially if you've had a couple of small dishes as a run-up. The tapas is nicely varied, from refreshing baby anchovies to crisp pig's ears. Service is spirited and the room comes alive later in the evening as the locals return from work and wander over.

Azou

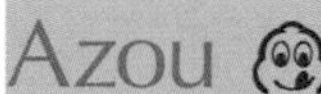

North-African S2

Hammersmith

375 King St ✉ W6 9NJ

✆ (020) 8563 7266

www.azou.co.uk

⊖ Stamford Brook

Closed 1 January and 25 December – booking essential – (dinner only)

Carte £20/38 

You'll probably walk past the first time and not notice this unassuming little place but, once visited, you won't walk past again. Inside is all silks, lanterns and rugs but it is also very personally run; the owner will often pop out from his kitchen to offer guidance – and his advice is well worth listening to. The cooking skips across North African countries – order some Algerian olives while you choose from the wide choice of main courses. Understandably, most of the regulars come here for a tajine, especially the Constantine with its tender lamb and triple-steamed couscous. Highlights to start include the terrific baba ganoush with homemade bread and fresh briouat. It's the perfect food to share as the dishes come in large portions.

Brackenbury

Mediterranean

Hammersmith

S1

129 - 131 Brackenbury Rd ✉ W6 0BQ
✆ (020) 8741 4928
www.brackenburyrestaurant.co.uk
⊖ Ravenscourt Park

Closed Christmas, Easter, Monday and dinner Sunday

Menu £22 (lunch) – Carte £28/36

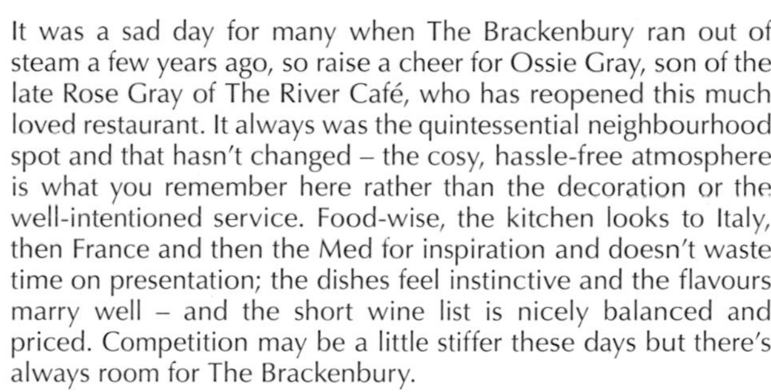

It was a sad day for many when The Brackenbury ran out of steam a few years ago, so raise a cheer for Ossie Gray, son of the late Rose Gray of The River Café, who has reopened this much loved restaurant. It always was the quintessential neighbourhood spot and that hasn't changed – the cosy, hassle-free atmosphere is what you remember here rather than the decoration or the well-intentioned service. Food-wise, the kitchen looks to Italy, then France and then the Med for inspiration and doesn't waste time on presentation; the dishes feel instinctive and the flavours marry well – and the short wine list is nicely balanced and priced. Competition may be a little stiffer these days but there's always room for The Brackenbury.

Crabtree

modern

Hammersmith

T2

4 Rainville Rd ✉ W6 9HA
✆ (020) 7385 3929
www.thecrabtreeW6.co.uk
⊖ Barons Court

Carte £25/38

A/C

On a sunny day few things in life beat being by the river in a London pub and The Crabtree certainly makes the most of its location. Its beer garden, with its barbeque-style menu, can seat over 80, while the dining room boasts its own terrace overlooking the river – and if you haven't yet booked for lunch on Boat Race day then you're probably already too late. A variety of ploys are used to fill the equally large interior of this Victorian beauty, from BYO Mondays to quiz nights on Tuesdays. For lunch the selection varies from ciabatta sarnies to shepherd's pie; the evening menu is more adventurous. The kitchen does things properly – parfaits and terrines are highlights and fish is perfectly timed – but vegetarians are also looked after.

Dartmouth Castle

Mediterranean

Hammersmith

S2

26 Glenthorne Rd ✉ W6 0LS

✆ (020) 8748 3614

www.thedartmouthcastle.co.uk

⊖ Hammersmith.

Closed 24 December-5 January

Carte £19/30

Plenty of locals pop into this Victorian pub just for a drink so you may find one of them has nabbed your table. It's worth biding your time though, as it's better than decamping to the upstairs room where the atmosphere isn't a patch on the bustling ground floor with its worn-in look and etched mirrors. Simply hand over your credit card and order at the bar to enjoy dishes from the well-priced and quite lengthy Mediterranean-influenced menu which is the same lunch and dinner. The antipasti platter for two is a winner and pasta dishes appear to come in two sizes – big or even bigger. The blackboard wine list is also a cut above your average pub list and uses the reliable Italian orientated merchant Liberty.

Hampshire Hog

British modern

Hammersmith

S2

227 King St ✉ W6 9JT

✆ (020) 8748 3391

www.thehampshirehog.com

⊖ Ravenscourt Park

Closed 24-25 December

Menu £10/28 – Carte £24/43

For many years the owners ran The Engineer, a much loved pub in Primrose Hill, before their lease ran out. They subsequently moved west, took over what was the Ruby Grand, did it up and gave it back its original name. The Hampshire Hog is a big old place and calls itself a 'pub and pantry' – the pantry is open for breakfast, tea and cakes and doubles as a private party room; the bright bar serves cocktails and snacks like Scotch quail eggs and pork boards; and the large dining room focuses on freshness and seasonality. So, in spring, that means asparagus or broad bean risotto; a choice of daily salads and popular main courses like marinated leg of lamb. Like The Engineer, The 'Hog' comes with a terrific terrace and garden.

Havelock Tavern

Mediterranean

T1

Hammersmith

57 Masbro Rd, Brook Grn ✉ W14 0LS
✆ (020) 7603 5374
www.havelocktavern.com
⊖ Kensington Olympia.
Closed 25-26 December

Carte £19/29 s

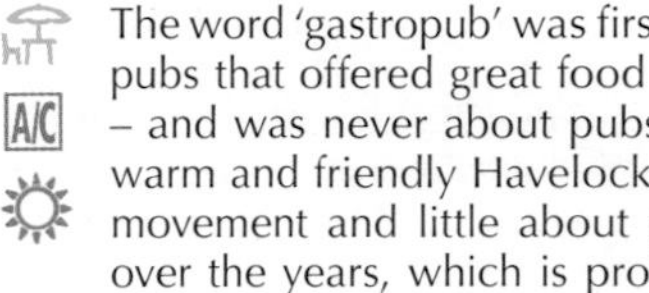

The word 'gastropub' was first coined in the early '90s to describe pubs that offered great food while remaining true to their roots – and was never about pubs masquerading as restaurants. The warm and friendly Havelock Tavern was at the vanguard of this movement and little about its lived-in look has changed here over the years, which is probably why it's as busy as ever. Put your name down for a table at the bar, order a drink and then place your order from the blackboard menu which changes with each service and reflects the seasons. The food is comforting and prices fair, while the freshness is underlined by the fact that dishes often run out; there could be grilled mackerel or goujons of coley alongside a tagine or roast pork belly.

Indian Zing

Indian

S1

Hammersmith

236 King St. ✉ W6 0RF
✆ (020) 8748 5959
www.indianzing.co.uk
⊖ Ravenscourt Park

Menu £12/27 – Carte £20/41

The menu tells you all you need to know: this is not your typical high street Indian restaurant. Chef-owner Manoj Vasaikar seeks inspiration from across the country and his cooking cleverly balances the traditional with the more contemporary. Evident care goes into the preparation of the fragrant dishes, which deliver many layers of flavours – lamb dishes are particularly good, as are the various breads. However, you'll see many customers giving the menu no more than a cursory glance – that's because they're regulars who know what they want before they get here, and is the reason why Karwari fish curry, lamb Rogan josh and the thalis can never be taken off the menu. Service is courteous and unhurried and the room judiciously lit.

Potli

Indian

Hammersmith

S2

319-321 King St ✉ W6 9NH
✆ (020) 8741 4328
www.potli.co.uk
⊖ Ravenscourt Park

Menu £20 (lunch and early dinner) – Carte £18/28

Potli is the latest Indian restaurant to try its luck on King Street. The two close friends behind it spent their formative years training with the Oberoi hotel group and they have created a smart and warmly run restaurant. It's named after a sort of spiced version of a bouquet garni which is apt as spicing plays a huge part here: the spices are ground – and the pastes made – in-house. The classically trained kitchen uses food markets from across India as their inspiration; some dishes are smaller-sized and inspired by street food while others are more traditional. 'Chicken 65' – spiced breast with black pepper – has quickly become a firm favourite, while the rich curries are often a highlight. Be sure to order a freshly made lassi.

Kew Grill

meats and grills

Kew

R2

10b Kew Grn. ✉ TW9 3BH
✆ (020) 8948 4433
www.awtrestaurants.com/kewgrill
⊖ Kew Gardens

Closed 25 December-4 January – booking essential

Carte £27/54

The canopy may be a little faded and the front door rather creaky, but don't be put off – inside, the welcome will be warm, the steaks are good and this long, narrow room will be full with locals. The lunch menu is a scaled down version of dinner but with better prices, along with sandwiches and snacks – you can even build your own burger. At dinner most customers go straight for steaks – Aberdeen Angus and hung for 35 days – which are expertly cooked and come with a wide choice of toppings, butters and sauces. There are daily specials too which could be a Dover sole, duck confit or lamb rump. Unreconstructed carnivores should consider pre-ordering the mixed grill; and puds are largely of the nursery variety.

River Café ✿

Italian

T2

Hammersmith

Thames Wharf, Rainville Rd ✉ W6 9HA
✆ (020) 7386 4200 – **www**.rivercafe.co.uk
⊖ Barons Court
Closed Christmas and New Year, Sunday dinner and bank holidays – booking essential

Carte £57/87

River Cafe

They should run a shuttle service from local catering colleges to the River Café so that the students can learn the secret of good cooking: good ingredients. There's a vigour and honesty to the kitchen and, with the chefs all on view as they go about their work, there seems to be more of a relationship here between cook and customer than is found in most restaurants. The big wood-fired oven really catches the eye and the restaurant seems to attract a wonderfully mixed bunch of customers, united in their appreciation of what makes a restaurant tick. That includes charming service: on looks alone, the team can rival those in glossier and glitzier restaurants but they break ranks here by actually smiling and caring about their customers. The menu is still written twice a day and head chef Sian Wyn Owen brings an added sparkle to the cooking. Things taste just the way you want them to taste. Ordering a pasta dish ought to be made compulsory and the Chocolate Nemesis dessert should be a recognised treatment for depression.

First Course

- Wood-roasted langoustines, chilli and oregano.
- English pea salad with 12 year old balsamic vinegar.

Main Course

- Roast turbot with broad beans and an anchovy and rosemary sauce.
- Veal chop roasted with salsa verde and braised violetta artichokes.

Dessert

- Panna cotta with champagne rhubarb.
- Chocolate Nemesis.

The Glasshouse ✿

modern

Kew

R2 

14 Station Par. ✉ TW9 3PZ
✆ (020) 8940 6777
www.glasshouserestaurant.co.uk
⊖ Kew Gardens
Closed 24-26 December and 1 January

Menu £28 (weekday lunch)/43

The Glasshouse

The Glasshouse is the very model of a modern neighbourhood restaurant. It sits in the heart of lovely, villagey Kew, always seems to be busy and is known for the quality and reliability of its cooking. The food is confident yet unshowy – much like the locals themselves, who are the restaurant's biggest fans – and comes with distinct Mediterranean flavours along with the occasional Asian hint. The kitchen is also using more Welsh ingredients these days, especially beef and lamb, as the chef is from north Wales. The wine list is well worth closer examination as it offers an interesting range by the glass and a particularly good selection of grower champagnes. The floor to ceiling windows create a feeling of space which cleverly distracts you from realising that actually the place is quite cramped – just don't let the staff sit you in the middle of the room as you'll feel surrounded by diners and staff rushing by. Service is eager and youthful.

First Course

- Octopus terrine with mussels, aioli, fennel and citrus dressing.
- Spring pea and mint soup with vermicelli and smoked ham hock.

Main Course

- Rump of lamb, pie, tongue, Lyonnaise onions and rosemary jus.
- Steamed hake with chicken wings, asparagus and pea raviolo.

Dessert

- Coconut semifreddo with alphonso mango and pineapple carpaccio.
- Cherry clafoutis with bay leaf ice cream.

Linnea

British modern

R2

Kew

12 Kew Grn. ✉ TW9 3BH

✆ (020) 8940 5696

www.linneakew.co.uk

⊖ Kew Gardens

Closed Christmas, Easter, 2 weeks August, Sunday and Monday

Carte £24/47

A/C Horticulturists will not be surprised to learn that the chef-owner of this attractive neighbourhood restaurant is from Sweden as Linnea is his country's national flower. It's also a rather apt name for a restaurant overlooking The Green and so close to Kew Gardens. The room, designed by Jonas's wife Elia, has a pared down yet elegant look and a Scandic feel, with candlelight casting a warm glow at night. The monthly changing menu offers a range of modern, unfussy, classically influenced dishes with Scandinavian techniques of pickling, curing and air-drying in evidence; go for any dish that includes mushrooms or berries. Flavours are clear and fresh and presentation is as pretty as the flower. Linnea is a restaurant that deserves to blossom.

Bibo

Italian

T2

Putney

146 Upper Richmond Rd ✉ SW15 2SW

✆ (020) 8780 0592

www.biborestaurant.com

⊖ East Putney

Closed 25-26 December and bank holiday Mondays

Carte £24/31

Few restaurateurs are as adept as Rebecca Mascarenhas in creating great neighbourhood restaurants and, with Bibo, she's hit the bullseye once again. This fun Italian restaurant has all the right component parts, from an appealing environment and clued-up service to food that's well priced and effortlessly easy to enjoy. It also ticks the accessibility box as it's somewhere you can just pop into for a drink and a plate of great nibbles. The same appealing menu is served at lunch and dinner, the top notch British and imported Italian produce is treated with care and dishes are refreshingly uncomplicated yet full of flavour. As the Latin name means 'to drink', it's no surprise that the wholly Italian wine list is also worth exploring.

Enoteca Turi

Italian

T2

Putney

28 Putney High St ✉ SW15 1SQ
✆ (020) 8785 4449 – **www.**enotecaturi.com
⊖ Putney Bridge
Closed 25-26 December, 1 January, Sunday and lunch bank holiday Mondays

Menu £19/34 – Carte £26/46

There is a corner of Putney that is forever Italy. Giuseppe Turi's restaurant has been warming the hearts of Putney residents for nearly 25 years and he shows no signs of slowing down. One reason for its longevity – apart from Giuseppe himself obviously – is that it has had the same ethos since the day it opened: top quality produce, cooked with care and considerable pride. The emphasis is on Northern Italy and while the dishes are certainly appealing to the eye, they are also full of flavour. The restaurant itself seems to be unique in that there are no bad tables and the room has an appealing Mediterranean feel. Service is slick and smooth and wine plays a huge part in the experience, with lesser known Italian producers to the fore.

Prince of Wales

British modern

T2

Putney

138 Upper Richmond Rd ✉ SW15 2SP
✆ (020) 8788 1552
www.princeofwalesputney.co.uk
⊖ East Putney.
Closed 23 December-1 January and Monday lunch except bank holidays

Carte £25/39

Idiosyncratic decoration and good food make this substantial Victorian pub stand out. Its deep green walls are lined with tankards and its ceiling is covered in playing cards; head further in and you'll find the dining room in the old billiard room. Here lights are fashioned from antlers and its walls are decorated with vintage farming photos and a little taxidermy; mind you, it's so dimly lit you'll be pushed see anything. The kitchen is out to impress and its daily changing menu reads well, ranging from rabbit and pork terrine to Cornish sardines and even a plate of Spanish delicacies. Although the ingredients are top-notch, the plates are sometimes a little too busy which perhaps explains the popularity of the simpler bar menu.

Bingham Restaurant

modern

Richmond

R3

Bingham Hotel, 61-63 Petersham Rd. ✉ TW1O 6UT
✆ (020) 8940 0902
www.thebingham.co.uk
⊖ Richmond
Closed Sunday dinner

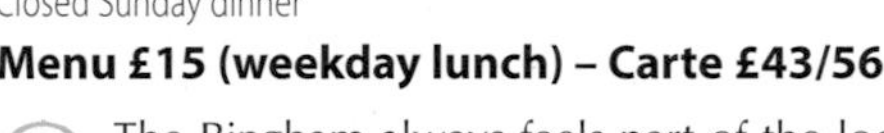

Menu £15 (weekday lunch) – Carte £43/56

The Bingham always feels part of the local community and has lots of supporters in the neighbourhood who use it for a variety of different occasions. Perhaps its location, within a relatively unremarkable looking building, does it a favour as the restaurant has something of a 'hidden jewel' feel about it and the décor is surprisingly swish and comfortable. Come on a warm summer's day and you could find yourself having lunch on the balcony terrace, looking out over a garden and the Thames – and you don't get that everywhere. The cooking is contemporary and displays some original touches, however, dishes don't always deliver the flavours promised by the impressive presentation.

Dysart Arms

modern

Richmond

R3

135 Petersham Rd ✉ TW10 7AA
✆ (020) 8940 8005
www.thedysartpetersham.co.uk
Closed Sunday dinner – booking advisable

Menu £19 (weekdays) – Carte £30/51

Overlooking Richmond Park and built in the early 1900s as part of the Arts and Crafts movement, the Dysart Arms is named after the family who once lived in Ham House. The owners decided to run it as a restaurant rather than a pub and have created a bright and fresh space that successfully blends its period features with more contemporary design elements. Service comes with a formality that seems somewhat at odds with this environment yet the formula clearly pleases the locals. The menu is also a blend of styles – the young chef uses top-notch ingredients and his cooking comes with a classical base to which he adds subtle Asian tones to create quite refined, delicately flavoured dishes. Look out for the occasional musical recital evening.

Matsuba

Japanese

Richmond

10 Red Lion St ✉ TW9 1RW
(020) 8605 3513
⊖ Richmond
Closed 25-26 December, 1 January and Sunday

R2

Carte £21/39 

A/C

Matsuba is a small, family-run place that is so understated it's easy to miss – look out for the softly lit sign above the narrow façade. The interior is equally compact and low-key, with just a dozen or so tables along with a small counter at the back with room for four more. In fact the biggest thing in the room is the menu, which offers a comprehensive tour through most recognisable points in Japanese cooking. The owners are Korean so you can also expect to see bulgogi, the Korean barbecue dish of marinated meat that comes on a sizzling plate. All the food is fresh and the ingredients are good; lunch sees some very good value set menus. The service is well-meaning and it's hard not to come away thinking kind thoughts.

Petersham Nurseries Café

modern

Richmond

Church Ln (off Petersham Rd) ✉ TW10 7AG
(020) 8940 5230
www.petershamnurseries.com
Closed 25-26 December and Monday – booking advisable – (lunch only)

R3 

Carte £31/52 

On a summer's day there can be few more delightful spots for lunch than the Café at Petersham Nurseries. Buy into the whole Sunday-supplement charm of the place and you'll find that, whether you're on the terrace or inside the greenhouse with its wobbly tables and soil floor, the hustle and hassle of modern life seem a world away. The cooking is a perfect match for this rural retreat: it uses the freshest of seasonal produce in unfussy and flavoursome dishes. Nothing – apart from the daily sorbet – is frozen here and fridges are nigh on empty at the end of each day. Many herbs and leaves come from their own gardens and dishes, like shoulder of lamb with cime di rapa and anchovies, come with a subtle Italian accent.

Swagat

Indian

Richmond

R2

86 Hill Rise ✉ TW10 6UB
✆ (020) 8940 7557
www.swagatindiancuisine.co.uk
⊖ Richmond
Closed 25-26 December – booking essential – (dinner only)

Menu £25 – Carte £18/31

This likeable little Indian restaurant is run by two friends; they met while training with Oberoi hotels in India before coming to London to work in the capital's best Indian restaurants. One organises the warm, well-meaning service while the other partner ensures his kitchen delivers the authentic and satisfying dishes, some of which come with North Indian influences. Dishes display a pleasing degree of lightness and subtlety so the first taste is always that of the prime ingredient rather than the spice; there's a health dividend to some of the dishes, such as sea bass with chilli with ginger; and vegetarians have plenty of choice. Add in complimentary poppadoms and chutneys and you can see why it's a hit with the locals.

Princess Victoria

British traditional

Shepherd's Bush

S1

217 Uxbridge Rd ✉ W12 9DH
✆ (020) 8749 5886
www.princessvictoria.co.uk
⊖ Shepherd's Bush.
Closed 24-27 December

Menu £13 (weekday lunch) – Carte £21/45

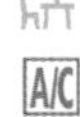

London has a wealth of fine Victorian gin palaces but few are as grand as Princess Victoria. From the friezes to the etched glass, the portraits to the parquet floor, the last restoration created a terrific pub. Mind you, that's not all that impresses: there's a superb, wide-ranging wine list, with carafes and glasses providing flexibility; enticing bar snacks ranging from quail eggs to salt cod croquettes; a great menu that could include roasted skate wing or homemade pork and herb sausages; and, most importantly, cooking that's executed with no little skill. Those with proclivities for all things porcine will find much to savour – charcuterie is a passion here and the board may well include pig's cheeks and rillettes.

Earl Spencer

Mediterranean T3

Southfields

260-262 Merton Rd ✉ SW18 5JL
✆ (020) 8870 9244
www.theearlspencer.com
⊖ Southfields
Closed 25-26 December

Carte £23/30

The owner worked at this Edwardian pub over a decade ago and so jumped at the chance of actually buying it himself – he felt he had "unfinished business" here. It's a handsome pub, standing a baseline lob away from the All England Tennis Club and its small terrace overlooks a showroom of the finest 4-wheel thoroughbreds. Inside is bright and welcoming, with many of the original features and fittings restored, but it's the cooking that really sets it apart. The experienced brigade are strict apostles of seasonality – the menu can sometimes change twice a day – and everything is homemade. Flavours are assured and ingredients marry well. The one entry in the debit column is that you have to keep going up to the bar to order everything.

Al Borgo

Italian R3

Teddington

3 Church Rd. ✉ TW11 8PF
✆ (020) 8943 4456
www.alborgo.co.uk
Closed 1-9 January, Sunday and bank holidays

Menu £18 (weekdays) – Carte £25/45

Aside from being home to Ted, love rival to Ernie the Fastest Milkman in the West, Teddington has rarely featured in the national consciousness – but a few more restaurants like Al Borgo may start to change people's perceptions. This refreshingly unpretentious Italian eatery, owned and keenly run by Brescia born Marco and his partner Nikola, exudes warmth and bonhomie in the way that only a true neighbourhood restaurant can. The menu cleverly appeals to both traditionalists and those who are a little more adventurous. The focaccia is homemade, as is the pasta; try the tagliolini with scallops or the pumpkin tortelli with sage. Special seasonal offerings such as a black truffle menu prove popular and there's a great value lunch menu too.

King's Head

modern

Teddington

123 High St ✉ TW11 8HG
(020) 3166 2900
www.whitebrasserie.com
⊖ Teddington (Rail).
Closed 25 December

R3

Menu £12/14 – Carte £19/34

Britain has its pubs and France its brasseries; The King's Head does its bit for the entente cordiale by combining both. Raymond Blanc's team has given this Victorian pub a tidy makeover and, although there might not be much character left, they have created a suitably warm environment. The brasserie at the back is run by a pleasant, enthusiastic team and the menus offer all comers plenty of choice. Classic brasserie dishes such as Toulouse sausages and beef stroganoff come with a satisfyingly rustic edge, while the dual-nationality element is maintained through the inclusion of a ploughman's board alongside the charcuterie. Steaks on the charcoal grill are popular and families are lured in by the decent kiddies menu.

Rétro Bistrot

French

Teddington

114-116 High St ✉ TW11 8JB
(0208) 9772 239
www.retrobistrot.co.uk
Closed first 2 weeks August, first 10 days January and Sunday dinner

R3

Menu £13/23 – Carte £27/48

There's substance as well as style to this classic French bistrot. The kitchen brigade were once teammates at the much missed Monsieur Max, so they know their way around a French menu. Moules marinière, coq au vin, foie de veau and crème brûlée – all the classics of bourgeois cuisine are here and all are prepared with innate skill and understanding. Lunch and early evening menus are a steal, and the service team display equal commitment to the cause as cheeks are kissed and cries of "bon appétit" ring out. The mix of fabrics, exposed brick walls, simple tables and art for sale creates a very genial environment. The best seats are in the room at the back with the partially open kitchen, which adds aroma and a little more noise.

Simply Thai

Thai

Teddington

R3

196 Kingston Rd. ✉ TW11 9JD
(020) 8943 9747
www.simplythai-restaurant.co.uk
Closed 25-26 December – (dinner only)

Menu £16 – Carte £21/32

A/C

Over the years, this simple Thai restaurant in the heart of suburbia has built up a loyal clientele. They describe the cooking as 'a healthy approach to eating' and there's a bewildering array of dishes to choose from; if you're struggling to decide, pick one of Patria's signature dishes. What the cooking lacks in authenticity (it's adjusted for Western tastes), it makes up for in its commendable use of British ingredients. You might find cod dumplings in green curry sauce or rack of lamb marinated with Thai spices. The budget conscious should come on a Sunday for the street food selection, while the dipping sauces, made in house, are good any day of the week. Service is friendly but don't be surprised if things slow down as the place fills up.

Chicken Shop

meats and grills

Tooting

T3

141 Tooting High St ✉ SW17 0SY
(020) 8767 5200
www.chickenshop.com
⊖ Tooting Broadway
Bookings not accepted

Carte £15/18

These days everyone is looking for a restaurant concept to 'roll out' across the capital. When Soho House's Chicken Shop opened in Kentish Town it was fairly obvious that it was only a matter of time before a second branch popped up, although few guessed that Tooting would be the chosen location. Success, though, seems assured once again, thanks largely to their ingenious idea of just offering a whole, half or quarter chicken with a few sides and a couple of puddings. The chickens are plump and succulent, the wine is served in jugs and the corn on the cob is painted with garlic butter – who hasn't just licked their lips? The other element they get spot on is the service: staff have clearly bought into the concept and are very engaging.

A Cena

Italian

Twickenham

R2

418 Richmond Rd. ✉ TW1 2EB
✆ (020) 8288 0108
www.acena.co.uk
⊖ Richmond
Closed Sunday dinner, Monday lunch and bank holidays

Carte £17/46

The constantly evolving menu at this bigger-than-you-first-think Italian restaurant, just over Richmond Bridge, covers all parts of the country, although you can expect more of a nod to the north in the colder months when dishes become a little heartier. The cooking is fresh and tasty; pasta is most certainly a highlight and desserts, although limited in choice, are usually done well too. The front section of the restaurant can feel a little cramped and it's at the back where it all seems to be happening. The owners are not actually Italian but his mother is and she clearly exerted quite an influence because his passion and enthusiasm are obvious. They also own a nearby foodstore and butcher's.

Brula

French

Twickenham

R3

43 Crown Rd., St Margarets ✉ TW1 3EJ
✆ (020) 8892 0602
www.brula.co.uk
Closed 26 December, Sunday dinner and Monday – booking essential

Menu £15/20 – Carte £24/44

Brula is already well past its tenth birthday and this relative longevity can be put down to a combination of reliable cooking, sensible prices and personable service. This pretty Victorian building has been both a pub and a butcher's shop in the past but now thoroughly suits its role as an authentic looking bistro. France remains at the heart of the cooking but over the past couple of years influences from Spain and Italy have started to appear on the menu, which is priced per dish rather than per course as it once was. Cooking is also more exact in its execution. The cheeses and the thoughtfully arranged wine list remain exclusively French. The friendly and helpful service also extends to those using one of the private rooms.

Crown

British traditional

Twickenham

R3

174 Richmond Rd, St Margarets ✉ TW1 2NH
(020) 8892 5896
www.crowntwickenham.co.uk
⊖ St Margarets (Rail)
Closed 26 December

Carte £23/36

Much to the delight of St Margarets residents, this fine-looking Georgian pub has been revived and revitalised. Setting the scene are an old lantern hanging above the entrance and a mosaic floor inlaid with the pub's name, while inside it feels relaxed and stylish, with parquet floors, feature fireplaces and bright colours; sit in the airy, elegant rear restaurant, with its high vaulted ceiling and garden view. There's something for everyone on the global menus, from sharing boards and classic pub dishes to Mediterranean-influenced fish stew or Asian-inspired Tom Yum Thai prawns and squid. Portions are ample and cooking fresh, tasty and reliable. Service is enthusiastic and the pretty beer garden is popular with drinkers and diners alike.

Cannizaro House

modern

Wimbledon

S3

Cannizaro House Hotel,
West Side, Wimbledon Common ✉ SW19 4UE
(020) 8879 1464
www.cannizarohouse.com
⊖ Wimbledon

Menu £45

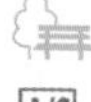

London can offer the curious epicurean a vast number of dining options and, with Cannizaro House, that now includes a part-Georgian mansion in 34 acres of parkland. There is a choice to be made once you're here: you can sit in the elegant and classically dressed main room or the more intimate, glass fronted Loggia overlooking the Italian sunken garden. The set price menu offers a range of carefully prepared and appealing British dishes with a modern edge – some dishes are quite simple, others more ambitious, but flavours and textures always work well together and presentation is appealing. A preponderance of business types can sometimes lend too much of a corporate feel to proceedings but staff keep things light and relaxed.

Chez Bruce ✿

French

U3

Wandsworth

2 Bellevue Rd ✉ SW17 7EG

✆ (020) 8672 0114

www.chezbruce.co.uk

⊖ Tooting Bec

Closed 24-26 December and 1 January – booking essential

Menu £28/45

A/C

Chez Bruce

Not only did Chez Bruce weather the choppy waters of recession better than most but it finally expanded into the old deli next door. What this meant for its merry band of dependable followers was nothing more than 'business as usual', as Chez Bruce has had a successful formula for years. That means flavoursome and uncomplicated food, sprightly service, sensible prices and an easy-going atmosphere. Matthew Christmas is the head man in the kitchen, having worked closely with Bruce Poole for over 10 years. His cooking provides an object lesson in the importance of flavours and balance: dishes are never too crowded and natural flavours are to the fore. The base is largely classical French but comes with Mediterranean tones, so expect words like parfait, pastilla, brandade and confit. The menu offers an even-handed selection, with a choice of around seven dishes per course. Cheese is always worth exploring and coffee comes with shortbread at lunch and terrific palmiers at dinner.

First Course

- Calf's brains with dressed Puy lentils, sauce gribiche and capocollo.
- Red mullet with sauce vierge, courgette flower fritter and tapenade.

Main Course

- Sea bass with morels, garlic leaves, crushed potatoes and asparagus.
- Crisp pork belly with borlotti beans, boudin blanc and salsa verde.

Dessert

- Lemon meringue ice cream sandwich with lemon curd and poppy seeds.
- Hot chocolate pudding with praline parfait.

Fox and Grapes

British modern

Wimbledon

S3

9 Camp Rd ✉ SW19 4UN
✆ (020) 8619 1300
www.foxandgrapeswimbledon.co.uk
⊖ Wimbledon.
Closed 25 December

Carte £20/46

The Fox and Grapes is discreetly tucked away on the south side of the common, amongst a row of old workers' cottages, and is surprisingly spacious inside, with a low-ceilinged snug and a vaulted room complete with leaded windows and chandeliers. The menu is concise, offering simply cooked dishes which let the ingredients do the talking. Pies and burgers sit alongside Mediterranean-inspired dishes and the likes of Tandoori hake, while steaks cooked on the Josper grill will satisfy those with the heartiest of appetites. To start, the avocado prawn cocktail has become something of a speciality; to finish, the puddings are of the proper, no-nonsense variety and come with a port or sherry recommendation. Three modern bedrooms complete the picture.

Lawn Bistro

modern

Wimbledon

T3

67 High St. ✉ SW19 5EE
✆ (020) 8947 8278
www.thelawnbistro.co.uk
⊖ Wimbledon
Closed 18 August-2 September, Sunday dinner and Monday

Menu £15/25 – Carte £26/44

Those disheartened by the homogenised look of most UK high streets will be cheered by the prominent position of Lawn Bistro in Wimbledon Village. This attractive room is comfortable and relaxed, with leather seating down one side facing the well-stocked bar. A personable Frenchman is at the helm in the kitchen and those who know their south London restaurants will recognise the signs of a previous engagement at La Trompette: his menu is an appealing mix of modern European dishes and his cooking is clean and well-defined. The kitchen does its own butchery and uses ingredients wisely: lunchtimes' saddle of rabbit with offal becomes a rabbit and ale casserole at dinner; similarly, it's leg of guinea fowl leg for lunch, breast for dinner.

Light House

Mediterranean

Wimbledon

75-77 Ridgway ✉ SW19 4ST
✆ (020) 8944 6338
www.lighthousewimbledon.com
⊖ Wimbledon

Closed 25-26 December, 1 January and Sunday dinner

T3

Menu £15/24 – Carte £25/44

The façade may have been smartened up but one's first impression is of being in a branded operation. Fortunately, that notion is quickly dispelled by the quality of the food. While they still have the odd Thai dish, it is in Italy where the majority of the menu and the kitchen's strengths lie, with a roll-call of favourites that include tagliatelle, gnocchi, saltimbocca and panna cotta. The food is wholesome and confident, with plenty of bold flavours and prices at lunch and early evening are attractive, which ensures that it is often very busy. The result is that the young team can sometimes struggle to keep up, but they remain admirably calm and cheery. As this was once a shop selling lights and fittings, it is fittingly well lit.

Good food without spending a fortune? Look for the Bib Gourmand ☺.

Thierry Burot/Fotolia.com

Where to **stay**

▸ *These 50 recommended hotels are extracted from the Great Britain & Ireland 2015 guide, where you'll find a larger choice of hotels selected by our team of inspectors.*

Ampersand

10 Harrington Rd ✉ SW7 3ER
✆ (020) 7589 5895
www.ampersandhotel.com
⊖ South Kensington.

E6

111 rm – †£155/170 ††£174/216, ☕ £14 – 5 suites

The Ampersand hotel is an elegant, converted Victorian hotel surrounded by some of the world's greatest museums, in the heart of London's cultural centre. Its bedroom decoration is inspired by five themes which inform these museums: botany, music, geometry, ornithology and astronomy. This undoubtedly adds some personality to the bedrooms, which come in all sorts of different categories: some have balconies, others free-standing baths. All are thoughtfully lit and although they are far from being the largest rooms around, they do all have smart bathrooms and a good number of extras. Snacks, coffee, tea and cakes are served in the brightly decorated Drawing Rooms, while Apero is the intimate restaurant in the basement offering a Mediterranean-influenced menu. Traditionalists may need time getting used to seeing staff wearing jeans but they'll also find that this is a professionally run, smart and comfortable hotel in a terrific location.

Andaz Liverpool Street

40 Liverpool St. ✉ EC2M 7QN
✆ (020) 7961 1234
www.andaz.com
⊖ Liverpool Street
🍴 **1901** *(See restaurant listing)*

M2

267 rm – ♂£144/402 ♂♂£180/438, ☕ £18 – 3 suites

Andaz Liverpool Street

The philosophy behind Hyatt's Andaz brand is to create luxury hotels with a less structured, less formal feel. On a practical level, this means that there is literally no barrier between arriving guest and receptionist, nor between cocktail-drinker and barman – it's all central islands and general mingling. This does create a more relaxed environment – being served a drink while someone checks you in on their iPad does come as a nice change – but you do subsequently find yourself trying to work out who are the guests and who are the staff. The bedrooms are modern and slick; those in the older Victorian part of the hotel are the best, with high ceilings and quite a masculine feel. The hotel is a labyrinth of corridors, floors and different areas which means there is also a plethora of dining options available to discourage you from ever leaving: there's the ersatz pub called George, the grandiose 1901, the rather sweet little Japanese Miyako restaurant and a big brasserie that specialises in the grilling of red meats.

Aster House

3 Sumner Pl. ✉ SW7 3EE
✆ (020) 7581 5888
www.asterhouse.com
⊖ South Kensington

E6

13 rm☕ – †£90/135 ††£120/295

Michelin

If you made a mathematical calculation to find the best location for a tourist in London, then chances are the X would mark a spot somewhere near Aster House on Sumner Place. You've got all the best museums within strolling distance; Hyde Park mere minutes away; all the famous shops and, above all, you're staying in a charming Victorian house in a typical Kensington street where people actually live rather than in a faceless hotel district. Mr and Mrs Tan keep the house commendably shipshape and are enthusiastic hosts. The bedrooms at the front of the house benefit from larger windows while those at the back are quieter and overlook the garden, but all boast fairly high ceilings and room to breathe. Wi-fi is available without charge in all the rooms, while L'Orangerie, a first floor conservatory looking down over Sumner Place, doubles as the breakfast room and guests' sitting room. Prices are also kept within the parameters of decency so bookings need to be made plenty of time in advance.

Berkeley

Wilton Pl ✉ SW1X 7RL
✆ (020) 7235 6000
www.the-berkeley.co.uk
⊖ Knightsbridge
Koffmann's and Marcus *(See restaurant listing)*

G4

210 rm – †£270/720 ††£330/840, ☕ £32 – 28 suites

The Berkeley

You'd have thought that having Marcus Wareing's luxury restaurant on one side of the hotel would be enough, but the hotel then coaxed Pierre Koffmann out of retirement and his restaurant now provides the bookend on the other side. In the middle you have the Blue Bar which is as cool as the name suggests and, on the other side of the lobby, the Caramel Room whose target audience is obvious when you consider that tea is called "Prêt-à-Portea" and the biscuits look like mini handbags. The most unique area of the hotel must be the 7th floor, with its rooftop pool, treatment rooms and personal training services to satisfy the most slavishly health-conscious traveller. By using a number of different designers, bedrooms have been given both personality and a sense of individualism; the most recent have softer, calmer colours and a lighter, more contemporary feel while the classic rooms feel richer, thanks to their deeper, more intense colours. All the rooms are immaculately kept and several of the suites have their own balcony.

Blakes

33 Rowland Gdns ✉ SW7 3PF
✆ (020) 7370 6701
www.blakeshotels.com
⊖ Gloucester Road

D6

47 rm ☕ – 🚹£215/300 🚹🚹£263/359 – 8 suites

Blakes

Following a couple of years of uncertainty, Blakes is now back in private hands and the young owner is busy investing considerable funds in its upgrade and upkeep. Created by Anouska Hempel in the early '80s, this was one of London's original 'boutique' hotels. It was exuberantly decorated then and remains so now; it also represents the perfect antidote to the plethora of generic corporate hotels that seemingly pop up overnight. The lavish decoration, the dramatic four-poster beds and the rich fabrics remind you that staying in a hotel can be a thrilling, erotic and sensual experience – this isn't the sort of hotel for those who get excited by the sight of a trouser-press and a miniature kettle. That being said, the mod cons are all here, but they're camouflaged and concealed. Downstairs is a slick and stylish affair, from the dark and mysterious Chinese Room and bar, to the intimate restaurant with its ambitious Asian-influenced menu – and there is a charming courtyard at the back, perfect for hiding out.

Brown's

Albemarle St ✉ W1S 4BP
✆ (020) 7493 6020
www.roccofortehotels.com
⊖ Green Park
🍴 **Hix Mayfair** *(See restaurant listing)*

H3

117 rm – †£420/905 ††£460/945, ☕ £32 – 12 suites

Brown's

Opened in 1837 by James Brown, Lord Byron's butler, Brown's has a long and distinguished history and has been the favoured hotel of many a visiting dignitary: it was here that Alexander Graham Bell first demonstrated his telephone and The Kipling Suite is just one named after a former guest. It reopened in 2005 after a full face-lift, with Olga Polizzi personally overseeing the design and her blending of the traditional with the modern works well. The bedrooms have personality and reflect the character of the hotel, albeit with all of today's required gadgetry. One thing that has remained constant is the popularity of the afternoon teas – the selling point, apart from the pianist, is that the waiter replenishes all stands and pots without extra charge. The wood-panelled restaurant took slightly longer to bed in and now goes by the name of Hix at The Albemarle; the menu features British comfort food. The Donovan Bar is probably the hotel's best feature and celebrates the distinguished work of British photographer Terence Donovan.

Bulgari

171 Knightsbridge ✉ SW7 1DW
✆ (020) 7151 1010
www.bulgarihotels.com/london
⊖ Knightsbridge
🍴 **Rivea** *(See restaurant listing)*

F4

85 rm – †£528/1,128 ††£528/1,128, ☕ £24 – 7 suites

Bulgari

Having wowed them in Milan, Bulgari waited until they'd found the perfect location before creating this London jewel. This is a hotel that shouts style, with silver its underlying theme in homage to the brand's silversmith origins. Actually, it is so cool, so impeccably tailored, it wouldn't possibly be caught shouting anything. The dark lobby, with its camouflaged staff, sets the tone of restrained elegance and leads into the sleek bar. From there it is down a sweeping staircase to the Alain Ducasse restaurant, where the Italian and French small plates are bursting with colour and freshness. The hotel is on 15 floors but six of those are underground and used for a state-of-the-art spa, a ballroom and a terrific cinema. The bedrooms are stunning and all about sensual curves, polished mahogany, silks and black marble; the bathrooms are worth the price of admission alone and there are some delightful touches, such as minibars hidden within upright trunks. Unlike other fashion-led hotels, there is real substance behind the style here and an emphasis on comfort.

The Capital

22-24 Basil St. ✉ SW3 1AT
(020) 7589 5171
www.capitalhotel.co.uk
⊖ Knightsbridge
Outlaw's at The Capital *(See restaurant listing)*

F5

49 rm – £200/340 ££250/430, £17 – 1 suite

The Capital

The Capital is one of London's most enduringly discreet and comfortable hotels and is thoroughly British in its feel. It is owned by David Levin, who opened it in 1971, and it is this continuity which has lead directly to there only being five head chefs in over 40 years. The restaurant is as elegant as ever, with a menu filled with classic British dishes and an extensive wine list that includes selections from the Levins' own winery in the Loire. Bedrooms remain classically chic and the contemporary embellishments are restrained and in keeping with the general atmosphere. Each floor is slightly different and uses designs from the likes of Mulberry, Ralph Lauren and Nina Campbell. What has always raised The Capital to greater heights than similarly styled hotels has been the depth and detail of the service. No one can walk through the small lobby without being greeted and the concierge is old-school in the best sense of the word and can arrange anything for anyone.

Charlotte Street

15 Charlotte St ✉ W1T 1RJ
(020) 7806 2000
www.charlotteestreethotel.co.uk
⊖ Goodge Street

I2

52 rm – †£264/330 ††£360/492, ☕ £20 – 4 suites

A/C

Firmdale

Expect the lobby and bar to be full of men with man-bags and horn-rimmed specs, for Charlotte Street is the hotel of choice for those in the advertising industry. But even if you've never pitched, promoted or placed a product and are just after a stylish, contemporary hotel in a street thronged with bars and restaurants then get on the mailing list here. Oscar is the busy bar and restaurant that spills out onto the street in summer; its sunny, contemporary European menu and vivid mural brighten it in winter. Film Club is on Sunday evening: dinner followed by a film in the downstairs screening room. Those after some quiet can nab one of the sofas in the Drawing Room or Library. The bedrooms are, as with all hotels in the Firmdale group, exceptionally well looked after. Every year, three or four are fully refurbished and one thing you'll never see is a bit of dodgy grouting or a scuff mark. They are all decorated in an English style but there is nothing chintzy or twee about them. Bathrooms are equally immaculate and the baths face little flat screen TVs.

ⓝ Chiltern Firehouse

1 Chiltern St ✉ W1U 7PA **G2**
✆ (020) 7073 7676
www.chilternfirehouse.com
⊖ Baker Street
🍴 **Chiltern Firehouse** *(See restaurant listing)*

26 rm – †£480/900 ††£540/1,020, ☕ £20 – 6 suites

Anyone familiar with André Balazs' portfolio of properties will know that where he goes, the celebrity world follows. From Chateau Marmont in Hollywood to The Mercer in New York, his group of hotels are so effortlessly cool that they exist beyond the mere vicissitudes of fashion. For his grand London entrance, he has taken a gothic Victorian former fire station in Marylebone and sympathetically restored and extended it. Compared with the frenzy that is the Chiltern Firehouse restaurant, this is a veritable sanctuary of calm and tranquility. From the snug sitting room to the handsome cocktail bar, the style is accompanied by an easy elegance and the real joy of the place is that it hardly feels like a hotel at all. The 26 rooms are a striking mix of modern and art deco forms, in a mix of colours and styles – there is no uniformity to be found anywhere in this building. Even the staff were chosen for the care they would give, rather than for the experience they have garnered.

Claridge's

Brook St ✉ W1K 4HR
✆ (020) 7629 8860
www.claridges.co.uk
⊖ Bond Street
🍴 **Fera at Claridge's** *(See restaurant listing)*

G3

203 rm – †£480/780 ††£540/900, ☕ £32 – 67 suites

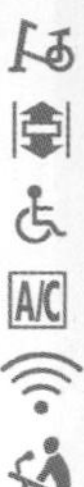

Claridge's

Claridge's has a long and very illustrious history dating back to 1812 and this iconic and very British hotel has been a favourite of the royal family over generations. The hotel has kept its place at the top table of London addresses by recognising that reputations are forged because of the quality of the service rather than mere longevity or striking architecture. That being said, no modern, purpose-built hotel could afford the extravagance of having such wide corridors, such ornate decoration or such sumptuous bedrooms. Art deco is the hotel's most striking design feature and it is kept suitably fresh and buffed. Despite its glittery past, Claridge's has never been in danger of becoming a museum piece; the David Collins designed bar attracts a more youthful crowd and The Foyer, with its eye-catching light sculpture, proves that afternoon tea need not be a stuffy or quaint affair. Even the restaurant has been re-launched – it is now called Fera and is under the aegis of chef Simon Rogan.

Connaught

Carlos Pl. ✉ W1K 2AL
✆ (020) 7499 7070 – **www**.the-connaught.co.uk
⊖ Bond Street
🍴 **Hélène Darroze at The Connaught**
(See restaurant listing)

G3 

121 rm☕ – †£400/840 ††£450/990 – 26 suites 

The Connaught

The restored, refurbished and rejuvenated Connaught still retains a sense of effortless serenity and exclusivity – but has now been discovered by a new generation. These sprightlier guests should take the stairs up to their room, that way they'll see the largest mahogany staircase in the country. The bedrooms are now more contemporary in style; they have wooden floors, leather worked into the soft furnishings and come with larger marble bathrooms; some overlook a small oriental garden, others peer down on mews houses. All rooms have full butler service and use linen specially woven in Milan and toiletries from Daylesford. The Coburg Bar honours the hotel's original name and its seats are so deep it's a wonder anyone ever leaves. In contrast, the Connaught Bar attracts a more youthful clientele. Hélène Darroze oversees the restaurant with her refined French cooking and Espelette is an all-day venue just off the lobby that offers a weekly changing list of classic French and British dishes. If you need anything, just ask one of the hotel's 300 members of staff.

Covent Garden

10 Monmouth St ✉ WC2H 9HB
✆ (020) 7806 1000
www.firmdalehotels.com
⊖ Covent Garden
🍴 **Brasserie Max** *(See restaurant listing)*

I3

58 rm – †£282/348 ††£342/420, ☕ £20 – 1 suite

Firmdale

The Covent Garden Hotel has always been hugely popular with those of a theatrical bent, whether cast or audience member, not least because of its central location, a mere saunter away from the majority of playhouses and productions. The hotel was once a French hospital – the words 'Nouvel hopital et dispensaire francais' are still etched into the brickwork – but the style is essentially British. Mannequins, soft fabrics and antique furniture are juxtaposed with crisp lines and contemporary colours to create a very stylish and comfortable environment. The first floor residents-only wood-panelled sitting room is a delight and so is occasionally used by a visiting grandee for a backdrop to an interview; the presence of an honesty bar adds further to the appeal. The Screening Room holds weekend dinner-and-a-film nights, while Brasserie Max feels much more like a proper restaurant than a mere addendum; its menu is appealingly accessible and afternoon tea is a popular event.

Dorchester

Park Ln. ✉ W1K 1QA G4
(020) 7629 8888 – **www**.dorchestercollection.com
Hyde Park Corner
Alain Ducasse at The Dorchester and China Tang
(See restaurant listing)

250 rm – †£355 ††£415, £34 – 50 suites

The Dorchester

The Dorchester has been a byword for luxury and elegance since it opened in the 1930s and constant reinvestment over the decades has ensured that this grandest of hotels has remained one of London's finest. For many, The Promenade is the first port of call: afternoon tea in its gilded surroundings is as popular as ever, so much so that there's now a mezzanine level above the lobby. If you're coming here to dine you have the choice of three restaurants: The Grill, which was being redesigned as we went to press, is for all things British; the luxuriously adorned Alain Ducasse restaurant, with its exceptional cuisine, waves Le Tricolore, while downstairs China Tang celebrates the cuisine of China. The bedrooms are constantly being upgraded and each floor has its own colour scheme. There's an elegance to all the rooms, whether they're traditionally decorated or in a more contemporary style; park-facing bedrooms must be some of the most sought after real estate in the capital. But comfort is nothing without service – and standards here remain impeccable.

Dukes

35 St James's Pl. ✉ SW1A 1NY
✆ (020) 7491 4840
www.dukeshotel.com
⊖ Green Park

H4

90 rm – ♦£234/250 ♦♦£276/496,☕ £24 – 6 suites

Dukes

Every hotel needs a little reinvention now and again and Dukes has been steadily changing its image over the last few years. It has enjoyed a constant presence in St James's for over a century and traditionally had a clubby, very British feel but this has given way to a brighter, fresher look which seems to suit it equally well. What hasn't been lost is the discreet atmosphere which is largely down to the very central, yet surprisingly quiet, location. The basement restaurant, which looks out at street level thanks to the vagaries of local topography, now offers an ambitious, modern menu with dishes that are original in look and elaborate in construction. The comfortable sitting rooms still do a brisk trade in afternoon tea but there is now also an outside cigar lounge. The bar is something of a London landmark (and was reputedly one of Ian Fleming's old haunts). Bedrooms are devoid of chintz and come in warm, calming colours; they have smart marble bathrooms and are decently proportioned.

Egerton House

17-19 Egerton Terr ✉ SW3 2BX
✆ (020) 7589 2412
www.egertonhousehotel.com
⊖ South Kensington

F5

28 rm☕ – †£310/440 ††£325/455

Egerton House

In challenging economic times hotels can either panic and cut staff and rates – a course of action which usually ends in ruin – or they can hold their nerve and provide greater value for their guests. Anyone wondering what more a hotel can do should get along to Egerton House. This is a townhouse whose decorative style is at the lavish end of the scale; the fabrics are of the highest order and the colours neatly coordinated. The ground floor Victoria and Albert Suite comes with its own little decked terrace and a row of filled decanters for company. All the rooms are slightly different; the marble bathrooms are very neat and the hotel has made the best use of limited space – ask for one of the quieter rooms at the back overlooking the little garden. What really makes this little place stand out, though, is the service and the eager attitude of the staff. Lots of hotels spout tosh about being 'a home from home' but here they do make a genuine effort to make their guests feel part of things by, for example, arranging complimentary admission to events at the V&A.

Four Seasons

Hamilton Pl, Park Ln ✉ W1J 7DR
(020) 7499 0888
www.fourseasons.com/london
Hyde Park Corner
Amaranto *(See restaurant listing)*

G4 

193 rm – £384 £384, £32 – 33 suites

Four Seasons

These days competition is pretty fierce at the luxury end of the hotel market so, to stay ahead of the game, contenders need to do more than just tinker with the cosmetics. The Four Seasons, which was the group's first hotel outside the US, closed for a couple of years and in that time was stripped right back, before being put together again. The result is that Park Lane now has a hotel that's really raised the bar in the comfort stakes. The bedrooms, trimmed with plenty of walnut, sycamore, marble and shiny steel, are particularly striking and come with all the latest wizardry like self-regulating ambient heating. They also occupy impressive square footage, as do the suites, the number of which has been greatly increased. Dining is a flexible feast – Amaranto is divided into a three areas: a bar, restaurant and lounge and you can eat what you want, where you want it, and that includes on the secluded outdoor terrace. The stunning top-floor spa, with its fantastic views, caps off this hotel's dazzling renaissance.

45 Park Lane

45 Park Ln ✉ W1K 1PN
✆ (020) 7493 4545
www.45parklane.com
⊖ Hyde Park Corner
🍴 **Cut** *(See restaurant listing)*

G4

46 rm – †£595/834 ††£595/834, ☕ £21 – 10 suites

45 Park Lane

It was the original site of the Playboy Club and has also been a car showroom but now 45 Park Lane has been reborn as The Dorchester's little sister and, lit up at night, her art deco façade makes her look rather cute. The style is certainly different from her famous sibling but the quality and depth of service come from the same top drawer. On each floor you'll find the work of a different contemporary British artist as well as a couple of hosts to take care of everything from unpacking your bags to booking you a restaurant. The bedrooms, which all have views over Hyde Park, are wonderfully sensual, with velvet walls, leather-wrapped doors and warm, heavy fabrics and the marble bathrooms are beautiful. Suites take up great positions on the corners of the building and have the best views, while the penthouse occupies the entire top floor. The red leather makes the cocktail bar on the mezzanine level a very sexy spot, while on the ground floor sits Wolfgang Puck's glamorous restaurant Cut which specialises in steaks.

The Gore

190 Queen's Gate ✉ SW7 5EX
✆ (020) 7584 6601
www.gorehotel.com
⊖ Gloucester Road

D5

50 rm – †£126/246 ††£168/546, ☕ £15

The Gore

Being the nearest hotel to the Royal Albert Hall makes The Gore a popular choice for performers as well as attendees and the bright, casual bistro is always busier early and late in the evening than it ever is at 8pm. The hotel clearly stands out at the top of Queen's Gate with its fluttering Union flag and gleaming brass plaque and who needs a fitness room when you've got Kensington Gardens just yards away. If you were in any doubt that this is the part of London most closely associated with Queen Victoria, then just step through the door because the walls are covered with pictures and paintings relating to her reign. But, despite the plethora of antiques and all that Victoriana, this is a hip little hotel with a large element of fun attached. Rooms like Miss Fanny and Miss Ada are as camp as they sound; the Tudor Room has a secret bathroom and minstrel's gallery, and many of the bathrooms give meaning to the expression 'sitting on the throne'. Bend down in the rooms and you might find a card saying "Look, we've cleaned here too".

Goring

15 Beeston Pl ✉ SW1W 0JW
H5
✆ (020) 7396 9000
www.thegoring.com
⊖ Victoria
Dining Room at The Goring (See restaurant listing)

69 rm – †£310/630 ††£310/1,025, ☕ £32 – 8 suites

The Goring

Not only has The Goring celebrated its centenary, but it is still owned by the family who built it. Jeremy Goring, the great-grandson of the founder, is now at the helm and this lineage is clearly welcomed by the staff – many of whom have been working at the hotel for years – as well as being appreciated by regular guests, who benefit from the excellent service. The hotel still has a pervading sense of Britishness, which designers like Nina Campbell fully respected when they were asked to update its look. There has been a clever introduction of new technology, from the TVs that rise from the desk to the touch panels that control everything but, reassuringly for those less familiar or enamoured with the modern world, one can still get a proper key with which to open one's bedroom door. The ground floor restaurant is a bright, discreet and comfortable affair and its menu celebrates Britain's own culinary heritage; the bar is colonial in its feel and the veranda overlooks the hotel's surprisingly large back garden.

Halkin

5 Halkin St ✉ SW1X 7DJ **G5**

✆ (020) 7333 1000
www.comohotels.com/thehalkin
⊖ Hyde Park Corner
Ametsa with Arzak Instruction *(See restaurant listing)*

41 rm – †£280/795 ††£280/795, ☕ £28 – 6 suites

Halkin

There may be glossier and glitzier hotels around these days but there aren't many that can be considered quite as dapper as The Halkin. When it opened back in the early '90s, its boutique style and modern design were considered quite ground-breaking as the majority of London hotels at that time were still exhibiting a feverish devotion to all things chintz. In the intervening years the hotel has retained its reputation as a preferred London address of those who like a little comfort and calmness to go with the cool. The hotel is big enough to provide all the desired services yet small enough to feel familiar. The bedrooms have an enduring quality and hide their technology well – touchscreen panels control everything from the curtains to the temperature; those rooms overlooking the garden at the back are particularly quiet. The Armani-clad staff glide around the place with calm assurance and know all their regulars well, while Ametsa, with its modern Spanish food, is the latest in a long line of impressive restaurants to grace the ground floor.

Ham Yard

1 Ham Yard, ✉ W1D 7DT
✆ (020) 3642 2000
www.firmdalehotels.com
⊖ Piccadilly Circus
Ham Yard *(See restaurant listing)*

I3

89 rm – †£318 ††£318, ☕ £14 – 9 suites

Ham Yard is the thoroughfare that links Denman and Archer streets and having lain empty for years is now home to a stylish new hotel from the Firmdale group. The U-shaped building is set around a tree-lined courtyard which is a little haven of tranquillity bang in the middle of the West End. Unsurprisingly, the hotel itself is very pleasing on the eye and, with decorative influences ranging from Africa to India, there's a talking point on every turn. Each of the very luxurious and generously proportioned bedrooms is different – one can be lime green, another bright red – but the best ones are those with floor-to-ceiling windows overlooking the courtyard. That said, you can't go wrong with any of the rooms – the emphasis here is very much on comfort. Along with a large restaurant is a basement 'Dive Bar', a terrific rooftop terrace with a little vegetable garden, a 190-seater theatre and even a four-lane bowling alley; the fully stocked library and drawing room is for the exclusive use of hotel residents.

Haymarket

1 Suffolk Pl. ✉ SW1Y 4HX
✆ (020) 7470 4000
www.haymarkethotel.com
⊖ Piccadilly Circus
Brumus *(See restaurant listing)*

I4

50 rm – †£368 ††£368, ☕ £20 – 3 suites

Firmdale

Created out of one of the finest examples of a John Nash building and next to his celebrated Haymarket Theatre Royal is this elegant hotel from the Firmdale group. The contemporary interior provides a striking contrast to the traditional Regency façade and is the most arresting feature of the hotel. It was a gentleman's club for a while – a Shooting Gallery once used by chaps checking their aim is now a private dining room – but there is certainly nothing fuddy or even duddy about the place these days. An eclectic collection of artwork and furniture runs through the hotel and the bedrooms are spacious, designed with an eye for detail and decorated with a contemporary palette – they are also very well soundproofed but ask for one overlooking the inner courtyard if you're a light sleeper. Brumus manages the trick of feeling like an independent restaurant rather than a hotel dining room and does a roaring trade pre- and post-theatre. The huge pool and bar in the basement doubles as a great party venue.

Hazlitt's

6 Frith St ✉ W1D 3JA
✆ (020) 7434 1771
www.hazlittshotel.com
⊖ Tottenham Court Road

I3 

30 rm – †£199/222 ††£227/288, ☕ £12

Hazlitt's

Along with its central Soho location, one of the best features of Hazlitt's has always been its intimate and chummy atmosphere, which even the addition of eight rooms in 2009 failed to disrupt. The building dates from 1718 and was named after the essayist and critic William Hazlitt, whose home it was. Appropriately, it still attracts plenty of writers, but while there is much character to be found in all the bedrooms – from the wood panelling and busts to the antique beds and Victorian fixtures – you do also get free wi-fi. Duke of Monmouth is the most striking of the newer rooms: it's spread over two floors and has its own terrace with a retractable roof. Madam Dafloz, named after another of Soho's former roguish residents, is also appealing, with a sultry, indulgent feel. The Library, with its 24/7 honesty bar, is the hotel's only communal area and was slightly enlarged when the newer rooms were added. This is also one of the few hotels where breakfast in bed really is the only option – and who is going to object to that?

K + K George

1-15 Templeton Pl ✉ SW5 9NB
✆ (020) 7598 8700
www.kkhotels.com
⊖ Earl's Court

C6

154 rm☕ – †£150/330 ††£150/375

K&K Hotels

Providing a model lesson on the importance of keeping on top of your product, the K+K George hotel spent time during the recent economic turndown refurbishing all its bedrooms; they now boast fast internet, 320 thread count linen, American cherry wood panelling, flat screen TVs, full minibars, and underfloor heating in the bathrooms; and the hotel is reaping the rewards. It occupies seven houses of a stucco-fronted terrace; its interior in contrast to the period façade, is colourful and contemporary, and fresh flowers and bowls of fruit are scattered around the lobby. The unexpectedly large rear garden, for which most hotels would give their eye teeth, has won local horticultural prizes and hosts breakfast on warm summer days. A simple menu is served in the bar but most guests take advantage of the central location and go out to eat. The hotel may be part of an international chain but there are plenty of staff on hand to add a personal touch and it also manages to feel part of the local community.

Knightsbridge

10 Beaufort Gdns ✉ SW3 1PT
✆ (020) 7584 6300
www.knightsbridgehotel.com
⊖ Knightsbridge

F5

44 rm – †£234/252 ††£264/894, ☕ £19

Firmdale

Firmdale Hotels all seem so quintessentially British and The Knightsbridge, converted from a row of Victorian terraced houses in an attractive square, is another typical example of what they do so well: it proves style and comfort are not mutually exclusive and that a hotel can be fashionable without being fuzzy. The work of British artists, such as Carol Sinclair's slate stack and Peter Clark's dog collages, sets the tone and the bedrooms are constantly being refreshed and rearranged. Those facing the square on the first floor benefit from floor to ceiling windows, while the Knightsbridge Suite stretches from the front to the back of the building. All rooms are so impeccably tidy and colour coordinated it'll make you question your own dress sense. The Library Room differs from many similarly named hotel sitting rooms by actually containing books, along with an honesty bar which holds everything from fruit and snacks to champagne and ice cream.

Langham

1c Portland Pl., Regent St. ✉ W1B 1JA
(020) 7636 1000
www.langhamhotels.com
⊖ Oxford Circus
Roux at The Landau *(See restaurant listing)*

H2

380 rm – †£288/780 ††£288/780, ☕ £30 – 25 suites

Langham

The Langham was one of Europe's first purpose-built Grand hotels when it opened in 1865. Since then it has been owned by all sorts, including at one stage the BBC – they used it as their library and was where 'The Goon Show' was recorded. In 2009 it emerged from an extensive refurbishment programme that didn't provide much change from £80 million and it is now competing with the big boys once again. Pride of place must be the Palm Court, a twinkling ersatz art deco space, which serves light meals and afternoon teas. The Artesian bar is a stylish affair and does interesting things with gin; there's a small courtyard terrace named in honour of a BBC radio gardener and the striking restaurant is under the aegis of the Roux organisation. The bedrooms have personality and, for a change, the furniture is free-standing rather than fitted; the boldly decorated Club rooms are particularly distinctive. The health and fitness club is impressively kitted out and includes a swimming pool in what was once a bank vault.

The Levin

28 Basil St. ✉ SW3 1AS
✆ (020) 7589 6286
www.thelevinhotel.co.uk
⊖ Knightsbridge

F5

12 rm☕ – †£240/399 ††£295/499

The Levin

Its bigger sister, The Capital, is a few strides down the road and may be better known, but The Levin still does the (Levin) family proud. Here you'll find a different decorative style but still the same level of care and enthusiasm in the service. The eye-catching fibre optic chandelier dominates the staircase, while the collection of Penguin paperbacks reminds you that this is a fundamentally British hotel. All 12 bedrooms are light and fresh-feeling; there are subtle nods in the direction of art deco in the styling but these are combined with a cleverly contemporary look which blends in well with the building. The best room is the top floor open-plan suite. Mini-bars are stocked exclusively with champagne - along with some helpful hints on how to prepare an assortment of champagne cocktails. In the basement you'll find Le Metro which provides an appealing, all-day menu with everything from quiche and salads to shepherd's pie and sausage and mash, along with selections from the family estate in the Loire.

Mandarin Oriental Hyde Park

66 Knightsbridge ✉ SW1X 7LA F4

✆ (020) 7235 2000 – **www**.mandarinoriental.com/london
⊖ Knightsbridge
Bar Boulud and Dinner by Heston Blumenthal *(See restaurant listing)*

194 rm – †£390/870 ††£450/942, ☕ £26 – 25 suites

Mandarin Oriental Hyde Park

When the bewilderingly expensive new apartments next door went on sale things could finally quieten down in this part of town for a while. That said, during their construction there was also plenty of work being done on the hotel too. Bar Boulud, celebrated New York based chef Daniel Boulud's first European venture, occupies what was previously the hotel's housekeeping storeroom and proved a hit from day one. But that was nothing compared to the frenzy caused by Heston Blumenthal's enigmatically named restaurant with its thrilling menu of rediscovered and re-imagined British dishes. Meanwhile, the hotel continues to constantly upgrade and redecorate its bedrooms which all offer every imaginable luxury and extra. They are decorated in a classic English country house style and come in either beige and blue or red and gold – although the TVs do seem to be incongruously large. If evidence were still needed that the hotel is keen to remain one of the most luxurious in the capital, it comes in the fact that it recently spent a mere £1 million just on doing up its Royal Suite.

Mayflower

26-28 Trebovir Rd. ✉ SW5 9NJ
✆ (020) 7370 0991
www.mayflowerhotel.co.uk
⊖ Earl's Court

C6

47 rm – †£89/129 ††£119/350

Mayflower

The Mayflower shares the same ownership as Twenty Nevern Square just around the corner and it too offers good value accommodation. It is also twice the size so the chances of actually getting a room are somewhat greater. Some of those rooms can be a little tight on space but this is also reflected in the room rates. Rooms 11, 17 and 18 are the best in the house and the general decoration is a blend of the contemporary with some Asian influence; some of the rooms have jet showers and others balconies. But what makes the hotel stand out is that the owner is nearly always on the property and his enthusiasm has been passed to his staff. This may not be a glitzy West End hotel but they really do make an effort to get to know their guests and help in any way they can. There is no restaurant, but then it doesn't need one: there are plenty of places in which to eat that are no more than a vigorous stroll away. A plentiful breakfast is provided and, on summer days, can even be taken on the small terrace.

Metropolitan

Old Park Ln ✉ W1K 1LB
G4

✆ (020) 7447 1000
www.metropolitan.com/metropolitanlondon
⊖ Hyde Park Corner
🍴 **Nobu** *(See restaurant listing)*

144 rm – †£318/534 ††£366/582, ☕ £28 – 3 suites

Metropolitan

The Metropolitan is inextricably linked to its über-cool hang-out, The Met Bar. If you've never managed to blag your way past the doorman at night you can now secure entry by grabbing yourself some 'Afternoon Delight': a healthy version of afternoon tea with low-fat cakes and breadless sandwiches. The Metropolitan Hotel is well over a decade old now; in design terms, there are more contemporary competitors around but it still holds its own in the fashion stakes by letting its guests create their own atmosphere. The bedrooms are neutral in colour and gadgets are discreetly integrated; all get regular licks of paint or, following an overnight stay from the occasional wannabe rock star, a full redecoration. Plenty of rooms overlook the park but the more interesting views are those facing east over the rooftops. The spa promises plenty of holistic treatments while London's original Nobu on the first floor ensures a further sprinkling of stardust. Even better, the staff are more inclined to provide good service instead of just standing at an angle, looking cool.

The Milestone

1-2 Kensington Ct ✉ W8 5DL
✆ (020) 7917 1000
www.milestonehotel.com
⊖ High Street Kensington

D4

62 rm – ♦£342/504 ♦♦£342/504, ☕ £27 – 6 suites

The Milestone

Behind the striking Gothic red-brick façade is a little gem of a hotel. Fashioned out of three houses dating from the 16C, which were joined together early in the 20C, The Milestone is discreet, cosy and sumptuously decorated. It is also very well soundproofed so you can enjoy the location opposite Kensington Gardens without being disturbed by the traffic on Kensington Road. There's a thoroughly British feel to the hotel, especially the sitting room where you can have afternoon tea beneath a painting of a youthful Noel Coward. The Jockey Bar is so named because this was where the horses were once stabled and the basement leisure club is a useful little facility for those who like to exercise their way out of jetlag. For others, there's the wood-panelled Cheneston's restaurant for modern British food. Entry level bedrooms can be a little on the small size but there's impressive attention to detail in all the rooms, especially the suites which display greater levels of whimsy. Every room has enough Penhaligon's toiletries to stock a small shop.

Number Sixteen

16 Sumner Pl. ✉ SW7 3EG
✆ (020) 7589 5232
www.numbersixteenhotel.co.uk
⊖ South Kensington

E6 

41 rm – †£209 ††£302, ☕ £20

Firmdale

Number Sixteen opened back in 2001 and was the first one in Tim and Kit Kemp's Firmdale Group of hotels not to have its own restaurant. This actually suits it because it feels more like a private house than the others and, with repeat business standing at around 55%, they've clearly got it right. Attention to detail underpins the operation, whether in the individual styling of the bedrooms or the twice-daily housekeeping service. Breakfast is in the conservatory overlooking the little garden – don't miss the smoothie of the day – and is served until midday: welcome acknowledgement that not every guest has an early morning meeting. Firmdale also operates its own laundry service which explains how the bed linen retains such crispness. Rooms 2 and 7 have their own private patio terrace and all the first floor rooms benefit from large windows and balconies. The drawing room, with its plump sofa cushions and pretty butterfly theme, is a very charming spot and there's the added bonus of a nearby honesty bar.

One Aldwych

1 Aldwych ✉ WC2B 4RH
✆ (020) 7300 1000
www.onealdwych.com
⊖ Temple
Axis *(See restaurant listing)*

J3

105 rm – ♦£306/564 ♦♦£342/594, ☕ £26 – 12 suites

One Aldwych

Things have gone all green down at One Aldwych. The hotel is hoping to take a lead within the hospitality industry on matters environmental (without, of course, neglecting its duties as a luxury hotel) and has appointed a 'green team' to oversee and coordinate procedures. The swimming pool is chemical and chlorine free; bath products are organic; and the chocolate on your pillow has been replaced by a book called 'Change the World'. As far as guests are concerned though, it's business as usual, which means extremely comfortable bedrooms and plenty of polished staff. Fruit and flowers are changed daily in the rooms, which are awash with Bang & Olufsen toys and also come with Frette linen; deluxe rooms and corner suites are particularly desirable. There's a choice of restaurant: the first floor Indigo offers a light, easy menu while Axis boasts more personality and greater ambition in its cooking. The lobby of the hotel is perhaps its most well-known feature; not only does it double as a bar surprisingly successfully but it also changes its look according to the seasons.

The Pelham

15 Cromwell Pl ✉ SW7 2LA
✆ (020) 7589 8288
www.thepelhamhotel.co.uk
⊖ South Kensington

E6

51 rm – †£180/335 ††£260/480, ☕ £18 – 1 suite

The Pelham

Owned by the people who have The Gore in Queensgate, The Pelham boasts a stylish look derives from juxtaposing the feel of a classic English country house with the contemporary look of a city townhouse. Originally three houses, the hotel has a pleasing lack of conformity in its layout. Bold pastel colours, fine fabrics and a housekeeping department that could satisfy Howard Hughes combine to create bedrooms that are pristine, warm and comfortable. Spend too long in the panelled sitting room or library, with all those cushions, an honesty bar and a fridge full of ice cream and the world outside will seem positively frenzied. Downstairs you'll find Bistro Fifteen, a relaxed all-day affair which becomes a cosy and romantic dinner spot. Its menu is mostly centred on Europe with an extra Gallic element – a nod to the high number of French émigrés in the neighbourhood. There's a genuine helpfulness and an eagerness to please amongst the staff.

Ritz

150 Piccadilly ✉ W1J 9BR
✆ (020) 7493 8181
www.theritzlondon.com
⊖ Green Park
🍴 **Ritz Restaurant** *(See restaurant listing)*

H4

134 rm – †£315/865 ††£345/995, ☕ £35 – 45 suites

The Ritz

Henry James considered that, "There are few hours in life more agreeable than the hour dedicated to the ceremony known as afternoon tea". Such is the popularity of Tea at the Ritz, which is served daily in the grand surroundings of the Palm Court, that the ceremony begins at 11.30 am – an hour before lunch is served in their restaurant – and doesn't cease until 7.30pm. Meanwhile, the rest of the hotel, built in 1906 in the style of a French chateau, remains in fine form thanks to constant re-investment by its owners, the Barclay Brothers. The William Kent Room must be the most ornate private dining room in London and the bedrooms are all immaculately kept. The Royal and Prince of Wales Suites both have enormous square footage and are often booked for long stays by those for whom the credit crunch is no more than a mild irritant. The Ritz Restaurant, with its dinner dances, lavish surroundings and brigades of staff, evokes images of a more formal but more glamorous age and the art deco Rivoli bar remains a veritable jewel.

The Rockwell

181-183 Cromwell Rd. ✉ SW5 0SF
✆ (020) 7244 2000
www.therockwell.com
⊖ Earl's Court

C5/6

40 rm☕ – †£108/135 ††£150/180

The Rockwell

The Rockwell is steadily establishing itself on the London hotel scene and is building up quite a loyal client base. They certainly get a lot of things right: the reception is manned 24/7 and staff are imbued with sufficient self-confidence to make eye-contact with their guests and offer help when needed; the housekeeping department also do an evening service of all the rooms. The lobby is a comfortable space, with its fireplace and generous scattering of newspapers. The hotel is made up of two Victorian houses; the best two rooms are the split level 104 and 105 and those on the lower ground floor have their own private patios. All rooms have showers rather than baths, and come with top-brand toiletries, mini bars and free internet – you can even borrow a laptop. Meals are relaxed affairs with plenty of favourites and decent cocktails. Freshly baked croissants and homemade breads are a feature of breakfast; sometimes served on the south-facing garden terrace which is the hotel's most appealing feature.

The Rookery

12 Peters Ln, Cowcross St ✉ EC1M 6DS
✆ (020) 7336 0931
www.rookeryhotel.com
⊖ Farringdon

L2

33 rm – †£168/222 ††£210/312, ☕ £12

The Rookery

The mere fact that the original opening of the hotel was delayed because the owner couldn't find quite the right chimney pots tells you that authenticity is high on the agenda here. Named after the colloquial term for the local area from a time when it had an unruly reputation, the hotel is made up of a series of Georgian houses whose former residents are honoured in the naming of the bedrooms. Its decoration remains true to these Georgian roots, not only in the antique furniture and period features but also in the colours used; all the bedrooms have either half-testers or four-poster beds and bathrooms have roll-top baths. However, with the addition of all mod cons, there is no danger of the hotel becoming a twee museum piece; Rook's Nest, the largest room, is often used for fashion shoots. Breakfast is served in the bedrooms and there is just one small sitting room which leads out onto a little terrace - its mural of the owner herding some cows goes some way towards blocking out the surrounding sights of the 21C.

St James's Hotel and Club

7-8 Park Pl. ✉ SW1A 1LS
(020) 7316 1600
www.stjameshotelandclub.com
⊖ Green Park
Seven Park Place *(See restaurant listing)*

H4

60 rm – £260/3,000 ££260/3,000, £24 – 10 suites

St James's Hotel & Club

The liveried doorman and a plethora of concierges immediately tell you that this is a hotel with an eye for service. Staff make concerted efforts to note down guests' preferences for future visits and the housekeeping department ensure that bedrooms are so immaculate you feel you're sullying the room just by being in it. The building dates from 1892 and there can be few better positions for a London hotel: it is bang in the heart of the metropolis and yet because Park Place is a cul-de-sac, it's very quiet. For those who like a little exercise, there's a cut-through to get to Green Park. Before being a hotel this was a private club and there remains a discernible clubby feel. Granted, it's quite a compact place but they've made good use of the space – the bar doubles as a simple brasserie and this leads into the intimate, gilded restaurant. However, perhaps the greatest aspect is the vast collection of art from the Rosenstein collection scattered around the building and covering the 1920s to the 1950s.

St Martins Lane

45 St Martin's Ln ✉ WC2N 3HX
✆ (020) 7300 5500
www.stmartinslane.com
⊖ Charing Cross

I3

206 rm – †£222/479 ††£222/479, ☕ £26 – 2 suites

St Martin's Lane

If you're uncomfortable with the idea of hotel staff calling you by your first name or have never considered working out in a gym wearing a pair of stilettos then St Martins Lane is probably not the hotel for you; nor you the right guest for them. Philippe Starck's design of the modern juxtaposed with the baroque creates an eye-catching lobby. The bedrooms are decorated in a blizzard of white, although you can change the lighting according to your mood. The views get better the higher you go but all have floor to ceiling windows. Thanks to the paparazzi, readers of the more excitable magazines will be familiar with Bungalow 8: Anne Sacco's London outpost of her hip New York club is a favoured hang-out for the already-famous, the would-be-famous and the related-to-someone-famous-famous. Asia de Cuba is Scarface meets Dr No: fiery Floridian Cuban mixed with teasing influence from across Asia – dishes are designed for sharing. The Light Bar is sufficiently hip and the Gymbox is a branded gym with a nightclub vibe – what else?

Sanderson

50 Berners St ✉ W1T 3NG
(020) 7300 1400
www.morganshotelgroup.com
Oxford Circus

H2

150 rm – †£234/538 ††£234/538, ☕ £18

Sanderson

When the doorman greets you with a "how ya doing?" you know this is not a hotel that stands on ceremony. The staff do now smile here, something that was all too rare in the early days when they were mostly recruited from model agencies and had a somewhat disdainful attitude towards the whole concept of service. The Sanderson has always worn its exclusivity with confidence but now there's some substance to it. The Philippe Starck designed bedrooms still impress, with their celestial whiteness, sleigh beds in the middle of the room and idiosyncrasies such as the framed print hung on the ceiling – its actually the same print in all the rooms, is called 'Pathway to Heaven' and is designed to encourage heavenly thoughts before sleep. Some bedrooms have their own treadmills while others boast small terraces; the top two suites have their own lifts. On the ground floor the Purple Bar has over 75 different vodkas, miniature chairs and a selective door policy; the Long Bar is more accessible and leads into Suka, their modern Malaysian restaurant.

Savoy

Strand ✉ WC2R 0EU
✆ (020) 7836 4343
www.fairmont.com/savoy
⊖ Charing Cross
🍴 **Savoy Grill** *(See restaurant listing)*

J3

268 rm – †£445 ††£445, ☕ £30 – 45 suites

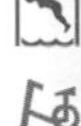

The Savoy

The Savoy is one of the grande dames of the London hotel scene. The comprehensive restoration took nearly three years but the best news for the hotel's legions of regulars was that many of the familiar Edwardian and art deco features were retained. The lobby still offers a welcoming air and adds to the sense of expectation, with plenty of staff on hand to offer help or directions. Afternoon tea is served in the Thames Foyer, which remains at the heart of the operation – although it now has a steel gazebo beneath a glass dome. There is a choice of two bars: the world famous American Bar and the Beaufort Bar which occupies the space from which the BBC once broadcast. However, the hotel were clearly not happy with everything because in 2013 they replaced the legendary River restaurant with Kaspar's, a more informal seafood bar and grill – tables here are easier to secure than those in the famous Savoy Grill. They did get it right first time with the bedrooms though: they remain true to the hotel's origins and are split between Edwardian and art deco styles.

Shangri-La

The Shard, 31 St Thomas St ✉ SE1 1RX
✆ (020) 7234 8000
www.shangri-la.com/london
⊖ London Bridge

M4

202 rm – †£450/575 ††£450/575, ☕ £20 – 17 suites

When your hotel occupies floors 34-52 of The Shard, you know there's already plenty of wow factor. Shangri-la was the most eagerly anticipated hotel opening of 2014 and when one considers how much marble they've used, it's a wonder Renzo Piano's iconic building is still upright. Due to the building's shape and configuration, the bedrooms vary in size, although the hotel judges the best ones – ergo, the most expensive ones – to be those facing north across the river. Modern Chinese abstracts and calming shades feature throughout the hotel; London's highest swimming pool is on level 52 and sits alongside the Gong bar where one side serves champagne, the other cocktails. Lang is a small all-day patisserie at ground level and Ting is the comfortable restaurant where classic British dishes with the odd Asian twist are made using plenty of produce from nearby Borough Market. This fusion of East and West extends to afternoon tea, where you have a choice of traditional English or Asian style with dim sum.

Soho

4 Richmond Mews ✉ W1D 3DH
✆ (020) 7559 3000
www.sohohotel.com
⊖ Tottenham Court Road
Refuel *(See restaurant listing)*

I3

91 rm – †£353/402 ††£353/402, ☕ £20 – 5 suites

Firmdale

It's almost as if they wanted to keep it secret. The hotel is on a relatively quiet mews – not something one readily associates with Soho – and, even as you approach, it gives little away. But inside one soon realises that, if it was a secret, it wasn't very well kept as it's always buzzing with people. Their guests' every dietary whim or food mood should find fulfilment in 'Refuel', the restaurant with its own bar as a backdrop. Whether your diet is gluten-free, vegetarian, vegan, carnivorous or organic you'll discover something worth ordering and, if you're off out, you'll find the early dinner menu a steal. It's also worth checking out the Film Club for a meal and a movie in the screening room. Upstairs and the bedrooms are almost celestial in their cleanliness. From jazzy orange to bright lime green, from crimsons to bold stripes, the rooms are vibrant in style and immaculate in layout; those on the top floor have balconies and terraces. Add infectiously enthusiastic service and it's little wonder the hotel has so many returning guests. And to think this was once an NCP car park.

South Place

3 South Pl ✉ EC2M 2AF
✆ (020) 3503 0000 – **www**.southplacehotel.com
⊖ Moorgate
Closed 26-31 December
Ⓧ **Angler** *(See restaurant listing)*

M2

80 rm – †£185/350 ††£185/350, ☕ £15 – 1 suite

Restaurant group D&D's first venture into the hotel business is a very stylish looking affair, and for that credit goes to their erstwhile boss, in the shape of Conrad & Partners, who designed the interior. The bedrooms are a treat for those with an eye for aesthetics and a great advert for how design can enhance one's mood. They are understated, uncluttered and cool yet no detail has been forgotten, from blackout blinds to all manner of high-tech gizmos; contemporary artwork lines the walls and the bathrooms are a great balance between form and function. On the food front you have a choice of two restaurants: 3 South Place is a bustling bar and grill on the ground floor, with a good range of modern brasserie dishes and food-inspired pop art on the walls; Angler, a more formal seafood restaurant is on the top floor. The hotel is actually fashioned out of two former offices but you wouldn't know it from the exterior – the atmosphere is relaxed yet animated, helped along by service that is discreet and professional.

Stafford

16-18 St James's Pl. ✉ SW1A 1NJ
✆ (020) 7493 0111
www.kempinski.com/london
⊖ Green Park

H4

105 rm – †£336/700 ††£336/700, ☕ £25 – 15 suites

Stafford

The Stafford has, for a few years, been a mix of the new and the more traditional. Recently, the owners have been busy injecting considerable amounts of money into its refurbishment; something which no doubt terrifies many of its loyal and longstanding guests who appear to like things just the way they are. Thanks to some judicious lighting, the lobby and lounge appear brighter and more inviting. The dining room now opens out more into the drawing room and has changed its name to the Lyttleton, after a family who once lived here, but it has wisely kept its traditional British menu. The relatively recently created suites in the Mews House, a converted office block in the rear courtyard of the hotel, are the most impressive of all the bedrooms. What will never change at The Stafford is the celebrated American Bar, which is festooned with an impressive collection of assorted ties, helmets and pictures and is one of the best in London for those who like their bars with chairs and without music.

Twenty Nevern Square

20 Nevern Sq. ✉ SW5 9PD
✆ (020) 7565 9555
www.twentynevernsquare.co.uk
⊖ Earl's Court

C6

20 rm ☕ – †£80/200 ††£100/350

Michelin

It's wise to book well in advance here, as this small but friendly hotel – with its quiet location in a typical Victorian Square – represents decent value for money and gets booked up pretty quickly. The two best rooms are the Pasha and the Ottoman Suites and both have their own terraces, but all rooms are well looked after and given regular refits. Ten of the rooms overlook the gardens opposite; those at the front of the house tend to be larger, while those on the top floor are better suited to individual travellers. Hand-carved Indonesian furniture is found throughout which, together with the elaborately draped curtains, adds a hint of exoticism. You'll find gratis tea, coffee, water and a pile of daily newspapers laid on in the pleasant lounge. Continental breakfast comes included in the room rate; it can be taken in one's bedroom or in the bright conservatory. The hotel's other great selling point is the genuine sense of neighbourhood one feels. Its sister hotel, the Mayflower, is around the corner.

The Wellesley

11 Knightsbridge ✉ SW1X 7LY
✆ (020) 7235 3535
www.thewellesley.co.uk
⊖ Hyde Park Corner

G4

36 rm – †£450/550 ††£450/550, ☕ £34 – 14 suites

It may once have been one of the entrances to Hyde Park Corner tube, but for nearly three decades this site was occupied by the legendary Pizza on the Park, which was celebrated by its fans less for the pizzas and more for being a great venue for live jazz. It was subsequently gutted and rebuilt and emerged as the very end of 2012 as this very stylish, intimate boutique hotel named after Sir Arthur Wellesley, the first duke of Wellington. The owners were not blind to the building's past: not only were some of the decorative features inspired by the jazz age but live music is also performed in the Jazz Lounge. The discreet restaurant serves modern Italian food and, in perhaps another nod towards the appetite of your typical jazz fan, the hotel has a great cigar lounge and a bar with a superb selection of whiskies and cognacs. The smart, elegant bedrooms have been beautifully finished and come with every conceivable facility, including full butler service; those most in demand are the ones facing the park.

Westbury

Bond St ✉ W1S 2YF **H3**
(020) 7629 7755
www.westburymayfair.com
⊖ Bond Street
Alyn Williams at The Westbury *(See restaurant listing)*

246 rm – †£335/599 ††£335/599, ☕ £26 – 13 suites

Westbury

The Westbury opened in the 1950s and caused quite a commotion with its New York sensibilities. Over recent years, considerable funds have been spent restoring it to its former glory with the result that this is now one of Mayfair's more comfortable hotels. It is traditional without being staid and discreet without appearing precious; the staff are suitably enthusiastic and clearly proud of their hotel. There is no doubt that its location is also a huge draw: there are enough exclusive designer brands just outside the front door to satisfy even the most committed disciple of Edina and Patsy. The bedrooms are sleek and comfy and each floor is decorated with photos from the corresponding decade (so 1960s style icons adorn the 6th floor). The suites are particularly smart, especially those with art deco styling. The iconic Polo bar is elegantly dressed in Gucci and Fendi and its celebrated cocktail list ensures it's busy at night. Along with a sushi bar the hotel now offers sublime dining courtesy of chef Alyn Williams' creative and elaborate cuisine.

Zetter

St John's Sq, 86-88 Clerkenwell Rd. ✉ EC1M 5RJ **K1**
(020) 7324 4444
www.thezetter.com
⊖ Farringdon
Bistrot Bruno Loubet *(See restaurant listing)*

72 rm – †£115/235 ††£115/235

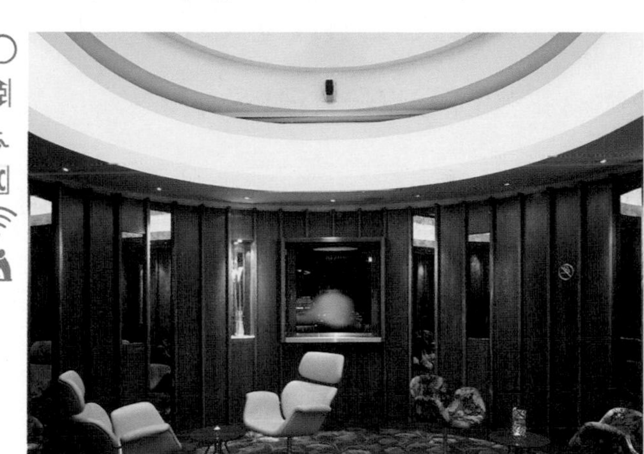

The Zetter

It doesn't matter how good looking and coolly dressed you are – if you never crack a smile no one will want to know you. What makes the Zetter more than just another hip hotel lies in the friendliness of its staff: instead of checking their pose or practising their pout they'll actually greet you with a warm smile and this is one of the reasons why guests keep returning. The main part of the hotel is within a converted Victorian warehouse, although the Bistrot on the ground floor adds a little continental element. Not only does the hotel have impressive eco-credentials – it bottles the water from its well – it also comes with some nice touches, like affordable vending machines on each floor; you can even borrow a folding bike from reception, complete with helmet and map. The rooms in this part of the hotel are understated and come with a cool retro edge; the more idiosyncratic Townhouse across the road acts as an overflow with more colourfully decorated rooms and a cocktail bar that has become a destination in its own right.

Michelin is committed to improving the mobility of travellers

ON EVERY ROAD AND BY EVERY MEANS

Since the company came into being - over a century ago – Michelin has had a single objective: to offer people a better way forward. A technological challenge first, to create increasingly efficient tyres, but also an ongoing commitment to travellers, to help them travel in the best way. This is why Michelin is developing a whole collection of products and services: from maps, atlases, travel guides and auto accessories, to mobile apps, route planners and oneline assistance: Michelin is doing everything it can to make travelling more pleasurable!

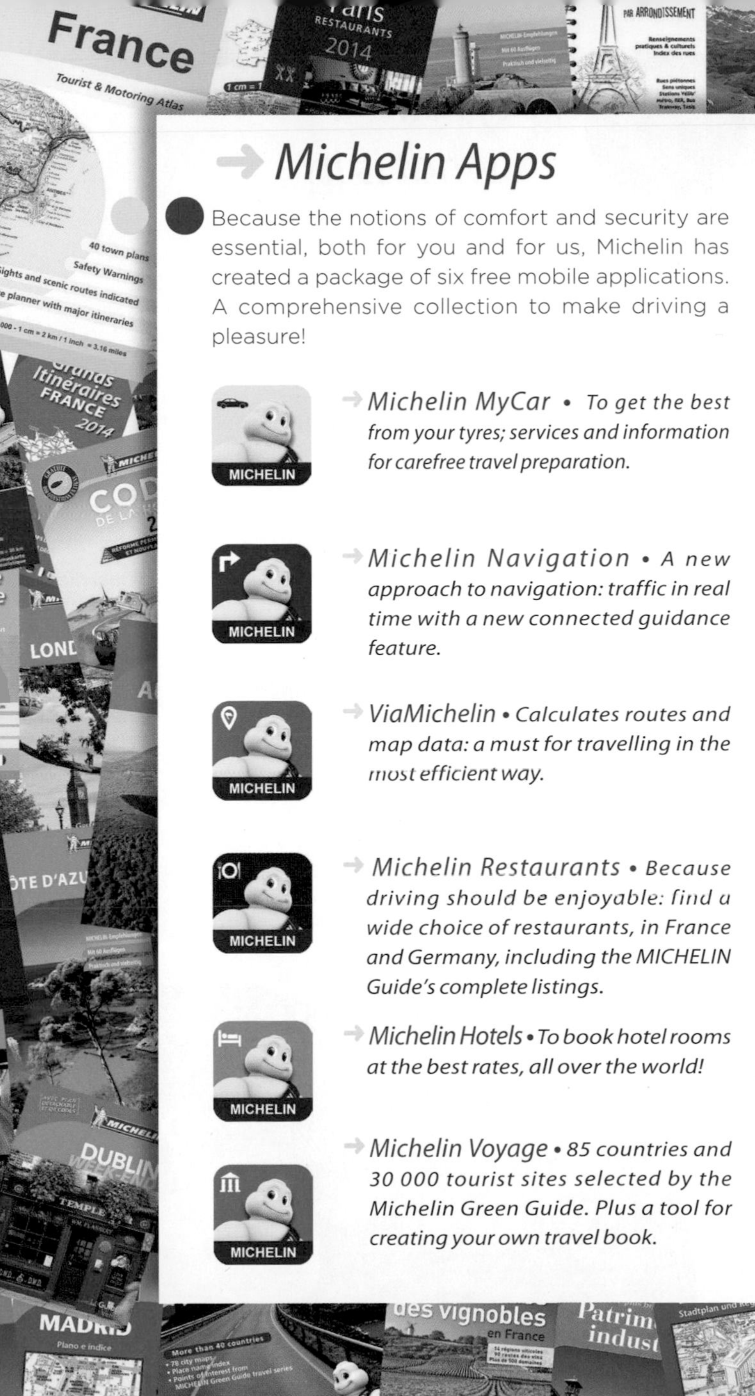
Michelin Apps
Because the notions of comfort and security are essential, both for you and for us, Michelin has created a package of six free mobile applications. A comprehensive collection to make driving a pleasure!
MICHELIN
Michelin MyCar • To get the best from your tyres; services and information for carefree travel preparation.
MICHELIN
Michelin Navigation • A new approach to navigation: traffic in real time with a new connected guidance feature.
MICHELIN
ViaMichelin • Calculates routes and map data: a must for travelling in the most efficient way.
MICHELIN
Michelin Restaurants • Because driving should be enjoyable: find a wide choice of restaurants, in France and Germany, including the MICHELIN Guide's complete listings.
MICHELIN
Michelin Hotels • To book hotel rooms at the best rates, all over the world!
MICHELIN
Michelin Voyage • 85 countries and 30 000 tourist sites selected by the Michelin Green Guide. Plus a tool for creating your own travel book.
France
Tourist & Motoring Atlas
40 town plans
Safety Warnings
Sights and scenic routes indicated
Route planner with major itineraries
RESTAURANTS
2014
PAR ARRONDISSEMENT
Itinéraires
FRANCE
2014
DUBLIN
TEMPLE
MADRID
Plano e índice
More than 40 countries
des vignobles
en France
Patrim
indust
Stadtplan und

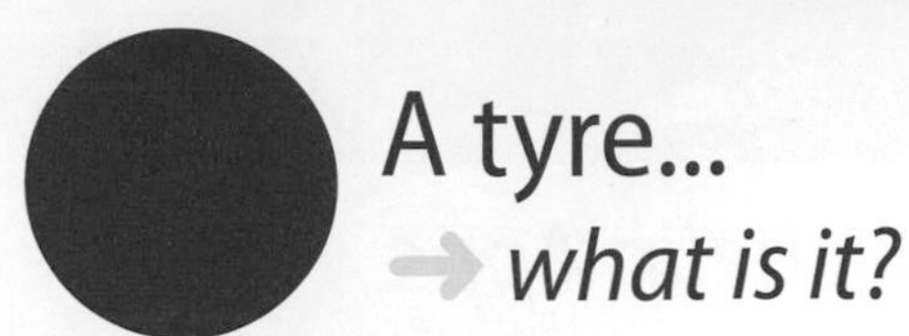

A tyre... → *what is it?*

Round, black, supple yet solid, the tyre is to the wheel what the shoe is to the foot. But what is it made of? First and foremost, rubber, but also various textile and/or metallic materials... and then it's filled with air! It is the skilful assembly of all these components that ensures tyres have the qualities they should: grip to the road, shock absorption, in two words: 'comfort' and 'safety'.

1 *TREAD*
The tread ensures the tyre performs correctly, by dispersing water, providing grip and increasing longevity.

2 *CROWN PLIES*
This reinforced double or triple belt combines vertical suppleness with transversal rigidity, enabling the tyre to remain flat to the road.

3 *SIDEWALLS*
These link all the component parts and provide symmetry. They enable the tyre to absorb shock, thus giving a smooth ride.

4 *BEADS*
The bead wires ensure that the tyre is fixed securely to the wheel to ensure safety.

5 *INNER LINER*
The inner liner creates an airtight seal between the wheel rim and the tyre.

Michelin

→ *innovation in movement*

Created and patented by Michelin in 1946, the belted radial-ply tyre revolutionised the world of tyres. But Michelin did not stop there: over the years other new and original solutions came out, confirming Michelin's position as a leader in research and innovation.

→ *the right pressure!*

One of Michelin's priorities is safer mobility. In short, innovating for a better way forward. This is the challenge for researchers, who are working to perfect tyres capable of shorter braking distances and offering the best possible traction to the road. And so, to

support motorists, Michelin organises road safety awareness campaigns all over the world: «Fill up with air» initiatives remind everyone that the right tyre pressure is a crucial factor in safety and fuel economy.

The Michelin strategy:
→ *multi-performance tyres*

Michelin is synonymous with safety, fuel saving and the capacity to cover thousands of miles. A MICHELIN tyre is the embodiment of all these things – thanks to our engineers, who work with the very latest technology.

Their challenge: to equip every tyre – whatever the vehicle (car, truck, tractor, bulldozer, plane, motorbike, bicycle or train!) – with the best possible combination of qualities, for optimal overall performance.

Slowing down wear, reducing energy expenditure (and therefore CO_2 emissions), improving safety through enhanced road handling and braking: there are so many qualities in just one tyre – that's Michelin Total Performance.

Every day, **Michelin** is working towards sustainable mobility

OVER TIME, WHILE RESPECTING THE PLANET

Sustainable mobility

is clean mobility... and mobility for everyone

Sustainable mobility means enabling people to get around in a way that is cleaner, safer, more economical and more accessible to everyone, wherever they might live. Every day, Michelin's 113 000 employees worldwide are innovating:

- by creating tyres and services that meet society's new needs,
- by raising young people's awareness of road safety,
- by inventing new transport solutions that consume less energy and emit less CO_2.

Michelin Challenge Bibendum

Sustainable mobility means allowing the transport of goods and people to continue, while promoting responsible economic, social and societal development. Faced with the increasing scarcity of raw materials and global warming, Michelin is standing up for the environment and public health. Michelin regularly organises 'Michelin Challenge Bibendum', the only event in the world which focuses on sustainable road travel.

MICHELIN
CHALLENGE
BIBENDUM

Index & Maps

Alphabetical list of restaurants

C

K

L

M

T

U – V

W

X – Y

Z

Map Index

Central London

Greater London

MAYOR OF LONDON

tfl.gov.uk

24 hour travel information 0343 222 1234*

*Service and network charges may apply. See tfl.gov.uk/terms for details.

Sign up for email updates tfl.gov.uk/emailupdates

@TfLTravelAlerts

UNDERGROUND

TRANSPORT FOR LONDON

EVERY JOURNEY MATTERS

 Reg. user No. 14/2681/P Version C 05.2014

Improvement works may affect your journey, please check before you travel Correct at time of going to print

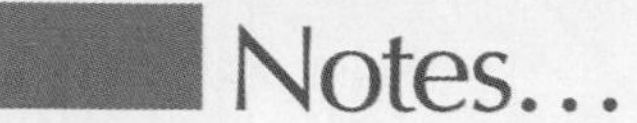

Michelin

Notes...

Michelin

Cover photography: Palomar

Michelin Travel Partner
Société par actions simplifiées au capital de 11 288 880 EUR
27 Cours de l'Ile Seguin - 92100 Boulogne Billancourt (France)
R.C.S. Nanterre 433 677 721

Dépôt légal August 2014

Printed in Italy - August 2014
Printed on paper from sustainably managed forests

Compogravure: Nord Compo à Villeneuve d'Ascq (France)
Impression et Finition: Printer Trento (Italie)

Our editorial team has taken the greatest care in writing this guide and checking the information in it. However, practical information (prices, addresses, telephone numbers, internet addresses, etc.) is subject to frequent change and such information should therefore be used for guidance only. It is possible that some of the information in this guide may not be accurate or exhaustive as at the date of publication. We therefore accept n liability in regard to such information.